D0610383

LOS ANGELES
AND
NEARBY ATTRACTIONS

HOW TO USE THIS GUIDE

The first section consists of useful general information—Facts at Your Fingertips—designed to help you plan your trip, as well as local facts, business hours, local holidays, time zones, and customs that will be of use while you are traveling.

Next are essays to help you with the background of the area that this Guide covers—the cultural scene, some historical insights, regional food and drink, and so on.

Following these essays comes the detailed breakdown of the area, geographically. Each chapter begins with a description of the place or region, broadly describing its attraction for the visitor; this is followed by Practical Information to help you explore the area—detailed descriptions, addresses, directions, phone numbers, and so forth for hotels, restaurants, tours, museums, historical sites, and more.

Two vital ways into this book are the Table of Contents at the beginning and the Index at the end.

FODOR'S TRAVEL GUIDES

are compiled, researched, and edited by an international team of travel writers, field correspondents, and editors. The series, which now almost covers the globe, was founded by Eugene Fodor in 1936.

OFFICES
New York & London

Fodor's Los Angeles:

Area Editor: JANE E. LASKY

Editorial Contributors: STEPHEN ALLEN, CHRIS BARNETT, JANICE WALD HENDERSON, MURRAY HERTZ, MARY JANE HORTON, JAYNE LEVANT, MARIE MONEYSMITH, TONY PEYSER, DIANA RICO, NORMAN SKLAREWITZ

Research: WILLIAM PATRICK BROWN, GERRY COHEN, MARY PAT FUCHS, HEIDI GORDON, JENNIE MOFFITT, ELIZABETH RIVIERA, MELISA SANDERS, BELINDA VIDAURRI.

Editor: TOM SZENTGYORGYI

Editorial Associate: PAUL BUSBY

Illustrations: TED BURWELL

Maps and Plans: BURMAR, PICTOGRAPH

FODOR'S

LOS ANGELES

AND
NEARBY ATTRACTIONS
1984

FODOR'S TRAVEL GUIDES
New York

All the following Guides are current (most of them also in
the Hodder and Stoughton British edition.)

CURRENT FODOR'S COUNTRY AND AREA TITLES:

AUSTRALIA, NEW ZEALAND
AND SOUTH PACIFIC
AUSTRIA
BELGIUM AND
LUXEMBOURG
BERMUDA
BRAZIL
CANADA
CARIBBEAN AND BAHAMAS
CENTRAL AMERICA
EASTERN EUROPE
EGYPT
EUROPE
FRANCE
GERMANY
GREAT BRITAIN
GREECE
HOLLAND
INDIA
IRELAND

ISRAEL
ITALY
JAPAN
JORDAN AND HOLY LAND
KOREA
MEXICO
NORTH AFRICA
PEOPLE'S REPUBLIC
OF CHINA
PORTUGAL
SCANDINAVIA
SCOTLAND
SOUTH AMERICA
SOUTHEAST ASIA
SOVIET UNION
SPAIN
SWITZERLAND
TURKEY
YUGOSLAVIA

CITY GUIDES:

BEIJING, GUANGZHOU, SHANGHAI
CHICAGO
DALLAS AND FORT WORTH
HOUSTON
LONDON
LOS ANGELES
MADRID
MEXICO CITY AND ACAPULCO
NEW ORLEANS
NEW YORK CITY

PARIS
ROME
SAN DIEGO
SAN FRANCISCO
STOCKHOLM, COPENHAGEN,
OSLO, HELSINKI, AND
REYKJAVIK
TOKYO
WASHINGTON, D.C.

FODOR'S BUDGET SERIES:

BUDGET BRITAIN
BUDGET CANADA
BUDGET CARIBBEAN
BUDGET EUROPE
BUDGET FRANCE
BUDGET GERMANY
BUDGET HAWAII

BUDGET ITALY
BUDGET JAPAN
BUDGET MEXICO
BUDGET SCANDINAVIA
BUDGET SPAIN
BUDGET TRAVEL IN AMERICA

USA GUIDES:

ALASKA
CALIFORNIA
CAPE COD
COLORADO
FAR WEST
FLORIDA

HAWAII
NEW ENGLAND
PENNSYLVANIA
SOUTH
TEXAS
USA (in one volume)

MANUFACTURED IN THE UNITED STATES OF AMERICA
10 9 8 7 6 5 4 3 2 1

CONTENTS

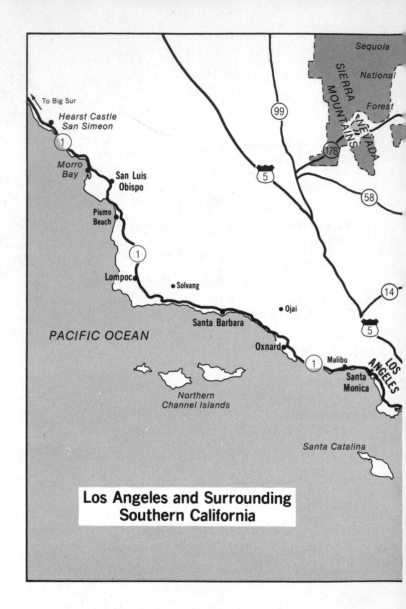

Los Angeles and Surrounding
Southern California

FOREWORD

Los Angeles has long been dubbed the "Entertainment Capital of the World." More than twelve million people spend some time in the "Big Orange" and in the surrounding Southland every year.

Fodor's *Los Angeles* is designed to explain just what this stimulating city is all about. It is written to help you decide what to do and where to go once you're there. The book is intended to be your tool for making some order from the chaos of possibilities. We have therefore concentrated on presenting the broadest *range* of choices offered by the city and within that range to offer *selections* that will be safe, reliable, and of value to you. We think that our descriptions will provide you with enough information on which to make intelligent choices based on your own tastes and pocketbook.

All selections and comments in Fodor's *Los Angeles* are based on the editors' and contributors' personal experience. We believe that our first responsibility is to inform and protect you, the reader. Changes are bound to affect any travel guide, however. We go to press in the early winter of every year, and many changes can occur in Los Angeles while we are on press and during the succeeding twelve months or so when this edition is on sale. We cannot, therefore, be responsible for the sudden closing of a restaurant, a change in an amusement park's admission fees, days, or hours, a shift of chefs (for the worse), and so forth. We welcome letters from readers on these changes or from those whose opinions differ from ours. We will revise our entries for next year's edition when the facts warrant it.

Send your letters to the editors at **Fodor's Travel Guides, 2 Park Avenue, New York, NY 10016.** Continental or British Commonwealth readers may prefer to write to **Fodor's Travel Guides, 9–10 Market Place, London W1N 7AG, England.**

Finally, a word about the "nearby attractions": Los Angeles is the major port of entry for Southern California. This book would have to be published in several volumes if we tried to cover it all. Instead, we have selected only a few of the most popular or rewarding side trips a visitor might want to add to an itinerary after arriving in the city.

FACTS AT YOUR FINGERTIPS

 FACTS AND FIGURES. The third largest state in size, California's population topped 26 million in 1981. It hosts millions of visitors yearly, and tourism has replaced agriculture as the state's number one industry. California stretches almost 1,000 miles from the Oregon border in the north to the Mexican border in the south. It is an exciting blend of Spanish–Mexican, European, Asian, and Yankee spirits.

Los Angeles and environs are certainly an integral part of our largest western state. It's home to the aerospace industry, the glamour industries of film and television and a focal point for our nation's fashion and music. It is in fact the center for industry and agriculture in the west and boasts the largest and busiest harbor on the West Coast.

The boundaries of Los Angeles encompass more than 464 square miles and combine urban, desert, mountain, and coastal landscapes. This area is large enough to hold the cities of St. Louis, Cleveland, Milwaukee, Boston, Pittsburgh, and San Francisco, as well as the borough of Manhattan in New York City. More than 6,500 miles of roads and freeways make the Big Orange the most modern city in the United States for land transportation.

The population of Los Angeles proper is nearly three million; approximately thirteen million inhabitants live in the four-county metropolitan area.

 PLANNING YOUR TRIP. If you don't want to bother making your own reservations a travel agent won't cost a cent, except for specific charges like telegrams. He gets his fee from the hotel or carrier he books for you. A travel agent can also be of help for those who prefer to take their vacations on a "package tour"—thus keeping their own planning to a minimum. If you prefer the convenience of standardized accommodations, remember that the various hotel and motel chains publish free directories of their members. Such directories will enable you to plan and reserve everything ahead of time.

If you don't belong to an auto club, now is the time to join one. It can be very helpful about routings and providing emergency service on the road. If you plan to route yourself, make certain the map you get is dated for the current year. (Highways and thruways are appearing and being extended at an astonishingly rapid rate.) Some of the major oil companies will send maps and mark preferred routes on them if you tell them what you have in mind. Try: *Exxon Touring Service,* Exxon Corporation, 1251 Avenue of the Americas, New York, NY 10020; *Texaco Travel Service,* P.O. Box 1459, Houston, TX 77001; or *Mobil Oil Corp. Touring Service,* P.O. Box 25, Versailles, KY 40383. In addition, most areas have their own maps that pinpoint attractions, list historical sites, parks, and so on. City chambers of commerce are also good sources of information. Specific addresses are given under *Tourist Information.*

1

Plan to board the pets, discontinue paper and milk deliveries, and tell your local police and fire departments when you'll be leaving and when you expect to return. Ask a kindly neighbor to keep an eye on your house; protect your swimming pool against intruders. Have a friend keep your mail, or have it held at the post office. Look into the purchase of trip insurance (including baggage), and make certain your auto, fire, and other insurance policies are up to date. Today most people who travel use credit cards for important expenses such as gas, repairs, lodgings, and some meals. Consider converting the greater portion of your trip money into traveler's checks. Arrange to have your lawn mowed at the usual times, and leave that kindly neighbor your itinerary (insofar as is possible), car license number, and a key to your home (and tell police and firefighters he has it). Since some hotel and motel chains give discounts (10–25 percent) to senior citizens, be sure to have some sort of identification along if you qualify. Usually AARP or NRTA membership is best. (See below at the end of the *Hotels and Motels* section.)

VISITOR INFORMATION. In 1979 the *California Office of Tourism* (P.O. Box 1499, Sacramento 95805, tel. 916–322–1396) was established. Visitor information is available through that office and at the many convention and visitors' bureaus or chambers of commerce throughout the state. See individual sections for listings.

TIPS FOR BRITISH VISITORS. Passports. You will need a valid passport and a U.S. visa (which can only be put in a passport of the ten-year kind). You can obtain the visa either through your travel agent or directly from the *United States Embassy,* Visa and Immigration Department, 24 Grosvenor Sq., London W1 (tel. 01–499 7010/3443).

No vaccinations are required for entry.

Customs. If you are twenty-one or over, you can take into the U.S. 200 cigarettes, 50 cigars, or 2 kilos of tobacco; 1 U.S. liter of alcohol; duty-free gifts to a value of $100. Don't take in meat or meat products, seeds, plants, fruits, and so on. And avoid narcotics like the plague.

Insurance. We recommend that you insure yourself to cover health and motoring mishaps with *Europ Assistance,* 252 High St., Croydon CRO 1NF (tel. 01–680 1234). Their excellent service is all the more valuable when you consider the possible costs of health care in the U.S.

Tour Operators. The price battle that has raged over transatlantic fares has meant that most tour operators now offer excellent budget packages to the U.S. Among those you might consider as you plan your trip are:
American Express, 6 Haymarket, London SW1.

Thomas Cook Ltd., P.O. Box 36, Thorpe Wood, Peterborough, PE 3 6SB.
Cosmos, Cosmos House, 1 Bromley Common, Bromley, Kent BR2 9LX.
Cunard, 8 Berkeley St., London W1.
Jetsave, Sussex House, London Rd., East Grinstead RH19 1LD.
Page and Moy, 136–140 London Rd., Leicester LE2 1EN.
Speedbird, 152 King St., London W6 OQU.

Air Fares. We suggest that you explore the current scene for budget flight possibilities. All the main transatlantic carriers have standby tickets available a short time before the flight only, as well as APEX and other fares at a considerable saving over the full price. Quite frankly, only business travelers who don't have to watch the price of their tickets fly full price these days. They usually find themselves sitting right beside an APEX passenger!

Hotels. You may have need of a fast booking service to find a motel room. One of the very best ways to do this is to contact *HBI-HOTAC*, Globegate House, Pound Lane, London NW10 (tel. 01–451 2311). They book rooms for most of the large chains (Holiday Inns, Hilton, Ramada, and others), and so you can have multiple choices with only one contact. HBI-HOTAC specializes in booking for business firms but also deal with the general public.

 WHEN TO GO. With the Humboldt Current (cold) swirling toward the north of this region and the Japanese Current (warm) nudging northern coastal strips, with America's highest, coolest mountains and its deepest, sun-sizzled valleys, the humidity and temperature readings in this region are as varied as the patterns on your grandmother's favorite patchwork quilt. Here and there sea breezes cause a temperature variance of as much as 5 to 15 degrees within the limits of a single city.

Nonetheless, Los Angeles normally has a pleasant and mild year-round climate. In the summer the city's renowned smog will cause a problem for some who have respiratory ailments.

Average summer temperature is 79.5 degrees Fahrenheit; the winter average is 69.3 degrees Fahrenheit.

The rainy season usually runs from November through March. In January there usually occur the heaviest downpours, even though thunderstorms are infrequent. Summers are practically rainless. The coast may be overcast in late spring.

In fall, winter, and early spring occasional descending Santa Ana foehn winds rage from the northeast, picking up a considerable amount of dust. These winds reach speeds of 35 to 50 mph and cause a heat cover to envelope the city and surrounding areas. The most discomfort occurs in the valley regions.

PACKING. *What to take, what to wear.* Make a packing list for each member of the family. Then check off items as you pack them. It will save time and reduce confusion. Time-savers to carry along include extra photo film (plenty), suntan lotion, insect repellent, toothpaste, soap, and so on. Always carry an extra pair of glasses, including sunglasses, particularly if they're prescription ones. A travel iron is always a good tote along, as are some plastic bags (small and large) for wet suits, socks, and so on. They are also excellent for packing shoes, cosmetics, and other easily damaged items. If you fly, remember that despite signs to the contrary, airport security X-ray machines do in fact damage film rolls in about 17 percent of the cases. Have them inspected separately, or pack them in special protective bags. Fun extras to carry include binoculars, a compass, and a magnifying glass to read fine-print maps.

All members of the family should have sturdy shoes with nonslip soles. Keep them handy in the back of the car. You never know when you may want to stop and clamber along a rocky trail. Store the family raingear in a separate bag in the back of the car so that no one will have to get out and hunt for it in a downpour en route.

Women will probably want to stick to one or two basic colors for their holiday wardrobes so that they can manage with one set of accessories. If possible, include one knit or jersey dress or a pants suit, and for the winter months take a *lightweight* coat. For dress-up evenings, take along a few "basic" dresses that you can vary with a simple change of accessories. In that way you can dress up or down to suit the occasion.

Be sure to check what temperatures will be like along the route. Traveling in mountains can mean cool evenings, even in summer, and so can traveling through the desert. An extra sweater is always a safe thing to pack even if only to protect you from the air conditioning.

Men will probably want to take a jacket along for dining out, especially for Los Angeles. T-shirts are now accepted almost everywhere during the daytime; in some resort areas they're worn evenings as well. Don't forget extra slacks.

Pack lightly, but keep weather extremes in mind. The morning and evening fogs and frequent windy gusts suggest the advisability of having a sweater or a jacket available, plus a scarf for special hairstyles.

Planning a lot of sun time? Don't forget something to wear en route to the pool, beach, or lakefront and for those few days when your tender skin is getting reacquainted with the sun.

CLIMATE. Seasons in Los Angeles and the Southland are not as defined as in most other temperate areas of the world. November through March brings rain, so count on needing an umbrella during a winter trip. But in June, July, August, and September there is virtually no rain at all. Smog is common during the summer months of July, August, and September.

The Pacific Ocean is the primary moderating influence; however, coastal mountains along the north and east sides of the Los Angeles coastal basin act as a buffer against extreme summer heat and winter cold occurring in desert and plateau regions. Between mild sea breezes and either hot (the Santa Ana wind) or cold winds from the interior, a variety of weather conditions results. An unusual aspect of Los Angeles' climate is the pronounced difference in temperature, humidity, cloudiness, fog, rain, and sunshine over short distances.

	Average High Daily Temp.
January	65° F
February	67°
March	68°
April	69°
May	72°
June	75°
July	82°
August	84°
September	83°
October	78°
November	73°
December	69°

WHAT WILL IT COST? This is obviously a crucial question and one of the most difficult to answer. The American Automobile Association estimates that expenses for a couple driving across the country should average around $48.00 per day for meals, $48.00 for lodging, and about $8.00 for each 100 miles for gasoline (at 20 miles to the gallon). Though our own figures are slightly higher, we hope you can do it for less, and have included a number of concrete and practical suggestions for cutting costs wherever you can. A couple can travel comfortably in California for about $125 a day (not counting gasoline or other transportation costs), as you can see in the table below.

In some areas you can cut expenses by traveling off season, when hotel rates are usually lower. The budget-minded traveler can also find bargain accommodations at tourist homes or family-style YMCAs and YWCAs. Both California state and national parks offer limited lodgings; book early. Colleges offer dormitory accommodations to tourists during the summer vacations at single-room rates of $2.00–$10.00 per night, with meals from $0.60–$3.50. A directory of some 200 such opportunities all over the U.S. is *Mort's Guide to Low-Cost Vacations and Lodgings on College Campuses, USA-Canada* from Mort Barrish Assoc., Inc., Research Park, State Rd., Princeton, NJ 08540.

Another way to cut down on the cost of your trip is to look for out-of-the-way resorts. Travelers are frequently rewarded by discovering very attractive areas that haven't as yet begun to draw quantities of people.

If you are budgeting your trip (who isn't?), don't forget to set aside a realistic amount for the possible rental of sports equipment (perhaps including a boat or canoe), entrance fees to amusement and historical sites, and so on. There are no tolls on the highways, but allow for modest bridge tolls, extra film for cameras, and souvenirs.

Typical Expenses for Two People

Room at moderate hotel or motel	$50.00
Breakfast at hotel or motel, including tip	12.00
Lunch at inexpensive restaurant, including tip	9.00
Dinner at moderate restaurant, including tip	30.00
Sightseeing bus tour	17.00
Evening drink	4.00
Admission to museum or historic site	5.00
	$127.00

After lodging your next biggest expense will be food, and here you can make very substantial economies if you are willing to get along with only one meal a day (or less) in a restaurant. Plan to eat simply and to picnic. It will save you time and money, and it will help you enjoy your trip more. That beautiful scenery does not have to whiz by at 55 miles per hour. There are picnic and rest areas, often well-equipped and in scenic spots, even on highways and thruways, and so finding a pleasant place to stop is usually not difficult. Before you leave home, put together a picnic kit.

If you like a drink before dinner or bed, bring your own bottle. Most hotels and motels supply ice free or for very little, but the markup on alcoholic beverages in restaurants, bars, lounges, and dining rooms is enormous, and in some areas peculiar laws apply regarding alcohol consumption. In any case, a good California dry white wine makes a fine apéritif and can be far cheaper than a cocktail.

 HINTS TO THE MOTORIST. Probably the first precaution you will take is to have your car thoroughly checked by your regular dealer or service station to make sure that everything is in good shape. Second, you may find it wise to join an auto club that can provide you with trip-planning information, insurance coverage, and emergency and repair service along the way. Third, if you must have your car serviced, look for a repair shop displaying the *National Institute for Automotive Service Excellence* seal. *NIASE* tests and certifies the competence of auto mechanics in about 10,000 repair shops nationwide.

Driving in California is probably more unpredictable and challenging than in any other part of the nation. With an auto registration of some nine million, the Golden State easily outranks its two closest contenders, New York and Texas, each of which issues five and one-half million license plates. If you enter a California freeway, be sure you have a full gas tank.

California speed limits comply with federal law—55 mph. Tops for cars hauling trailers is 50, but lower limits sometimes are posted. General speed limit for school zones and residential and business districts is 25, again, except when posted. And there are special speed zones ranging from 25 to 55, depending on what the sign says at the entrance to such zones. Watch the signs: There is no state requirement for posting warning signs on radar, mechanical, or electrical speed-checking devices.

DESERT DRIVING

If you are driving to the southeast from Los Angeles into southern California, you will encounter some stretches of desert driving. Service industries across the desert have grown in number during the past decade to the point that the hazards of desert driving have been minimized. A principal point to check before crossing the hot desert should be your tires. Put them at normal driving pressure or slightly below. Heat builds pressure. If your car seems to be bouncing too readily, stop to let your tires cool. If you have a good radiator, don't bother about extra water—except for Death Valley—but keep an eye on the water gauge. Be alert for sudden sandstorms and rainstorms. If you have a car radio, keep it tuned to local stations for information about unusual weather conditions.

MOUNTAIN DRIVING

Unless you venture onto exotic mountain roads, you should have little trouble with mountain driving. Today's mountain roads are engineered for the ordinary driver. They are normally wide, well graded, and safe. Be especially wary of exceeding the speed limit posted for curves. Keep to the right. If your normal driving is at low altitudes, have a garage mechanic check your carburetor. It may need adjusting for mountain driving. If your car stalls and your temperature gauge is high, a vapor lock may be the problem. Bathe the fuel pump with a damp cloth for a few minutes.

If you get stuck on any kind of road, pull off the highway onto the shoulder, raise the hood, attach something white (a handkerchief, a scarf, or a piece of tissue) to the door handle on the driver's side, and sit inside and wait. This is especially effective on limited-access highways, usually patroled vigilantly by state highway patrol officers. A special warning to women stalled at night: Remain inside the car with doors locked, and make sure the Good Samaritan is indeed a Good Samaritan. It's easier to find telephones along the major highways these days since their locations are more frequently marked than they used to be.

PULLING A TRAILER

Most states have special safety regulations for trailers, and these change frequently. If you plan to operate your trailer in several states, check with your motor club, the police, or the state motor vehicle department about the rules. Also, talk it over with the dealer from whom you buy or lease your trailer. Generally, speed limits for cars hauling trailers are lower, the parking of trailers (and automobiles) is prohibited on expressways and freeways, and tunnels often bar trailers equipped with cooking units that use propane gas.

 WHAT TO DO WITH THE PETS. Traveling by car with your pet dog or cat? More and more motels and hotels accept them. Some turn them down, some want to look first, some offer special facilities. Check first before you register. If it's a first trip with your pet, accustom it to car travel by short trips in your neighborhood. And when you're packing, include its favorite food, bowls, and toys. Discourage your dog from riding with its head out the window. Wind and dust particles can permanently damage its eyes. Dogs are especially susceptible to heat stroke. Don't leave your dog in a parked car on a hot day while you dawdle over lunch. Keep your dog's bowl handy for water during stops for gas; gasoline attendants are usually very cooperative about this. Make sure your pet exercises periodically; this is a good way for you and the kids to unwind from unbroken traveling, too.

 HOTELS AND MOTELS. *General Hints.* Don't take potluck for lodgings. You'll waste a lot of time hunting and often won't be happy with the accommodations you finally find. If you are without reservations, by all means begin looking early in the afternoon. If you have reservations but expect to arrive later than 5:00 or 6:00 P.M., advise the hotel or motel in advance. Some places will not, unless advised, hold reservations after 6:00 P.M. And if you hope to get a room at the hotel's minimum rate, be sure to reserve ahead or arrive very early.

In Los Angeles or any resort area in southern California, try to reserve *well* in advance. Include a deposit for all places except motels (and for motels if they request one). Many chain or associated motels and hotels will make advance reservations for you at affiliated hostelries of your choosing along your route.

A number of hotels and motels have one-day laundry and dry-cleaning services, and many motels have coin laundries. Most motels but not all have telephones in the rooms. If you want to be sure of room service, however, better stay at a hotel. Many motels have swimming pools, and even beachfront hotels frequently have pools. Even some motels in the heart of large cities have pools. An advantage at motels is the free parking. There's seldom a charge for parking at country and resort hotels.

Hotel and motel chains. In addition to the hundreds of excellent independent motels and hotels throughout the state, there are also many that belong to national or regional chains. To many travelers a major advantage of the chains is the ease of making reservations en route or at one fell swoop in advance. If you are a guest at a member hotel or motel one night, the management will be delighted to secure a sure booking at one of its affiliated hotels at no cost to you. Chains also usually have toll-free WATS (800) lines to assist you in making reservations on your own. This, of course, saves you time, money, and worry. For directory information on (800) lines, dial (800) 555–1212 to see if there is an (800) number for the hotel you want to reach.

Since the single biggest expense of your whole trip is lodging, you may well be discouraged and angry at the prices of some hotel and motel rooms, particularly when you know you are paying for things such as a heated swimming pool, wall-to-wall carpeting, a huge color TV set, two huge double beds for only two people, meeting rooms, a cocktail lounge, maybe even a putting green you neither need nor want. Nationwide motel prices for two people now average $60.00 a night; hotel prices start at $70.00, with the average around $75.00. This explains the recent rapid spread of a number of budget motel chains whose rates average $40.00 for a single and $50.00 for a double, an obvious advantage.

The main national motel chains are Holiday Inn, Howard Johnson's, Quality Inns, Ramada Inns, Sheraton Motor Inns, and TraveLodge. Other popular family-type motel chains include Best Western, Friendship Inn Hotels, Rodeway Inns, Vagabond Motor Hotels, and Motel 6.

HOTEL AND MOTEL CATEGORIES

Hotels and motels in all the Fodor's guidebooks to the U.S.A. are divided into five categories and arranged primarily by price but also taking into consideration the degree of comfort, the amount of service, and the atmosphere that will surround you in the establishment of your choice. Occasionally an establishment with *deluxe* prices will offer only first-class service or atmosphere, and so we list it as *expensive*. On the other hand, a hotel that charges only *moderate* prices may offer superior comfort and service, and so we list it as *expensive*. Our ratings are flexible and subject to change. In every case, however, the dollar ranges for each category are clearly stated before each listing of establishments. We should also point out that many fine hotels and motels had to be omitted for lack of space.

Super Deluxe: This category is reserved for only a few hotels. In addition to giving the visitor all the amenities discussed under the deluxe category (below), the super deluxe hotel has a special atmosphere of glamour, good taste, and dignity. Its history will inevitably be full of many anecdotes, and it will probably be a favored meeting spot of local society. In short, super deluxe means the top.

Deluxe: The minimum facilities must include bath and shower in all rooms, valet and laundry service, suites available, a well-appointed restaurant and a bar (where local law permits), room service, TV and telephone in room, air conditioning and heat (unless locale makes one or the other unnecessary), pleasing décor, and an atmosphere of luxury, calm, and elegance. There should be ample and personalized service. In a deluxe *motel* there may be less service rendered by employees and more by automatic machines (such as refrigerators and ice-making machines in your room), but there should be a minimum of do it yourself in a truly deluxe establishment.

Expensive: All rooms must have bath or shower, valet and laundry service, restaurant and bar (local law permitting), at least some room service, TV and telephone in room, attractive furnishings, heat and air conditioning (locale not precluding). Although décor may be as good as that in deluxe establishments, hotels and motels in this category are frequently designed for commercial travelers or for families in a hurry and are somewhat impersonal in terms of service.

As for *motels* in this category, valet and laundry service will probably be lacking; the units will be outstanding primarily for their convenient location and functional character, not for their attractive or comfortable qualities.

(**Note:** We often list top-notch, ultramodern hotels in this category in spite of the fact that they have rates as high as deluxe hotels and motels. We do this because certain elements are missing in these hotels. Usually the missing element is service. In spite of automated devices such as ice-cube-making machines and message-signaling buzzers, service in these hotels is not up to the standard by which we judge deluxe establishments. Room service is incredibly slow in some of these places, and the entire atmosphere is often one of expediency over comfort, economy of manpower and overhead taking precedence over attention to the desires of guests.)

Moderate: Each room should have an attached bath or shower; there should be a restaurant *or* a coffee shop, a TV and a telephone in room, heat and air conditioning (locale not precluding), a relatively convenient location, clean and comfortable rooms, and public rooms. *Motels* in this category may not have attached bath or shower, may not have a restaurant or a coffee shop (though one is usually nearby), and, of course, may have no public rooms to speak of.

Inexpensive: Nearby bath or shower, telephone available, and clean rooms are the minimum.

Free parking is assumed at all motels and motor hotels; you must pay for parking at most city hotels, though certain establishments have free parking, frequently for occupants of higher-than-minimum-rate rooms. *Babysitter* lists are always available in good hotels and motels, and cribs for young children are always on hand—sometimes at no cost but more frequently at a cost of $3.00 or $4.00 per night. The cost of a cot supplementing the beds in your room will also be around $3.00 per night, but moving an extra single bed into a room will cost from $7.00 in better hotels and motels.

Senior citizens may in some cases receive special discounts on lodgings. The Days Inn chain offers various discounts to anyone 55 or older. Holiday Inns give a 10 percent discount year round to members of the NRTA (write to National Retired Teachers Association, Membership Division, 215 Long Beach Blvd., Long Beach, CA 90802; 213–432–5781) and the AARP (write to American Association of Retired Persons, Membership Division, 215 Long Beach Blvd., Long Beach, CA 90802). Howard Johnson's Motor Lodges give 10 percent off to NRTA and AARP members (call 800–654–2000); and the ITT Sheraton chain gives 25 percent (call 800–325–3535) to members of the AARP, the NRTA, the National Association of Retired Persons, The Catholic Golden Age of United Societies of U.S.A., and the Old Age Security Pensioners of Canada.

Los Angeles' Bed-and-Breakfast Inns offer a rather new approach toward visitor accommodations but are not as popular as they are two hours north of the city in Santa Barbara, as well as in other northern spots between Los Angeles and San Francisco, where the custom has really caught on.

The bed-and-breakfast establishments in and around Los Angeles County are priced conservatively, most in the moderate range. All offer highly personalized service to their guests. They're small and reservations are always required.

Ambience in these hideaways includes Victorian and Art Deco, highlighted daily by fresh southern Californian flowers and fluffy towels. Breakfast, usually special, may consist of tasty croissants or San Francisco sourdough toast, fresh fruits and juices, and wonderful coffee and teas.

More information on these charming hostelries is available from *California Houseguests International*, 6051 Lindley Ave., #6, Tarzana, CA 91356; (213) 344–7878. This organization represents the best locations of this kind in Los Angeles and throughout California; staff members in these homes are sometimes multilingual, speaking French, German, and Spanish. Prices range from $45 to $125 for two, with breakfast. The average charge is $65.

Throughout California, bed-and-breakfast accommodations can be arranged by *International Friends*, 5819 Green Oak Dr. in Los Angeles; (213) 465–8331. A small deposit is required; prices start at $20 per person, double occupancy. This company also can arrange group dinners in private homes, picnics, and other outings reflecting the California lifestyle. For those specifically interested in bed-and-breakfast establishments in and around Santa Barbara, write the *Bed-and-Breakfast Innkeepers Guild of Santa Barbara*, P.O. Box 20246, Santa Barbara, CA 93120.

Styles and standards vary widely, of course; generally private baths are not common, and rates are often moderate. In many small towns such guest houses are excellent examples of the best a region has to offer. Each one is different so that its advantage is precisely the opposite of that "no surprise" uniformity that motel chains pride themselves on. In popular tourist areas, state or local tourist information offices or chambers of commerce usually have lists of homes that provide spare rooms for paying guests, and such a listing usually means that the places included have been inspected and meet some standard of cleanliness and comfort and reasonable pricing. A nationwide *Guide to Guest Houses and Tourist Homes USA* is available from Tourist House Associates of America, Inc., P.O. Box 355-A, Greentown, PA 18426.

Youth Hostels. Hostels are a budget-minded alternative to hotel and motel accommodations. One must be a member of the American Youth Hostel/International Youth Hostel Federation to use its facilities at a discounted rate, but nonmembers may also stay at hostels for a slightly increased rate. There are two main hostels in the Los Angeles area, and they are open to all ages.

The *American Youth Hostel* is located in Harbor City, south of Los Angeles and close to such South Bay cities as Palos Verdes and Redondo Beach. Although sleeping bags are recommended, sheets and blankets are available to rent. There's a communal kitchen for cooking your own meals. The hostel sleeps seventy, and you may stay three days as a nonmember, five as a member.

The *Hollywood YMCA Hotel and Youth Hostel* is close to the core of the city, although the area is not safe during the evening hours. Hostelers are taken on a first-come, first-served basis. Rates are under $10.00 per person. Bring your own sleeping bag.

Both hostels offer simple accommodations. Dormitories are segregated by sex. In season it is wise to reserve space ahead; write or phone the hostel. Check with the Los Angeles Visitors Bureau (213–488–9100) or check a library for a copy of the *Official American Youth Hostels Handbook* by Michael Frome. It lists 240 or more U.S. hostels and includes maps. As an alternative (and you need not be a member), write to American Youth Hostel Association, Inc., 1332 L Street, N.W., 8th Floor, Washington, DC. 20005. If you join the association, a copy of the hostel guide and handbook will be sent to you.

 DINING OUT. The best advice for evening meals is to make reservations in advance whenever possible anywhere in the Southland but certainly in Los Angeles and in some of the resort areas, including Palm Springs.

Some restaurants, particularly in the evening, are fussy about customers' dress. For women, pants and pants suits are now almost universally acceptable. For men, tie and jacket remains the standard. Shorts are almost always frowned on for both men and women. Standards of dress are becoming more relaxed, and so a neatly dressed customer will usually experience no problem. If in doubt about accepted dress at a particular establishment, call ahead.

If you're traveling with children, you may want to find out if a restaurant has a children's menu and commensurate prices. (Many do.)

When figuring the tip on your check, base it on the total charges for the meal, not on the grand total if that total includes a state sales tax. Don't tip on tax.

RESTAURANT CATEGORIES

Restaurants located in Los Angeles proper are categorized in this volume by type of cuisine: French, Chinese, and so on, with restaurants of a general nature listed as Continental-International. Restaurants in less populous areas are divided into price categories as follows: *deluxe, expensive, moderate,* and *inexpensive.* As a general rule, expect restaurants in metropolitan areas to be higher in price than nonmetropolitan areas, although many restaurants that feature foreign cuisine are often surprisingly inexpensive. We should also point out that limitations of space make it impossible to include every establishment. We have therefore included those that we consider the best within each type of cuisine and price range.

Although the names of the various restaurant categories are standard throughout this series, the prices listed under each category may vary from area to area. In every case, however, the dollar ranges for each category are clearly stated before each listing of establishments.

Deluxe: This category will be pertinent to Los Angeles and a few select resort areas. This designation indicates an outstanding restaurant that is lavishly decorated and may delight in the awe that it inspires among the humble. Sometimes overpriced and overrated, it charges the customer at least $15.00 for soup, entrée, and dessert. The average price is apt to be closer to $20.00, although some run much higher than this. As in all our other categories, this price range *does not include* cocktails, wines, cover or table charges, tip, or extravagant house specialties. The price range here indicates a typical roast beef (prime ribs) dinner. A restaurant in this category must have a superb wine list, excellent service, immaculate kitchens, and a large, well-trained staff. Many fine restaurants around Los Angeles fall into this category. Each has its own well-deserved reputation for excellence, perhaps a house specialty or two for which it is famous, and an atmosphere of elegance or unique décor.

Expensive: In addition to the expected dishes, it will offer one or two house specialties, a wine list and cocktails, air conditioning (unless locale makes it unnecessary), a reputation for very good food and an adequate staff, an elegant décor, and an appropriately dressed clientele.

Moderate: Cocktails and/or beer, air conditioning (when needed), clean kitchen, adequate staff, better-than-average service. General reputation for good, wholesome food.

Inexpensive: The bargain place in town, it is clean even if plain. It will have air conditioning, when necessary, tables (not a counter), and a clean kitchen and will attempt to provide adequate service.

Chains: There are now several chains of restaurants, some of them nationwide, that offer reliable eating at excellent budget prices. Some of the ones that operate in California are *Denny's; Shakey's Pizza Parlors,* 21 kinds of pizza; *Sizzler;* and *Sambo's,* simple food, surprisingly inexpensive. *Sheraton* and *Holiday Inn* motels and hotels have all-you-can-eat, fixed-price buffets on certain days.

 TIPPING. Tipping is a personal expression of your appreciation of someone who has taken pleasure and pride in giving you attentive, efficient, and personal service. Because standards of personal service are highly uneven, you should, when you get genuinely good service, feel secure in rewarding it, and when you feel that the service you got was slovenly, indifferent, or surly, don't hesitate to show your reaction by withholding or reducing your usual tip. Remember that in many places the help are paid very little and depend on tips for the better part of their income. This practice is supposed to give them incentive to serve you well. These days the going rate on *restaurant* service is 15 percent on the amount *before* taxes. Tipping at counters is not universal, but many people leave 25¢ on anything up to $1.00 and 10% on anything over that. For *bellhops,* 50¢ per bag is usual. However, if you load him down with all manner of bags, hatboxes, cameras, coats, and so on, you might consider giving an extra quarter or two. For one-night stays in most *hotels* and *motels* you leave nothing. If you stay longer, at the end of your stay leave the maid $2.00–$3.00 per day or $5.00 per person per week for multiple occupancy. If you are staying at an *American Plan* hostelry (meals included) $1.50 per day per person for the waiter or waitress is considered sufficient and is left at the end of your stay. However, if you have been surrounded by an army of servants (one bringing relishes, another rolls, etc.), add a few extra dollars and give the lump sum to the captain or maître d'hotel when you leave, asking him to allocate it.

For the many other services you may receive in a big hotel or resort, figure roughly as follows: doorman, 50¢ for taxi handling, $1.00 for help with baggage; bellhop, 50¢ per bag, more if you load him down with extras; parking attendant,

$1.00; bartender, 15 percent; room service, 10–15 percent of that bill; laundry or valet service, 15 percent; pool attendant, $1.00 per day; snackbar waiter at pool, beach, or golf club, 50¢ per person for food and 15 percent of the beverage check; locker attendant, 50¢ per person per day, or $2.50 per week; golf caddies, $1.00–$5.00 per bag, or 15 percent of the greens fee for an 18-hole course, or $3.00 on a free course; barbers, $1.00; shoeshiners, 50–75¢; hairdressers, $3.00; manicurists, $1.50.

Transportation: Give 25¢ for any taxi fare under $1.00 and 15 percent for any above; however, drivers in Los Angeles *expect* 20 percent, limousine service, 20 percent, car rental agencies, nothing. Bus porters are tipped 50¢ per bag, drivers nothing. On charters and package tours, conductors and drivers usually get $25–$30 per day from the group as a whole, but be sure to ask whether this tip has already been figured into the package cost. On short, local sightseeing runs, the driver-guide may get $1.00 per person, more if you think he has been especially helpful or personable. Airport bus drivers get nothing; redcaps in resort areas, 50¢ per suitcase; elsewhere, 40¢. Tipping at curbside check-in is unofficial, but same as above. On the plane, no tipping.

Railroads suggest that you leave 10–15 percent per meal for dining-car waiters; the steward who seats you is not tipped. Sleeping-car porters get about $1.50 per person per night. The 40–50¢ that you pay a railway station baggage porter is not a tip but the set fee that he must hand in at the end of the day along with the ticket stubs he has used. Therefore his tip is anything you give him above that, 50–75¢ per bag depending on how heavy your luggage is.

SENIOR CITIZEN AND STUDENT DISCOUNTS. Some attractions throughout the Southland offer considerable discounts to senior citizens and students. Some may require special city-issued senior-citizen identification, but in most cases showing a driver's license, passport, or some other proof of age will suffice—"senior" generally being defined as sixty-five or over for men and sixty-two or over for women. Museums, first-run and neighborhood movie theaters, and even some stores often post special senior-citizen rates. Those places offering student discounts are generally somewhat more stringent in their proof requirements—a high school or a college ID, international student traveler card, or evidence of age may be requested. Unfortunately, there is no uniformity on these matters.

DRINKING LAWS. In California the minimum age for the consumption of alcohol is twenty-one. In Los Angeles alcoholic beverages—by the bottle or by the drink —can be purchased from 6:00 A.M. to 2:00 A.M. daily. Package sales are made in liquor stores, some groceries, and drugstores. Most restaurants, bars, nightclubs, and pubs are licensed to serve a full line of beverages, whereas some have permits to serve beer and wine only. The legal age for the purchase of alcoholic beverages is also twenty-one; proof of age is required.

One quart of alcohol can be imported or transported from another state or country.

BUSINESS HOURS, HOLIDAYS, AND LOCAL TIME. Los Angeles and the areas up and down the coast, like the rest of the United States, are on Standard Time from the last Sunday in October until the last Sunday in April. In April the clock is advanced one hour for Daylight Savings Time and in October is turned back an hour. The entire state lies within the Pacific Time Zone, which is three hours earlier in the day than the Eastern Time Zone, eight hours earlier than Greenwich Mean Time, and eighteen hours earlier on the clock and calendar than Sydney when Sydney is on Daylight Savings Time.

Business hours for banks are pretty much the same as those in the rest of the country, by and large 9:00 A.M. to 3:00 P.M., with some opening earlier or staying open later. Shops open at 9:00 A.M. and department stores at 10:00 or 10:30 A.M. Offices operate from 8:30 A.M. to 4:30 P.M. or from 9:00 A.M. to 5:00 P.M..

Most businesses, banks, and many restaurants close for the following holidays (the dates are for 1984): New Year's Day, January 1; Washington's Birthday (observance), February 22; Easter Sunday, April 22; Memorial Day (observance), May 28; Independence Day, July 4; Labor Day, September 3; Thanksgiving Day, November 22; and Christmas Day, December 25.

In addition, banks and some businesses may be closed on Lincoln's Birthday, February 12; Good Friday (from noon), April 20; Columbus Day (observance), October 8; Election Day (partially), November 6; and Veterans Day, November 11.

SPORTS. Southern California offers a wide variety of spectator sports throughout the year. January brings the most famous parade, the Tournament of Roses on New Year's Day. The Rose Bowl football game is held that afternoon. Although reserved seats can be bought, many people camp out on the sidewalk, using stoves, sleeping bags, chairs, and so on, a day in advance to secure ideal viewing sites. Other exciting January events include the Chinese New Year Parade, the Mounted Police Rodeo and Parade in Palm Springs, and the Triple Crown Women's Golf Tournament in Palm Springs.

February is the month of the famous Bob Hope Desert Golf Classic in Palm Springs, and in March the Long Beach Grand Prix features International Formula 1 race cars passing through the city in a 161-mile competition.

The Dodgers open the **baseball** season in April.

Del Mar Turf Club begins its **racing** season in July; it runs through September.

September ushers in the famous Los Angeles **County Fair** in Pomona as well as the Concours d'Elegance, the **antique car parade** in Santa Barbara.

The holiday season begins with the Los Angeles Times' NASCAR 500 at the Ontario Motor Speedway in November.

All along the coast there are **sportfishing** landings and public fishing piers. Marina del Rey has dock fishing as well as charter-boat fishing (13759 Fiji Way; 822–3625). The Malibu pier has both dock and boat fishing (23000 Pacific Coast Hwy.; 456–8030). The Redondo Beach Pier in the South Bay offers local off-shore fishing (end of Harbor Dr. and Portofino Way; 372–3566). Hermosa Beach Pier has a municipal pier (end of Pier Ave., Hermosa Beach; 372–2124).

Horseback riding is popular at guest ranches in Santa Barbara and Palm Springs. Griffith Park in Los Angeles has 43 miles of horse trails. Commercial stables on the outskirts of the park, including Bar "S" Stables, Livingston Stables, Studio Stables and Sunset Ranch, offer horses for rent.

Offered up and down the coast, participant sports include swimming, surfing, sailing, skin diving, and fishing. Southern California's climate facilitates a year-round sports season. Besides the ocean, Southern California has lakes such as Big Bear, June Lake, and Lake Arrowhead for freshwater fishing, swimming, and boating. Hiking is also popular in these areas.

Golf is another popular Southern California sport. The small, well-known resort of Palm Springs alone has at least thirty-seven golf courses. See individual sections on practical information for details about each area.

Bicycling. For free maps or information regarding bike routes in the state, write to: Bicycle Facility Unit, Division of Highways, P.O. Box 1499, Sacramento, CA 95807; or call (916) 322–4314. For a copy of the 100-page guide of the Pacific Coast Bicentennial Bike Route, send $1.00, plus 6¢ tax (total $1.06) to: Caltrans, 6002 Folsom Blvd., Sacramento, CA 95817.

Los Angeles' Wheelman's Association has information on numerous bike trails; (213) 533–1707. A free bike-trail map is available to visitors at bike shops, City Hall, and the Convention and Visitors Bureau counter in the airport terminal. Rentals at bicycle shops around town and at many independent rental locations, especially along the coast, are abundant.

WINTER SPORTS. Despite the mild climate there are more than twenty established **ski** areas in southern California, half within a two-hour drive of Los Angeles. Depending on the weather, the season runs from November through March. North of Los Angeles, try the slopes of June Lake at June Mountain, Lake Isabella at Shirley Meadows, Mammoth Lakes at Mammouth Mountains, or at Sequoia National Forest at Montegicto–Sequoia, or Wolverton Ski Bowl east of Los Angeles. There is also skiing at Big Bear Lake at Crystal Ridge, Goldmine, or Snow Summit, at Running Springs at Ski Green Valley, or Snow Valley, or at Wrightwood at Holiday Hill, Mountain High, or Ski Sunrise.

Ice skating is a popular sport, especially in Los Angeles proper. Of course, skating takes place in indoor rinks where participants, dressed in summer attire, sometimes embellish their skating outfits with woolen scarfs and mittens to suggest a winter environment.

ROUGHING IT. More and improved camping facilities are springing up each year in California in national parks, national forests, state parks, private camping areas, and trailer parks, which by now have become national institutions.

A current *California State Park Camping Guide* is available for $2.00 at most State Park units or from the Department of Parks and Recreation, P.O. Box 2390, Sacramento, CA 95811, (916) 445–6477. This comprehensive brochure pinpoints all sites throughout the state and includes specific details concerning whether the campsites are developed, primitive, or contain trailer hookups. Sites especially set aside for hikers and bicyclists are noted. Parks able to accommodate group camping and those that have boat landings are designated.

For information on camping in the national park system in California, the Department of Interior offers a free booklet, available from the U.S. National Park Service, 22900 Ventura Blvd., Suite 140, Woodland Hills, CA 91364; (213) 888–3770.

Reservations are recommended for the state parks, especially in summer. There is a reservation charge plus campsite fees. Call Ticketron, (213) 642–3888 for information, but reservations must be made in person at a Ticketron outlet.

To camp in a national park or forest, there is a small fee; people are usually taken on a first-come, first-served basis. Yosemite is an exception, and in summer the valley campgrounds are on a reservation basis. Reservations are taken at the Western Regional Office, National Park Service, 450 Golden Gate Ave., San Francisco, CA 94102, (415) 556–4196, or through Ticketron, P.O. Box 26430, San Francisco, CA 94126.

For information on national forest camping write: U.S. Forest Service, 630 Sansome St., San Francisco, CA 94111, (415) 556–0122. Other useful addresses are the National Campers and Hikers Assoc., 7172 Transit Rd., Buffalo, NY 14221; and Kampgrounds of America, Inc., P.O. Box 30558, Billings, MT 59114—a very helpful commercial camping organization. Adventure Guides, Inc., 36 East 57th St., New York, NY 10022, publishes a book, *Adventure Travel (Source Book for North America)*, which gives details on guided wilderness trips, backpacking, canoeing, rock climbing, covered-wagon treks, scuba diving, and more. The AAA publishes a *California-Nevada Camping Guide*, available to all members; it is revised annually.

 RECREATIONAL VEHICLE PARKS. Inglewood: *Rolling Homes, Inc.,* 5875 Rodeo Rd.; 673–6868. **Desert Hot Springs:** The *Golden Lantern Trailer Lodge,* Dillon Rd., has therapeutic pools. **North Hollywood:** *Valley Trailer Park,* 8250 Lankershim, takes adults only; no pets. **Oxnard:** *Wagon Wheel Trailer Lodge,* 2851 Wagon Wheel Rd. **Santa Monica:** *Beck's Deluxe Trailer Park,* 2818 Colorado Ave., adults only. **Anaheim:** *Vacationland Ltd.;* 1343 S. West Street, across from Disneyland. **Santa Barbara:** *Rancho Santa Barbara,* 333 Old Mill Rd., adults only; no pets.

FARM VACATIONS, GUEST RANCHES, HEALTH SPAS, AND RESORTS. Farm vacations continue to gain adherents, especially among families with children. Some accommodations are deluxe, some extremely simple. Here and there a farm has a swimming pool, whereas others have facilities for trailers and camping. For a directory of farms that take vacationers (including dates, accommodations, rates, etc.), write to Adventure Guides, Inc., 36 East 57th St., New York, NY 10022, for their 240-page book *Farm, Ranch, and Country Vacations.*

Circle Bar B Guest Ranch, situated in the midst of the Santa Ynez Mountains, offers an unusual combination of country living and city amenities. During the day swim, fish, horseback ride, or cook outdoors, and in the evening enjoy live theater or a private cabin with the luxuries of home. For information, write 1800 Refugio Rd., Goleta, CA 93117; or phone (805) 968–1113.

A different approach is taken at *San Ysidro Rancho,* just outside Santa Barbara, where luxury is the key to ranching. Heated swimming pools and a French-Continental restaurant decorate the area around the stables. Celebrities often seek out the Rancho because of the beauty and solitude to be found at San Ysidro. Write 900 San Ysidro Lane, Montecito, CA 93108, (805) 969–5046.

At *Zaca Lake Resort* in the Los Padres National Forest near Santa Barbara the ranching way of life mixes with what you'd normally find in a resort area. Boating and horseback riding are the main activities at Zaca Lake, the site of many of the more memorable Western films made in America. Write P.O. Box 187, Los Olivios, CA 93441, (805) 688–4891.

Spas have been popular for several centuries in Europe, and in California they are now the rage. More and more clients of both sexes, who seek relief from high-stress jobs, are vacationing at luxury spas. Some spas are directed toward pampering their clientele, whereas others are more spartan and offer highly disciplined schedules, enabling their clientele to get back into shape or to keep the ones they have.

As an example of the former, try the *Golden Door,* a superdeluxe establishment in Escondido, California. Write to The Golden Door, 3085 Reynard Way, San Diego, CA 92103, or call (619) 295–3144. Opened in 1958, the nation's smallest, most exclusive, and most expensive fitness center sits serenely in the Escondido Valley. Impressive Japanese architecture and gardens and an air of tranquillity have drawn patrons from all over the world.

A more moderate establishment is the *Oaks* at Ojai. Low-cal meals, personalized weight control, and medical supervision constitute the name of the game. About an hour away from Santa Barbara in a picturesque setting, this elegant hotel, built in 1920, was recently reconstructed. Write 122 East Ojai Ave., Ojai, California 93023.

The *Bermuda Inn* is a no-frills fat farm located on the edge of the Mojave Desert, a little more than an hour's drive from Los Angeles. Weekly and daily rates include low-cal meals, exercise classes, the use of a gym, a jogging track, and a pool, as well as medical supervision. Write Joan Applegate, 43019 Sierra Highway, Lancaster, CA 93534.

HUNTING. For current information on fees, which animals you may hunt, and seasons, write to the Department of Fish and Game, 1416 9th St., Sacramento, CA 95814, or phone (916) 445-7613. Some of the state's wildlife is protected. Deer and black bear hunting licenses are required. Pheasant, dove, and grouse shoots are often in private shooting reserves. No firearms are allowed in either the national or state parks. Big-game hunting is usually confined to national forests or public lands.

 FISHING. Fishing is an all-season sport and business in the Golden State. Commercial fishermen netted over $230 million in 1980. For the sportsfisherfolk, the state's lakes and rivers abound with a great variety of freshwater fish. Several varieties of trout, salmon, bass, and catfish are especially plentiful. Saltwater catches include salmon, yellowtail, rockfish, and bass. For information, write to the Department of Fish and Game in Sacramento, listed under *Hunting*.

 STATE PARKS. Reservations for state parks may be made through the central reservation system. For forms write the Department of Parks and Recreation, P.O. Box 2390, Sacramento, CA 95811. Reservations must be made two weeks in advance of the dates requested.

Reservations may also be made by applying in person to a local Ticketron outlet. In Los Angeles the phone is (213) 642-3888.

California's state park system involves more than 200 units spread over 850,000 acres of mountains and valleys, lakes and plateaus, rivers and deserts, forests and beaches. It also embraces many famous landmarks of the state's heritage.

Two kinds of **campgrounds** exist in the parks. Developed sites include hot showers, laundries, stoves, tables, piped drinking water, and flush toilets. The maximum stay is fifteen days; less in smaller camping areas and during peak summer months. Dogs on leashes are permitted during daylight hours only. At night your dog must stay inside your tent or in an enclosed vehicle.

About half the state's parks are in Southern California. They are strung along the Pacific Coast as beach parks. These beach parks form a chain from San Simeon Beach down to San Diego's Silver Strand and Imperial Beach next to Mexico.

The park closest to Los Angeles proper is the *Will Rogers State Historic Park*, 14253 Sunset Blvd. in Pacific Palisades. This park enshrines the beloved cowboy philospher's ranch home and mementos. "Never met a man I didn't like," said Will. Folks seem to share that feeling, for more than 225,000 visitors come callin' at his house yearly. Free polo games; more details on the park are in the *Practical Information* section.

Information on all state parks is available from the Department of Parks and Recreation, P.O. Box 2390, Sacramento, CA 95811, or phone (916) 445-6477.

NATIONAL PARKS AND MONUMENTS. California numbers among its blessings five national parks and eight national monuments. The precise number located in Southern California depends on whose north–south demarcation is considered. (Many writers, historians, and politicians use the east–west Tehachapi Range, northeast of Santa Barbara, as the dividing line. Others claim the ten counties whose northern boundaries are parallel and slightly to the north of the 36-degree latitude. And there are those who include the four counties bordering the southern ten. *The California Information Almanac,* a state textbook, excludes Santa Barbara and San Luis Obispo counties and a portion of Kern County. It includes Inyo and part of Mono County. This interpretation extends the panhandle of southern California on the east all the way north to the same latitude as San Francisco.)

Sequoia and *Kings Canyon National parks* are considered in Southern California when one of the more generous measures mentioned above is applied. Sequoia has a visitors' center that will provide sightseeing advice. Helpful data and photographs are displayed. Campfire gatherings take place at night. Housekeeping cabins (European plan) are available at Camp Kaweah, where there also exist a coffee shop, a grocery store, a gift shop, and a gas station, all open all year. Giant Forest Lodge (American and European plan) is open from about May 24 to October 25. At Kings Canyon, the lodge, cabins, and housekeeping cabins follow the same schedule and have similar facilities. For additional information write Sequoia Kings Canyon National Parks, Three Rivers, California 93271.

Death Valley National Monument, awesome and historic, is up in the Southern California panhandle that pokes northward to the east of Los Angeles. It's weird, spooky, and memorable, covering almost two million acres. Death Valley is actually a lively place; it has many facilities ranging from rough to resort. The Mesquite Spring Campground has sixty campsites (thirty-day limit), water, and sanitary facilities. Texas Spring Campground, with eighty-five campsites, provides a trailer-parking area, water, fireplaces, and sanitary facilities. The Visitors' Center is open year round.

Joshua Tree National Monument, a 557,992-acre sprawl, preserves the unique yucca species, named by pioneering Mormons to whom its arms seemed raised in supplication in the manner of Joshua in the Bible. The Visitors' Center is at Twenty-nine Palms, and there are eight campgrounds on the valley floor. Fill your car's tank before entering.

The Channel Islands of Anacapa, Santa Barbara, Santa Cruz, Santa Rose, and San Miguel now form California's newest national park, the *Channel Islands National Park,* consisting of approximately 18,000 acres. At park headquarters in the Ventura Harbor there is a small visitors' center. All-day boat trips are scheduled from the Central Harbor aboard Island Packer Cruises (P.O. Box 993, Ventura, CA 93301, tel. 805–642–1393).

Cabrillo National Monument is without doubt within the boundaries of Southern California. It's a memorial, in the form of the Old Point Loma Lighthouse, to Juan Rodriguez Cabrillo, the Portuguese mariner who, in the service of Spain, discovered what is now San Diego Bay. The ocean view is top mast, and whale watching is another exciting pleasure from mid-December through mid-February. Pack a picnic; it'll never taste better.

For information on weather, road conditions, and campground information concerning any national park, call Parkcast, the National Park Service's recorded message at (213) 688–2902.

 THEME PARKS. Within a sixty-mile radius of Los Angeles, you will find more theme or amusement parks than in any other area of the United States. Included are *Disneyland, Knott's Berry Farm, Movieland Wax Museum, Lion Country Safari,* and the *Kingdom of Dancing Stallions,* all in Orange County. (For more information on the aforementioned, see the "Anaheim/ Orange County" chapter.) Closer to the city proper, one can visit *Six Flags Magic Mountain, Marineland,* and *Universal Studios.* (See "Children's Activities" section under *Practical Information* for Los Angeles.) For a more extensive list of other such attractions, see "Sightseeing Checklist."

 HINTS TO HANDICAPPED TRAVELERS. In July 1978 California's new laws concerning special privileges for handicapped people became effective. Handicapped people are now issued license plates allowing special parking privileges. The law also applies to vehicles carrying blind passengers and to people with serious heart problems. Handicapped people are now permitted to park in special blue-marked parking spaces, to park for unlimited periods in limited-time spaces, and to park free in metered spaces.

To find out what historic sites can accommodate wheelchair travelers in Los Angeles, write to the Junior League of Los Angeles, 3rd & Fairfax Sts., Los Angeles, CA 90036 for a free copy of *Round the Town with Ease.* Be sure to include a self-addressed, stamped envelope.

For general travel tips for the handicapped, write to the Consumer Information Center, Pueblo, CO 81109. Hints include requesting specially equipped hotel and motel accommodations and making reservations. Allow plenty of time if meeting bus, train, or plane schedules. Be sure the wheelchair is clearly identified if it is carried with other luggage. Check out restroom facilities, and if driving, allow frequent, refreshing breaks. Travel lightly and informally.

Additional information can be obtained by writing to the Society for the Advancement of Travel for the Handicapped, 26 Court St., Brooklyn, NY 11242. This organization has presented awards to both Ramada and Holiday Inns for their programs for handicapped guests.

Access to the National Parks, a handbook for the physically disabled, describes facilities and services at all U.S. national parks and costs $3.50. *Access Travel,* a brochure, provides information on 220 worldwide airport facilities. These publications are available from U.S. Government Printing Office, Washington DC 20402. A booklet especially for people with lung problems is available for $1.25 from George Washington University, Rehabilitation Research and Training Center, Ross Hall, Suite 714, 2300 Eye St., N.W., Washington, DC 20037.

For a free copy of Amtrak's *Access Amtrak,* a guide to their services for elderly and handicapped travelers, write to Amtrak, National Railroad Passenger Corporation, 400 North Capitol St., N.W., Washington, DC 20001. Handicapped travelers and senior citizens are entitled to 25% off regular coach fare, when the one-way coach fare is at least $40.00. A special fare is also available for handicapped children aged 2 to under 12 years. The fare is a special savings —37.5% of the applicable one-way regular adult coach fare.

The following hotels and motels will make special efforts to comply with the needs of handicapped guests. Phone or write in advance for reservations and mention any special needs or requests.

Downtown: *Alexandria Hotel,* 501 South Spring St.; The *Biltmore Hotel,* 515 South Olive St.; *Best Western Kent Inn Motel, Downtown,* 920 South Figueroa St.; *Dunes Motel,* 5625 W. Sunset Blvd.; *Holiday Inn Golden State,* 1640 Marengo Dr. at Mission Rd.; *Hyatt Regency Los Angeles,* 711 South Hope St.; *Los Angeles Hilton,* 930 Wilshire Blvd.; *Mayflower Hotel,* 535 South Grand Ave.; *Milner Hotel,* 813 South Flower St.; *Mitchell Hotel,* 1072 West 6th St.; The *New Otani Hotel and Garden,* 120 South Los Angeles St.; *Olympian Hotel,* 1901 West Olympic Blvd.; *Sheraton Grande Hotel,* 333 South Figueroa St.; *University Hilton,* 3540 South Figueroa; The *Westin Bonaventure, Los Angeles,* Fifth and Figueroa Sts.

At the airport: *Airport Century Inn,* 5547 West Century Blvd., P.O. Box 92080; *Holiday Inn–LAX,* 9901 S. La Cienega Blvd.; *Hyatt Hotel–LAX,* 6225 West Century Blvd.; *Manchester House Hotel,* 901 West Manchester; *Skyways Airport Hotel,* 9250 Airport Blvd.; *Pacifica Hotel,* 6161 Centinela Ave., P.O. Box 3200; *TraveLodge International Hotel,* 9750 Airport Blvd.; *Vista Motel,* 4900 Sepulveda Blvd.

Marina Del Rey: *Marina City Club Hotel,* 4333 Admiralty Way; *Marina International Hotel,* 4200 Admiralty Way; *Marina del Rey Hotel,* 13534 Bali Way; *Marina del Rey Marriott,* 13480 Maxella Ave.

Santa Monica–Malibu: *Hotel Carmel,* 201 Broadway, Santa Monica; *The Huntley Hotel,* 1111 2nd St., Santa Monica; *Inn at Santa Monica,* 530 Pico Blvd., Santa Monica; *Miramar-Sheraton Hotel,* 101 Wilshire Blvd., Santa Monica; *Palm Motel,* 2020–14th St., Santa Monica; *SeaShore Motel,* 2637 Main Street.

Hollywood: *Franklin Motel,* 1824 N. Beachwood Dr.; *Holiday Inn–Hollywood,* 1755 N. Highland Ave.; *Cine Lodge/Howards Weekly Apartments,* 1738 North Whitley; *Ramada Inn–Hollywood,* 1160 North Vermont Ave.

Mid-Wilshire, Los Angeles: *The Ambassador,* 3400 Wilshire Blvd.; *Executive Motor Inn–Mariposa,* 457 South Mariposa Ave.; The *Hotel Chancellor,* 3191 West 7th St.; *Hyatt Wilshire Hotel,* 3515 Wilshire Blvd.; *Wilshire Dunes Motor Hotel,* 4300 Wilshire Blvd.; *Wilshire–Orange Hotel,* 6060 West 8th St.

Beverly Hills/West Los Angeles: *Bel Air Sands Hotel,* 11461 Sunset Blvd.; *Beverly Wilshire Hotel,* 9500 Wilshire Blvd.; *Century Plaza,* 2025 Avenue of the Stars; *Holiday Inn Westwood Plaza Hotel,* 10740 Wilshire Blvd.; *Los Angeles*

West TraveLodge, 10740 Santa Monica Blvd.; *L'Ermitage Hotel,* 9291 Burton Way; *Ramada Inn–Beverly Hills,* 1150 South Beverly Drive; *Westwood Marquis Hotel,* 930 Highland Ave.

 POSTAGE. At press time, rates for international mail from the United States are as follows: *Surface* letters to Canada and Mexico are at the U.S. domestic rate: 20¢ for 1 ounce or under, 37¢ for 2 ounces or under, but these rates actually involve airmail carriage to those countries. Surface letters to other foreign destinations are 30¢ for the first ounce and 47¢ for up to 2 ounces. *Airmail* letters to foreign destinations other than Canada, Mexico, and some Caribbean and South American countries are 40¢ for ½ ounce, 80¢ for 1 ounce, $1.20 for 1½ ounces, $1.60 for 2 ounces. *Postcards* (except to Canada and Mexico, which go airmail for 13¢) are 19¢ for surface mail and 28¢ for airmail to any foreign destination. Standard international *aerogram letters,* good for any foreign destination, are 30¢ but, of course, nothing may be enclosed in them. Postal rates are no exception in periods of inflation; so check before you mail in case they have gone up since press time.

METRIC CONVERSION

CONVERTING METRIC TO U.S. MEASUREMENTS

Multiply:	by:	to find:
Length		
millimeters (mm)	.039	inches (in)
meters (m)	3.28	feet (ft)
meters	1.09	yards (yd)
kilometers (km)	.62	miles (mi)
Area		
hectare (ha)	2.47	acres
Capacity		
liters (L)	1.06	quarts (qt)
liters	.26	gallons (gal)
liters	2.11	pints (pt)
Weight		
gram (g)	.04	ounce (oz)
kilogram (kg)	2.20	pounds (lb)
metric ton (MT)	.98	ton (t)
Power		
kilowatt (kw)	1.34	horsepower (hp)
Temperature		
degrees Celsius	9/5 (then add 32)	degrees Fahrenheit

CONVERTING U.S. TO METRIC MEASUREMENTS

Multiply:	by:	to find:
Length		
inches (in)	25.40	millimeters (mm)
feet (ft)	.30	meters (m)
yards (yd)	.91	meters
miles (mi)	1.61	kilometers (km)
Area		
acres	.40	hectares (ha)
Capacity		
pints (pt)	.47	liters (L)
quarts (qt)	.95	liters
gallons (gal)	3.79	liters
Weight		
ounces (oz)	28.35	grams (g)
pounds (lb)	.45	kilograms (kg)
tons (t)	1.11	metric tons (MT)
Power		
horsepower (hp)	.75	kilowatts
Temperature		
degrees Fahrenheit	5/9 (after subtracting 32)	degrees Celsius

 SECURITY. Take a good look at a map before exploring Los Angeles. This is an extremely seductive city, and it looks safer than it really is. There are some areas, in fact, that should be avoided—especially after daylight hours.

Stay away from south-central Los Angeles along the Imperial Highway and around the Sports Arena and Colliseum in Watts unless absolutely necessary. When you must be in that part of town, ride with your car doors locked, and park in secured parking lots.

Hollywood Blvd., with all its neon and bright lights, is also a haven for pickpockets and street criminals. Although a stroll along the Walk of Stars shouldn't be discouraged, take caution.

Don't leave money or valuables in your hotel room. Be sure to lock your door—even when you intend to stay in your room briefly. Use safe-deposit boxes offered by hotels for valuables; they are usually free.

Carry most of your funds in traveler's checks, and be sure to record the numbers in a separate, secure place. Watch your purse or wallet. Enjoy casual acquaintances—but at a distance. Never leave your car unlocked or valuable articles in plain sight in the car even if it is locked. Terminal counters and hotel check-in desks are also favored spots for lurking opportunists.

Since it isn't hard to have a safe vacation in Los Angeles, it would be too bad to let a little carelessness spoil it.

 EMERGENCY TELEPHONE NUMBERS. In Los Angeles during emergencies, dial "0" and ask the operator to connect you immediately with the appropriate agency. The direct-dial number for the police in Los Angeles is 625–3311; the sheriff's office is 855–8850; for paramedics and fire call 623–3473.

AN INTRODUCTION
TO LOS ANGELES

by
JANE E. LASKY

Jane Lasky is a contributor to the Los Angeles Times Syndicate and a columnist for the in-flight magazines for both Continental and Republic airlines. She writes for such publications as Palm Springs Life, Los Angeles *magazine,* Travel Agent, Bon Appetit, Emmy, *and many other magazines. She is a resident of Los Angeles.*

On an acclaimed public television documentary called "LA, LA, Making it in LA," which chronicles struggling performers, a particularly naive yet charmingly enthusiastic actor observed: "Los Angeles

26

is a place you dream of coming to and yet when you get here, you can still keep dreaming."

The surrounding landscape—towering skyscrapers, sun-baked deserts, rambling mountain ranges, miles of beaches, and the ubiquitous palm trees—is so unbelievably diverse that it enhances the unreal quality of the region. When you take account of the fact that this is the home of the movie and television industry, the mass producers of Technicolor dreams for the entire world, you can understand why so many visitors pinch themselves during their first encounter with Los Angeles.

This is a metropolis that possesses urban statistics that may well jolt back into consciousness the sun-and-fun-besotted mind:

- The city contains more cars than Detroit.
- Some 6,500 miles of road and freeways exist within city limits.
- Los Angeles alone is bigger than the entire state of Rhode Island; it comprises about 464 square miles.
- More than 100 legitimate theaters, 36 dance companies, 29 symphony orchestras, 35 museums, 17 opera and light opera companies, and 74 movie theaters enrich the life of Los Angeles.
- Los Angeles boasts 46 colleges and 15 universities.
- Every year 12.1 million people visit the city, and 75 percent of them come back for a second look.

Although these statistics may seem overwhelming, one fact may help the visitor relax and enjoy his or her visit: It's virtually impossible to do everything during one trip to Los Angeles. After all, as the city's slogan suggests, "LA's the place"—just do it at your own pace.

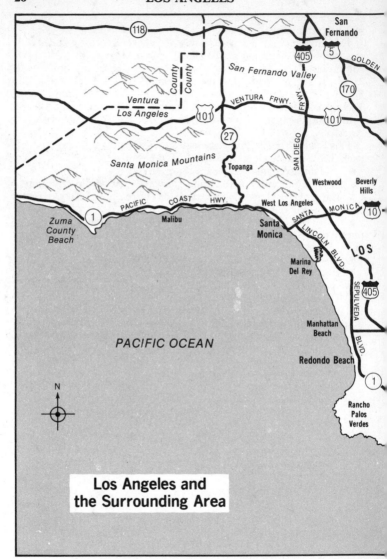

**Los Angeles and
the Surrounding Area**

THE HISTORY OF
LOS ANGELES

by
JANE E. LASKY

The earliest known inhabitants of what is now called the Los Angeles Basin were members of a tribe of Shoshone Indians who coexisted peacefully with other, larger Indian nations to the north and to the south of them. The Shoshone were primarily hunters and gatherers who lived well off the rolling grassy hillsides that were abundant with seeds and nuts of many varieties. The Shoshone women wove baskets and fashioned soapstone vessels; craftsmen made "sewed plank" boats suitable for expeditions to the coastal Santa Barbara Islands.

For several generations after the initial influx of outsiders, the Shoshone continued to be the area's most numerous residents. And "though they were taken advantage of, they learned to perform much useful work at the Missions, in town, and on the Ranchos," surmised John and Laree Caughey in their historical book on Los Angeles, *Biography of a City.*

In 1769 a Spanish army expedition led by Gaspar de Portola, en route from San Diego to Monterey, discovered a river flowing through a beautiful valley and named it Nuestra Señora de Los Angeles de Porcuincula, after a religious feast celebrated the day before. A member of the expedition, Father Juan Crespi, wrote of the discovery: "A spacious valley, well grown of cottonwoods and alders, among which ran a beautiful river . . . All the soil is black and loamy and is capable of producing every kind of grain and fruit which may be planted."

By this time, the Spanish, intending to deter both British and Russian expansionism in the area, were proceeding with the full scale colonization of Alta, or northern, California. Baja California, today part of Mexico, had already been placed under Spanish control. California's Spanish Governor Felipe de Neve, acting on reports that he had received, chose Los Angeles as the site of a small agricultural community because of the quality of its soil and its proximity to a water supply.

Three main forms of Spanish colonization existed: the missions, the presidios, and the pueblos. The missions, which eventually numbered twenty-one throughout colonial California, were outposts of Spanish Catholicism run by monks of the Franciscan Order. Self-sufficient units, the missions were the focal point of Spanish colonial rule in the New World. The presidios (of which there were four in Alta California) were military bases filled with soldiers to protect Spanish interests, namely, the missions and pueblos. The pueblos were agricultural communities designed to support the presidios.

On September 8, 1771, the first mass was said at Los Angeles, and the following morning construction began at Mission San Gabriel, founded by Father Junipero Serra. Father Serra's closest associate, Father Francisco Palow, wrote that work progressed quickly, "with the pagans themselves cutting and dragging in a greater part of the wood." The Franciscans were highly encouraged in their endeavors, "seeing that, from the very beginning, there was no opposition to the gentle yoke of our Evangelical law." The Indians eventually became known as the Gabrielinos and became dependent on the Spanish even for their identity.

When Mission San Gabriel was established and apparently thriving, Governor de Neve, together with a small group of farmers recruited in

Sonora, founded El Pueblo de Nuestra Señora Reina de Los Angeles in September 1781.

Located on the west bank of the Porciuncula River, the pueblo was set up to provide food for the garrisons at Santa Barbara and San Diego. The recruits from Sonora had traveled seven months to get to their new homeland. By the time they arrived, land allotments were ready for the eleven families consisting of forty-four people; the distribution of the 28 square miles of the pueblo was quick and troublefree. Each family received two fields for planting corn and for farming equipment, cattle, horses, and mules.

Soon their temporary thatched willow huts gave way to more permanent adobe housing, which was later reinforced with tar roofing. The tar came from the La Brea tar pits, eight miles to the west.

Shoshone from nearby Yang-Na Village were trained and employed as cheap labor at the pueblo and at the mission, thus beginning a trend that led eventually to the almost total extinction of California's Indians. Exposed for the first time to nonnative diseases and racially based prejudice and practices that promoted inequity, the Indians all but vanished within 100 years of the first Spanish settlements.

During the first five years of the pueblo, the Pobladores built a dam on the river. Irrigation ditches brought water to their burgeoning fields. In September 1786, on the fifth anniversary of the founding of the pueblo, Governor Pedro Fages granted title to the land to the settlers; each new owner also received a registered branding iron with which to mark and identify his cattle and livestock. Significantly, this date also marks the start of land taxation for the new landowners. Unfortunately, little is known of the day-to-day existence of the Pobladores. The settlers themselves were mostly illiterate, and visitors to the pueblo were still few and far between.

In 1790, the year of the first U.S. census, 148 persons belonged to the pueblo, only twenty-eight of whom were men and only nine of whom were over the age of fifty. The total picture indicates a harmonious community of twenty-nine adobe houses inhabited by a racially mixed group (one European, seventy-two Spaniards, seven Indians, twenty-two mulattos, and thirty mestizos) and surrounded by a safe and hospitable countryside. There was no concern about traveling alone or in small parties with valuable pack trains; records indicate a good deal of churchgoing in this pleasant community. In the first forty years of its existence, the pueblo grew at a steady rate. By 1820, the last year of Spanish rule, 650 people lived within the boundaries of El Pueblo.

In 1810 the pueblo elected a mayor, or *alcalde,* Don Francisco Avila, whose adobe home still stands today on Olvera Street. It is now the oldest surviving structure in the city. The plaza, centered on the adobe church, was the focal point of the community. And so the town grew in size as it grew in independence. Floods in 1815 caused the relocation of the church and other plaza buildings to their present location, slightly northwest of the original town square.

Spanish rule came to an end in 1821, precisely forty years after Felipe de Neve founded El Pueblo, but word of the end of the Mexican Revolution did not reach Alta California until the following year. With the relaxation of the enforcement of statutes pertaining to individual land ownership that came with the end of Spanish rule, small independent ranchos began to spring up all over the area.

The rancho period was a time of great prosperity, a flourishing frontier city where parties, festivals, and annual rodeos were commonplace. El Pueblo de Los Angeles rapidly became an important social and commercial center. Between 1833 and 1836, the missions were secularized, religious authority being replaced by civil administration. Again, the Gabrielinos got the short end. As much as 50 percent of the newly available land should have been awarded to the Indians under the Mexican secularization plan; in actuality, they received very little. The majority of the land went to the more wealthy settlers and new arrivals from the East.

During the Mexican, or "rancho," period, commerce boomed, and business was conducted on a grand scale. An especially flourishing trade existed in animal hides bought by ships' pursers and traders from Boston. This commercial activity naturally led to economic dependence on U.S. tradesmen, including trappers and fur hunters who traveled overland, crossing the Rocky Mountains.

The first Americans to arrive via the overland route consisted of a party of beaver trappers in 1826. They were greeted warmly by the leaders of the missions, thus opening the doors for the Americanization of Alta California. The fur trappers were followed by pioneers and settlers of many ethnic backgrounds. As trade and cattle production increased, the land opened up, and El Pueblo de Los Angeles achieved a legendary pastoral perfection.

Eventually the strong trade ties with the United States brought about a virtual American economic annexation of California. As John and Laree Caughey concluded in their history of Los Angeles, "American takeover signaled as drastic a change for Los Angeles as had occurred to the Gabrielino with the coming of the Spaniards."

In September 1846 Commodore R. F. Stockton met with little or no resistance as his troops took possession of Los Angeles. They had experienced similar good fortune forty days earlier in taking Monterey and San Francisco Bay. With the advent of U.S. rule, the situation in Los Angeles began to change very rapidly.

On January 13, 1847, the Treaty of Cahuenga put a formal end to the Mexican–American War, and the subsequent Treaty of Guadalupe Hidalgo ratified the official surrender of California to the United States. In the following year gold was discovered in northern California; San Francisco and the Mother Lode areas experienced what many have referred to as "instant Americanization."

Over the next two decades Los Angeles steadily grew from a tough frontier town into a real city, afflicted with such prototypical Western problems as gambling, drinking, and, sadly, murder. The Los Angeles of the 1850s and 1860s was a city "long on saloons and guntoting and violence." Common aspects of Angelino existence seem to have included racial tension and frequent shooting incidents. By this time, the gold rush was winding down, and prospectors from the north, both successful and not so successful, descended on Los Angeles. There was a sizable Chinese population, along with the American settlers and speculators and the descendants of the Pobladores.

By the end of the violent 1850s, the gold rush was a thing of the past up north, and as the boomtown communities dispersed, so did the huge demand for beef that had bouyed the Los Angeles economy during the gold rush years. The rancheros met hard times, and, like many others, some of the wealthy old Mexican families were forced to sell parcels of land to the American newcomers—marking the end of the idyllic rancho days.

Violence and lawlessness came to an awful culmination with the Chinese incident of 1871. One observor wrote in a local paper: "A shooting scrape in Chinatown expanded into a mass assault on the Celestials in which 19 persons were killed, many in execution style." Lynchings, beatings, and preemptory justice meted out by ad hoc "vigilante committees" had been a way of life and death in Los Angeles for twenty years. The tide was turning, though, for in 1874, when a celebrated bunch of bandits were captured, there were no lynchings or vigilante style of justice. Instead, the captives were routinely sent to San Jose for trial.

With the end of this distasteful era, efforts were made to rejuvenate the city, particularly the plaza area that had fallen prey to gamblers, vagrants, and misfits. Ex-governor Pio Pico built a hotel, the Pico House, on the corner of Main and Plaza, and the Merced Theater, constructed by William Abbott, opened next door on New Year's Eve 1870.

Los Angeles was growing rapidly, still attracting settlers from the East. In March 1876, the San Pedro Street Railway Company completed a rail line from central Los Angeles to the San Pedro docks. Funded by the county, this development spurred the onset of other local lines in the region.

In September 1876 Southern Pacific Railroad completed the San Francisco–Los Angeles line; six years later, the link with El Paso, Texas, was made. The Santa Fe Railroad, completed in 1885, was in direct competition with Southern Pacific, resulting in a price war and ultimately very low fares. This was a boon to commerce, for California was in a position to enjoy easy contact with the Midwest and the Eastern Seaboard.

In about the mid-1880s, a new publication, *The Los Angeles Times,* began to appear on the streets of Los Angeles. Harrison Gray Otis was the editor. In 1894 his daughter married Harry Chandler, then an employee in the Circulation Department but soon to become a partner. Together the two men built the vast empire that became the city's largest newspaper.

Oil was discovered in the Los Angeles Basin in 1891 by Edward Doheny and Charles Canfield. In the following ten years more than 600 oil wells were drilled, and petroleum became an important local product. Ironically, the oil refineries that naturally followed hot on the heels of the wells are now known to have been major contributors to Los Angeles' smog problem.

By the turn of the century, San Pedro Harbor had been completed and was in full operation, somewhat to the dismay of the powerful Southern Pacific Railway, which had lobbied to have the harbor built in Santa Monica. Also, an event of no minor significance occurred in 1897, when the first automobile using the internal-combustion engine was driven in Los Angeles, a city that was to become dependent on this form of transportation. In the early 1900s Los Angeles had the world's largest mass-transit system. Controlled by Henry Huntington and run by the Pacific Electric Company, the city's "red cars" were immensely popular streetcars, carrying passengers over routes that covered much of the incorporated area.

Citrus groves had long replaced cattle as the region's predominant agricultural enterprise, and the population had swelled enormously when William Mulholland began construction of the Owens Valley— Los Angeles Aqueduct in 1902. A reliable water supply, one of the city's oldest problems, had long necessitated such a development. The aqueduct, which stretched 240 miles across hot desert sands to the San Fernando Valley, enraged those residents of Owens Valley who opposed it vocally and sometimes violently for the next twenty years. During that time, the city of Los Angeles quietly bought all Owens Valley land that came up for sale.

Los Angeles continued to annex land for the city, and by the mid-1920s it was the largest city, by area, in the world. Industry was flourishing, and the harbor led the world in oil exports. Another aqueduct was under construction, this time bringing water from the Colorado River, about 250 miles away. Many leading manufacturers were moving to Los Angeles, and in the thirties Donald W. Douglas, along with Lockheed, Goodrich, and Firestone, built plants in the area. The film industry also began to blossom during this period, shortly after the advent of the talking motion picture.

World War II played a major role in the development of Los Angeles as a leader in commerce and industry and, sadly, as a hub of racism and paranoia. Although the war constituted an undisputed gold mine for the aircraft and shipping industries, as well as for electronics and armaments, it was a living nightmare for many Californians—the Japanese-Americans. After Pearl Harbor, feelings on the West Coast ran high; there was a general sense of alarm and a fear of an invasion or an air attack. This near panic led to one of our darkest episodes, one of America's greatest wartime mistakes.

The Los Angeles Times, in its first editorial after Pearl Harbor, referred to California as "a zone of danger" and showed thereafter that even such an objective institution as a newspaper was not immune to a wave of racism and fear sweeping through the city. The *Times* and the rest of the California press corps spewed out daily a stream of racist venom across its editorial pages, soon turning all Japanese-American citizens into scapegoats and encouraging the subsequent policy of "relocation." This whole segment of the population was uprooted and sent to concentration camps.

Americans had only one goal in mind throughout those awful years: Win the war. Heavy industry churned day and night, venting gases and smoke into the atmosphere; the refineries' daily stream of noxious by-product filtered into the air. On September 8, 1943, a midday dimout similar to an eclipse of the sun focused attention on the issue of air quality: What Los Angeles had was smog.

Industry cannot take all the blame for the air pollution problem, though. The geography of the area and the warm, windless days combine to create an inversion layer, a boiling cauldron of deleterious gases and vapors that burn eyes, sear lungs, and send vulnerable persons, especially asthmatics, to hospitals. At its worst, in the forties and fifties, the severe smog conditions lasted for weeks. Eventually, the Air Quality Management District was established. So far it has achieved only mixed results.

During the last years of the war and immediately afterward, the State Highway Commission began to subsidize and construct the famous Southern California freeway system, ultimately encompassing 6,500 miles of roadway. The freeways not only became an integral part of the life of the city but its trademark too.

The fifties were a time of prosperity in the United States. In 1954 Disneyland opened in Anaheim. Since then it has attracted millions of visitors, becoming perhaps the world's best known amusement park.

All was not roses, however. As the fifties progressed, Senator Joe McCarthy's communist witch hunt stirred deep feelings everywhere but perhaps nowhere so much as in Los Angeles. Many creative members of the Hollywood film community were accused of being communists; many were blacklisted without ever having the opportunity to face their detractors.

Civil rights became a major issue in the early sixties; racial tension was again on the rise in the City of Angels. Urban unrest culminated in the Watts riots of 1965. Much of south-central Los Angeles was in flames when the National Guard arrived to quell the rioting and the looting. Today Watts is still a ghetto substantially unchanged in the years since the riots erupted.

Los Angeles was a major center of the youth movement in the middle sixties. The legendary Sunset Strip attracted hippies and musicians from all over the country. Violence and bloodshed continued to be part of the Los Angeles scene in the late sixties. Robert Kennedy's assassination here in 1968 and, in the following year, the Manson Family murders were the most notorious incidents.

However, these unsavory incidents are only a small part of the history of this bustling metropolis. By the late sixties, Los Angeles had become what New York City was one hundred years earlier: the main port of entry for immigrants coming into the United States. Huge numbers of Korean, Vietnamese, Japanese, and Latinos swelled the population; today large immigrant communities exist. Although they are assimilating into the mainstream, they are maintaining their cultural independence. Current estimates state that by the year 2000, half the population of Los Angeles will be of Mexican-American or of Latino descent.

A major earthquake (6.4 on the Richter Scale) occurred in 1971, heightening the awareness among the multitude of Angelinos that such devastation and destruction, while probably not imminent, could occur again. Earthquake preparedness is another issue that faces the LA City Council and local government.

Even though the citrus crown has long been passed on to Florida, about 90,000 acres are still under cultivation in the county. The entertainment industry is booming, producing 90 percent of the world's recorded entertainment within a five-mile radius of the intersection of Hollywood and Vine. The aerospace industry is enjoying a resurgence, fueled by the new military spending hikes that are reaching the production line.

Today Los Angeles is a thriving metropolis of widely varied ethnic groups, diversified industry, and all the tinsel and glitter, glamour and excitement that any major city should possess.

THE LOS ANGELES
WAY OF LIFE

by
TONY PEYSER

Tony Peyser writes about the entertainment industry and life in Los Angeles for such publications as The Los Angeles Herald Examiner, The Los Angeles Times, *and* California, Los Angeles, *and* American Film *magazines.*

The West has always been a beacon of the future, of hope, of probability. It is the place one goes when possessed of the need to go some place.

The American West of the late 1800s was pretty much a thing of the past when Los Angeles began to develop its identity in the years before World War I. At that time the town wasn't exactly swinging. In 1915 writer S. S. Van Dine observed, "The tourist in search of urban pleasure will find himself thwarted by some ordinance, the primary object of which is to force Middle West moralities upon all inhabitants. Puritanism is the inflexible doctrine of Los Angeles."

Oddly enough, the city was undergoing quite a change right around the time that Van Dine made that comment. The movies were having a big impact. A fitting irony is that some of the first pioneers in this film frontier were cowboys; some were even Indians.

Since a lot of the early silent movies were set in the Wild West, producers found it expedient to hire real Western types to be in their fictional adventures. However, these fun-loving, rowdy guys didn't whoop it up only when the cameras were rolling. Their offscreen antics were not appreciated by the locals. Signs emphatically stating "No Dogs or Actors" began popping up at various apartments and hotels, and a general disdain for movie people developed. (This unfriendly attitude was nothing new to actors, who were accustomed to being regarded as pariahs by the outside world.)

As the names of silent-film stars became household words, Los Angeles found itself being carefully scrutinized by people from all over the world. The general consensus seemed to be that even though the movies were wonderful, the rest of the town didn't have much to offer. Visitors found a short supply of museums, legit theaters, concert halls, art galleries, and other amenities expected of a major city. Los Angeles was having enough trouble just dealing with the onslaught of people from the picture business and consequently was not prepared to accommodate the needs of visiting onlookers. The result was that the City of Angels got a devilish reputation as being uncivilized, uninhibited, and uncultured, the undisputed Un-capital of the planet.

It is far easier to say what this unique city *isn't* than to define what it is. Perhaps a good way to start is by isolating some of its special characteristics in an attempt to understand how each contributes to shaping the Los Angeles way of life.

"The famed climate has one major flaw," wrote Dickson Hartwell in a 1946 issue of *Liberty* magazine. "You can't eat it." Aside from this curious culinary shortcoming, the climate in Los Angeles is outstanding. Even with the smog, the preponderance of sunny days and blue skies for the greater part of the year promotes a discernibly easy style of living. However, this style does not make Los Angeles an easy place to *make a living*. Regardless of how relaxed the inhabitants may appear, they are working just as diligently as people in other big cities.

Having a tan does not render one immune to ulcers, headaches, and other physical ailments related to trying to make ends meet.

Although the weather is unusually kind most of the time, it does have some flaws other than its inedibility. In *Slouching Towards Bethlehem,* Joan Didion observed: "The climate is characterized by infrequent but violent extremes: two periods of torrential subtropical rains which continue for weeks and wash out the hills and send subdivisions sliding toward the sea; about twenty scattered days a year of the Santa Ana [wind], which, with its incendiary dryness, invariably means fire."

These most peculiar winds, whenever they blow, also cause a strange anxiety that tends to make tempers shorter and bouts of depression longer. Didion suggests, "The violence and unpredictability of the Santa Ana affect the entire quality of life in Los Angeles, accentuate its impermanence, its unreliability. The wind shows us how close to the edge we are."

Another way in which this sense of being on the edge is manifested concerns the omnipresent threat of earthquakes. The two biggest ones occurred in Long Beach in 1933 and in the Sylmar area in 1971. The likelihood of "The Big Quake" is a subject most frequently discussed by visitors, new residents, and local newscasters whenever a catchy story is needed during crucial ratings periods. A lot of people regard earthquake data in the same way that television executives look at the ratings of shows. TV shows have the Nielsens; quakes have the Richter Scale. In fact, some people have shown their disappointment on learning that a particular seismic jolt did not register as high on the Richter Scale as they'd hoped. "By and large," famed *Los Angeles Daily News* columnist Matt Weinstock once noted, "Los Angeles takes its earthquakes the way it takes its weather: with a great deal of conversation but not much else."

Another topic that generates much conversation is the automobile. Some visitors to Southern California probably assume shortly after arriving that most Los Angelenos have been surgically attached to their cars. Of course this isn't the case, but locals do have an extraordinary attachment to whatever vehicle they're driving for a number of reasons: A car is an absolute necessity given the vastness of the city. Take a car away from an L.A. resident, and he will look as silly as Sammy Davis Jr. without jewelry or as helpless as Rod Stewart without a mirror. Since folks who live in L.A. spend a lot of time driving, they spend a lot of time fixing up their cars. This preoccupation has to do with the overall vanity of the city, but it is also an expression of the domesticity that cars seem to acquire. A friend once confessed to me that the one place in the city in which he felt most comfortable was not his apartment but behind the wheel of his bright yellow VW convertible. Not only do cars get you where you have to go, they also provide a kind of home away from home. Automobiles have another symbolic meaning. In a city in which many residents have no relatives in the area and where whirlwind affairs are fairly common, people are eager to hold onto anything that gives them a sense of continuity. As a result, some of the longest relationships in Los Angeles are between people and their cars.

This vehicular addiction has more or less been put into law. Public transportation bond issues have been voted down for decades, and when the first freeway was completed in 1953, Los Angelenos became hooked. The system of byzantine ramps and interchanges that evolved was imposing, but the overall effect served to link the sprawling collection of little Southland cities. The freeways magically leveled distances, making everything in Los Angeles twenty minutes away from everything else except, of course, during rush hour.

Although they have been encouraged for quite a while to form car pools, most residents prefer commuting alone. Time spent in solitude on these high-speed highways is either regarded as a refreshing period of privacy or as further proof of the willful separation of Southern Californians from one another. In his book *Californians,* James D. Houston has an interesting thought on this subject. He writes, "In L.A., the freeway is a form of entertainment, a form of commitment, a form of engaging the environment on its own terms and, if you survive, a source of infinite satisfaction."

With respect to the other ways residents get around, you will find them on skateboards, bicycles, roller skates, or running; they rarely walk. Los Angelenos have an overriding sense of hurry even if they've set out to do nothing in particular. Los Angeles is not a city that has developed a leisurely approach to leisure.

Although cars and freeways have conspired to reduce the city to a manageable size, Los Angelenos often spend much of their free time in the general neighborhood in which they live. If they know people living across town, chances are that they will *hear* from those folks more often than they will *see* them. "In Los Angeles," novelist Carolyn See insists, "the best place to hang out is on the phone." Locals may unintentionally go for months at a time without actually getting together with their friends, but they maintain close ties by socializing on the phone.

It can be argued that the one location where people hang out the most is the beach. It is a place where people in swim suits not only show off their bodies but where others in not so revealing attire can show up to watch the showing off. Gazing out across the vast blue expanse of the Pacific Ocean, one is aware of seeing one of nature's most enduring creations in the same condition it has been in for centuries. For people living in Los Angeles, this sight is a reminder of why they came to Los Angeles and are putting up with whatever they're putting up with.

Apart from the beach, the weather, and the freedom of the freeways, there is also the entertainment industry. Even when its money is bad, the money is good. Everyone in Los Angeles knows someone who is *somebody,* or at least they know someone who knows someone who is *somebody.* Association is the first step toward being initiated into the fold. Who you know is often essential to where you will go, for show business is not unlike football: It is a contact sport. Nevertheless, the business is primarily made up of people who arrived knowing no one, people who packed whatever they had besides their dreams and decided to cut a wedge out of The Big Orange. Their unshakable belief that those who came before them were not unlike themselves sustains all those magnetically pulled toward Hollywood.

The old clichés about Los Angeles persist even though enormous cultural changes have rectified the obvious shortcomings that the city experienced in its infancy. The theater community is quite active. Two of its plays in particular—*Children of a Lesser God* and *The Shadow Box*—received national recognition as well as Tony Awards and a Pulitzer Prize. The museums are accumulating great collections, and the local art and music scene is thriving as well. Nevertheless, there is a tendency to belittle anything that comes out of L.A., and the usual jokes recycle tired references to hot tubs, Perrier, and poolside conferences.

Living in Los Angeles is like eating at the kid's table; it is made fun of by some but envied by many more. If you're in the former category, we'll laugh along with you. If you're in the latter, pull up a chair and pass the guacamole.

FUGITIVES IN PARADISE

The Movie and Television Business
in Los Angeles

by
TONY PEYSER

"Hollywood itself is not an exact geographical area, although there is such a postal district. It has commonly been described as a state of mind, and it exists wherever people connected with the movies live and work."
— Anthropologist Hortense Powder-
maker from her book, *Hollywood, the
Dream Factory.*

In 1908 nine film-producing companies got together and formed an organization called the Motion Picture Patents Company. Its founder and most distinguished member was the wizard of Menlo Park, Thomas Alva Edison. The ostensible aim of the MPPC (known to industry insiders as the Trust) was to protect Edison's patents on the various kinds of movie equipment he had invented. However, according to film historian Robert Sklar in *Movie-Made America,* this was not the only motive: "Edison wanted complete domination of the motion picture field. But instead of driving his competitors out of business, he tried to force them to use only his cameras under license and to sell or rent films only to the exchanges and exhibitors who agreed to use licensed products exclusively." In other words, Edison's Trust was trying to monopolize the young but developing film industry.

A number of independent movie companies didn't accept the many stringent rules and regulations of the trust; the ensuing dispute between these two factions became known as the Patents War. Although fierce feuding and some incidents involving both weapons and violence did occur, the term *war* was a bit extreme. Nevertheless, its usage presaged a penchant for hyperbole that soon became synonymous with the name *Hollywood.*

In order to avoid harassment from representatives of the Trust, many companies left New York and headed west. Although some settled in Chicago, Florida, and even Cuba, the majority wound up in Los Angeles. What they saw on arriving stunned them. The weather was sunny and wonderful and was apparently that way year round. The geography offered mountains, deserts, and beaches, all easily accessible by car.

These film industry fugitives realized they had come to the solar plexus of paradise. The entire region seemed to have been created for location filming. In addition, it was easy enough to take off for Mexico if any Trust enforcers showed up.

Despite the fact that the Trust had the venerable Mr. Edison behind it, some political sentiments were brewing that signaled its demise. Sklar observes, "In July 1912 the Democratic Party picked as its candidate Woodrow Wilson, who accused the incumbent Republicans of favoring big business and promised a return to competition and opportunities for the little man. Six weeks later, almost as if in response to Wilson's nomination, the Republican Administration filed suit against the Motion Picture Patents Company, charging it with restraint of trade and violation of the 1890 Sherman Antitrust Act."

In 1915 the federal court announced its decision that the Trust was illegally conspiring to restrain trade. The Trust was broken, and a new movie era began.

While all these matters were being argued in the courts, filmmakers were not holding their breath. Movies were being made in no small numbers. With the first showings of D. W. Griffith's *Birth of a Nation* (also in 1915), the medium was suddenly regarded as art, and controversial art at that. But it was in fact primarily a business that had an annual payroll of twenty million dollars that year. With stars such as Charlie Chaplin, Mary Pickford, and Douglas Fairbanks earning thousands of dollars a week, people from across the country (and all over the world, for that matter) brought dreams of making it or, at the very least, of taking hold of the glitter and the glamour of this brassiest of brass rings. The hoards of Hollywood hopefuls migrating to Los Angeles increased the labor pool available to the business. Many of these people were more than willing to work in any capacity for little money, a fact that was not lost on producers always looking for ways to cut corners.

Until that time, Los Angeles had been a fairly straitlaced and conservative town, but the movies changed all that. The role that movies played in defining the young city's personality was enormous.

In *Southern California Country,* Carey McWilliams clarified this special relationship by asserting that if the movies had arrived either earlier or later, the impact of the industry on the city might not have been as significant. "Lacking socially prominent first families or deeply rooted social traditions," he wrote, "Los Angeles quickly adopted the motion picture elite as its arbiters of taste and style." Whatever stars were wearing became the fashions of the day, and since many of their elegant homes were built by studio carpenters, it is no accident that certain parts of Los Angeles started to resemble the sets where movies were made. Add to this already fantasy-laden terrain the fact that the location shooting of films was an everyday occurrence, and you can see that those who lived in Los Angeles at this time were surrounded by an unmistakable aura of unreality.

The fanciful bubble burst in the early 1920s, when Hollywood was rocked by a series of scandals involving top names such as Fatty Arbuckle, Wallace Reid, William Desmond Taylor, and Mabel Normand in notorious escapades, including murders, orgies, and drugs.

Attempting to prove their skill in both leadership and civic responsibility, a number of studio heads formed an organization called the Motion Picture Producers and Distributors Association. The man they brought in to head this new operation was Will H. Hays, who resigned from his post as postmaster general to take the job. Hays proved so effective in his new capacity that the MPPDA wound up being known as the Hays Office. Not only did he help give Hollywood a badly needed moral facelift, but he also worked with representatives from different crafts to establish full-fledged unions. He also involved himself with the creation of the Academy of Motion Picture Arts and Sciences.

Just as Hollywood was trying to adjust to all these changes, another bombshell hit: The movies began to talk. In a peculiar assault on the senses, sound actually affected how the city *looked.* "The circus and carnival atmosphere completely vanished when sound was first introduced in 1925, " McWilliams asserted. "Tourists and visitors were not welcome in the new double-walled, soundproof studios. Location trips were reduced to a minimum and the movies became an indoor industry. Before sound was introduced, well-known actors and actresses could be seen throughout the city, on the streets and on location. But after 1925 guides began to put up signs along the boulevards offering to take tourists on a tour of the studios and to point out the homes of the stars. The carnival atmosphere survived only in the gaudy premieres, with their blazing klieg lights."

Having acquired a certain physical respectability with the innovation of sound, the picture business proceeded to wall itself off from the surrounding community. To a large extent, that wall has never been lifted, and its presence, however elusive it may seem, is a fundamental source of frustration for visitors to Los Angeles who hope to get a glimpse of "Hollywood."

While the making of motion pictures was becoming a more private enterprise, the general public was going to the movies in record numbers. The nation was in the midst of a terrible Depression, and people went to movies to escape from the many troubles their daily life presented. They took solace in lavish musicals, screwball comedies about the rich, and two-fisted stories about gangsters. Movie attendance in the early 1930s averaged sixty to seventy-five million people a week.

In an effort to meet this incredible demand for product, the Hollywood hierarchy initiated the contract system: Studios established stables of performers, writers, directors, and producers who worked under contract. They made whatever films were assigned. Hundreds and hundreds of movies were churned out each year.

The heyday of Hollywood lasted through the 1940s. In the 1950s, however, allegations of monopoly were again heard, and the result was major surgery on the body of Hollywood. At the behest of the federal government, the studios were forced to sell their theaters and end what the government regarded as their monopoly of both film production and exhibition. The rise of television further eroded the clout of the film industry, putting the studio system on its last legs. By the time it finally collapsed in the early 1960s, directors, writers, and performers were selling their services to the highest bidders and were structuring deals that gave them not only higher salaries but percentages of the overall profits as well. The power base of the industry shifted from the studios to independent production companies.

In an attempt to combat TV, which provided people with free entertainment in their own homes, the movies began to develop strategies to regain viewers. They began to use such gimmicks as 3-D, stereo sound, the wide screen, and Technicolor, and simultaneously started to produce big-budget extravaganzas that they hoped would demonstrate that TV could never touch movies.

The gimmicks proved to be just that, and although some of the expensive films were hits (*Ben-Hur, The Sound of Music*), many others were fiascos (*Cleopatra, El Cid*).

The movie business was undergoing a state of transition, but so was the culture. Student protest against the war in Vietnam, the rise of the counterculture, and a general questioning of society as a whole was causing a crisis of the American spirit. In 1968 a survey sanctioned by the movie industry indicated that almost half the people going to movies were between the ages of sixteen and twenty-four. Even though one could argue that it wasn't essential to be an eight-year-old to make movies for children, it did seem more logical that movies for young people be made by those closer in age to the target audience. The result was that studio doors were thrown open in an attempt to accommodate the young talents that it hoped would revitalize the industry.

Although *Bonnie and Clyde* broke ground with its graphic depiction of violence and by ennobling the antiheroics of its subjects, and *The Graduate* showed a frankness about sex and the plasticity of modern life, it was probably *Easy Rider* (1969) that best captured the alienated feelings of the period. Made for a mere five hundred thousand dollars, it grossed over forty million dollars and proved that there was an audience that was eager to connect with movies dealing with their lives.

Over the next several years a particular group of movies was made not necessarily *about* young people but by talented, young directors who had arrived with a vengeance. Francis Ford Coppola did *The Godfather,* William Friedkin offered *The French Connection* and *The Exorcist,* George Lucas made *American Graffiti* and *Star Wars,* and Steven Spielberg directed *Jaws* and *Close Encounters of the Third Kind.* Needless to say, virtually all these movies generated some of the highest revenues ever made.

The extraordinary success of these films earned for those and other directors as well virtual free reign on their next projects. However, a number of their subsequent efforts—*1941, Sorcerer,* and Michael Cimino's infamous *Heaven's Gate*—turned out to be colossal financial failures. As a result there was a swing toward smaller budgeted films that focused on the intimate problems of lovers, families, and strangers. Some of these movies include *On Golden Pond, Diner, Ordinary People,* and *Kramer vs. Kramer*. Although these films were quite well received and became quite successful, it was ironical that they were frequently compared to the kinds of personal stories that were popular in the early days of live TV on such programs as "Playhouse 90" and "Studio One." However, blockbuster films such as *Raiders of the Lost Ark* and *Superman* are proof that big-budget movies will always be around, even though they are regarded as high-risk propositions.

Most of the major studios today are owned by conglomerates that produce and distribute over one hundred films a year. Their budgets are going up: At last count a single feature film cost in excess of ten million dollars. On some of the larger films, that sum of money is spent just on advertising and promotion.

Hour-long programs for television run close to five hundred thousand dollars per show; half-hour shows cost in the vicinity of two hundred thousand dollars. Outside prime time, a whole week of soap operas costs two hundred fifty thousand dollars, and five days of game shows cost a little less, around two hundred thousand dollars.

Other numbers worth noting pertain to how many people belong to the various show business guilds. The Writers Guild of America has 6,000 writers in its western division and 2,000 in its eastern branch. Rough estimates of western membership in the other guilds include 6,500 in the Directors Guild, 5,000 in the Screen Extras Guild, and 25,000 actors and actresses in the Screen Actors Guild.

Once again, the movie and television business is going through a metamorphosis. Pay TV has arrived in town, and it seems to be the new wave in the entertainment industry, causing much controversy with the major studios that up until now monopolized the film industry. One of the most influential services is Home Box Office, a subsidiary of Time Inc. The fees by paid subscribers to HBO, Showtime, and the Movie Channel have increased ten times in the last five years, to an expected total of $2.4 billion, compared to $3.5 billion at the box office. There is talk of creating a pay-per-view situation in which viewers would be charged only for what they watched.

The movie business has not faced such dramatic change since the 1940s, when TV arrived. The potential for cable TV to become a common household addition is quite good. But, as in most new ventures, there are many problems to be ironed out before it is perfected.

One of the fundamental conflicts in Tinseltown goes back to that old issue of art versus business. Studio heads claim that filmmakers are often irresponsible with their money, and filmmakers claim that studio heads are not responsive to their creative needs. This battle is not a new one. Anthropologist Hortense Powdermaker observed, "The domination of the business executive over the artist in Hollywood is not surprising either in view of the history of movies or in terms of American culture. Movies began as a small business, an extension of the Coney Island type of entertainment. The men who started them were usually small entrepreneurs, some from the field of cheap entertainment, some from other small businesses. The artist was not even present. Later, when he arrived on the scene, he came as the employee of those men, who by this time were big business."

A common criticism made about contemporary Hollywood, as well as other American industries, is that the people running it are themselves unable to make the products that they are in charge of manufacturing. Many studio heads today are former talent agents who have knowledge of the business but do not necessarily have hands-on experience making movies. In *American Film Now,* James Monaco discussed this condition with writer–director Paul Mazursky, who declared, "In any other business, acting the way they do, they'd fold immediately. Hollywood can survive all that with one hit." And, after all, hits are what Hollywood is all about. Whether a producer used to be selling shoes or working as somebody's hairdresser, if his movie is raking it in at the box office, he's an instant industry expert. Succeeding in the business often depends on such fortuitous events as timing and dumb luck, and failure, as the *New York Times* has recently reported, can result from living in the wrong section of town, yet people still flock to Hollywood, recalling those defiant moviemakers who came here over seventy years ago to try their hand in the land of bilk and money.

CREATIVE LOS ANGELES

by
JANE E. LASKY and DIANA RICO

Cultural life in Los Angeles has never had very good press. Dismissing the city as a cultural Siberia, a lotusland under the palm trees, critics of Tinseltown as far back as H. L. Mencken—who, more than forty years ago, called LA "Moronia"—continue to put down the place. More recently, Woody Allen, in his film *Annie Hall,* made the flippant observation that the Big Orange is a city "where the only cultural advantage is that you can turn right on a red light." This criticism reflects the prejudices of LA's detractors, not the facts.

Los Angeles has long been a crossroads of creativity, a place where some of the most talented artists of this and earlier decades have lived and worked. The names of those who came to work in the film studios during the golden years of the Hollywood film read like a *Who's Who*

51

of modern culture. Bertolt Brecht, Kurt Weill, William Faulkner, Thornton Wilder, Lillian Hellman, Dashiell Hammett, F. Scott Fitzgerald, Dorothy Parker, John O'Hara, Aldous Huxley, S. N. Behrman, and Raymond Chandler are numbered among the extraordinarily talented people who worked in Hollywood's dream factories. In fact, there never has been—and probably never will be again—such a dense aggregation of talent concentrated in such a relatively small space as there was in the writers' community of Hollywood during its heyday.

Hollywood, however, does not hold the franchise on talent. Stravinsky, Schoenberg, Thomas Mann, Rubinstein, and Heifeitz all lived (or still live) in Los Angeles or its environs, and they had no connection whatsoever with the studios.

Even today Los Angeles attracts creative people because of its rich mingling of ethnic groups, its permissive cultural atmosphere, its wealthy patrons, and its colonies of kindred spirits struggling to extend their artistic boundaries.

Los Angeles may not have the bohemian mystique of San Francisco or the heady traditions and resources of New York, but there is important theater here, innovative art, fine music, and ground-breaking experimentation in all the arts. What has become increasingly apparent is that the creativity once channeled into the film industry is spreading throughout the region, as evidenced by the growth of small theater groups and independent filmmaking. Los Angeles is a city that will continue to attract talent from all over the world.

In the beginning there were Hollywood and the Studios, as well as the writers who arrived when the industry was feeling its early growing pains. Writers were a resource in great demand in the period after the advent of talking pictures. The scramble was on to find those who could put words in the mouths of luminous figures on the silver screen. The most famous playwrights of the Broadway stage—Elmer Rice, Moss Hart, Robert Sherwood, Maxwell Anderson, S. N. Behrman, Clifford Odets, George S. Kaufman—were wooed by the studios in an endeavor to get them to contribute their own brands of literary finesse to the movies.

The film moguls probably understood commerce better than creativity, having ears more attuned to the ring of box-office figures than to sparkling dialogue, but they liked the snob value of having blue-ribbon literary talent attached to their studios. They spared no expense in attracting the heavyweights. At one time Samuel Goldwyn even tried to lure George Bernard Shaw to Hollywood. Shaw's reply to the offer was short and ironical: "The trouble, Mr. Goldwyn, is that you are only interested in art, and I am only interested in money."

After the playwrights came the short story writers and the novelists, along with a new generation of socially conscious playwrights, many of whom left Hollywood during the years of the blacklist. Writers such as William Faulkner and Aldous Huxley, James M. Cain and Raymond Chandler, Eric Ambler and Dashiell Hammett, Christopher Isherwood and Erskine Caldwell, Dorothy Parker and John O'Hara sojourned in the sun, adapting their muses to the marketplace.

The writers settled in the Hollywood hills, the canyons of Santa Monica, or the flatlands of Beverly Hills. Lured by handsome contracts, they arrived in Hollywood in the thirties and the forties—despite the dominant feeling that their film work would be considered slumming. These talented writers played a prominent role in fashioning those movies that typify the golden era of film history: *A Star Is Born, Body and Soul, The Big Sleep, Double Indemnity, Gone with the Wind, The Thin Man, Dinner at Eight, Animal Crackers, Rebecca.* These are only a few of the films that reveal the signatures of writers who had come to Hollywood with laurels from the New York stage or from the ranks of the serious literary world.

Many incorporated their observations and experiences of Los Angeles life into their novels and short stories. Aldous Huxley did not write directly about the film business, but his impressions of Los Angeles provided the raw material for both *After Many a Summer Dies the Swan* (1939) and *Ape and Essence* (1949). Huxley, who is perhaps best known for his novel *Brave New World,* lived in Los Angeles from 1939 until his death in 1963, working at various times for MGM and Universal Studios. His film work includes the screenplays for *Pride and Prejudice,* starring Greer Garson and Laurence Olivier, and *Jane Eyre,* another elegant and romantic period piece, which featured Orson Welles and Joan Fontaine.

Perhaps the classic book to come out of Hollywood during this period is Nathanael West's *Day of the Locust.* West had been a screenwriter who worked on many "B" movies from 1933 until 1940. A gifted novelist with a talent for grotesque satire, West, like so many serious writers, moved west during a low point in his financial fortunes. During his early days in Los Angeles, he stayed in a cheap hotel called the Pa-Va-Sed on North Ivar Street near Hollywood Boulevard. While waiting for a job to open up at the studios, he spent hours observing the local scene, watching the ebb and flow of stuntmen, bit players, extras, and screen hopefuls making their rounds. He also observed the subculture of call girls, gamblers, and pushers who had set up shop within the shadow of the studios. He incorporated a large chunk of this moving carnival of Tinseltown street life into the satirical masterpiece, *Day of the Locust,* published in 1939. West, however, never got a chance to bask in the critical acclaim that the book eventually received; tragically, he died in a car accident only a few months after the publication of the book.

During the 1940s Hollywood became a popular haven for refugees from Hitler's Europe. Film directors such as Max Ophuls, Fritz Lang, and Alfred Hitchcock came to Hollywood during this storm-tossed period, refining their own particular sensibilities and political convictions through their work.

One of these refugees was the celebrated German playwright Bertolt Brecht, a great innovator of the modern theater. He left Germany the day after the Reichstag fire, realizing that his creative freedom—not to mention his life—was in danger under Nazi rule. Brecht eventually settled in Santa Monica in the summer of 1941, and for the next four years he moved primarily in that small community of German and Austrian refugee intellectuals who had found sanctuary in Los Angeles.

Brecht wrote with his friend, the director Fritz Lang, the screenplay for *Hangmen Also Die,* an eloquent indictment of Nazi oppression. Brecht abruptly ended his residence in Santa Monica in 1947 after being subjected to an inquisition directed by the House Un-American Activities Committee, which was investigating subversive activities in Hollywood. Sensing the changing political climate in this country, he left for Switzerland to escape the hobgoblins of anticommunism.

Many other artists, writers, and musicians who fled the upheavals in Europe to settle in California remained outside the film business and its influence. Among this group were the great modern composers Schoenberg and Stravinsky, along with Thomas Mann and his brother Heinrich, another widely respected writer. During his exile in Santa Monica, Thomas Mann continued to fight Nazism. In 1940 he began a series of radio broadcasts to Germany for the BBC, appealing to his countrymen to come to their senses. These California years were productive for Mann. The hours of quiet and concentrated writing culminated in the publication of the most popular of his later works, *Dr. Faustus* and *Joseph the Provider.* The great author returned to Europe in 1952. He died three years later in Zurich.

Faulkner

William Faulkner is today considered one of the giants of modern literature. But when he moved to Hollywood in 1932, after having written four books, including his masterpiece, *The Sound and The Fury,* he was teetering on the edge of bankruptcy. Although it's hard to imagine now, Faulkner's books were languishing on the remainder shelves and in the mid-thirties, during the Depression, sold on the average of roughly two thousand copies a title.

Besides providing for his wife and child, Faulkner supported his brother's widow and children (and he and they weren't doing very well on his earnings as a writer). Not surprisingly, he was deeply relieved when his agent sold *Sanctuary* to Paramount and secured a contract for the novelist to work as a screenwriter at MGM.

A year later, Faulkner returned to his real home, Oxford, Mississippi. Eventually he produced a total of four years' worth of work in Hollywood during various periods between 1932 and 1955.

However, Faulkner and Hollywood proved to be an incompatible combination. A shy, courtly, unpretentious man with a wide streak of eccentricity, Faulkner felt sorely out of his element in the flamboyant and highly commercial atmosphere of the studios. His wry and laconic style, prickly independence, and heroic drinking spawned many colorful stories around the film community.

It is said, for example, that Faulkner was so unnerved by his initial days in Hollywood that during his first week, he decided to quit. It is reported that he fled in panic, spending several days wandering around the wilds of Death Valley. Another story has him receiving producer Jack Warner's approval to work at home rather than at the writer's building at MGM. This occurred during the making of *The Big Sleep* (screenplay by Raymond Chandler, directed by Howard Hawks). Midway through the early stages of script development, Warner called Faulkner to find out how the work was going and discovered that the writer could not be reached in California. Warner panicked until one of his assistants suggested that he try contacting Faulkner at his Oxford, Mississippi, home. When he finally got Faulkner on the line, Warner asked with great distress why Faulkner had skipped town in the middle of an assignment. "This *is* my home," the writer answered patiently. "I live in Mississippi."

Faulkner's drinking bouts did not help endear him to studio heads. Screenwriter and producer Nunnally Johnson met Faulkner to discuss a film based on a book called *The Road to Glory*. Painfully shy, Faulkner sat silent for a long time. Finally, to loosen up, he took out a pint of whiskey and proceeded to share with Johnson, a hard-drinking Southerner himself. According to legend, this was the beginning of a three-week drunk that ended after studio sleuths found both Faulkner and Johnson in an Okie camp, sobered them up, and got them back to work.

Faulkner was not one to play star struck. One time he went hunting with Clark Gable and director Howard Hawks. While driving along, Gable turned to Faulkner and to make conversation, asked him, "I hear that you write books, don't you?" To which Faulkner laconically replied, "Yes, and I hear that you make movies, don't you?"

Faulkner's residences in Los Angeles consisted of a series of nondescript motels. A private man, he made few friends; among the few were Howard Hawks and Nathanael West. West introduced him to Stanley

Rose's bookstore on Hollywood Boulevard, a favorite meeting place for many Hollywood writers.

Rose was a legendary local personality, a colorful self-styled con man who had a soft spot for writers and literature. He often filled huge briefcases with the latest books written by his friends and then peddled them from door to door in all the writers' buildings at the various Hollywood studios. Rose was also a conduit for that floating, low-rent society of call girls, small-time gangsters, and drug pushers that existed on the fringes of the film community. West and other writers drew inspiration for characters and situations from Rose and his underground network of friends.

It was in a separate back room of Rose's bookstore that Faulkner met many of the talented writers who had moved west to work in the studios. John O'Hara, Erskine Caldwell, Dashiell Hammett, Lillian Hellman, S. J. Perelman, Ben Hecht, F. Scott Fitzgerald, and Christopher Isherwood were only a few of the literary legends who hobnobbed in the smoke-filled back room of Rose's bookstore. Most, expatriates from the New York theater or literary world, had been lured to Hollywood by handsome wages and now drew together in a spirit of cynical camaraderie. Many were also great storytellers. Faulkner sat quietly and listened while these high-flying wits and raconteurs performed.

Faulkner did not have the "light touch" considered necessary for screenwriting. Much of his work was scrapped, although his partnership with director Howard Hawks, another iconoclast, did pay off. The two fashioned some of the most memorable films of the period, including *To Have and Have Not* and *The Big Sleep*. Undoubtedly, the rakish flavor and understated wit of these two films, which paired Bogart and Bacall to such a memorable effect, owed something to the handiwork of Faulkner.

Of most importance, Faulkner's short time in the dream factory of Hollywood helped provide the financial resources that he needed to resume writing in Mississippi, enabling him to write the books that eventually earned him his place in the pantheon of great American writers.

The Beloved Infidel

F. Scott Fitzgerald spent his last three years in Hollywood as a screenwriter. The palmy days when he and Zelda were the darlings of the literary set, the glamourous personifications of the Jazz Age, were far behind when he went west to work for MGM. Zelda, a tragic casualty of a life squandered in fantasies and headlong excess, was in the sanatorium where she would spend the remainder of her life.

Fitzgerald began his stint as a screenwriter in the midst of a deep professional and personal descent. The tragedy of Zelda, his lack of faith in his own talent, and a serious drinking problem had propelled him into a destructive spiral. His work wasn't selling at all. By May 1939, his agent had proved unable to place any of his stories in any magazine for more than a year. The total yearly earnings for all of Fitzgerald's books—and they were all in print during the accounting period—came to less than one hundred dollars, a far cry from his heyday a decade earlier, when his short stories in the *Saturday Evening Post* and other magazines were earning him a princely income. During the Prohibition era, Fitzgerald's reckless and flamboyant life-style had made him the golden boy of the period. Now besieged by debt collectors and immobilized by despair, Fitzgerald pulled all kinds of strings to get his studio contract, realizing that movie work might be the only economic lifeline open to him.

The Hollywood period is usually viewed as Fitzgerald's last act, the shabby twilight of his life. But this perception is far from the truth. Although his screenwriting was certainly uninspired, Fitzgerald triumphed over adversity in many other ways. To his credit, he controlled his drinking; he met Sheilah Graham, the great romance of his later years; he pulled himself out of debt; and, most important, he began to write again, mining the rich ore of his Hollywood experience to create a book that, although incomplete at his death, is an extraordinary achievement.

Fitzgerald stayed at the famed Garden of Allah on Sunset Boulevard (no longer extant), a collection of Hollywood bungalows that served as a hive of social activity attracting some of the city's most interesting people. Here, surrounded by old friends and New York literary colleagues such as Dorothy Parker and Robert Benchley, Fitzgerald met journalist Sheilah Graham. As she subsequently described in her book *Beloved Infidel,* a celebration of their life together, Graham helped pull Fitzgerald out of the emotional limbo associated with the long and debilitating disintegration of his marriage to Zelda.

Fitzgerald began to come out of his shell in other ways during this period. He began spending time with some of the other writers, besides Benchley and Parker, in captivity at the film studios, including Nathanael West. He met with them at such eateries as Musso and Frank Grill, a popular restaurant to this day, at 6667 Hollywood Blvd.

Fitzgerald applied himself conscientiously to the craft of screenwriting. And although he displayed no real gift for the medium, his efforts were often heroic. At MGM in early 1938 he toiled to develop a screenplay for producer Joseph L. Mankiewicz for a film that was eventually released as *Three Comrades.* He wrote seven versions of the script, devoting six months to the assignment, only to have the whole project deteriorate into a bitter series of arguments with the producer. During this time, Fitzgerald worked on more than a dozen films, receiving screen credit for only one.

Despite these bitter encounters, Fitzgerald began to experience a rebirth of his talents. From his experiences as a vassal to the studio lords, he began fashioning a book that revealed a new depth and assurance in his writing. After exhausting the material of his flapper era days, he found a new subject that would engage his considerable talents. This book, *The Last Tycoon,* ranks with Nathanael West's *Day of the Locust* as a brilliant exploration of the dark underside of the storybook façade of Hollywood during this whirlwind period. To many critics, *The Last Tycoon* reflects maturity and control in Fitzgerald's work, a stunning finale to this great writer's work.

MGM producer Irving Thalberg was the model for the hero, Monroe Stahr. Besides its ironic and sophisticated narrative, *The Last Tycoon* offers a fascinating backstage portrait of how movies were made during this period. The book, however, is actually only a provocative fragment; Fitzgerald died before completing it, on December 21, 1940, at the age of forty-four.

A Novel Pioneer

Raymond Chandler shares the honor with Dashiell Hammett of being the pioneer of the modern detective novel. His central character, Philip Marlowe, has become the model for succeeding generations of gumshoes—insouciant and streetwise, cycnical yet gallant, a knight-errant in a rumpled trench coat. Marlowe became a culture hero after Humphrey Bogart portrayed him in *The Big Sleep.*

Southern California and Los Angeles in particular were the settings for most of Chandler's books, which include, in addition to *The Big Sleep* (1939), *Farewell, My Lovely* (1940), *The High Window* (1942), *The Lady in the Lake* (1943), *The Little Sister* (1949), and *The Long Goodbye* (1953).

Chandler was certainly no ordinary mystery writer. He had a unique gift for wry dialogue and intricate plotting and a remarkable talent for description. One of the pleasures of reading his work is the way he evokes, with a few deft and ironical strokes, the world of Los Angeles and its purlieus during this gaudy and rough-and-tumble period. The Hollywood studios were then in their full flowering, and Los Angeles was a city imbued with a frontierlike spirit, an expansive and wide open town filled with emigres from all over and laced with corruption in both high and low places.

The palm-shaded bungalow cottages and the sun-drenched streets, the fairy-tale mansions with their surreal blends of architectural styles, and the smoky nightclubs with their fancy-dressed revelers, along with the small-time hoods and predatory showgirls caught up in the expansive and entrepreneurial atmosphere of a now vanished way of life, were an inextricable part of this scene.

Chandler described a blond ex-showgirl, a typical member of his low-life cast of characters, in the following way: "From thirty feet away she looked like a lot of class. From ten feet away she looked like something made up to be seen from thirty feet away." With one final phrase, Chandler pinned the specimen, like a captive butterfly, to the wall, noting that her hair looked "as artificial as a nightclub lobby."

A powerful sense of atmosphere was conveyed in his sentences: "There was a hot desert wind blowing that night. It was one of those hot, dry Santa Anas that come down through the mountain passes and curl your hair and make your nerves jump and your skin itch. On nights like that every booze party ends up in a fight. Meek little wives feel the edge of the carving knife and study their husbands' necks. Anything can happen."

Born in Chicago in 1888, Chandler went to England with his mother when he was seven. He was educated there and contributed to various literary weeklies in his early twenties. At twenty-three he returned to the United States, where he eventually found employment in the oil business. He worked primarily for Dabney Oil Syndicate as an office manager and later as the director of its subsidiaries. During those years Chandler and his wife, Cissy, lived in various Los Angeles locations—on Melrose Avenue, on South Highland Avenue, and in Redondo Beach. In the mid-1940s, when he went to work for Paramount, the Chandlers moved to Drexel Avenue in the southern part of Hollywood near the Fairfax District. He spent his final years in La Jolla, California, where he died in 1959.

Chandler didn't begin writing mystery stories until he was in his early forties, after he found himself out of a job when the oil business collapsed during the Depression. His writing apprenticeship was short, however, for he proved that he had an extraordinary talent for his vocation. After the success of his first novel, *The Big Sleep,* in 1939, he was able to make a good living through his writing.

A collaboration with Billy Wilder on the film script for James Cain's *Double Indemnity* led him to work for Paramount in mid-1943. Much of the enduring appeal of that film, with its atmosphere of dark violence and fast-moving chicanery, can be traced to Chandler's contributions. During the mid-1940s and early 1950s, Chandler worked sporadically as a screenwriter. After leaving Paramount, he moved to MGM and later to Universal. His work on such films as *Blue Dahlia* (1946) and Hitchcock's *Strangers on a Train* (1951) showed that he had a real aptitude for screenwriting. Many of his books were adapted for the screen, including *The Big Sleep*.

Despite his long residence in Los Angeles, Chandler had a peculiar love-hate relationship with the city. Although he described it as "a big, dry, sunny place with ugly homes and no style," he was also fascinated by the various layers of its society from the glamorous reaches of the Hollywood community to the lowest depths of its criminal element. The gritty and languorous atmosphere of Los Angeles in that halcyon period before superfreeways and glass-and-steel highrises permeated his work and helped make him one of America's finest mystery writers.

Art in Los Angeles

Los Angeles's movie industry has created extraordinary job opportunities for writers, but the written word is not the only art form that has flourished here. In the 1930s artist Lorser Feitelson, whose early years were spent absorbing cubism and surrealism in New York and Paris, brought knowledge of these art movements to the area. As a member of the faculty at the Art Center School, Feitelson became very influential in Los Angeles during the next two decades. At the same time, art dealers were bringing the works of major European painters (including Matisse, Picasso, the Surrealists, and some German Expressionists) into the city, and such transplanted painters as Rico Lebrun and Stanton Macdonald-Wright were disseminating a modernist aesthetic in their art classes. The painting that dominated the 1940s and 1950s mixed European modernism with perceptions of local color.

McCarthyism gave rise to attacks on modern art in the Fifties. Communist symbols were read into the most innocuous imagery; the Los Angeles County Museum of Art was picketed by protesters crying out against subversive art. June Wayne, a sophisticated artist, who had traveled to Paris and learned the rigorous, exacting technique of lithography, was a significant figure in fighting these attacks.

The 1960s gave birth to several important art movements. At the start of the decade, Wayne opened the Tamarind Lithography Workshop at her studio in Hollywood, which revived interest in this traditional art form and did much to dignify the position of printmaking in the fine arts.

Other important activities centered around the Ferus Gallery, which showed the work of Edward Kienholz (a Ferus cofounder), Billy Al Bengston, Edward Ruscha, and numerous other artists who are now internationally acclaimed. The Ferus group, as they came to be known, were the first to create a significant body of artworks that could be called indigenous to Los Angeles; one of their products was the so-called LA Look, characterized by a cool technological/industrial aesthetic and relying on such materials as plastics (especially polyester resin), glass, chrome, and lacquer for its effects.

Performance and process art, much of it with pointed political and social overtones, came to the fore in the 1970s. Allan Kaprow, a student of musician John Cage, became an inspiring force in the "happenings" of the period, which were staged presentations combining music, dance, art performance, and elements of the visual arts and emphasizing sensory overload and experiential excitement. An important related movement was feminist art, which was born with the feminist-art program at California Institute of the Arts in Valencia and continued with the establishment of the Women's Building in downtown LA, at 1727 N. Spring St. Judy Chicago, a central figure in the CalArts program, created her monumental environmental sculpture *The Dinner Party* in Los Angeles.

Large-scale public mural activity was also high in the 1970s. A major contributor was the LA Fine Arts Squad, composed of two painters whose murals commented on the essence of the city. *The Isle of California,* off Santa Monica Blvd. in West LA, depicts a ravaged freeway hanging over a cliff, as if destroyed by nuclear war or an earthquake; *St. Charles Painting,* off Windward St. in Venice, appears to reflect the surrounding buildings with their Italianate arcades.

Today the city's art scene revolves largely around downtown. In recent years, hundreds of young artists have rented old industrial spaces and converted them to studios, and gallery activity in the area has intensified. The projected Museum of Contemporary Art, due to open in its downtown Bunker Hill location in late 1985 or early 1986, has generated excitement in art circles all over the world. (The Temporary Contemporary, two warehouses in downtown's Little Tokyo that have been renovated by post-modern architect Frank Gehry, is scheduled to open its doors earlier, in October 1983.) With plans for this major art museum on the boards, all eyes are on Los Angeles, and it is believed that the city is at last well on its way to becoming a world center for the visual arts.

ARCHITECTURE
IN LOS ANGELES

An Eclectic Collection

by
DIANA RICO

Diana Rico is a Hollywood-based journalist specializing in the arts. Her articles have appeared in California, Architectural Digest, Arts & Architecture, The Los Angeles Herald Examiner, The L.A. Reader, *and many other magazines and newspapers.*

In *The Day of the Locust,* Nathanael West's hero, Tod Hackett, is fascinated by the collection of "Mexican ranch houses, Samoan huts,

Mediterranean villas, Egyptian and Japanese temples, Swiss chalets, Tudor cottages, and every possible combination of these styles" that pass for dwellings in the canyon where he lives.

There's only one city in the world to which his description can apply: Los Angeles.

Architecture in Los Angeles is an eclectic mixture of the functional and the funny, the sleekly modern and the wildly fantastic, the intensely serious and the intentionally silly. It is the physical manifestation of thousands of dreams, fantasies, illusions, and desires. It contains such elements as Hispanic, Norman, Italianate and Moorish; Victorian, Craftsman, International, and Post-Modern; pop cultural, dingbat suburban, high commercial, and low vernacular. For many years Los Angeles architecture was not taken seriously by so-called scholars of the art. But the same city that has produced a restaurant in the shape of a brown derby, a Coca Cola factory disguised as a 1930s Streamline Moderne ocean liner, and Hansel and Gretel houses in which people actually *live* also has served as a creative haven for such major names in the field as Frank Lloyd Wright, Rudolph Schindler, and Richard Neutra in the 1920s and the 1930s, Craig Ellwood and Charles Eames in the 1940s and the 1950s, and Charles Moore and Frank Gehry in the most recent decades.

Although the city is thought of as young, it has a visual tradition going back about 200 years to its Spanish roots. El Pueblo de la Reina de Los Angeles ("the Village of Our Lady, the Queen of the Angels") was founded in 1781 by Governor Felipe de Neve and was first governed by Spain and then by Mexico until 1847. Sprawling adobe missions and ranchos, low stuccoed structures with exposed beam ceilings, red tile roofs, rhythmically arcaded galleries, and cool interior gardens planted with brilliant azaleas and bougainvilleas were the architectural results of Spanish–Mexican rule. The visual features of these self-sufficient minicommunities reflected the rough raw materials and the rough, raw way of life that characterized the region. The San Gabriel Mission (1771; 537 W. Mission Dr., San Gabriel; 282–5191) and the San Fernando Mission (1797; 15151 San Fernando Mission Blvd., San Fernando; 361–0186) still stand as local examples of this primarily ecclesiastical architecture, whereas Olvera Street (downtown between N. Main and Alameda Sts.) is the oldest surviving fragment of secular Spanish Colonial architecture. It is filled with early Spanish–American houses and commercial buildings that now serve as shops and restaurants.

The initially religious life-style gradually gave way to a secular one as ranchers and then, with the introduction of water from the Owens Valley, intensive-crop farmers prospered. By the end of the nineteenth century, writes Reyner Banham in *Los Angeles: The Architecture of*

Four Ecologies, much of the land had been subdivided and was being sold "as residential plots in a landscape that must have appeared to anyone from east of the Rockies like an earthly Paradise." In fact, it was "this promise of an ecological miracle that was the area's first really saleable product—'the land of perpetual spring.'"

In this period occurred the flourishing of the Victorian style of architecture, characterized by steeply pitched and gabled roofs, elaborate wood ornamentation, asymmetrical floor plans, decorative shingle work, and porches or verandas. Today Heritage Square (3800 N. Homer St., Highland Park; 222-3150) contains Victorian homes that have been moved to the site and restored. The area surrounding the University of Southern California, on and around Bonnie Brae Street, is also a pocket of Victorian dwellings. And at 304 S. Broadway in downtown stands one of the finest specimens of Victorian commercial architecture in the country: the Bradbury Building (489-1411), designed in 1893 by George Wyman. This building's unremarkable exterior gives no hint of what one will find inside: soft natural light filtering through a massive glass skylight into open interior corridors facing an interior court, lacy wrought-iron balcony rails, elevators, and staircases, warm brick walls, and frothy interior foliage.

A turn-of-the-century trend that was picked up and refined by major architects in Southern California was the Craftsman movement (after Gustav Stickley's *Craftsman* magazine), a response to the mass production of the Industrial Revolution. Craftsman perpetuators valued the visible celebration of craftsmanship and natural materials. The style reached its apex in the Gamble House in Pasadena (4 Westmoreland Pl.; 793-3334), a spacious "winter cottage" designed by Charles and Henry Greene for the wealthy Gamble family in 1908. It incorporates projecting hand-finished end beams, jewellike stained glass fixtures, and fine Greene and Stickley Craftsman furnishings. The Gamble House's loose plan of informally interlocking rooms, its open-air sleeping porches, and the tranquillity implied by its horizontal massing and wide, low overhangs are expressive of the relaxed life-style for which the Southland was becoming known.

The Craftsman style also became translated into a vernacular architectural form that was something like a working person's version of the Gamble abode: the California bungalow. This modest type of dwelling, described by David Gebhard and Robert Winter in *A Guide to Architecture in Los Angeles and Southern California,* "was the closest thing to a democratic art that has ever been produced," for it could be afforded without too much difficulty by "a young family on the make, a sick family on the mend, or an old family on meager savings." Usually made of wood, with low-pitched roofs, extended eaves, irregular floor plans, and a porch or a veranda joining inside and outside spaces, the

California bungalow appeared in dozens of different variations: the "airplane" bungalow (so called because of its elevated central section resembling a cockpit), the Japanese style (with upturned eaves), the Swiss chalet type (with gingerbread-cutout vented gables), and many others. The residential parts of Hollywood, Silverlake, and Echo Park are still studded with hundreds of examples of this indigenous form of architecture.

At the turn of the century there also occurred the birth of Southern California's first attempt to acknowledge its historical roots in visual terms. The Mission Revival style, which later evolved into the Spanish Colonial Revival style, encompassed a variety of visual references, from the unadorned stucco walls, red tile roofs, and rough wooden balconies of Casa Laguna (5200 Franklin Ave., Hollywood; a handsome example of the Spanish courtyard housing that became popular in the 1920s and the 1930s) to the elaborate Churrigueresque ornamentation of the St. Vincent De Paul Roman Catholic Church (Albert C. Martin, 1923; Adams Blvd. and Figueroa St.; 749–8950).

Architect Irving Gill, working at the same time as the Greenes, took the Mission Revival idiom and stripped it down to its most basic elements: clean, bare expanses of white or light colored walls, smooth planes pierced only by simple strips of glass, arched doorways and arcades—almost an abstraction of the Hispanic tradition. Gill's Horatio West Court of 1919 (126 Hollister Ave., Santa Monica), flat-roofed apartments arranged around a central patio axis, is still remarkable for its upstairs living rooms, glassed in on three sides to overlook the beach three blocks away.

Another major pioneer in the world of architecture came here in the 1920s and drew from historical sources to create fresh, innovative forms. Frank Lloyd Wright had already developed a solid theory of architecture and an extensive oeuvre (he had been working in Chicago for almost thirty years) when he met oil heiress Aline Barnsdall in Japan. She offered him a commission in Los Angeles. Between 1918 and 1920 he built what was to become known as Hollyhock House (4800 Hollywood Blvd., at Barnsdall Park; 662–7272), so called because he incorporated a hollyhock motif (the flowers grew wild on the site) into the cast concrete walls, lamp posts, carpets, drapes, and furniture. Barnsdall's former residence seems to emerge organically from its hilltop site. Its heavy, terraced concrete tiers, reminiscent of the Mayan pyramids, reflect Wright's interest in pre-Columbian art, a theme that he used again in several other houses in the Hollywood Hills, Griffith Park, and Pasadena.

Two young European architects who became prominent in Los Angeles were allied with Wright during this period. Rudolph Schindler and Richard Neutra, both Viennese born, took the Modernism that was emerging from Europe—an attempt to create a style that would transcend historical references by reflecting directly the new materials, technological changes, and social attitudes of the twentieth century—and adapted it to the Southern California environment and way of life.

In 1921, after working with Wright on the Barnsdall commission, Schindler built a house in West Hollywood for himself, engineer Clyde Chase, and their wives (835 N. Kings Rd.; 651–1510), "perhaps the first [floor] plan to give women equality with men," according to Esther McCoy in *Vienna to Los Angeles: Two Journeys.* Schindler perceived each of the four occupants "as an artist who needed a studio to work in, so the house was four beautiful cells of equal size, of equal importance"—a system of interlocking studios, sleeping porches, and small garden courtyards blending indoor and outdoor spaces with walls of white tilt-slab concrete alternating with glass panels.

Neutra arrived in Los Angeles in 1925 and lived in the Schindler–Chase House for a short time. His Health House (4616 Dundee Dr.), built in 1929 for Philip Lovell in the hills above Griffith Park, is a masterful example of the European International style adapted to the Southland's climate, geography, and relaxed ambience. Its lightweight steel frame, horizontal prefabricated panels, random suspended balconies, and great sheets of glass divided into rhythmic rectangles—all a conspicuous use of the new construction materials and technologies—gracefully belie the building's monumental size and form.

A visual style with which the 1920s and the 1930s have become identified and which found an especially comfortable home in Los Angeles is Art Deco, named after the Paris Exposition des Arts Decoratifs of 1925. Bevis Hillier, in the introduction to *Façade: A Decade of British and American Commercial Architecture,* observed that Art Deco architecture as it was developed in the United States "was the first example of Americans coming to terms with their own environment and exploiting their own lusty traditions of commercial knock-'em-for-six and showbiz razmataz in art." In its extreme stylization of visual motifs and its streamlining of forms, Art Deco celebrates the glories of the Machine Age: speed, motion, and travel. The May Company Department Store (Albert C. Martin, 1939; 6067 Wilshire Blvd.; 938–4211), with thin triple strips of windows that speed toward a golden cylindrical tower cut into the façade's west corner, exemplifies the substyle of Art Deco that came to be called Streamline Moderne. And a few miles away stands a monument to elegance and conspicuous spending done in Zigzag Moderne, another substyle of Art Deco: Bullocks Wilshire Department Store (John and Donald B. Parkinson, 1928; 3050 Wilshire Blvd.; 382–6161), with cubelike masses clustered toward a central tower—a form reminiscent of some great chunk of crystalline rock—and beautifully detailed, golden-glowing Deco interiors designed primarily by Jock Peters.

The 1920s, 1930s, and 1940s were decades of phenomenal growth for Los Angeles. Easterners and Midwesterners, who had been attracted to the Southland since the turn of the century because, as Gebhard and Winter pointed out, it "provided an environment that, given water, fertilizer, toil, and imagination, could be transformed into almost anything that the human mind could conceive," came in droves, beckoned by the burgeoning movie industry. (The city's population jumped from 576,000 to 1,238,000 between 1920 and 1930.) The centrality of the film industry to Los Angeles cemented (probably forever) its already romanticized image as a paradise where dreams come true, where fantasy reigns supreme, where illusion and reality are interchangeable.

This image found expression in a type of building that is loosely referred to as "fantasy architecture"—portions of the built environment that embody fantasy visions and can be read on this symbolic level by the general public. Thus in Los Angeles one finds, for example, a hot dog stand in the shape of a hot dog, complete with mustard and bun (Tail o' the Pup, ca. 1930; 311 N. La Cienaga Blvd.; 652–4517); a movie theater imitating an elaborate Chinese pagoda (Mann's—formerly Grauman's—Chinese Theater, Meyer and Holler, 1927; 6925 Hollywood Blvd.; 464–8111); an urban family dwelling disguised as a thatched Hansel and Gretel cottage (Spadina House, Henry Oliver, 1925; Walden Dr. and Carmelita Ave., Beverly Hills); and even an entire planned fantasy environment: Disneyland (1955; Ball Rd. at Santa Ana Fwy., Anaheim; 626–8605), which bills itself as "the Happiest Place on Earth." Disneyland is the consummate example of the Angeleno penchant for creating seamless illusion, with its perfectly rendered African jungle, fairy-tale castle, Old West streets, Mississippi riverboat, pirate ship, haunted Southern mansion, dinosaur diorama, and outer space entertainment center.

In this period there also occurred the beginnings of another important part of the built environment of the city: the freeway system, officially dating from the opening of the Arroyo Seco Parkway in Pasadena in December 1939. In subsequent years there evolved a massive web of sleek, steel-reinforced concrete thruways that to visitors today seems like a confusing tangle but to Angelenos makes reassuring sense. (Joan Didion's protagonist in *Play It as It Lays* drives the freeways ritualistically every day to restore order to her frayed nerves.)

One cannot fully appreciate the built environment of Los Angeles without experiencing its freeways—preferably as the Angeleno does, for, as Mark Leviton pointed out in the *L.A. Reader,* "the native knows from experience that freeways have personalities: the exhilarating, wide turns of the Hollywood Freeway through Silverlake (and the watchful

Western Exterminator sign), the determined tabletop of the 210 Foothill Freeway, the serenity of the rising Ventura as it leaves the West [San Fernando] Valley, the straight, functional 405 in the Valley, becoming the car-killing Sepulveda Pass, the parking lot they call the Santa Ana Freeway, the time-saving practicality of the 57 in the East, the sheer terror of the Harbor during rush hour." Although Angelenos enjoy griping about the crush of rush-hour traffic, the massive blocks of commuting time whittled away daily in their cars, they show no signs of giving it up, for the freeway system makes possible that fluid, free, mobile life-style that is an integral part of the Los Angeles dream.

The fantasy-fueling freeways and the fantasy-expressive buildings of Los Angeles are all designed for the public. But private fantasies also find their expression in the Angel City's built environment, and nowhere is this more evident than in Beverly Hills. Here one sees, in the space of a few short miles, upright Tudor mansions and French chateaus, sprawling Spanish Colonial Revival stuccos and Western ranch houses, sparkling white neo-Classical temples and pink Arabian near-palaces—each, of course, with the requisite Rolls Royce in front and swimming pool out back. Frank Lloyd Wright correctly said of these houses, "They look like the boxes Disneyland came in"—but he might have gone one better, for the fantasies that are symbolized by this exclusive enclave are not the candy coated kid stuff of Walt Disney but the hard, glittering power plays of Hollywood's heyday, fantasies of money and stardom and sex.

Some of the city's finest "serious" architecture was built in its affluent residential areas—Pasadena, Pacific Palisades, the Hollywood Hills, Malibu, and elsewhere. Craig Ellwood's Smith House of 1955 (Crestwood Dr. in West Los Angeles), a single-level series of glass boxes supported on a steep hillside by a spare steel frame, is beautiful in its Modernist simplicity. And a picture of the often illustrated Eames House of 1949 (203 Chautauqua, Santa Monica), designed by Charles Eames, was published in the English magazine *Architectural Design* and thereafter, according to Banham, influenced a generation of architects with its Mondrian-like arrangement of alternating glass and opaque wall panels outlined in skinny dark steel.

In the 1960s and 1970s there occurred the rise of the commercial skyscraper, usually modeled after the designs of Mies van der Rohe: vertical slabs sheathed in glass, their surfaces modulated only by lightly etched window outlines. Century City (between Pico and Santa Monica Blvds. in West Los Angeles) contains recent commercial buildings by some of the country's best-known contemporary architects, including Skidmore, Owings and Merrill, Charles Luckman, Welton Becket, and I. M. Pei. After the sun sets, it's transformed into a fairyland—rows of brilliant lights gleaming behind glass, breathtaking against a night-black sky.

In the last decade the Angel City, with its longtime tolerance of experimentation and eclectic façade, has witnessed the growth of work by such important Post-Modernists as Charles Moore and Frank Gehry. Moore's design for the Burns House (1974; 230 Amalfi Dr., Santa Monica) combines skylights and shed roofs in an inventive reinterpretation of the Spanish Colonial Revival idiom, all in pink. Gehry's Cabrillo Marine Museum (1981; 3720 Stephen White Dr., San Pedro; 548–7562) is a delightful concoction of chain-link fencing, galvanized metal, glass, stucco, metal pipes, and lights that has undergone a sea change. Being inside the museum, observes *Los Angeles Times* architecture critic John Dreyfuss, is like "being underwater in a sea into which all manner of building materials have been dumped and are floating on the surface."

Moore's and Gehry's recent designs, characterized by a playful rearrangement of traditional architectural elements, an unabashed gusto toward colors and materials, and, most of all, an exuberant sense of fun, are especially appropriate in this always unconventional playground of the West Coast. Gebhard and Winter drew a telling analogy when they compared the Los Angeles of today with ancient Rome, whose perpetrators of taste took pleasure in both refined "high" art and gaudy "low." "Southern California is the New Rome," they concluded. "Whether or not it lasts is not the point. It will, like old Rome, influence popular conceptions of the good life for centuries to come." One might add that the city's architecture—whether "high" or "low," traditional or experimental, formal or casual, planned or impromptu—is, like the good life it symbolizes, here to be enjoyed.

THE FOOD OF SOUTHERN CALIFORNIA

by
JANICE WALD HENDERSON and JANE E. LASKY

Janice Wald Henderson is a member of the Los Angeles Restaurant Writers Association. She contributes to in-flight magazines and newspapers around the country and makes guest appearances on local television and radio shows on the subjects of food and travel.

The attention paid to the freshness of ingredients in Los Angeles restaurants borders on the fanatical. Many discerning restaurateurs raise their own poultry and beef or have them nutured to most particular specifications. The finest eateries would not consider serving canned vegetables; nor would most neighborhood delis.

The propensity for fresh ingredients does not end at the city limits. Even if it's the dead of winter, you can find fresh raspberries flown in from New Zealand at many of Los Angeles' top dining establishments. Florida red snapper can be served as fresh as the Pacific red snapper at the same seafood restaurant. Cheesecake made in New York is flown in to Los Angeles on a weekly basis for many restaurants.

And if there ever was a region of this country with a reputation for wonderful salad combinations, it would have to be Southern California. Romaine, escarole, and Bibb lettuce is tossed with jicama and alfalfa sprouts, and that's just for starters. Even the most moderately priced bistros have satisfactory salad bars with ten to fifteen ingredients; some restaurants claim up to fifty-five!

With such dedication to freshness, Southern California restaurants are fast becoming pacesetters as they develop a distinctive California cuisine. Local meats, fish, and dairy products are stressed, usually in a simple preparation with the most understated of sauces. Fresh herbs provide startling accents to dishes; and the proximity of the Mexican border often adds Spanish-style flair. A newer local trend, toward the combination of French and Oriental cuisines, evolved from the popular *nouvelle cuisine* that revolutionized cooking. Many in-vogue restaurants are now featuring French-style entrees prepared by traditional Oriental methods. It's not unusual to find sushi on the same menu as the Gallic coq au vin, but this chicken-in-wine dish will be made with American-grown Oriental mushrooms rather than French.

The New American Cuisine and its obsession with native American products is also prevalent. Restaurant menus strictly incorporate only American ingredients, substituting them for such formerly imported items as caviar, escargots, goat cheese, and wine, among others. It is predicted by food authorities that the impact of this trend is here to stay.

Southern California restaurants have created some restaurateur superstars along with innovative cuisine. Patrick Terrail, the proprietor of Ma Maison, a chic Los Angeles bistro catering to many of Hollywood's celebrities, sees restaurants going through a revolution in the 1980s. He believes that the Mom-and-Pop concept will be reintroduced and that regional or provincial cooking will be a new area for restaurants to explore. Wolfgang Puck, former chef-owner of Spago, which features the California cuisine, claims, "It's the ingredients that typify the California cuisine. Restaurants will use them simply, without charging a fortune for the results. Los Angeles restaurants stand on their own. We do not imitate the restaurants of France." Another noted restaurateur who agrees with Terrail and Puck is Jean Leon, owner of

Beverly Hills' La Scala, a premier Los Angeles Italian restaurant. He believes that Italian and Oriental cuisines will be the two most exciting of the 1980s: "Italian food is the world's most civilized. A few fresh ingredients and you've got yourself an excellent meal."

Italian, French, and California-style cuisines are not the only styles of food preparation that you can find in Southern California. Not only is almost every type of cuisine in the world represented in bistros here, but there are specific neighborhoods that contain a bounty of authentic restaurants reflecting their ethnic origins.

The Fairfax district, which runs from Beverly Boulevard on the south to Melrose Avenue on the north and from La Brea west to La Cienega, is a predominantly Jewish community. Many residents are Israeli, but other Jewish communities throughout the world are represented. This neighborhood resembles the Lower East Side of New York at the turn of the century. Street markets and small cafés feature Kosher and Israeli food; New York-style delis also proliferate.

Chinatown in downtown Los Angeles runs along North Hill Street and North Broadway between Sunset Boulevard and the Pasadena Freeway. There are many Chinese markets and small Chinese restaurants, most of which are excellent. The Food Center is a new building in Chinatown that houses fifteen Chinese cafés; all feature specialized regional cuisines. Chinatown also contains many tea houses that serve the delicacies of *dim sum,* tiny dumplings with meat or sweet fillings.

Little Tokyo (from Los Angeles Street to San Pedro Street on 1st, 2nd, and 3rd Streets) is a community filled with sushi and tempura bars and tiny cafés. The Restaurant Plaza, built on a farmer's market concept, houses six Japanese restaurants. You can walk from one to another and sample different dishes.

The Oriental communities of Los Angeles have expanded to include Little Korea, a newer ethnic center along Olympic Boulevard between Alvarado and Western Avenues. Korean restaurants in this area specialize in Korean barbecue and assorted pickled vegetables.

Although the largest Vietnamese community is in Orange County, the area of Chinatown closest to Sunset Boulevard contains a growing Vietnamese population. Vietnamese restaurants feature a cuisine that blends both French and Oriental culinary ideas, reflecting the history of the country, including the French colonization.

San Pedro, Los Angeles' main harbor, contains a large Greek and Yugoslavian population, and restaurants of these origins may be found nearby. Just outside Los Angeles is the city of Gardena with its large Japanese community. It offers many fine Japanese restaurants. Monterey Park, south of Pasadena, has some excellent Chinese restaurants, reflecting its large Chinese population.

When one speaks of the ethnic influence on the cuisine of Southern California, tribute must be given to the Spanish settlers and nearby Mexico. As excellent pizza stands abound in New York City because of its high incidence of Italian-Americans, taco stands flourish in Los Angeles because of the Mexican cultural influence. Mexican food is Los Angeles' most popular cuisine, and refried beans, enchiladas, and tostadas play an important role in this city's diet. But Mexican food amounts to much more than these American-style staples, and the combination of the exotic seasonings of Mexican Indian cooking with the texture and the intensity of Spanish cooking has worked together to create a cuisine that is unique in the world. Many Southern California restaurants prepare regional Mexican menus that are outstanding in their sophistication and charm.

Because Los Angeles is geographically diverse, one can expect to find restaurants that take advantage of nature's attributes. Many such establishments are located along the coastline and afford fine oceanfront dining. City office buildings and some hotels feature top-floor restaurants that provide dramatic panoramic views of the city.

It wasn't too many years ago that Los Angeles had few restaurants to write about, let alone categorize. One of the earliest prominent restaurants in this city was Lawry's Prime Rib, built on La Cienega Blvd. in 1938 by Walter Van De Kamp and Lawrence Frank. This award-winning establishment was based on Simpson's-on-the-Strand, a roast beef restaurant in London. The owners were originally going to call it Larry's, but Van de Kamp thought it was not a dignified name; he suggested Lawry's. In 1947 Lawry's moved to its present location across the street from the original site, and it is still one of Los Angeles' leading restaurants.

Lawry's success helped initiate the growth of La Cienega Boulevard (from Olympic Boulevard on the south to Santa Monica Boulevard on the north) as a mecca for other dining establishments. This area was nicknamed Restaurant Row because of the large proportion of restaurants developed on this strip.

The success of Restaurant Row was ostensibly due to its shopping-center concept—the idea of clustering a group of business developments—and the simple fact that there just weren't many restaurants in the city from which to choose. Restaurant Row lost its glamour in the early 1960s, when the restaurant industry in Los Angeles started to boom. Beverly Hills continued to build restaurants, imitation French bistros became the rage, and shopping centers with convenient dining spots were springing to life in both the city and the suburbs. Today Restaurant Row is more a tourist mecca than anything else.

The Pacific Dining Car, established in 1921 in downtown Los Angeles at the corner of 7th and Westlake, quickly earned the loyal following that it maintains today. The original owners, Fred and Grace Cook, decided to build a replica of a railroad dining car. It took its name from the Pacific Electric Company, which was busy laying railroad tracks all over the city. It could have boasted of more than 1,200 miles of railway across Southern California by the mid-1920s. The menu was basic American fare: steaks, homemade steak sauce, hearty soups, and flaky pies. In 1923 the restaurant was moved to 6th and Witmer, and it has been there ever since, open daily, 24 hours a day.

In the 1920s a special sirloin steak at the Pacific Dining Car was 65 cents, and a filet mignon was a mere $1.50. Film stars Mae West and George Raft and gossip columnist Louella Parsons dined there; today the clientele consists primarily of downtown business people.

Another leading food center with a colorful history is the Farmer's Market. In the 1930s the San Fernando Valley was the place to go to get fresh produce and poultry. Farmers operated small stands on street corners, which were not extremely profitable ventures until Roger Dahljelm came along. Dahljelm figured that if all the stands were in one place; they would do better. He located a field at West 3rd and Fairfax, enticed eighteen farmers to rent stalls, and the Farmers Market opened in July 1934. Today there are more than 160 stalls in the market featuring everything from fine produce to poultry, prime beef, and fresh ice cream. More than twenty-seven restaurants, offering dishes representing many foreign cuisines, are included. It's entirely possible to eat a complete meal at different stalls offering food ranging from soup to nuts.

Los Angeles' fascination with food is annually demonstrated at the recently established Bon Appetit Gourmet Fair, which is held at the Los Angeles Convention Center every autumn. This is a three-day festival celebrating the culinary arts. It features samplings from top restaurants, cooking demonstrations, cookware exhibits, and representatives from the travel industry promoting tours pertaining to culinary exploration.

The combination of ingenuity and open-ended curiosity displayed by this city's restaurants will continue to make a pronounced mark on the American culinary scene by setting trends for the rest of the nation.

LOS ANGELES

Exploring the City over the Rainbow

by
MARIE MONEYSMITH

Marie Moneysmith, a Los Angeles based editor/writer, has contributed to the new Saturday Evening Post, New West *magazine,* The Los Angeles Times, *and many other publications.*

Los Angeles: The Big Orange, El Lay, Tinseltown, the City of Angels. Why does one place have so many different names? Perhaps because Los Angeles is not just one city; it's a collection of towns, villages, neighborhoods, and other assorted places, all connected by geography and freeways, where you can find practically anything. For instance, although Los Angeles is the entertainment capital of the world, the city also offers a growing list of cultural attractions. Los Angeles is one of the few cities in the world where people are able to choose between lying on a sunny beach or going skiing. Looking for something more stimulating than leisure-time activities? There is the possibility of visiting state-of-the-art computer technology centers and firms where aerospace research is underway that just might put a man (or a woman) on Mars in the next few years.

Maybe a fantasy diversion is what you had in mind. Here again, Los Angeles is the place for you. Less than an hour away is the world-famous Disneyland, and in the surrounding area are many other amusement parks filled with all kinds of rides and attractions. Just want to see a movie? Well, you can do that, or you can see how they're made by taking the Burbank or Universal Studios tour. Or get tickets to a prime-time television show and watch your favorite stars go through their paces.

There are the usual kinds of visitor pastimes here, too—such things to do as shopping and sightseeing. If you'd care to do a little gambling, you don't have to go all the way to Las Vegas: the race track circuit in Los Angeles is always active. At any time of the year you can find thoroughbreds racing at Santa Anita, Hollywood Park, or Del Mar. In addition, quarter horse races and trotters can be seen throughout the year at Los Alamitos Race Track.

If you'd prefer not to be a spectator, plenty of small shops offer roller skates or bicycles for rent. You can even rent a Rolls Royce if you like to travel in style.

When you get hungry, you'll have to do some choosing. There are about 16,000 restaurants in Los Angeles, *not* counting franchises and fast food parlors. They range from pure fun to extremely fine. Because of the ethnic mix in the city, one can find cuisine from all over the world in Los Angeles, as well as good old American fare.

Why does Los Angeles offer so much variety? Possibly because the city has attracted people from all over the world. Most have brought with them their dreams for a better life. Los Angeles is a city built on fantasy, hope, and wishes, a place beyond the rainbow, where even today dreams really do come true—sometimes.

The Early Days

Most people are surprised to learn how big Los Angeles is. Founded in 1769 by Spanish missionaries, the village in its early days was a sleepy little farming community that flooded every time a sizable rain came.

Although Los Angeles served briefly as the capital of California, most of the growth in the state took place in the north, especially during San Francisco's gold rush days in the mid-1800s. During those years, the fertile Los Angeles valleys provided miners up north with food, but the city, hampered by lack of water, grew only modestly.

It was another kind of "gold" that brought settlers to Los Angeles: citrus fruits. Cheap railroad fares and the promise of easy-to-grow, easy-to-sell citrus fruits attracted thousands to Southern California at the turn of the century. Black gold, in the form of rich oil deposits, was discovered in the area at about the same time and further increased the influx of would-be settlers.

Oddly enough, it was a development on the East Coast that eventually gave Los Angeles its most famous industry. Shortly after Thomas Edison developed valuable motion picture equipment in his New Jersey studio, it became apparent that the mild weather and the good sunlight of Southern California formed a more suitable environment for producing movies. And ever since the early 1900s, the Los Angeles area has been the center of the world's film business.

Los Angeles continued to thrive as its economy diversified and its population grew. Today it is the second largest metropolitan area in the United States. Yet, despite its growth, Los Angeles has managed to retain much of its early charm.

An Overwhelming Experience

"It's so spread out!" If you find yourself exclaiming about the vastness of the city during a visit to Los Angeles, don't be surprised. It's true. Los Angeles city proper isn't all that big (64 square miles as opposed to San Francisco's 49), but the Greater Los Angeles Basin, which encompasses the other towns as well, extends from the Pacific Ocean's shores 60 miles inland to the San Bernardino and San Jacinto mountain ranges and takes in all the territory between Santa Barbara and San Diego, a range of about 464 square miles. Now *that* is big, but not intimidating. The people and the pleasant weather combine to make Los Angeles one of the easiest places in which to live.

Los Angeles has been maligned on several counts: its size, the intricately entangled freeway system, the smog, and the shallow "sun worshipper" mentality. Some of these criticisms are based on fact: The place is large, no doubt about it. The freeways can be confusing, but, on the other hand, what better way to get around such a vast area than via huge arteries that keep the traffic flowing? A good map and paying attention to the roadsigns will enable you to find your way around. The smog, a natural by-product of the freeways and the geography of the city, which is located between an ocean and several mountain ranges, is another story. Fortunately, not every day is smoggy, and many Angelenos seem to be immune to the effects of unclean air. As for being

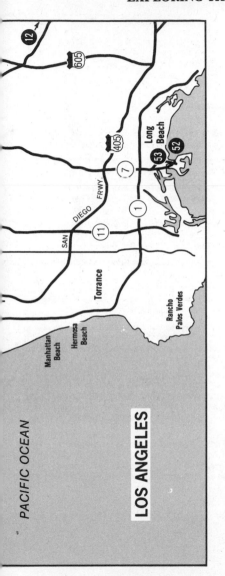

LOS ANGELES

PACIFIC OCEAN

Points of Interest
(Add'l info. on following 2 pages)

1) Rose Bowl
2) Norton Simon Museum
3) Pasadena Civic Auditorium
4) Santa Anita Racetrack
5) Mt. Wilson Observatory
6) Huntington Library Gallery
7) Descanso Gardens
8) USC Campus & Medical Center
9) Little Tokyo
10) Chinatown
11) Dodger Stadium
12) Anaheim Stadium, Disneyland, Knott's Berry Farm, Anaheim Convention Center
13) L.A. Zoo
14) Barnsdall Park
15) Griffith Park
16) Greek Theater
17) Civic Center
18) Music Center
19) City Hall
20) Watts Towers
21) Griffith Park Observatory
22) Hollywood Sign
23) Hollywood Bowl
24) Pantages Theater
25) Mann's Chinese Theatre
26) Universal Amphitheatre
27) Universal Studios
28) NBC Studios
29) Huntington Hartford Theatre
30) Union Station
31) Coliseum
32) Exposition Park
33) Hollywood Park Racetrack
34) The Forum
35) Shrine Auditorium
36) L.A. County Art Museum
37) La Brea Tar Pits
38) Farmer's Market
39) CBS TV City
40) Pacific Design Center
41) Shubert Theater
42) ABC Entertainment Center
43) UCLA
44) Santa Monica Civic Auditorium
45) J. Paul Getty Museum
46) Mormon Temple
47) Los Angeles Convention Center
48) California Museum of Science and Industry
49) Forest Lawn Memorial Park
50) Paramount Studios
51) Olvera St.
52) Queen Mary/Spruce Goose
53) Long Beach Convention Entertainment Center
54) L.A. Int'l Airport
55) Beverly Center

LOS ANGELES AREA
(Italic numbers refer to map and legend on previous pages)

Olvera Street. Cobblestoned, historic Olvera Street is a bustling strip of shops and open booths selling souvenirs and mementos of all kinds, many imported from Mexico. *(51)*

Little Tokyo. A short hop away from Olvera Street between 1st and 3rd Streets is Little Tokyo, with a wealth of restaurants, shops—and even a Buddhist temple. *(9)*

Chinatown. Close to Little Tokyo is Los Angeles' Chinatown, an active area along North Broadway where hundreds of tiny shops, restaurants, and food stores share only a few blocks of space. *(10)*

Downtown. Bordered by 1st Street, Olympic Blvd., Alameda, and Figuero Streets lies the city's downtown district, which includes the Music Center, the flower market, the garment district, the Bonaventure Hotel, and the ARCO Plaza (shops and restaurants).

Exposition Park. Close to the downtown area, Exposition Park is the site of the Los Angeles Museum of Natural History. *(32)*

The Boulevard. Wilshire Boulevard takes you from downtown Los Angeles to the Pacific Ocean, showing off lots of the city in between. Along the way to the beach, the sixteen-mile street passes Beverly Hills, Westwood, and Santa Monica.

Miracle Mile. The stretch of Wilshire Blvd. between Vermont Ave. and La Brea Ave. is known as the Miracle Mile. At the mile's end is Hancock Park, location of the famous La Brea Tar Pits, along with the George C. Page Museum, devoted to displays of prehistoric relics, many retrieved from the nearby tar.

Hollywood. The most well-known street in Hollywood is Hollywood Blvd., where the star plaques embedded in pavement beneath your feet make up the notable Walk of Fame, commemorating the greats of the entertainment industry. At the end of this walk is a monument to movies, Graumann's (now Mann's) Chinese Theatre. Also in Hollywood are Paramount Studios, ABC and CBS Studios, Griffith Park, the Hollywood Bowl, and the highly visible Hollywood sign.

West Hollywood/Fairfax Area. The Farmer's Market is located at 3rd Street and Fairfax Avenue: 20 acres of sights, including souvenir shops, restaurants, and fresh-produce stands. The Fairfax area is considered to be the heart of Los Angeles' Jewish community, and also has loads of open-air markets featuring fresh produce and baked goods. *(38)*

Beverly/La Cienega. At Beverly and La Cienega is a mammoth shopping mall, the Beverly Center, which houses more than 100 shops, 18 movie theaters, and seemingly endless eating establishments. *(55)*

Sunset Strip. A scenic view of a different kind can be found along Sunset Blvd.'s infamous strip, located between Crescent Heights Blvd. and Doheny Drive in Beverly Hills. Found on the Strip are some of the most creative billboards in the world, advertising current motion pictures or recently released record albums. The Strip is the location of the legendary Hollywood hotel favored by celebrities, Chateau Marmont, and also of a large number of restaurants catering to a wide range of tastes.

Beverly Hills. The glitz of the Strip ends as suddenly as it begins at Doheny Blvd. where Sunset Blvd. enters the glamorous and world-renowned city of Beverly Hills. Suddenly the sidewalk gives life to perfectly manicured lawns and the palatial homes of movie stars and entertainment-industry biggies.

Century City. Once the backlot of Twentieth Century Fox Studios, today Century City is a 180-acre tribute to modern architecture and the Los Angeles business world.

Westwood. Here nationalities of all kinds meet and mix creating an interesting street life. Westwood has much to offer, such as the University of California at Los Angeles (UCLA) and the actual village itself, with a dozen movie theaters, nearly as many book stores, and all manner of restaurants.

Bel Air. While not as well known as Beverly Hills, this area is equally spectacular in terms of real-estate. Upon driving through the white wrought-iron gates, you'll see some of the gigantic homes beyond—some of them, of course, owned by the stars who rule in Hollywood.

Santa Monica. This portion of town offers an interesting juxtaposition of the old and the new on its Main Street. You'll find some of the trendiest shops, restaurants, and bars anywhere, while nearby you will catch glimpses of the good old days. Take a walk along Santa Monica pier, which juts out into the Ocean.

Venice. There is no shortage of street life along the three-mile stretch of beach in Venice; sidewalk cafés, street vendors, roller skaters, bike riders and sidewalk entertainers. Canals in the area slightly remind the visitor of the Italian Venice.

Marina del Rey. A recently developed area, the Marina is home to thousands of boats, everything from sampans to yachts and schooners. The marina's harbor—one of the largest on the West Coast, and completely man-made—offers scenic boat tours.

Malibu. North of Santa Monica lies a city that is virtually synonymous with California: Malibu. Surfing here is a religion. On this stretch of the Pacific Coast Highway there are several restaurants where one can sit out over the water's edge and absorb some of the Malibu state of mind.

San Fernando Valley. For years, the Valley was considered suburbia, but now it has come into its own right, boasting fine restaurants, shopping, and several major movie studios—not to mention Beautiful Downtown Burbank.

Pasadena. Several of the main streets are lined with quaint little shops and architecture reflecting the city's early days. Some of Pasadena's claims to fame are the Norton Simon Museum, the Pasadena Library, the Rose Bowl, and Pasadena Center.

San Marino. South of Pasadena lies San Marino, home of magnificent homes and one of Southern California's most remarkable landmarks, the Huntington Library, Botanical Gardens, and Art Gallery.

inhabited by people who do nothing but sip drinks at their poolsides, that assessment is far from the truth. Some of the finest universities in the world are located here, as are some of the nation's best museums and art galleries. Although the film and television industries often overshadow it, Los Angeles has a bustling theater community that consists of a large number of Broadway-type theaters and a seemingly endless number of smaller showcases, which feature hopefuls who sometimes go on to stardom.

In addition to the universities, museums, art galleries, and theaters, there are innumerable bookstores that specialize in everything from fine first editions to pulp paperbacks and comic books. That should be enough nonalcoholic pleasure to keep anyone satisfied.

The Angeleno

Over the years, thanks to television and films depicting the southern California area, a stereotypical Angeleno has emerged: blond, tanned, athletic, and clad in swimwear. This image of the Southern Californian seems to persist for good reason. Just one visit to a beach area and you'll see why. Because of the magnificent weather, sun lovers in Southern California can enjoy their favorite pastime nearly every day. And they do. It's only during the few cool, cloudy days each year that the beaches aren't occupied by sun-streaked blond surfers and sunbathers.

But the stereotypical Angeleno is only one member of the Los Angeles population. If you travel inland, you'll find a wide-ranging mix of people, and most of them are from somewhere else. Surprising as that sounds, you'll rarely meet a native Southern Californian. The city is primarily made up of people from other places who've come here to find the good life.

Does it exist? Is the quality of life here better than it is elsewhere? It's a difficult question to answer, but most residents seem quite content with their lives. Feel free to take a poll of your own, however. Angelenos love to talk about their city and their lives.

Besides serving as a second home for transplanted Easterners and Midwesterners, Los Angeles is a melting pot comprising a substantial foreign-born population. The largest group is Mexican-Americans, and the city also has a number of Chinese, Japanese, Korean, Filipino, South American, English, Armenian, Israeli, and Polish residents, a rich assortment of ethnic communities scattered throughout the city.

The Original Los Angeles

Because of the city's vastness, it's difficult to get a clear idea of how to approach it. But if you think of it as a giant meal and try to take it just one course at a time, you'll find it easier than trying to cover too much territory in one day. Remember that Los Angeles is a basin more or less circular in shape. The best way to see the area, therefore, is to go in circles.

A convenient place to begin is at one of Los Angeles' oldest streets, now named Olvera Street. Although Los Angeles isn't a city suited to walking, this downtown district—encompassing Olvera Street, Chinatown, and Little Tokyo—lends itself to daytime walking tours.

Olvera Street is where the first settlers established a homestead, which still stands. Tours go through the Avila Adobe, built in 1818, the city's oldest extant home. One can see the furnishings of an early California family. Cobblestoned Olvera Street itself is now a bustling strip of shops and open booths selling souvenirs and mementos of all kinds, many imported from Mexico. Here you can get a colorful serape, a pinata, a first-rate enchilada, or tooled leather goods without crossing the border. Often there is outdoor entertainment such as folk dancers and mariachi bands performing in the plaza. It's no wonder that Olvera Street ranks as the city's number one tourist attraction.

A short walk from Olvera Street is Union Station Passenger Terminal, the city's central train station. Nearly fifty years old and covering 50 acres of ground, Union Station retains its historic charm. Still used today, it is filled with original furnishings. When you step inside the doors, however, don't be surprised if you experience *déjà vu:* Union Station has been seen in many films and television shows.

Another short hop away from Olvera Street, between First and Third Streets, is Little Tokyo, which contains a wealth of Japanese restaurants, shops, and even a Buddhist temple. The Japanese Village Plaza provides a mall setting for a number of shops. Nearby is the New Otani Hotel, which contains several fine restaurants serving sushi and other traditional Japanese fare. Next to the hotel is Weller Court, a retail shopping area of department stores and boutiques. At the Japan Cultural Arts Center is the new Japan America Theater, which showcases Kabuki and koto presentations. Nisei Week is celebrated here every August.

Not far from Little Tokyo is Los Angeles' Chinatown—an active area on North Broadway where hundreds of tiny shops, restaurants, and food stores share only a few blocks of space. One can sample *dim sum,* tiny traditional Chinese pastries, sip some tea, and perhaps buy a silk kimono or hand-painted fan. At night Chinatown takes on another aspect when several of the city's premier punk rock clubs open their doors and the plaza fills with an assortment of colorful young people. (Most of the older citizens seem to have gone home.) Chinese New Year, featuring parades and festivities, is celebrated here in February.

DOWNTOWN
LOS ANGELES

Points of Interest

1) Chinatown
2) Union Station
3) Olvera Street
4) Los Angeles Mall
5) City Hall
6) Music Center
7) Federal Building
8) Little Tokyo
9) Grand Central Market
10) Bradbury Building
11) World Trade Center
12) Bonaventure Shopping
   Gallery
13) Arco Plaza Visitors
   Information Center
14) Central Library
15) Pershing Square
16) RTD/Greyhound Bus
   Terminal
17) California Mart
18) Convention Center

Yes, There Is a Downtown

Many people (some of them are Los Angeles residents) claim that there is no downtown Los Angeles. But there is. In the area roughly bounded by First Street on the north, Olympic Boulevard on the south, and Alameda and Figueroa on the east and west, respectively, lies the city's center.

Like many city centers, it has its share of unsavory characters. But don't let that stop you from visiting it; it has plenty of interesting sites.

At the north end of the district is one of the renowned landmarks, the Music Center. A forty million dollar monument to Los Angeles' cultural community, it consists of three theaters. At the Dorothy Chandler Pavilion, the Los Angeles Philharmonic Orchestra, the Civic Light Opera, and the Joffrey Ballet perform. The Ahmanson Theater offers entertainment in a Broadway vein. And the Mark Taper Forum is home for some of Los Angeles' experimental plays, as well as more conventional fare.

The Los Angeles Times Building, taking up an entire city block at First and Spring Streets, houses the West's largest newspaper operations. Tours are offered.

The Los Angeles Mall on North Main Street is two blocks of double-decker shopping, plus dining and convenient parking facilities. The Los Angeles Children's Museum, with its wonderful "hands-on" displays, is at the north end of the mall.

On Wall Street near Eighth is the Los Angeles Flower Market, one of the largest in the nation. Although most business is transacted in the wee hours of the morning (when there's also the most excitement), there is still plenty to see throughout the day.

Also worth a visit in the downtown area is the Pacific Stock Exchange, a miniversion of the one in New York. The visitors' gallery on the second floor overlooks the often frenetic activities.

Also downtown is the garment district on Los Angeles Street between Fourth and Tenth, where clothing of all sorts (some by major designers, others not) is sold at cut-rate prices.

The oldest library in Los Angeles, built in 1926, is downtown on Fifth Street. This central library features beautiful Spanish tiles, a second-floor rotunda, and an outstanding collection of Californiana.

There are two very good spots in the downtown area to get one's bearings. One is the observation area on the 27th floor of City Hall. The other is at the Westin Bonaventure Hotel's rooftop lounge, which revolves, displaying different vistas of the city as you relax and take in the view. Downtown Los Angeles boasts many old architectural won-

THE
SUMMER
OLYMPICS
SUPPLEMENT

July 28 - August 12, 1984

The Summer Olympics

It all seemed so simple back in 776 B.C. The first Olympiad was held in Greece and had only one event—a 200-yard sprint for which the winner received a crown of laurel leaves. Not until 52 years later did the Greeks feel bigger might be better, adding another sprint race to the competition, this one twice as long as the first.

The modern Olympic Games, revived from the ancient tradition in 1896, have since become much bigger and, some would say, only debatably better. In recent years political acrimony and propaganda, host-city bankruptcies and human tragedy have clouded the triumphant gathering of nations. Los Angeles, host of the 1984 Summer Games, is hoping—and working hard—to avoid such problems.

History

The City of Angels has lived up to its name as corporations and other private donors have contributed the millions of dollars necessary to create a setting for the Olympics. It is the first time in Olympics history that private enterprise has financed the Games. The financial misfortunes of Montreal had much to do with the Los Angeles city fathers' refusal to fund what they feared could be another fiasco.

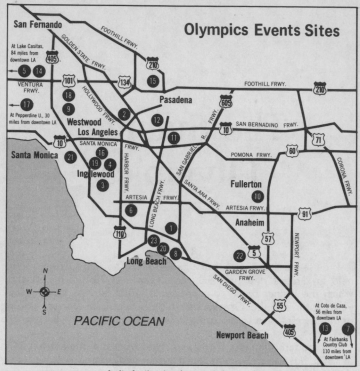

A site for the shooting events has not been chosen at press time

Events

1) Archery
2) Baseball
3) Basketball
4) Boxing
5) Canoeing
6) Cycling
7) Equestrian
8) Fencing
9) Gymnastics
10) Handball
11) Hockey

12) Judo
13) Modern Pentathlon
14) Rowing
15) Soccer (Football)
16) Swimming
17) Water Polo
18) Tennis
19) Track and Field
20) Volleyball
21) Weightlifting
22) Wrestling
23) Yachting

But it is not Los Angeles' first time as an Olympic host. The 10th Summer Olympics, held in 1932, took place in Depression-struck Los Angeles. At that time, 50 percent of the city's people were unemployed; two and three dollar tickets to the athletic events went unsold until just days before the Games; and angry unemployed workers hurled stones through shop windows decorated with the five-ring Olympic symbol. William May O'Garland, chief organizer of the Los Angeles Athletic Club which coordinated the 1932 Olympics, had to fight a committee vote which would have killed the whole event.

Public sentiment in 1984 has not been quite so hostile to the Olympics; after all, California has become the sporting center of the U.S. But Peter Ueberroth, president of the Los Angeles Olympic Organizing Committee, has fought his share of battles to bring the Games to town. He has had some convincing arguments: This year's Olympics will likely generate close to 70,000 jobs and more than $3 billion in visitor spending in Los Angeles.

Los Angeles provided the first Olympic Village when it hosted the 1932 Games. In 1984, the city will provide the first *triple* -village: three college campuses specially secured for the record-breaking 12,000 foreign athletes who will be coming from nearly 150 countries. Moreover, the Olympic torch relay planned for Los Angeles, will be the longest ever in Olympic history and the first time the flame has been kindled twice at the same stadium (except for ancient Olympia). From its lighting in Olympia this year, the torch will be carried by young athletes to Athens, then by plane from Greece to New York City, and finally by more than 10,000 Americans across the continent from New York to Los Angeles. The 12,000-mile course, including the District of Columbia, will begin May 8, 1984 and reach the Los Angeles Memorial Coliseum 82 days later on July 28.

The Olympics have grown considerably from that original 200-yard sprint in ancient Greece and from the 10 sports and 42 events staged at the first "modern" Olympics in Athens in 1896. This year there will be 23 competition or "medal" sports and 220 events. And despite tough times for the economy and international political tension, everyone close to the planning of the Olympics expects Los Angeles to be decked out with Olympic fever—that excitement that grips every host city as flags fly and the Olympic flame reaches its goal. Problems with unsold tickets seem unlikely: The opening and closing ceremonies, as well as two major events were sold out a year in advance.

5

Visitor Information

The Los Angeles Olympic Organizing Committee (LAOOC) is constantly updating the situation in Los Angeles as the time nears for the XXIIIrd Olympiad in the Big Orange in July. The Information Brochure, compiled by the Committee, will answer many questions. A copy of the brochure is available by writing: Public Information, Los Angeles Olympic Organizing Committee, Los Angeles, CA 90084; telephone (213) 305–1984.

In addition, six to eight weeks prior to the Games, Trans America will begin a hotline of prerecorded messages covering major events. Former Olympic athletes will provide the voices for these recordings, pointing out street festivals, openings and Olympic-related art activities. Call: (213) FUN IN LA (or 213–386–4652.)

Tickets

Some eight million tickets to the XXIIIrd Olympiad have been made available—the largest number in Olympic history. Seventy percent of these will be sold in the ensuing months through the mail, while thirty percent are reserved for the Olympic "family"—the news media, officials, athletes and coaches.

To order tickets for the 1984 Games, pick up a ticket order form at any of the official outlets. The largest is Sears, Roebuck and Company which includes some 3,300 retail and catalog sales outlets nationwide. In Southern California, applications may be found at any of the 204 branches of the First Interstate Bank, and in the New York City metropolitan area, at any of the branches of Manufacturers Trust. You can also obtain a ticket order form and catalog by writing LAOOC—1984 Ticket Orders, P.O. Box 60728, Los Angeles, CA 90060.

At press time, both opening and closing ceremonies were sold out as were all gymnastics, synchronized swimming and cycling events. Other events, however remained open (though tickets for swimming, diving, volleyball and weightlifting were growing scarce).

Ticket costs range from $3 to $95. The average price is $17. Some 4.5 million of the 8 million tickets are priced at or below $10. Tickets sales, the primary source of revenue available to the nonprofit Los Angeles Olympic Organizing Committee, are expected to bring in about $90 million.

Free events include men's marathon (except for the finish for which admission will be charged), women's marathon (same), men's 190-kilometer individual cycling road race, women's 70-kilometer cycling road race team time trial, selected weightlifting events and yachting.

Payment for tickets, which must accompany each order, may be made by check, money order or charge card (American Express, Visa or MasterCard).

Acknowledgement of ticket orders will be received by applicants within 60 to 90 days of the order. Olympic tickets will be delivered in June 1984.

For further information on tickets and other details, contact the Los Angeles Olympic Organizing Committee, Los Angeles, CA 90084; telephone (213) 209–1984.

Transportation

For the Olympics nearly five hundred buses will be added to the 2,940 buses in the Southern California Rapid Transit District (RTD) fleet. This special service is designed to expedite movement to and from the Games, with forty percent of the new buses primarily serving Exposition Park and UCLA. In addition, specially designed bus lanes, and on and off ramps, are being created to facilitate speedier movement to each Olympic site and Olympic Village.

The added bus service will fall into three categories:

SHUTTLE. This bus service will transport riders short distances from downtown to Exposition Park or from the Federal Building to UCLA. The fare will be $2.

EXPRESS. For longer rides, the express service will transport riders from downtown Los Angeles to UCLA, and back, for a $4 fare.

PARK AND RIDE. For motorists who wish to leave their cars in outlying suburbs, this helpful service will provide transportation to various Olympic sites. There is a $6 fare.

(A $10 ticket may be purchased to combine both regular daily RTD service with any special Olympic bus service.)

This auxiliary service is expected to start approximately two weeks before the Games begin, on July 14, 1984.

For further information, call RTD at (213) 626–4455 or write RTD, Los Angeles, CA 90001.

Olympic Housing

Despite the abundance of hotel space in Los Angeles (some 65,000 rooms), chances are accommodations will be tight during the 1984 Games. Those hotel and motel rooms that can be found, moreover, are likely to be extraordinarily expensive. Many hotels are planning to raise their room rates from 50–100% for the duration of the Olympics. As an alternative to the Best Western crowd, many independent entrepreneurs—most of them with a background in real estate or travel planning—have set up shop in the Big Orange to provide sleeping space for visitors during the Olympics. Accommodations may range from bed and bath in homes, and condominiums, to houseboats and private museums. Keep in mind that these companies listed below, although members of the Greater Los Angeles Visitors & Convention Bureau, are not endorsed by either the Bureau or the Olympic Committee, so pick a service at your own discretion.

Accommodations-Prime Locations '84, P.O. Box 80678, San Marino, CA 91108; telephone (213) 570–1746 or (213) 304–9380.

Action Housing, P.O. Box 91815, Los Angeles, CA 90009; telephone (213) 451–1166.

Apartments & Houses for Rent, 9348 Santa Monica Blvd. #101, Beverly Hills, CA 90210; telephone (213) 395–4078; telex 698475.

Association of Olympic Accommodations (Div., S.I.I.), 9107 Wilshire Blvd., #600, Beverly Hills, CA 90210; telephone (213) 275–5580 or (714) 439–4481.

California Houseguests International, 6051 Lindley Ave., #6, Tarzana, CA 91356; telephone (213) 344–7878.

Executive Home Leasing, 9100 Sepulveda Blvd., #129, Los Angeles, CA 90045; telephone (213) 649–0305.

Home Exchange International Inc., 22458 Ventura Blvd., Ste. E, Woodland Hills, CA 91364; telephone (213) 992–8990.

Homes Away From Home, P.O. Box 84384, Los Angeles, CA 90073; telephone (213) 291–3539.

Homes by Roberts, 1915 Leman Street, South Pasadena, CA 91030; telephone (213) 682–3254.

House Guests USA, Inc., 7368 Center Avenue, Huntington Beach, CA 92647; telephone (213) 598–3790 or (714) 891–3736. Telex: RCA 277709 TIUR.

Housing '84, 11581 W. Olympic Blvd., Los Angeles, CA 90064; telephone (213) 477–6007.

Housing Unlimited Inc., 1221 N. Avalon Blvd., Box 1062, Wilmington, CA 90744; telephone (213) 548–1403 or (213) 548–1664.

LA Housing for 1984, 27665 Forbes Road, Ste. D, Laguna Niguel CA 92677; telephone (714) 831–6870.

LA '84 Spectator Services, P.O. Box 1984, Rolling Hills Estates, CA 90274; telephone (213) 541–9084.

Los Angeles Gold Medal Housing, 11693 San Vincente Blvd., Ste. 1984, Los Angeles, CA 90049; telephone (213) 459–2625.

Lodgings International, 19944 Lemarsh Street, Chatsworth, CA 91311; telephone (213) 993–4000.

Lodging Unlimited of Southern California, P.O. Box 1984, Los Angeles, CA 90053; telephone (213) 877–1984, (714) 675–1984 or (800) 521–5860.

1984 Los Angeles Hotel Corporation, P.O. Box 36M09, Los Angeles, CA 90036; telephone (213) 936–6385.

1984 Los Angeles Housing, 461 Prospect Avenue, Manhattan Beach, CA 90266; telephone (213) 376–0994.

Merrill Lynch Realty-Summer Leasing '84, 11828 San Vicente Blvd., Los Angeles, CA 90049; telephone (213) 394–5033.

Olympic Accommodation Services Ltd., 415 Herondo Street, #258, Hermosa Beach 90254; telephone (213) 379–6972.

Rental World, 201 W. Colorado Blvd., Glendale, CA 91204; telephone (231) 507–1139.

Roommate Finders, 3402 Pacific Avenue, Marina del Rey, CA 90291; telephone (213) 822–5548.

Royal American Hospitality, 7002 Moody, Ste. 219, La Palma, CA 90623; telephone (714) 826–2373.

R.V. Property Management, P.O. Box 4461, Carson, CA 90746; telephone (213) 635–4583.

Southern California Vacation Housing (Division, South Bay Limousine Service, Inc.), 19323 Andmark Ave., Carson, CA 90746; telephone (213) 604–8096.

Summer Olympia Housing, Inc., 3345 Newport Blvd., #210, Newport Beach, CA 92663; telephone (213) 202–8074 or (714) 673–1271.

Century 21, Camino Real Inc., LA Olympic Housing, 7189 N. Figueroa St., Los Angeles, CA 90042; telephone (213) 258–8268.

Home or Yacht Olympic Accommodations, 1800 Broadview Avenue, Montrose, CA 91020; telephone (213) 957–5688.

OLYMPIC CALENDAR OF EVENTS

	July 28	29	30	31	Aug. 1	2	3	4	5	6	7	8	9	10	11	12
Opening Ceremony	•															
Archery												•	•	•	•	
Baseball		•	•	•	•	•	•	•	•	•	•	•	•			
Basketball		•	•	•	•	•	•	•	•	•	•	•	•	•		
Boxing		•	•	•	•	•	•	•	•	•	•	•	•	•	•	
Canoeing															•	•
Cycling		•	•	•	•	•	•	•	•							•
Equestrian Sports		•	•	•	•	•	•	•			•	•	•	•	•	
Fencing			•	•	•	•	•	•	•	•	•	•	•			
Gymnastics			•	•	•	•	•	•	•						•	
Handball			•	•	•	•	•	•	•	•	•	•	•	•	•	
Hockey		•	•	•	•	•	•	•	•	•	•	•	•	•	•	
Judo					•	•	•	•	•	•	•	•	•	•	•	
Modern Pentathlon		•	•	•	•	•										
Rowing		•	•	•	•	•										
Shooting		•	•	•	•	•	•	•		•					•	
Soccer (Football)		•	•	•		•	•		•		•		•		•	
Swimming		•	•	•	•	•	•	•								
Diving												•	•	•	•	•
Synchronized										•	•	•	•	•		
Water Polo						•	•		•	•	•	•	•	•		
Tennis							•	•	•	•	•	•	•	•	•	•
Track and Field						•	•	•	•	•	•	•	•	•	•	•
Volleyball		•	•	•	•	•	•	•	•	•	•	•	•	•	•	
Weightlifting		•	•	•	•	•	•	•	•	•	•	•			•	
Wrestling				•	•	•	•	•	•	•	•	•				
Yachting						•	•		•							
Closing Ceremony																•

10

OLYMPIC EVENTS

Like the city of Los Angeles itself, events for the XXIIIrd Olympiad are spread far and wide. From downtown Los Angeles, south to San Diego and north to Lake Casitas, the Olympics will take advantage of beach-front, lake-side, and urban locations. Here is a run-down of these Olympic game sites and the events hosted at each:

Opening and Closing Ceremonies, Track and Field

The Los Angeles Memorial Coliseum, in downtown Los Angeles, brings an interesting historical flavor to the 1984 Games. The Coliseum was built back in 1923, and was used for the 1932 Olympic Games. The Coliseum will host all track and field events, in addition to the opening and closing ceremonies. The fact that these two important ceremonies will be held at the same place is a history-making arrangement, as are the plans for the President of the United States to officiate at the opening festivities for the first time. The lighting of the Olympic torch and the parade of the athletes are mainstays of the opening ceremony, which this year promises to be especially innovative under the direction of movie and television producer, David Wolper. The closing ceremony, on August 12, will feature bands, performers, choirs, fireworks, and the extinquishing of the Olympic flame. Extensive refurbishing of the Coliseum has been sponsored by the Atlantic Richfield Co. (ARCO), and includes the addition of a world-class, synthetic track.

The Opening Ceremony will take place on July 28. Track and field events are scheduled for August 3–6, and August 8–12. Ticket prices for track and field events range from $8 to $60; and for the opening and closing ceremonies from $50 to $200.

HOW TO GET THERE. Take the Santa Monica Fwy (10) east to the Harbor Fwy (11) south, exit at Martin Luther King Blvd. (formerly Santa Barbara Ave.) left, to Figueroa, make a right and follow signs to the Coliseum.

Swimming Sports

The University of Southern California (USC), site of the Mac-Donald's Corporation's Swim Stadium, will host the swimming, diving, and synchronized swimming competitions. Pepperdine University, in Malibu, will host the water polo competition. The swimming and diving events are traditionally among the most popular, and the new world-class facility at USC should add to the excitement of these events. Synchronized swimming, or choreographed aquatic ballet, is a new discipline for women and a much-heralded addition to the games.

Swimming events are scheduled for July 29–31, and August 2–4. Diving events are set for August 5–12; synchronized swimming for August 6, 8, and 9; and water polo for August 1–3, 6, 7, 9 and 10. Tickets for diving range from $10 to $75; for swimming $15 to $95; for synchronized swimming from $5 to $35; and for water polo from $7 to $30.

HOW TO GET THERE: For USC, take the Santa Monica Fwy (10) to Vermont, exit, go to Exposition and make a left; this borders USC. Pepperdine University is in Malibu on Pacific Coast Hwy (1); make a right at Malibu Canyon Rd, and the campus is on your left.

Boxing

The Los Angeles Sports Arena, site of the boxing competition, is well known to moviegoers as the backdrop for "Rocky" and "Rocky II," as well as to boxing fans for its many championship bouts. This was also the site of the 1960 Democratic Convention at which John F. Kennedy was nominated. The boxing events will feature 400 of the world's best amateur boxers in 12 weight categories.

Boxing events are scheduled for July 29–August 9, and August 11. Ticket prices for boxing range from $10 to $95.

HOW TO GET THERE: Take the Santa Monica Fwy (10) east to the Harbor Fwy then head south to the exit at Santa Barbara Ave., make a left, and then a right on Figueroa, and a left on South Coliseum Dr.

Basketball

The Los Angeles Forum, in Inglewood, has been called one of the world's most beautiful basketball arenas. Home of the Los Angeles Lakers Basketball team, this stadium will host the Olympic basketball competition, as well as part of the handball competition. The Forum has played host to the National Basketball Association Professional Basketball Championships six times since its opening in 1966. Furious competition is expected at the Olympic basketball games, which should prove to be one of the most popular events.

Games are scheduled for July 29–August 10. Ticket prices for basketball range from $5 to $95.

HOW TO GET THERE: Take the San Diego Fwy (405) south to Manchester Blvd. (42), go east about two miles to the corner of Manchester and Prarie.

Weightlifting

The Albert Gersten Pavilion at Loyola Marymount University, will be the site for the weightlifting competition. This newly built facility is in the midst of the lush greenery of the campus, and will be a respite for those weary of more congested areas. Weightlifting traditionally measures power, both mental and physical.

Weightlifting events are scheduled for July 29–August 2, and August 4–8. Tickets for events range from no charge to $25.

HOW TO GET THERE: Take the San Diego Fwy (405) south to the Centinela/Sepulveda exit, go right on Sepulveda to 80th St., make a right and the campus is about a mile away on the right.

Cycling

California State University, Dominquez Hills, in Carson, is the site of the new velodrome, specially built for the Olympic cycling events. The $3 million facility is the only world-class cycling track in the western states and touted to be the perfect shape for its purpose. Bicycle racing offers the spectator a fascinating look at a unique combination of strategy and athletic ability.

Cycling events are scheduled for July 29–August 3, and August 5. Ticket prices for cycling range from no charge for road races in Mission Viejo to $30.

13

HOW TO GET THERE: Take the San Diego Fwy (405) south to Avalon Blvd., make a right and the college is a few miles away on the right.

Archery

El Dorado Park, in Long Beach was built in 1972. The only facility of its kind in southern California, it will host the archery competition. The range is approximately 275 meters wide and can accommodate 50 targets. During the four days of archery competition each competitor will shoot a total of 288 arrows. In recent years, Americans have dominated this sport in both the men's and women's events.

Archery events are scheduled for August 8–11; prices for tickets to the events range from $5 to $40.

HOW TO GET THERE: Take the San Diego Fwy (405) south to the 605 Fwy, go north and exit at Spring St. The park is visible from the freeway to the west.

Soccer

The world-famous Rose Bowl, in Pasadena, will play host to the soccer competition, in which 16 teams will participate. This facility was the site of the cycling competition in the 1932 games, and is currently home to the Los Angeles Aztecs. Soccer fans in over 150 nations have made this game the most popular spectator sport in the world. One hundred of those countries will vie in pre-Olympic competition for the 16 places.

Soccer games are scheduled for July 29–August 3, and August 5, 6, 8, 10 and 11. Ticket prices range from $3 to $20.

HOW TO GET THERE: Take the Pasadena Fwy (11) north to the junction of routes 134 and 210; the Rose Bowl is in Brookside Park.

Equestrian Sports

Santa Anita Park, in Arcadia, will be the site of the Olympic equestrian competitions, except for a three-day event which will be held at Fairbanks Ranch Country Club, in San Diego. Santa Anita Park, with its distinctive Spanish flavor, opened on Christmas day in 1934. Its opening spurred renewed interest in racing in southern California; that interest has been going strong ever since. The 1984 competition will include: show jumping; dressage, a test of the horse's skill; and the three-day event which is a combination of jumping, dressage, and endurance over cross-country, flat, and steeplechase courses.

Events are scheduled for July 29, 30, August 1, 3, 4, 7–10, and 12. Tickets for these events range from $5 to $110.

HOW TO GET THERE. For Santa Anita Park take the Ventura Fwy (134) south to the Foothill Fwy (210); go south to Baldwin Rd., exit and make a right. The park is on the right near Santa Anita Fashion Park. For the Fairbanks Ranch Country Club, take the San Diego Fwy (405) south to Route 5, exit near Del Mar at Via de la Valle, go east to El Camino Real, turn right and you will see a sign that says Fairbanks Estates. Go to San Dieguito Rd. and make a left. The golf course on which the events will take place is on your left.

Gymnastics

Pauley Pavilion, on the University of California, Los Angeles (UCLA) campus, will host the gymnastic events. The ease and grace of Olympic gymnasts makes for spectacular viewing. This year a new discipline, rhythmic gymnastics, will be offered; hoops, balls, ribbons and clubs are used in these eye-catching routines.

Scheduled dates of competition are July 29–August 5, and August 9–11. Tickets for gymnastic events range from $10 to $95.

HOW TO GET THERE: Take the San Diego Fwy (405) to Wilshire Blvd., follows signs to Westwood, make a left on Westwood Blvd.; this takes you directly to Westwood Plaza and the campus.

Fencing

The Long Beach Convention Center will be used for the fencing competition. Fencing was introduced into the Olympics at the 1896 games and has appeared ever since.

Events are scheduled for August 1–5 and August 7–11. Ticket prices for the fencing events range from $5 to $20.

HOW TO GET THERE: Take the San Diego Fwy (405) south to the Long Beach Fwy (7), then go south to the end of the freeway, and make a left on Linden St.

Handball

California State University at Fullerton is the site, along with the Forum, of handball competitions. This team sport, which resembles basketball, was first developed in Denmark at the turn of the century as a way for soccer players to keep in shape during the winter. It is very fast: Handball has been called hockey without the sticks.

Handball events are scheduled for July 31–August 11. Tickets for the events range from $3 to $30.

HOW TO GET THERE: See above (Basketball) for the Forum. To get to California State University at Fullerton take the San Diego Fwy (405) south to the Artesia Fwy (91), go east to the Orange Fwy (57), and go north to the Nutwood Ave. exit; turn left and the campus is a block away on the right.

Judo

California State University, Los Angeles, will be host to the Olympic judo competition. A relatively new Olympic sport, judo was first introduced into the games in 1964. The popular sport includes competition in eight different weight categories. Throws, locks, and strangleholds are all used to get an *ippon,* or full point, which ends the match.

Judo events are scheduled for August 4–11. Tickets range from $20 to $25.

HOW TO GET THERE. Take the San Bernadino Fwy (10) east to Eastern, exit, make a right on State University Dr., which borders the campus.

Canoeing and Rowing

Lake Casitas, in Ventura County, is the site for the canoeing and rowing competitions. This marks the first time that a natural setting has been used for an Olympic event since 1960. When driving to this particular site, along Route 101, Olympic goers will be treated to numerous beaches: Carpinteria; Emma Wood; and Buenaventura State beaches, among others. Ventura is also a good stepping-off point for the Channel Islands.

Canoeing and rowing events are scheduled for July 30—August 11. Tickets for canoeing range from $5 to $10, and for rowing also from $5 to $10.

HOW TO GET THERE: Take the Santa Monica Fwy (405) north to the Ventura Fwy (101), go north to Route 150 which surrounds the lake.

Hockey

East Los Angeles College will host the Olympic hockey events. Located less than 10 miles from the Coliseum, and USC, the East Los Angeles College Stadium has been the scene of numerous sporting activities, including football and athletics. Field hockey is a rugged game that requires speed and agility. The United States will make its first appearance with a team in this sport since the 1956 games in Melbourne. This is also only the second time that a women's team will compete in field hockey.

Hockey games are scheduled for July 29—August 11. Tickets for hockey events are priced from $3 to $15.

HOW TO GET THERE: Take the Long Beach Fwy (7) north to the Pomona Fwy (60), go east and exit at Atlantic Ave., make a left, go to Brooklyn Ave., make a left and the college will be on your right.

Pentathlon

The Modern Pentathlon will be held at Coto de Caza resort in Trabuco Canyon. In rural surroundings, all-around athletes will compete in a demanding series of contests: riding, on an unfamiliar horse; swimming, in a 300-meter course against the clock; fencing; shooting, with a .22 caliber pistol; and running a 4-kilometer cross country course. All of these events are contested on both a team and individual basis.

Pentathlon events are scheduled for July 29—August 1. Tickets are $14.

HOW TO GET THERE: Take the San Diego Fwy (405) south to 5, continue south to El Toro Road, exit and go east 6 miles to Live Oak Canyon Road; make a right and follow it to the end and the entrance to Coto de Caza.

Volleyball

The Long Beach Arena is the location of the volleyball competition. This sport is considered one of the fiercest around. The game originated in America, and the American women's team is one of the best in the world today. Volleyball is second only to soccer in international popularity. The Arena is part of the Long Beach Convention Center Complex and was built in 1962.

Volleyball games are scheduled for July 29–August 8 and August 10 and 11. Tickets for the games range from $5 to $60.

HOW TO GET THERE: Take the San Diego Fwy (405) south to the Long Beach Fwy (7), go south to the end of the freeway and make a left on Linden St.

Yachting

Olympic Yachting will be held at the Long Beach Marina and Harbor. This is the first time that this particular competition will be held close by other activities, and will include boardsailing. Long Beach has been the scene of Olympic class regattas for many years.

Yachting events are scheduled for July 31–August 3 and August 6–8. Admission is free.

HOW TO GET THERE: Take the San Diego Fwy (405) south to Long Beach Fwy (7), take it to the end and make a left on Linden St. The marina is behind the Entertainment Center Complex.

Wrestling

The Anaheim Convention Center is the site for wrestling matches. This sport has its roots in ancient times, when it served as a test of endurance. Two styles are featured in Olympic competition—Greco-Roman and freestyle. The difference is that in Greco-Roman style rules prohibit attacking one's opposition below the waist.

Bouts are scheduled for July 30–August 3 and August 7–11. Tickets range from $5 to $25 for wrestling events.

HOW TO GET THERE: Take the San Diego Fwy (405) to the Garden Grove Fwy (22), go east to Harbor Blvd., make a left and follow signs to the Convention Center; it is up the road on the left.

Shooting

The site for the Olympic shooting competition has yet to be determined at press time. This sport requires concentration, coordination, and control. Competitors take into consideration such factors as the earth's rotation, and their own heartbeats. Competitions include air rifle, trap, skeet, running game, rifle and pistol matches. For the first time the 1984 Games will have women-only shooting events.

Events are scheduled for July 29–August 4. Tickets for shooting competitions are $10.

Demonstration Games

In addition, two Olympic sports-to-be will be on display at Los Angeles: Baseball and tennis. Both are slated to become full competition events in future Olympics (tennis, in fact, has already been granted that status for the 1988 games), but for the present are played for demonstration only. No medals are given.

Baseball

Dodger Stadium will be the site of the baseball demonstration games. At press time, six nations were scheduled to compete: South Korea, Italy, Cuba, Nicaragua, Chinese Taipei (Taiwan), and the U.S. This is the seventh time that baseball has been included in the Olympics.

Games are scheduled for July 30 through August 6. Prices for baseball tickets range from $5 to $20.

HOW TO GET THERE: Take the Santa Monica Fwy (10), east to the Harbor Fwy/Pasadena Fwy (11), go north, exit on Stadium Way, and follow signs.

Tennis

Tennis will be played on the UCLA campus. At press time it was uncertain which countries would be competing.

Matches are scheduled for August 6 to 11. Tickets range from $5 to $15 for the preliminary matches, $20 to $50 for the finals.

HOW TO GET THERE: See directions under "Gymnastics."

THE OLYMPICS ARTS FESTIVAL

The affiliation of the arts with the Olympics began in 1906 when a movement to develop the complete person—not just athletic ability—was established. To underline this commitment and philosophy during the XXIIIrd Olympiad, a ten-week international celebration of the arts has been scheduled to coincide with the Games.

The Olympic Arts Festival will present more than fifty performing arts companies from eighteen countries and six continents. Beginning June 1, 1984, this city-wide celebration will feature some of the best theater, music and dance in the world today.

Dance

Dance, the performing art most closely tied to sports, is widely and diversely represented at the Festival. Bowing June 1 is Pina Bausch und das Wuppertaker Tanztheater, one of Europe's most exciting and dynamic groups. This is the first time this evocative choreographer and her troupe will perform in the United States. The work is presented dance/theater style.

Among other major dance masters to be included in the Festival are Twyla Tharp, known for her eclectic use of American popular music; Merce Cuningham, a pioneer of modern dance; and the Feld Ballet, whose themes reflect on social criticism through the use of vaudeville. Others slated for performances during the Olympics in Los Angeles are the Dance Theatre of Harlem, the Joffrey and the L.A. Dance Company—collectively exploring the many variations of the classical side of the art form.

Among international companies confirmed or invited to the Festival are Canada's Royal Winnipeg Ballet; Japan's Sankai Juker and Kodo—the "demon drummers"; Guinea's famed Les Ballet Africains (in their first performance in the U.S. in thirteen years); the London Contemporary Dance Company; Ballet Folklorico de Mexico; and the Korea National Dance Company.

All in all, more than 70 performances by dance companies will take place, primarily at the *Pasadena Civic Auditorium* (300 E. Green St., Pasadena 91101) and the *Japan America Theater* (244 S. San Pedro, LA 90012).

Theater

There will be many forms of theatrical presentations at the Olympics Arts Festival, including the performance of Shakespeare in four languages (English, French, Italian and Russian). Among those companies invited are Brazil's Macunaima, staging large scale spectacles combining erotic imagery with political overtones; Italy's 1 Colombaioni, presenting two clowns performing in the commedia dell'arte tradition; Canada's Theatre Sans Fil, which uses larger-than-life puppets and Belgium's Radeis, staging the gentle satire of street theater. Other countries to survey world theater during the Olympics include Australia, China, Mexico, Japan and, of course, the United States.

(Dates and locations had not been determined at press time.)

Music

On July 27, the night preceeding the beginning of the Games, the Los Angeles Philharmonic—lead by Michael Tilson Thomas—will salute both international and American artists at the *Hollywood Bowl*. Contemporary American tunes will be featured in several concerts blending jazz and country with blues and folk music.

HOW TO GET THERE. Heading north, take the Hollywood Fwy (101), exit at Barham, bear right and signs will lead to the Hollywood Bowl. Heading south, take the Hollywood Fwy (101), exit at Highland to 2301 N. Highland.

And in keeping with the Olympic's theme, the Festival will present winners of the 1984 International Chamber Music competitions, including Banff, Naumburg, Evian and Coleman. On hand as well will be the highly regarded Sequoia Quartet. Neither a date nor a site had been set for the concert at press time.

Art

In conjunction with the Louvre, the *Los Angeles County Museum of Art* (LAOMA) (5905 Wilshire Blvd,) will present "A Day in the

Country: Impressionism and the French Landscape." The exhibition of 140 paintings, including 45 borrowed from the Louvre, will be on view from June 28 through September 16, 1984.

HOW TO GET THERE. Take the Santa Monica Fwy (10) to Fairfax exit, head north to Wilshire Blvd., turn right and then two blocks east to the museum at 5905 Wilshire.

Tickets. Price of admission to the L.A. County Museum of Art is normally $1.50 but due to the unusual nature of this exhibition, authorities at the museum say prices may escalate to $3. For more specific details closer to the time of the exhibition, call (213) 857–6201.

Although the *Museum of Contemporary Art* (MOCA) is not scheduled for completion in the Bunker Hill area until 1986, a major exhibition will be erected a mile down the street at the Temporary Contemporary Museum (at 152 N. Central; telephone: (213) 621–2766.) This museum will serve as exhibit space for the not-yet-completed MOCA.

The first exhibit to line the walls of the Temporary Contemporary Museum is *In Context,* mounted in November 1983, and scheduled to run through the Olympics. Twelve works of contemporary art form this exhibit in both the museum and in various locations throughout the city. Represented will be Robert Therrian, Mariea Nordman, Michard Heizer, Betye Faar and Mark Cere.

Another exhibit to coincide with the Olympics at the Temporary Contemporary is *The Automobile and Culture,* to be mounted in June 1984.

HOW TO GET THERE. Take the Santa Monica Fwy East to the Harbor Fwy (11) North, exit at Second Street, head east, make a left at Central. From the Hollywood Fwy South, take the Harbor Fwy (11) North. Exit at Second street, head east and take a left at Central.

At the *Craft & Folk Art Museum* (5814 Wilshire Blvd.) from June 1 through August 2, an exhibit called *Masks In Motion* will highlight the masking traditions of many of the 151 nations participating in the XXIIIrd Olympiad. For more information, call the Craft & Folk Art Museum at (213) 937–5544. A Festival of Masks is scheduled for July 20, 21 and 22 to be held in a park outside the Craft & Folk Art Museum. Choreographed as a dance production, the Festival will feature the use of masks in theater.

HOW TO GET THERE. Take the Santa Monica Fwy (10) to Fairfax, head north to Wilshire Blvd. Make a right to 5814 Wilshire Blvd.

A ceremonial gateway will be placed at the front of the **L.A. Memorial Coliseum** (3939 South Figueroa St.). Created by Robert Graham, it will greet athletes of the 151 participating nations as they pass through for the Olympic ceremonies.

HOW TO GET THERE. Take the Santa Monica (10) Fwy east to the Harbor (11) Fwy South, exit at Martin Luther King Jr. Blvd.; make a left at Figueroa, turn right and follow signs to Coliseum.

Other programs being planned include exhibits at the L.A. Municipal Art Gallery, Barnsdall Park (4804 Hollywood Blvd.) featuring ceramics by Carlos Almaraz and Judd Fine; "The Pursuit of Excellence," a multi-media history of the Olympics at the L.A. County Museum of Natural History (900 Exposition Blvd); "Blacks in the Olympics 1904–1980" at the new California Museum of Afro American History; "Folk Arts Mexico—L.A." at the Plaza de la Raza in East Los Angeles; "Rowing—Art and Artifact" at the Art Museum at UCSB (Art Building, 1626B University of California-Santa Barbara), as well as a 75-foot mural along the Tujunga Wash documenting the roles of women and minorities in the Olympic Games.

Film

Since Los Angeles is the movie capital of the world, it is only appropriate that film be well represented. The largest public film event in the world—Los Angeles's International Film Exposition (Filmex)—will schedule its annual festival in July 1984 to coincide with the Olympic Games.

A special Sports Film Festival will be included along with the regular showcases of documentaries, classics and short films. The Olympiad of Animation presents new films especially created for the festival, keeping the Olympic theme at the forefront.

ders, but the shimmering cylinders of the Bonaventure are certainly one of the most dramatic constructions of recent origin.

Other sights in the downtown area include the Bradbury Building, an architectural wonder built in 1893 on S. Broadway, the Arco Plaza, which features some fine art displays, shops, restaurants, and the World Trade Center. For something with more of an ethnic flavor—almost any ethnic flavor in the world—check out the Grand Central Market, a vast cavern filled with shops for food and delightful oddments of all kinds, on Third Street. A less well-known downtown spot is St. Vincent's Court on Seventh Street, a lovely little courtyard where you can buy a book and a bouquet and even enjoy them both at an open-air coffee shop.

Near Downtown

Although not strictly downtown, two of the city's finest museums are only a short drive south. The California Museum of Science and Industry honors achievements in aviation, space technology, mathematics, electricity, and industrial design. Some learning, "hands-on" types of exhibits are fun and instructional for both children and adults.

Close by in Exposition Park is the Los Angeles Museum of Natural History. Its displays focus on mammal, bird, and artifact exhibits from all over the world. The development of motion pictures is also the subject of a fascinating exhibit here.

In the same vicinity is the campus of the University of Southern California, a leader in both education and sports. Many of the buildings on the spacious campus are reminiscent of Ivy League schools, with their brick and ivy-covered buildings. The school has a leading film studies department, as well as medicine, dentistry, and pharmacy. One of the few gerontology departments in the nation is located here as well. The university's Fisher Art Gallery houses sixteenth- and seventeenth-century Flemish and Dutch paintings.

Also in this area are three of Los Angeles' major stadiums. The Los Angeles Memorial Coliseum is the site of football games, motorcycle racing, rodeos, and other competitive sports. The coliseum was built in 1932 to house the Olympic events of that year.

Nearby is the Sports Arena, a modern, enclosed structure where indoor sporting events, such as basketball and tennis, are held. Farther north is Dodger Stadium, home of Los Angeles' most famous National League baseball contenders.

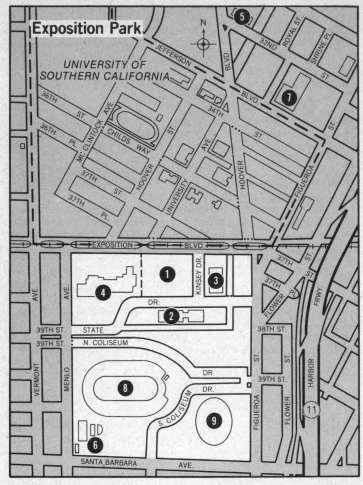

Points of Interest

1) Exposition Park Rose Garden
2) California State Museum of Science and Industry
3) The Space Museum
4) Los Angeles County Museum of Natural History

5) Hebrew Union College and Skirball Museum
6) Swimming Stadium
7) The Shrine Auditorium
8) Los Angeles Memorial Coliseum
9) Sports Arena

The Boulevard

Since the Los Angeles Basin is round in shape and not everyone wants to traverse the entire circumference of the place, there is an alternative. You can take Wilshire Boulevard from downtown Los Angeles to the Pacific Ocean. Along the way to the beach, the 16-mile street passes by Beverly Hills, Westwood, and Santa Monica before it runs to the ocean. Like New York's Fifth Avenue or Chicago's State Street, Wilshire is filled with banks, shops, department stores, and myriad stop offs. (In fact, a neat little four-hour capsule tour of Los Angeles can be accomplished by taking Wilshire from its point of origin to the beach, continuing on the Pacific Coast Highway up to Sunset Boulevard, and then following Sunset all the way back downtown.)

The stretch of Wilshire between Vermont and La Brea referred to as the Miracle Mile—the world's only linear downtown—contained the city's first commercial establishments adapted to motorized transport in the 1920s. At the end of Miracle Mile is Hancock Park, the location of the famous La Brea Tar Pits and the George C. Page Museum, devoted to displays of prehistoric relics, many of them retrieved from the nearby tar.

Adjacent to Hancock Park is the Los Angeles County Museum of Art, a worthwhile stop. A major collection of Impressionist paintings and an excellent sculpture garden are permanently on display. In addition, major national exhibits are frequently booked. The museum consists of three buildings and the sculpture garden. The four-story Ahmanson Gallery displays collections spanning the history of art and culture. Among its offerings are works by Picasso, modern-day American painters, and early Asian artisans. The Frances and Armand Hammer Wing features contemporary art and visiting exhibitions. The Leo S. Bing Theater shows retrospectives of Hollywood classics.

Hollywood

Following Wilshire will provide you with a pleasant overview of the city; but to get to the main sights, other routes are required. In Los Angeles, the foremost sight and the "city within the city" is Hollywood. Once synonymous with glamour, Hollywood is now a shadow of its former self.

The area is roughly bounded by Vermont Avenue on the east, La Brea on the west, Melrose on the south, and Franklin on the north. The best known Hollywood street within the city, though, is Hollywood Boulevard. It still offers a wealth of sights. Beginning at the eastern edge, at Vermont and Hollywood Boulevard, the first attraction is

Points of Interest

1) Mann's Chinese Theatre
2) Hollywood Bowl
3) Pantages Theater
4) Huntington Hartford Theatre
5) Capitol Records, Inc.
6) Hollywood Memorial Park

7) Hancock Park
8) CBS Studios
9) ABC TV
10) Los Angeles Convention and Exhibition Center
11) Greek Theatre
12) Observatory
13) Hollyhock House, Barnsdall Park

14) Burbank Studios
15) Universal Studios
16) CBS Television Studios
17) Farmer's Market
18) Los Angeles County Museum of Art
19) La Brea Tar Pits

Barnsdall Park, a former estate designed by Frank Lloyd Wright. It now houses the municipal Art Gallery and a Junior Arts Center where exhibits by local artists and festivals celebrating creativity are held. There are tours of Hollyhock House, oil heiress Aline Barnsdall's former residence, which still contains some of the original furnishings from the 1920s. Hollyhock House was recently restored.

Farther west along the boulevard is the Pantages Theater, a former movie palace that has been refurbished and now presents Broadway musicals.

Continuing west: The famous intersection of Hollywood and Vine is nearby, but visitors may notice that it is not quite what it used to be. Nevertheless, this stretch of Hollywood Boulevard between Vine and La Brea is fun to stroll. North on Vine is an architectural wonder, the Capitol Records building, shaped like a stack of records with a needle on top. In addition, there are endless novelty and book shops, as well as lots of movie memorabilia and poster shops. The stars embedded in the pavement beneath your feet, commemorating the greats of the entertainment industry, make up Hollywood's Walk of Fame. At the end of this walk is a monument to the movies, Grauman's (now Mann's) Chinese Theater. Even the most jaded traveler can have fun trying to match foot- and handprints with those of their favorite stars. And even if you're not going in to catch a movie, take a peek at the lobby of the theater. It's a wonderful reminder of the splendor that once was Hollywood.

The equally extravagant Egyptian Theater is located across the street from the Chinese. Also nearby, just one block east, is the Hollywood Wax Museum, containing lifelike replicas of immortal stars.

Speaking of movies, where is the industry that once made Hollywood great? A fair share of it is still in Hollywood. Paramount Studios is just south of Hollywood Boulevard, at Melrose and Valentino. And in that neighborhood there are many small, independent studios, film-developing labs, and other auxiliary services—such as plant rental outlets that can create a whole jungle on a soundstage—that supply the film industry with its magic.

There are two major television studios on the edges of Hollywood: ABC is located on Prospect Street, at the eastern fringe, and CBS is on Beverly Boulevard, to the south.

Griffith Park

Just north of Hollywood Boulevard is one of the city's jewels—Griffith Park. Comparable to New York's Central Park or Chicago's Lincoln Park, this quiet haven contains a zoo, lovely scenic drives, playgrounds, an observatory, and all the other amenities traditionally associated with a major city park. It also offers some extravagant vegetation and, from its high points, vistas unmatched anywhere else in the city.

Farther west a bit, a familiar Hollywood trademark can be seen up in the hills. The world-famous Hollywood sign spells out the name of the city in 45-foot high letters that weigh a total of 480,000 pounds. Erected in 1928, the sign originally read, "Hollywoodland"—an advertisement for Hollywoodland Realty. The *land* fell off, and what was left was simply *Hollywood*—which stuck. The sign fell into further disrepair over the years but was refurbished and rededicated in 1978.

Just to the west of the sign is another of Los Angeles' major cultural attractions: the Hollywood Bowl, a home of the Los Angeles Philharmonic Orchestra. Busiest in the summer, the bowl, a natural amphitheater set in a hillside, sponsors concerts by some of the greatest conductors and musical performers in America. Most of the performances are in the evening, under the stars, and picnicking on the grounds before a concert is one of the supreme summer pleasures in Los Angeles.

West Hollywood

In the area known as West Hollywood, between Hollywood and Beverly Hills, run Fairfax and La Cienega Boulevards, two streets that offer a number of diversions.

At Third Street and Fairfax Avenue is the Farmer's Market, a novel shopping area that once served the Depression-era farmers of Los Angeles. Today the Farmer's Market offers convenient parking and 20 acres of sights, including souvenir shops, restaurants featuring many kinds of cuisines, and fresh produce stands—as well as a small wine-tasting room.

Continuing north on Fairfax, you'll find a lot of open-air markets featuring fresh produce and baked goods. Fairfax is considered to be the heart of Los Angeles' Jewish community, and many of these stores offer kosher products.

At Beverly and La Cienega is an absolutely mammoth shopping mall, the Beverly Center, which houses more than 100 shops, 18 movie theaters, and endless eating establishments—including the landmark Hard Rock Café. The rest of La Cienega is made up of restaurants, shops, and art galleries that encourage browsing.

If you are interested in the unusual, check out the shops along Melrose Avenue, which runs between Hollywood and West Hollywood. This area has recently blossomed as a novel shopping district. It is filled with one-of-a-kind and imported items from all over the world. The merchandise includes everything from funky antiques to sophisticated clothing to new wave and high-tech home furnishings. Melrose Place, a short street that branches off the main thoroughfare near La Cienega Blvd., is known for its high-quality antiques.

Another "must see" on Melrose Avenue is the stunning "blue whale"—officially known as the Pacific Design Center, an all-glass-panel building of the brightest blue that caused quite a controversy when it was unveiled. The dust has since settled, but the design center still attracts its share of attention. Although it is full of shops specializing in interior furnishings, the proprietors sell only to registered interior designers and decorators. It's a fun place to window-shop.

A glimpse of "how the other half lives" can be seen in two nearby areas. The first, Laurel Canyon, is located at the borderline of Hollywood and West Hollywood. The street itself, also named Laurel Canyon, winds its way along the foot of several small mountains. By turning off on any of the smaller residential streets and continuing to the top of the mountain, you can see not only some prime examples of expensive California real estate but also some exceedingly lovely views.

Another nearby scenic drive is Mulholland Drive. This area is divided by impressive mountains where fabulous views of both the flat San Fernando Valley and the flat Los Angeles Basin can be simultaneously enjoyed. These views extend for miles both to the left and to the right.

A scenic view of a different kind can be found along Sunset Boulevard's infamous "strip," between Crescent Heights Boulevard and Doheny Drive. It is here that some of the most creative billboards in the world are located. Most advertise current motion pictures or new record albums. At the Strip's east end is the Chateau Marmont, a legendary Hollywood hotel still favored by celebrities.

The Strip is also the location of a number of restaurants catering to a wide range of tastes. Nightclubs are numerous in this area, too. They run the gamut from ultrafashionable, private watering holes to punk and heavy metal rock clubs.

Beverly Hills

The glitz of the Strip ends as suddenly as it begins at Doheny Drive, where Sunset Boulevard enters the world-famous city of glamorous Beverly Hills. Suddenly the sidewalk street life gives way to expansive, perfectly manicured lawns and palatial homes, all representative of what the name Beverly Hills has come to mean.

The fabulous Beverly Hills Hotel is located here, right off Sunset. Its quiet Spanish Colonial Revival architecture and soft pink exterior belie the excitement inside, where Hollywood moguls make deals over margaritas in the Polo Lounge and where such stars as Warren Beatty keep permanent bungalows as second homes.

Selected Areas of
WEST HOLLYWOOD/
BEVERLY HILLS/
WEST LOS ANGELES

It is on this stretch of Sunset, especially during the daytime, that you'll see hawkers peddling maps of stars' homes. Are the maps reliable? Well, that's a matter of debate. Stars do move around, and so it's difficult to keep any map up to date. But the fun of looking at some of these magnificent homes, irrespective of whether they're owned by a star at the moment, makes many people buy such maps and embark on tours.

Any map of stars' homes will almost certainly include a drive up Beverly Glen, which is not actually in Beverly Hills. The homes along this street are a lot more posh than the Laurel Canyon variety. This is where many of the people you'll see in Beverly Hills actually live.

Beverly Hills itself was incorporated as a city early in the century and has been thriving ever since. As a vibrant, exciting city within the larger city, it has retained its reputation for wealth and luxury, an assessment with which you will agree as you drive along one of its main thoroughfares, Santa Monica Boulevard. Rolls Royces, Mercedes Benzes, and Bentleys are as common as Chevrolets might be in another town. The same can be said for the shops. Within an area of only a few square blocks are some of the most exotic, not to mention high-priced, stores in southern California. Here one can find such items as $200 pairs of socks wrapped in gold leaf and stores that take customers only by appointment.

On Wilshire Boulevard in Beverly Hills are a number of fine department stores, including Neiman-Marcus, Bonwit Teller, and Saks Fifth Avenue, as well as an Abercrombie and Fitch.

A fun way to spend an afternoon is to stroll famed Rodeo (pronounced ro-DAY-o) Drive between Santa Monica Boulevard and Wilshire. Some of the names of shops may be familiar to you since several of them supply clothing for major network television shows, and their names often appear among the credits. Others such as Gucci have a worldwide reputation. Fortunately, browsing is free (and fun), no matter how expensive the store. Several nearby restaurants have outside patios where you can sit and sip a drink while watching the fashionable shoppers striding by.

Santa Monica Boulevard splits into two portions in Beverly Hills. The southern route, known as Little Santa Monica, runs through the heart of the shopping district. The other—"Big Santa Monica"—is one of the city's main thoroughfares. As you drive along, take a look at the attractive and varied landscaping at the north side of this street. Each block deploys different plants: cactus, roses, and so on. The landscaping enhances the attractive drive and provides pleasing diversion for the numerous joggers who run through the "park."

Century City

West of Beverly Hills is a new "city"—Century City. Once the back lot of the Twentieth Century Fox film studio (before that it was cowboy star Tom Mix's ranch), today Century City is a 180-acre tribute to modern architecture and the Los Angeles business world. Although most of Century City contains office buildings, there is much here for the visitor to see. The huge Century City Shopping Mall houses major department stores, such as Bullock's and the Broadway, and smaller, boutique-type shops.

The three-level ABC Entertainment Center is located near the prestigious Century Plaza Hotel, where many political functions are held. The entertainment center is a complex of shops, restaurants, and theaters. Here you can dine on anything from a hot dog to fine French or Italian cuisine. Then drop by the Shubert Theater for a Broadway play, or take in a film at one of the twin movie theaters. There is a branch of the Playboy Club located here, and ABC has a ticket booth offering tickets to shows to be taped that week.

Near Century City—just around the corner, in fact—is the lot of Twentieth Century-Fox Studios. Production is still undertaken here, and the public is not permitted inside. You might be able to get a glimpse of the sets from the studio driveway.

Just west of the Century City area is a magnificent building in a style completely different from most others in the city. The Mormon Temple, located on Santa Monica Boulevard, is situated on a hilltop where it projects over a picture-perfect lawn. At the Visitors Center you can watch a movie about the interior of the temple, but visitors are not permitted inside the building.

Westwood

Continuing west on Santa Monica Boulevard, you'll come to Westwood, an exciting area that includes the University of California at Los Angeles (UCLA). Here nationalities of all kinds meet and mix, creating an interesting street life. In fact, it is in Westwood that many people encounter what they consider to be a city—an area containing a lot of milling people, day and night.

Indeed, Westwood has a lot to offer, which explains why it attracts so many people. Not only is there the fine university, which sponsors a vast number of extension courses for those who cannot attend school full time, but there is also the "village" itself, which houses a dozen movie theaters, nearly as many book stores, and restaurants of all sorts. This is also one of the few places in Los Angeles where you can enjoy

UCLA and WESTWOOD

Points of Interest

1) Pauley Pavilion
2) Dykstra Hall
3) Franklin Murphy Sculpture Garden
4) Dickson Art Center
5) Spaulding Field
6) Stein Eye Institute
7) Tennis
8) Botanical Gardens
9) Center for Health Sciences
10) Westwood Plaza
11) Women's Gym
12) Men's Gym
13) Athletic Field
14) Drake Track Stadium
15) Central Tickets Office

New York City-type sidewalk entertainment: Strolling minstrels, mimes, and magicians perform for the crowds and can be enjoyed at all hours.

The UCLA campus is located just north of the village. It is an enormous parklike area that's fun to explore. The Dickson Art Center, for example, has an outdoor sculpture garden where visitors can admire some fine works of modern art. The Student Union is open to all, and so if you're a Bruin buff, you can pick up souvenirs of all kinds. Free maps are available at the entranceways to the campus.

North of Westwood, just off Sunset Boulevard, is the legendary neighborhood of Bel Air. Although not as well known as Beverly Hills, it is equally spectacular in terms of real estate. Just take a drive through the white wrought-iron gates marking the entrance, and you'll see why. Some of these palatial estates are, of course, owned by stars, but again, it's difficult to tell which ones. Unfortunately, many of the houses are screened from public view by lush vegetation and clever landscaping.

Santa Monica

West of Westwood is Santa Monica, a pleasant town bordered on its west side by Palisades Park. This two-mile stretch of green offers magnificent views of the ocean and the beaches below. Picnicking here is a wonderful way to spend an afternoon.

Although the city of Santa Monica is known for its clear air and proximity to the ocean, it has an abundance of shopping opportunities. Santa Monica Place is an enclosed mall containing hundreds of shops, and the downtown city itself was converted to a pedestrian mall, with plenty of room to stroll.

Santa Monica offers an interesting juxtaposition of the old and the new. On its Main Street you'll find some of the trendiest shops, restaurants, and bars. Nearby you can get a glimpse of the good old days by taking a walk along the Santa Monica Pier, which juts out into the ocean. Here, where the Redford–Newman film, *The Sting,* was filmed, are arcades, bumper cars, and merry-go-rounds, all the kinds of amusements not usually found in cities any more. Fishing from the end of the pier is permitted, and anglers can be found there day and night.

Venice

South of Santa Monica is an area that has achieved a distinctive reputation. Venice, California, has frequently been the subject of discussion for several reasons. At one time, Venice was a typical ocean beach community, then it was developed by Abbot Kinney, a well-to-do man with a dream. Kinney decided to build in Southern California another Venice modeled on the city in Italy. At the turn of the century, he did just that, replicating even the canals.

The area prospered in the early days when the amusement parks, gondola rides, and seaside hotels drew large numbers of tourists. Then the place lost its importance as newer attractions were developed in other places and oil interests caused a major shift in the city's economic base. Eventually Venice fell into disrepair. Attracted by the low rents, a large number of senior citizens and artists moved there and enjoyed the peaceful little community until the Los Angeles real-estate boom eventually attracted developers to Venice again. The construction of several high-rise condominiums displaced long-time Venice residents, and the citizens protested vehemently that a way of life was being destroyed.

Although development has not stopped, Venice has managed to retain its great charm and color. There is no shortage of street life along the three-mile stretch of beach in Venice; here one can find sidewalk cafés and street vendors, as well as roller skaters and bicycle riders acting out fast-paced performances. Although rents have gone up, artists still favor the pleasant climate of Venice, and art galleries abound. It's fun to walk here; roller skates and bicycles can be rented. Weekends are the busiest but also the most lively times.

Marina Del Rey

In contrast to Venice, Marina Del Rey is not a beach community; it's a boat community. A recently developed area, the marina is home to endless numbers of boats, including everything from sampans to yachts and schooners. During the Christmas holidays there is a night-time parade featuring many of the marina's boats emblazoned with lights and other holiday decorations.

The marina's harbor—one of the largest on the West Coast and completely man-made—offers tours, or you can rent any one of a variety of boats and tour independently. There are some lovely restaurants offering seaside dining, but since the windowside tables fill up fast, reservations, when accepted, are advised.

Marina Del Rey's Undersea Gardens on the waterfront offers an unusual view from more than one fathom below the sea, where fish and divers put on a show in a natural environment.

South Bay and Beyond

At this point, it is necessary to leave the circle that encompasses the Los Angeles Basin for a tour of the magnificent south coastline. Traveling south from Marina Del Rey, you should arrive at the South Bay

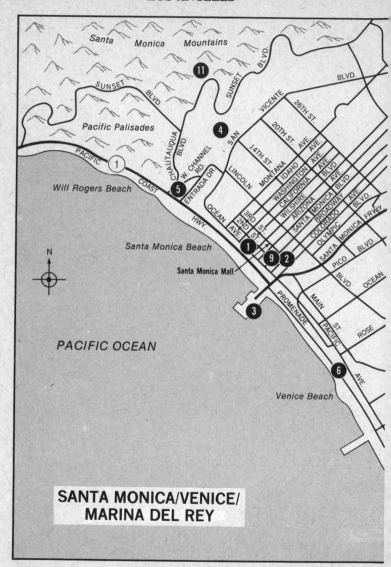

SANTA MONICA/VENICE/
MARINA DEL REY

Points of Interest

1) Palisades Park
2) Santa Monica Place
3) Santa Monica Pier
4) Santa Monica Canyon
5) Castle Rock
6) Ocean Front Walk
7) Santa Monica College
8) Santa Monica Airport
9) Mayfair Music Hall
10) Fisherman's Village and Undersea Gardens
11) Will Rogers State Park
12) U.C.L.A.
13) Century City

in about twenty minutes. This area is known primarily for offering, on a smaller scale, all the kinds of beach activities that are so popular in Los Angeles. The South Bay area consists of three small cities: Redondo Beach, Hermosa Beach, and Manhattan Beach. Each one contains a series of small shops and restaurants and a stretch of beach offering great opportunities for light surfing, swimming, and sunbathing.

Since the South Bay is close to the Los Angeles International Airport, a number of aviation and aerospace firms are based here. Some, such as TRW, permit tours.

An old and famous jazz club, the Lighthouse, is located in Hermosa Beach, and in Redondo Beach there is the King Harbor marina complex, with restaurants, a jazz club, and a lot of boats.

A bit farther south of the South Bay is an area that even some residents of Los Angeles aren't familiar with. The Palos Verdes Peninsula, comprised of five cities, is considered to be something of a bedroom community for the Los Angeles area. But it is more than that, and one trip along Palos Verdes Drive will tell you why. It contains some of the area's most beautiful scenery. Here visitors will see unparalleled seacoast vistas highlighted by rocky cliffs, a most unusual glass and redwood building named the Wayfarer's Chapel (designed by Frank Lloyd Wright), and nearly inaccessible beaches.

Besides its natural beauty, Palos Verdes is also known for its amusement park, Marineland. Now owned by Hanna-Barbera, Marineland is hosted by many of that firm's cartoon characters, such as Yogi Bear and Fred Flintstone. There are dozens of rides and entertaining displays here. Visitors can even go snorkeling if they wish.

Farther south is Los Angeles Harbor, where both the Port of Los Angeles and the Port of Long Beach are located. In Los Angeles Port is a shopping center done in a rustic seaside motif. Nearby is the *Queen Mary* ocean liner providing tours as well as hotel rooms for those who would like to stop and investigate the area further. Alongside is the world's largest airplane, Howard Hughes' *Spruce Goose,* also a touring facility.

Only twenty-one miles from Los Angeles Harbor is the jewellike Santa Catalina Island. This lovely little place can be reached by sea or by air. Although automobiles are not allowed on the island, tours of all kinds are available. They afford a wide variety of scenery, including oceanfront as well as mountainous terrain and even a charming seaside city, Avalon. Two things not to be missed here are the grounds of the Wrigley Estate, once owned by the chewing gum king, and the Avalon Ballroom, a relic from the island's glamourous past. Diving buffs rave about the clear water off Catalina and the many coves where they can practice their favorite sport without interruption. The nighttime harbor tours are spectacular. (Santa Catalina is covered in the chapter *Long Beach South to San Clemente.*)

Malibu

North of Santa Monica, our coastal starting point, lies a city that is virtually synonymous with California: Malibu. The subject of movie and television cameras, Malibu is less a city than a state of mind. As they drive up the coast, visitors are often perplexed when they realize that much of Malibu is invisible. And indeed it is.

Malibu Colony, a residential area noted for its extraordinary wealth, isn't visible from the road. But the natural beauty of the place makes a drive up the coast well worth the time. The beaches of Malibu are spectacular. Surfing here is a daily ritual—even on cold days, when surfers wear wetsuits. On this stretch of the Pacific Coast Highway there are several restaurants where one can overlook the water's edge and absorb some of the Malibu "state of mind."

You can also view some magnificent artwork at the J. Paul Getty Museum in Malibu. As part of the estate of the "richest man in the world," this museum features a multitude of pieces from Roman and Greek antiquity and is itself a replica of an ancient Italian villa.

The San Fernando Valley

Just over the Santa Monica Mountains, which separate Malibu from the Los Angeles Basin, lies the San Fernando Valley, a 220-acre expanse that was once an agricultural center. Only in the last half century or so have the orange groves and family farms yielded way to subdivisions and shopping centers.

The Valley, as it's known to locals, is now home to more than one million people. For many, this area is idyllic; it contains neat bungalows and ranch-style homes situated on tidy parcels of yard. The shopping center is only a block or two away. For years the Valley was considered suburbia, a bedroom community and nothing more. But now the San Fernando Valley is coming into its own: It boasts fine restaurants, a shopping center, and even several major movie studios— in short, all the things that used to belong exclusively to Los Angeles proper.

As remote as the Valley may seem, it is well connected to the rest of Los Angeles via the extensive freeway system, the lifeline used by residents to get to the city itself. If you are planning a trip to the Valley, try to avoid the rush-hour freeway traffic jams, which can be brutal. The Ventura, Hollywood, and San Diego freeways connect the Valley to various other parts of Southern California. Remember that residents travel to the city in the morning until about 10 A.M. and return home between the hours of 3:30 P.M. and 6:30 P.M. Although a resident may not mind spending an hour and a half driving a twenty-mile stretch, you may.

The Valley sounds like one entity, but it encompasses many small communities that are related only by proximity. The following account contains a sampling of sights selected from some of them.

At the far northwestern corner of the Valley is the village of Calabasas. This little town has retained some of the flavor of its early days as a stagecoach stop. Many present-day residents own horses (the real estate ads read "Minirancho, 1½ acres"), and the feed store is one of the town's most active spots. The rural, homey atmosphere of Calabasas blooms every autumn during the annual Pumpkin Festival, which brings out the locals in celebration of the city's rural roots.

Continuing eastward, you will come to the city of Encino, where Indian tribes settled more than 200 years ago. These settlers left behind the adobe buildings where they lived and raised livestock. The buildings at Los Encinos State Historic Park on Moorpark Boulevard are open for touring.

Continuing our circular tour to the area north of Encino will lead to the Saugus–Newhall area where a number of sites of interest are found. Perhaps the best known is Magic Mountain, an amusement park. Here you can wander through 200 acres of entertainment, including live stage shows featuring name performers, super roller coasters, water slides, and a host of other attractions. There are plenty of places where you can stop off for a bite to eat or to pick up a souvenir.

In nearby Newhall is the William S. Hart Park, where the silent-screen cowboy once lived. There are numerous items of interest focusing on the star's film career, and there are displays associated with the early days of the American West.

In Valencia, to the south, is a noted school, the California Institute of Arts, established by Buena Vista (a Disney company) as a place devoted to the study of the arts. It contains an art gallery and represents a striking example of contemporary architecture.

Returning to the San Fernando Valley: The next area of interest is Studio City, which is indeed the home of a major studio. CBS has deployed a major portion of its operations here, and both television movies and television shows are filmed on the premises.

Universal City, the home of Universal Studios, as well as of numerous record companies and businesses related to films, has one prominent landmark that serves as a guide for visitors. "The Black Box," as the tower is known to locals, is actually the studios' executive office building. But because it towers above the landscape, it looks like a futuristic monolith.

The Universal Studios Tour offers an all-inclusive introduction to the way in which motion pictures are made. Included are demonstrations covering makeup, stunts, special effects, trained animals, and other treats. The tour, conducted by a guide, is kept up to date. It gives glimpses into the making of current motion pictures and television programs. Stars often participate in the tour, and audience participation is encouraged. Camera-rental facilities are available, and a number of gift shops, snack bars, and several restaurants are located on the tour grounds.

Just a mile or so east of Universal City is Burbank, a city made famous because of the many references made to it by comedians. Beautiful downtown Burbank is the home of a number of record studios and film companies, including Disney, Warner Brothers, and Columbia, as well as the NBC Television Studios on Olive Avenue. NBC offers tours and tickets for those who would like to attend a taping of a television show.

Next door to Burbank is Glendale, the location of the world-famous Forest Lawn Cemetery, where reproductions of entire churches from all around the world decorate the magnificent grounds. Although Forest Lawn is a cemetery, it's also a tourist attraction because of its many copies of art treasures. Don't hesitate to stop here.

Griffith Park's Travel Town, containing outdoor displays of classics in transportation, and the Los Angeles Zoo, with its "cast of thousands," are located in Glendale. Like the famous San Diego Zoo, the one in Los Angeles keeps animals in environments as similar to their natural ones as possible. The zoo boasts a large number of endangered species among its extraordinary collection. Another special feature is the baby animal nursery, where visitors can see tiny animals being cared for.

San Gabriel Valley

Although it seems like one continuous stretch, the San Fernando Valley gives way to the San Gabriel Valley in the Pasadena area. The San Gabriel Valley has a number of museums, magnificent gardens, and stately homes reflecting the gracious life-style of an earlier era.

Pasadena is perhaps most famous because it is the site of the annual Tournament of Roses Parade and football game. The Rose Bowl, where the tournament is held, is actually part of the larger Brookside Park, where picnicking, hiking, and golfing facilities are available.

The city of Pasadena represents an interesting blend of yesterday and today. Several of the main streets are lined with quaint little shops whose architecture reflects the city's early days. The library is a monument to buildings of another era. Several blocks away from the downtown district is the Pasadena Center, a contemporary cluster of buildings housing shops and conference areas.

Another expression of Pasadena's claims to fame is the Norton Simon Museum, 411 W. Colorado Blvd., with its wide-ranging collection of fine art. There is something here from almost every culture in the world, and most centuries are well represented, too. Besides the art collection, there is the building itself, a modern-day architectural statement that evokes a feeling of timelessness.

In the neighboring city of La Canada are the lovely Descanso Gardens, where camellias bloom spectacularly during the spring months. Besides the veritable cornucopia of camellia bushes, there is a rose garden, endless bulb flowers, and a small Japanese tea house, dispensing souvenirs and, of course, tea.

South of Pasadena is the city of San Marino, the site of magnificent homes and one of Southern California's most remarkable landmarks, the Huntington Library, Botanical Gardens, and Art Gallery. Once a tycoon's estate, the Huntington grounds are now devoted to some of the finest plant collections in the world, including a Shakespeare garden, one of the most complete cactus gardens to be found anywhere, and an herb garden. The Art Gallery is home to Gainsborough's *Blue Boy* and other well-known pieces. In addition, the library contains a Gutenberg Bible and first editions of works by Shakespeare, Ben Franklin, and others.

Another remarkable garden lies just to the east of the Huntington in the city of Arcadia: the Los Angeles State and County Arboretum containing more than 100 acres of plants, flowers, and trees. A number of films and television shows have been shot at the arboretum's gardens.

Nearby is the Santa Anita Race Track, where a string of snowcapped mountains provides the backdrop for some of the area's finest thoroughbred racing. The clubhouse is of Spanish architecture and tiling. Those who arrive early in the day can take a tram ride through the stable area conducted by a guide who provides a running commentary on the horses and the people "backstage" at the track.

Above the San Gabriel Valley, in the San Gabriel Mountains, is Mt. Wilson Observatory. The site of the 100-ton Hooker telescope provides outstanding views of the surrounding area, and displays set forth an explanation of the science of astronomy.

To the east of the San Gabriel Valley is the Pomona area, where the annual Los Angeles County Fair is held. Once a prime winemaking region, the Pomona area is now known because of the fair and the fine Arabian horses housed at the Kellogg Ranch. Nearby, on Foothill Boulevard, is Rancho Santa Ana Botanic Gardens displaying exclusively California vegetation, with nature trails.

The Mountain Resorts

Continuing east, you will come to the San Bernardino Mountains. At their peak is one of Southern California's prime recreation areas: the resorts of Lake Arrowhead and Big Bear Lake, which provide year-round opportunities for boating, swimming, and water- and snow-skiing in an atmosphere of fresh, pine scented air reminiscent of an alpine resort. All kinds of cabins, motels, and condominiums can be rented through realtors in the area. Almost any kind of sporting goods can be rented in the area. Lake Arrowhead, the more urbanized of the two, has a lakeside shopping mall. Although the winding mountain roads are not for everyone, don't miss Rim of the World Drive. The stretch of road at the edge of the mountain offers some of the finest vistas available anywhere.

The Desert Resorts

Just below the mountains of Lake Arrowhead–Big Bear lies one of California's most publicized attractions, Palm Springs, where swimming pools nearly outnumber the residents, and golf courses abound. Graceful, tree lined Palm Canyon Drive offers sophisticated shopping opportunities and some very fine restaurants as well as nightlife. (See the chapter on Palm Springs in this book.)

Actually, Palm Springs is the best known of the string of cities, including Rancho Mirage, Cathedral City, La Quinta, and Palm Desert, in this desert oasis. At the end of the string is Indio, where an annual Date Festival, featuring camel races and date flavored milkshakes, is held every winter.

While in Palm Springs, don't miss the aerial tram that takes a handful of people on a long climb to the top of Mt. San Jacinto. In the wintertime snow is usually very much in evidence, even though the temperature at the tram's origin might have been 80 degrees.

In the Palm Springs area there are exhibits of interest to those who would like to learn more about the desert. At the Desert Museum elaborate dioramas show desert life; the museum also houses fine collections of art and Indian artifacts.

At the Living Desert Reserve in Palm Desert are all kinds of desert vegetation, along with explanations of how many of the plants are used today and how many were used in the past.

Heading back toward Los Angeles from the desert communities, you will approach two state parks worthy of a visit. Anza Borrego Desert State Park is an enormous desert preserve encompassing more than 600 miles of roads, plenty of camping and hiking trails, and historic spots, including old stagecoach stations. At the nearby Joshua Tree National Monument, picnicking, camping, hiking, and rock climbing are permitted, but the main attraction is provided by thousands of majestic Joshua trees. Although these high-desert plants appear to the casual observer to resemble cactus, they are members of the lily family. Joshua Tree encompasses more than 800 square miles of varied terrain and includes wildlife preserves and self-guided nature trails.

Back to the Beginning

If you continue west on Interstate 10 when you leave the desert areas, you will end up right back at our starting point, downtown Los Angeles. The circle is complete, although by now it is more of an irregularly shaped ellipsis. But at least, our overview should have given you a general feel for the area that should help you in deciding which areas you'll be going back to visit.

 SIGHTSEEING CHECKLIST. We believe that the following attractions or experiences should rate "10" on everyone's what-to-see-and-do list, although we recognize that many visitors will not have enough time to follow all these suggestions. Throughout the guidebook we will provide more extensive information about these places of interest.

ABC Entertainment Center. 2020 Ave. of the Stars, Century City 90067; (213) 557–7777. Gourmet restaurants, shops, athletic facilities, and top-draw night spots and clubs complement the center's twin cinemas and the Shubert Theater. Open daily.

Alpine Village. 833 W. Torrance Blvd., Torrance 90502; (213) 323–2872. This charming village, reminiscent of Bavaria, is a marketplace for twenty-eight Old-World shops, a German restaurant, and a beer garden, plus an animal farm and old-fashioned amusement rides for the children.

Barnsdall Park. 4800 Hollywood Blvd., Los Angeles 90027; (213) 460–2200. A gracious hilltop park, home of the Frank Lloyd Wright-designed Hollyhock House and a gallery offering a changing program of contemporary art by local talent. Open 12:30 P.M. to 5:00 P.M.

Bradbury Building. 304 S. Broadway, Los Angeles 90013; (213) 489–1411. Erected in 1893, this is the only office building listed on the National Register. Noted for its turn-of-the-century wrought iron and marble trappings, ornate elevators, and Victorian flourishes. Also, the set for many famous movies. Open 10:00 A.M. to 5:00 P.M., Monday through Saturday.

Burbank Studios Tour. 4000 Warner Blvd., Burbank 91522; (818) 954–1008. Take a look at the behind-the-scenes activities on the sound stages of Warner Brothers and Columbia Pictures. Summer hours: Monday through Friday, 10:00 A.M. to 2:30 P.M.; winter hours: 10:00 A.M. to 2:00 P.M.

Chinatown. 900 Block of North Broadway, Los Angeles 90012. The aromas of delectable Cantonese cuisine are sensed as one walks through the streets and shops; evocative of Old China and the charm of the Far East.

Descanso Gardens. 1418 Descanso Dr., La Canada 91011; (213) 790–5571. The Descanso Gardens provide the setting for a Japanese teahouse and garden, picnic area, and extensive rose gardens. There are also 100,000 camellia bushes set in a forest of native oaks, providing sheer beauty in the spring. Open 9:00 A.M. to 4:30 P.M., daily.

Disneyland. 1313 Harbor Blvd., Anaheim 92803; (714) 999–4565. Nearly sixty attractions are contained in a magical kingdom of yesterday, tomorrow, adventure, and fantasy. The park is designed around seven imaginative themes. Disneyland's entertainment and originality are unparalleled. Summer: 9:00 A.M. to midnight; Winter: 10:00 A.M. to 6:00 P.M., Wednesday through Friday, 9:00 A.M. to 7:00 P.M., Saturday and Sunday.

Exposition Park. Figueroa at Exposition Blvd., Los Angeles 90037. Near downtown, Exposition Park contains the Los Angeles Museum of Natural History, which focuses on mammal, bird, and artifact exhibits from all over the world.

Farmer's Market. 6333 W. Third St., Los Angeles 90036; (213) 933–9211. A sprawling and unique marketplace that boasts 160 individually owned shops and stores plus numerous dining patios and remarkable food selections. Open Sunday, 9:00 A.M. to 8:00 P.M., Wednesday, 9:00 A.M. to 7:00 P.M.

Forest Lawn Memorial Park. 1712 S. Glendale Ave., Glendale 91209; (818) 254–3131. Spacious grounds display precise reproductions of Michelangelo's major statuary, historic churches, and the world's largest permanent mounted painting.

Griffith Observatory, Planetarium Theater, and Laserium. 2800 E. Observatory Rd., Los Angeles 90027. Located atop Mt. Hollywood is the world-famous Griffith Observatory, which houses a 500-seat planetarium theater, the Hall of Science, and a telescope with twin refractors. The colorful Laserium show features two screenings of laser images accompanied by pulsating music. Summer hours: 1–10:00 P.M., Sunday through Friday, 11:30 A.M. to 10:00 P.M., Saturday; Winter hours: 2–10:00 P.M., Tuesday through Friday, 11:30 A.M. to 10:00 P.M., Saturday, and 1:00 P.M. to 10:00 P.M., Sunday.

Griffith Park. Los Feliz Blvd., at Vermont Ave., Los Angeles 90027. This beautiful park rests on 4,063 acres of natural mountainside greenery, which forms the foremost entertainment center for golf, tennis, picnicking areas, and an educational center for children. Located on the hillside setting is the Greek Theater, a leading amphitheater presenting top performers throughout the summer.

Hancock Park. Curson Ave. at Wilshire Blvd., Los Angeles 90036. One of the loveliest areas in Los Angeles, with its attractively landscaped park that is the home of major cultural, anthropological, and art facilities.

Hanna-Barbera's Marineland. 6610 Palos Verdes Dr., South, Rancho Palos Verdes 90274; (213) 377–1571. Marineland, situated on beautiful Pacific coastal cliffs, presents shows of performing killer whales, sea lions, and dolphins, plus a unique swim-through aquarium. Summer hours: 10:00 A.M. to 7:00 P.M., daily; winter hours: 10:00 A.M. to 5:00 P.M., daily.

Heritage Square. 3800 Homer St., Los Angeles 90031; (213) 222–3150. Historic Victorian-era structures have been relocated here from various Los Angeles neighborhoods and have been lovingly restored to their original grandeur. Open 11:00 A.M. to 3:00 P.M., every second Sunday and third Wednesday of the month.

Hollywood Wax Museum. 6767 Hollywood Blvd., Hollywood 90028; (213) 462–8860. More than 170 famous persons are uncannily recreated in fleshlike wax, alongside a continuous screening of scenes from award-winning films produced from 1927 to the present. Open 10:00 A.M. to midnight, daily.

Japanese Village Plaza. 327 East Second St., Los Angeles 90012; (213) 620–8861. Twenty-four specialty shops and fourteen restaurants are charmingly set off by a fountain, rock sculpture, and traditional Japanese Village architecture. Open 10:00 A.M. to 8:00 P.M., Tuesday through Sunday.

Kingdom of Dancing Stallions. 7662 Beach Blvd., Buena Park 90620. Dancing stallions from the best breeds of various countries perform daily in this lavish new ten-million-dollar entertainment complex. There is also an Antique Carriage Plaza with an extensive collection of fully restored horse-drawn carriages. Open 10:00 A.M. to 10:00 P.M., Tuesday through Sunday. Closed Monday except on holidays.

Knott's Berry Farm. 8039 Beach Blvd., Buena Park 90620; (714) 827–1776. Knott's roaring-twenties area, Ghost Town, and Fiesta Village offer live entertainment, thrill rides, and family attractions. Adding to the zest are the renowned Chicken Dinner Restaurant and many colorful shops.

Lion Country Safari. 8800 Irvine Center Dr., Laguna Hills 92653; (714) 837–1200. Lion Country Safari exhibits hundreds of untamed animals roaming freely in natural bushveld settings. This amusement park is a 240-acre drive through a wildlife preserve.

Little Tokyo. First St., at San Pedro St., Los Angeles 90012; (213) 620–0570. Little Tokyo serves as the social, economic, cultural, and religious center of the largest Japanese community in mainland United States.

Los Angeles Times. 202 West 1st St., Los Angeles 90053; (213) 972–5757. A one-hour tour can be taken of the nation's largest non-tabloid daily newspaper. The tour includes the Times' pressroom, newsroom, and photocomposition facilities; minimum ten years of age. Open 3:00 P.M., Monday through Friday.

Los Angeles World Trade Center. 350 S. Figueroa, Los Angeles 90071; (213) 489–3330. The World Trade Center offers to the traveler the U.S. Passport Office, visa services, travel agencies, a currency exchange, and passport photo services amid international shops and restaurants. Open daily.

Los Angeles Zoo. 5333 Zoo Dr., Los Angeles 90027; (213) 666–4650. Two thousand animals from all over the world live in divided continental areas. The facility includes a complete children's and 80-acre main zoo. Summer hours: 10:00 A.M. to 6:00 P.M., daily; Winter hours: 10:00 A.M. to 5:00 P.M., daily.

Mann's Chinese Theater. 6925 Hollywood Blvd., Hollywood 90028; (213) 461–3331. Hollywood's most famous landmark, the Chinese Theater's courtyard, records the hand- and footprints of more than 150 famous motion-picture stars. Open daily.

Movieland Wax Museum and Palace of Living Art. 7711 Beach Blvd., Buena Park 90620; (714) 583–8025. One hundred spectacular sets, with more than 200 lifelike wax figures, immortalize favorite motion picture and television stars. The Palace of Living Art brings new dimensions to the world's most treasured paintings. Open 9:00 A.M. to 9:00 P.M. daily (summer); 10:00 A.M. to 10:00 P.M., daily (winter).

NBC Studios Tour. 3000 Alameda Ave., Burbank 91523; (818) 840–4444. For those who want a glimpse of the behind-the-scenes world of television here is the world's only "backstage" tour of a major television facility. It offers a look at set construction, makeup, and wardrobe. Summer hours: 8:30 A.M. to 5:00 P.M., Monday through Friday, 10:00 A.M. to 5.00 P.M., Saturday and Sunday. Winter hours: 10:00 A.M. to 5:00 P.M., daily.

Olvera St. Downtown. Known as "Little Mexico," this quaint marketplace is one of Los Angeles' first thoroughfares. It bustles with Mexican shops, restaurants, and evening entertainment, and hosts frequent fiestas.

Queen Mary Tour and Museum. Pier J, Long Beach 90801; (213) 435-4747. This 1934 luxury liner offers a tremendous insight into one of history's most famous ships. Summer hours: 10:00 A.M. to 5:00 P.M., daily; winter hours: 10:00 A.M. to 4:00 P.M., Monday through Friday, 10:00 A.M. to 5:00 P.M., Saturday and Sunday.

Redondo Beach Marina. 181 N. Harbor Dr., Redondo Beach 90277; (213) 374–3481. Varieties of ocean-view restaurants, dancing, and boat cruises are showplaced in this delightful waterfront setting.

Santa Catalina Island. The famous scenic isle resort offers many diversions, ranging from glass-bottom coastal cruises and flying-fish boat trips to hiking, swimming, fishing, and cycling, for the whole family. The cruises to the island depart daily from Long Beach, Newport Beach, and San Pedro.

Six Flags Magic Mountain. 26101 Magic Mountain Pky., Valencia 91355; (805) 992–0884. This lushly landscaped, 260-acre entertainment complex and family amusement park is only twenty-five minutes north of Hollywood by car. Just one ticket brings a whole day of fun. Summer hours: 10:00 A.M. to midnight, Monday through Friday, 9:00 A.M. to midnight, Saturday and Sunday; winter hours: 10:00 A.M. to 6:00 P.M., Saturday, Sunday, and holidays.

South Coast Botanic Garden. 26300 Crenshaw Blvd., Palos Verdes Peninsula 90274; (213) 377–0468. California natives, ground covers, flowering fruit trees, and a man-made lake provide a remarkable 87-acre environmental transformation. Open 9:00 A.M. to 5:00 P.M., daily.

Spruce Goose. Pier J, Long Beach 90801. Self-guided tour of this "flying boat," the world's largest airplane. Free video films on construction, life of Howard Hughes, exhibits of Hughes's flying accessories. Open 10:00 A.M. to 6:00 P.M., weekdays, 9:00 A.M. to 6:00 P.M., weekends. Part of the Londontowne Village complex.

Universal Studios Tour. 100 Universal City Plaza, Universal City 91608; (818) 877–1311. If you've wondered how a movie is made, take the Universal

Studios tour. You'll take a peek behind the scenes of movie-style mayhem and observe special effects on a tram tour full of surprises. Summer hours: 8:00 A.M. to 6:00 P.M., daily, Winter hours: 10:00 A.M. to 3:30 P.M., daily.

Wild Goose Yacht Charters. Suite 208, 2412 Wilshire Blvd., Santa Monica 90403; (213) 828–4614. Take a charter on the Wild Goose, the yacht once owned by John Wayne; it still contains the Duke's personal effects, awards, and furnishings—perfect for large or small groups.

Will Rogers State Historic Park. 14253 Sunset Blvd., Pacific Palisades 90272; (213) 454–8212. The noted humorist's ranch, containing the original furnishings, is preserved on lovely acreage, including a stable, corrals, a riding ring, and a roping arena. Open: 8:00 A.M. to 7:00 P.M., daily.

OUTSIDE LOS ANGELES

Beaches. Along the coast both north and south of Los Angeles are some of the most uncrowded beaches in the country, such as the noteworthy Avila Beach, Laguna Beach, and Wood's Dove.

Channel Islands. A tiny chain of islands, untouched by modern times; they display a wealth of cliffs and caves and lush vegetation.

Guest Ranches. Within a three-hour radius of Los Angeles is a multitude of guest ranches, such as Alisial and San Ysidro, which offer guests everything from homey dinners to horseback riding.

Health Spas. There are probably more health spas in this area of the country than any other; Golden Door, the Oaks at Ojai, La Costa, and Rancho La Porta are some of the best.

High Sierras, including Sequoia and King's Canyon National Parks. A breathtaking experience of crystal-clean air, sparkling lakes, giant redwoods, and jagged mountain peaks—unspoiled nature at its best.

Laguna Beach. An artist's colony of sorts, Laguna Beach is one of the most attractive coastal towns in the country, and has one of the nicest beaches.

Mojave Desert and **Death Valley.** The stark desert scenery is only a short drive from Los Angeles and features ghost towns as well as spectacular rock formations, sagebrush, and exotic desert wildlife.

Missions. There are 21 in California, established around 1800 by the Spanish to convert the native Indians to Christianity. Today they are active churches and museums filled with antiques and artifacts.

Ojai. A relaxed, rural community with a gamut of activities from camping and country inns to health spas and gourmet restaurants.

Palm Springs. One of the country's most luxurious resorts; tennis, golf, good food—the good life.

Santa Barbara. One of the most representative cities of the California lifestyle. Santa Barbara has beaches, mountains, clean air, and a wealth of boutiques and cultural activities.

PRACTICAL INFORMATION FOR LOS ANGELES

 HOW TO GET THERE. There are, of course, four common ways to get around in the United States: plane, train, bus, and car. Usually, if you plan to travel long distance, it is cheaper to go by plane than by rail. But for distances under 300 miles, the train is cheaper and may be faster too because the station is often in the middle of town and you won't have to take a long ride to and from the airport. Another benefit of rail travel is seeing the scenery, which can't be observed when flying.

For short trips between cities, buses offer the same sightseeing advantage as trains but are usually cheaper and may provide more frequent service.

By bus. *Continental Trailways* and *Greyhound* bus routes provide a vast array of scheduled trips, allowing travelers from all U.S. areas to come close to their vacation destinations and often to reach them directly. Focal points to consider are the same as those for trains. Currently both offer unlimited train passes at $186—7 days; $240.00—15 days; $347.00—30 days. Children under 12 pay half-price and under 5, they travel free. The great distance involved in traveling around southern California may make these passes advantageous.

Contact your travel agent or a nearby Greyhound or Trailways office for information about special tours to and in the area you would like to visit. Also, ask your travel agent about special tours to the area you plan to see. Keep in mind that you will be alloted only a certain amount of time in any one place, and the allocation of time depends on your tour itinerary.

By air. In the Los Angeles area, two major airports bring in visitors: Los Angeles International Airport (LAX) is the larger; Burbank operates a smaller domestic terminal in the San Fernando Valley. Among major airlines serving either or both of these airports are *American, Capitol Air, Delta, Eastern, Republic, TWA, United,* and *Western.* Some of the international carriers serving LAX are *Air Canada, Air France, AeroMexico, Air New Zealand, UTA, British Airways, Continental, China Airlines, Qantas, Mexicana, World Airlines,* and *Pan American.*

Also serving the Los Angeles area are regional airlines, which offer many scheduled flights from the cities mentioned above as well as from other metropolitan areas. Regional airlines include *Air Cal, PSA (Pacific Southwest Airlines),* and *Western.*

Discounts are usually available to members of the family who are traveling together. Thirty-day excursion fares, youth fares for college students, and special low fares for senior citizens as well as for members of the armed forces are also offered by many airlines that may also offer stand-by reduced rate fares. All special fares are subject to restrictions requiring the traveler to make the trip when the airlines are least busy, usually midweek. Savings can range from 15 to 50 percent over regular coach fares, but since discounts change frequently, it is best to consult your travel agent for the most recent exact rates.

To accommodate those travelers who require transportation to and from LAX, try the *Flyaway Service*. This ground transportation line has two locations: in West Los Angeles, at 1401 S. Sepulveda Blvd., and in San Fernando Valley, at 7610 Woodley Ave. Both locations offer nonstop service to the airport at a nominal fee. Otherwise, unless your hotel has an airport shuttle-bus service, you will be better off with a car rental. A new helicopter service, *Airspur* (9841 Airport Blvd., Suite 714, Los Angeles; 417–2222), offers hourly flights from Los Angeles International Airport to Fullerton. Flights run daily from 7:00 A.M. to 10:00 P.M. Flight time is 15 min. Some joint fares are offered by such larger carriers as American, Delta, Northwestern, TWA, and Western.

By train. Amtrak's *Coast Starlight* is a superliner train that offers service to Seattle–Portland and Oakland–San Francisco and south to Los Angeles. A special bedroom is available for handicapped passengers traveling with a companion. Superliner sleepers offer an economy bedroom for two, family bedroom accommodations for two adults and two children, and deluxe bedrooms with sofa and reclining swivel chair. Connecting with the *Coast Starlight* in Martinez, Amtrak's *San Joaquin* train travels through the Central Valley, the gateway to three national parks: Yosemite, Kings Canyon, and Sequoia.

For more information, see your local travel agent or Amtrak for details on discounts and excursion fares; Family-A-Fare and discounts for the handicapped and senior citizens are also available. Ask for the "Rail America" West tour book that lists many different plans that will enable travelers on a budget to save money.

Also available on the *Coast Starlight* are one- and two-day tours to Yosemite National Park and a two-day train tour to Hearst Castle. Daily service is available to Stockton, Merced (Yosemite), Fresno, Bakersfield, and San Joaquin Valley points.

Los Angeles' Amtrak Union Station, one of the last grand railroad stations to be built in this country, is located at 800 N. Alameda St.

TELEPHONES. The area code for Los Angeles proper is 213. You do not need to dial the area code if it is the same as the one from which you are calling. Information (known as directory assistance) is 411 locally. When trying to find a number, be aware of which section of the city you are seeking—Los Angeles has many different sections with so many different telephone books and different telephone companies (two: Pacific Telephone and General Telephone). When direct-dialing a long-distance number from anywhere in Los Angeles, you must dial the number "1" (one) *before* you dial the area code and the number itself. An operator will assist you on person-to-person, credit-card, and collect calls if you dial "0" first. Pay telephones still start at 10 cents.

On January 7, 1984, area was split off the 213 area code and given a new code: 818. The communities to go into 818 of interest to visitors are the San Fernando Valley, Glendale, Pasadena, and Burbank.

HOTELS AND MOTELS. Los Angeles offers almost any kind of accommodation, from a simple motel room, which permits you to park right in front of your room, to a posh hotel such as the Beverly Hills, where an attendant will park your car and whisk you off to a spacious room or to your own bungalow.

Because Los Angeles is so spread out—the city is actually a series of suburbs connected by freeways—it is possible to obtain clean, decent accommodations at low priced motels that place you only a little distance from the mainstream of the city.

The best known Los Angeles hotels—the Century Plaza, the Beverly Wilshire, the Beverly Hills, and the Westin Bonaventure among them—are sleek, fashionable establishments in the hub of the city; they are high-priced luxury hotels providing many restaurants and conveniences.

European-style hotels are also prospering here; they provide personalized attention, rooms that are often minisuites, and a concierge to perform services. These hotels are usually small and gracious and often present you with baskets of fruit, bottles of wine, and/or place fine chocolates on your pillow at night. L'Ermitage Hotel is high on the list, in both price and amenities; it offers elegant suites, original artwork, and a gourmet dining room for guests only. The Westwood Marquis offers similarly intimate accommodations.

It is best to plan ahead and reserve a room; hotels usually offer special prices for weekend visits or may offer tickets to amusement parks or plays. A travel agent or the Sunday Travel Section of *The Los Angeles Times* can aid you in your efforts.

Rates are generally priced for double occupancy, that is, two persons. You can expect that there will be more rooms available at the higher end of the range of prices listed.

All hotels take all major credit cards, unless otherwise noted.

Hotels are categorized according to location, style, service, and distinction of accommodations. Public transportation in Los Angeles is generally inconvenient and slow; it's best to stay close to where you plan to sightsee, unless you have access to an automobile.

As a general guideline, the *deluxe* category refers to the top hotels in Los Angeles. In fact, these few pinnacles of service and elegance rank with the finest hotels in the world. They are, however, the product of their environment, a genuine reflection of the California way of life.

The *expensive* category often caters to business travelers and includes many of the convention-oriented, "brand name" hotels that are perfectly suitable for tourists. All hotels in this range provide the full spectrum of services you'd expect to find away from home and are usually situated in the most desirable areas.

Moderate hotels provide fewer services but are priced to reflect the sacrifice in comfort; *inexpensive* hotels in the guide are just that: inexpensive. They are clean, responsible properties that are modest but pleasant; they are especially appreciated by young travelers and travelers on a budget.

Most hotels in Los Angeles and the surrounding area boast the proverbial swimming pool and are often air conditioned to provide relief from the climate.

DOWNTOWN

Deluxe

The Biltmore Hotel. 515 S. Olive St.; 624–1011; (800) 421–0156 nationwide; (800) 252–0175 in California. This Los Angeles historical landmark near beautiful Pershing Square has recently undergone renovation and restoration to the tune of $35 million. Since the Biltmore first opened in 1923, this impressive property has hosted such dignitaries as Mary Pickford, J. Paul Getty, Eleanor Roosevelt, Princess Margaret, and several of our nation's Presidents, including Ronald Reagan. Award-winning European architecture. Bernard's is a critically acclaimed Continental restaurant. Private, swank health club in a Roman bath motif. Modern updated guest rooms. Banquet and meeting rooms serve up to 1,200; special club floor boasts library, wide-screen television theater, and pocket-billiards room. 1,022 rooms. No CB. *$90—$142.*

Los Angeles Hilton Hotel. 930 Wilshire Blvd; 629–4321. On Los Angeles' most accessible street, this hotel offers a restaurant, a lounge, a 24-hour coffee shop, a pool, and large banquet and meeting rooms. One-hour airport bus service at $4.00; parking at $4.00 per day. 1,200 rooms. *$65.90 and up.*

Sheraton Grande Hotel. 333 South Figueroa St.; 617–1133; (800) 325–3535. New 14-story, 550-room mirrored hotel near Dodger Stadium, Chinatown, Music Center, in the Bunker Hill district downtown. Three restaurants, outdoor pool, movie theaters, 23 meeting rooms, limo service available. Privileges at Los Angeles Racquet Club. *$85 and up.*

Westin Bonaventure Hotel. Fifth and Figueroa; 624–1000; (800) 228–3000. John Portman's striking masterpiece, this 35-story, circular towered, mirrored glass high rise is situated in the heart of downtown. This superstructure includes outside elevators, five acres of ponds and waterfalls in the lobby, several restaurants, including Beaudry's Gourmet, and the Bona Vista revolving lounge at the top. Pool, five-level shopping gallery inside. Popular Sunday brunch in atrium lobby. Parking at $8.00 per day. 1,474 rooms. *$85 and up.*

Expensive

Best Western Inn Towne. 925 S. Figueroa St.; 628–2222; (800) 421–6222 nationwide; (800) 528–1234 in California. A three-story hotel located one and one-half blocks from the Convention Center and right down the street from the famous 24-hour Pantry Restaurant. Room service, pool, facilities for the handicapped. Parking is free. 170 rooms. *$51–$65.*

Holiday Inn Convention Center. 1020 S. Figueroa; 748–1291; (800) 238–8000; (800) 465–4329. Various athletic teams visiting the city stay at this newly renovated hotel. Next door to the Convention Center. It offers the lovely Courtyard Restaurant, a pool, a laundry room, and complimentary garage parking. Amtrak offers a weekend package at this Holiday Inn. 193 rooms. *$50–$54.*

Hyatt Regency, Los Angeles. 711 S. Hope St.; 683–1234; (800) 228–9000. One of the largest downtown hotels, it prides itself on its "atmosphere" and "service." Each room has a wall of windows that takes advantage of the city view. Atop this 25-story building is Angel's Flight, a revolving restaurant and lounge. Glass-enclosed skylight. The hotel is part of downtown's Broadway Plaza comprising 35 fine shops and restaurants, including Hugo's V, offering gourmet fare. There also is the Los Angeles Racquet Club. Parking is $8.00 per day. 500 rooms. *$85–$115.*

Mayflower Hotel. 535 S. Grand; 624–1331; (800) 421–8851; (800) 421–8852. This fashionable hotel is located in the center of downtown. 24-hour coffee shop, room service, valet laundry. Multilingual staff. 350 rooms. *$75–$90.*

The New Otani Hotel and Garden. 120 S. Los Angeles St.; 629–1200; (800) 252–0151. A fusion of international design and human-scale concepts, this ultramodern hotel surrounds a beautiful Japanese garden with running stream and waterfalls. Visitors at the hotel especially like the fine restaurants: A Thousand Cranes, offering classic Japanese cuisine; Commodore Perry's, boasting steak and lobster; and the Genji Bar with notable jazz entertainers. Each room has a refrigerator, an alarm clock, a phone in the bathroom, and concrete walls for great noise control. Large conference center inside. 446 rooms. *$83 and up.*

University Hilton, Los Angeles. 3540 S. Figueroa St.; 748–4141. If you're doing business at USC, the Coliseum, or the Sports Arena, you will find that this is the best hotel in the area. All rooms have a view of the pool area, the lush garden, or the nearby USC campus. Coffee shop, Trojan Horse Restaurant, lounge. Courtesy shuttle service to both LAX and the Amtrak train station. The hotel is well equipped to handle banquet meetings and conventions. Parking at $2.00 per day. 241 rooms. *$80–$100.*

Moderate

Alexandria Hotel. 501 S. Spring St.; 626–7484; (800) 421–8815. This turn-of-the-century charmer has recently undergone a three-million-dollar facelift that preserved all its Old World elegance. Pleasurable Victorian accommodations at reasonable rates; lovely nightclub; fine restaurant. This landmark hotel is located in the heart of the financial district close to the Convention Center and City Hall. Room service, facilities for the handicapped. 500 rooms. *$45 and up.*

Best Western Kent Motel. 920 S. Figueroa; 626–8701; (800) 528–1234. This Best Western motel is two blocks from the Convention Center and near the famous Pantry Restaurant. Inside: an Italian Restaurant and cocktail lounge. Pool. Parking is free. *$45 and up.*

City Center Motel. 1135 W. Seventh Street; 628–7141 (hotel gives permission to call collect for reservations). Near the downtown Hilton, this small hotel allows small pets. Pool, laundry rooms. Quiet rooms. Parking on premises. 42 rooms. No CB. *$35–$38.*

Executive Motor Inn—Mariposa AAA. 457 S. Mariposa; 380–6910. This Spanish-style hotel is relatively new. Pool, sauna. Offers refrigerators. AAA members discount. Spanish, Chinese staff. *$44–$54.*

Figueroa Hotel. 939 S. Figueroa; 627–8971; (800) 421–9092. This charming 55-year-old Spanish-style hotel is situated across the street from the historic

Variety Arts Theater. There's a 24-hour coffee shop in the building and a pool with a Jacuzzi. On the Gray Line Sightseeing tour route. Parking is free. Airport service every hour. 280 rooms. *$45–$55.*

Friendship Inn—Motor DeVille. 1123 W. Seventh; 624–8474. Well located downtown, near the Hilton, this reasonably priced hotel boasts a coffee shop and a pool and is on the Gray Line tour bus stop. Parking is free. 63 rooms. *$28–$35.*

Holiday Inn—Chinatown. 1640 Marengo Dr.; 223–3841; (800) 238–8000; (800) 465–4329. This Holiday Inn is about as close as one can get to Dodger Stadium and, of course, Chinatown. Restaurant and lounge, laundry service, babysitting service. Parking is free. *$40–$48.*

Holiday Inn, L.A. Downtown. 750 Garland Ave.; 628–5242; (800) 238–8000; (800) 465–4329. Restaurant, cocktail lounge, pool. Pets allowed. Plenty of free parking. Holiday Inn's usual professional staff. 201 rooms. *$45–$50.*

Holiday Lodge Motel. 1631 W. Third; 483–4920. One of the only downtown hotels with an outdoor garden complete with trees. Tourists will find the atmosphere friendly. Coffee shop, pool, free parking. 60 rooms. *$25–$26.90.*

Los Angeles Huntington Hotel. 752 S. Main Street; 627–3186. Situated one block from main Greyhound Bus depot, this hotel is inexpensively priced. Not many services but very clean. Vending machines off main lobby for 24-hour quick-food service. No parking. 200 rooms. MC, V. *$11.30–$13.*

Oasis Motel. 2200 W. Olympic; 385–4191. Near Little Korea, this hotel is a favorite with Korean tourists. Also, sports enthusiasts find the Oasis convenient to the Sports Arena. Pool, free parking. 70 rooms. *$38–$42.*

Vagabond Motor Hotel. 1904 W. Olympic; 380–9393; (800) 854–2700 nationwide; (800) 522–1555 in California. Near the Convention Center. This hotel is also convenient to several area restaurants. On the Gray Line sightseeing tour route. Free parking. 54 rooms. *$47–$52.*

Inexpensive

Milner Hotel. 813 S. Flower at Eighth; 627–6981. Across the street from the Broadway Plaza, three blocks from the Central Library and four blocks from the Convention Center. A very clean building. Coffee shop, hotel restaurant; popular bar decorated in old Hollywood theme: Scarlett O'Hara adorns the wall. 175 rooms. MC, V. *$30–$40.*

Orchid Hotel. 819 S. Flower St.; 624–5855. One of the smaller downtown hotels, this brick hotel is very reasonably priced. No frills but clean; a laundromat on the premises. No parking at the hotel but plenty of public lots close by. *$35.*

Royal Host Olympic Motel. 901 W. Olympic; 626–6255. Clean, friendly atmosphere. Convenient to Convention Center. 52 rooms. *$25–$35.*

Stillwell Hotel. 838 S. Grand; 627–1151. One of Los Angeles' oldest hotels, the Stillwell has kept its charm throughout the years. For those who like Indian cusine, the on-premises restaurant offers just that. No parking at the hotel but plenty nearby. 250 rooms. AE. *$28–$30.*

MID-WILSHIRE

Deluxe

The Ambassador. 3400 Wilshire Blvd.; 387–7011; (800) 241–0182, nationwide; (800) 252–0385 in California. Aptly called the city within a city, this hotel is situated on 160 acres and is surely one of the most exquisite in Los Angeles. The "city within"—built in 1921—includes a health club, three restaurants, a putting green, a jogging track, a travel agency, post office, 17 shops, . . . and the list goes on. The hotel is well equipped to handle conventions and banquets in a number of meeting rooms. (Check with reservations regarding group rates). For film buffs: On occasion the Ambassador is used as a set for filming television shows and feature films. Overnight security parking at $2.50. 500 rooms. *$76 and up.*

Expensive

Hyatt Wilshire. 3515 Wilshire; 381–7411; (800) 228–9000. One of the larger hotels on Wilshire Blvd., this 12-story building has a recently renovated interior. The lobby is enhanced by a grand piano manned by a concert pianist. The Hyatt's corporate clients often utilize the property's large banquet and meeting rooms (up to 400 people). Extras include the Hyatt Regency Club, a full security floor, a lounge, a disco, room service, and same day laundry service. Parking costs $4.75 per night. Sunday Champagne brunch. 397 rooms. *$65 and up.*

Sheraton Towne House. 2961 Wilshire; 382–7171; (800) 325–3535. Howard Hughes slept (and lived) here. One of Sheraton's finest establishments, this hotel was built in the 1920s. It prides itself on its country-estate setting, with marble fireplaces and cedar lined closets. Tennis and swimming in an Olympic-sized pool. Two restaurants on the property: a coffee shop and the Garden Room for fine dining. Right across the street from Bullocks Wilshire, a fine example of the city's best Art Deco architecture. Parking at $4.00 per day. 300 rooms. *$59 and up.*

Moderate

Best Western Executive Motor Inn—Mid-Wilshire. 603 S. New Hampshire. 385–4444; (800) 528–1234. This Best Western hotel is a block away from the Wilshire financial district. Pool, sauna, Jacuzzi, laundry. Parking is free. 90 rooms. *$39 and up.*

Cloud Motel. 3400 W. Third Street; 385–0061. This hotel is centrally located between downtown Los Angeles and Hollywood. Business types especially find the hotel convenient, for it is near the Wilshire commercial district but not situated on the busy boulevard. Rooms done in a modern decor, coffee shop, pool, free parking. 130 rooms. *$36–$40.*

Hotel Chancellor. 3191 W. Seventh; 383–1183; (800) 421–8260. Near the Wilshire Center, this hotel provides an intimate atmosphere at a low price. Coffee shop and the award-winning Cove Restaurant satisfy guests' appetites. Heated pool year round. The Chancellor is a popular hotel with Japanese and Asian tourists. 114 rooms. *$35–$45.*

Royal Viking Motel. 2025 W. Third Street; 483–8691. Near St. Vincent's Hospital, the Royal Viking is quite small in terms of the number of rooms available but big in terms of friendliness. Large security parking lot for guests at no extra charge. American–Chinese restaurant. On the Gray Line tour bus line. Car rentals, laundry service. Pool. Large suites available to accommodate up to 6 guests. 38 rooms. *$32.25–$38.70.*

HOLLYWOOD

Deluxe

Le Dufy Hotel. 1000 Westmont Drive, West Hollywood; 657–7400. New 121-suite property boasting a lot of luxury: rooftop heated pool, whirlpool, spa, sauna, and sundeck, among other things. Great for business travelers. Near Restaurant Row. *$75–$90 and up.*

Sunset Marquis Hotel. 1200 Alta Loma Rd.; 657–1333; (800) 421–4380 (U.S.); (800) 858–7125 (Canada). This three-story property near La Cienega and Sunset offers nightly entertainment. Jacuzzi, complimentary breakfast, garden area with lovely landscaping. Parking is free. 115 rooms. *$80–$105.*

Le Valadon Hotel. 900 Hammond St., West Hollywood. 653–0560. Opened July 1983. 138 suites, most with lovely fireplaces. Quite fashionable with lighted rooftop tennis, pool, and spa. Massages available. Complimentary Continental breakfast. *$75–90, and up.*

Expensive to Deluxe

Beverly Sunset Hotel. 8775 Sunset Blvd.; 652–0030; (800) 421–3323. You'll find people in the music business frequenting this high-service hotel offering the beautiful Café Chez Pierre overlooking Sunset Blvd. Recently renovated. Pool, free parking. 60 rooms. *$85–$120.*

Chateau Marmont Hotel. 8221 Sunset Blvd.; 656–1010. Despite its location on the Sunset Strip among giant billboards and a lot of glitz, this castle of Old World charm and French Normandy design is offered to its guests as a secluded hideaway convenient to all Hollywood's hot spots. All kinds of accommodations are available, including fully equipped cottages, bungalows, and a penthouse (at $200–$250 per night; monthly rates available). Garden, swimming pool, patios. 62 rooms. No CB. *$60–$250.*

Expensive

Hollywood Holiday Inn. 1775 N. Highland Ave.; 462–7181; (800) 238–8000; (800) 465–4329. You can't miss this one. It's one of the tallest buildings in the heart of Hollywood. Twenty-three stories, topped by Windows, a revolving restaurant lounge. Features include a safekeeping box in each room. The location is minutes from the Hollywood Bowl and Universal Studios and only fifty paces from Hollywood's Walk of Fame. Gray Line Sightseeing tour bus stop. Free parking. 468 rooms. *$67.*

Hollywood Roosevelt. 7000 Hollywood Blvd.; 469–2442. The site of the first presentation of the Academy Awards, this charming hotel is state-of-the-art Hollywood. From its famous star-studded sidewalk on the exterior to a lush

Olympic-sized pool and Tropicana Bar in the courtyard, it never lets guests forget where they are. A magnificent lobby is enhanced by ornate fountains and a gallery of famous movies stars' photographs. Airport bus service, car rentals on premises, free parking, group rates. 380 rooms plus 90 poolside lanais. *$51–$63.*

Hyatt on Sunset. 8401 W. Sunset Blvd.; 656–4101; (800) 228–9000. Located in the heart of the Sunset Strip, this Hyatt is a favorite of music business executives and rock stars. Penthouse suites and some rooms with private patios. Rooftop pool, garage, parking lot. Daisy's Restaurant features everything from hamburgers to steak and lobster; cocktail lounge. *$60 and up.*

Moderate

Dunes Motel. 5625 Sunset Blvd.; 467–5171. Across the street from two television stations, so you'll find studio people around and about this hotel. American Restaurant and cocktail lounge. Parking is free. 56 rooms. *$38–$54.*

Farmer's Daughter Motel (Best Western). 115 S. Fairfax; 937–3930. Across the street from the fabulous Farmers Market shopping and CBS Television City, the hotel is especially proud of its good service. Steak house, swimming pool. Free parking. Cantor's 24-hour New York-style deli is down the street. *$48.*

Franklin Motel. 1824 N. Beachwood Dr.; 464–1824. This fairly new hotel has an AAA rating and is immaculate. Close to Bronson Canyon and Griffith Park. Weekly rates available for rooms with kitchenettes. 24 rooms. *$40–$45.*

Hallmark House Motor Hotel. 7023 Sunset Blvd.; 464–8344. Near the Wax Museum, this hotel offers free security parking, which is not easy to find elsewhere in Hollywood. Pool, small pets allowed. 24-hour coffee shop nearby. 72 rooms. *$38–$45; lower winter rates.*

Hollywood Highland Motel. 2051 N. Highland Ave.; 851–3000. Here's something unusual—a free Continental Chinese breakfast is offered at this hotel. Located just steps away from the Hollywood Bowl, with a pool, laundry rooms, and free parking. 53 rooms. *$39 and up.*

Sunset–LaBrea TraveLodge. 7051 Sunset Blvd.; 462–0905; (800) 255–3050. Just around the corner from the Chinese Theater, this hotel offers friendly service. The rooms have recently been refurbished. Facilities for the handicapped, babysitting service. Free parking. 43 rooms. *$36–$40.*

Sunset Plaza Hotel. 8400 Sunset Blvd.; 654–0750; (800) 252–0645 in California; otherwise (800) 421–3652. Located on the Sunset Strip, this hotel is a favorite with show business people. Rooms are modern in design, in the mode of the Los Angeles open air style. Parking is free. AE, MC, V. *$48–$58.*

Vermont Sunset TraveLodge. 1401 Vermont Ave.; 665–5735; (800) 255–3050. This hotel is situated in East Hollywood, right next to Children's Hospital and in the vicinity of Griffith Park. Pool, direct dial phones, near several restaurants. Free parking. 71 rooms. *$36–$44.*

Inexpensive

Bevonshire Lodge Motel. 7575 Beverly Blvd., near Fairfax in West Los Angeles–Hollywood; 936–6154. Close to CBS and the Farmers Market, this

25-room family-style motel has a pool and free parking. On Gray Lines bus route. *$28.*

Hollywood Downtowner Motor Hotel. 5601 Hollywood Blvd.; 464–7191. Located in the heart of Hollywood. You'll find this hotel to be one of the most reasonably priced in the area. Swimming pool, babysitting service. *$28–$32.*

Hollywood La Brea Motel. 7110 Hollywood Blvd.; 876–8000. Conveniently located near all Hollywood Blvd. attractions. A pool and free parking. 30 rooms. *$28–$30.*

Hollywood Premier Hotel. 5333 Hollywood Blvd.; 466–1691. Near Western Ave., this hotel is just down the street from Griffith Park's loveliest spot, Ferndell, a perfect place to have a picnic or just relax. The hotel offers room service from their coffee shop. Pool, free parking. *$30–$32.*

Howard's Weekly Apartments. 1738 N. Whitley; 466–6943. A popular hotel with Oriental visitors. You'll find this hotel quite reasonable. Charges are by the week exclusively, but there is a three day/three night miniweek special. The apartments are located one block off Hollywood Blvd. Laundry room. Reservations are a must. 138 units. MC, V. *$100 per week for rooms with kitchenettes.*

Saharan Motor Hotel. 7212 Sunset Blvd.; 874–6700. Near La Brea Ave., this hotel has a babysitting service, facilities for the handicapped, and allows small pets. Pool, plenty of free parking. 63 rooms. *$30–$32.*

BEVERLY HILLS

Deluxe

Bel Air Hotel. 701 Stone Canyon Rd.; 472–1211. Charming, secluded hotel, lovely gardens, trees, flowers, and a creek complete with swans. This celebrity mecca contains a dining room with Old-World atmosphere, a cocktail lounge, and entertainment. Fine service. Distinctively furnished rooms and suites. Heated pool. *$100 and up.*

Beverly Hills Hotel. 9641 Sunset Blvd.; 276–2251. Beautiful grounds with tropical plants on 12 acres. A California landmark. Lovely rooms, quiet location. Movie stars often occupy the bungalows. Breakfast and lunch are served on the Loggia and adjoining outdoor patio. Lunch and dinner served in the Lanai Restaurant overlooking the pool. The famous Polo Lounge is here. Tennis courts, poolside service. Heated swimming pool. Screening room, country club feeling. Parking at various prices. *$120 and up, up, up to $1,200.*

Beverly Wilshire Hotel. 9500 Wilshire Blvd.; 275–4282. European in atmosphere and decor with personal service and extras to match. The garden swimming pool is lovely. Sauna bath. Great restaurants, including El Padrino, Hernando's Hideaway, and La Bella Fontana. Limousine service to airport. Multilingual staff. *$135 and up.*

Century Plaza Hotel. 2025 Ave. of the Stars, Century City; 277–2000; (800) 228–3000. One of the area's largest hotels offers fine style and amenities. Handsomely designed by Minoru Yamasaki. Each room has a refrigerator, a lanai, and a view. The hotel has several restaurants, including Yamato and the Vineyard. Dancing and entertainment. Pool. In the heart of Century City. No pets. *$103 and up.*

L'Ermitage Hotel. 9291 Burton Way; 278–3344; (800) 282–4818 in California; otherwise (800) 421–4306. This hotel of Old-World charm offers all the modern conveniences to ensure the highest standards in accommodations and services. Opened in 1976, it has won the Mobil Five-Star Award and the AAA Five-Diamond Award, the only West Coast hotel to garner both. Near Beverly Hills, elegant shopping, and 20th Century-Fox, this gem offers 117 suites with parquet entries, sunken living rooms with fireplaces, wet bars, and private balconies. Café Russe, a fine dining place, is reserved exclusively for hotel patrons and their guests. The café offers French cuisine amid a collection of nineteenth- and twentieth-century oils by European masters. Twenty-four-hour in-suite service, complimentary Continental breakfast. Chauffeured limousine within the city of Beverly Hills. Rooftop garden available for dining. Swimming pool, whirlpool, spa, and private solariums. Overnight shoeshine, basket filled with fresh fruit, newspapers, mineral water. Parking underneath building for guests only. *$155 and up, for one bedroom; $345–$455 for two bedrooms; $850 for three-bedroom townhouse.*

Le Parc Hotel. 733 North West Knoll in West Hollywood (in the area between Beverly Hills and Hollywood); 855–8888; (800) 421–4666, nationwide; (800) 252–2152 in California. This intimate European-style hotel is housed in a modern low-rise building in a lovely residential area. Received a presidential citation in recognition of superior design from the Society of American Registered Architects. Each of the 154 suites includes a living room with a fireplace, a kitchenette, a stocked cocktail cabinet, and a private balcony. Near Farmers Market, the Los Angeles County Art Museum, and CBS Television City. Guests will especially enjoy their own private eaterie, Café Le Parc, which is reserved exclusively for them. In-suite service from 7:00 A.M. to 10:30 P.M.; complimentary Continental breakfast. Colorful rooftop garden, lighted tennis, heated pool, whirlpool spa, sauna, and exercise room. Complimentary covered security parking and chauffeured limo to Hollywood and Beverly Hills from 9:00 A.M. to 9:00 P.M. Special "Le Weekend" consists of accommodations for two nights, a champagne brunch, a basket of fruit, and cocktails to welcome guests to the hotel. *$90–$135.*

Expensive to Deluxe

The Beverly Hilton. 9876 Wilshire Blvd., at Santa Monica; 274–7777. Large hotel complex, 600 well-decorated rooms, a broad selection of restaurants and shops. Trader Vic's and L'Escoffier are two of the city's renowned restaurants. Theater ticket desk, limousine service, pool. Free coffee in lobby for hotel guests. Underground parking at $6 a day. *$84 and up.*

Expensive

Beverly Comstock. 10300 Wilshire Blvd.; 275–5575. Small, well-appointed fifty-room hotel. All suites. *$75 and up.*

Beverly Rodeo. 360 N. Rodeo Dr.; 273–0300. With modern elegance throughout its 100 units, this small Beverly Hills hotel features Café Rodeo, an outdoor eaterie popular with the locals. Newly renovated, the hotel contains a sun deck, a free garage, and an intimate bar and lounge. Convenient to fashionable shopping. 100 rooms. *$70–$82 and up.*

Holiday Inn of Beverly Hills. 9360 Wilshire Blvd.; 273–1400; (800) 238–8000. In the heart of Beverly Hills, this property is popular with commercial clients. Parking is free. Pool, restaurant, laundry. 109 rooms. *$69–$81 and up.*

Ramada Beverly Hills. 1150 S. Beverly Dr.; 553–6561; (800) 228–2828. A large high-rise property in the heart of Beverly Hills. Affordable rates. Room service, meeting rooms, cocktail lounge. Close to Rodeo Drive, Century City, and 20th Century Fox. Parking adjacent at no extra charge. Haunt of movie stars and musicians. 260 rooms. *$75–$88.*

Moderate

Beverly Terrace Motor Hotel. 469 N. Doheny; 274–8141. Pentagon shaped hotel with a roof terrace. The hotel attracts an international clientele. Scully's Restaurant. Pool. Good security. Parking is free. *$42 and up.*

Inexpensive

Beverly House Hotel. 140 S. Lasky Dr., Beverly Hill; 271–2145. Small and friendly establishment near Century City. Parking is free. Laundry. 50 rooms. *$28 and up.*

WEST LOS ANGELES
(INCLUDING WESTWOOD AND BRENTWOOD)

Deluxe

Westwood Marquis. 930 Hilgard Ave.; 208–8765; (800) 352–7454 in California; otherwise (800) 421–2317. Corporate and entertainment personalities like this elegant property. Breakfast and lunch are served on the Garden Terrace. The Dynasty Room features Continental cuisine. European teas are served in the afternoon in the Westwood Lounge. Pool, sauna, phones in bathrooms, laundry, banquet and meeting rooms. Parking $6 per day. Near UCLA campus. 225 suites (and no two are alike). *$140 and up.*

Expensive to Deluxe

The New Bel Air Sands Hotel. 11461 Sunset Blvd.; 476–6571; (800) 421–6649, nationwide; (800) 352–6680 in California. Recently renovated. There you'll find "a bit of the Bahamas in Bel Air." A putting green, tennis courts, a cocktail lounge with live entertainment, and a pool. DC, MC, V. *$75 and up.*

Expensive

Best Western Royal Palace Hotel. 2528 S. Sepulveda Blvd., West LA; 477–9066; (800) 528–1234. Pool and sauna are both available in this small, 32-room hotel right off the 405 freeway. All suites. Parking is free and so is morning coffee. *$57–$65.*

Century Wilshire. 10776 Wilshire, West LA; 474–4506. A European-style hotel offering mostly suites, many with kitchenettes. Near UCLA and Westwood. The clientele is mostly European. Pool, laundry. Room service but no restaurants. Parking is free. *$50 and up.*

Holiday Inn–Brentwood Bel Air. 170 N. Church Lane, West LA; 476–6411. Near UCLA and the 405 Freeway, this 17-story, round establishment is popular with corporate and college clients. Van shuttle to UCLA. Outdoor kennels for animals. Parking is free. *$62–$78.*

Holiday Inn of Westwood. 10740 Wilshire Blvd.; West LA; 475–8711. Near UCLA. Pool, laundry, restaurant. Free parking. Nineteen-story property. *$67 and up.*

Moderate

St. Regis Motor Hotel. 11955 Wilshire Blvd.; West LA; 477–6021. Near UCLA and Westwood Village. Many restaurants close by. Cocktail lounge and El Capote Restaurant inside. Pool. Parking free to guests. 50 rooms. *$26–$50.*

Stardust Motor Hotel. 3202 Wilshire Blvd., West LA; 828–4584. Near UCLA and Westwood Village, this hotel offers a pool and ample parking for guests and guests of guests. Multilingual staff. 33 rooms. *$25–$50.*

SANTA MONICA

Deluxe

Miramar Sheraton. 101 Wilshire Blvd.; 394–3731. This hotel is located "where Wilshire meets the sea," close to all area beaches and across the street from Pacific Palisades Park. Landscaping incorporates the area's second largest rubber tree. Group rates available. Two restaurants and a lounge. 276 rooms. *$95–$175.*

Expensive

Holiday Inn. 120 Colorado Ave.; 451–0676. Close to many restaurants, major shopping centers, the beach, and the Santa Monica Pier, this hotel offers a heated pool, laundry facilities, meeting and banquet rooms, and room service. Free guest parking. 128 rooms. *$50–$150 for suites.*

Huntley House. 111 Second St.; 451–5971. One block from miles and miles of magnificent white sand beaches, this hotel has 17 floors and is located on a quiet street overlooking the ocean. The area is hopping with restaurants (one on the roof), nightclubs, and 350 shops and boutiques. Also available are facilities for swimming, jogging, biking, tennis, and boating. Room service, laundry facilities, banquet and meeting rooms. Free guest parking. 210 rooms. *$68–$150.*

Pacific Shore. 1819 Ocean Ave., 451–8711; (800) 241–3848, nationwide; (800) 532–3733 in California. Formerly the Royal Inn of Santa Monica, this modern building is one-half block from the beach. Attractive rooms, heated pool, sauna, laundry facilities and same-day valet services. Therapy pool and Jacuzzi, Ajax Rent a Car, gift shop, lounge bar. Surrounding the hotel is a variety of restaurants. Parking is available in a security patroled lot at no fee to guests. 172 rooms. *$62–$88.*

Moderate to Expensive

Breakers Motel. 1501 Ocean Ave.; 451–4811. This two-story building with large, luxurious rooms is a haven for Europeans. It is only a minute from the beach and is known for its well-maintained rooms. Heated pool, color TV, free parking. 34 rooms. *$32–$75.*

Moderate

Carmel Hotel. 201 Broadway; 451–2469. Built in the 1920s, this charming hotel offers fun and excitement for the entire family. Very close to the beaches, shopping, and theaters. Color TV, free parking. Restaurants specializing in seafood are nearby. 110 rooms. No CB. *$42–$48.*

Inexpensive

Stardust Motor Hotel. 3202 Wilshire Blvd.; 828–4584. Friendly hotel service at motel rates. Multilingual staff. Located a distance from the beach in the heart of the Santa Monica shopping area. Amenities include color TV, room service, and laundry facilities. No charge for parking. 33 rooms. *$30–$32.*

AIRPORT

Expensive

Airport Park Hotel. 600 Ave. of Champions; 673–5151. "Lets be friends" is the motto of this hotel, which is located on the grounds of the Hollywood Park Racetrack, next door to the Forum, and close to major freeways. There is live entertainment in the Picadilly Circus Lounge; the Thoroughbred coffee shop offers superb eating for the casual diner; pool; 24-hour shuttle to LAX. 350 rooms. *$56–$68.*

Amfac Hotel Los Angeles. 8601 Lincoln Blvd.; 670–8111; (800) 227–4700, nationwide; (800) 622–0838 in California. This hotel is located in a quiet residential area perfect for jogging, tennis, and golf. Full services are provided; excellent dining in the Bistro Restaurant. Airport transportation, shuttle service to Fisherman's Village. 754 rooms. *$66–$125.*

Holiday Inn–LAX. 9901 La Cienega Blvd.; 649–5151; (800) 238–8000; (800) 654–4329. This newly decorated, international-style hotel is ideal for families as well as business types. Full group facilities. Dining room; the 2001 Lounge has live entertainment featuring acts from Las Vegas, San Francisco, and the East. Multilingual telephone operators, tour information. 403 rooms. *$64–$67.*

Howard Johnson's Airport Hotel. 5990 Green Valley Circle, Culver City; 641–7740; (800) 654–2000. Another fine Howard Johnson accommodation, just two miles north of LAX. Just right for the commercial traveler. Close to the Fox Hills Shopping Mall. 24-hour restaurant, pool, laundry, banquet facilities, and meeting rooms. Free airport transportation. 200 rooms. *$62–$70.*

Hyatt Hotel–LAX. 6225 W. Century Blvd.; 670–9000; (800) 228–9000. An elegant, 12-story hotel decorated in earth tones with brass. The hotel closest to LAX, Hollywood Park, and Marina Del Rey. With business travelers in mind, it boasts large meeting rooms with ample banquet space. Bilingual staff; con-surroundings are enhanced by trees and foliage, and a goldfish pond makes Sunday brunches by the water exceptionally nice. Meeting and banquet rooms, game room, restaurant, Jacuzzi. 281 rooms. *$99–$110.*

Expensive

Marina Del Rey Hotel. 13534 Bali Way; 822–1010; (800) 421–8145. Completely surrounded by water, this deluxe waterfront hotel is located on the marina's main channel, making cruises and charters accessible. It houses five meeting rooms and is within walking distance to shopping and Don the Beachcomber's Restaurant. Full catering. Beautiful Gazebo area for parties. *$86–$94.*

Marina International Hotel and Villas. 4200 Admiralty Way; 822–1010; (800) 421–8145. Directly across from an inland beach, this hotel is unique for its village style of luxury decor featuring such rooms as "The African Queen," "The King Tut Hut," and "Old Hollywood." Very private accommodations; boat charters available for as many as 90 people. Dining in the elegant Crystal Fountain Restaurant for Continental cuisine. Jacuzzi. 110 rooms, 25 villas. *$86–$92 and up.*

Marina-Pacifica Hotel and Apartments. 1697 Pacific Ave., Venice; 399–7770; (800) 421–8151. Quaint European intimacy is the only way to describe Los Angeles' only contemporary beachfront hotel. On Venice Beach, it features rooms with fireplaces and kitchens and an indoor-outdoor café. For the active traveler, there's ocean swimming, roller skating along the strand, racquetball, and tennis. Centrally located. 92 rooms, one-bedroom apartments available. *$50–$75;* apartments rented by the month.

SOUTH BAY BEACH CITIES

Deluxe

Barnabey's Hotel and Restaurant. 3501 Sepulveda Blvd. at Rosecrans, Manhattan Beach; 545–8466. More than $4 million was spent to transform this hotel into a 19th-century English inn. Rooms contain four-poster beds, lace curtains, and antique decorations. Enclosed greenhouse pool. Rosie's Bar resembles a cozy pub with live entertainment. The restaurant features Continental cuisine and curtained, private booths. Afternoon tea. Adjacent health club; $2 per day use. Weekend packages. 128 rooms. *$98–$115.*

Expensive to Deluxe

Portofino Inn. 260 Portofino Way, Redondo Beach; 379–8481. A complete resort in the middle of the harbor, this inn is located on a man-made finger of land near King Harbor. Attractive rooms, most with kitchenettes. Heated pool, room service, restaurants, laundry facilities, meeting rooms. Bike rentals and tennis nearby. 136 rooms. *$63–$225.*

Expensive

Hacienda Hotel. 525 N. Sepulveda Blvd., El Segundo; 615–0015; (800) 421–5900, nationwide; (800) 262–1314 in California. Uniquely designed, the Hacienda provides tour advice, free transportation to two shopping malls in the area,

24-hour limousine service, Jacuzzi, two pools, 24-hour room service, and complete meeting and banquet facilities with the finest audio equipment available for any business assembly. 660 rooms. *$57–$63.*

Moderate

Hi-View Motel. 100 S. Sepulveda Blvd., Manhattan Beach; 374–4608. Quaint and simple, with kitchenettes available in several rooms; only one mile from the beach. Small pets allowed. 22 rooms. *$34–$50.*

Inexpensive

Malahini Motel. 14329 E. Whittier Blvd., Whittier; 698–6731. This modern building offers laundry facilities, a heated pool, and color TV. Convenient to many ethnic restaurants, including Chinese, Mexican, and Italian. Not far from a major shopping center; easy freeway access. 31 rooms. V, MC, AE. *$21–$28.*

SAN FERNANDO VALLEY

New Area Code (818)

Expensive

Beverly Garland's Howard Johnson Resort Lodge. 4222 Vineland Ave., North Hollywood; 980–8000. Popular with business and entertainment types, this seven-story property suggests a country club atmosphere; private balcony patios and sliding view-windows. The lodge is located on the historic El Camino Real; all rooms have AM–FM radio and color TV. Swimming and wading pool, children's playground. Cocktail lounge. Parking is free. 258 rooms *$64–$72.*

Burbank Airport Hilton. 2500 Hollywood Way, Burbank; 843–6000. Directly across the street from the Burbank-Glendale-Pasadena Airport. Close to major television and movie studios. Pool, saunas, and whirlpool spa. Video-game room, gift shop, babysitting service. Premier floor features special amenities. Meeting facilities. Free parking. 280 rooms. *$74–$110.*

Holiday Inn–Burbank. 150 E. Angeleno St., Burbank; 841–4770; (800) 465–4329. This newly opened Holiday Inn is very large and is near all major Burbank studios. It features full service, including a restaurant and lounge with fireplace. This hotel, according to the management, has the most sophisticated fire-control system available. 45 banquet and meeting facilities, the largest accommodating up to 300. The five-story converted parking structure is free. 375 rooms. *$62–$66.*

Holiday Inn of Van Nuys. 8244 Orion Ave., Van Nuys; 989–5010; (800) 238–8000. Next to the Busch Brewery (tours conducted), this hotel is located off the Roscoe exit of the 405 freeway near Magic Mountain and Universal. Cable television with current movies. Pipers Restaurant and a lovely outdoor pool. Parking is free. 126 rooms. *$50–$55.*

Sheraton Universal. 333 Universal Terrace Pkwy., Universal City; 980–1212. A large, 23-story hotel located at Universal City (Studios). You're likely to see the stars here. Two restaurants, a rooftop pool, sauna, whirlpool spa, and exercise room. On the grounds of Universal City, where you'll see the newly renovated Universal Amphitheater and tour the world's largest movie studio. Overlooks Hollywood. 500 rooms. *$75–$115*.

Sportsman Lodge Hotel. 12825 Ventura Blvd., Studio City; 769–4700. An English country-style establishment with a resort atmosphere. Stroll along the grounds through beautiful gardens with waterfalls and an unusual mountain pool stocked with live trout. Guest rooms are quite large, and the pool is Olympic size. Restaurant with American and Continental cuisine and coffee shop providing room service. Studio suites with private patios are available. 196 rooms. *$60–$75*.

The Valley Hilton. 15433 Ventura Blvd.; 981–5400. One great feature of the hotel is location: It's situated at the intersection of the 405 San Diego and 101 Ventura Freeways. Like all Hiltons, this hotel stands behind its excellent service and comfort. Aside from being a great location for tourists, this hotel is also well equipped for conventioneers. Its banquet and meeting rooms accommodate up to 500 people. 210 rooms in all, including plush executive suites. *$65–$80*.

Moderate

Burbank TraveLodge, L.A. 1112 N. Hollywood Way, Burbank; 845–2408; (800) 255–3050. Near the NBC, Universal, and Warner Bros. studios, this small hotel dishes up a warm, friendly atmosphere. Courtesy services include coffee in each room and a bus to the Hollywood-Burbank Airport. 28 rooms. *$35–$45*.

Mission Hills Inn (Best Western). 10621 Sepulveda Blvd., Mission Hills; 891–1771. At the northern end of the San Fernando Valley; get a true taste of the California life-style at this hotel, with its 120 spacious rooms surrounding a large pool with flower gardens and palm trees. This resort atmosphere is just 10 minutes from Magic Mountain and blocks away from the San Fernando Mission. Restaurant, cocktail lounge, room service. *$45–$50*.

Safari Inn. 1911 W. Olive, Burbank; 845–8586. Used frequently for location filming, this hotel offers high standard services. There is a fine French restaurant, Leserene, on the premises, along with a pool and Jacuzzi. Suites available with wet bars. 110 rooms. *$45–$60*.

St. George Motor Inn. 19454 Ventura Blvd., Tarzana; 345–6911. This English Tudor-style hotel is located near the southwest end of the San Fernando Valley close to the Warner Studios ranch. Services available include TV, a heated pool, Jacuzzi, suites with kitchenettes at reasonable rates, and parking for both cars and RVs. Near such restaurants as Victoria Station, Charlie Brown's, and several fast food outlets. 57 rooms. AE, MC, V. *$45; $65 for suites*.

Inexpensive to Moderate

Chase House Motel. 8525 Sepulveda Blvd., Sepulveda; 894–5721. You'll find this fine hotel just down the street from Western Bagel (open 24 hours and offering the best bagels in town). Very clean; swimming pool and restaurant on property. Laundromat nearby. Parking is free. *$30–$50*.

SAN GABRIEL VALLEY

Expensive

Holiday Inn–Pasadena. 303 E. Cordove St., Pasadena; 449–4000; (800) 238–8000; (800) 465–4329. Situated next to the Ice Capades Ice Rink and convenient to the Rose Bowl and Super Bowl. (To obtain a room during those times, please make reservations well in advance of your arrival.) Tennis courts and swimming pool; a popular Champagne brunch is available every Sunday. *$66–$74.*

Huntington–Sheraton Hotel. 1401 South Oak Knoll, Pasadena; 792–0266. A picturesque, old resort hotel situated on 23 landscaped acres in a beautiful, quiet neighborhood near the Huntington Library. This establishment is more than 70 years old and is one of Pasadena's most spectacular buildings. Recreational facilities include a putting green, tennis courts, and an Olympic-sized pool. In addition to the main building, the hotel offers poolside cottages comprising one to seven bedrooms. Daily to monthly rates available. First-class restaurant, lounge. 525 rooms. *$80–$105.*

Pasadena Hilton. 150 S. Los Robles Ave., Pasadena; 577–1000. This Hilton prides itself on "rich fabrics, fine woods, lush plants, and a distinct European ambience." Enter the lobby, where you'll find Fanny's piano bar, and ride the elevator to Skylights, a gourmet penthouse restaurant with panoramic views of the city and the mountains. A full-service hotel close to the Rose Bowl and Pasadena's historical Civic Center. Convention facilities. 264 rooms. *$79–$95.*

Moderate

Holiday Inn Montebello. 7709 E. Telegraph Rd., Montebello; 724–1400; (800) 238–8000; (800) 465–4329 Conveniently located near the Santa Ana Freeway and next to the City of Commerce, this hotel caters to the businessperson as well as the tourist. Restaurant, pool, cocktail lounge. Parking is free. 148 rooms. *$40–$48.*

Rodeway Inn and Valley Racquet Club. 840 S. Indian Hill Blvd., Claremont (in Los Angeles County); (714) 621–4831. Off San Bernardino Freeway. Reservations necessary during the L.A. County Fair and the Ontario Races. Sauna, swimming pool, Jacuzzi. AE, V, MC. *$39 and up.*

Inexpensive

El Dorado Motor Inn. 140 N. Azusa Ave., West Covina; 331–6371. Located just off Freeway 10 in West Covina. A moderate motor inn, with many of the luxuries of a hotel, set in a garden atmosphere. Newly refurbished interior with a Spanish-style decor. Equipped with a therapy pool, swimming pool, wading pool, restaurants, banquet and meeting rooms. Daily valet service. Cocktail lounge. Free parking for guests. 85 units. *$31.50–$36.50.*

YOUTH HOSTELS

For those on tight budgets, Los Angeles youth hostels offer clean accommodations, a communal atmosphere, and reasonable rates. Youth hostels are available to American Youth Hostels/International Youth Hostel Federation (AYH/IYHF) members at discounted rates and to nonmembers at rates averaging less than $10 per night.

A false impression about youth hostels is that they are offered only to students. On the contrary, hostels welcome people of all ages who have an adventuresome spirit—students and nonstudents alike. The only requirement for registration may be willingness to perform a simple chore or a task.

The two main hostels in Los Angeles are located near popular places of interest. Both are accessible to public transportation lines.

The American Youth Hostel for Los Angeles. 1502 Palos Verdes Drive North, Harbor City, CA 90710; (213) 831–8109. Located in a hilly area that was once a reservation for the Suangna tribe, the hostel overlooks the Long Beach Harbor area. Once serving as a naval barracks, the structure was renovated four years ago to accommodate hostelers. It is minutes away from Redondo, Hermosa, and Palos Verdes beaches and Port O'Call Village. The #232 bus takes you from LA International Airport to the hostel.

It's recommended that visitors bring sleeping bags, but bed sheets and blankets are available for a rental charge of $1 per night. The hostel has separate men's and women's dormitories, with toilet and shower facilities. The communal building consists of a fully equipped kitchen where hostelers can save money by cooking meals, a dining area, a reading room, a lounge area, a television room, and a large patio area—the only place smoking is allowed.

Dutch, French, German, and Spanish are spoken by staff members who are great conversationists eager to give information on Los Angeles or hostel services. It is best to make reservations if you plan to stay during the summer or if you will be traveling with a large group. The hostel sleeps 70 and has a tendency to reach maximum occupancy during July and August. Check-in time is between 7:30 and 9:30 A.M. and 4:00 and 11:00 P.M. Nonmembers are allowed to stay up to three days and members up to five, but arrangements can be made ahead of time for a longer visit. Rates are $7.25 for nonmembers and $5.25 for members.

Most of hostel visitors are in the 18–30 age range, usually cross-state or cross-country travelers. A sign in the hostel reads "The basic premise of hosteling is to leave a place better than one found it." In this regard, simple chores such as wiping a table or sweeping a floor are expected to be performed by hostelers. No maid service is offered and so hostelers are continually encouraged to pick up after themselves.

The hostel is between Western Avenue and Gaffey Street near Pacific Coast Highway and is two miles from the Harbor (#11) Freeway. It is a 25-minute walk from bus #232's stop.

The Hollywood YMCA Hotel and Youth Hostel. 1553 N. Hudson Ave., Hollywood; (213) 467–4161. Unwinding in the saunas, floating in the pool, or, if you feel up to it, exercising with weights in the gymnasium is one way to end a day of sightseeing in Hollywood. All this, along with aerobic classes and other programs, are available to guests of both the hotel and the youth hostel. In a strategic location for those touring via public transportation, the Hollywood

YMCA is accessible to several bus lines going to Disneyland, Universal Studios, or the beaches and is less than a mile from the Hollywood Greyhound Bus Terminal.

The hotel consists of single and double rooms available for both men and women. The decor is modest but clean. Guests share the bathroom and shower facilities located in the hallway. Check-out time is 11:00 A.M., and it is best to make reservations between mid-May and late August. Rooms are not offered on a weekly basis.

The youth hostel provides separate sleeping quarters for men and women. Blankets are available, but it is best to bring your own sleeping bag. Check-in time is 7:45 P.M. and all are required to check out by 8:00 A.M. because the rooms used as sleeping quarters are also used for YMCA activities during the day and evening. Hostelers are taken on a first-come-first-served basis and allowed to stay up to seven days. Longer visits can usually be worked out. Showering facilities are in the men's and women's locker rooms. Women must shower before 11:00 P.M. or after 7:00 A.M. Belongings can be stored in closets available to hostelers.

There are no kitchen facilities, but the YMCA has a patio restaurant on the premises. It serves Middle Eastern dishes, Turkish coffee, pastries, healthful drinks, and sandwiches. Umbrella-covered tables and plants make up the Garden Café's decor. The restaurant is open from 7:30 A.M. to 8:30 P.M.

Vending machines, a TV set, and computer games are in the patio areas—the only place smoking is permitted. The hostel lounge contains a piano, chess and backgammon games, tables, and large sofas and is reserved exclusively for hostelers who want to meet and enjoy one another's company. Hotel and hostel guests are encouraged to use all the facilities, including the gym and spa areas, and to participate in YMCA services and programs, such as exercise classes, weight control programs, and psychological counseling provided at no additional charge. Tourist information is available at the front desk or from the hostel attendant.

Hotel rates are $14.75 per night for a single room and $22.00 for a double. Hostel rates are $4.50 per night for Youth Hostel members and $6.25 for nonmembers. Proper I.D. is required and used as collateral when checking out equipment.

The neighborhood of the Hollywood YMCA is not safe during the evenings. Hotel and hostel guests, especially women, are asked to be extremely cautious when walking in the area and not to walk unaccompanied.

 HEALTH SPAS. Southern California is probably *the* fitness capital of the country, boasting more health and reducing spas per potbelly and double chin than any other state in the nation. There's a spa tailored to fit every bulging waistline and budget and to cater to almost all needs. If your shape could use some remodeling—and your body a little rejuvenation—a visit to one of the area's top spas could be just what you need.

From The Ashram, with its spartan regimen of hard exercise and good, natural eating, to La Costa, with its luxurious amenities, to an inexpensive hotel in the beautiful countryside offering outdoor activities and hiking, the choices are endless.

A month is optimum for a stay at the serious health resort; but since this time span is unrealistic for most people, weekly programs are designed to provide the most benefit within that length of time. Many spas also offer daily rates for quick pick-me-ups. Even though the selection is large, these spas—especially the more popular ones—fill up quickly, so book as far in advance as possible. And check prices: They change frequently.

Prices can be steep—up to $2,275 at The Golden Door—but health spas offer invaluable benefits. Clients invigorate their systems, release the tensions of the everyday world, and get their bodies in shape. Here is a sampling of spas within a day's drive (many much closer) from Los Angeles. Go out and get healthy!

La Costa Hotel and Spa. *Super Deluxe.* Rancho La Costa, Carlsbad, CA 92008; (619) 438–9111. At this world-famous, posh health resort do as much or as little as you like. Rates vary, but a full spa program, with individualized exercise and diet programs, is $405 a day, double occupancy (there are a 15% service charge and a four-night minimum). Guests hobnob with stars such as Ava Gardner and Ali McGraw. The usual amenities, such as exercise classes, massage, sauna, and swimming, are available. There is an impressive sports complex offering tennis courts and golf.

Night life at La Costa is more active than at most spas. Guests dine among strolling violinists and dance or converse to music. Movies are available both in the theater or in the rooms. Located 40 minutes from San Diego, a few minutes from the Pacific Ocean, and not far from Mexico.

The complete spa program for men and women offers not only a medical evaluation and a special diet, but also skin analysis and review, herbal wraps, yoga, the daily use of sauna, whirlpool, solarium, and gym facilities. The food gets rave reviews; executive chef Willy Hauser creates such lunches as broiled sherried grapefruit, cucumbers vinaigrette, braised chicken chasseur, fresh carrots with fine herbs, and peach parfait—all totalling only 284 calories.

The Golden Door. *Super Deluxe.* Escondido, CA. Contact: The Golden Door, 3085 Reynard Way, San Diego, CA 92103; (714) 295–3144. The "creme de la creme" of health spas, this one is the model for many other such establishments around the world. Founded by its present owner, Deborah Szekely, in 1959 and in its present home since 1975, The Golden Door is a posher version of Rancho La Puerta, also founded by Szekely and her husband.

Beautiful people such as actress Christina Ferrare (who has been visiting the spa for nearly a decade), her friend Joanna Carson, and designer Bill Blass frequent The Golden Door. Small classes allow for a great deal of supervised exercise and health programs centered on the individual. The hefty price tag of $2,500 per week is thought to be well worth it by guests. The Golden Door is predominantly for women, although there are special men's weeks nine times a year and couples' weeks about seven times a year.

A typical day at The Golden Door can include any number of activities and treatments: body contouring, water exercises, back-strengthening exercises, yoga, steam, meditation, and herbal wraps. The atmosphere here—although relaxing—is one of serious work and serious pampering.

The physical environment also adds to the relaxed atmosphere: The spa complex includes one of the largest Japanese-style buildings outside Japan. It was constructed in the spirit of a classic honjin inn that has served the nobility in Japan since feudal times. The graceful, low buildings have exotic roof lines and tiles that reflect the blue of the sky. The gem-studded golden door is reached by a 141-foot wooden footbridge. The grounds, with citrus trees and thickets of evergreen, encompass 157 acres, with 1,000 feet of outdoor walkways and three courtyards. The entrance gates are surrounded by camellias, fuschias, and spring flowers. A teahouse and Koi pond on the grounds complete the picture.

Another inviting aspect of The Golden Door is its cuisine. Large selections of natural foods are prepared gourmet style. Much of the menu—fresh vegetables, fruits, and herbs, is grown in The Golden Door's gardens. The diet is low calorie, low sodium, and low cholesterol.

The Ashram. *Deluxe.* P.O. Box 8, Calabasas, CA 91302; (213) 888–0232. *Deluxe* in the context of The Ashram does not denote the meaning that we usually attach to that word, even at $1,200 a week. Guests do not go to The Ashram to be pampered; they go there to work *hard.* Ashram directors Anne-Marie Bennstrom and Catharina Hedberg know how to get the body in shape, and they do not fool around.

Everyone entering The Ashram is put through a cardiovascular stress test (included in the fee) to determine how far he or she can exert himself/herself. Then a specialized program is prescribed. The diet consists of raw foods and various kinds of therapeutic fasting. All the attire that a guest will need, except for personal items and sneakers, is provided. The Ashram encourages guests to bring books and hobby items, but the real emphasis here is spiritual renewal—best attained by taking yourself away from the world for a couple of days.

"During your short stay with us," says a letter from the directors, "we would like you to receive the optimum program conducive to your physical, mental, and spiritual well-being. To insure this please plan to retreat from the world for this one time in your life, and let your business associates, family, and friends know ahead of time. Even a phone call has proven a disruptive influence in our daily routine at The Ashram."

A typical day at the Ashram begins with morning meditation at 6:30, breakfast at 7:30, followed by a 2–2¼ mile walk. At 11:00 A.M. there is a weight class; at 12:00 P.M. water exercise; at 1:00 P.M., lunch; at 4:00 P.M., jogging, and at 5:30 P.M., walking. In the evening, at 7:00, is yoga, and finally, at 8:00, dinner. The evening program, from 9:00–10:00, consists of movies, discussions, tips on home follow-up.

Dennis' Canyon Villas. *Expensive.* 520 Murray Canyon Drive, Palm Springs, CA 92262; (714) 320–6841; toll free in California (800) 472–1253 and toll free in the U.S. (800) 854–1288. $85 a day and up, double occupancy; special weekly rates. Villas and luxury hotel combined with a health resort. Also features the

Aida Grey Beauty Center for massages, pedicures, and so on. The daily fitness program offers approximately seven exercise classes. Sauna, swimming pool, Jacuzzi, and game room. Nearby golf, tennis, horseback riding, and sightseeing are available.

The Oaks at Ojai. *Expensive.* 122 East Ojai Ave., Ojai, CA 93023; (805) 646–5573. This spa is run by another physical fitness "celebrity," Sheila Cluff. A noted expert in the field of physical fitness, Cluff's philosophy about exercise and fitness is employed in this spa and at the Palms.

A two-hour drive from Los Angeles, the Oaks' rates are $65 a day for a double, $69 a day for newly renovated triple-occupancy cottages, and $95 a day for a single. The prices are flexible, and there is a two-day minimum. The usual extras—massage, facials, makeup, hair salon, and so on—are available at extra cost; the fitness program combines a diet of low-calorie gourmet food and a choice of twelve fitness classes per day. Tennis and golf are available nearby.

The Palms at Palm Springs. *Expensive.* 572 No. Indian Ave., Palm Springs, CA 92262; (619) 325–1111. Also run by Sheila Cluff, this spa is similar to the Oaks. The rates are slightly higher: from $69 a day for an adjoining double to $140 a day for a single cottage. Special deals are often offered. The location is a big plus for the Palms: All the shopping, sports, and sightseeing activities in Palm Springs are easily accessible. The Palms offers twelve fitness programs each day together with personalized attention and healthy food.

Rancho La Puerta. *Expensive.* Tecate, Baja, CA 92080, (619) 478–5341. One of the oldest spas, established by spa pioneers Deborah and Edmond Szekely in 1940. Rancho La Puerta is a more humble version of The Golden Door. A European philosopher and chemist, Edmond Szekely was one of the first to show an interest in preventive medicine.

Today Deborah Szekely is one of the most respected experts in her field—health spas. She personally directs Rancho La Puerta and The Golden Door. Also known for her work with the President's Council on Physical Fitness, Szekely has earned many nationwide honors.

Rates for the one-week program range from $600 per person in a double-occupancy cabana to $1,000 each for a double- or triple-occupancy villa. This spa offers a complete exercise program from sunup until sundown, along with a low-cholesterol, low-sodium, low-calorie, and high-energy diet that contains minimal artificial chemicals and preservatives. After-hours activities include a camera clinic, Indian pot painting, and pottery; seminar topics include transactional analysis, behavior modification, assertiveness training, and more.

Zane Haven. *Expensive.* P.O. Box 2031, Palm Springs, CA 92263; (619) 323–7486. $550 double occupancy (subject to change) for five days and four nights. Program based on weight training and fitness; a selection of weight-training regimens, as well as aerobic exercises and stretching, is offered in a fully equipped gym. Nutritional counseling is also available. Each session is limited to only eight people.

Swimming pool, sunbathing facilities, and a sauna. Zane Haven is a 15-minute walk from downtown Palm Springs. It is a place that will enable you to combine a vacation with an introduction to weight training and healthful living.

Alive Polarity Murrieta Hot Springs. *Expensive.* 28779 Via Las Flores, Murrieta, CA 92362; (714) 677–7451. Murrieta Hot Springs, in the European health spa tradition, offers mud baths in mineral waters, healthy vegetarian cuisine, and beautiful surroundings. The 46-acre facility, near Lake Elsinore, has two mineral pools and an Olympic-size swimming pool; various special programs—Feel Alive, Self-Growth, Fit 'n' Trim, among others—add to the attractiveness of this place. Prices vary depending on the program.

A typical weekly rate is $595, double occupancy. Available at extra cost, although sometimes part of a special package, are massage, facial, tennis, gravity balancing, and medical services.

Bermuda Inn. *Moderate.* 43019 Sierra, Lancaster, CA 93534; (714) 942-1493; in Los Angeles (213) 625-3115. The Bermuda Inn, about an hour's drive north from Los Angeles, is essentially a weight-reduction resort. The program, supervised by a medical doctor, offers an exercise schedule including water exercises in both indoor and outdoor pools. Additional activities include jogging, bicycling, badminton, tether ball, and evening entertainment. Rates are $63 a day, or $441 a week, double occupancy.

The Grove. *Moderate.* 32281 Riverside Drive, Lake Elsinore, CA 92330; (714) 674–1501. Daily rates range from $49 to $99; special weekly rates are available. Located 75 miles south from Los Angeles, it is a modern spa dedicated to helping guests take off weight and condition their bodies. Low-calorie meals, behavior modification, and exercise help attain these goals. Indoor and outdoor pools, a sauna, a whirlpool, and tennis available nearby.

Meadowlark Health and Growth Center. *Moderate.* Friendly Hills Fellowship, Meadowlark, 26126 Fairview Ave., Hemet, CA 92343; (714) 927–1343. Since 1959 Meadowlark has been reestablishing a balance in their clients' lives through diet, nutrition, and exercise. The program costs from $365 to $435 a week, per person, not including such extras as nutritional counseling. This facility focuses on holistic health under the guidance of Evarts Loomis, M.D., F.A.C.S., a health practitioner in the field. Activities include walking, swimming, lectures on body awareness, yoga, and discussions on journal keeping. Guided fasting is featured. Outdoor activities also include jogging and bicycling. Located on a 20-acre estate at the foot of the San Jacinto Mountains.

Glen Ivy Hot Springs. *Inexpensive.* 25000 Glen Ivy Road, Corona, CA 91720; (714) 737–4723. At the base of the Santa Ana Mountains and the Temescal Valley, Glen Ivy Hot Springs is a good place for a day visit. The Luiseno Indians nicknamed this area temescal (meaning sweathouse) after the mud saunas they built around the hot springs. Established in 1890, the spa has changed with the times. Reproductions of old pictures trace the history of the spa. The same mineral springs are still flowing, and the mud is thought to be good for skin and circulation. Be careful though; bring some old clothes because the mud can stain. Extras include massage, eucalyptus blanket-wrap treatments, private mineral baths, and chiropractic treatment by appointment. The daily rate is $6.75 for adults, $5.75 for seniors, and $4.75 for children 12 and under.

Jacumba Hotel Hot Springs Resort. *Inexpensive.* P.O. Box 466, Jacumba, CA 92034; (619) 766–4333. This reasonably priced resort is located between Tijuana and Mexicali. Weekly rate, double occupancy, is $198; daily and monthly rates are also available. Jacumba is a quiet village in a high desert oasis 70 miles east of San Diego. Visitors bathe in mineral waters, swim, and explore such attractions as an old stagecoach trail, a mine, and tunnels. The hotel features two hot springs mineral pools and two outdoor pools. Good desert hiking. Exercise classes only on the weekends.

Wheeler Hot Springs. *Inexpensive.* 16825 Maricopa Hwy. (just north of Ojai); (805) 646–8131. Both hot and cold mineral baths are offered here, in redwood tubs. There is a staff of masseurs and a century-old restaurant serving organically prepared food. Private tubs are $10 an hour, and a tub and massage combination is $30.

 GUEST RANCHES. Travelers looking for a more unusual vacation might be interested in checking the guest ranches that are located in the area surrounding Los Angeles. Although the accommodations vary widely, most offer a glimpse of California country living, complete with horses, unspoiled acreage, and fresh air. Those listed here are not more than three hours away from Los Angeles, and in all cases the drive itself is memorable. A word of caution: Plan a guest ranch vacation in advance; many of these facilities are booked months ahead of time.

San Ysidro Ranch. *Expensive.* 900 San Ysidro Lane, Montecito, CA 93108; (805) 969–5046. Just outside Santa Barbara, it offers a taste of the luxurious side of ranch living. Peace, quiet, and privacy are in abundance here, along with three tennis courts, a heated swimming pool, stables, and a French-Continental restaurant. Celebrities often seek out San Ysidro Ranch because of the solitude it offers. In fact, John and Jacqueline Kennedy honeymooned here. Rates range from $98 to $239, double occupancy.

Apple Valley Inn. *Moderate.* P.O. Box 5, Apple Valley, CA 92307; (619) 247–7271. Near Victorville in the scenic Apple Valley, it offers a taste of Western-style ranch life with none of the inconveniences. Visitors here can browse through the Roy Rogers and Dale Evans memorabilia on display or take part in activities that range from horseback riding and hayrides to swimming and boating, tennis and volleyball. Campfire cookouts and stagecoach rides through the desert trails round out the experience. Rates are $53–$55, double occupancy.

Cholame Creek Ranch. *Moderate.* P.O. Box 8-R, Cholame, CA 93431; (805) 463–2320. A 5,000-acre homestead about a three-hours' drive north from Los Angeles, it gives guests a choice of lodging in either a ranch house or a cowboy-style bunkhouse. Horseback riding is a featured activity here, with summers being devoted exclusively to teaching children (ages 8–16) all about equitation. All ages are welcome the rest of the year. Among the activities are all kinds of ranch "chores," including branding, as well as camping, cookouts, and the chance to pick up bits of history from nearby Indian sites. Rates are $49 to $69 daily, American Plan.

Circle Bar B Guest Ranch. *Moderate.* 1800 Refugio Rd., Goleta, CA 93117; (805) 968–1113. Situated in the midst of the magnificent Santa Ynez Mountains, one of Southern California's most lovely natural settings, the Circle B offers an unusual pairing of both country living and city amenities. By day, visitors can enjoy swimming, outdoor cooking, mountain hikes, and horseback riding (at an extra charge). Evening offerings include live theater presentations in the barn-style theater. Dinner, a show, overnight accommodations, and breakfast are $115 for two.

Zaca Lake Resort. *Moderate.* P.O. Box 187, Los Olivos, CA 93441; (805) 688–4891. In the Los Padres National Forest near Santa Barbara, it is not strictly a guest ranch, but a blending of resort and ranch, where movie crews used to come to film Westerns in a California environment. Zaca Lake Lodge, built in the 1920s, sits on the very edge of the natural lake, with the guest cabins a short walk away. Boating and horseback riding are the two main activities, or you can just stroll through the pine forests where squirrels and deer play. Privacy is assured; there are no phones in the cabins. Cabins are $69; day use is $3.00 ($1.50 for children 12 or younger).

 HOW TO GET AROUND. Los Angeles takes up 464 square miles, and so, needless to say, there's a lot of ground to cover. Whether you are walking, busing, or driving, it is a good idea to become familiar with a map of the city before venturing out on your own. Take notes on how to get to and from each destination so that you will avoid getting lost, and always travel with telephone numbers of the hotel concierge or friends so that they can talk you back to your original destination should you lose your way.

By bus. You may have heard that a tourist in Los Angeles is helpless without a car. Well, **the Southern California Rapid Transit District** (otherwise known as RTD) believes differently. RTD offers a tourist pass that will enable you to see Los Angeles on $2.00 a day. Since RTD believes that public transit is an effective way for visitors to get where they want to go, they have introduced this tourist pass. From three days for $6.00 to a fifteen days for $30.00, the RTD tourist pass is quite a good transportation bargain.

To purchase the pass you must show proof that you live outside the following areas: Los Angeles, Orange County, Ventura, Riverside, or San Bernardino counties (in California). You may buy as many passes as you need for you and your family. If you are traveling to Los Angeles by bus, you can purchase the tourist pass seven days a week at the downtown RTD Greyhound Station at 6th and Los Angeles Streets. Many other locations offer the pass; among them: downtown at 425 S. Main, at 1016 S. Main, and in the ARCO Towers, and in Hollywood at 6249 Hollywood Blvd.; information call (213) 626–4455 or 972–6000. A tourist kit prepared by the RTD will be mailed on request. Write to the Tourist Kit Department, RTD Marketing, Los Angeles, California 90013.

RTD also has bus service to *Los Angeles International Airport.* All airport-bound bus lines run to and from a point located just outside LAX at 98th Street and Vicksburg, where a line 608 Minibus picks up passengers and takes them to their terminals within the airport complex. Line 608 operates in and out of LAX from 5:00 A.M. to 1:00 A.M. the following day. Buses make trips approximately every fifteen minutes throughout the day and about every twenty minutes in the late evening. As a passenger traveling on the regular bus lines to the airport, you should ask the operator for a free transfer to line 608. For more information, call RTD at (213) 626–4455, or, for timetables, write RTD, Los Angeles, California 90001.

Touring Los Angeles by bus is easiest if you obtain the RTD self-guided tours brochure. Experiencing Los Angeles by bus could be the best way for a first time visitor. The RTD self-guided tour outlines Los Angeles and explains in detail the RTD bus system. Every major attraction in Los Angeles is available via the bus. In 1984, more buses will be added to the system to accommodate the increased influx of tourists due to the Olympics. (See *Olympics* section.)

Hop on the #202 minibus for 25 cents and tour the downtown area of the city. Each ethnic section such as Chinatown, Olvera Street, and Little Tokyo, is covered. You will also see City Hall, the Music Center for the Performing Arts, Arco Plaza, and the California Mart, where you can do some shopping at bargain prices. From this point, board RTD Line #83 and head westbound, stopping off along the way at any one of Los Angeles' major attractions. To find out more about the self-guided tours, phone RTD at (213) 626–4455, or visit any of the ten RTD Customer Service Centers: Arco Plaza, 505 S. Flower Street, Los Angeles; RTD/Greyhound Station, 208 E. 6th Street, Los Angeles; RTD Headquarters, 425 S. Main Street, Los Angeles; RTD El Monte Station, 3501 N. Santa Anita Ave., El Monte; Hollywood, 6249 Hollywood Blvd., Hollywood; S. Central L.A., 5425 Van Ness Ave., Los Angeles; in Van Nuys at 14435 Sherman Way; South Bay, 1811 Hawthorne Blvd., Redondo Beach; in the Wilshire area at 5738 Wilshire Blvd.; and in Long Beach at 18 Long Beach Blvd., Long Beach.

By car. While visiting Los Angeles it really is helpful to have a car at your disposal if possible. Many car rental agencies operate around town, especially on Century Blvd., the street opposite Los Angeles International Airport. Car rental rates charged by a given company are the same regardless of the location from which you rent; so pick up your car at the most convenient spot. It would also be best to arrange for car rentals before visiting Los Angeles to ensure that you will be able to rent the car of your choice.

Once you've secured a car, the next step is to learn to drive in Los Angeles, really an experience in itself. Maps outlining the freeway system are essential; the Southern California Automobile Club has put together "Triptiks" to Los Angeles, guides that will take you to your destination. AAA provides special area maps that give useful details about all kinds of recreational activities. Also available are county maps, city maps, and special guide publications that blend accurate map coverage with information on campgrounds, golf courses, parks, boat-launching sites, coastal surfing areas, and other points of interest.

The next step in learning to drive in Los Angeles is to understand the city's extensive *freeway system.* Los Angeles is served by more than thirty freeways; eight radiate from the downtown freeway loop and, with the exception of the

Golden State Freeway, are named for their major destinations. By traveling the freeways, you will also familiarize yourself with the metropolitan Los Angeles area.

The #405, or San Diego, Freeway runs north to south, stretching from the San Fernando Valley south down to San Diego. This is an excellent freeway to use as an approach to Los Angeles from LAX, for it runs parallel to the coastline from Santa Monica on south.

The #10, or Santa Monica Freeway, runs east/west and loops off the San Diego Freeway (#405) beginning in Santa Monica and then continues east toward San Bernardino, where it is then called the San Bernardino Freeway. This freeway is particularly effective when your destination is somewhere between Santa Monica and the downtown area.

Beginning in the northwest area of Los Angeles (San Fernando Valley) and diagonally dividing the city is the #5, or Golden State, Freeway. You can travel on this freeway as far north as San Fernando Valley; however, the name of the Freeway changes at the intersection of the #10 Freeway, for you will be heading south at this point. The new name, the Santa Ana Freeway, reflects the fact that your direction at that point has changed.

Also traveling north to south is the Harbor Freeway, or #11. It stems from the #11 Pasadena and finishes at Los Angeles Harbor.

Other freeways traveling into the Pasadena/Glendale area are the Glendale Freeway, which runs north to south, and the #210, or Foothill Freeway, which intersects with the #2 and runs east to west. Stretching from Ventura County on east is the Ventura Freeway, or the #134 East/West. You can use this freeway to travel to the San Fernando Valley or north/east to Pasadena.

The #101, or Hollywood, Freeway runs north to south in Hollywood and then shifts direction and heads east to west out toward Pasadena, merging with the #134 Freeway. This freeway can take you to the San Fernando Valley as well as connect you to the necessary freeways to take you west to the beach.

At the beach, Route 1, also called the Pacific Coast Highway (PCH), runs right along the coastline and is one of the world's most beautiful drives. Many freeways will lead you to this highway.

There is a method to this madness on the freeway system. AAA has many maps to assist visitors driving to Los Angeles, an exceptionally good one being *The Guide to Los Angeles Freeway System.* Now you're ready to drive in Los Angeles. Gather up your maps and start driving.

By limousine and cab. Los Angeles is an unusual city; although the four-county metropolitan area is home to thirteen million people and about eleven million visitors come here year after year, the cab system is not like that of any other major American city. You will probably not be able to hail a cab on the street, unless by chance you happen to be in Hollywood or on a major boulevard.

To call a cab, you must phone one of the many taxi companies that operate in Los Angeles. A few of the more reputable companies are: *Independent Cab Co.* at (213) 385–5397 or 385–TAXI. *United Independent Taxi* at (213) 653–5050. United Independent accepts MC and V.

For total luxury and a real taste of the Los Angeles way of life, try a limousine. It's the most relaxing way to view a city of this caliber. Limousines come equipped with everything from a full bar and telephone to a hot tub and a double bed—depending on your needs.

Most travel agencies will be able to suggest a reputable limo service suited to your requirements. Contrary to popular knowledge, a limo service is not all that much more expensive than other forms of transportation. Consider hiring a limo if you have a group of eight or fewer that want to travel together. (The fare can be split, making it extremely reasonable.) After all, since you're here on vacation, you might as well let someone else do the driving if you possibly can.

A few limo services suggested by the Greater Los Angeles Visitors Bureau are: *Dav-El Livery* at (213) 550–0070; *Grayline Tours Co.* at (800) 421–8921 or (213) 481–2121; and *Limousine for Hire, Inc.* at (213) 659–3903.

TOURIST INFORMATION. *The Greater Los Angeles Visitors and Convention Bureau* has multilingual aides to assist you in making your sightseeing plans. The Bureau operates in four convenient locations.

The Downtown Visitors Information Center, (213) 488–9100), located in the Atlantic Richfield Plaza at 6th and Flower Streets, L.A. 90071, is open Monday through Friday, 9:00 A.M. to 5:00 P.M. and Saturday, 10:00 A.M. to 4:00 P.M. In addition to walk-in service, this center will also mail the bureau's vacation-planning material to soon-to-be visitors to the city.

The Hollywood Visitors Information Center, (213) 466–1389, is open Monday through Thursday, 9:00 A.M. to 4:00 P.M. and Friday from 9:00 A.M. to 6:00 P.M. in the Pacific Federal Bank Building at 6801 Hollywood Boulevard, on the corner of Hollywood and Highland.

The Westchester Visitors Information Center, (213) 645–5151, is located in the Westchester Chamber of Commerce building at 8833 South Sepulveda Blvd. in Westchester. This information center is open from 9:00 A.M. to 5:00 P.M., Monday through Friday.

A new information center has just opened this year at the airport. Located at 201 Worldway, LAX, room 205, it's open Monday through Friday, 10:00 A.M. to 6:00 P.M., and can offer advice on accommodations and similar subjects of concern to a first-time visitor. Multi-lingual assistance is also available.

All four locations offer free information on attractions, public transportation, hotel and motel accommodations, restaurants, and Los Angeles nightlife. In addition, bimonthly special calendars, climate information, and information on self-guided tours of Los Angeles and Southern California are available to aid the uncertain traveller.

Beyond the Greater Los Angeles Visitors and Convention Bureau, each community in this sprawling metropolis maintains either a specialized tourism bureau or a chamber of commerce. Here is a sampling; for those areas not listed, consult directory assistance.

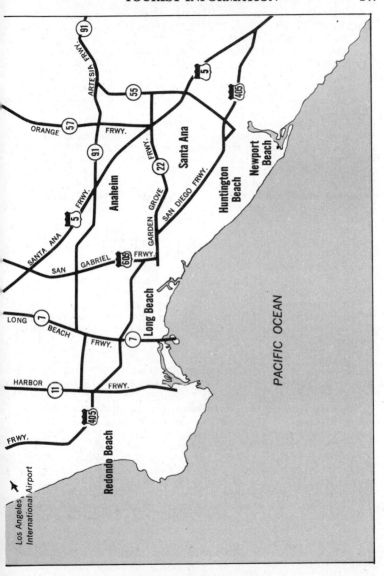

Beverly Hills Visitors and Convention Bureau, Chamber of Commerce, 239 South Beverly Dr., Beverly Hills 90212; (213) 271–8126; open 9:00 A.M. to 5:00 P.M., Monday through Friday.

Santa Monica Tourist Information Center, Santa Monica Blvd. at Ocean Ave. in Palisades Park; (213) 393–7593. Open 10:00 A.M. to 4:00 P.M., seven days a week.

Pasadena Convention and Visitors Bureau, 300 East Green St., south of the Pasadena Mall; (213) 795–9311. Open 9:00 A.M. to 5:00 P.M., Monday through Friday.

Because Los Angeles covers such a large area, telephone assistance can save the visitor considerable time and energy. For beach and surfing conditions, call (213) 451–8761; for national park information, call (213) 688–2902; for road conditions, call (213) 626–7231; for the weather, call (213) 554–1212; and for a general orientation to the city, call (213) 628–5857.

California magazine and *Los Angeles* magazine are published monthly and incorporate extensive listings of restaurants, shopping, museums, children's activities, theater events, and films, as well as happenings in the world of art, dance, and music. All reflect the true pulse of the city.

This sprawling city also offers three daily newspapers, *The Los Angeles Times, The Daily News,* and *The Los Angeles Herald Examiner.* They keep up with city goings-on from day to day. The *Times'* Calendar Section gives information on films, theater events, and so on, and that information is also provided in the *Herald's* Style Section. On Sunday these papers offer their most complete coverage of the Los Angeles way of life through listings and feature articles.

Two free newspapers, *The Los Angeles Weekly* and the *Los Angeles Reader,* are excellent sources of information on scheduled events. These publications can be found in many stores and neighborhood restaurants as well as in bookstores and movie theaters.

RECOMMENDED READING

A selection of books and pamphlets for visitors with specialized interests:

For families coming to town, a good source of information is *In and Around Los Angeles for Kids.* Written by Stephanie Kegan, it is published by Chronicle Books and can be found at most bookstores in the area, at $4.95.

Two titles of books on Los Angeles architecture worth picking up are *A Guide to Architecture in Los Angeles and Southern California* by David Gebhard and Robert Winter (Santa Barbara and Salt Lake City: Peregrine Smith, 1977), 728 pages for a mere $13.95; and *Los Angeles: The Architecture of Four Ecologies* by Reyner Banham (Baltimore: Penguin Books, 1971), 256 pages, at $5.95.

For art lovers, a new book on the subject is *The Los Angeles Art Review,* a comprehensive look at the museum and gallery scene. Edited by Hank Baum, it is published by The Krantz Company for $7.95 and can be found in most art book shops in the area.

A guide to museums and galleries from Santa Barbara to San Diego that's useful to the tourist is *Inside L.A. Art* by Deborah Ashin, published by Chronicle

Books/San Francisco. It contains 150 listings of the best in fine-art, natural-history, and science museums as well as the finest university and contemporary galleries and costs $6.95.

On a budget? *Try 200 Things to Do In Los Angeles for Free* by Carol Mac-Conaugha. It's published by Jim Hargrove Book Productions, Ltd., and is available at many book shops (look around, you'll find it) for $3.95.

For an in-depth look at the city's history, pick up *Los Angeles: Biography of a City* by John and LaRee Caughey. Published by the University of California Press, it's available in most major book stores for $6.95.

A directory to discount fashions in L.A. and Orange Counties, published by Chronicle Books, is *Glad Rags II* by Leigh Charlton and Annette Swanberg. Price: $8.95.

Those seeking off-beat services in Los Angeles may want to pick up *Only in Los Angeles* by Doni Sue Malin and Judy Ruderman ($5.95). Published by Chronicle Books, this publication directs you to some of the more unusual services L.A. has to offer.

 SEASONAL EVENTS. Whatever the season, the weather in Los Angeles is usually summerlike. Thus the traveler will find continuous outdoor as well as indoor special events. The weather and landscape of Los Angeles contribute to a great number of sporting events ranging from celebrity golf tournaments and horse racing to volleyball tournaments and stock-car racing. And the city's streets lure crowds of people to attend such events as the Rose Parade in January, Chinese New Year and Mardi Gras at Olvera St. in February, the Los Angeles Street Scene in October, and the Hollywood Christmas Parade in November.

As a general rule, outdoor happenings are free, but be prepared to buy food and souvenirs. Indoor events usually take place at either the *Los Angeles Convention Center* (Pico and Figueroa), the *Music Center* (135 N. Grand), or at the *Sports Arena* (3939 S. Figueroa).

The phone numbers listed below are in the 213 area code unless otherwise indicated.

January. On the first day of the year, Pasadena is the place to be. Get there before sunrise, or rough it and spend the night on Colorado Blvd. (between Orange Grove and Sierra Madre) to be assured a good view of the *Tournament of Roses Parade.* Grandstand seats are available, but reservations must be made at least a month in advance. Write the Tournament of Roses Association, 391 S. Orange Grove Blvd., Pasadena, CA 91105. The parade begins at 8:40 A.M. and is followed by the Rose Bowl football game. Call (818) 449–ROSE. The Convention Center hosts two events this month: the *Greater Los Angeles Auto Show* and the *Southern California Boat Show.* Call 748–8531. The *Beverly Hills Dog Show* is held at the Sports Arena. Call 748–6131. At the end of the month, the *Harlem Globetrotters* do their basketball tricks at various locations. Call 906–1234.

February. Crowds gather in Chinatown for the *Chinese New Year* celebration, a colorful display of costumes and great fireworks. Call 617–0396. Later in the month is the *Mexican Mardi Gras* down Olvera St. Call 625–5045. For a leisurely stroll, there's the *Glen Campbell LA Open Golf Tournament* in Pacific Palisades. Call 482–1311. And at the Convention Center, hot rodders will enjoy the *Custom Car and Hot Rod Show.* Call 588–1934 or 748–8531.

March. The world's largest *Camellia Show* takes place all month at Descanso Gardens, where more than 100,000 camellia plants are in full bloom. Call 790–5571. *Filmex* in Century City presents film buffs with a marathon of films, including premier releases as well as some classics. Call 469–9400. Runners gather at City Hall downtown to begin the *L.A. Lite Marathon,* a 26-mile race to Burbank Studios and back. First Sunday in March. Call (818) 485–4871.

April. A parade of colorfully decorated animals takes place for the *Blessing of the Animals* at Olvera St. Call 625–5045. On Easter Sunday the traditional *sunrise service* is held at the Hollywood Bowl. Call 972–7200. Hollywood Park *thoroughbred racing* begins its run in Inglewood through mid-July. Call 677–7151. Orchids, cacti, and other exotics are on display to commemorate the *L.A. Zoo Plant and Garden Day.* Call 666–4650. Artists and musicians gather for a weekend at Beverly Hills Park on Santa Monica Blvd. for an *Affaire in the Gardens.* Art work on sale, live music, and a lot of food. Call 550–4864. Near the end of the month, see the *Ice Capades* skate for ten days at the Forum. Call 469–2767.

May. The *Los Angeles Civic Light Opera* begins its stay at the Music Center (through November). Call 972–7200. Every Saturday and Sunday of the month the *Renaissance Faire* celebrates in Agoura. (From Los Angeles, take the Ventura Freeway to the Agoura offramp). Find a costume and prepare for a day in the life of Renaissance Man. Call 889–3150. On the first weekend of the month is the *Westwood Sidewalk Arts and Crafts Show.* Call 475–4574. Olvera St. presents the *Cinco de Mayo* celebration on the fourth and the fifth. Call 625–5045. Beginning on about the tenth is *Auto Expo/LA* at the Convention Center. Call 748–8531. Catch a free boat ride and tour the harbor at San Pedro during *World Trade Week.* Call 519–3508. The *Armed Forces Day Parade* strides along the streets of Torrance in mid-May. Call 540–5858. See the stars hook and slice their way to even greater fame at the *Celebrity Golf Tournament* at Rancho Park. Call 485–3281.

June. The *Greek Theater* begins its season of outdoor concerts at Griffith Park (through September). Call 460–6300. The *Whale Festival* is at Cabrillo Beach. Call 548–7562. The *Playboy Jazz Festival* takes place at the Hollywood Bowl. Call 972–7200. An equestrian's delight is the *Santa Anita Horse Show* in Arcadia, from the last week in June through first week in July. Call 574–6384.

July. *Ringling Bros./Barnum and Bailey Circus* occupies the Forum in Inglewood from mid-July through mid-August. Call 673–1300. *Symphonies Under the Stars* concerts begin at the Hollywood Bowl and are highlighted by a Fourth of July celebration by the Los Angeles Philharmonic. Another way to spend American Independence Day is to lounge in the sun at Venice Beach. When the sun goes down, you can see spectacular *fireworks* over the Pacific Ocean. For biking fans, the *Coca Cola Super Bowl of Motorcross* comes to Anaheim Stadium. Call (714) 553–3333. Another beach event is the *Malibu Festival of Arts and Crafts* during the last weekend of the month. Call 456–9025.

August. The *San Fernando Valley Fair* at Devonshire Downs takes place early in the month. It features rides, games, crafts, animals, and a lot of food. Call 363–8181. Surfers from all over gather at such beaches as Hermosa, Manhattan, Redondo, and Torrance for the *International Surf Festival.* Call 545–4502. In Santa Monica, take in the *Sports and Art Festival* during the last two weeks of the month. Call 393–9975.

September. Los Angeles celebrates *its birthday* on the sixth by holding festivities at Olvera St. Call 625–5045. The *Los Angeles County Fair* in Pomona has everything from livestock judging and pie tastings to carnival rides and game booths. Call (714) 623–3111. More than 100 *gymnasts* perform in outdoor competition on the beach just south of the Santa Monica pier. Call 393–9825. Another *Affaire in the Garden* takes place in Beverly Hills Park (see listing under April). The horses are running for the *Oak Tree Thoroughbred Horse Races* at Hollywood Park in Inglewood from late September through October. Call 677–7151.

October. At the beginning of the month is the *Budweiser Grand Prix* at the Riverside International Raceway (714–653–1161) and the *Westwood Arts and Crafts Show* (475–4574). Recently the *LA Street Scene* has become a tradition downtown in the streets adjacent to City Hall. Artisans and cultural groups from the city gather to present their exhibits and goods. Musicians play, people dance in the streets, exotic foods are served, all enhancing your enjoyment during the second weekend in October. Call 626–0458. The *Los Angeles Chamber Orchestra* begins its series of performances in Pasadena (796–2200) and the *Glendale Symphony* and the *Los Angeles Philharmonic* begin their six-month schedules at the Music Center. Call 972–7211. If you would rather ski but can't find any snow, at least have a look at the latest equipment and clothes for the slopes at the *Ski Show* at the Convention Center. Call 748–8531. During the last weekend of the month, witches and goblins gather at Hancock Park for the *Festival of Masks* Parade and the Masquerade Ball. Call 937–5544.

November. The Dorothy Chandler Pavilion at the Music Center features the *New York City Opera.* Call 972–7211. For philatelists, the *Stamp Expo Pacific* is at the Convention Center in the middle of the month. Call 748–8531. The holiday festivities begin the Sunday after Thanksgiving down Hollywood Blvd. See your favorite stars and celebrities join Santa Claus at the *Hollywood Christmas Parade,* a motor arcade of vintage vehicles. Call 469–2337.

December. The closing of the year marks a month of parades. *Christmas parades* are in abundance during the first half of the month in Los Angeles, Covina, El Monte, San Pedro, Glendora, Pacoima, and El Segundo. Call the Chamber of Commerce of each city to find out when and where. There's the *City of the Christmas Story* in Santa Monica along Palisades Seaside Park, where lighted Nativity scenes are set up to be viewed by motorists. Call 393–9825. A beautiful show of lights reflecting on the water takes place at the *Christmas Lighted Boat Parades* in San Pedro (832–7272) and Marina del Rey (821–0555). At Olvera St. on each evening from the sixteenth through the twenty-fourth at

7:00 P.M. is *Las Posadas.* This nightly event begins with a children's choir singing carols, followed by a candlelight procession through the decorated street, which depicts the journey of Joseph and Mary. Each evening is climaxed by children breaking a piñata full of goodies. Call 625–5045. The day after Christmas *thoroughbred horse racing* begins at Santa Anita in Arcadia. It continues through mid-April. Call 574–7223.

 FREE EVENTS. In Los Angeles every day is a free event in terms of nature; The sun, sand, and ocean alone can fill a vacation. But there are plenty of other free activities, events, and cultural attractions to keep busy even those with limited budgets. (All telephone numbers listed below are in the 213 area code.)

Free concerts take place at the *Triforium* (at the Los Angeles Mall, corner of Temple and Main Sts.). This building was originally designed to symbolize the city of Los Angeles; here, right near City Hall, free noontime concerts are offered every day. Many feature recorded music from a tape library, but at least once a week there is live entertainment.

Even though winter in Los Angeles is not at all harsh, the outdoor concert scene thrives a bit more during the summer months. Outdoor *Concerts on the Green* in Barnsdall Park, 4800 Hollywood Blvd., are held on Sunday afternoons in the summer at 4:00 P.M. Classical concerts are sponsored by the Cultural Affairs Department of Los Angeles, and there are also free performances—drama, dance, comedy—at the Gallery Theater in the same park.

On Sunday evenings during July and August, *Stough Park* in Burbank is the site of free evening concerts at 7:30. The big band sound and smaller musical groups are the bill. *Concerts in the Sky,* on top of the ARCO Center garage, at 400 S. Flower St., take place on Wednesdays and Fridays at noon throughout the summer. Several artists are featured. (To find out who is appearing, call 972–7211.)

Another summer concert series, the *Watts Towers Jazz Concerts,* is offered on Sunday afternoons at 1765 East 107th St. The towers of Simon Rodia provide a splendid backdrop for some of the best sounds in jazz. Because the schedule is a bit uneven, call 485–2433 for more information. The Los Angeles State Historical Park at the Plaza in *El Pueblo de Los Angeles* has Mexican music and celebrations on Thursday evenings during the summer. The festivals, which serve to encourage the audience to sing and dance, take place at 6:30 and 8:30.

In Santa Monica at Lincoln Park on 7th St. and Wilshire Blvd., Sunday afternoon concerts are held. The *Outdoor Summer Band Schedule* features many different kinds of music from marches to jazz. (Call 393–9975, ext. 311, for further information.) From mid-June through mid-August, free noon concerts are held downtown at the Bonaventure Hotel at the pool plaza level; call 972–7211. Summer musical entertainment can also be heard for four consecutive Saturdays in August at the *William Grant Still Community Arts Center* at 2520 West View St., Los Angeles. Jazz, big band, and other kinds of music are sponsored by this community center. (For details call 734–1164.)

Finally, a fall musical series takes place at the *John Anson Ford County Cultural Arts Theater* at 2580 Cahuenga Blvd., East, in North Hollywood. This multifaceted presentation offers dance, jazz, and many other kinds of music. It is sponsored by the Los Angeles Board of Supervisors, the Performing Arts Commission, and the Department of Parks and Recreation. For more information call 485–2433.

Free festivals, including musical events, abound in Los Angeles throughout the year (see *Seasonal Events*). Some, such as the Pasadena *Tournament of Roses Parade* on the first of the year, are real "California events," and others, such as the Chinese New Year in February, are special events in many cities. March marks the *Return of the Swallows* to San Juan Capistrano; and also in March is *National Mime Week;* although it is celebrated in various areas of the city, the closing celebration occurs in Venice (call 463–1404 for details). *Cinco de Mayo* is an especially Californian, or southwestern, celebration. This day of Mexican Independence is celebrated throughout the city; one of the largest gatherings takes place at the El Pueblo de Los Angeles State Historical Park.

Another Los Angeles celebration devoted to one of its special ethnic groups is *Nisei Week* in August. This Japanese festival in Little Tokyo at First and San Pedro Sts. offers tea ceremonies, dances, martial arts demonstrations, and other examples of Japanese cultural traditions.

Another southern California festival takes place at the San Gabriel Mission in September. At the *Community Fiesta* such traditional rites as blessing the animals are performed. For more information call 282–5191. One of the most exciting celebrations in the city is the *Los Angeles Street Scene,* which takes place in October on all the downtown streets around City Hall. Eleven stages are set up, and the entertainment is nonstop. For information call 626–0485. *Christmas parades* in cities and in harbors fill the month of December. There are boat parades in Los Angeles Harbor, Marina del Rey, Newport Harbor, and Dana Point.

In addition to festivals and musical entertainment, Los Angeles offers a variety of visual art. Throughout the year communities open their streets to displays of local artists. *The Los Angeles Times* and *The Herald Examiner,* as well as local papers such as *The LA Reader* and *The LA Weekly,* have information on these shows as well as other free events that might be available when you are in town. Art in progress is one of the attractions at the *Santa Monica Fine Art Festival* in August at Palisades Park. The *Santa Monica Art Show* in October takes place in the open-air Santa Monica Mall. There are street entertainers as well.

At Century City in April the *Spring Festival* hosts an exhibition of art for four days. And one of the well-attended showings is the *Westwood Sidewalk Art and Craft Show* in May. Strolling musicians will serenade you as you look at the art displayed throughout the streets of Westwood Village.

As you might expect of the capital of the movie business, Los Angeles offers free movie showings. Here is a list of the places where you can see *free films: The Academy of Motion Picture Arts and Sciences* has retrospectives, 278–8990; for free films at *The Natural History Museum,* check *The Los Angeles Times* or call 746–0410; *the Beverly Hills Library* shows screen classics; *the UCLA Meinitz Auditorium* often shows offbeat films, 937–5544; *the Hearst Theater* in the Museum of Science and Industry offers old movies, 744–7400; *the Norris Theater* at USC shows classics on Saturdays and Sundays, 743–2311; and *the Santa Monica Community College District* at 1900 Pico Blvd. offers "Sunday Afternoon at the Movies" at which classic movies are shown on Sundays at 2:00 P.M.

There is more. Live theater freebies can also be had. The *Free Public Theater Festival* from mid-July to the end of August is the largest free theater offering. Productions take place at the Gallery Theater in Barnsdall Park as well as at smaller parks in communities around town. Call 485–2433.

Works in progress are sometimes read by the *Los Angeles Actors' Theater.* Call 464–5500. And the *Hollywood Actors Theater,* 464–0300, often presents free performances.

In addition to scheduled free events, many things in Los Angeles can be experienced. The *Walk of Fame* on Hollywood Blvd. from Vine to Orange is one of the most popular attractions. Over a thousand stars, each with a plaque of his or her own, are represented on this walk. In the same vein, a visit to the famous *Chinese Theater* at 6925 Hollywood Blvd. will enable you to view famous hand and foot imprints. Elizabeth Taylor, Shirley Temple, and Clark Gable are only a few of the stars whose imprints are immortalized.

For present-day stargazing, charity sports activities are a good choice. An *Arthritis Run-a-Thon* is held in Griffith Park each December. The *Beverly Hills–Perrier 10K* is also held in December. It pits local celebrities against each other in various unique events. The *All Star Celebrity Softball League* begins practice in April at Rancho Park at Motor Ave. and Pico Blvd. Stars playing raquetball can be caught at the *Motion Picture/Television Industry Raquetball Classic* in October. The Greater Los Angeles Visitors and Convention Bureau can provide additional information on these events.

And for those who are not satisfied with watching celebrities but want to see the "business" firsthand, there are opportunities to attend the taping of *television shows.* Most networks prefer to process ticket requests sent through the mail. Write to CBS at 7800 Beverly Blvd., LA 90036, and to NBC at 3000 W. Alameda, Burbank 91523. ABC makes things easier by providing ticket booths at ABC TV Center, 4151 Prospect Dr., ABC Vine Street Theater, 1313 N. Vine, ABC Entertainment Center, Plaza Level, 2040 Ave. of the Stars and Glendale Galleria in Glendale. You can call 557–7777 to see what is available.

TOURS. By bus, car, or boat there is a lot to see in and around Los Angeles. All forms of transportation provide a good overview of this vast city and its surrounding environment. Motor travel provides an excellent way to discover what the Big Orange is all about.

By bus. The largest of the sightseeing companies in the Southland is *Gray Line Tours Co.* of Los Angeles. Offices, branches, and travel desks are operated in hotels throughout Southern California.

TOURS

For a large enough group, Gray Line will tackle any special tour any the group wants to go. All Gray Line Tours make pickups at major hotel... Hollywood and Beverly Hills and then join other sightseers for a mass departure from Gray Line, 1207 W. 3rd St. in Los Angeles (downtown).

Among Gray Line tours are *Pasadena and Huntington Library, Hollywood, Beverly Hills Movie Star Homes, Farmers Market, Twentieth Century-Fox Universal Studio Tour,* including studios and sites of interest in Hollywood and Beverly Hills.

Listed under "Sightseeing Tours" in the yellow pages are a number of small companies offering individualized tours, multilingual guides, and personal chauffeurs who will drive your car or theirs. Two examples: *Tourcoach* (1930 Wilshire Blvd., Los Angeles; 384–4911) is one of Los Angeles' newest tour operators. Deluxe air-conditioned buses take tourists to Universal Studios, Knotts Berry Farm, Disneyland, the Getty Museum, and a number of coastal areas.

L.A. Today Tours focuses on seven areas of Greater Los Angeles, each of which includes scenic beauty, art, shopping, and historical development: the downtown area, Wilshire West, Hollywood, Pasadena and East, the Valley, South to Long Beach, and West to the Pacific Ocean. For reservations, phone or write Elinor Oswald, LA Today, 14964 Camarosa Dr., Pacific Palisades, CA 90272; 454–5730.

By boat. Sightseeing boat trips leave from the piers and docks at Malibu, Pierpoint Landing at the Port of Long Beach, from the foot of Magnolia Ave. in the city of Long Beach itself, and from Fisherman's Wharf in Redondo Beach.

Catalina Terminals, Inc. (P.O. Box 1948, San Pedro CA 90733; 213–514–3838) has tours via ship from San Pedro to Santa Catalina Island. The tour offers a glass bottomed boat, inland motor trips, a seal colony, and scenic drives.

Long Beach/Catalina Cruises (same address as Catalina Terminals, Inc., above) offer one of three modern boats to Catalina Island. There are also harbor tours at Long Beach, including a close-up water view of the *Queen Mary* and Howard Hughes's *Spruce Goose.* For information call *Starline,* 6843 Hollywood Blvd., Hollywood CA 90028, at (213) 463-3131. *Long Beach Harbor Helicopters* (same address as Catalina Terminals, Inc., above) tour the area after lift-off from San Pedro's Ports o'Call Village.

SPECIAL-INTEREST TOURS AND SIGHTSEEING

As a major American city with all the corresponding attributes, Los Angeles offers quite a diversified array of attractions to the visitor no matter what his or her tastes. From the many cultural activities here to the host of major universities and the galaxy of famous people in their architecturally amazing homes, the Big Orange is a city that has something for everyone. Below is a sampling of unique, special-interest tours in and around Los Angeles. (For Long Beach, see the chapter *Long Beach South to San Clemente* at the end of the book.)

Public tours of the *Music Center* downtown at 135 N. Grand are sponsored by The Music Center Operating Company and conducted by the Symphonians, a dedicated group of volunteers who offer this service to visitors at no charge. During the week, the tour will take you inside all three theaters (the Mark Taper, the Dorothy Chandler Pavilion, and the Ahmanson), where history and architecture, as well as the artwork decorating the hall and the wall of these beautiful buildings, will be discussed. On Saturdays, the tour is centered on the Dorothy Chandler Pavilion. From May through October, tours can enjoyed Monday, Tuesday, Thursday, and Friday at 10:00 A.M., 10:30 A.M., 11:30 A.M., 12 noon, 1:00 P.M. and 1:30 P.M. On Saturdays throughout the year tours are given every half hour beginning at 10:00 A.M. and ending at 12:30 P.M. For information and reservations, call 972–7211.

A tour of the *California Institute of Technology* (Cal-Tech) at 1201 E. California St. in Pasadena provides a general walking tour of the grounds. The first stop along the walk is the Campus Building, where student life is discussed. As the tour progresses through the grounds, tour guides will point out interesting sites and the history of the school. Also mentioned on the tour is an overview of the vast research conducted on this lovely campus. One especially interesting stop at Cal-Tech is the Seismological Building, where semiprecious stones and minerals found not only in California but all over the world are displayed. Tour hours are Monday, Thursday, and Friday at 3:00 P.M. and Tuesday and Wednesday at 11:00 A.M. The duration of the tour is one hour. For more information, call 356–6811.

Located in the heart of downtown Los Angeles on one hundred fifty acres of rolling green hills is the *University of Southern California* (USC). Here specially trained tour guides give walking tours of the campus, which is known for its exceptional athletic department. A few points of interest on the tour are the Tommy Trojan Statue, notorious for its appearance at football games as the USC symbol; the Annenberg School of Communications; and renowned Heritage Hall, a building dedicated to athletes.

Another portion of the tour takes the visitor through the school's multimillion dollar performing arts center, which was dedicated by George Lucas and Steven Spielberg. The equipment in these buildings is comparable to that found on professional soundstages. The Mudd Hall of Philosophy may look familiar to you; it has been used quite often in a number of films. Tours, which are free, last approximately forty-five minutes; they are held on the hour Monday through Friday from 10:00 A.M. to 2:00 P.M. Call 743–2983 and prearrange your tour. Parking instructions will be given on the phone.

At the *University of California, Los Angeles* (UCLA), in Westwood at 405 Hilgard Ave., many different kinds of general public tours are offered. A Day at UCLA is one; ten tours featuring the serene Japanese Gardens, as well as the beautiful Botanical Gardens, are conducted every Friday. For art enthusiasts, the Frederick Wight Art Gallery is open for viewing.

Materials for a self-guided tour are available in the UCLA tour office located on campus. This kind of do-it-yourself tour enables the visitor to choose what to see on campus. A self-guided tour of the Japanese Gardens is also available, but a reservation is necessary. These special tours can be prearranged on Tuesdays between 10:00 A.M. and 1:00 P.M. or Wednesdays between 12 noon and 3:00 P.M. For a group of ten or more, tours are conducted on Friday between 10:00 A.M. and 3:00 P.M.

Minilecture discovery tours at UCLA are conducted on Thursdays. On this walk, one department is visited each week. The Green Thumb Tours in the spring and fall focus on the beautiful landscape and foliage.

Other points of interest during a general UCLA tour are the Ackerman Student Union, the Student Store, the Bookstore, and the campus's eighteen libraries. For information and reservations, call 825–5574 or 825–4338.

On the *Stars' Homes Tours* you can peek at the celebrities' hideaways in a few hours. Plan this self-guided tour through charming Beverly Hills and Bel Air residential areas by consulting maps that can be purchased from street vendors and from Hollywood specialty shops. A sneak preview: Judy Garland once lived at 1231 Stone Canyon Rd. in Bel Air; Rudolph Valentino lived at *Falcon's Lair*, 1436 Bella Dr. in Beverly Hills; Charlie Chaplin lived at Breakaway House at 1085 Summit Dr. in Beverly Hills; Douglas Fairbanks and Mary Pickford lived at Pickfair, 1143 Summit Dr. in Beverly Hills; and Lionel Barrymore lived at 802 North Rexford Dr. in Beverly Hills.

Inside Hollywood Tours brings visitors face to face with stars of the silver screen. Designed for groups (minimum size: twenty), these tours can be arranged through American Express Tours or Trade Wind Tours. On one of these tours, participants take a walking tour of NBC and then dine in the studio commissary. Then they view an NBC television taping and are given personalized gifts or door prizes.

Inside Hollywood Tours' "Spotlight on Beverly Hills" is operated weekdays only. Visitors see selected homes of the stars and spend some time at the Academy of Motion Picture Arts and Sciences.

For further information on Inside Hollywood Tours write P.O. Box 283, Tarzana, California 91356, or call 346–1211.

Hollywood Fantasy Tours runs a two-hour excursion covering dozens of Hollywood highlights. Included are Charlie Chaplin's old studio and Rudolf Valentino's grave. The open-air double-decker buses leave every hour starting at 8:30 A.M. from 1721 North Highland Ave., Hollywood 90028. Phone 469–8184.

Architecture is an intriguing aspect of Los Angeles. From older edifices to sleek, handsome, high-rise buildings to fantasy architecture, there is quite a diversity that reflects the tastes and styles of the city during different stages of growth. Many of the city's buildings, designed by such world-famous architects as Frank Lloyd Wright and Richard Neutra, are exceptional.

You may want to consider self-guided tours of some of these fascinating buildings: Frank Lloyd Wright's Hollyhock House, built from 1917 to 1920, at Barnsdall Park, 4800 Hollywood Blvd. in Hollywood; the Bradbury Building, at 304 S. Broadway, downtown, with its outstanding iron decoration; the ornate Byzantine architecture of the Cathedral of Saint Sophia at 1324 S. Normandie Ave. in Los Angeles; the Gamble House at 4 Westmoreland Pl. in Pasadena (luncheon is served; reservations necessary)—a charming example of the Greene and Greene California bungalow style; Los Angeles' first brick house, La Casa Pelanconi at 33–35 Olvera St., now a restaurant; Lovel House, 4616 Dundee Ave.; Queen Anne Cottage, 301 N. Baldwin, part of the Los Angeles State and County Arboretum; fabulous Watts Towers at 1765 E. 107 St. in Los Angeles, which was thirty-three years in the making; Casa de Adobe, 4603 N. Figueroa St. in Los Angeles, which replicates a Spanish hacienda.

Each spring, home tours of private homes designed by master builders and architects can be arranged. Check with information at the Los Angeles County Museum of Art (857–6111) to find out when this tour is scheduled.

To see the architecture as well as an overview of the artwork and the performing arts in Los Angeles, try the *Los Angeles Cultural Connection* at 2228 Benecia Ave. in Los Angeles. Group tours.

Art Tours of Los Angeles at 2864 Motor Ave. (870–2549), helps visitors experience the contemporary art explosion in the city. Tours take you to Venice and Melrose Ave., art communities and melting pots of current trends, styles, and influences. Reservations are necessary.

Los Angeles Conservancy Cultural Tours at 623-CITY offers a guided walking tour of downtown Los Angeles to view the city's historical architecture, California's Broadway Theater district, and the lavish movie palaces of the 1920s. Reservations are necessary; the fee is $5.00.

MOVIE AND TELEVISION TOURS

Before Los Angeles became one of the nation's largest and fastest growing cities in the 1920s, it had been a kind of rural nirvana. Surrounded by bean fields and orange groves, its climate was temperate all year long; grassy plains, snow-capped mountains, ocean, and even the desert were easily accessible.

The first settlers found themselves on a flat plain that ended at the Pacific Ocean. Cooled in summer by an offshore breeze, the temperature seldom climbed above 85 degrees F., and in the winter the daytime temperature often reached the 60s and 70s.

This was the Hollywood that Cecil B. De Mille, a struggling actor turned director from New York, found when, a few days before Christmas in 1913, he arrived in Hollywood. He came to film *The Squaw Man* for the Jesse Lasky Feature Play Company, a notable movie in that it was the first feature ever made. De Mille rented a barn on the southeast corner of Selma Ave. and Vine St.

The Squaw Man changed Hollywood. It marked the beginning of a new era for Los Angeles and the fledgling moving-picture business. Within a few years, Hollywood replaced New York as the capital of the film industry and became a symbol of glamour, fame, and riches to millions. Today movie studios look nothing like De Mille's barn (which still stands at Vine near Yucca—see *Historical Sites* for further details.) They are huge, technically sophisticated production centers and account for one of Los Angeles' most important industries. A few of them, along with the newer television studios that flourish here, are the public.

Universal Studios. 100 Universal Pl., Universal City. Call 877-1511 for information. Discover what really goes on behind the scenes in Hollywood. The five-hour Universal tour is an enlightening and amusing day at the world's largest television and movie studio. (It stretches across more than 400 acres, many of which are traversed during the course of the day by trams featuring witty running commentary provided by enthusiastic guides.)

Visitors experience the parting of the Red Sea, an avalanche, and a flood. They live through an encounter with a runaway train and an attack by the ravenous killer shark of *Jaws* fame. They endure a confrontation by aliens armed with death rays—all without ever leaving the safety of the tram.

Visitors are taken through a New England village, an aged European town, and the same New York street that Kojak and Columbo once walked. They examine giant props and see children lift up "automobiles." Also on display are a mobile forest and a Western jail. At this point in the tour, visitors relax in the snack bar and picnic area before going on to the Entertainment Center, the longest and the last stop of the day.

At the Entertainment Center visitors stroll around to enjoy various shows. In one theater animals beguile you with their tricks. In another you can pose for a photo session with the Incredible Hulk. Visit Castle Dracula and confront a variety of terrifying monsters. At the Screen Test Theater, visitors may find themselves being filmed as extras in films already released and now recut to include them.

Recent additions to the tour include access to more of the back-lot filming areas. Another attraction, which opened in the summer of 1982, is the Comedy Screen Test Theater.

Admission fees: $10.50 for adults, $7.75 for children ages three–eleven. For children under three, admission is free. Summer hours: open daily from 8:00 A.M. to 6:00 P.M. and during the other seasons, Monday through Friday, 10:00 A.M. to 3:30 P.M., Saturday and Sunday from 9:30 A.M. to 4:00 P.M.

Burbank Studios. Warner Brothers and Columbia Pictures share the lot at Burbank Studios, 4000 Warner Blvd., Burbank. A guided walking tour is available. Called the VIP tour, it is limited to groups of twelve adults. Reservations are essential; no visitors are allowed without them. (Call 213-954-1008.)

Because the tours involve a lot of walking, dress comfortably and casually. This tour is somewhat instructional, more technical, and more centered on the actual workings of filmmaking than the tour at Universal.

Visitors can also make reservations to dine in the studio commissary, the Blue Room, after the tour.

NBC Television Studios. NBC Television Studios (3000 W. Alameda Ave., Burbank, 840–4444 or 840–3572), offers a one-and-one-half hour guided tour of the largest color TV facilities in the United States. During the tour, visitors will have communication satellite and videotape processes explained to them. Studio I, where the *Tonight* show is filmed, is also part of the tour, as is the huge prop warehouse.

Tickets are available for tapings of NBC shows (see below).

Tours take place daily, 9:00 A.M. to 4:00 P.M. except in the summer when the studio opens at 8:30 A.M. Admission fees are $3.50 for adults, $2.75 for children ages five–eleven. Children under five are admitted free when accompanied by an adult. Free parking.

KCET: Los Angeles' Public Television Station. A behind-the-scenes look at television production is available to the general public at KCET, Los Angeles' public television station, located at 4401 Sunset Blvd. in Hollywood. On this tour you will walk through sound stages where special television productions (such as Steve Allen's *Meeting of the Minds* and Carl Sagan's *Cosmos*) were taped for nationwide broadcast. KCET's satellite system has an instantaneous feed throughout the world, which allows the station to pull any information occurring twenty-four hours a day. This satellite, along with the many different kinds of television cameras and equipment found on the sound stages, will be discussed in detail during the tour. Also seen on the tour is KCET's legitimate theater, which dates to the early 1920s.

Free tours are available Tuesday through Thursday at 10:00 A.M. and at 10:30 A.M. These tours should be prearranged by contacting the volunteer department of the station at 667–9242.

Television Shows. There's no better opportunity to see a television show being produced than in Los Angeles, and TV show tickets are easily obtained throughout the Los Angeles area.

Each network maintains a ticket booth located at its respective studio, and each is open during the hours of 9:00 A.M. and 5:00 P.M. The studios suggest that those interested in seeing a particular show phone ahead to be assured of ticket availability and show times.

Phone numbers for each network are:

    ABC: 557–4396
    CBS: 852–2345
    NBC: 840–3537
    KTLA (Channel 5 in Los Angeles): 460–5500
    KTTV (Channel 11 in Los Angeles): 856–1425.

Most tickets can be obtained the day of the performance; however, on shows such as *Johnny Carson,* NBC will mail tickets if you live more than 150 miles outside Los Angeles and if you allow six weeks for delivery. Write to NBC Ticket Office, 3000 W. Alameda Ave., Burbank, CA 91523.

Free tickets are also available outside Mann's Chinese Theater in Hollywood, at the Universal Studios Tour, and at the Hollywood Greater Los Angeles Visitors Bureau (see *Tourist Information,* above).

Mann's Chinese Theater. A no fuss, self-made tour at Mann's Chinese Theater (at 6925 Hollywood Blvd.) is on the top of most movie buffs' sightseeing lists. Opened by Sid Grauman in 1927 for the premiere of Cecil B. De Mille's *King of Kings,* this theater was the subject of much fanfare.

Mann's Chinese is famous for its courtyard filled with the impressions of more than 150 movie stars' handprints, footprints, and signatures sealed in concrete—a tradition that began accidentally (or so the legend goes) when

Norma Talmadge stepped in wet cement at the first premiere. Modern-day celluloid stars (including R2D2 and Darth Vadar of *Star Wars*) and long-ago lovelies (such as Marilyn Monroe and Judy Garland) are remembered in this historical Hollywood setting. For information, call 646–8111.

INDUSTRIAL TOURS

So much is heard about Los Angeles being a show-business capital that visitors might overlook the fact that it is also the West Coast's major industrial and commercial center. Here the nation's aerospace industry has its home, as can be seen from the exotic looking radar dishes and special antennae mounted atop factory buildings, particularly in the South Bay area, near the Los Angeles International Airport, and in parts of the San Fernando Valley. Most electronics and aircraft companies have defense contracts, which means that their plants are off limits to outsiders. Nevertheless, visitors are welcomed at facilities representative of the city's varied commercial and industrial life.

Fans of television's old "Lou Grant" will want to tour *The Los Angeles Times* plant for a close look at what goes on in the city room of a metropolitan daily newspaper. Two free tours are offered daily, Monday through Friday, except holidays, at 11:15 A.M. and 3:00 P.M. The minimum age for children is ten. Visitors see the complete process involved in producing a paper, from the editorial room, where stories are written, through the gigantic press room, where the papers are printed. Tours begin at the Bicentennial Exhibit in the main lobby, First and Spring Sts. in downtown Los Angeles.

If you can get up early enough, you can catch the bustling world of commercial florists. The two *wholesale flower markets* near downtown Los Angeles open at 2:00 A.M. each Monday, Wednesday, and Friday and close at 11:00 A.M. Things are relatively quiet on Tuesday and Thursday and thus hours are limited to between 6:00 A.M. and 11:00 A.M., but visitors are still welcome. A visitor's card costs $1.00 and can be obtained at the offices of the Southern California Floral Association, 745 Wall St., Los Angeles, CA 90014, or at the markets from 6:00 A.M. to 2:30 P.M., Monday through Friday. The days just before a major holiday are so frantic that visitors are discouraged then.

A rare chance to watch commercial jetliners being produced is provided by the *Douglas Aircraft Company,* a division of McDonnell Douglas Corporation, at its Long Beach plant. After a short introductory briefing, visitors go out to the huge manufacturing building to see DC 9 and DC 10 jets being made. The ninety-minute tour ends at the flight line, where just completed planes are prepared for delivery. Tours are conducted each Tuesday and Thursday at 10:30 A.M.; the minimum age is thirteen. No photos are permitted. For reservations, write External Relations Department, Douglas Aircraft Co., Mail Code 18A–54, 3855 Lakewood Blvd., Long Beach, CA 90846.

No sugar but plenty of spices are part of the forty-five minute guided tour of the *Lawry's Foods* spice-blending and food-products plant at Lawry's California Center, 570 W. Ave. 26. Tours start at 11:30 A.M., 1:30 P.M., and 2:30 P.M. each weekday. Free parking is available. No reservations are required; group tours of thirty are accepted on a first-come basis. The California Center also features an outdoor restaurant, shops, and gardens.

Visitors interested in modern retail merchandising and promotion will find valuable a one-hour tour of *The Broadway Plaza* in downtown Los Angeles. Groups of fifteen or more begin the visit to the forty retail shops and the Broadway Department Store by listening to an introductory explanation. Then they tour the mall to see how the store's marketing activities are carried on.

This tour may be taken in conjunction with one that goes to the 500-room *Hyatt Regency Los Angeles,* which is part of the same skyscraper complex. The hotel tour includes a peek at the exclusive Regency Club Floor, which has its own butler and maid service for guests. A behind-the-scenes look at the Hyatt's kitchen and convention facilities concludes this tour. Only group reservations are accepted. Write at least two weeks in advance to Nann Miller Enterprises, 800 W. First St., Los Angeles, CA 90012. Indicate day and time desired.

 PARKS. The extensive Los Angeles park system provides a welcome oasis after the myriad concrete freeways and urban sprawl. The Los Angeles Department of Parks and Recreation provides helpful information on locating and identifying park facilities. Call 485–5555.

The vast park system offers everything from small, grassy knolls for picnicking and relaxing to huge wilderness areas offering a wide spectrum of recreation facilities, including tennis courts, golf courses, and lakes.

The Parks Department also sponsors various activities such as marathon races, interpark sports contests, poetry readings, art shows, and chess tournaments. During the summer months the Los Angeles Free Public Theater sponsors performances in the parks featuring a roving troupe of players offering Shakespeare and contemporary plays. For a schedule of events and activities, check *The Los Angeles Times* Sunday "Calendar" section, *The Herald-Examiner's* Friday "Style" section, or *Los Angeles* or *California* magazines. Each has special listings on upcoming activities.

Barnsdall Park. 4800 Hollywood Blvd., Los Angeles. The Hollyhock House, the first California residence designed and built by Frank Lloyd Wright, is hidden amid the bustle of Hollywood by a hillside olive grove. There is an ample picnic area, and tours of the remarkable house are free. Also located in the park is the Junior Arts Center, a facility offering arts and crafts classes and theater arts instruction to children. The Municipal Art Gallery exhibits feature a changing lineup of local talent primarily in a contemporary vein.

El Pueblo de Los Angeles State Historical Park. 420 N. Main St. (Mailing address: 845 N. Alamita St., Los Angeles, 90012). Tours are offered at the historic buildings that make up this park, the founding site of Los Angeles in 1781. Adjacent to Olvera St., the city's oldest thoroughfare, is the park itself, also known as the Old Plaza, a cobblestone square filled with shops, restaurants, and entertainment facilities—all suggestive of the atmosphere of a real Mexican village.

Elysian Park. Entrances on Academy Rd., Stadium Wy., Scott Ave., Los Angeles. This 575-acre park is on hilly acreage overlooking downtown Los Angeles and the San Gabriel Valley. Much of the park is still wilderness, and there is a 10-acre rare-tree grove completely labeled for convenient identification. The recreation center has volleyball and basketball courts. Plentiful play areas for the children, nature trails for hiking, plus nine picnic spots round out the park's offerings. Perched on the southeast corner, high above the smog, is Dodger Stadium, home of the Los Angeles Dodgers professional baseball team.

Ernest E. Debs Park. 4235 Monterey Rd., Los Angeles. A 306-acre wooded park that includes a 1½-acre lake available for boating and fishing. The park is also designated a bird sanctuary. Picnicking is welcomed.

Exposition Park. Figueroa at Exposition Blvd., Los Angeles. This beautiful park was the site of the 1932 Olympics, and the impressive architecture still stands. Adjoining the University of Southern California, Exposition Park is the location of two major museums: the California Museum of Science and Industry and the Natural History Museum. Also included in this 114-acre park is the Los Angeles Swimming Stadium (home of Los Angeles aquatic competitions), which is open to the public during the summer, and the Memorial Coliseum, the site of college football and soccer games. There are plenty of picnic areas on the grounds, as well as a sunken rose garden that is lovely for strolling. (See the map of Exposition Park in the *Exploring Los Angeles* section, above.)

Forest Lawn Memorial Park. 1712 S. Glendale Ave., Glendale. This 300-acre formally landscaped area features a major collection of marble statuary and art treasures, including a replica of Leonardo da Vinci's *The Last Supper* done entirely in stained glass. In the Hall of the Crucifixion–Resurrection is one of the world's largest oil paintings incorporating a religious theme, *The Crucifixion* by artist Jan Styka. The picturesque grounds are perfect for a leisurely walk. Forest Lawn was the model for the setting of Evelyn Waugh's novel *The Loved One*.

Forest Lawn Memorial Park—Hollywood Hills. 6300 Forest Lawn Dr., Hollywood. Just west of Griffith Park on the north slope of the Hollywood Hills, this 340-acre "sister" park to Forest Lawn Glendale is dedicated to the ideal of American liberty. Featured are bronze and marble statuary, including Thomas Ball's 60-ft. Washington Memorial and a replica of the Liberty Bell. There are also reproductions of Boston's Old North Church and Longfellow's Church of the Hills. A film entitled *The Many Voices of Freedom* is shown daily, and Revolutionary War documents are on permanent display.

Griffith Park. Entrances on Los Feliz Blvd. at Vermont, Western, and Riverside Dr. and off the Golden State Fwy. at the Los Feliz exit. Donated to the city in 1896 by mining tycoon Griffith J. Griffith, this is the largest city park in the United States. It contains 4,000 acres. There are seemingly endless picnic areas, as well as hiking and bridle trails. Travel Town, with its miniature railroad, is a favorite for kids. Pony riding is also available. The park is home to three major golf courses, a driving range, and tennis courts. A swimming pool and soccer fields are nearby. The world-famous Los Angeles Zoo, which includes the Children's Zoo, is on the park's north side. Here animals can be seen in environments as close to their natural habitat as possible. The Griffith Park Observatory and Planetarium is located on the park's south side, high atop the Hollywood Hills, where visitors can enjoy stargazing or view the various astrological exhibits on display. The Western Ave. entrance is the location of Fern Dell, a half mile of shaded area that includes paths winding their way amid waterfalls, pools, and thousands of ferns. A small nature museum is centered on the many species of ferns growing there. (Map overleaf.)

Hancock Park. Curson Ave. at Wilshire Blvd., Los Angeles. This attractively landscaped park is the location of the La Brea Tar Pits, the George C. Page Museum, and the Los Angeles County Museum of Art. At the bubbling asphalt of the Tar Pits, replicas of prehistoric beasts recreate fateful ventures into the tar. The George C. Page Museum houses discoveries from the pits and other sites in the park. During the summer months there are usually ongoing excavations for fossilized animals on the grounds, and visitors are welcome to watch the painstaking search. Fossilized animals aren't the only type to be found here; look for rabbits that hide among the shrubs and trees.

Highland Park. 6150 Piedmont Ave., Los Angeles. Located in a suburban area also called Highland Park, this spot has plenty of picnic space amid the sycamores. It's a favorite for family get-togethers.

Hollywood Bowl. 2301 N. Highland Ave., Los Angeles. Nestled in the Hollywood Hills is a natural amphitheater, the Hollywood Bowl, famous for its outstanding cultural events ranging from free symphony concerts on Sundays to the three-day Playboy Jazz Festival. There are picnic tables in the surrounding area; baskets of sandwiches, salads, and wine can be purchased on the premises. Bring sweaters and a blanket for night performances because no matter how hot it is during the day, nights tend to get chilly. For program information call 876–0232.

John Anson Ford Theater. 2580 Cahuenga Blvd., East Los Angeles. Just a short distance from the famed Hollywood Bowl in Hollywood, near the Universal Studios lot, is this amphitheater and picnic area. The outdoor theater hosts theatrical events and concerts and is the home base for the Free Public Theater Foundation's Shakespeare productions, available in the summer months at no charge. Sometimes a deer or a raccoon will venture into the park from the nearby hillsides. As with the Hollywood Bowl, performances are outside; bring warm clothing in the evenings.

Lincoln Park. 3501 Valley Blvd., Los Angeles. Located in a predominately Mexican–American neighborhood, this park offers bilingual activities and has basketball and tennis courts. Picnicking under the trees.

Los Encinos State Historical Park. 16756 Moorpark, Encino. Located in the San Fernando Valley, this park's main attraction is the early California dwelling, complete with grounds, all of which are furnished with historically accurate furniture, household goods, and tools. Tours are available Wednesday through Sunday.

MacArthur Park. 2230 W. 6th St., Los Angeles. This lovely park, sprawling under majestic palm trees, features a large lake that is available for boating in the summer months. During the 1920s and 1930s, MacArthur Park was the

Griffith Park

FREEWAY
ROAD
TRAIL

Points of Interest

1) Observatory and Planetarium
2) Greek Theater
3) Los Angeles Zoo
4) Travel Town
5) Golf Course
6) Tennis Courts
7) Picnic Grounds
8) Griffith Park camp
9) Hollywoodland Camp
10) Ranger Visitor Center
11) Driving Range
12) Stables, Pony and Stage Ride
13) Miniature Railroad
14) Merry-Go-Round
15) Los Angeles Live Steamers, Inc.
16) Bird Sanctuary
17) Park Nursery

hangout for the elite, a favorite spot for a leisurely stroll, boating, or an afternoon concert. Unfortunately, the park now suffers from urban blight and is frequently the gathering place for loiterers—who have been unable, however, to diminish the park's beauty. On Sunday afternoons impromptu music played by jazz musicians who gather to "jam" is still offered. The park is, of course, the inspiration for the famous song "MacArthur Park."

North Hollywood Park. 11430 Chandler Blvd., North Hollywood. Just off the Hollywood Freeway at Magnolia, this impressive park has baseball diamonds, a swimming pool, lighted tennis courts, and a beautiful Spanish-style library. In front of the library stands a bronze statue of Amelia Earhart, the famed aviatrix. There are many picnic spots under the trees and plenty of open space for volleyball nets.

Palisades Park. 851 Alma Real Dr., Pacific Palisades. Between West Los Angeles and the Pacific Ocean, just off Sunset Blvd., is this exclusive area where many stars and entertainment moguls reside. The park is lush with palms and eucalyptus trees, and there are plenty of picnic areas, and hiking trails.

Plummer Park. 1200 N. Vista, Los Angeles. This small 6-acre park in West Hollywood is especially geared to the elderly. There is a senior citizen center where organized activities take place. Most days horseshoes, shuffleboard, checkers, and croquet matches are scheduled. The park also contains tennis courts, a children's playground, and a bird sanctuary, plus the historic Plummer House that is open for tours on Sundays. Picnic tables are available.

Roxbury Park. 471 S. Roxbury Dr., Beverly Hills. This centrally located park is under the Beverly Hills Parks and Recreation's jurisdiction. It offers a softball diamond, tennis courts, and lawn bowling, as well as excellent youth programs, including monthly summer theater productions performed on a portable stage. Shaded picnic areas surround the grassy park.

Silverlake Park. 1850 W. Silverlake, Los Angeles. Adjacent to a reservoir, this park offers grassy picnic areas, volleyball and basketball courts, tennis courts, and plenty of space for soccer or jogging, favorite activities here.

Sycamore Park. 4702 N. Figueroa Ave., Los Angeles. Near Highland Park, this area offers shaded picnicking amid the towering sycamores.

REGIONAL PARKS

Banning Mansion and Park. 401 E. M St., Wilmington. An 1864 mansion built by General Phineas Banning, founder of the city of Wilmington, sits on the grounds of this landscaped park, complete with gardens. Tours on Wednesday, Saturday, Sunday, 1:00, 2:00, 3:00, and 4:00 P.M. Park and children's playground are open daily. Picnic areas are plentiful. No fee, but small donations are requested.

Brookside Park. Pasadena. At the junction of Hwys. 134 and 210, or Colorado Blvd. and Orange, lies the Arroyo Seco Glen, a valley that is the home of Brookside Park and the world-famous Rose Bowl. The park rambles along a sparkling creek and offers many hiking trails in the hillsides. Tennis, basketball, and volleyball courts are located at the park's recreation facilities.

Will Rogers
State Historic Park

- PAVED ROADS
- - - TRAIL – RIDING HIKING
- ••• TRAIL – HIKING ONLY

Topanga State Pk.

BACKBONE TRAIL

WILL ROGERS STATE PK. RD.

Entrance

Exit

To Los Angeles

SUNSET BLVD.

Points of Interest

1) Picnic Area
2) Inspiration Point
3) Roping Arena
4) Heart Canyon
5) Mitt Canyon
6) Riding Arena
7) Stables
8) Bone Canyon Corral
9) Nature Center
10) Lawn Area
11) Will Rogers' Home
12) Visitor Center Store
13) Tennis Courts
14) Contact Station
15) Parking
16) Polo Fields

Catalina Island. Officially Santa Catalina Island could be called a park. The Wrigley Foundation donated most of the island to the federal parks system, and it has been designated a wildlife preserve. There are plenty of outdoor activities here, including tennis courts, golf courses, riding stables, and a beautiful cactus garden, plus guided tours of the bays in glass-bottom boats and tours of the island's interior, where wildlife, some of which is endangered, and indigenous vegetation are abundant. To help preserve the natural habitat, a regional park of 41,000 acres is being developed for backpacking, hiking, camping, and general public use.

Chatsworth Park. Off Hwy. 118 in the San Fernando Valley, west on Chatsworth St., is this unusual park made up of scattered boulders and rocks. The area has served as the location of many Western movies and television shows. The children's playground includes a stockade, a log house, and a cannon, all of which have often formed the background for films.

Jesse Owens Park, 9651 S. Western Ave. This park of twenty acres features a gymnasium, a field house, an indoor swimming pool and basketball, volleyball, badminton, and tennis courts, plus a senior citizen's center with shuffleboard and horseshoes. Picnic sites are plentiful. The park also has a three-par golf course.

Malibu Creek State Park. Santa Monica Mountains, about six miles north of Malibu. This park features a nature walk guided by a ranger who will point out native animals and vegetation. Birds are plentiful, which should delight those who like to identify species. Because the nature walks are leisurely paced, children and the elderly can join in. Bring a picnic lunch to enjoy at the stops along the way.

Placerita Canyon County Park. 19150 Placerita Canyon Rd., Newhall. This 350-acre park is perfect for hiking. There are eight miles of trails through both flat and hilly terrain along a stream and through oak trees. Overnight or day camping and picnicking are available. There is an equestrian area for horseback riding and a ½ mile ecology trail centered on flora and fauna. Gold was discovered in the park, and the site is designated by the so-called Oak of the Golden Dream. Naturalists are available at the park headquarters to answer questions.

Oak Grove County Park. 4550 N. Oak Grove Dr., Pasadena. Picnic areas are nestled in the oak trees next to the Devil's Gate Reservoir. An eighteen-hole frisbee course is located here; bring your plastic discs.

William S. Hart County Park. 24151 Newhall Ave., Newhall. This park is the ranch and former home of legendary silent film star William S. Hart. Western and cowboy mementos and art are on view. This 259-acre facility includes picnic tables and barbecue braziers as well as overnight camping accommodations.

Will Rogers State Historic Park. 14253 Sunset Blvd., Pacific Palisades 90272. In the Pacific Palisades, this twenty-seven-acre park was once the home of the famed humorist Will Rogers. The ranch house is open to the public, and displays of mementos and manuscripts are arranged exactly as if Rogers still lived there. There is also a horse-exercising ring with stable; polo matches are held on Sundays. There are fields for softball or soccer and a lot of grassy, wooded acreage for hiking and roaming. Sorry, there's no picnicking. (See map in this section.)

 ZOO. The **Los Angeles Zoo,** one of the major zoos in the United States, is noted for its breeding of endangered species. An Indian rhinoceros was born as recently as 1982. Koala bears and white tigers are the latest addition. This 113-acre compound holds more than 2,000 mammals, birds, amphibians, and reptiles. Animals are grouped according to the geographical areas where they are naturally found—Africa, Australia, Eurasia, North America, and South America. A children's zoo features a baby animal nursery where small, newborn mammals can be seen in incubators. At the baby animal compound, larger newborn mammals can be seen at close range. Another area popular with children is the barnyard, where they can walk among gentle animals such as lambs, goats, and chickens.

There are also a couple of new features at the zoo: A walk-through bird exhibit with more than 50 different species from all over the world; and, for a dollar, you can actually ride a camel, elephant, or Clydesdale horse.

Located in Griffith Park, at the junction of the Ventura and Golden State Fwys. Open daily, 10:00 A.M. to 6:00 P.M. (summer), and 10:00 A.M. to 5:00 P.M. (the rest of the year). No one is admitted an hour before closing. Adults $4.00; children ages 5 through 15 and senior citizens, $1.50. Children under 5, free. Baby strollers and wheelchairs can be rented. There is tram service around the perimeter of the zoo. Snack stands and two picnic areas are located on the grounds. Recorded general zoo information can be obtained by calling 666–4090; guided tours and further information are available by calling 664–1100.

Marineland. 6600 Palos Verdes Drive South, Rancho Palos Verdes; (213) 541–5663. This seaside zoo and theme park offers an unusual view of aquatic animals in beautiful surroundings. Live shows star sea animals and birds such as Orky and Corky in the whale show. Other animal-actors include sea lions, macaws, and dolphins. The Marineland Animal Care Center affords the curious a view of the care of sick or wounded animals. The Baja Reef, the newest attraction at Marineland, is the first man-made aquarium in which you can swim among the fish. Visitors are given a wet suit, snorkel, mask, and fins to use and swim in the tank with 2,000 fish; there are viewing ports for those who would rather just watch. Also worthwhile is the Sky Tower—an elevator ride that lifts 344 feet above the sea for a panoramic view of the coastline.

 GARDENS. Although Los Angeles is known primarily for its sunny weather, movie stars, and freeways, a closer look reveals, among other things, some of the finest botanical gardens in the world. Not merely collections of cacti and palm trees, these gardens include exotic flowers, plants, and trees from all over the world. Several of the gardens have provided backdrops for many films and television shows. Others are the focal point of important botanical research.

The Huntington Library, Art Gallery, and Botanical Gardens. On Oxford Road in San Marino. The Huntington has been a landmark ever since it was founded by rail tycoon Henry E. Huntington in the early 1900s. The Huntington has established a reputation as one of the most extraordinary cultural complexes in the world, annually receiving more than half a million visitors—and for good reasons. The library contains six million items, including such treasures as a Gutenberg Bible. In the library's hallway are five tall hexagonal towers displaying important books and manuscripts. Other rooms contain books dating to the 11th century.

The art gallery, devoted to British art from the 18th and early 19th centuries, possesses the original *Blue Boy* by Gainsborough and Lawrence's *Pinkie*.

The Huntington's awesome 130-acre garden, formerly the grounds of the estate, now includes a twelve-acre Desert Garden featuring the largest group of mature cacti and other succulents in the world, as well as a Japanese Garden with traditional Japanese plants, stone ornaments, a moon bridge, a Japanese house, a walled Zen Garden, and a Bonsai Court.

Besides these gardens, there are collections of azaleas and 1,500 varieties of camellias, the world's largest public collection. The 1,000-variety rose garden displays its collection historically so that the development leading to today's roses can be observed. There are also herb, Shakespeare, and palm gardens, plus a newly completed jungle garden.

Because of the Huntington's vastness, a variety of tour options is available for visitors. They include: a 12-minute slide show introducing the Huntington; an hour-and-a-quarter guided tour of the Gardens; a 45-minute audio tape about the art gallery (which can be rented for a nominal fee); a 15-minute introductory talk about the library; and inexpensive, self-guided-tour leaflets.

In 1980 the first major facility constructed on the Huntington grounds in more than sixty years opened. The five million dollar Huntington Pavilion offers visitors unmatched views of the surrounding mountains and valleys, while housing a bookstore, displays, and information kiosks as well. Both the east and the west wings of the pavilion display paintings on public exhibition for the first time. The Ralph M. Parsons Botanical Center at the pavilion includes a botanical library, a herbarium, and a laboratory for research on plants.

Open Tuesday through Sunday, 1:00 P.M. to 4:30 P.M. Reservations are required for Sunday visits (818–449–3901). Call 792–6141 for general information and public programs.

To get there: From the west take the Ventura Fwy. (#134) and exit at the Hill St. offramp. Follow this street east to Allen, and proceed south to the Huntington. From the east take the 210 Fwy. to the Allen offramp and continue south to the Huntington.

Los Angeles State and County Arboretum. 301 N. Baldwin Ave., Arcadia. Contains 127 acres of native and exotic plants. The rotunda inside the main entrance features displays of those currently in bloom, including rare orchids and other flowers seldom seen. The Arboretum's demonstration home gardens were designed to provide homeowners with ideas for gracious outdoor-living landscaping. Other attractions at the Arboretum include the begonia house, with about 200 varieties of begonias, and the nearby tropical greenhouse, featuring orchids, bromeliads, ferns, and other exotics in a rainforest setting.

To simplify things for the visitor, many of the more than 5,000 kinds of plants on the Arboretum's grounds are arranged in geographical sections, based on the plants' place of origin. In these individual areas you can see vegetation thriving as it does in its natural habitat. Included are plant life from Australia, South Africa, North America, Asia, the Mediterranean, and South America.

The Arboretum's historical section features buildings, along with appropriate flowers and plants, from different times in California's colorful past. The result is a colorful mixture of Victorian, adobe, and railroad-depot architectures.

One of the most popular sites at the Arboretum is Lasca Lagoon, one of the few natural freshwater lakes in southern California. The lagoon may look familiar: It has been used as a jungle setting for movies and television series, including *Tarzan* and *Fantasy Island.*

Open daily from 9:00 A.M. to 4:30 P.M. Adults, $1.50; senior citizens and students with ID, 75¢; children under 5, free. Third Tuesday of each month, all admissions free. Call (213) 446–8251.

How to get there: From the east or west, take the Foothill Fwy. (#210) to Baldwin Ave. and go south to the entrance. From the south, take the San Bernardino Fwy. (# 10) to Baldwin Ave. and go north to the entrance.

Descanso Gardens. 1418 Descanso Dr., La Canada. Once part of the vast Spanish Rancho San Rafael that covered more than 30,000 acres. Descanso Gardens now encompasses 155 acres of native chaparral-covered slopes. A forest of California live oak trees furnishes a dramatic backdrop for thousands of camellias, azaleas, and a four-acre rose garden. Descanso's Tea House features pools, waterfalls, and a gift shop, as well as a relaxing spot to stop for refreshments. Flower shows, including chrysanthemum, daffodil, camellia, and bonsai competitions, are held at various times of the year. Guided tours are available; trams traverse the grounds.

Open daily from 9:00 A.M. to 4:30 P.M. Tea House open Tuesday through Sunday, 11:00 A.M. to 4:00 P.M.; closed Mondays.

How to get there: Take the Glendale Fwy. (# 2) to Verdugo Blvd., exit. At second light—Alta Canada Rd.—turn right and proceed to Descanso Gardens parking lot.

South Coast Botanic Garden. 26300 Crenshaw Blvd. on the Palos Verdes Peninsula. (213) 377–0468. A study in recycling. This eighty-seven acre garden environment has been transformed from a landfill into a place of serenity and beauty. Visitors will find guided bird walks (more than 240 different bird species have been sighted here), plant identification photos, exhibits and display materials, and small wildlife at the man-made lake. There are plenty of trails and paths, as well as a tram. Among the plants to be found at South Coast Botanical Garden are flowering trees, palms, ornamental figs, legumes, redwoods, succulents, and eucalyptus.

Open daily from 9:00 A.M. to 5:00 P.M. Closed Christmas. Adults, $1.50; senior citizens and students with ID, 75¢; children under 5, free. Tram tours, $1.50 per person. Third Tuesday of each month, all admissions free.

How to get there: From the north, take the San Diego Fwy. (#405) to the Crenshaw offramp. Continue south on Crenshaw to the gardens.

Exposition Park Rose Garden. Menlo Ave. near Exposition Blvd. A rose lover's dream come true. Here, in a seven-acre sunken garden, more than 17,000 roses are on display. During the months of April and May, the height of the flowering season, the fragrance coming from the rose garden and the array of magnificent flowers attract more than 45,000 visitors *weekly*.

Many all-American award-winning roses grow at Exposition Park; the range includes everything from miniature tea roses to six-inch diameter blooms, in every hue imaginable. A magnificent fountain and four summery gazebos provide respite from the busy city that surrounds the garden.

Open daily from 9:00 A.M. to 5:00 P.M.

How to get there: Take the Harbor Fwy. (# 11) south to the Santa Barbara Ave. exit. Then follow signs to Exposition Park.

Wrigley Memorial and Botanical Garden. 1400 Avalon Canyon Rd. in Avalon on Catalina Island. A living tribute to William Wrigley Jr., the chewing-gum magnate who helped develop Santa Catalina Island. The Wrigley Memorial, with its spectacular circular staircase leading to the top of the eighty-foot observation tower, is constructed almost completely of materials obtained from the island itself. Surrounding the memorial is the garden, a thirty-seven acre showcase for Catalina's native plants. Surprisingly enough, this little island has an even better climate than the Southern California mainland, and so plants, including St. Catherine's lace and the wild tomato, that cannot survive at any of the Los Angeles gardens grow here. Cars are not permitted on Catalina Island, but a tram connects the garden with downtown Avalon island plaza. Open daily from 8:00 A.M. to 5:00 P.M. Admission is 50¢; children under 12, free.

The Virginia Robinson Gardens. In Beverly Hills, 6.2 acres of terraced gardens surrounding the former home of Virginia Robinson of the J. W. Robinson Department Store clan. A trained guide will take you on an hour tour of the gardens and the exquisite exteriors of the main house, guest house, servants' quarters, swimming pool, and tennis court. A highlight of the tour is the collection of rare and exotic palms.

Two tours daily, Tuesday through Friday at 10:00 A.M. and 1:00 P.M. Adults, $3.00; children, students, and senior citizens, $2.25. Phone (213) 466–8251. Since the garden's administration is trying to keep a low profile to avoid congestion in the cul-de-sac where this garden is situated, visitors must call for reservations and be told the address and how to get there.

Rancho Santa Ana Botanic Garden. 1500 N. College, Claremont (714) 626–3922. Now more than 50 years old, Rancho Santa Ana specializes in plants native to California. Here an extensive library, research labs, classrooms, and systematic collections contribute to research, conservation, and graduate work in botany. Although these functions are not open to the public, the grounds of the garden are. Located at the foot of the San Gabriel Mountains, with Mount

Baldy looming on the horizon, the gardens are perhaps at their best between February and June, when desert plants such as manzanitas, California lilacs, tree poppies, and bush anemones burst forth in an array of colors seldom seen anywhere.

A home demonstration garden here offers homeowners suggestions on how to use California native plants in landscaping. Other attractions include a rock garden, a coniferous forest, Joshua tree woodland, and a desert and dune garden. Open daily from 8:00 A.M. to 5:00 P.M. Closed Christmas, New Year's Day, July 4th, and Thanksgiving. Admission free.

How to get there: Take the San Bernardino Fwy. (#10) east to the Indian Hill Blvd. exit. Go north on Indian Hill to Foothill. Take Foothill east to College Ave. Turn left into the grounds there.

 BEACHES. More so, perhaps, than even Disneyland or Hollywood, Los Angeles beaches are memorable. Each has its own mood and flavor. Histories vary, as do sizes and locations, but all are within an hour's drive of downtown Los Angeles in normal (non-rush-hour) traffic.

Take any main east/west street (such as Wilshire, Santa Monica, or Olympic Blvds.), travel as far west as possible, and eventually you'll reach the Pacific Ocean. Pacific Coast Highway (PCH), California Route 1, follows the coast. Starting at the northern end is illustrious Malibu, the home of dozens of stars. The scenery here, including miles of rugged cliffs, is spectacular. It is a city by the ocean that offers plenty to do and see and is a welcome magnet for both residents (many of whom also have homes in the city proper) and visitors.

South along the cliffs on PCH, all the southerly beaches spread before your eyes. Santa Monica is the next stop; as beach communities go, this city has one of the strongest reputations. Scene of the famous Muscle Beach of the "beach blanket" movie genre and hangout for the perennial beach boy in a wet suit, Santa Monica seems the essence of the beach experience. This beachiness, however, takes a different turn as you leave family-oriented Santa Monica.

Although Venice Beach has recently been subject to a bad press, it boasts one of the most fascinating histories of the area. A bit similar to SoHo in New York City and other artists' habitats, Venice seems somewhat sinister but electric. During the day the boardwalk is congested with all manner of rollerskaters, hippy types, street entertainers and other folk having all kinds of fun.

South from Venice is Marina del Rey, one of the largest man-made venues of its type. Thousands of colorful boats are surrounded by residences, hotels, and restaurants. Beaches here are scarce, but the area is still fascinating to explore. Playa del Rey, farther south, is an old-fashioned beach town. Connecting Playa del Rey with El Segundo is Dockweiler State Beach, which is surrounded by a bizarre-looking steam-generating plant. Dockweiler is the unofficial home of area hang gliders.

The communities farther south—Manhattan, Redondo, and Hermosa—are old beach cities that, through the years, have added to California's reputation for surf, sand, and fun. These communities swarm with visitors all summer long.

On any given evening after surfers have grounded their boards, the main strip—Manhattan Beach Blvd.—looks like a scene out of the movie *American Graffiti.* The cruising culture here is still built on fast cars, loud radios, and knowing everyone who drives by. It is an interesting place in which to watch and mingle.

MALIBU

World famous Malibu Beach stretches twenty-seven miles along the coast from Ventura County to Santa Monica. Old Beach Boy songs and Frankie Avalon movies depict Malibu as a swinging, surfing town—a teenager's paradise —but it is really much more.

The Malibu Colony is actually a community of well-to-do and well-known people. With coastal homes ranging from one million dollars to over four million dollars and as the home of residents such as Barbra Streisand, Johnny Carson, and Larry (J. R.) Hagman, this city resembles a beachfront version of Hollywood.

Malibu is a physically arresting environment. It is surrounded by the stunning Santa Monica Mountains and canyons and valleys that sweep inland to the beach. Although rock slides are common here during the rainy season, residents seem to remain undaunted.

Most beaches along the Malibu coast are private. But where there are accessways, it is legal to be on the beach—despite the lack of rest room facilities and lifeguards. A better bet is to try the public beaches. (A listing follows.) Approximately six, all great for surfing, sunning, and swimming, exist along the Malibu stretch of ocean. Most have lifeguards and health facilities, concession stands, and water fountains. If you want to give surfing a try, surfboard rentals are available at *Zuma Jay,* 22775 Pacific Coast Hwy. (456–8044).

To take in a little of Malibu's local color, visit the *Malibu Pier,* 23000 Pacific Coast Hwy. Fisherman, tourists, and locals mingle here. For a meal or just a bite to eat, *Alice's Restaurant* (456–6646) at the beginning of the pier is a local favorite.

In Ventura County and heading south toward Santa Monica, the following Malibu beaches are public:

The County Line Beach (half in Malibu and half in Ventura County) is good for surfing; a rocky ocean floor, however, makes it impossible to swim or body surf. There is also no lifeguard, so confine your visit to walking and looking.

Leo Carillo State Beach, quite an active beach, is divided into three separate areas: two with no name, and one, called Secos, known for its surfing. Camping is allowed on part of the beach; and Leo Carillo has the added attraction for the younger folks of caves to explore and crawl through. Scuba diving, surfing, body surfing, and swimming are also good at Leo Carillo. Rock piles form on the shore in interesting configurations, making intimate spots perfect for a picnic.

Zuma Beach, about 5 miles long, is the largest of the Malibu beaches. Many people come here from "the Valley"; it is a good family recreational area that contains a large parking area, concession stands, rest rooms, showers, and drinking fountains. In terms of the ocean, body surfing and swimming are good—and there are lifeguards on duty during the days in season. Zuma Beach is also the site of the Los Angeles County lifeguard exhibition.

Paradise Cove, a private beach at Point Dume, costs $3 to enter. Point Dume, with its red sandstone cliffs, is a beautiful spot, and the beach is clean and sandy. The *Sandcastle Restaurant* is a local favorite for breakfast, lunch, and dinner.

The section of **Paradise Cove** on the other side of Point Dume is the county's notorious nude beach. The focus of much controversy in recent years, it is actually not very secluded, and voyeurs and photographers have been troublesome. The police department watches this area closely for illegal doings; nonetheless, many people congregate here, especially on weekends.

Corral Beach is a narrow strip of land two miles west of Pepperdine University. Parking and other facilities are scarce, but this beach is usually less crowded than most others and is a good place to retreat to from the packed beaches.

Malibu's **Surfrider Beach,** near the pier, is a world-famous beach, with some of the best surfing in Southern California. This is also the site of the International Surfing Contest at the end of September, when waves usually reach from three to five feet. (During the summer the waves are usually only one to three feet.) This beach is sometimes very crowded, but it is a good place for people watching.

Las Tunas Beach, just left of Las Tunas Canyon, is a good surf-fishing beach. Sunbathing is good, too, but be careful of the steel groins set in the water to hold the sand. The last Malibu beach, closest to Santa Monica, is **Topanga Canyon Beach.** At the foot of Topanga Canyon and near the illustrious Getty Museum, this beach is good for swimming and has some fishing areas.

Besides the beaches, Malibu contains many establishments for fine food and interesting atmosphere: The *Showboat,* 22718 W. PCH, has a counter that overlooks the ocean; the *Charthouse,* 18412 W. PCH, and *Moonshadow,* 20356 W. PCH, also have great views. A wonderful jazz club, *Pasquales* (22724 W. PCH), has gained in popularity recently.

SANTA MONICA

You'll notice the family flavor of the Santa Monica beach area, particularly on weekends. When the local masses take to the waves, there is a good chance you will find most of them here.

Temescal Canyon, below Pacific Palisades, is the entrance for the main section of **Will Rogers State Beach.** This beach, three miles long, contains volleyball courts, rest rooms, showers, and lifeguards. It is extremely clean. Pack your own volleyball and be sure to arrive early on weekends; the parking areas fill up quickly.

Castle Rock—the section of Will Rogers north of the junction of Sunset Blvd. and PCH—is small and cozy. There is very good body surfing in this area. Farther south, at Santa Monica Canyon, is where you will find many famous people whiling away the hours between jobs. Will Rogers attaches to **Santa Monica city beaches** here for miles and miles of oceanfront fun.

Los Angeles Area Beaches

Avila Beach
● San Luis Obispo
Pismo State Beach

● Guadalupe

Lompoc

US 101

1

LOS PADRES NATIONAL FOREST

166

Gaviota State Beach
● Solvang
Gaviota

Refugio State Beach
El Capitan State Beach

Isla Vista
● Goleta
● Santa Barbara

San Miguel I.
Santa Rosa
Carpinteria State Beach
Seacliff

Santa Cruz

CHANNEL

Emma K. Wood State Beach
San Buenaventura Beach
● Ventura
McGrath State Beach
● Oxnard

ISLANDS

Anacapa I.

1

5

PACIFIC OCEAN

LOS ANGELES

San Nicholas I.

Area of map on facing page

● Long Beach

Seal Beach (Natl. Wildlife Ref.)

Santa Catalina I.

Huntington Beach

Newport Beach

Dana Point

Doheny State Beach

San Clemente

San Clemente State Beach
San Onofre State Beach

N W E S

0   30
Miles

San Clemente

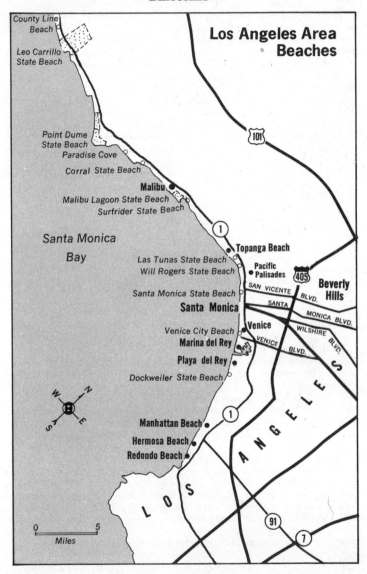

County Line
Beach

Leo Carrillo
State Beach

Point Dume
State Beach
Paradise Cove

Corral State Beach

Malibu

Malibu Lagoon State Beach
Surfrider State Beach

Santa Monica

Bay

**Los Angeles Area
Beaches**

101

1

Las Tunas State Beach
Will Rogers State Beach

Topanga Beach

Pacific
Palisades

405

**Beverly
Hills**

Santa Monica State Beach

SAN VICENTE BLVD.

Santa Monica

SANTA

MONICA BLVD.

Venice

WILSHIRE BLVD.

Venice City Beach

Marina del Rey

VENICE BLVD.

Playa del Rey

Dockweiler State Beach

LOS ANGELES

Manhattan Beach

1

Hermosa Beach

Redondo Beach

LOS

W N E S

0 5
Miles

91

7

Presently and historically Santa Monica is a beach haven. Families seeking solace from their daily routine and pleasure seekers have come here for many years. The old pier is standing, although almost a third of it has been washed away in severe winter storms. The pier and carousel (which is open on weekends) bring the visitor back to the time when beaches were synonymous with saltwater taffy and striped bathing costumes. Although updated with the latest electronic games, this is an interesting place in which to wander and imagine what it was like when movie stars and famous people came here for vacations. The movie *The Sting* used this pier as a backdrop to convey a sense of the past; it is still a great place to watch people. Fish eateries dot the pier; *The Lobster* at the beginning of the pier is one of the most popular.

Santa Monica also has Palisades Park, on a cliff above the ocean. Joggers, skaters, and walkers can enjoy a respite from the bright sun and a picnic amid this lush greenery. Just as Santa Monica is a beach community, it is also a thriving business community. Although many stores sell surfboards and bathing suits, others sell sophisticated "worldly" items. The recent revitalization of Main Street, which starts just blocks away from the beach area, has made Santa Monica an exciting place to spend a rainy afternoon.

For those who favor active beach sports more than rambling along the shore, there is the bike path. Bike-rental outlets and roller skate rentals can be found along the boardwalk. (See Venice section for bike and skate rental stores.) The bike path that goes for miles and miles starts in Santa Monica. This path follows the ocean, detours in Marina del Rey, then goes back to the ocean, and continues along the coast all the way south to Redondo Beach.

VENICE

If Santa Monica is where to go with the family for a peaceful day of fun, Venice is where to go for excitement and the exotic. People do not go to Venice to sit on the beach; instead, they take in the throng of people and activities on the boardwalk.

Venice began as the dream of Abbot Kinney who wanted to turn it into a replica of Venice, Italy. And for a while his dream came true. (There are still some canals to attest to this.) Hollywood stars used to flock here to take advantage of the romantic gondoliers and one of the largest roller coasters ever built.

Over the years the flavor of Venice has changed. It is a West Coast version of New York's Greenwich Village, and many of the same kinds of people live here—actors, writers, poets. There is also a large contingency of punk rockers sporting pink, green, and other lively shades of hair. The weekend is the best time to visit the boardwalk, which follows miles of beach, but it can be hard to find a place for your feet among a thousand others. Every inch of boardwalk seems filled with a roller skate or a bicycle wheel, or another intrepid pedestrian. The place is abuzz with street performers—musicians and comedians—in the summer. Swami X is a popular fellow; he spends some of his time here and the rest in Washington Square Park in Greenwich Village. There are also people in booths selling clothing, jewelry, souvenirs, and art. And when you get tired from all the walking, the *Sidewalk Café,* 1401 Ocean Front Walk, right near the Venice Pavilion, is a great indoor–outdoor café in which to sit and take in all the activity. And if you feel like treating yourself to lunch, dinner, or a pleasant drink, the *Sidewalk Cantina,* at 205 Ocean Front Walk, is a recent addition to the area.

If you'd like to join in the confusion, bicycle rentals are available at the *Venice Pier Bike Shop,* 21 Washington St. (399–8518), where they rent everything from five-speed two wheelers to tricycles.

For wheels that go directly on your feet, *Roller Skates of America,* 64 Windward Ave., and *Skatey's,* 22 Washington St., offer roller skates by the hour or by the day.

MARINA DEL REY

South a bit from Venice is the illustrious home of the "swinging singles," Marina del Rey. An extremely young and vibrant residential area and a visitor's delight, the marina is made up of a maze of boats, restaurants, shopping, great walking paths, and a beach. The main road through the marina—the largest man-made marina in the world—is Admiralty Way.

On one end is Via Marina, and just as the road curves is the location of the only public beach in the marina. A small crescent in the harbor area, this is a good beach for children because there are no waves. It can get very crowded on summer weekends, but the rest of the time it is fine. There is a public parking lot here, and it is a good place to start a walk around the area.

On the other end, on Fiji Way, is Fisherman's Village—a recreation of a Cape Cod-type fishing village. Interesting shops and restaurants line the street, and on the other side is the water and a good view of the thousands of boats docked in Marina del Rey.

The marina channel (near the beach—continue on Via Marina) is another great vantage point. Walk down the pier into the water, and you can see planes taking off from nearby LAX Airport every couple of minutes. To the right you can see north to Santa Monica and farther. And all around all kinds of sailboats and yachts are entering and leaving the channel. The area just north, known as the Marina Peninsula, boasts a wide beach that goes all the way to Venice. But during the summer the parking situation is impossible.

Admiralty Way is an oasis filled with many restaurants to refresh you after a busy day of walking, sightseeing, and sports activities. As a result of being filled with young professionals and many visitors from all over the world, the range of restaurants and the types of cuisine in the marina are staggering. From the exclusive, members-only (unless a guest of the hotel) Marina City Club to the new *Red Onion* for good Mexican food and dancing afterwards, this street is called Restaurant Row.

PLAYA DEL REY

Just south of Marina del Rey is Playa del Rey. At the turn of the century this was the site of one of the most popular seaside resorts in the area. It had a three-story pavilion, a restaurant, a bowling alley, a 50-room hotel, an automobile speed-racing track, and a boat-launching harbor. Holiday crowds used to rush here to ride two cable cars that offered a magnificent aerial view of the beach and mountains. This ended in 1913 when a fire destroyed everything.

Today Playa del Rey is still a popular beach community. The beach is wide and the surf is usually calm. Facilities include lifeguards, rest rooms, showers, drinking fountains, basketball courts, picnic tables, and barbeque grills. Ten yards from the beach is the lovely Del Rey Lagoon. This is a large plot of green grass surrounding a pond; and there are basketball courts and barbeque pits.

Outside Playa del Rey, going south to El Segundo, is **Dockweiler State Beach.** The landscape here is an eerie reminder of the industrial nature of Southern California: There is a steam-generating plant out in the water, a green structure with imposing smoke stacks. Perhaps not the most peaceful of beaches, with this view and the jets taking off from nearby LAX, this beach has one definite attraction: It is the unofficial site of hang gliding in southern California. It is thrilling to watch these daring men and women glide through the air on wings. Another reason to go to Dockweiler is the fact that it is the only Los Angeles beach with fire rings; if you want a primitive beach barbeque, this is the place. Firewood is sold along the beach, which has ample parking.

MANHATTAN BEACH

The South Bay communities begin here, and these beaches offer some of the cleanest sand and nicest settings in the area. Manhattan Beach is a small, young community, a health-oriented place; joggers, skaters, and runners can be seen on the street at all times.

It is said that when the Beach Boys went to the beach, this is where they came. They lived in nearby Hawthorne. The Manhattan Beach pier offers fishing; the pier pavilion, a roadhouse built in 1921, is covered with stucco and roofed with Spanish tile. Today the roadhouse is used by biology, geology, and chemistry students as an ocean-study center.

The beach is clean and has lots of room to spread out, but the only drawback is the parking—available only on the street. This beach is a hangout for teenagers in the summer. At night Manahattan Beach Blvd. becomes *the* cruising street. Just as the Beach Boys sang, the street is packed with cars of people who know each other, and the air buzzes with the sound of hundreds of radios.

There are a few establishments that have been around a long time and are almost a part of the community. Beach bars with a real local flavor include *Grunions, Brennan's* and *La Paz.* And for dining with a terrific view of the ocean there is *Orville and Wilbur.*

HERMOSA BEACH

Hermosa Beach (*hermosa* means beautiful in Spanish) is appropriately named: It stretches two miles along a lovely section of the coast. After the turn of the century this area was a summer haven for movie stars and other wealthy people. Today single-family homes and condominiums, along with some businesses and restaurants, line the Strand.

The beach itself is great for swimming and body and board surfing. Pole, bait, and tackle rentals are available at the Hermosa Beach Pier. Again, parking is only on the street.

The community of Hermosa Beach is artistically oriented. Small shops with unusual items line Pier Ave., one block east of the beach. And there are many good food establishments. *The Lighthouse,* 30 Pier Ave., offering great acts nightly, is the oldest jazz club in Southern California.

Twice a year, on Memorial Day and Labor Day weekends, local artists and artists from around the country come out en masse to the Fiesta de Las Artes—an arts and crafts festival.

REDONDO BEACH

The next stop along the beach is Redondo. Its marina is its main distinction. Although not quite as well known as Marina del Rey, *Kings Harbor* is quite similar, with boats, restaurants, and apartments overlooking the colorful port.

During the 1800s much of the shipping trade in Los Angeles was centered here, but with the opening of the harbor at San Pedro, that changed. Today Redondo's marina and beach area attracts sailing, swimming, and fishing enthusiasts from all over Southern California. Shops, restaurants, and fresh-fish stores abound on the Redondo Beach pier alongside the harbor. The *Murata Pearl Company,* 233K Fisherman's Wharf on the Redondo Pier (379-4915), is a unique jewelry store featuring pearls, rings, and pendants. Choose an oyster from the tank near the store window. Each one has a cultured pearl in it—sometimes two!

The beach itself starts at the pier and extends south about two and a half miles. Condominiums and single-family units line the Esplanade. This is where the bike path from Santa Monica ends. There are fire pits on the sand and volleyball courts at the beach.

Also near the marina is Seaside Lagoon, a warm saltwater pool dug out of the sand. Besides swimming, the lagoon area offers picnicking, a playground, and volleyball courts. Private parties can be arranged here for day or evening. There is an admission charge.

 WATER SPORTS. Los Angeles has abundant and diverse water recreation, including skin diving, snorkeling, surfing, sailing, pleasure boating, swimming, and wind surfing.

There are many **swimming pools** located throughout the area. Two of the most popular are Griffith Park Pool, at the intersection of Riverside and Los Feliz; and the Magnolia Pool at Magnolia Park, just off the Hollywood Fwy. at Magnolia, in the San Fernando Valley. Both are Olympic-sized; Magnolia Park also offers a second, smaller pool. Moreover the Magnolia Pool is in the middle of a lovely tree-lined park. Another popular pool, located in Exposition Park near downtown Los Angeles, is also Olympic size; in fact it was used in the 1932 Olympics. This pool is used for summertime recreation and for college meets.

If **paddle boating** is your idea of fun, you can do just that at MacArthur Park during the summer months. Loll about this man-made lake in the beautiful setting of palm and sycamore trees and dream to your heart's content. You can also rent small boats on Echo Lake, just a few minutes from downtown. Take the Echo Park exit from the Hollywood Fwy., and you'll find a small lake surrounded by eucalyptus and sycamore trees.

The Los Angeles City Department of Parks and Recreation (485–5515) will provide information on locations, fees, and hours of these city facilities.

For the intrepid sports person, **wind surfing** is at the height of popularity in Los Angeles. Rentals and lessons are available at *Wind Surfing West,* 4047 Lincoln Blvd., Marina del Rey (821–5501), and *South Bay Windsurfing,* 2027 Pacific Ave., San Pedro (519–1159).

Sailing enthusiasts can rent boats all around the Marina del Rey area. Among others: *Rent-A-Sail,* 13560 Mindanao Way (822–1868), offers 14- to 25-foot sloops, Hobie 16 catamarans, gas-powered boats, and lessons. Rent-A-Sail also has an outlet at 13757 Fiji Way in Fisherman's Village (822–2516). Here, again, they have sailboats for rent (no catamarans or lessons though) and electric power boats for public use.

For high-budget travelers, *Charter Concepts,* 13757 Fiji Way (823–2676), charters yachts, 40 to 140 feet long. Skippers are available for hire.

Fun Fleet, 13727 Fiji Way (822–1151), offers harbor cruises all year round. Boats leave every hour.

Boats offering sport fishing and sightseeing tours leave daily from the Redondo Beach Marina, 181 N. Harbor Drive (374–3481). Boat rentals are available here, but the reservation office is open Monday through Friday only, so be sure to call weekdays for a weekend boat.

 FISHING is a common pier activity in Los Angeles. *Malibu Pier Sport Fishing* (456–8030) offers two boats, both approximately 60 feet, for a group fishing experience. The full-day boat, leaving at 7:00 A.M. each day, features deep-sea fishing for rock cod in the winter and surface fishing during the summer. Surface fish such as halibut and bonita are regulars here, whereas warm summer waters attract bass and occasionally yellowtail and barracuda as well. Half-day boats, leaving at 8:00 A.M. and 1:00 P.M. daily, take you surface fishing all year around.

The *Pier Shop,* on the Venice Pier (399–0425), has pole rentals and live and frozen bait. And at the *Redondo Sport Fishing Company,* 233 N. Harbor Drive (372–2111), you can arrange half-day and full-day charters, excursions, and pole rentals.

A real California activity—grunion hunting—takes place on the beach from March through August. These small fish spawn on the beach at night, and finding them can be quite an experience. On the first day they are spotted each year, local tradition dictates that everyone meet them on the beach for a party. Grunions are edible, but they have a hard time swimming for miles and miles to spawn, so people interested in the environment go only to witness an interesting natural phenomenon.

See also *Water Sports,* above.

 PARTICIPANT SPORTS. Los Angeles is an athlete's paradise. Year-round sunshine, geographic variety, and a near-perfect climate combine to create the sport activist's haven. From hiking (or skiing in winter) in the mountains to surfing and swimming at the beaches, outdoor enthusiasts are certain to find ample recreation here.

Because Los Angeles is such a sprawling metropolis, it is advisable to do some planning with a map before attempting your sporting adventure. For instance, if you want to drop the kids at the beach and buzz on over to the San Fernando Valley for golf, you may find yourself spending the greater part of the day just traveling between activities. There are two excellent resources that will inform you of what activities are available in the area in which you are staying or the part of town you would like to see: The City of Los Angeles Dept. of Recreation and Parks, 200 N. Main Street, 13th floor, City Hall East, Los Angeles (485–5515), and Los Angeles County Parks and Recreation Dept., 433 S. Vermont Ave., Los Angeles (738–2961). These agencies are more than happy to assist in locating recreational areas for tennis, hiking, bridle paths, golf, swimming, basketball, soccer, shuffleboard, and so on.

Because the Los Angeles area is so large, and space in our book is so limited, listed below are only some of the more popular recreation facilities.

Golf. Golf courses abound in the Los Angeles area. In urban Griffith Park alone there are three public golf courses: *Harding Golf Course,* an eighteen-hole course at the entrance of Los Feliz Ave. and Riverside Dr.; *Wilson Golf Course,* another eighteen-hole course, also to be found by entering the park at Los Feliz and Riverside Dr.; and *Roosevelt Golf Course,* a very popular nine-hole course at the Vermont entrance. The Griffith Park courses are quite hilly.

Near Beverly Hills is the *Rancho Park Golf Course,* an eighteen-hole course at 10460 W. Pico Blvd., Los Angeles. Nearer the beach is *Penmar Golf Course,* a popular flat nine-hole course at 1233 Rose Ave., Venice.

In the San Fernando Valley, in what is referred to as the Sepulveda Dam Basin, lie perhaps the longest, straightest, flattest, fairways you might ever encounter. It is advisable to keep in mind that these courses have very little shade in summer. The courses include *Woodley Golf Course,* eighteen holes—

pure heaven for those who are prone to losing balls; there are no trees, brush, or water hazards on this course, which is located at 6331 Woodley Ave., Van Nuys. *Balboa Golf Course* at 16821 Burbank Blvd., Encino, offers eighteen holes. Here you will also find *Encino Golf Course,* an eighteen holer, Balboa's twin.

Other popular courses listed in "Golf Digest" include the *Riviera* at Pacific Palisades and *Brookside* in Pasadena.

Special pitch 'n' putt golf courses include *Holmby Hills,* an eighteen-hole course, at 601 Club View Dr., Los Angeles, and *Rancho Park,* a nine-hole, three-par course, at 10460 W. Pico Blvd., Los Angeles, alongside the regular course near Beverly Hills.

Driving ranges are available at the Balboa, Encino, Rancho Park, and Wilson courses, above.

Contact the Los Angeles City and County Parks and Recreation Depts. for more information, fees, availability, and additional courses.

Tennis. Courts, most of which are lighted at night, are located in most parks. Try Griffith Park's ample, well-lit courts at the intersection of Los Feliz and Riverside Dr. These courts, except for the daytime hours between 11:00 A.M. and 3:00 P.M., are rarely unoccupied. Be prepared to pay an hourly fee anywhere, unless courts are available at your accommodations. A popular pay-by-the hour tennis club, available to the public, is the *Racquet Center* in North Hollywood, at the intersection of Vineland and Ventura Blvd., near Universal Studios. For reservations, call 985–8686. You might also try The Racquet Center of Pasadena; for reservations, call 258–4178.

A few hotels offer tennis clinics, weekend classes, and make courts available to guests. The Century Plaza in Beverly Hills has eight outdoor rooftop courts featuring John Gardiner's famous clinics. The Sheraton Town House, at 2961 Wilshire Blvd., offers four indoor courts; Al Secunda, pro. The Ambassador Hotel, on the Wilshire Corridor at 3400 Wilshire, shares ten outdoor courts with a local private tennis club and offers clinics on weekends. The Los Angeles Bonaventure, downtown Los Angeles, reserves eight courts from the Los Angeles Racquet Club. The Marina City Club in Marina Del Rey has six outdoor courts for guests.

For additional club or tournament information, contact the Southern California Tennis Association, 609 N. Cahuenga Blvd.; 467–5151.

Racquetball and Handball. Rapidly becoming the most popular participant sport in the area. Courts for the sports are offered at most YMCAs for an hourly rate, and courts are also available at the *Racquet Center of Pasadena,* 258–4178, and at the *Racquet Center in North Hollywood,* 985–8686. Both centers are clean, fairly new, and offer equipment and locker rental. They have small sport shops in the lobby areas. Their courts are well lighted and clean.

Jogging. A national mania has swept everyone onto their feet. Angelenos jog everywhere: on sidewalks, along busy streets, in parks, or at high school and college tracks. The best place to jog, however, is definitely at the beach. There are miles and miles of sandy strand, and the air is not congested with smog, a real problem for visitors not conditioned to it. Redondo Beach maintains an area along the beach called "the Strand," designated especially for runners. Several marathons feature this course throughout the year.

Great Shape, a health club in Beverly Hills, offers free coed hiking and jogging clinics weekly. Clinics, featuring world-class marathoners, are also available twice a week. For information, call 820–6602. Great Shape is advertised as a women's health club, but classes are for both men and women.

Besides the beach, favorite places for jogging include San Vicente Blvd. from Brentwood to Santa Monica, where runners jog along a wide, grassy meridian under the shade of coral trees. This path ends at the Palisades high above the Pacific Ocean, where there are benches and grassy lawns to rest. Griffith, Will Rogers, and Elysian parks are all good places to run unobstructed from most traffic. Griffith Park is very hilly and crowds of motorists arrive on weekends. Generally, you will find the least amount of traffic on the valley side. Elysian and Will Rogers have light traffic, especially on weekdays. These roadways are also hilly. The *Sepulveda Dam Recreation* area in the San Fernando Valley offers jogging near the golf courses. This area is very flat, and the smog can be troublesome. For information and updates on races, pick up a copy of *Runner's World,* California Edition, at any newsstand.

Bicycling and Roller Skating. Both these sports are extremely popular and often vie with each other for the right of way, especially in the famous beach walkway between Venice and Santa Monica. The area is crowded, especially on weekends when everyone tries to crowd onto the paved pathways extending along the beach from the Santa Monica pier to the Venice pier. (The bike path actually ends farther south, to Redondo Beach.) There are plenty of rental shops in Venice and right under the Santa Monica pier.

Other areas are not recommended; bicycling and roller skating in unprotected areas can be dangerous.

There are, however, many roller skating rinks in the area: *Moonlight Rollerway Skating Rinks,* 5110 San Fernando Rd., Glendale, 241–3630; *Skateland* 18140 Parthenia St., Northridge, 885–1491 or 885–1142.

There is an excellent source book for the bicycle trouper who insists on cycling about the city: *Bicycle Touring in Los Angeles* by Weltman and Ellis; it's available in public libraries or in bookstores.

Exercising and Weightlifting. All the beautiful bodies on the beach in Los Angeles weren't born that way, they worked hard at it. If you wish to partake of some of that hard work here are a couple of places to do it: *Gold's Gym,* 364 Hampton Drive, Venice, (213) 392–3005 is world famous. The gym, open from 5 A.M. to 10 P.M. Monday through Friday, and 8:00 A.M. to 6:00 P.M. on weekends has a clientele of hard-core body builders. Nautilus machines and free weights are featured. The daily rate is $7.00, and the weekly rate is $20.00.

Exercising classes, from Jane Fonda's Workout (213–652–9464 in Beverly Hills or 986–1624 in Encino), to Holiday Health Spas, to YMCAs and YWCAs, are available all over the Los Angeles area. Check the local phone books for information about the gym or salon nearest you. (Remember that each area has separate phone books: North Hollywood, Glendale, Los Angeles, Beverly Hills.)

Horseback Riding. Horses are popular in the Los Angeles area, especially in the valleys, where most of the horse owners and stables are located. *Griffith Park* maintains bridle paths, and a free map is available at the Ranger Headquarters in the park, 4730 Crystal Springs Dr., 665–5188.

Azusa Canyon Stables rent horses and feature both western and English saddles; call 334-7000 for information and directions. Other stables for horse rental include *Hansen Dam Equestrian Center* in Lakeview Terrace, 896–6514; *Livingston Stables* in Burbank, 843–9890; and Sunset Hollywood Stable in Hollywood, 469–5450 (the latter offers at dusk a special "starlight" ride through Griffith Park over to Burbank on Fridays only).

Many more exciting adventures such as hang gliding (see also *Beaches,* above), soaring, glider flying, and hot-air ballooning can be found in the Riverside County and San Bernardino sections near the cities of Hemet, Perris, Antelope Valley, and Victorville. These areas are only a day's trip from Los Angeles.

Enjoy your stay and take advantage of our year-round sunny playground. Be certain to contact the state, city, and county park systems to ensure that you enjoy the 800,000 acres of recreational facilities available for fun and adventure in and around Los Angeles. (For further details, refer to the *Parks* section of this guide.)

HIKING. Most of the large city parks such as *Griffith, Brookside, Elysian,* and *Will Rogers* have wilderness paths. Griffith and Elysian perch atop the Hollywood Hills and offer spectacular views of downtown and Hollywood to the south or the Valley and the mountains to the east. When hiking, keep in mind that these are wilderness areas and that you may be hiking in an area that does not provide drinking water. Elysian Park features a wooded botanical area with a wide variety of trees. Please check the *Parks* section for further information.

Placerita Canyon Park in Newhall is especially geared to the hiker, for it has well-marked trails of varying length for the amateur hiker as well as the more seasoned hiker. Information is available on the natural wildlife and flora, and rangers are available for any questions. This canyon park is in dry, oak tree, rocky terrain typical of the San Gabriel Mountains.

In the Angeles National Forest are several hiking trails, including Spruce Grove, Mt. Lowe, and Altadena. These trails are in dry, mountainous regions, and drinking water is not available. For information on hiking in these areas, contact the National Forest Service Parks at 790–1151.

For further information on area hiking, outings, and so on contact the Sierra Club, 2410 Beverly Blvd., 387–4287.

WINTER SPORTS. Los Angeles area mountains offer many fine skiing opportunities from December to April. There are a dozen ski areas offering more than 150 ski runs and nearly 70 lifts and tows within a two-hour drive of downtown Los Angeles. With fickle California weather, the natural snowfall may not suffice, so most resorts have on hand artificial snow machines to ensure winter skiing. The resorts that use snow-making machines are Snow Summit, Snow Forest, Goldmine, Snow Valley, Mountain High, and Holiday Hill. Big Bear's snow-making operation is one of the largest in the world.

Regular runs can be found at *Mammoth* to the north and *Mt. Waterman, Mt. Baldy,* and *Kratka Ridge* much closer to home, a scant two-hours drive into the San Bernardino Mountains. A bit farther south in the San Bernardinos are *Goldmine, Snow Summit, Snow Valley, Big Bear, Arrowhead,* and *Table Mountain.* Most offer lifts and beginner's, moderate, and advanced runs. Rates tend to be somewhat lower than most resorts around the country.

Summit Express bus service to the Big Bear area departs from several Los Angeles locations. Combination fares are available for combination lifts and transportation at Ticketron. For information, call 460–6960. Advance lift tickets are a must for the Big Bear area. Also available is airport–ski transportation; call Mountain Air Service, (714) 585–2511. For reservations, package deals, or information, contact Big Bear Chamber of Commerce at (714) 866–4601 or Big Bear Lake's Tourist and Visitor Bureau at (714) 866–5878.

For any information on other ski area resorts, feel free to contact any sporting goods store; they are helpful and have the latest information on skiing and road conditions. *Sport Chalet,* at 951 Foothill Dr., La Canada (near Pasadena), (213) 684–0545, is very knowledgeable.

Ice Skating. This sport is very popular in the dry basin that has never experienced an icy winter. Try *Ice Capades Chalet Ice Arena,* 6100 Laurel Plaza, North Hollywood, 985–5555; also in Pasadena (818–578–0800) and Palos Verdes (541–6630); *Pickwick Ice Arena,* 1001 Riverside Dr., Burbank, 846–0032. Rinks have adjacent skating shops for rentals and sharpening and refreshment areas.

 SPECTATOR SPORTS. Angelenos are people on the move, whether it be jogging, running, surfing, playing tennis, or on through the whole gamut of indoor and outdoor sports. But when not participating themselves, they are avid fans, and there is never a day when you can't settle down into a stadium seat and see sporting action. Take your pick.

Baseball. Get the Dodger Blue Fever at the Dodger Stadium. The season starts early in April and runs through early October. For ticket information, call 224–1500.

Golf. The Glen Campbell Los Angeles Open will be played in late February at the Riviera Golf Course in Los Angeles. It starts on Wednesday with the pro-am. The big-money tourney starts on Thursday and runs through Sunday.

Thoroughbred Racing. At Santa Anita Park in Arcadia, the Los Angeles Turf Club continues the 1983–1984 meeting through April 23, Wednesday through Sunday. Then the Oak Tree Racing Association has its meeting October 3 through November 5. The $500,000 Santa Anita Handicap is run around late April. The 320-acre park is located at the junction of Huntington Dr. and Colorado Pl.

Starting late April and continuing through mid-July, Hollywood Park in Inglewood near Los Angeles International Airport offers sixty-six days of racing. Races are run Wednesday through Sunday, with special promotions on Memorial Day, the Fourth of July, and closing day. Post time is 2:00 P.M. The 350-acre park includes such features as picknicking in the infield, a fully supervised children's playgroup, gift shop, and a variety of restaurants. Total seating capacity is 34,000, with parking for 31,000 cars. For ticket information, telephone 419–1574.

Harness racing is at Los Alamitos. Prearranged group tours are available.

Basketball. The Los Angeles Lakers represent the NBA at its best at the Los Angeles Forum in Inglewood.

Boxing. At the Olympic Auditorium in downtown Los Angeles and at the Forum.

Boat Racing. Marinas in Los Angeles host all classes of sailboat races, and, on special occasions, powerboat competition and surfing contests.

Auto Racing. Long Beach Grand Prix, April 1–3, draws more than thirty of the world's top Formula One drivers and close to two hundred thousand spectators for the three days of celebrity and pro-racing. The course snakes around twelve turns and covers 2.13 mi. through the city's streets. Prize money tops $1.5 million. Ticket information is available from Long Beach Grand Prix Association, 110 W. Ocean, Suite A, Long Beach, CA 90802.

Collegiate athletics are not only big in Los Angeles but offer visitors the opportunity to see top-flight teams in action. The Bruins teams of the **University of California at Los Angeles** (UCLA) go nonstop virtually year round.

Basketball. Intersectional as well as Pacific 10 competition played at Pauley Pavilion at the UCLA campus in Westwood.

Football. First home game September 17 against Arizona State through the November 19 intercity clash with the University of Southern California (USC). All UCLA home games played at the Rose Bowl, Pasadena.

Baseball. Late January through mid-May; home games are played at the Jackie Robinson Stadium on campus.

Fencing. Late January through late March at the UCLA Men's Gym.

Rugby. On campus at the North Athletic Field, early January through early April.

Swimming. At the Sunset Canyon Recreation Center, early January through mid-February.

Volleyball. At Pauley Pavilion, late January through early April.

Track and Field. At Drake Stadium on campus, late February through late April. (Some meets are dual events with the women's track team.)

For UCLA ticket information and schedule details, call (213) UCLA 101.

The Trojans of the **University of Southern California** (USC) offer a full slate of collegiate athletics for visitors. Telephone: (213) 743–2620.

Basketball. Remaining 1983–84 season games start early in January; home games are played at the Sports Arena adjoining the USC campus and continue into early spring.

Football. The Trojans kick off their season on September 10 and wrap up against UCLA on November 19.

Baseball. Begins at Dedeaux Field on campus in late January and continues on through mid-May.

Volleyball. At the campus gym starting in late January and continuing through late April.

Regatta. Starts in March with crew races for men and women at the Los Angeles harbor, Berth 192, or Bellona Creek, and continues through May.

 BABYSITTING SERVICES. Don't be reluctant to bring the children to Los Angeles. Daytime activities are plentiful, and for those evenings when parents want to be out on the town, the city offers reliable babysitting sources.

Babysitters Guild, Inc., Agency. 469–8246. The largest babysitting agency covering the greater Los Angeles area, including the San Fernando and San Gabriel valleys and Beverly Hills. The agency, in business for over thirty-five years, is bonded and licensed by the state. There is a minimum fee of $17.50, travel included, with a four-hour minimum. The base rate after the first four hours is $5.50 per hour.

Finigan's. 393–0314. This babysitting guild covers Los Angeles beach areas, including Pacific Palisades and Santa Monica south to Playa Del Rey, plus West Los Angeles and Beverly Hills. There is a four-hour minimum at $4.00 an hour plus a $3.00 transportation fee. Babysitters are mature.

Babysitter's Guild. 797–7792. Servicing the Pasadena area, La Canada, and parts of the San Gabriel Valley, this guild charges a four-hour minimum of $20.50 (transportation included) and slightly higher fees for more than two children. The hourly base rate is $5.00 per hour.

We Sit Better. 997–1421. Covers the San Fernando Valley, Bel Air, and Brentwood. Four-hour minimum, $14; each additional hour, $3.50. Transportation fee, $3.50.

 CHILDREN'S ACTIVITIES. From the area's many amusement parks to the simple pleasures of a day swimming or playing in the sand at the beach to a trek to one of Los Angeles' excellent museums, this city will not fail to delight children. (For *Long Beach* and *Orange County* attractions, see the separate chapters at the end of the book.)

Places listed below are popular year-round attractions of special interest to children. The beauty of these southern California attractions is that they are not strictly kiddie oriented; adults will undoubtedly find as much pleasure in experiencing most of these activities as will the children.

A more comprehensive source of information on weekly children's activities is *The Los Angeles Times'* Sunday Calendar section that contains listings in the Family Activities column. This column includes announcements of special events oriented toward children, museum hours, exhibitions, and other current events that would be of interest to the entire family.

MUSEUMS

Beulah Hawkins Doll Museum and Hospital. 1437 Sixth St., Santa Monica; 394–2981. Nine rooms in one of Santa Monica's old mansions contain this doll museum and hospital. More than 3,000 dolls, including a 1765 Queen Anne Doll, French fashion dolls, and a Japanese samurai doll, are displayed. An animated doll house over 150 years old is a delight. Half-hour tours are conducted daily. If your child's doll gets "injured" traveling, this is the place to bring it to be mended. Open Friday and Saturday, 1:00 P.M. to 5:00 P.M. Call for current tour hours. Fee $2.50 for adults; $1.50 children.

Cabrillo Marine Museum. 3720 Stephan White Dr., San Pedro; 548–7562. A multilevel marine and nautical museum featuring aquariums with live sealife and exhibits of stuffed sharks, whales, and marine history. Children will love maneuvering nautical equipment and rummaging through old whale bones. The museum is adjacent to a grassy picnic area, playground, and the beach. Open Tuesday through Sunday, noon to 5:00 P.M. Closed Monday. Free.

California Museum of Science and Industry. 700 State Dr., Exposition Park, Los Angeles; 744–7400. With one section geared solely to children, this museum is also of great interest to adults. Each exhibit demonstrates a scientific or a mathematical principle, clearly labeled and explained. Children can operate the exhibits by punching buttons, twisting knobs, or pulling levers.

Children's Playce. Sherman Oaks Galleria, Ventura and Sepulveda Blvd., Sherman Oaks; 995–6031 or 995–3469. A hands-on museum with exhibits, workshops, an arts-and-crafts center, and Saturday-morning films. Parents get to shop in the giant mall, and children get to play—a fair trade. Monday through Friday, 9:00 A.M. to 5:00 P.M.; Saturday and Sunday, noon to 5 P.M. Admission free.

George C. Page Museum of La Brea Discoveries. 5801 Wilshire Blvd., Hancock Park, Los Angeles; 936–2230. In conjunction with the La Brea Tar Pits, the Page Museum houses the prehistoric fossils recovered from the Tar Pits. Excellent displays, films, and exhibits recreate the skeletons and histories of the prehistoric animals that once roamed the Los Angeles basin and have been perfectly preserved for thousands of years in natural asphalt. In the lab area, everyone is welcome to view the ongoing painstaking recovery of the fossils from the tar. During summer months an excavation on the grounds is usually in progress and can be viewed from a roped-off area. Open Tuesday through Sunday, 10:00 A.M. to 5:00 P.M. closed Monday. Adults, $1.50; 75 cents for students, children and senior citizens.

Kidspace. 390 S. El Molino Ave., Pasadena; 449–9143. A museum where kids can experiment with running a newspaper, talking to a robot, directing a radio or television station, or test skills in observation and changing environments. A special "Human Habitrail" challenges children by changing architectural environments and "Illusions" teases one's ability to perceive what is real and what is an illusion. Summer hours: Monday through Saturday, 10:30 A.M. to 1:00 P.M.; Saturday, 9:00 A.M. to 1:00 P.M. Closed in September. Winter hours (beginning October 4th): Monday, Wednesday, Friday, 2:00 P.M. to 5:00 P.M.; Saturday, 11:00 A.M. to 4:00 P.M. Adults, $2.00; children, $1.50.

Los Angeles Children's Museum. 310 Main St., Los Angeles; 687–8800. Near downtown, City Hall, and other government buildings, this museum offers art, science, and technology exhibits where children, for once, are asked to "Please Touch." This is a learning center where children participate in such adventures as "City Streets"; they are encouraged to crawl through a mock manhole cover and discover what goes on beneath the pavement or visit a replica of Los Angeles' KNXT newsroom. There is a large "Lego" room for kids to experiment with building. Huge fabric blocks are used for construction. Art and science projects are tactile, and all exhibits are geared toward participation. Summer hours: Tuesday through Friday, 11:30 A.M. to 5:00 P.M.; Saturday and Sunday, 10:00 A.M. to 5:00 P.M. Winter hours (beginning in late Sept.): Wednesday and Thursday, 2:30 P.M. to 5:00 P.M.; Saturday and Sunday, 10:00 A.M. to 5:00 P.M. Summer hours are observed during school vacations. Wednesday: Free. Saturday and Sunday: adults, $3.50; children and senior citizens, $1.75.

Lomita Railroad Museum. 2135 250th St., Lomita; 326–6255. Don't be surprised if you think you've gotten lost in this typical suburban neighborhood before you find the museum. Look closely, and you'll discover a replica of a turn-of-the-century Massachusetts train station. Beyond the gate, discover one of the largest collections of railroad memorabilia in the West. Climb aboard a real steam engine and take a look at the immaculate interior of the cab itself. Open Wednesday through Sunday, 10:00 A.M. to 4:30 P.M. Admission 50 cents.

Los Angeles County Museum of Natural History. 900 Exposition Blvd; 744–3430. See the skeletons of prehistoric animals, including the saber-tooth tigers, bison, mastedons, and camels, uncovered in the La Brea Tar Pits. There are also artifacts and relics of prehistoric man. In the "Hall of Gems" discover jewels in their natural forms as well as cut and polished. There's a stunning exhibit of diamonds, rubies, and sapphires. Open daily except Monday, 10:00 A.M. to 5:00 P.M. Admission: adults, $1.50 children, students and senior citizens, 75 cents.

Museum of Rock. 6427 Sunset Blvd., Hollywood; 463–8979. Located on the famous Sunset Strip, this small museum houses art, cover illustrations, and other artifacts of rock-and-roll. Changing exhibits feature photos and album covers of prominent rock artists. A video gallery offers a changing program of video disc performances ranging from the Doors to Rod Stewart. Call for admission and hours.

Southwest Museum. 234 Museum Dr., Los Angeles; 221–2163. If you enter this museum from Museum Dr., it will appear as if you're entering a cave or catacombs. Enjoy the displays and niches along the walls depicting native American Indian art and artifacts from west of the Mississippi. An elevator will take you to the main floor. There is parking on the ground floor level as well. The museum houses a fine collection of clothing, tools, pottery, bows and arrows, and dolls. Children will especially enjoy an authentic tepee set up in the center room. Free. A park is conveniently located nearby for relaxation. Open Tuesday through Saturday, 11:00 A.M. to 5:00 P.M.; Sunday, 1:00 to 5:00 P.M. Adults, $1.50; children and students, 75¢; children under 7, free.

FUN AND GAMES

Bob Baker Marionette Theater. 1345 West First St.; 642–3973. Two hours of charming puppet and marionette shows delight both children and adults. Watch fairy tales come to life on stage as the brightly costumed marionettes enact the stories. Children sit close to the stage and after the show are served refreshments. As a special treat, visitors are invited backstage to see how the puppets are operated. The staff is especially patient and attentive to children and even show the workshop where the puppets and marionettes are made. Reservations are necessary. Admission $4.00 children, $5.00 adults, $3.50 senior citizens.

Griffith Park Observatory. Atop the hill, on the south side of Griffith Park. The entrance at Los Feliz and Vermont is most convenient; 664–1191. One of the world's largest telescopes is open to the public for viewing every clear night. Exhibits display models of the planets with photographs from satellites and spacecraft. The adjoining Planetarium has dazzling daily shows that duplicate the starry sky. A guide narrates the show and points out constellations. A Laserium show is featured nightly, and other special astrology shows are offered frequently. Call the Planetarium for scheduling. The Observatory sits high above Los Angeles and from the outside decks and walkways offers a spectacular view of the city. Free. Shows: Adults, $2.25; children, $1.25.

Let's Put on a Show. The Roxy Theatre, 9009 Sunset Blvd.; 204–KIDS. In the San Fernando Valley, this unique afternoon club is strictly for kids. Children can enjoy assorted snacks and a two-act show by the "Too Short for Prime Time Players." Sundays only. Admission, $6.50. Reservations are recommended. Showtime, 2:00 P.M.

Los Angeles Philharmonic Symphonies for Youth. Dorothy Chandler Pavilion, Music Center, 135 N. Grand Ave.; 972–0703. January and February hour-long concerts with appearances by young guest artists. Call for fees and scheduling. Summer programs in conjunction with the Hollywood Bowl called Open House. 2301 Highland Ave., Hollywood; 850–2077. Weekday mornings. $2 per person. Call for scheduling.

Santa Monica Pier. At the end of Main St., Santa Monica, jutting out into the ocean, this pier, built in 1875, holds myriad fun and games places. Visit the arcade for old-fashioned amusement games or new electronic games. Ride on the merry-go-round, or purchase a bag of freshly fried potato chips. At the end of the pier you can rent bait and tackle to try your hand at fishing off the pier.

(You don't need a license to fish off this pier.) Many eateries and refreshment stands. Roller skates can be rented from shops in front of the pier, and paved paths for rollerskaters run alongside the beach to Venice pier about three miles away. Another option is to park your family on the beach and enjoy the ocean. A children's park is planned for the east end of the pier, to be completed by summer 1984.

Magic Mountain. Also known as Six Flags Magic Mountain, Valencia; 992–0884. 260 acres of rides, shows, and amusement-park entertainment. Colossus, the world's largest roller coaster, thrills adventure seekers. (See "Theme Parks" section, below, for details.)

Travel Town. 5200 Forest Lawn Dr., Los Angeles; 662–5874. Located on the east side of Griffith Park. A collection of airplanes, trains, and other early transportation replicas onto which the children can climb and play. The area is situated in a pleasant grassy park with ample picnic areas. A miniature train and one of Los Angeles's old trolleys take children for rides around a small track. Open daily 9:00 A.M. to 5:00 P.M. Free.

Treehouse Bookstore. 17322 Ventura Blvd., Encino; 986–7374. A vast bookstore catering to imaginative kids. Offers a wide selection of books for ages ranging from infants to fourteen-year-olds. An intriguing highlight of the shop is the collection of dollhouses and dollhouse furniture. Children can visit the workshop where the tiny furnishings and the dollhouses are built. Open Tuesday through Saturday from 10:00 A.M. to 5:00 P.M.

ZOOS

Los Angeles Zoo. Ventura and Golden State Fwys. intersection, Griffith Park; 666–4090, 666–5133, or 666–4650. The Los Angeles Zoo features five "continents" where the animals are grouped. A tram is available for stops at all areas. The zoo is beautifully landscaped, and areas for picnicking are available. The animals are in well-kept, spacious areas with imaginative settings for roaming or climbing. The *Children's Zoo* features a petting pen and an animal nursery. Spend a day and enjoy the zoo's newest family, koala bears from Australia housed in an area resembling their natural habitat, each with its own eucalyptus tree. (See main "Zoo" section, above, for further information.)

Marineland. 6610 Palos Verdes Dr., S., Rancho Palos Verdes; 377–1571. An aquatic zoo with shows featuring killer whales, sea lions, and dolphins. This park is a combination research facility and tourist attraction. Colorful tropical fish, sea horses and other seafaring creatures reside in aquariums simulating their natural habitat. Children can romp freely in the playground-and-games area. At Sea Lion Point, view sea lions in their natural habitat. At Baja Reef visitors swim with more than 2000 varieties of fish. (Adults must accompany children for swimming.) Open daily from 10:00 A.M. to 5:00 P.M.; mid-April through mid-June 10:00 A.M. to 6:00 P.M.; rest of the summer, 10:00 A.M. to 7:00 P.M. Admission adults, $9.50; senior citizens, $8.05; children, $6.85 (ages 3 to 11), free for children under 3.

SIGHTSEEING

Catalina Island. Take the two-hour boat trip from San Pedro or Long Beach and land in port at Avalon, Catalina's main city. There is so much to do in one day that you may want to consider staying in one of the many hotels. There are tours such as the glass-bottom boat tour (make certain that it's a sunny day), a boat cruise to see the seals on Seal Rock, or the all-day inland tour spotting wild goats and buffalo and a visit to the Arabian horse ranch. There are restrictions on automobiles, but Avalon is small enough to wander about on foot. Enjoy the beach and the many shops. Rent an electric cart or walk out to the Wrigley Botanical Gardens, an extensive cactus garden, or rent a horse for a scenic ride through the hills. Be prepared to spend the day; boats arrive in the morning and do not return to the mainland until afternoon. There is also air service to the island. (See "Long Beach to San Clemente," below, for details.)

Chinatown. Between Broadway and Hill Sts., Los Angeles. Wait until dark and enjoy the colorful hanging lanterns and lighted ornate buildings; shops are open until 9:00 P.M. Stroll through the shops or have dinner in a neighborhood bistro. A great opportunity to teach children how to use chopsticks.

Grand Central Market. Hill St. between 3rd and 4th, Los Angeles. Wander through this large marketplace with over fifty stalls containing everything from fresh fruit, vegetables, dairy products, meats, fish, and eggs to exotic spices. The fixtures are still intact from the 1930s. Glass cases display noodles and legumes of every kind. The mix of customers and vendors is as colorful as the produce. Expect to hear many languages. Don't eat before you visit, for you'll find something you can't resist.

Mann's Chinese Theater. Hollywood Blvd., Los Angeles. The famous Chinese Theater with a dramatic exterior that resembles a Chinese pagoda. Stand before the footprints, handprints, and signatures of the stars engraved in the cement sidewalk in front of the theater. Every member of the family will enjoy comparing feet and hands with the cement impressions. On Hollywood Blvd. is the famous "Walk of the Stars," where golden stars with the names of the famous are imbedded in the sidewalk. The "stars" continue to the intersection of Hollywood and Vine.

NBC Studio Tour. 3000 W. Alameda Ave., Burbank; 840–4444. A backstage tour of this huge studio complex takes you through sets and the makeup and wardrobe departments. Don't be surprised if you spot a celebrity on the way to a show's taping or rehearsal. (See "Tours," above.)

Olvera St. Near Sunset and Main, Los Angeles. The first settlement in Los Angeles. You can walk down the brick street and enjoy the buildings, some of which are authentic. Others were built to replicate an authentic, bustling Mexican village. Watch colorful dancing or tortilla making; have your picture taken in a fruit cart or astride a burro. Shop to your heart's content among the bounty of Mexican merchandise. Don't be surprised to hear English only as a second language; Spanish is predominant.

Universal Studios Tour. Universal City; 877–1311. This tour takes you on a tram to see sets, mock cities, special effects, and other aspects of the movie industry. Shows, which include talking birds, a Wild West fight with real stuntmen, and a trained animal show, are included with the tour. (See "Tours," above.)

THEME PARKS

Most of the area's amusement parks, including *Disneyland* and *Knott's Berry Farm*, are in and around Orange County. (See the separate chapter for Orange, below.) But the city proper does boast one large park worth checking out.

Six Flags Magic Mountain. Located in Valencia, this 260-acre park is one minute's drive west of Interstate 5 on Magic Mountain Pkwy., approximately one-half hour north of Hollywood; 992–0884. Open daily, Memorial Day to Labor Day, from 10:00 A.M. to midnight; rest of the year on Saturdays, Sundays, and school holidays: mid-September through October from 10:00 A.M. to 10:00 P.M.; November to Memorial Day from 10:00 A.M. to 8:00 P.M.

The roster of major rides includes the Roaring Rapids, a simulated white-water wilderness adventure complete with whirlpools, waves, and real rapids; the Colossus, the largest dual-track wood roller coaster ever built, offering two "drops" in excess of 100 ft. and experiencing speeds up to 62 mi. per hour; the Revolution, a steel coaster with a 360°, 90-ft. vertical loop; and the Electric Rainbow, an illuminated, revolving ride in a giant circle tilting upright almost 50°.

Children can enjoy Wizard's Village, a playground of bright colors, shapes, and textures, including a punching-bag forest, a rope bridge to the Wizard's Castle, and a giant "Swiss cheese" with a maze of tunnels. Children's World is a minipark with scaled-down rides, such as the Red Baron's Airplane and the Little Sailor Ride. Reservations can be made for a child's birthday party, complete with cake, ice cream, and punch, at the Birthday House.

Other attractions of this park include a puppet theater, celebrity musical revues, Dixieland jazz, rock-and-roll concerts, and the Aqua Theater high-diving shows. Spillikin's Handcrafters Junction is a four-acre compound in which craftsmen exhibit skills and wares from blacksmithing to glassblowing.

There are many styles of food service available for dining pleasure. The Timber Mill offers hearty American food; Old El Paso's menu travels throughout Mexico; Valencia Terrace features farm-style breakfasts; and the Potato Patch serves fried chicken and fresh French fries crisped in almond oil. Also at your service are countless stands for munching hot dogs, hamburgers, cotton candy, and beverages.

Admission fees for adults are $11.95; for children under 48 inches in height the fee is $5.95; under two are admitted free. Admission includes all rides, attractions, shows, and special events. Major credit cards are accepted. From late May to early September the park is open daily; during the remainder of the year, it's open weekends and school holidays.

HISTORIC SITES. When Los Angeles celebrated its bicentennial in 1981, the event came as something of a shock to many Americans. Until then most people had assumed that Los Angeles came into being in the 1920s or thereabouts.

The city's historical heritage has not only been carefully preserved, but active restoration projects are taking place all the time. There is a great deal to be seen that pre-dates the arrival of moving pictures.

On busy Broadway in downtown Los Angeles is the amazing **Bradbury Building** (304 S. Broadway), built in 1893 and among the city's most remarkable architectural achievements. Inside the Italian Renaissance building is a Victorian world of elaborate grillwork, French-made wrought-iron railings, and decorations with Belgian marble and Mexican tile.

Also downtown is **El Pueblo de Los Angeles State Historical Park,** site of the founding of the city in 1781. It is located in the middle of today's modern city. Spread around the Old Plaza is Olvera St., which recalls the city's rich Mexican beginnings. Historical buildings include the Pelanconi House (now a restaurant), the Old Plaza Church, the Garnier Building, and the Merced, the city's first theater, which has a Bicentennial exhibit inside. Avila Adobe at 14 Olvera St., a historic house with antique furnishings, was built in 1818. Free walking tours of the area are available on an hourly basis, from 10:00 A.M. to 1:00 P.M., Tuesday through Saturday. Meet at 130 Paseo de la Plaza.

Watts Tower, 1765 E. 107th St., is the folk art legacy of an Italian immigrant tile setter, Simon Rodia. From 1920 until 1954, without helpers, he erected three cement towers embellished with bits of colored glass, broken pottery, and assorted discards. Plans are underway to stabilize and protect this unique monument, often compared to the twentieth-century architectural wonders created by Barcelona's Antonio Gaudi. Well worth a pilgrimage for art and architectural buffs (or anyone else, for that matter).

In Hollywood, the **Hollywood Studio Museum,** once known as the Lasky Barn, is directly across from the Hollywood Bowl, in the Fairfield parking lot. In December 1913, an upstart movie company rented part of a barn at Vine and Selma Ave. in what was then a quiet, rural Hollywood and began production on *The Squaw Man,* Hollywood's first feature film. The movie was completed on February 15, 1914, and the credit was given to the Jesse Lasky Play Co., which later became Paramount Studios. Sam Goldwyn was the producer and Cecil B. De Mille was the director. As the Lasky company grew, part of the barn was torn down and the remainder was used for storage. In 1926 the structure was moved from Selma and Vine to Paramount's Marathon St. lot, where it became the studio gym. In 1956 it was designated a California state landmark, and in 1980 Paramount donated it to the Hollywood Chamber of Commerce, which moved the barn to its present location. Now, aged and decrepit, the barn faces an uncertain future.

The **Banning Residence** in Wilmington is an interesting twenty-four-room Greek Revival mansion. In Pasadena is the Renaissance-style *Wrigley Mansion,* now home of the Pasadena Tournament of Roses Association. Free guided tours of the 18,500 sq-ft mansion at 391 S. Orange Grove Blvd. are held every Wednesday from 2:00 to 4:00 P.M., February through September. The surrounding Wrigley Gardens cover four and one-half acres and are open to the public daily. Free parking on nearby streets.

Gamble House, a noted Pasadena landmark built in 1908, is an outstanding design by Greene and Greene. It reflects a heavy Oriental influence. Also in Pasadena, the **Huntington-Sheraton Hotel,** built in 1907, features the Viennese Room containing duplicates of King Ludwig's Bavarian chadeliers. On the twenty-three acres of landscaped grounds are the Horseshow and the Japanese Gardens and the Picture Bridge. Admission free. For reservations, call the Concierge Desk, 792–0266.

Antiques are among the collection of functional fine art at the **Merle Norman Classic Beauty Collection** at Sylmar, California, which includes a collection of 100 antique, classic, and luxury automobiles; a music room filled with music boxes, mechanical instruments, a watch collection, and the Louis XV Dining Room, featuring a muraled ceiling and crystal chandelier, circa 1680. Free tours daily, Tuesday through Saturday. For tour information and reservations, call 367-1085.

MISSIONS

In 1768, when the Russian interest in Alaska was perceived to be a possible prelude to southward expansion, King Charles of Spain ordered the colonization of California. The king's decree launched the missions, which provided the seminal growth for California.

Under the astute leadership of Father Junipero Serra and Father Fermin Lausen (each founded nine missions), the gray-robed Franciscans moved slowly northward. By 1823 a chain of twenty-one missions extended 600 mi. from San Diego to Sonoma. Approximately a day's travel apart in those days (30 mi.), the missions dotted the coastal route called El Camino Real. Today US 101 parallels the historic Mission Trail, one of the state's most popular tourways.

Two of these missions are found in Los Angeles County. The first, **Mission San Fernando Rey de Espana,** is located at the north end of the San Fernando Valley in Mission Hills, 15151 San Fernando Mission Blvd.

This mission was established and named in honor of the thirteenth-century King Ferdinand III of Spain in 1797. Fifty-six Indians joined the mission to make it a self-supportive community. Soon wheat, corn, beans, and olives were grown and harvested there. In addition, the mission workshops produced metal-work, leather goods, cloth, soap, and candles. Herds of cattle, sheep, and hogs also began to prosper.

By 1833, after Mexico extended its rule over California, a civil administrator was appointed to the mission, and the priests were restricted to religious duties. The Indians began leaving, and what had been flourishing one year before became unproductive. Thirteen years later the mission, along with its properties (the entire San Fernando Valley, as we know it today), was sold for $14,000.

During the next forty years, the mission buildings were neglected; settlers had stripped roofing tiles, and the adobe walls were ravaged by the weather.

Finally, in 1923, a restoration program was initiated that resulted in a recovery of the rustic elegance and the feeling of history within the mission walls.

Today, as you walk through the mission's arched corridors, you may experience *deja vu*—that feeling of having been there before—and you probably have, vicariously, through an episode of *Gunsmoke, Dragnet,* or dozens of motion picture epics. The large two-story convent building is the largest adobe structure in California today. The mission plaza consists of a grand fountain, lushly planted gardens, and a bell tower. The church's interior, especially its walls, are decorated with Indian designs and artifacts of Spanish craftsmanship depicting the mission's eighteenth-century culture. Also at the mission is a small museum and gift shop.

The Mission San Fernando Rey de Espana is open every day from 9:00 A.M. to 5:00 P.M. Admission: for adults, 75 cents; for children ages seven to fifteen, 25 cents; children under seven are admitted free.

Self-guided tours of the mission are possible, as are group tours, which can be arranged on Monday and Thursday afternoons. For information, call 361-0186.

How to get there: From downtown Los Angeles, take the #5 Fwy. north approximately fifteen mi to San Fernando Mission Blvd. Exit west, and follow San Fernando Mission Blvd. one mi directly to the mission.

The other old mission, the **Mission San Gabriel Arcangel,** is located west of downtown Los Angeles in San Gabriel at 537 W. Mission Dr.

Over 200 years ago, Father Junipero Serra dedicated this mission to the great Archangel and messenger of God, Saint Gabriel. As the founders approached the mission site, they were confronted with savage Indians. In fear of battle, one of the padres produced the canvas painting *Our Lady of Sorrows.* This so impressed the Indians that they laid down their bows and arrows. This miracle produced a painting, which is on display at the mission today. Within the next fifty years, the San Gabriel Arcangel became the wealthiest of all California missions.

In 1833 the Mexican government passed the "Decree of Desecularization," and following their confiscation of the mission, it began to decline, as did the Mission San Fernando Rey. In 1855 the United States government returned the mission to the church. Unfortunately, by this time the Franciscans had departed. Not much happened until 1908, when the Claretian Fathers (the Missionary Order of the Sons of the Immaculate Heart of Mary) took charge. In the following years much care and respect was poured into the mission.

Today Mission San Gabriel Arcangel's adobe walls preserve an era of history unchanged by the outside world. The magnificent cemetery tells the history of the mission through the people that lived, died, and were buried there. Over 6,000 Indians stricken by horrible cholera and smallpox epidemics in 1825 are buried in the cemetery.

You may walk through the grounds and admire such utilitarian spots as the soap and tallow vats, the tannery, the aqueduct, the kitchen, and the winery.

The magnificent church and museum house relics reflecting the history of the padres and early visitors to San Gabriel.

And, to give visitors some sense of the scope of the California mission chains, the Court of Missions established in 1921 has models of each of the twenty-one missions still standing today. There is a gift and souvenir shop.

Hours at the museum are from 9:00 A.M. to 4:00 P.M. every day of the week. Admission is $1.00 for adults; 50¢ for children. For further information, call 282–5191.

How to get there: Take Interstate 10 (San Bernardino Fwy.) from Los Angeles to New Ave. Follow New Ave. and Ramona St. north to the mission.

 LIBRARIES. The public libraries are composed of the city, the county, and the metropolitan cooperative library systems. As a result of these combined systems, one can find public libraries in most neighborhoods. At the hub is the *Central Library* in downtown Los Angeles; 626–7555, 630 W. 5th St. (at Flower); 626–7461; it's the largest library west of Chicago. It offers such specialties as local business information, a California history room, U.S. patent information, music scores, published plays, and a special children's library. It might be interesting to spend a couple of hours in the genealogy room and trace your family tree. The building itself, designed by Bertram Goodhue in 1925, is an interesting mix of Art Deco and International syles, with interior murals depicting the history of California. Walking tours are conducted every Saturday at 12:30 P.M. and on weekdays by reservation.

The *Huntington Library, Art Gallery, and Botanical Garden.* 1151 Oxford St., San Marino; 792–6141 or 681–6601. Formerly magnate Henry E. Huntington's estate, it became a public institution in 1928. The Art Gallery's prize collection of eighteenth-century paintings includes Gainsborough's *Blue Boy,* Lawrence's *Pinkie,* and works by Reynolds, Turner, and Blake. The library is open for scholarly research only, but it does feature a public exhibit of literary treasures, including a Gutenberg Bible, the earliest known manuscript of Chaucer's *Canterbury Tales,* a first edition of the King James' Bible, and Benjamin Franklin's original autobiography. The Botanical Garden has the world's largest cactus collection, a Japanese garden, and a camellia garden (in bloom February through April). No picnics or pets. A refreshment room is open to the public. Maps can be acquired at the main gate.

The *UCLA Library System.* 405 Hilgard Ave.; 825–1323. It is made up of eighteen campus libraries, including the University Research, Architecture and Urban Planning, Dickson Art (specializing in Renaissance art and da Vinci), Biomedical, Chemistry, Geology–Geophysics, Music (orchestration and scores), and Theater Arts (motion picture and television scripts, motion picture poster collection, and the entire British Film Institute catalog on microfilm).

Take Sunset from the 405 Fwy. east two miles to Hilgard; turn right (south) to Wyton and turn right into the parking lot, where there is an information booth. Parking, $2.00. Ask for the University Research Library, where at the reference desk you can obtain a free guide to the entire library system.

The *Brand Library* in Glendale. 1601 W. Mountain (near Grand View); 956–2051. It specializes in the arts. The library has an art gallery (the exhibit changes monthly) and a small auditorium for recitals and lectures (with a fall concert series). The Brand also contains a vast record collection, including full-length plays on records, as well as art exhibition catalogs and an historic calendar collection.

An excellent library on the east side of town is the *Pasadena Public Library*. 285 E. Walnut; 577–4037. Its specialties are an extensive architectural book collection, with an emphasis on Pasadena and California architecture, and collections of dance and photography materials. The library is part of the Pasadena Civic Center. Built in the late 1920s, this complex includes some of the city's most beautiful examples of Mediterranean-style architecture. Ask about group tours.

And on the west side is the *Santa Monica Public Library*. 1343 6th St.; 451–5751. It features a Santa Monica history section and an art gallery with displays of works by local artists.

Another library specializing in the arts is the *Beverly Hills Public Library*. 444 N. Rexford; 550–4721. It houses a large collection of books on nineteenth- and twentieth-century art and also has many artists works on slides. Various films, video, cassettes, audio cassettes and records are available for circulation. There is a special section on classical ballet.

SPECIAL-INTEREST LIBRARIES

Los Angeles has a great number of special-interest libraries. Some of the more notable ones (listed below) are swayed toward the life-style of Los Angeles. They emphasize art, film, and sports.

Art. *Los Angeles County Museum of Art Library.* 5905 Wilshire Blvd.; 857–6118. Books covering the collection in the museum, including Indian and Southeast Asian art, Islamic art, and European sculpture. Research only.

Los Angeles Insitute of Contemporary Art. 2020 S. Robertson Blvd., Beverly Hills; 559–5033. Slides on contemporary artists (mostly Californian).

Craft and Folk Art Museum Library. 5814 Wilshire Blvd.; 937–5544. Local, national, and international folk arts and crafts. Artists' slide registry. Also, an audio tape series of living folk artists in Los Angeles. Reference only.

Film. *Margaret Herrick Library,* Academy of Motion Picture Arts and Sciences. 8949 Wilshire Blvd.; 278–4314. Numerous periodicals and scripts relating to the film industry. Research only.

The Warner Library. 110 N. Glenoaks Blvd., Burbank; 847–9743. General historical information on people, fashion, and life-styles, including a vast number of historical and current newspaper clippings. Of particular interest to costumers, decorators, and writers. Research only. A fee is charged by the hour.

Handicapped. *Braille Institute of America Library.* 4205 W. Melrose Ave. (at Vermont); 660–2880. Books in Braille, records, and cassettes for the blind, including the most current best sellers on tape.

Law. *The Law Library.* 301 W. 1st St.; 629–3531. Laws and codes of all fifty states and the federal government. Extensive foreign law coverage.

Medicine. *USC Medical Library.* 2025 Zonal Ave. (near Exposition Park); 224–7231. One of the finest medical resources, specializing in drug abuse and pharmacology.

UCLA Biomedical Library. 405 Hilgard Ave.; 825–6375. A fine medical library, part of the UCLA Library system.

Natural History. *Natural History Library.* 900 Exposition Blvd.; 744–3387. Located in Exposition Park, this Los Angeles County facility offers information on zoology, botany, earth sciences, and anthropology. Research only.

Sports. *First Interstate Bank Athletic Foundation Sports Library.* 2141 W. Adams Blvd.; 614–2995. Books on sports from archery to yachting. Sports guides dating back to the 1880s. Olympic Games coverage.

Ralph Miller Golf Library. 1 Industry Hills, City of Industry; 965–0861. History of golf from its beginning through today. Memorabilia on exhibit.

 MUSEUMS. When referring to the visual arts of Los Angeles, moving pictures rather than those of canvases and sculpture come to mind. The varied collections in the county's museums and galleries have long been overshadowed by its celluloid counterpart of the movie and television industry.

From the Norton Simon Museum of Art in Pasadena, celebrated for its collection of Old Master paintings, sculpture, and tapestries, to the avant-garde exhibits of its many galleries, Los Angeles offers a broad range of art forms. (Art Galleries are covered in a separate section, below.)

The permanent collections housed at the Los Angeles County Museum of Art (LACMA), Norton Simon, and J. Paul Getty Museums can be enjoyed in a variety of architectural and landscape creations. LACMA offers a lovely garden featuring sculpture by Rodin, Calder, and Lieberman (to name a few) and the La Brea Tar Pits, imprinted by prehistoric dinosaur paws. The sleek, wood paneled halls of the Norton Simon create a wonderful environment to view art.

The Getty is an ambitious reproduction of the Villa dei Papiri, a first-century Roman villa excavated in 1750 from the slopes of Mount Vesuvius. A member of the Los Angeles art scene controversial for its $1.3 billion endowment by Getty Oil, the museum's power in the American art market is unparalleled.

Soon to be added to this exciting museum scene is the $700 billion project for the development of the Museum of Contemporary Art, proposed for an eleven-acre Bunker Hill site in downtown Los Angeles. Expected to open in late 1984, the 100,000 sq ft will contain the first permanent modern collection in this very modern city.

The following Los Angeles museums are all in the 213 area code.

The California State Museum of Science and Industry. 700 State Dr. in Exposition Park; 744–7400. The second largest museum of its kind in the country (the Smithsonian in Washington, DC, is first). Fourteen exhibition halls present mind-boggling scientific concepts in a stimulating way that all ages can understand. Visitors participate in making machinery work by pushing buttons

The J. Paul Getty Museum

Upper Level

The J. Paul Getty Museum

Main Level

West Porch

Greek Masterpieces

Attic Memorial Sculpture

Study Collection

Late Classical & Hellenistic Sculpture

Hall of Aphrodite

Atrium

Room of Colored Marbles

Etruscan Vestibule

Basilica

Book Store

Villa Display

Temple of Herakles

South Porch

Entrance

Vestibule

Mosaics

East Vestibule

Changing Exhibits

and pulling levers. IBM's mathematics exhibit simplifies theories of multiplication and probability through the use of moving displays. General Motor's turning wheel demonstrates the workings of an automobile through the use of visual aids and visitor participation. Pacific Telephone and Southern California Edison both offer fascinating permanent exhibits relating to their respective industries. The Hall of Health illustrates the workings of the human body with an elaborate arrangement of visuals describing blood circulation, the nervous system, and the reproductive system, among others. Watch more than 150 baby chicks hatch every day in the Animal Husbandry Hall. Open every day, 10:00 A.M. to 5:00 P.M. Free.

Craft and Folk Art Museum. 5814 Wilshire Blvd.; 937–5544. This museum was established in 1973 for the study, the preservation, and the exhibition of the world's contemporary crafts and folk arts. The museum's collections include Japanese, Mexican, American, and East Indian folk art, folk textiles, Indonesian masks, and contemporary crafts. Six to eight major exhibitions are planned each year. The museum Library and Media Resources Center are open to the public. The Museum Shop carries displays of merchandise relating to each current exhibition as well as quality work by expert craftspeople, folk art from around the world, original postcards, and educational materials. Located on the mezzanine of the museum, overlooking the exhibitions, is the Egg and the Eye Restaurant, which serves soups, salads, desserts, and forty exotic varieties of omelettes. The museum's educational programs present classes, films, lectures, and concerts in the museum and in the community. Open Tuesday through Sunday, 11:00 A.M. to 5:00 P.M. Free.

Francis E. Fowler Jr. Museum. 9215 Wilshire Blvd., Beverly Hills; 278–8010. Beyond a simple, modern façade is housed an outstanding collection of European and Asiatic decorative arts assembled by Francisco E. Fowler Jr. over a period of nearly sixty years. More than twenty categories of objects ranging from a collection of extremely rare and unusual firearms to ship models and one of the world's finest silver collections are displayed. The last spans four centuries and contains a variety of English, early American, and Continental silver. Also on display are ceramics, glass, shells, paperweights, and other *objets d'art.* Open Monday through Saturday, 1:00 P.M. to 5:00 P.M. Free.

The J. Paul Getty Museum. 17985 Pacific Coast Hwy., Malibu; 459–8402. Founded by oil magnate J. Paul Getty, the museum contains one of the country's finest collections of Greek and Roman antiquities in a classical building that is a recreation of a first-century Roman villa. The Main Level houses the Greek and Roman antiquities collection, which includes marble and bronze sculpture, mosaics, vases, and examples of various minor arts, such as household items. Of particular interest are the fourth-century Attic stelai (funerary monuments) and Greek and Roman portraits. The decorative arts collection (Upper Level) features furniture, carpets, tapestries, clocks, chandeliers, and small decorative items made for the French nobility and the royal household from the early years of the reign of Louis XIV to the age of Napoleon. Some of the objects are displayed in paneled rooms of the period. All major schools of Western art from the late thirteenth to the early twentieth centuries are represented in the painting collection, which emphasizes Renaissance and Baroque art. The collection includes works by Masaccio, Rembrandt, Rubens, de la Tour, Van Dyck, Gainsborough, and Boucher.

The museum itself has an interesting history. Getty began collecting art in the 1930s, concentrating on the three distinct areas that are represented in the museum today: Greek and Roman antiquities, Baroque and Renaissance paintings, and eighteenth-century French decorative arts. Between 1945 and 1946 he purchased a large Spanish-style home on sixty-five acres of land in a canyon just north of Santa Monica, near Los Angeles. In December 1953, the J. Paul Getty Museum was officially established in part of the house to display the many art objects Getty had collected. But by the late 1960s the museum could no longer accommodate Getty's collection, and he began to review proposals for expansion. He finally decided to build an entirely new museum building. Completed in 1974, this building and its gardens cover about ten acres of the total Getty property; the remaining fifty-five acres and the original house have been inherited by the museum as part of Getty's estate. Indeed, with the receipt of Getty's estimated $1.3 billion bequest upon his death in 1976, the museum became the most richly endowed art museum in the United States.

The new museum building is a recreation of the Villa dei Papiri, a luxurious first-century Roman villa that stood on the slopes of Mount Vesuvius overlooking the Bay of Naples. Located just south of the ancient city of Herculaneum, the villa was the home of wealthy patrician families and is thought to have once belonged to Lucius Calpurnius Piso, the father-in-law of Julius Caesar. The two-level, thirty-eight-gallery building and its extensive gardens (which include trees, flowers, shrubs, and herbs that might have grown 2,000 years ago at the Villa dei Papiri) provide an appropriate and harmonious setting for Getty's collection of Greek and Roman antiquities. (Museum plan on preceding pages.)

The museum offers concerts at 1:30 P.M. every third Thursday of the month in the upstairs Baroque Painting Gallery. The bookstore carries art books, reproductions, calendars, and a variety of scholarly and general-interest publications. A self-service lunch is available in the indoor/outdoor Garden Tea Room. Open Tuesday through Sunday, mid-September through mid-June, 10:00 A.M. to 5:00 P.M., Monday through Friday, mid-June through mid-September. Closed major holidays. Free. Parking reservations are necessary. They should be made one week in advance by telephoning or writing to the museum's Reservations Office.

Hebrew Union College and Skirball Museum. 3077 University at 32nd St. and Hoover St.; 749–3424. An important museum that opened in Los Angeles in 1972, the collection comprises Judaic art, Palestinian archaeology, and anthropological material from the Negev Desert. Also in the collection are rare manuscripts, historic coins and medals, ceremonial art, ancient Israeli artifacts, and an extensive display of paintings, graphics, and sculptures. The museum offers a unique opportunity to explore Judaiism and its history and culture through esthetic and material treasures of the Jewish people. The museum itself is of architectural note because of its series of arches representative of the ten commandments. Open Tuesday through Friday, 11:00 A.M. to 4:00 P.M. Closed Monday and Saturday. Free.

The Huntington Art Gallery. 1151 Oxford Rd., San Marino; 792–6141. On 207 acres that also include the Huntington Library (see the *Library* section) and the Huntington Botanical Gardens (see the *Garden* section), this art institution is devoted primarily to British art of the eighteenth and early nineteenth centuries. French furniture, decorative objects, and sculpture of the same periods are also included in the collection. Displays existing as domestic settings of the appropriate era are inside the original Huntington residence. The collection consists of such world-famous paintings as Gainsborough's *Blue Boy,* Lawrence's *Pinkie,* and Constable's *View of the Stour.* A new 37,000-sq-ft pavilion, complete with orientation center, information kiosks, an introductory slide show, bookstore, a conservation center for rare books, and a garden court, serves as an entrance to the grounds. Open Tuesday through Sunday, 1:00 P.M. to 4:40 P.M. Reservation tickets required for Sunday only by writing to the address above (zip code 91108). Free.

Los Angeles County Museum of Art. 5905 Wilshire Blvd.; 937–2590. Founded in 1913 as part of the Los Angeles County Museum of History, Science, and Art, the Museum of Art became a separate county institution in 1961. The museum is a complex of three major buildings—the Ahmanson Gallery, the Frances and Armand Hammer Wing, and the Leo S. Bing Center—surrounded by the B. G. Cantor Sculpture Garden. The four-story Ahmanson Gallery, built around a central atrium, houses a permanent collection of paintings, sculptures, graphic arts, costumes, textiles, and decorative arts from a wide range of cultures and periods, prehistoric to present. Included are works by Picasso, Rembrandt, Veronese, Dürer, Hals, de la Tour, and Homer. One of the Western world's largest collections of Indian, Nepalese, and Tibetan art is housed here. A two-level addition to the gallery, completed in the fall of 1982, has provided an additional 30,000 sq ft of space for exhibiting items from the museum's ever-growing collection. Major changing exhibitions are presented in the Frances and Armand Hammer Wing, which also houses the museum's Contemporary Art Galleries.

Currently under construction, the Robert D. Anderson Building will be completed by 1985. This 75,000 sq ft gallery will be located at the front of the present museum complex in what is now the Lower Plaza. Special exhibitions of 20th Century art from the museum's permanent collection will be housed on the 2nd and 3rd floors. The new building will increase the museum's available exhibition space by 50 percent. Another addition (planned completion: 1985) is the Pavilion for Far Eastern Art, which will house paintings of the Edo Period (17th-18th Centuries.)

The Leo S. Bing Center contains the Art Rental Gallery, the Bing Theater, the Art Research Library, and the indoor/outdoor cafeteria-style Plaza Café. The museum offers the community many cultural activities, including film series (with special senior citizens matinees), concerts, lectures, tours of the collections, and student programs. The Art Research Library, with more than 75,000 volumes and an extensive collection of slides, is open for scholarly research. The

Museum Shop features a selection of books, magazines, postcards, posters, antiquities, jewelry, and gifts. Family Weekend, sponsored monthly by the museum, offers demonstrations of crafts, workshops, plays, and mime performances. Open weekdays 10:00 A.M. to 5:00 P.M. (except the second Tuesday of each month, when hours are noon to 9:00 P.M.) and weekends 10:00 A.M. to 6:00 P.M. Closed Mondays, Thanksgiving, and Christmas. Adults, $1.50; children and senior citizens, 50 cents. Free admission second Tuesday of each month.

The Natural History Museum of Los Angeles County. 900 Exposition Blvd. in Exposition Park; 744-3411. The fourth largest natural history museum in the United States covers a span of history ranging from the prehistoric to the present. So many aspects of history are presented here that all couldn't possibly be absorbed in one visit. Opened in 1913, the 400,000 sq ft museum contains more than thirty-five halls and galleries displaying permanent as well as special, temporary exhibits. The main building is an attraction in itself. Spanish Renaissance in structure, the museum contains travertine columns, walls, and domes. An inlaid marble floor heightens the overall effect of magnificence. The museum is rich in its collection of prehistoric fossils, both reptile and mammal. It also houses an extensive bird and marine-life exhibit, as well as a vast display on insect life. A brilliant array of stones can be seen in the museum's *Hall of Gems and Minerals.* In addition, the museum features an elaborate taxidermy exhibit of North American and African mammals in their natural habitats. The settings are excellent replicas of the real thing.

Exhibits typifying various cultural groups include myriad African masks and tribal art, artifacts of the Western American Indians, and a display of crafts from the South Pacific. *The Hall of American History* presents everything from the paraphernalia of prominent historical figures to old American cars.

A gift shop features ethnic arts. Other facilities include a bookstore, parking, access for the handicapped, and a cafeteria. Free documentary films are shown every Saturday at 2:00 P.M., and free chamber music concerts are presented every Sunday at 2:00 P.M. Open Tuesday to Sunday, 10:00 A.M. to 5:00 P.M. Closed Monday. Admission: adults, $1.50; senior citizens, sixty-two and over, students with ID, and children from five to seventeen, 50 cents. Free admission the first Tuesday of every month.

Pacific Asia Museum. 46 N. Los Robles Dr., Pasadena; 449–ASIA. Built in the 1920s, this museum is listed in the National Register for Historic Places. Designed in the style of a Chinese imperial palace courtyard, it is highlighted by a traditional Chinese garden. The museum's collection contains a group of objects from Pacific and Asian cultures, including Australia, Japan, and China. Most of the objects are on loan from private collections and other museums; there is a constant flow of changing exhibits. A bookstore and a gourmet food center, which deals in foods, spices, and kitchen implements from the Pacific–Asian world, are also on the premises. The extensive research library there can be used by appointment only. Open Wednesday through Sunday, 12 noon to 5:00 P.M. Donation requested; no set fee.

George C. Page Museum and **La Brea Discoveries.** 5801 Wilshire Blvd.; 936-2230. A satellite of the Los Angeles County Museum of Natural History,

Los Angeles County Museum of Art

Ahmanson Gallery contains the permanent collections, special exhibitions, and an information desk.

Frances and Armand Hammer Wing contains changing major exhibitions, contemporary art, and the Conservation Center.

Leo S. Bing Center contains the Bing Theater, Plaza Cafe, education programs, Junior Art Workshop, travel programs, research library, slide library, art rental gallery, and ticket sales for concerts, films, and lectures.

Los Angeles County Museum of Art
AHMANSON GALLERY

Atrium Level

Pre-Columbian Art

Atrium

Chinese Art

Southeast Asian Art

African Art

Japanese Art

Ancient Art

Assyrian Reliefs

Ancient Near Eastern Art

Japanese Art

Plaza Level

16th-18th Century European Art

European Art

European Art

16th-18th Century European Art

16th-18th Century European Art

16th-18th Century European Art

Atrium

Information Desk

European Art

Indian Art

Curator's Gallery

Los Angeles County Museum of Art

Third Level
AHMANSON
GALLERY

European Art
1850-1950

European Art
1850-1950

Early
20th Century

Late 19th, Early
20th Century

Middle
19th Century

Early
19th Century

18th and early
19th Century

American Art

Atrium

European Art 1850-1950

New York School
Painting

Rodin
Sculpture

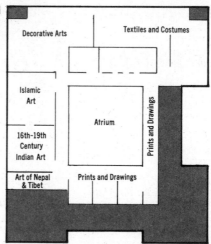

Fourth Level
AHMANSON
GALLERY

Decorative Arts

Textiles and Costumes

Islamic
Art

16th-19th
Century
Indian Art

Atrium

Prints and Drawings

Art of Nepal
& Tibet

Prints and Drawings

La Brea Discoveries
George C. Page Museum

Points of Interest

1) Hancock Park
2) Dual image Saber-Tooth
3) Large Ground Sloth
4) Tar pits
5) Antique Bison
6) Fossil bones
7) Mastodons
8) American Camel
9) Fossil exhibit
10) Small Ground Sloth
11) 9,000-year-old La Brea Woman
12) Imperial Mammoth
13) Fossil Birds
14) Giant Condors
15) History of Rancho LaBrea
16) Wall of Dire Wolf Skulls
17) American Lion
18) California Saber-Tooth
19) Excavation and research
20) Fossil Exhibit
21) Fossil Dating
22) Plant evidence
23) Ice Age Horse
24) Saber-Tooth family
25) The George C. Page Story
26) Paleontology Laboratory

the George C. Page Museum is located at the site of the La Brea Tar Pits formed about 35,000 years ago when deposits of oil rose to the earth's surface, collected in shallow pools, and coagulated into sticky asphalt. Animals fleeing predators stumbled into these pools and became trapped. The deposits have proved to be the richest source of Pleistocene (Ice Age) fossils in the world: Over 100 tons of fossil bones have been removed in the seventy years since excavations began there. Exhibits include reconstructed, life-size skeletons of mammals and birds whose fossils were recovered from the pits—saber-toothed cats, mammoths, wolves, sloths, eagles, and condors. Several large murals and colorful dioramas depicting the history of the Pleistocene are displayed in the well laid out museum building. The glass-enclosed Paleontological Laboratory permits easy observation of the ongoing cleaning, identification, and cataloging of fossils excavated from the nearby asphalt deposits. *The La Brea Story* and *Dinosaurs, the Terrible Lizards* are fifteen-minute documentary films shown every twenty minutes in the museum's two one hundred twenty-five-seat theaters. The Children's Concepts Exhibit displays letters and drawings sent by children who have toured this intriguing museum. Open Tuesday through Sunday, 10:00 A.M. to 5:00 P.M. Closed Mondays, Thanksgiving, Christmas and New Year's Day. Admission: adults, $1.50; children and senior citizens, 75 cents. Free admission the second Tuesday of each month.

Norton Simon Museum of Art. 411 W. Colorado Blvd., Pasadena; 449–6840. The museum's contemporary, clean design is in direct contrast to the vast display of European masterpieces it houses. The spaciousness enhances viewing of the tasteful, uncrowded, and often intimate display of top-class paintings, prints, tapestries, and sculpture. Originally the Pasadena Museum of Modern Art, the institution was reorganized by businessman Norton Simon in 1974 and through his family and corporate foundations has assembled one of the world's finest collections, rich in the works of Rembrandt, Goya, Degas, and Picasso.

Three Rembrandt oils—*The Bearded Man in the Wide Brimmed Hat, Self-Portrait,* and *Titus*—illustrate the development of the artist's painting style. The collections contain an extensive selection of Rembrandt etchings as well as Goya prints. Goya is also represented in two important oils: his dramatic painting *St. Jerome* and the three-quarter length portrait of *Dona Francisca Vicenta Chollet y Caballero.* On descending the expansive walnut and steel curved staircase, you enter the Degas gallery, which contains his paintings and enchanting ballerina modèles.

A comprehensive Picasso collection, including paintings, drawings, sculptures, and prints, exhibits memorable examples dating from 1899 to 1971. The well-known *Woman with Book* is one of many outstanding oils in the collection.

For those who love Impressionist painting, the Norton Simon Museum provides a collection containing choice works by van Gogh, Matisse, Cezanne, Monet, Renoir, and others. Picasso's *Point de la Cité,* Braque's *Still Life with Pipe,* and Gris' *Still Life with a Poem,* plus other Cubist paintings, represent the museum's modern schools of the twentieth-century collection.

The oldest works in the museum's collection are from Southeast Asia and date from 100 B.C. Bronze, stone, and ivory sculptures are from India, Kashmir,

Cambodia, Thailand, and Nepal. The controversial tenth-century Indian bronze *Shivapuran Nataraja*, believed stolen and smuggled out of India, highlights the Asian collection and is on loan from the Indian government until 1986.

The earliest pieces of Western art are works from the Early Renaissance. Among them are magnificent panels by Pietro Lorenzetti, Guariento's altarpiece, and Giovanni de Paolo's *Branchini Madonna*. Raphael's *Madonna and Child with Book* and other paintings by masters of the fifteenth and sixteenth centuries, such as Filipino Lippi, Memling, Bassano, and Lucas Cranach, illustrate the esthetic and technical developments of the Renaissance.

Of the Baroque style are several fine works by the well-known master Sir Peter Paul Rubens. Dutch masters of the seventeenth century are represented by excellent works of notable landscapes, portraits, still lifes, and genre scenes by Frans Hals, Jacob van Ruisdael, and Jan Steen. The Zurban *Still Life with Lemons, Oranges, and a Rose* is a superb example of Spanish Baroque and is one of the collection's great masterpieces.

The Norton Simon also boasts delightful works by the major artists of the Rococo period, notably, the impressive Tiepolo ceiling and works by Chardin, the popular eighteenth-century French still-life painter.

A welcome respite halfway through an afternoon of picture gazing is the sculpture garden, with its elegant fountain and reflecting pool, as well as monumental pieces by Maillol and Matisse's *The Backs*. At the entrance you are greeted by a larger-than-life (Rodin) sculpture, one of many displayed outside the museum and occasionally between galleries.

The Norton Simon is a nonprofit corporation operated for the cultural benefit of the community at large; it does not house touring exhibits. Distinctive lighting and imaginative displays reflect the museum's pride, as do its personable and eager-to-help staff.

An extensive bookstore at the museum offers art books of all periods. Of particular interest are books on Oriental art for the collector and contemporary photography, fine selections of original prints, posters, and greeting cards, including reproductions from the collection.

Because the museum has no dining facilities, it is best to lunch before venturing in. Private group tours are offered at $250.00 per group; the museum recommends arrangements for groups of approximately twenty-five, and so the cost can be divided into a more affordable amount.

Open Thursday through Sunday from 12 noon to 6:00 P.M. Admission: adults, $2.00, for students and senior citizens, 75 cents. General admission on Sundays: $3.00. Admission includes a free art reproduction from the collection. Parking is free.

The Norton Simon Museum of Art is located at the corner of Colorado and Orange Grove Blvd., Pasadena, near the junction of the Foothill (I-210) and Ventura (SR-134) Fwys. and can be easily spotted upon exiting the freeway.

Southwest Museum. 234 Museum Dr.; 221–2163. Set atop Mt. Washington and built in the early California Mission style with a commanding view of the city. A respected collection of Indian artifacts. Notable is a collection of prehistorical rock art and tools and Poole Indian baskets. Also worthwhile are Navajo

Rugs and Pueblo pottery. Open Tuesday through Saturday, 11:00 A.M. to 5:00 P.M. Free.

OTHER MUSEUMS

Pasadena Historical Society and Museum. 470 W. Walnut St., Pasadena; 577–1660. Housed in the former Finnish Consulate (built in 1905) are original furnishings, antiques, and paintings owned by the Feynes–Paloheimo family. The art features works by Carl Oscar Borg, William Keith, and Benjamin Brown. Also on the premises is the Finnish Folk Art Museum in the Finlandia Gardens, with folk art and antique furnishings. Open Tuesday, Thursday, and the last Sunday of the month from 1:00 P.M. to 4:00 P.M. Admission is $2.00.

Will Rogers State Historic Park Western Art Collection. 14253 Sunset Blvd., Pacific Palisades; 454–8212. Each of the thirty-one rooms in this house once owned by the humorist Will Rogers is packed with examples of Western art, including works by Charles Beil, Charles Russell, Howard Chandler Christy, and Ed Borein. Indian crafts are also abundant here. (See the *Parks* section.) Open from 8:00 A.M. to 7:00 P.M., daily. Admission: $2.00 per vehicle; 50 cents for dogs.

The Los Angeles Children's Museum. 310 N. Main St.; 687–8800. Opened in 1979, this museum offers educational exhibits oriented to the environment of children. Located in a large, modern building in the Los Angeles Mall, the store has educational toys and children's books. Open Saturday and Sunday, 10:00 A.M. to 5:00 P.M.; Wednesday 2:30 P.M. to 5:00 P.M. Admission: adults, $3.50, senior citizens and children, $1.75. Children under 2 are free.

Kidspace. In 390 South El Molino, Pasadena; 449–9143. A participatory museum, this former school gymnasium is designed to provoke thinking and stimulate curiosity among the younger generation. A Space and Technology exhibit introduces the world of computers, and a ranger spacecraft shows how solar power works. Dr. Feelbetter's Clinic teaches about the human body. Open Monday, Wednesday, and Friday, 2:00 to 5:00 P.M., Saturday from 11:00 A.M. to 4:00 P.M.; during the summer, from 10:30 A.M. to 1:00 P.M., Monday through Saturday.

SPECIAL-INTEREST MUSEUMS

Hollywood Studio Museum (originally called the Lasky Barn). In Hollywood across from the Hollywood Bowl; 874–BARN. Hollywood's first major film-company studio, which produced the first feature-length film, *The Squaw Man,* starring Dustin Farnum. In 1927, the barn became Paramount Pictures, with the original company of Jesse Lasky, Cecil B. De Mille, and Samuel Goldwyn. The museum shows the origin of the motion-picture industry. Open 8–5 daily.

Dunbar Museum of Black Culture and History. 4233 S. Central Ave., Los Angeles; 233–7168. On the site of the Dunbar Hotel (named for the poet), this was America's first hotel built by and for black people. Since its dedication in 1976, each guest room has been dedicated to a different black personality. Hours: By appointment only. Free.

The Forest Lawn Museum. at 1712 S. Glendale Ave., Glendale; 254–3131. A small museum of original art and reproductions of art masterpieces. Included are works by Frederic Remington, Charles Russell, and Jesse Beasley. Open 8:00 A.M. to 5:00 P.M., daily. Free.

Hawkins Doll Museum. 1437 Sixth St., Santa Monica; 394–2981. There are more than 3,500 dolls in this museum. They date from the 1500s to the mid-1950s. Dolls of many countries are represented and presented in this 1890s home. Open Fridays and Saturdays, 1:00 to 5:00 P.M.; tours on the hour. Admission: adults, $2.50, children $1.50.

Simon Wiesenthal Center Holocaust Museum. At the Yeshiva University of Los Angeles, 9760 West Pico Blvd.; 553–9036 or 553–4478. Audio visuals, graphics, photomurals, and other exhibits portray the events of Nazi Germany from 1933 to 1945. A mechanized information center answers common questions about this period. Lectures and public outreach program. Open Monday through Thursday, 10:30 A.M. to 4:30 P.M.; Friday, 10:30 A.M. to 2:30 P.M.; Sunday, 11:00 A.M. to 4:00 P.M. Free.

Hollywood Wax Museum. 6767 Hollywood Blvd., Hollywood; 462–8860. Opened some forty years ago. Trailers of Academy Award films are shown in the Oscar Movie Theater. Open Sunday through Thursday, 10:00 A.M. to 12 midnight; Friday and Saturday, 10:00 A.M. to 2:00 A.M. Admission: adults $4.00, senior citizens and 13–17 $3.00, 6–12 $2.00; under 6 free with adult.

Museum of Rock Art. 6427 Sunset Blvd.; 463–8979. The city's newest special-interest museum (it opened in 1981). Rock-music works by rock artists, and album cover art, are on display. Exhibits change every four to six weeks. In the permanent collection are a Video Theater showing early rock concerts, interviews, and old television shows. Call for hours and admission.

Wells Fargo History Museum. 444 South Flower Street, Los Angeles; 683–7166. More than 1,000 items on display cover more than 130 years of Wells Fargo history. Old West artifacts, fine art, photographs, documents, and famous collections are arranged in five areas depicting the evolution of Wells Fargo. Hours: Monday through Friday, 9:00 A.M. to 4:00 P.M. Closed on bank holidays. Admission free.

 MOVIE THEATERS. Spending two hours in a movie while visiting Los Angeles is not, as one might think, taking time out from sightseeing. Some of the most historic and beautiful theaters in the country are found here. They host first-run and revival films worth seeing if only to visit the famed movie palaces.

Perhaps the most celebrated movie theater in the world, *Mann's Chinese Theater,* 6925 Hollywood Blvd.; 464–8111, preserves the legend of Hollywood in cement. Formerly owned by Sid Grauman, the Chinese pagoda structure still carries out the oldest of Hollywood traditions, the hand- and foot-printing ceremony.

From Burt Reynolds to *Star Wars'* robots C3P0 and R2D2, today's stars are immortalized in the spirit of Sid Grauman, who founded the theater in 1927.

There are many stories about the origin of the ritual. The one most frequently circulated is that Norma Talmadge was the first to leave her impression in cement when she accidentally stepped onto the wet pavement while attending the theater's grand opening in 1927. The romantic tale is faithful only to the stuff of which Hollywood legends are made; the truth being that the imprinting rite was actually inspired by the mason who supervised the construction of the theater's forecourt.

Grauman came upon Jean W. Klossner, a French immigrant, as he put his handprint in wet cement near the marquee after he finished laying the entrance to the theater. A descendent of generations of French masons, Klossner explained that his father, grandfather, and great-grandfather had placed their handprints and signatures at the curbstone of Notre Dame in Paris to mark their contributions to civilization. Inspired by Klossner's family tradition, Grauman immediately offered the Frenchman a thirty-four-year contract to place the imprints of Hollywood's greatest stars in the secret cement mixture that Klossner had devised to stand the test of time.

Mary Pickford and Douglas Fairbanks were the first to place their hand- and footprints at the entrance to the theater at the grand opening ceremonies on May 18, 1927. Today the Chinese houses three movies and still hosts many of Hollywood's gala premieres.

Also owned by Sid Grauman was the great *Egyptian Theater* down the street at 6712 Hollywood Blvd.; 467–6167. Built before the Chinese in 1922, this theater was the site of many premieres. Now run by United Artists, the theater features a triple-screen facility for first-run movies, and the lobby maintains the ornate Egyptian decor for which it was made famous.

A contrast to Grauman's theaters is the *Cinerama Dome* on Sunset Blvd., one block west of Gower Gulch; 466–3401. This futuristic, geodesic structure was the first theater designed specifically for Cinerama in the United States. The gigantic screen and multitrack sound system create an unparalleled cinematic experience.

Movie listings are advertised daily in the Calendar section of *The Los Angeles Times* and the Style section of *The Herald Examiner.* Capsule reviews and schedules are also found in *The LA Weekly* and *LA Reader,* two free weekly publications stacked in coffee shops and book and record store entrances. The most common price of admission to first-run movies, as of this writing, is $5.00.

The less prestigious movie houses usually offer a double bill for a good price. They may not feature first-run engagements, but chances are you'll find two movies close in theme (SciFi, suspense, romance, etc.) sharing a bill at the Chinese only months before. In Hollywood: the *Fairfax 1, 2, 3,* 7907 Beverly Blvd., Fairfax, 653–3117; the *Gordon,* La Brea and Melrose, 934–2944; the *Oriental,* 7425 Sunset Blvd.; 876–0212, and *Pan Pacific,* 7554 Beverly Blvd.; 938–7070. These theaters house interesting films that you might not have felt warranted the $5.00 admission upon their release but can't be passed up for $2.50. The same bargain can be found in West Los Angeles and the Wilshire district at the *Clinton,* 526 N. Western; 461–3064; *Culver 1,2,3,* 9820 W. Washington Blvd.; 838–1893; the *Palms,* 3751 Motor; 837–7171. The *Aero* in Santa

Monica on Montana at 14th St.; 395–4990, and the *Brentwood 1 and 2,* in Brentwood, 2524 Wilshire Blvd.; 829–3366, are comparable theaters found on the West side. The environment at these theaters varies from architecturally unique to not so desirable, but the price is the draw.

Los Angeles art houses bill revival, foreign films, and animation festivals on neon-decorated marquees preserved to convey the original feeling of the neighborhood movie theaters. On the West side, the *Nuart,* 11272 Santa Monica; 478–6379, the *Fox Venice,* 620 Lincoln; 396–4215, and the *Beverly Cinema,* 7165 Beverly Blvd.; 938–4038, celebrate Hollywood's greatest with mini-film festivals featuring certain directors or performers, controversial documentaries, or notable foreign films. The *Rialto Theater,* S. Pasadena, 1023 S. Fair Oaks Blvd.; 799–9567, is a richly decorated, spacious house that has not been converted into multiscreen theaters as have most large, older theaters in town. The *Vagabond Theater,* 2509 Wilshire Blvd.; 387–2171, specializes in musicals and vintage drama and comedy films. Programs change daily, though theme and foreign film festivals run one night a week over a six- to eight-week period.

In Hollywood the sixty-year-old *Vista Theater,* 4473 Sunset Dr. (Sunset Blvd. at Hillhurst Ave.); 660–6639, and the *Tiffany,* 8534 Sunset (on Sunset Strip); 659–6738, like other neighborhood houses, run nostalgic double bills and special late shows on weekends for trendy films. For the past three years the *Tiffany, Nuart,* and *Fox Venice* have been the homes of such midnight cult classics as *The Rocky Horror Picture Show, Pink Flamingos,* and *Eraserhead.*

Melnitz Hall at UCLA runs a mixture of the old, the avant-garde, and the neglected. And the true film purist should definitely check out the Los Angeles County Museum of Art's *Bing Theater,* at 5905 Wilshire Blvd.; 857–6201. It regularly runs exhaustive tributes to greats from America cinema, obtains the finest prints available, and provides well-researched program notes for all their double bills. Call for programs; admission price is $3.00. No talking or eating allowed during the films, which are presented for serious filmgoers, who prefer to watch without interruptions.

The Laemmle Theaters host the best of the latest foreign releases. *The Music Hall,* 9036 Wilshire Blvd., Beverly Hills; 274–6869 and the *Royal Theater* in West L.A., 11523 Santa Monica Blvd.; 477–5581 are the forerunners of the other foreign houses that include the *Westland Twin,* Pico and Overland Sts., West Los Angeles; 474–9589, and the *Los Feliz,* 1822 N. Vermont; 664–2169.

Los Angeles is a twelve-month film festival because of its variety of theaters and unique programs. Each year the Filmex Society brings innovative and controversial films to the capital of the film industry by presenting the *Los Angeles International Film Exposition.* The nonprofit organization was founded in 1971 by a number of industry faithfuls, including director George Cukor and actress Rosalind Russell. The annual event runs in the spring, usually March and April, although the 1984 festival will run just prior to the Olympics in early July. Plans are underway for a permanent film center with year-round programming. For information, call 469–9400.

DANCE. In the past ten years, dance has grown considerably in Los Angeles. Because of the geographics of the city, theaters that present this art form cannot be found in any specific location. There is no special season for dance in the city, but there is always someone dancing somewhere.

One delight found at the Dorothy Chandler Pavilion at the Music Center during the Christmas season is the *Los Angeles Ballet* performing *The Nutcracker Suite.* The Los Angeles Ballet Theater is a nine-year-old company with John Clifford as founder and artistic director. The company, with 30 dancers, has a repertoire including both classic and modern dance. Recently, however, the company has had some trouble finding a theater to call its own. At press time (mid-1983), the company was uncertain where it would be performing in the coming year. For more information call (213) 464–0444.

In the summer, the outdoor John Anson Ford Theater presents "Dance Kaleidoscope," a gathering of local dance companies (ballet, modern, and jazz), each performing one or two of their specialties and collectively making quite an impressive showing.

UCLA (405 N. Hilgard; 825–2953) has three performing halls; one can usually find dance being performed in one of them. Companies that appear regularly at UCLA include *Bella Lewitzky* (Los Angeles based modern dance; the Lewitzky company expects to move to the proposed California Plaza Arts Complex, downtown near the Music Center, in 1984.), the *Trokaderos,* and *Lar Lubovitch,* as well as many local modern and jazz dance ensembles. At the Dorothy Chandler Pavilion (the Music Center, 135 N. Grand; 972–7211), ballet predominates. Such companies as the *American Ballet Theater,* the *National Ballet of Cuba,* the *Royal Ballet,* the *Stuttgart Ballet, Twyla Tharp* (modern dance), and the *Ahman Folk Dance Ensemble* have been featured at the Dorothy Chandler. The *Joffrey Ballet,* formerly of New York City, is now Los Angeles' official resident dance company. The Music Center has been chosen as the new home of this most eclectic ballet company. The Joffrey is known as a company whose repertoire includes classic dances as well as innovative contemporary pieces. Some full-length ballets that are possible choices for the Joffrey's Los Angeles repertoire are "Taming of the Shrew," and, if funding is available, "Romeo and Juliet" and "Cinderella." The Shrine Auditorium (649 W. Jefferson; 749–5123) usually schedules a ballet program in March, but programs may vary from year to year. The American Ballet Theater and the Chinese Ballet are companies that have appeared there. In Pasadena, the Pasadena Civic Auditorium (300 E. Green; 449–7360) has staged the American Ballet Theater, whereas the Ambassador Auditorium (300 W. Green; 304–6161) has presented New York's Eliot Feld Ballet Company.

In the summertime, the Greek and John Anson Ford outdoor theaters are popular places to view dance. The Greek Theater (2700 N. Vermont; 460–6300), located in Griffith Park, has the *Royal Canadian Ballet* and several ethnic dance companies. The John Anson Ford Theater (2850 Cahuenga Blvd. East; 972–7200) presents "Dance Kaleidoscope" and various local dance companies that perform throughout the summer.

An extremely efficient source of dance information in Los Angeles is the *Los Angeles Dance Alliance.* Give the alliance a call at 937–9586 when you're in town and find out who's performing where; they are most helpful and can answer any questions regarding local dance companies.

For a weekly listing of dance performances, consult the Sunday Calendar section of *The Los Angeles Times.*

Dance in Los Angeles continues to grow. The Dance Gallery has been proposed for downtown Los Angeles. It is expected to contain five rehearsal studios and a theater for year-round performances.

The visiting dancer will find that Los Angeles has an abundance of worthwhile dance studios throughout the city. Here are a few of the major ones; they offer everything from ballet and jazz to tap and modern: The *Debbie Reynolds Studio* in the San Fernando Valley (6514 Lankershim Blvd.; 985–3193); the *Dupree Dance Academy,* Hollywood (8115 W. 3rd St.; 655–0336); the *Los Angeles Dance Center,* near downtown (3100 Wilshire Blvd.; 381–6003); the *Marinaccio School of Dance,* Hollywood (6535 Santa Monica Blvd.; 462–1816); the *Stanley Holden Dance Center,* Westwood (10521 W. Pico Blvd.; 475–1725); and *Studio A* in the Los Feliz/Silverlake area (1947 N. Hillhurst Ave.; 661–8311).

MUSIC. Los Angeles is no doubt the focus of America's contemporary music scene. Hundreds of recording studios and over twenty record companies are headquartered here. Performers and songwriters from all over the world converge on the city seeking gold-record manna in this musical mecca. As a result, the hills around Hollywood are quite literally alive with the sound of live music.

The Los Angeles Times Calendar section provides a daily listing of current as well as upcoming events, as does the Style section of *The Herald Examiner.* The *Times'* Sunday Calendar and the *Herald's* Friday Weekend sections are expanded forms that provide considerably more detail. There are also helpful listings of the wide variety of musical goings-on in southern California in *The LA Weekly, The LA Reader, Los Angeles* and *California* magazines. (All phone numbers listed, unless otherwise indicated, are in the 213 area code.)

CLASSICAL AND OPERA

After years of being regarded as a cultural invalid, Los Angeles has finally come into its own as a center for the performing arts.

The Music Center, 135 N. Grand Ave.; 972–7211, was opened less than twenty years ago and, along with the Hollywood Bowl, is the center of the city's classical music scene. The Music Center can be reached from the Hollywood Freeway (Route 101): northbound, exit on Grand Street, turn right. The Center is about a block and a half away; southbound, exit on Temple Street, turn left, then turn right on Grand Street. If traveling south on the Pasadena Freeway, exit on Hill Street, go through Chinatown, make a right on Temple, than a left on Grand.

Within the Music Center is the 3,000-seat *Dorothy Chandler Pavilion* (winter home of the Los Angeles Philharmonic and the showcase for the Los Angeles Master Chorale Group, the Los Angeles Civic Light Opera, and, in the fall, the Joffrey Ballet), the *Mark Taper Forum,* and the *Ahmanson Theater.* The Hollywood Bowl, 2301 Highland Ave. (87-MUSIC), is the Philharmonic's summer home.

Dorothy Chandler, wife of former *Los Angeles Times* publisher Norman Chandler, is the acknowledged prime mover behind the creation of the Music Center. *The Dorothy Chandler Pavilion,* opened in 1964, is noted for its outstanding acoustics, lighting, and staging capabilities. The building is rich with marble walls, sculptured columns, and crystal chandeliers. Facing the Pavilion across a reflecting pool is the 742-seat *Mark Taper Forum,* which features drama, recitals, and lectures. The 2,071-seat *Ahmanson Theater* presents musicals, ballet, and drama as well.

The Hollywood Bowl, open since 1920, is one of the world's largest natural amphitheaters. In a park surrounded by mountains, trees, and gardens, it is said to be acoustically perfect. A night at the Hollywood Bowl can be filled with fun, glamour, and romance. Summer concertgoers usually arrive early, bringing or buying picnic suppers. Picnic tables are available throughout the area, and box seat subscribers can reserve a table right in their own box. Dining styles range from eating picnic sandwiches while sprawled on a blanket to elaborate culinary feasts atop fancy tablecloths adorned with flowers, candelabras, crystal, and fine china. Restaurant dining is available on the grounds (reservations recommended). Call (213) 851–3588 for information. Concerts under the stars begin at 8:30 P.M. The seats are wooden, and so you may want to bring or rent a cushion. A convenient way to enjoy the Hollywood Bowl experience without the hassle of parking is to take one of the Park-and-Ride buses, which leave from various locations around town; Call 87-MUSIC for information. If you're driving, there may be a short walk to the theater; wear comfortable shoes and bring a sweater. The Hollywood Bowl can be reached from the Hollywood Freeway (Route 101): northbound, exit at Highland Ave., make a right onto Highland, and a left into the Bowl; southbound, exit at Highland Ave., make a left onto Highland, and a left into the Bowl.

The Los Angeles Philharmonic, over sixty years old, puts on a powerful performance under the musical direction of its conductor, Carlo Maria Guilini. Guilini was preceded by Zubin Mehta, who conducted here from 1962 to 1978. Recognized as one of the greatest symphony orchestras in the country, the Philharmonic performs at its winter home, the Dorothy Chandler Pavilion in the Music Center, from November to April and at its summer home, the Hollywood Bowl, from July through September. Prices usually range from $6.00 to $22.00 a seat at the Chandler and from $1.00 to $27.50 at the Bowl.

The Los Angeles Civic Light Opera sponsors productions at the Dorothy Chandler Pavilion from May through October.

The Los Angeles Chamber Music Society, formed in 1977, has been growing steadily: The number of concerts has increased yearly. Members of the Los Angeles Philharmonic Orchestra are featured along with guest musicians.

Other concert halls include *The Ambassador Auditorium,* Pasadena, 300 W. Green St.; 304–6161. This theater matches the Dorothy Chandler in its elegance and tone. World-renowned soloists and groups perform here from September to May.

The Shrine Auditorium, 665 W. Jefferson Blvd.; 749–5123, was built in 1926 by the Al Malaikah Temple, and the undeniably unique decor could be termed Basic Baghdad and Beyond. Touring companies from all over the world, along with assorted gospel and choral groups, appear here. When the silent French film epic *Napoleon* toured the country with a live orchestra a while back, its Los Angeles performances were in this one-of-a-kind, 6,400-seat theater.

The Wilshire Ebell Theater, 4401 W. Eighth St.; 939–1128, is a Renaissance-style building, Spanish in architecture and design, which was built in 1924. The Los Angeles Opera Theatre comes here as do a broad spectrum of other musical performers.

Royce Hall at UCLA; 825–9261, features internationally acclaimed performers in its 2,000-seat auditorium. The university's *Schoenberg Hall,* smaller but with wonderful acoustics, hosts a variety of concerts as well.

If you're looking for a complete cultural experience, don't miss the *LA Street Scene Festival;* 626–0485. Sponsored by the Joseph Schlitz Brewing Company, the event began in 1978 and is held the second week in October in the Civic Center Area. Ten square blocks around City Hall in downtown Los Angeles are closed to traffic. Stages are built, and the public is invited—for free. It is an event that features new talents (for the perusal of record company executives) and established performers, such as Chuck Berry and Helen Reddy, and veteran ensembles such as the Los Angeles Philharmonic. In addition, there are strolling Mariachi bands, soul groups, and enough ethnic food to feed a United Nations picnic.

For complete information on performances, check the listings in the afore-mentioned publications.

THE GREAT OUTDOORS

Located on the way in to Griffith Park, *The Greek Theater,* 2700 N. Vermont Ave.; 460–6488, offers concerts under the stars from June to October. It features everything from popular to classical music. Its Doric columns evoke the amphitheaters of ancient Greece.

The Hollywood Bowl, 2301 Highland Ave.; 87-MUSIC, seats four times as many people as the Greek does, which means around 17,000 picnic baskets. Tucked at the base of the Hollywood Hills, it is one of the most venerable of Los Angeles's bona fide landmarks. (For more information on the Bowl, see the *Classical and Opera* section.)

ROCK

The Roxy, 9009 Sunset Blvd., 276–2222, is Los Angeles's most elegant music-industry showcase. Decorated in an Art-Deco style, this hot spot offers legitimate and performance theater as well as rock 'n' roll.

Gazzarri's, 9039 Sunset Blvd.; 273–6606, is one of the Sunset Strip's senior citizens. Teenagers frequent the club, as their parents did in the early 1960s. Up-and-coming talent is showcased on Tuesday and Thursday nights; local bands are featured on the weekend. There are two stages and dance areas.

Doug Weston's Troubador, 9081 Santa Monica Blvd.; 276–6168, may be best known as the favorite hangout in the 1960s for many singers who helped define the Los Angeles sound: among others, Jackson Browne, Linda Ronstadt, and individual members of the Eagles before they took flight. Although the club does not now command nearly the attention it once did, it has achieved a certain landmark status.

Madame Wong's Restaurant, 949 Sun Mun Way at the Broadway Gate in Chinatown; 624–5346, is perhaps the most exotic club in town but not the safest. In addition to housing a curious assortment of Oriental antiques, the thatched hut stage decor inherited from earlier times is best described as Early Hawaiian. There are two shows each night of state-of-the-art rock and roll. *Madame Wong's West,* 2900 Wilshire Blvd.; 829–7361 or 828–4444, offers the same musical menu in not nearly as bizarre surroundings. Madame Wong West attracts a college crowd and is tamer than the original. What it lacks in atmosphere it more than compensates for with a downstairs area that features an assortment of video games, pinball, two cocktail bars, and a disco where you can boogie to local bands.

Lingerie Club, 6507 Sunset Blvd.; 466–8557, is one of the newest and hottest spots on the circuit. Curiously enough, the building has been around for ages in variously divergent nightclub incarnations. The consensus now is that the current Lingerie identity will be around for quite a while. With a couple of bars, an upstairs lounge eminently suitable for lounging, and a spacious dance floor, the place is terrific. Shows begin at 9:00. The somewhat eclectic music it presents is a pleasing combination of rock, reggae, rhythm and blues, and New Wave.

The Country Club, 18415 Sherman Way, Reseda; (818) 881–5601, is one of the newer venues in the area. The sound is superb and it's a delight to listen to such a wide spectrum of music.

Perkins Palace, 129 N. Raymond, Pasadena; 796–7001, has done its part to promote the mini-Renaissance of Pasadena by proving itself to be a most enjoyable place to see a diverse number of groups and individual performers. It has all the nostalgic charm of a renovated old movie theater, which is appropriate because that's just what it is. To their credit, the folks running Perkins have done such a good job that people have stopped complaining about the drive.

The Forum, Manchester and Prairie Ave., Inglewood; 673–1300, one of the largest indoor facilities in Los Angeles, attracts such superstar acts as the Rolling Stones, Fleetwood Mac and Michael Jackson. It is also home of Lakers basketball and Kings hockey. The *Santa Monica Civic Auditorium,* 1855 Main St.; 393–9961, former home of the Academy Awards, is the most intimate of the local concert halls, even though it can accommodate thousands of people.

Another place provoking some historical curiosity is *The Hollywood Palladium,* 6215 Sunset Blvd.; 466–4311, which has been swinging with swing music for over forty years. You can still hear big bands playing there, but now Latin dance music and New Wave bands are also featured. This is where Lawrence Welk used to perform on New Year's Eve.

The *Universal Amphitheater,* Universal City; 980–9421, received a $20-million face-lift in 1982 that transformed it into a spectacular, state-of-the-art hall. A roof was put on the highly successful amphitheater, which has increased the number of shows produced annually. Pop concerts, including heavy emphasis on rock, make up 70 percent of the schedule; the remainder fall into the categories of ballet and legitimate theater. Beautiful fountains enhance the amphitheater's new look, which has to be seen to be appreciated. The capacity is 6,200, an expansion of 1,000 seats.

The Universal Amphitheater was first used in the early 1970s as part of the Universal Studios Tour where stunt shows were performed. Today the arena offers year-round scheduling of big-name talent. The new amphitheater seems to sell out quickly, despite its increase in size. Check local listings and order in advance for any acts that you really don't want to miss.

JAZZ

Los Angeles features some of the best jazz concerts around. *The Playboy Jazz Festival* is presented at the Hollywood Bowl; 87-MUSIC, every June. It features a two-day lineup of jazz greats.

Donte's Jazz Supper Club, 4269 Lankershim Blvd.; (818) 877–8347, presents a mixture of the clearly and nearly famous. Chuck Mangione got his start here. Steak and seafood are offered at special dining tables. The show begins at 9:30 P.M. The club is closed on Sundays.

The Baked Potato, 3787 Cahuenga Blvd., West; 980–1615, is so named because of the many ways they serve this particular tuber. Top jazzmen such as Tom Scott and Larry Carlton played some of their first gigs here. Shows begins at 10:00 P.M. Go early, stay late (last show at midnight). No reservations.

The Parisian Room, located at the corner of La Brea and Washington Blvds.; 936–0678. is one of the city's most beloved jazz clubs. You can see top talent such as Ahmad Jamal and Willie Bobo. Monday nights provide an opportunity for newcomers to showcase themselves and be rescued from anonymity.

Marla'a Memory Lane supper club, 2323 W. Martin Luther King, Jr., Blvd.; 294–8430. Blues and jazz predominate here. Local favorites as well as top-name entertainers. Versatile dinner menu.

Pasquale's, Malibu, 22724 W. Pacific Coast Hwy. 456–2007, is owned by bassist Pat Senatore and located right on the water. You can often find him playing with the better jazzmen in town.

One of the real veteran jazz clubs that continually has appealing performers is the *Lighthouse* in Hermosa Beach on 30 Pier Ave.; 372–6911. Open Tuesday through Sunday, the place may look like a bit like a dive, but the music is divine.

You can find Horace Silver, Milt Jackson, and Carmen McRae at *Concerts by the Sea* at Fisherman's Wharf in Redondo Beach; 379–4998. An elegant little theater complete with chandeliers and red carpeting, the club is the top of every local jazz fan's list. The only thing bad about the place is that it's closed Monday through Wednesday.

COUNTRY AND WESTERN

Quite simply, *The Palomino,* 6907 Lankershim Blvd.; 764–4010, is *the* place. Three decades of national renown have brought everyone from Jerry Lee Lewis to Emmylou Harris here. Even if you're only remotely interested in country and western music, take this brief bit of advice: go.

McCabe's, 3101 Pico Blvd.; 828–4497, is living proof that the 1960s are not completely over. Although the emphasis is primarily on folk, you can also hear jazz, blues, and even pop music here. Doc Watson, Tom Waits, and John Fahey have passed through and return now and again, along with many other top folk folks. You can savor homemade cakes, along with herbal teas, during intermission.

 STAGE. Some say that Los Angeles has become "the Broadway of the West." The scope of theater here does not really begin to compare to that of the Great White Way, but there is a uniqueness of the offerings in this vast entertainment-oriented city that is worth any visitor's while.

The growth is astounding. In 1978 only about 370 professional productions were brought to stages in Los Angeles, whereas in 1982 more than 600 were scheduled. Small theaters are blossoming all over town, and the larger houses, despite price hikes accelerating to $35.00 for a single ticket, are full more times than not.

An important aspect of Los Angeles theater to keep in mind while searching the Calendar section of *The Los Angeles Times* or *The Herald Examiner's* "Style" section for an appealing choice is that even the smallest productions might boast the biggest names in "the Business" (Los Angeles's entertainment empire). Film and television actors love to work on the stage between "big" projects as a way to refresh their talents or regenerate their creativity. Working on the stage can indeed be a more demanding exercise than working in television and film, and taking a job in the legitimate theater represents a way for these actors and actresses to get back in touch with their craft. Also, since stage work is so different from film and television work (often done piecemeal, with no sense of sequence or time), it is the perfect busman's holiday.

Those hoping for their chance in television and film are also happy to be on stage in a legitimate Los Angeles theater. It is an excellent way to be seen by those who matter in the more glitzy end of show business. Through plays and showcases many casting agents, producers, and directors find the talent that they need for their next projects. Hence a need for not only large houses—which usually mount productions that are road-company imports of established Broadway hits or, on occasion, the place where Broadway-bound material begins its initial tryout phase—but also a host of small, intimate, sometimes out-of-the-way theaters for the talent that abounds in this city.

Travelers on a budget will especially appreciate a new addition to Los Angeles theater: the city's first half-price ticket booths. There are three: 1002 Westwood Blvd. in Hunter's Bookstore, Westwood; 824–4773; 1462 N. Stanley Avenue through First Impression, in Hollywood; 876–8481; 2049 Century Park East, Suite 825, Century City; 203–0974. Tickets go on sale the day of performance at a 50 percent discount (plus service charge). Most major theaters participate.

Ticket agents also operate in Los Angeles. Try either Al Brooks at 626–5863 or Ticketron at 642–5700.

To give you a feel for theater in Los Angeles, the following sampling includes some of the largest houses in the area:

Mayfair Music Hall, 214 Santa Monica Blvd., Santa Monica; 451–0621. This charming 282-seat house is decorated in an Old World style to highlight the many live revues that are staged there. Once an opera house, the Mayfair (built in 1911) once echoed the voices of many famous European performers. Ticket prices range from $7.00 to $9.00; MC and V are accepted.

Westwood Playhouse, 10866 Le Conte Ave, Westwood; 208–6500. The basic architecture of this 498-seat house is Egyptian, with mosaics and columns decorating the walls. An acoustically superior theater. Sightlines are perfect anywhere in the house. This playhouse prefers to be known as the theater of events, where new plays are generally showcased; primarily musicals and comedies in the summer. Most productions come in from Broadway; however, two— *Perfectly Frank* and *Passionate Ladies*—went on *to* Broadway. Jason Robards and Nick Nolte both got their start at this playhouse. Ticket prices range from $12.00 to $20.00 MC, V, and AE are accepted.

Ahmanson Theater, 135 N. Grand Ave.; 241–9413 or 246–7165. Part of a three-theater complex (with the Dorothy Chandler Pavilion and the Mark Taper Forum), this is a modern structure made of stone and mosaic. Material presented here under direction of Robert Fryer includes both classics and new plays. The list of distinguished artists who have worked at this theater reads like a Who's Who of stage and screen. 2,071 seats. Prices for tickets range from $5.00 to $18.00, and all major credit cards are accepted.

Dorothy Chandler Pavilion, 135 N. Grand Ave.; 241–9413 or 246–7165. Also part of the Music Center, this 3,200-seat house offers a smattering of plays in between performances of the Los Angeles Philharmonic. The theater opened in 1964. Tickets range from $4.00 to $15.00, and all major credit cards are accepted.

Mark Taper Forum, 135 N. Grand Ave.; 972–7353; charge-line, 972–7654. Also part of the three-piece Music Center complex, this house boasts 742 seats and excellent acoustics in an intimate setting. The theater, under Gordon Davidson, is committed to new works and to the development of a community of artists. Opened in 1964. Many plays, including *Children of a Lesser God,* have gone on to Broadway from the Mark Taper.

Huntington Hartford, 1615 N. Vine St., Hollywood; 462–6666; charge line, 851–9750. Centrally located in the heart of Hollywood, this house offers an intimate feeling despite its large capacity (1,038 seats). New plays, dramas, comedies, and musicals are presented here throughout the year. Tickets cost from $10.00 to $15.00; MC and V are accepted.

John Anson Ford Theater, 2580 Cahuenga Blvd.; 972–7428. This theater was built to show pilgrimage plays primarily, and the setting resembled the environment of Jerusalem. Today it is known for its Shakespeare and free summer jazz and ballet concerts. There is no general box office; fees depend on the company performing, and most summer presentations are free. Seating is 1,300.

Shubert Theater, 2020 Ave. of the Stars, Century City; 553–9000; telecharge, 553–8101. Broadway musicals are usually on stage here in this 1,824-seat house. All major credit cards are accepted; tickets cost from $16.50 to $32.50.

Pantages, 6233 Hollywood Blvd.; 462–3104. Once the home of the Oscar telecast and big Hollywood premiers, this house is massive (2,300 seats) and splendid. Musicals direct from Broadway are usually presented here. Stars such as Yul Brynner, Mickey Rooney, Ann Miller, and most recently Sandy Duncan have appeared at the Pantages, an elaborate place that has one failing—less than perfect acoustics. Tickets run from $14.50 to $27.50. MC, V accepted.

Wilshire Theater, 8440 Wilshire Blvd., Beverly Hills; 653–4490. The interior of the Wilshire Theater, a 1,900-seat house, is decorated in Art Deco and is located in a very nice section of town; there are many restaurants in the area. Musicals from Broadway are usually the fare here. Newly renovated. Tickets range from $14.50 to $27.50. MC, V accepted.

Smaller houses are more specialized in their offerings. Here are a few:

Groundling Theater, 7307 Melrose Ave.; 934–4747. Satirical sketches are the kinds of performances that you're likely to witness here. This theater is best categorized as a comedy/improvisional house. Larraine Newman (of *"Saturday Night Live"* fame) and other comedians got their start here, which is a showcase for comics. Ticket prices are $4.00 for the late show and $6.50 for early show.

Fountain Theater, 5060 Fountain Ave.; 669–9306 or 1525. Seating 80, this theater presents contemporary drama and comedies. Marianne Mearser and Rob Reiner both got their starts here. Most actors and actresses come here from television to do theater and then leave and go on to film work. Prices for tickets are from $7.00 to $8.00.

Japan America Theater, 244 South San Pedro, Los Angeles; 628–2725. This community-oriented, 880-seat theater is at the Japan Cultural Arts Center. It opened in April 1983 and is home to Kabuki troupes, local Japanese koto recitals, the East West Players, and numerous children's-theater groups.

Cast Theater, 804 N. El; 462–9872. Musicals, revivals, and avant-garde improvisional pieces are done here. The production of *Working* was picked up for PBS from this house, whereas *The Hasty Heart* went on to the Ahmanson from here.

Globe Theater, 1107 N. Kings Rd.; 654–5623. A replica of the original Shakespeare Globe Playhouse, this theater is the only one in the world to have produced all Shakespeare's works. Most performers from Broadway come to the Globe, and then leave and go on to either film or television. Talia Shire and John Ritter got their starts here. Tickets are priced from $6.00 to $12.50.

Some other ninety-nine-seat houses (comparable to Off-Broadway) are *Cast at the Circle,* 800 N. El Centro Ave., Los Angeles; 462–0265; *Cast-at-the-Hyperion,* 1835 Hyperion Ave., Los Angeles; 661–9188; *Pilot Theater I and II,* 6600 Santa Monica Blvd., Los Angeles; 469–6600; *Hollywood Actor's Theater,* 715 N. Cahuenga Blvd., Los Angeles; 464–0300; *On the Fringe Theater,* 3709 Sunset Blvd.; 667–9556.

 SHOPPING. Unlike New York, with its Fifth and Madison Avenues and Herald Square, and London, with its Bond and Oxford Streets, Los Angeles is a hodgepodge when it comes to shopping. Rodeo Drive comes to mind as the one recognizable shopping thoroughfare, but compared to the others, it is extremely short. Several cities or areas, with various shopping sections in each, exist within metropolitan Los Angeles. It can get very confusing.

For instance, you may ask someone where such and such a shop is and they may answer, "the Valley." Not much of a clue. Then they may add, "On Ventura Blvd." Still not much help since Ventura Blvd. runs for more than twenty miles from Universal City to Calabasas.

As you can see, the area covered by shopping in Los Angeles is staggering. But once you have followed some of the leads, through word-of-mouth suggestions or newspaper advertisements, you'll discover there is almost anything to be had in Los Angeles from a slew of imaginative and innovative shops in which to find them.

Beverly Hills and Rodeo Drive are the most famous in which to shop. Rodeo Drive, with the biggest name stores—and most likely, the biggest price tags, too—is similar to Fifth Avenue and Madison Avenue in New York. From Gucci to Georgette Klinger, from Cartier, Van Cleef and Arpels, to Ted Lapidus, all can be found here. What's more, the city's indigenous stores, such as Fred Jollier and Bijan—probably one of the only men's boutiques in the world where you need an appointment—are mostly found in Beverly Hills. Beverly Hills is not only a great shopping experience, but it is also one of the best places for stargazing.

A star was born recently in Beverly Hills: The *Rodeo Collection,* on Rodeo Dr. between Brighton Way and Santa Monica Blvd., is the epitome of opulence and high fashion. Many famous European designers who have never had free-standing stores on the West Coast have opened their doors in this piazza-like area of marble and brass. Among them:

Cerruti is a designer known in Europe for his own fabrics. Here you'll find one of several women's franchises he has opened up worldwide. Louis Vuitton, known throughout the world for fine luggage, has a light, airy shop. Nina Ricci, with everything from accessories to evening gowns, is in a dramatic setting complete with crystal chandelier. Yves St. Laurent Pour Homme, with luggage and umbrellas, as well as his classically styled clothing, has pictures of the designer to remind you where you are shopping. Trend-setting Italian designer Gianni Versace is represented by one of the largest collections of his clothes in the U.S. Emmanuel Ungaro, known for his fabulous prints, is here, as is Fendi, with exquisite leather goods.

Madras, an Italian store, is represented in the Rodeo Collection by everything from shoes and purses to skirts and dresses, all color coordinated. A gallery of archaeological artifacts, Barakat, is a maze of age-old glass, sculpture, and jewelry from all over the world; according to the owner, prices range from $100 to $1 million. Yland Ylang is a fantasyland of costume and precious jewelry; it is worth visiting just to look at the bright colors and glitter. For those who are shopping weary, there are Pastels, for outdoor dining, and the Excelsior, for more formal dining. And for those with a sweet tooth, Chocolate-Chocolat is a treat with chocolates from many countries, including Belgium and Italy.

Mall shopping is so important in Los Angeles, that it is actually a sociological phenomenon. The *Beverly Center,* bounded by Beverly Blvd., La Cienega Blvd., San Vicente Blvd., and Third St., has more than 900,000 sq ft—over seven acres—and room for 200 stores. It is one of the largest shopping complexes in the Los Angeles area. Since its opening in spring 1982, the mall has catered to an upscale market taste. Many French designers—Daniel Hechter, Rodier, and others—have opened retail outlets here, and there are some interesting restaurants, such as the Tea Room–St. Petersburg, an authentic Russian restaurant with a fantastic view of the hills, and Food for Thought (a restaurant/bookstore) and the finest cineplex in Los Angeles—14 individual movie theaters.

Another shopping area, further west, that has evolved into a unique shopping area from a concept, is *Main Street, Santa Monica.* It is part of a "renewal" phase in Los Angeles in which many older neighborhoods are changing their faces; this area has been made to look like "Main Street, USA" in days past. Many of the stores and restaurants, decorated with carved wood, cut glass, and cute striped canopies, evoke a feeling that you are walking down the main street of a small western town just after the cowboys and gold miners left and the town had gained a bit of refinement. From *Willy Tiffany's Saloon* to *Main Street U.S.A.,* there is a theme—a special feeling—and it works well. This area was once well known for its large selection of antiques. Now clothing and kitchen stores and a slew of unusual galleries have come in, making this a full-service shopping area. Many of the stores carry Californian and other kinds of crafts, from original clothing to pottery and oils, and you are very likely to find items that you will see nowhere else. The Gallery of Eskimo Art and Main Street Gallery are just two of these places; and for clothes there is the Main Street Ensemble, with *very* trendy clothing, and No Sweat, with great exercise fashions.

Another new shopping area, in keeping with the ever-important mall, is *Santa Monica Place.* It is the newest mall in this part of town. There are so many kinds of malls in Los Angeles that they have become an architectural as well as a social phenomenon. The new Santa Monica Place Mall is one of the best places to study the evolutionary progress of "the mall."

Next door to the new three-story enclosed mall is the old *Santa Monica Mall* —an open-air mall. This predecessor to the recent mall, which is environmentally controlled, was also innovative in its day. There are pedestrian walkways between the streets, and there is also a landscaped island. The minute you see the huge green palm tree on the side of the new building you can feel the link that this mall has with its surroundings. The light, airy atrium design allows a view of all three floors at once, and from particular points you can see the ocean in the background. *Robinson's* and *The Broadway* are the department stores.

Century City has another shopping mall, set among gleaming steel office buildings. Here, in the center of a thriving business atmosphere, is a city kind of mall—open air. Charles Jourdan shoes at I. Magnin and designer labels at Ann Taylor are for high-fashion enthusiasts. The whimsical boutique *Heaven*, with its name emblazoned on T-shirts, sweat shirts, and so on, is a great place from which to get a souvenir for someone back home. As well as the open-air mall, there is a shopping section right in the middle of the twin towers in the ABC Entertainment Center. One typical Los Angeles Store, because of the emphasis here on luxury cars, is the *Road Show,* which features antique and classic cars and all kinds of paraphernalia, books, and novelty items for any Porsche, B.M.W., Rolls Royce, and other car enthusiasts. Galleries, clothing stores such as *The City Rage,* and a *B. Dalton Bookstore* are among the other stores in this center.

Changing gears again, we move to Westwood Village, which, with the influence of the UCLA campus, is a young and lively area for shopping. On a Saturday night in the spring and summer the stores are open late; there is a movie line around every corner; cars and people cruise; and the whole place looks like a scene from *Animal House.* It is great fun, and many of the stores are open as late as 11:00 P.M.

The recent arrival of pedicabs—bicycle-carts—in Westwood adds to the merriment. At about $6 an hour, they aren't a bad deal.

One particularly unique little shopping area in Westwood is the *Contempo Westwood Center,* at 10886 Le Conte Ave., right across the street from the UCLA campus. A certificate of Historical Preservation and Restoration is the building's claim to fame, and there is a photographic display of the history of the area. Stores in this center include the *Tower Gallery* with Danish furniture, *Kirsten's Art in Clothing, The Image of the Inuit,* and more; and there is also the Westwood Playhouse and Stratton's restaurant to complete the picture.

Westwood has often been compared to New York's Greenwich Village. As in New York's "Village," you are likely to see anything while strolling down the streets of Westwood Village. You may see a mime marrying two passersby or a tap-dancing twelve year old.

Farmers Market at Fairfax and Third is the historical shopping area of Los Angeles. It is near the top of every list of tourist attractions. Originally it was an open field where farmers went to sell their crops; now it is a huge shopping area with some of the best produce for miles around. There are other wares and a few restaurants offered as well.

Hollywood and West Hollywood are two shopping areas that depict special aspects of the Southern California life-style. In Hollywood it is the star and dazzle style that goes along with the show business industry. This sparkle is especially apparent in Hollywood, on Sunset Blvd.—or the Sunset Strip. The stores here and on Hollywood and Santa Monica Blvds. offer ultrahigh fashion as well as intriguing furnishings and antiques. The male shopper has more innovative stores to chose from here than perhaps anywhere in the city. It's for those daring enough to be current.

West Hollywood is less bizarre and less intimidating than the "hard core" Hollywood; and there is a real feel for the newest and liveliest fashions—especially on popular Melrose Ave. Melrose Ave. is definitely one of the "hottest" shopping areas in Los Angeles; part of its attraction is the blend of different kinds of stores. A certain "hippiness" is depicted by such bookstores as *Zarathustra* and *The Bodhi Tree,* with their emphases on nature, religion, health, and mysticism; and there is the more avant-garde influence featuring hip clothing and furniture from stores such as *Melon's* and *Fantasy Lighting.* Once mainly an antique area, Melrose Ave. still has a varied selection of unique and high priced antique stores. And although all are not expensive, all are definitely worth a look.

Also in this area is the Blue Whale: the *Pacific Design Center,* a building that's hard to miss. A huge blue edifice on the corner of Melrose Ave. and San Vicente Blvd., this center houses everything from furniture to window coverings, from fixtures to accessories. More of the same kinds of design stores can be found on Robertson Avenue.

Downtown Los Angeles, with its impressive renovation project in the Bunker Hill area, is undergoing a dramatic face-lifting. In the past few years downtown has become a recognizable force in the art world. Like New York City's SoHo section, there are converted lofts and galleries everywhere between Fiqueroa and Mateo Sts., on Los Angeles Street, in the ARCO Center, and all over this area. On any weekend you can stroll through this area and probably find a show opening or two offering wine and cheese and good art viewing.

Many up-and-coming artists—the new breed of "young Turks"—hang around and show their art in this section. There is a renegade atmosphere that usually develops in an art-oriented urban area. There is also a great deal of innovative contemporary art worth seeing and buying. Also downtown is the clothing district—the *California Mart* at 110 East 9th St. On the last Friday of each month the wholesale showrooms are open to the public for great bargains on sample items.

Downtown also affords the visitor to Los Angeles a great view of the many ethnic influences that make up the city. On Olvera St., one of the oldest streets in Los Angeles, the Mexican influence is at its best. Lining this pedestrian alley, stores offer handmade crafts and foods from Mexico.

Little Tokyo is the largest Japanese shopping district in the country. Japanese businesses started coming here in 1884, and this section has been going strong ever since. The evolution has filled Little Tokyo with an interesting mix of Japanese architecture interspersed with the usual American urban architecture.

Japanese tradition is still very strong here, and the important festivals, which are all celebrated in community fashion, offer a good way for the visitor to get a glimpse into this intriguing culture. The stores in Little Tokyo offer the most modern of Japanese merchandise. All are representative of the delicate Oriental touch. Clothing, jewelry, home furnishings, and other kinds of stores offer an unlimited variety from which to choose. For instance, *Matsuzakaya* is the first American branch of the oldest department store in Japan (founded in 1611). Typical of a department store, it features china to watches, ladies' and men's clothing, and much more. This is just one store in Weller Court—on Weller St. between First and Second St., near the New Otani Hotel and Garden. The Weller Court area is representative of what Tokyo looks like today.

Leaving downtown and traveling as far west as possible, you will find quite a bit of shopping in the beach communities. The Pacific Palisades has chic, and expensive stores, such as *Jona* for women's clothing and fashion consultation. Farther down the coast are Santa Monica, Venice, and Marina del Rey. Santa Monica has particularly good shopping on Main St. and the Santa Monica Place Mall. Another great shopping area in Santa Monica is Montana Ave. With *Brenda Himmel* for stationery and gifts, *Weathervane I* and *II* for women's and men's clothing, and *Lisa Norman* for the finest lingerie, this short strip of shopping—from about 11th St. to 23rd—is chock full of possibilities.

Venice is probably the punk or New Wave headquarters of Los Angeles, and shopping reflects this style. West Washington St. is the place to shop for unusual items in Venice; *Choux Sale,* with vintage shoes and clothing, is only one of the shops to explore. In the Marina, on Admiralty Wy., *Blondie's,* with a selection of cute, punk clothing for women, typifies this style. *Mudra Naturals,* on Washington Ave. near the beach, with earthy natural cottons that reflect a beach look, is quite different. *Kroma,* in Venice, has some eye-catching stained-glass art. The glass is coated by means of a special chemical process and turns different colors as the light hits it; it is a treat to see. Such items sell from about $30.00 to $5,000.

The South Bay communities of Redondo Beach, Manhattan Beach, and Hermosa Beach also contain a variety of shops on their respective shopping streets. In Redondo the shopping is good in the Kings Harbor section. Other streets for shopping include Pacific Coast Hwy., Torrance Blvd., and Catalina Ave. (There is no real "downtown" in Redondo.) Hermosa has its pier and Hermosa Ave. with shops; and the "strand," which is connected to the pier, is another shopping attraction. In Manhattan Beach, the Manhattan Village Mall, on Sepulveda at Rosecrans, has stores such as *La Chemise,* with lingerie "goodies," and *Pappagallo,* the popular women's shoe and clothing store. *Del Amo Fashion Center,* at 3525 Carson, in Torrance, is said to be the world's largest shopping mall. It has 350 stores and 2.4 million square feet of space.

The Valley, which was briefly mentioned, is a great place to shop, but it is important to get your bearings and directions straight before you set out. It is a sprawling area. The Valley refers to the San Fernando Valley, which is north of Los Angeles; but there is a lot more "out there." East of Los Angeles is the

San Gabriel Valley and nearby are Pasadena, Glendale, and dozens of other communities.

There are hundreds of shopping areas within this section; but there are some, in the Valley especially, that stand out. Ventura Blvd., which runs through many different cities—Universal City, Sherman Oaks, Topanga—has shops scattered along the way to Calabasas.

Well-known shops such as *Importique*, with contemporary sportswear at reasonable prices, and the *1900's Company*, with great reproductions of American antiques, are spread out among newer shops. At least one shop is opening each week in this thriving area.

In addition to Ventura Blvd. and other shopping streets, the Valley has a surprising number of malls. The Sherman Oaks Galleria is the newest. This is an upper-market mall featuring such stores as *Crabtree and Evelyn*, the famous English store, with delightful perfumes and beauty items; the *Casual Gourmet*, with everything for the kitchen; and *Martin Lawrence* for art; it offers a good selection of Dali and Rockwell originals. The atrium-style mall with glass elevators has about 120 stores anchored by the May Company and Robinson's.

Other malls in the Valley and in other outlying areas include the *Woodland Hills Promenade*, the *Topanga Canyon Mall*, the *May Company Plaza* in North Hollywood, the *Town and Country Shopping Center and Plaza de Oro* in Encino, and the *Glendale Galleria*.

Pasadena—east of Hollywood—is a refreshing older community in the midst of all these modern shopping areas. Pasadena has a wide range of shops to chose from. Many are in the crafts and gifts area. *Los Angeles* Magazine (February 1982) called Pasadena " . . . a place where time seems to move a little slower and people smile as they pass each other on the street. It's relaxed. It's classy. It's even colorful. And across the board, it's a good deal less expensive than comparable areas of Southern California."

One of the stores that expresses this friendly feeling is *The Gold Company* on East Green St. The proprietor/designer Karen McGrary is a marvel who has a special gift for designing jewelry in unusual combinations—a tourmaline crystal with a peach-colored pearl—and other striking pairings. The *Holly Street Bazaar*, on Holly St, is a cooperative effort offering separate booths containing such items as plastic costume jewelry, beaded lamp shades, and chenille bedspreads. Then there is *Four Quarters*, with gifts for the host or hostess.

DEPARTMENT STORES

As in all big cities, department stores are an important part of shopping in Los Angeles. For instance, *J. W. Robinson* (Robinson's), one of the classy department stores, has branches in Arcadia, Beverly Hills, Cerritos, City of Industry, Glendale, Downtown Los Angeles, Panorama City, Pasadena, Thousand Oaks, Woodland Hills, and Santa Monica. And J. C. Penney has over thirty-five locations. Here are the department stores represented in the Los Angeles area: The Broadway; Buffum's; Bullock's; I. Magnin—a high-quality, California based store; May Company; Montgomery and Ward; Neiman Marcus—perhaps at the top of the list; Silverwoods; and in Beverly Hills are Bonwit Teller, Saks Fifth Avenue (also in Costa Mesa), and two Abercrombie and Fitch Stores (one in the new Beverly Center and the other in Beverly Hills proper).

Bullock's Wilshire, in the mid-Wilshire section at 3050 Wilshire Blvd., is the grandmother of department stores in Los Angeles, though the same could be said of the downtown Bullock's at 7th and Hill. The design of the store on Wilshire is what makes it so interesting. It is built with terra cotta, green copper, and glass; its design is extremely unusual; it is a sight as well as a store. All Beverly Hills department stores are posh; you might even see your favorite star amid the beautiful merchandise.

In terms of merchandise, *Bullock's, Neiman Marcus,* and *Robinson's* have especially good accessories for women—belts, purses, and other goods are top quality. *The Broadway* has an unusually well-stocked housewares department and a good china selection. And *Robinson's* is also known for its variety in men's clothing.

MEN'S AND WOMEN'S CLOTHING

In Beverly Hills are some of the country's most traditional, classic, and expensive men's and women's clothing stores, as well as some of the trendiest. *Camp Beverly Hills* is in the latter category. Located at 9640 Santa Monica Blvd., this is more than just a clothing store; it is an institution. The motto of the store (and not *all* stores have mottos) is: "Survival clothing for the most modern age"; this is where you will find the most recent in chic uniforms—fatigues, sailor's pants and tops, and painter's pants—in dozens of colors, all piled high. There are also socks, sunglasses. sweat shirts, T-shirts, and an extensive collection of cards. Camp Beverly Hills T-shirts and sweat shirts make great souvenirs and presents for people back home.

Changing gears swiftly, we turn to *Celine,* one of the most posh names in international circles. Fine Old World craftsmanship and classic design are the key concepts at this store. Luggage, shoes, and accessories, as well as traditionally tailored clothes of the finest fabrics, are featured.

Have you heard of the book *Scruples? Giorgio,* Beverly Hills, at 273 N. Rodeo Dr., is the setting for this famous novel. One does not merely shop at Giorgio's; one also refreshes oneself at the stunning Oak Bar that separates the men's and women's clothes. A Beverly Hills landmark, Giorgio's is one of the stores that dresses the stars. Available are the best in American and European clothing, as well as superbly fashioned accessories and footwear.

At 9699 Wilshire Blvd., *Jaeger Sportswear Ltd.* is one of the best known first-class British clothiers. A complete line of cashmere and woolen separates is available in traditionally designed fashions.

The *Lanvin Boutique,* 362 N. Rodeo Dr., is a big name in French *haute couture;* the full line of Lanvin fashions for men and women is featured here along with toiletries and gift items. The staff speak several languages and even takes foreign currency. *Theodore* and *Theodore Man* are two more impressive clothing stores at 453 N. Rodeo Dr. These stores offer trendy items in fabulous fabrics. Everything is done with a real eye for color. The *Leather Club* at 9526 Santa Monica Blvd has the best pants, jackets, skirts, and other items in leather and suede from French, Italian, and Spanish designers.

Carroll and Company, 466 N. Rodeo Dr., Beverly Hills, has been one of the finest clothing stores in Los Angeles for more than thirty-two years. Carroll and Company offers only the best in design, fabric, and fit.

On Melrose Ave. are other upbeat clothing stores, including the ever-popular *Fred Segal* at 8100 Melrose. Fred Segal has a reputation for providing the most innovative of styling in men's and women's clothing. Featured are many designers and manufacturers, including New Man, Ralph Lauren, and Calvin Klein, to name only a few. Children's clothing, accessories, and shoes are also stocked at the Melrose store. *Harrari,* at 8463 Melrose and at 1015 Ocean Front Walk in Venice, has very unusual styles, "clothes with a sense of humor," as they say in their ads.

Hardware, at 8620 Melrose Ave., is a unique store for men and women. The window display is always eye catching, and the shop offers some of the most daring American and European styles that can be found anywhere. Originally a men's shop, Hardware became so popular with women that it started carrying items in smaller sizes.

If you are interested in vintage clothes for men and women, try *Pinnacle Vintage* at 22917 Pacific Coast Hwy. in Malibu, across from the pier. The huge collection consists of clothing spanning the years from the 1890s through the 1960s, and the prices are reasonable. Avant-garde and punk clothing for men and women can be found at the *Main Street Ensemble* at 2803 Main Street in Santa Monica. This small shop is chock full of new designs.

In Westwood is *Chanin's* at 1030 Westwood Blvd., for the best in casual wear. The UCLA influence can be seen in the youthful and fun fashions featured here. *Gary's and Company,* at 4728 Admiralty Way in Marina del Rey, brings us back to the classics. A preppie's dream, Gary's has men's and women's fashions by Ralph Lauren and Southwick and shoes by Cole Haan, to name only a few of the lines. Gary's does alterations and tapers shirts for free—if you don't mind a bit of a wait.

Raffles, a Clothing Collection, at 17554 Ventura Blvd. in Encino, is one of the Valley's most extensive stores. It is a treat for the eye to see so many interesting fashions for men and women in one place. There are accessories and shoes here as well, and the staff offers wardrobe-coordination advice.

Echelon is another store that carries many lines, some better known in Europe than in this country. Located in the Courtyard, 550 Deep Valley Dr., Rolling Hills Estate, this boutique carries La Squadra, J.P.G., Mario Valentino shoes, Soo Young Lee, Crash, Christian Dior, and other lines.

North Beach Leather, through its nine stores in the Los Angeles area, offers limited-edition leather designs for discriminating men and women. Classic designs and more trendy styles fill the racks, and there is something for everyone in the finest of leathers and suedes. The *First Western Boot and Clothing Company,* at 602 Santa Monica Blvd. in Santa Monica, is in step with the recent proliferation of western styles. They specialize in American-made boots and clothing. Represented are Luchesse, Tony Lama, and Frye. They also have a line of Stetson hats, accessories and gift items, and silver belt buckles.

Maxfield Bleu, 9091 Santa Monica Ave. in West Hollywood, is a haunt of some of the most famous Hollywood residents. The store stocks the most recent European and American designer clothing. This is good place to see what is "in," even if you can't afford it.

WOMEN'S CLOTHING

The new Beverly Center features French designers' outlets including *Philippe Salvet, Rodier Paris,* and *Momdjian Freres.* In the same tradition is *Laise Adzer,* at 8583 Melrose Ave. This Moroccan designer makes free-flowing clothes in the most luxurious natural fabrics. Only pure vegetable dyes are used to make the luscious colors. This store, including its mosque-like design, is a real treat, as is her new store in the Century City Shopping Center.

Back to Beverly Hills for women's clothing. We start out at *Jag,* 9612 Brighton Way. At the forefront of the jeans revolution a few years ago, this store still has a good selection of well-styled jeans as well as other clothing. The *Right Bank Clothing Company and Tea Room* at 313 N. Rodeo has some of the highest quality, best designed, and highest priced clothing in town.

Alan Austin and Company offers traditional clothing in a wide selection of fabrics and colors. The store, located at 9533 Brighton Way, manufactures its own designs, so you can have your clothing made to order. *Lady Battaglia* is the women's version of the men's store; at 350 N. Canon, this store, like its counterpart, offers the most beautiful clothing from Italy.

Matthews, 309 Rodeo Dr., is run by Ruth Matthews. She has a good eye for fashion, which can be seen in the collection of clothing available in her store. Everything is well coordinated to provide you with "a look."

Ann Taylor, at 357 N. Camden Dr. and at several other locations around Los Angeles, offers the epitome of the young executive look for women; there is also a good selection of more casual clothing. Featuring such designers as Carol Horn and Perry Ellis, the store also carries a full line of Joan and David shoes.

Melons, 8750 Melrose Ave., and *Melons Shoes,* 8739 Melrose Ave., are two of the newest and hottest stores on this street. They have a wide selection of innovative designs from young designers. The store and its owners have received much attention from the Los Angeles press since its opening because of their impressive clothing selection.

Ellene Warren, 8590 Melrose Ave., offers its own original designs for women. One recent ad showed an unusual minidress with a print featuring musical notes—only one of many unusual designs you are likely to find on any given visit to this store. *All Seasons Clothing Company,* 8463 Melrose Ave., has a collection of exclusive designer clothing at reasonable prices. *Cowboys and Poodles Vintage Clothing,* 7379 Melrose Ave., attracts tourists from all over the world. Their collection of unused vintage clothes from the 1950s to the 1960s is worth a look; they also make some of their own designs.

Blondie's, 4732 Admiralty Way in the Marina, is full of punk and nearly punk styles. The owner Lynette Nagel, a blond, hence the name, searches the mart for the unusual, resulting in a selection of out-of-the-ordinary casual clothing. *Jona,* 12352 Ventura Blvd. in Studio City and at 1013 Swathmore Ave. in Pacific Palisades, is billed as a wardrobe-consultation service and store in one. They will outfit you from head to toe, using precisely the right style to enhance your personal look and tastes. They have a great selection of clothing from which to choose.

Also in the Valley, at 12642 Ventura Blvd., are *Van Tassell* for complete wardrobe counseling and the *Klassy Lady Boutique,* at 17064 Ventura Blvd.

Ferouchi, at 518 Wilshire Blvd., in Santa Monica, has designer clothing that changes with the seasons; among labels featured are DDDominick, Nancy Heller, and Terryl De Vino. *Nancee G.,* 943 Westwood Blvd., offers a great blend of domestic and European fashions. It has active sportwear as well as more dressy clothing by Leon Max and Marithe and Francois Girbaud among others.

More punk fashions can be found at *Domo,* 107 Washington Ave. in the Marina. This store carries the latest in punk fashions and accessories; there is an impressive selection of swimwear as well. Down the street, at 22½ Washington Ave., *Mudra Naturals* manufactures its own line of natural cotton, beachy clothing. Bright yellows, reds, and blues are the colors for this line of simple, well-styled skirts, pants, jackets, and tops of all kinds.

Nana, at 120 Broadway in Santa Monica, is another trendy store offering some of the most current of contemporary fashions. They claim that they have the best collection of tights and socks in town; and they also have jeans and swimwear. English T-shirts, magazines, and records will please the Anglophiles.

Weathervane II, 1209 Montana Ave., Santa Monica, is a large, bright shop. The friendly staff makes browsing among the beautiful fashions even more fun. Classic styles are mixed with the offbeat, and all are of the finest quality and best fabrics. Across the street, at 1134 Montana Ave., *Lisa Norman Lingerie, Etc.,* is almost too good to be true. This modern, elegant store houses one of the largest collections of high-quality lingerie from Europe and the United States. It concentrates on all natural fibers—silk and cotton—and designs its own items as well. Bins of bikinis, fine and expensive silk stockings, slips, camisoles, robes, and at-home clothes are only some of the items carried by Lisa Norman. *Trashy Lingerie,* at 402 N. La Cienega Blvd. in West Hollywood, has just what the name suggests. This is a place for the more daring; it carries sexy black-and-red garter belts and such.

Johnathan Lingerie, 1706 S. Catalina Ave. in Redondo Beach, carries loungewear and dancewear as well as some of the most beautiful imported lingerie from Europe, the Orient, and South America. *The Old Soft Shoe,* at 1242 Hermosa Beach Blvd., is a resale shop with "almost new," pampered designer clothing.

Hats are the thing at *Brown's,* at 68A N. Venice Blvd. in Venice. Straight from London, this store has nothing but hats in all shapes and sizes—berets, bowlers, large floppy hats, and small pillboxes.

Holly's Harp, 8605 Sunset Blvd., is among the most "in" stores in Los Angeles. Holly's creates fashions for many of the well-known people of the world. Five lines are created each year, and she also carries a selection of items from other designers.

MEN'S CLOTHING

One men's clothing store that has generated quite a bit of publicity lately is *Bijan,* at 420 N. Rodeo Dr. The store's shopping is by appointment only. It has made a splash by offering a line of bulletproof clothing. Bijan claims that many Arabian sheiks and other royalty shop here along with some of the wealthiest men in the United States. The most expensive and well-made clothing is available; many of the styles are designed especially for Bijan; they contain the best in leathers, cashmeres, silks, and other natural materials.

Abercrombie and Fitch, at 9424 Wilshire Blvd. and at the Beverly Center, is listed under men's clothing because it has been traditionally known for its fine men's clothing and sportswear. But there is also a great deal more available—women's clothing, accessories, and sporting equipment. The most elegant of sports clothes for safaris as well as tennis are stocked, in keeping with Abercrombie's ninety-year old tradition.

Battaglia, 306 N. Rodeo, recently celebrated its twentieth year on Rodeo. Featured here are the richest of Italian fashions in the most luxurious silks, wools, cottons, and cashmeres. Accessories, shoes, and men's apparel are shown in stylish surroundings. *Cecil Gee* came to 346 N. Rodeo Dr. directly from London's Bond St.; this shop is one of the most well-respected English shops. Cecil Gee offers the best in styling and materials, and shopping here will expose you to the amenities that go with English life; you can relax and have tea or a drink while the staff takes care of you.

Cyril's, 370 N. Beverly Dr., features fine clothing in the latest European styles. This elegant store carries such labels as Valentino, Cerruti, and Michale Axel. *Jerry Magnin,* at 323 N. Rodeo Dr., has one of the best reputations as a gentleman's clothier in the city. One of the largest men's stores, Magnin's has a large selection of dressy and traditional styles as well as casual styles. Shoes and accessories are also in good supply.

Mr. Guy, 369 N. Rodeo Dr., is known and well respected throughout the country. Mr. Guy offers tasteful and well-made clothing; all the needs of the well-dressed man can be obtained under one roof. *W. D. Silk* in the Century City Shopping Center is another fine name in menswear. "Low key" and good taste are watchwords here; there is nothing trendy about this store. Everything is classic: Aquascutum suits, Cole Haan shoes, and other respected labels are stocked.

Brooks Brothers, a men's tradition since 1818, is located at 530 W. 7th St., downtown. The store's reputation is worldwide, and deservedly so, for its own line of pure cotton shirts, suits, and neckwear. You cannot go wrong with these classically styled clothes. Business cases and other furnishings for the executive complete the Brooks Brothers profile.

Preferred Stock, 1914 Wilshire Blvd. in Santa Monica, is a new shop that offers the best that you can buy for your money. Their credo is that great fashion ought to be of good value as well as good looking. Their buyers scour the markets for merchandise that is just right. They offer the best in natural fabrics —cotton, wool, silk, linen, and tweed; and they create wearable fashions out of these fabrics. The staff is friendly and gives customers personal attention.

CHILDREN'S CLOTHING

Auntie Barbara's, 251 S. Beverly Blvd., Beverly Hills, keeps the kids busy while their mothers shop. The children play with various toys and the mothers survey the most recent designs in domestic and imported children's clothing.

Les Enfants, at 8332 Melrose Ave. in Hollywood, has some of the most chic children's clothes; they offer imports as well as custom-made items. At Bonwit Teller is *Bambola Children's Boutique,* with beautiful clothes imported from all over the world for infants to teens. *Adelaine, Boutique d'Enfants,* 350 N. Canon Dr. in Beverly Hills, has an irresistible collection of children's clothing from France, Italy, Germany, Israel, Denmark, England, and Sweden.

Pixie Town, at 400 N. Beverly Dr., Beverly Hills, has been dressing children for thirty years. Everything from baby's clothes and accessories to impeccably designed clothing for boys and girls is available at this pleasant shop.

SHOES

Many of the stores already mentioned in the *Clothing* section also carry shoes, but here are a few stores of note that carry only shoes:

The *Right Bank Shoe Co.,* 450 N. Camden, Beverly Hills, has an exciting collection of the most contemporary shoe styles by designers such as Maud Frizon and Andrea Pfister. *Di Fiori Ladies' Footwear,* at 363 N. Camden Dr., features the designs of Orson Mozes, who is said to be "shoemaker to the stars." Punk, classic, and New Wave designs are also featured in this stunning shop.

Vin Baker, with several locations, has staple shoes as well as fashion shoes for women at reasonable prices. *Richard's Shoes* has both men's and women's styles in the latest name-brand styles at 8106 Santa Monica Blvd. in West Hollywood and 1055 N. Broxton in Westwood.

Shoe de Ville, with stores in Hollywood at 7210½ Melrose Ave., and in Venice at 1601 W. Washington Blvd., has outrageous styles—though well designed and comfortable. *Roger Bowman's Footgear,* 370 N. Bedford Ave. in Beverly Hills, has the finest in high-fashion Italian footwear.

COSMETICS, PERFUMES, AND TOILETRIES

Crabtree and Evelyn at the Sherman Oaks Galleria (corner of Ventura and Sepulveda Blvds.) is a welcome treat for all the senses. This internationally famous English store is traditional and elegant; it offers the best in natural cosmetics, soaps, shampoos, and other cosmetic and gift items.

Hoffman Beauty and Barber Supply has several stores, including locations in Santa Monica, Brentwood, Hawthorne, Los Angeles, and Thousand Oaks. They offer treatment products used by hairdressers, as well as hair dryers, curling irons, and a wide range of cosmetics.

The *Lanvin Boutique* at 362 N. Rodeo Dr. is the only United States outlet for this famous designer; in addition to clothes, it offers an extensive selection of Lanvin toiletries, perfumes, and gift items. Also in Beverly Hills, at Le Grand Passage, 350 N. Canon Dr., is *Reflets de Paris,* a quaint French "parfumerie" offering imported fragrances and natural makeup.

Merle Norman Cosmetics has many locations; the staff will teach you, at no charge, to apply makeup-and they sell the extensive and well-known Merle Norman line of cosmetics and skin-care products.

BEAUTY SALONS

Because vacationing in Los Angeles is like being a star, you might as well act the part and pamper yourself a bit. If you decide you want to dye your hair green or yellow while you are here, you may want to try *Hot Cuts,* a punk haircutter on Pacific Ave. in Venice, but most likely you will only want a less drastic, more calming luxury.

Georgette Klinger, 312 N. Rodeo Dr., is a good place for pampering. The staff offers complimentary consultation and treats such as facials and masks that relax sun-drenched faces. It is well worth a visit before returning home.

The department stores are a rich source for beauty treatments. *Adrien Arpel,* who has set up shop at Saks Fifth Avenue, offers everything from facials to hair cuts to makeup consultations. *Christine Valmy* has skin-care centers at Bullock's department stores; they offer collagen and other treatments to promote younger looking skin. The flagship Christine Valmy salon is at 9675 Wilshire Blvd. in Beverly Hills.

Aida Grey, whose salons are in the Santa Monica Pl. Mall and at 9549 Wilshire Blvd. in Beverly Hills, is a Los Angeles celebrity. Grey often appears on local television and is known internationally as a skin-care expert. You will always find the latest skin-care techniques at her salons.

For hair, *Jon Peters Salon* in Beverly Hills and other locations is rumored to be the prototype for "Shampoo." And *Vidal Sassoon,* 405 N. Rodeo Dr., Beverly Hills, has been a trend setter for years. This branch is no exception. The Beverly Hills Vidal Sassoon has a top staff of international designers. *Odile Salons* at 1141 S. Beverly Dr. in Beverly Hills and 16161 Ventura Blvd. in Encino provide personal skin-care analysis to help you look and feel younger. Manicures, pedicures, massage, and makeup consultation are also offered.

As You Like It Haircutting salon at 7469 Melrose Ave. in West Hollywood caters to the young crowd. Hairstyling is relaxed and easy here.

Changes, a trendy hair salon at 175 Pier Ave., off Main St. in Santa Monica, is offering an "Olympic Special" California makeover; you get a manicure, pedicure, and haircut and conditioning.

LEATHER GOODS AND LUGGAGE

One of the best-known stores for luggage, handbags, business cases, and the like is *H. Savinar Luggage Company* at 4625 W. Washington Blvd., Los Angeles. For sixty-six years this store has offered exceptional service and fine leather goods. In Beverly Hills you will also find some of the finer leather goods chains, such as *Gucci*, 347 N. Rodeo, and *La Bagagerie*, at 445 N. Rodeo. The latter is part of a Parisian chain that designs and manufacturers its own leather goods and has fine leathers of all kinds.

Bottega Veneta, at 457 N. Rodeo, is another store with a familiar name to those who shop in the best stores. With its unique advertising slogan, "When your own initials are enough," this store provides the essence in understated luxury in handbags, luggage, business cases, as well as small items such as passport cases and wallets.

The *Bon Voyage Bazaar*, 348 N. Beverly Blvd., has been outfitting travelers for years. One of the largest selections of luggage, business cases, and anything you may need for traveling is available at this store; the service is top notch.

Le Sportsac, at 914 Westwood Blvd. and in the Santa Monica Place Mall, offers a huge selection of lightweight luggage and purses. Folding into neat little cases, these bags are great when you have bought more than you have room for and need another piece of luggage. Many styles and colors are stocked.

JEWELRY

The large chain jewelers such as Slavick's, Weisfields, and Zales are well represented at shopping areas and malls throughout the Southland. But there are also a number of individual jewelers of note. Whether you want posh and expensive or more artsy-craftsy jewelry, there is a store for all tastes. *Tiffany and Company*, at the Beverly Wilshire Hotel in Beverly Hills, hardly needs an introduction. Bearing the finest of reputations for the finest of jewelry, this store is a bit smaller than one might expect, but it is still full of the most well designed, most expensive jewels to be found. *Cartier* recently opened its doors at 370 N. Rodeo; and *Van Cleef and Arpels* has a large store one block west.

Perhaps the most prestigious jewelry store in Beverly Hills (or Los Angeles, for that matter) is *Fred Jolliar*. This is one of the classiest jewelry stores in the country, and the store at 401 N. Rodeo was the first U.S. branch of this famous Paris store. They design many of their own pieces and have a leather boutique as well.

Pepi, at Caritta, 411 N. Rodeo Dr. and at Fred Segal, 8100 Melrose, is a California-based jewelry designer who has made quite a name for herself throughout the country. With modern designs and a real flair for style, her collection is worth a look. *Shanes Jewelers*, in Westwood at 1015 Broxton, is a more youth-oriented jewelry store geared to the large number of college students in the area. They specialize in earrings, chains, and watches.

William Wasserman is someone whose middle name should be jewelry. After operating a successful upstairs "salon" in Beverly Hills, where he had a loyal following, he expanded to a store in the Santa Monica Place Mall. The store—William Wasserman Jewelers—was superbly designed using the best materials, and makes a stunning showplace for the exquisite selection of jewelry. He carries a complete line of watches, including Croton, Concord, Gucci, and more; he also specializes in pieces designed by the most innovative jewelry designers. Wasserman, as well as his entire staff, is extremely friendly and helpful.

Another name in California jewelry is the well-known *Morgan and Company Jewelers,* at 1131 Glendon in Westwood, and *Morgan on Main,* at 2721 Main St. in Santa Monica. Here estate jewelry and well designed, high-quality jewels are featured. *Denton Fine Jewelers,* at 11696 San Vicente Blvd. in Brentwood, and 15231 Sunset Blvd. in Pacific Palisades, offers the finest in rings, watches, and other jewelry. A small classic collection is offered in fashionable and comfortable surroundings.

Another store geared to younger tastes is *Fashionable Affordables,* 103 W. Washington Ave., Marina del Rey. Thin gold bracelets and chains are featured, and the prices are right; you can pick up a bracelet for less than $40.00.

Norman and Company, at 11640 San Vicente Blvd., is a light, airy, modern store with classic as well as more innovative jewelry. High price tags and very high quality are key words here. *The Gold Company,* at 951 E. Green St. in Pasadena, carries one-of-a-kind designs by Karen McGrary, proprietor-designer. Such combinations as tourmaline crystals and pearls are made by McGrary, who has a real flair for jewelry design. She will be happy to work with individual customers who have loose stones or want a piece of jewelry that is way out of the ordinary. She also has a line of more conventional pieces.

GIFTS AND STATIONERY

Many shops that do not fit into any other category fit here. Los Angeles has an abundance of individual gift stores with just the right present for someone at home: Here are a few:

Brenda Himmel, Fine Stationery and Gifts, at 1126 Montana Ave, Santa Monica, is a paper lover's heaven. Offering stationery, blank books, address books, and gift items, this store has an added attraction: the helpful and knowledgeable owner—Brenda Himmel. *Discovery, A Gift Boutique,* at 3835 Cross Creek Rd., No. 21, The Country Mart, Malibu, has a good selection of handicrafts from the United States and around the world. Accessories, jewelry, cards, and stationery are all available here. At 9634 Santa Monica Blvd., Beverly Hills, *Marshall Todd's Glass Menagerie* has a whimsical collection of glass from all over the world. Animals and limited-edition sculptures, as well as other decorative and useful glass pieces, are featured.

Richard–Ginori, 9555 Santa Monica Blvd., Beverly Hills, has been manufacturing fine china in Europe since 1735. This store, in addition to having a large stock of china, has *objets d'art* and other decorative items. *Geary's North,* 437 N. Beverly Dr., Beverly Hills, has been a well-respected name in Los Angeles for years. *Geary's*—the more traditional sister store down the street—carries china, silver, and crystal, whereas this store carries a hodgepodge of items—graphics, ceramic dishes, stuffed pillows, and other unusual gifts.

Homeworks, 2913 Main St. in Santa Monica, is a great place to go when you want to buy something but you are not quite sure what. From pens and address books to a great selection of housewares, this store is chock full of high tech merchandise. It also carries a whole line of Braun items—clocks, scales, and so on. Also on Main St., at 2801, is the recently expanded *Bobbi Leonard.* Packed with furniture, novelty items, and accessories such as fans, lacquer boxes, and silk flowers, this store is a fantasy land of things for the home.

The Rainbow, 434 N. Camden Dr., Beverly Hills, is a wonderful store filled with unusual gift items; all the profits go to a treatment center for children with cancer. A variety of toys, stationery, gifts, quilts, and more is carried.

TOYS

Probably because of the devotion of Los Angelenos to leisure time, there are about as many toy stores for adults as for children. *Chess and Games Unlimited,* in Beverly Hills, West Los Angeles, and Encino, carries beautiful wooden chess and backgammon sets and almost any other game you can imagine. These stores are for the child in all of us. They carry a stunning array of traditional games as well as video and computer games.

At *G.A.M.E.S.,* at 6626 Valjean Ave. in Van Nuys, and in Torrance and Fountain Valley, there are investments that you can play with: the world's largest selection of antique slot machines. Decoration as well as diversion, these slot machines come in endless sizes, styles, and colors. There are also video games, crap tables, and other gambling paraphernalia here. The staff is very helpful.

Toy Mart, at 301 N. Beverly Dr. in Beverly Hills, is for actual children. This fantasy world includes every toy your child has ever wanted. Stuffed toys, erector sets, and dolls, as well as carriages, strollers and other things, are stocked.

SPORTING GOODS AND SPORTS CLOTHING

With the emphasis on health and fitness so much a part of the way of life in Southern California, it would follow that there are many stores in this category. Because new stores in this field pop up all the time, here is just a smattering:

Naico's Tennis Shop, at 9441 Little Santa Monica Blvd. in Beverly Hills, is frequented by many stars and offers fabulous service. Twenty-four hour stringing service is available, and the store has a full selection of clothing and accessories. *Oshman's* sporting goods stores, with many locations in the Los Angeles area, are virtual supermarkets for sporting goods; from baseballs to volleyball nets, these stores have whatever you need to keep fit.

Big 5, a sporting-goods store with a loyal following, also has branches in various areas.

Smith's Sporting Goods has stores in the Marina, West Los Angeles, and the Pacific Palisades. With many brand names such as Adidas, Nike, K-Swiss,

Head, and more, this is another one-stop place to shop for sports items. *Phidippides Sports* call themselves, "your aerobic sports center," and all the personnel at the stores in Marina del Rey, Rolling Hills Estates, and Manhattan Beach are very well versed in athletic footwear. They can help you with any specific need and know what kinds of shoes you will need for the specific sport you participate in.

The Dance Center of London, with locations in Pasadena and Beverly Hills, is one of the best places for women's athletic and dance clothing. They have tremendous stocks of fashionable and colorful warm-up suits, leotards, and other dancewear. Price tags are a bit hefty; but this is the place to go when you want something that you won't see everyone else wearing.

No Sweat, 2910 Main Street in Santa Monica, has unique cotton exercise and dancewear from France. Stripes and unusual designs identify these innovative and comfortable styles.

ANTIQUES

As a relatively young city, compared to those on the East Coast, Los Angeles has a surprisingly good selection of antique stores. Probably the most popular and one of the best priced collections of antiques can be found at the *Antique Guild,* 8800 Venice Blvd. Here, amid three acres of showrooms, is a full stock of English, Danish, French, and Italian furniture, clocks, jewelry, and other collectibles. Other countries are often represented as well in this collection that spans several eras of antiques. The Guild carries books on antiques and small items such as glass and china. A group of buyers is employed by the store to acquire the best buys in Europe. Dealers and decorators, along with retail buyers, shop here so you can be assured that you will be getting a good buy.

In Beverly Hills, *The Lion's Lair,* 427 North Canon Dr., is a great place for antique silver, crystal, and china. Also found in this charming boutique are fantastic objects from all over the European market.

The Antique Center, 10532 E. Whittier Blvd., Whittier, is another huge store filled with clocks—the specialty—furniture, jewelry, and accessories.

Cricket Antiques, 2025 Pacific Ave., Venice, is a surprisingly elegant establishment for such a casual beach community. But herein is the attraction of shopping in Venice: It offers the unusual as well as the unexpected. This shop specializes in French and English items from the seventeenth through the nineteenth centuries. In addition to furniture there are dishes and whimsical accessories such as a life-sized, colorful carousel horse.

At *Beverly Antiques,* 8827 Beverly Blvd., West Hollywood, silver is the specialty. If you are looking for a spoon or fork from an obsolete pattern, this may very well be the place. *Le Garage Sale,* 322 N. La Cienega, is as intriguing as its name. It has an interesting selection of memorabilia and collectibles such as glassware, knickknacks, tableware, and clothing.

Both *King's Arts and Antiques,* 529–531 N. La Cienega, and *Y. C. King and Sons,* 308 N. Rodeo Dr., have fine selections of Oriental antiques, including cloisonne, porcelain, jade, and semiprecious stones. Architectural antiques and cash registers constitute the fare at *The Vintage Cash Register and Scale Company*, Sherman Oaks, 13448 Ventura Blvd. Brass cash registers of all kinds are displayed with antique scales and architectural fixtures and accessories. Brass ceiling fixtures, bank teller cages, and slot machines provide only a sampling of the unusual items stocked.

ART GALLERIES

Although large in number, the art galleries of Los Angeles are as spread out as the city itself. The highest concentration, however, exists in Hollywood and West Hollywood; the galleries in the newer areas of downtown and Venice are developing and may perhaps overtake the Hollywood galleries in importance in the future. The downtown gallery scene, in particular, is coming more and more into prominence because it offers a cheaper area in which to open a business simply for art's sake.

Most Los Angeles galleries offer Southern California art; others include a smattering of international works.

The following is a selected tour of galleries throughout the city. For further general information, contact the Los Angeles Convention and Visitors Bureau, or, for current information about showings, consult either local Los Angeles papers, such as *LA Weekly* and the *LA Reader*, or *The Los Angeles Times* and *Herald Examiner*.

With more galleries popping up all the time, the downtown art scene there is especially important.

The *ARCO Center for Visual Arts* is located on Level B of the ARCO Plaza, 505 S. Flower St., one of the largest subterranean shopping centers in the country; it contains more than sixty shops and restaurants. This particular gallery specializes in current photography; and the exhibits change regularly.

LA Artcore, 652 Mateo St., embodies an interesting concept as well as some of the best Los Angeles art. Its literature describes it this way: "LA Artcore is a nonprofit public benefit corporation established to further professional opportunities for artists and to bring art into the lives of the general public." But beyond this, LA Artcore is a active gallery: "We focus on bringing new artists to light in the Los Angeles area," notes gallery president Julie Belnick. The gallery shows predominately contemporary paintings and sculptures; besides the Los Angeles influence, they often have other kinds of exhibits—contemporary Korean drawings, for example.

A long-time fixture in the Los Angeles art world is the *Ankrum Gallery*, 657 N. La Cienega Blvd. This gallery shows abstract and figurative contemporary art and emphasizes California artists. Sculpture is also shown on a decked balcony upstairs. The *Richard Mann Gallery*, 665 N. La Cienega, features work by such famous artists as Chagall, Miro, Agam; Mann's own abstract expressionist paintings are also displayed. Sculpture, etchings, and other contemporary works are exhibited as well. *James Turcotte Gallery*, 4513 Santa Monica Blvd., shows contemporary art with an emphasis on California artists; there are artistic, musical, and fashion shows here; new show the first Tuesday of each month. Represented are: Marc Kreisal, Hamilton Phillips, and Jett Jackson.

Galerie Helene, 8232 W. 3rd St., is unique in that it specializes in primitive and naive art by American and European artists. *Z Gallerie,* with many locations—Santa Monica, Sherman Oaks, Redondo Beach, Malibu, Encino, and Marina del Rey—is a poster gallery that specializes in big, bright, contemporary graphics. Some of the artists represented include Brian Davis, Steven Kenny, James Paul Brown, Jerry Schurr, Marcus Vailevsky, Edward Hopper, and Robert Weil. It also carries Filmex posters and photographs by Ansel Adams and Richard Avedon. This chain offers reasonably priced art at its best.

In Beverly Hills, at 399 N. Rodeo Dr., *Wally Findlay Galleries* is *the* place for contemporary art. This gallery has been in business for over 100 years and carries all genres by American and European artists. The *Speaker Gallery,* 9025 Santa Monica Blvd., West Hollywood, often has unusual exhibits.

In addition to fine-art galleries, there are many crafts galleries around Los Angeles. The *Main Street Gallery,* 2803 Main St., Santa Monica, has an interesting collection. Japanese folk art, featuring porcelain, scrolls, and masks, among many other crafts, is offered. In Brentwood, at 11981 San Vicente Blvd., the *del Mano Gallery* carries contemporary American crafts. Jewelry, ceramics, blown glass, wearable art, fiberworks, woodworks, and more are available here at a wide range of prices—from $2.00 to $2,000.

The *Image of the Inuit Gallery,* specializing in Eskimo art from Canada and Alaska, is located in the *Contempo Westwood Gallery,* 10886 Le Conte Ave. A good selection of prints and soapstone carvings is featured and all are authenticated and numbered. Another similar gallery, *Wounded Knee Indian Gallery,* 2413 Wilshire Blvd., has old and new Indian crafts. From pottery to rugs to graphics and beadwork, a multitude is offered from many nations, including the Navajo and the Hopi. Another such gallery, *The Gallery of Eskimo Art,* is located at 2665 Main St. in Santa Monica.

The *Silver Man Gallery,* 11739 Barrington Court, Brentwood, features an extensive collection of American Indian jewelry and folk art and a potpourri of authentic gift items from the world over.

Last, but certainly not least, is *Sherwood Gallery* in the Santa Monica Place Mall (and in Laguna Beach). This gallery is a fantasy land of soft sculptures—a grandmother, kids, and even a flasher equipped with a raincoat—all stand waiting to be snatched up and taken home. Traditional graphics and other types of nonhuman soft sculpture, such as flowers and palm trees, are also shown. This gallery is especially fun during the holidays; and it is always enlightening just to watch kids' faces as they enter.

The following is a list of smaller galleries by area. Phone numbers are included, since it is often necessary to make an appointment at these places.

West Hollywood/Hollywood. *Gemini Graphics Editions Limited,* 8365 Melrose Ave.; 651–0513. Limited edition graphics and small sculptures. The shows change as the graphics are published. Established names offer their work here. *Flow Ace Gallery,* 8373 Melrose Ave.; 658–6980. Exhibits in this three-room gallery change every four to six weeks. Artists include Sam Francis, Robert

Rauschenberg, Mark Di Suvero, and Edward Ruscha. *Los Angeles Institute of Contemporary Art* (LAICA), 2020 S. Robertson Blvd.; 559–5033. This nonprofit museum was founded in 1973 to provide alternatives to visual arts from its laboratory for new art. Everything in the gallery, including international installations, along with paintings and sculpture, is related to video. *Stephen White Gallery,* 752 N. LaCienga Blvd.; 657–6995. One-man shows are the highlights of this vintage and contemporary photography gallery. Shows change every six weeks. *Molly Barnes Gallery,* 750 N. La Cienega Blvd.; 654–1966. Original Los Angeles contemporary, nonrepresentational art is the focus of this five-year-old gallery. *Janus Gallery,* 8000 Melrose; 658–6084. Skylights show off paintings, sculpture, and contemporary ceramics created by both West and East Coast artists. *170 S. La Brea Galleries* (contains Jan Baum Gallery; 972–0170; Roy Boyd Gallery; 938–2328; Swope Gallery; 938–2234; Art Works; 934–2205; and Prints and Art of Japan; 933–8382). Located in an old apartment building that has been renovated and now contains the three galleries, plus an outstanding bookstore (one of Los Angeles' best for art books) and Le Grand Buffet, a high-tech luncheon place with catered meals. *Municipal Art Gallery,* 4800 Hollywood Blvd., Barnsdall Park, Los Feliz; 660–2200. This city-owned gallery contains two separate spaces filled with work by Southern California artists. Exhibits change once a month. Admission is 50 cents; Free tours at 2:00 P.M. A gift shop and a bookshop are on the premises.

Downtown. *Kirk deGooyer Gallery,* 1308 Factory Pl.; 623–8333. Mostly American artists with a focus on California paintings, photographs, and some sculpture. Located on the fifth floor of a large, airy converted warehouse which includes artists' lofts. *Traction Gallery,* 800 Traction Ave.; 680–4743. American artists are featured here; the focus is on Southern California work. The gallery is diverse, with films, video and lectures, along with mixed media and paper shows. By appointment. Located in a converted warehouse. *Los Angeles Contemporary Exhibitions* (LACE), 240 S. Broadway, third floor; 620–0104. Painting, sculpture, and performance pieces are highlighted in this converted loft space. Also, an art periodical library. The entire concept leans toward the avant-garde. *Stella Polaris Gallery,* 303 Boyd St.; 617–2846. This is one of the city's most unusual galleries; it encompasses the largest space of its kind in Los Angeles. It's filled with international contemporary paintings, drawings, and graphics and focuses on one-person shows. Special shows for the Olympics.

Beach Area (Venice/Santa Monica). *Flow Ace Gallery,* 185 Windward Ave., Venice; 392–4931. Contemporary European and American art is presented in three galleries in a converted bank building. Art and architecture bookstore. *Los Angeles Louver Galleries,* 77 Market St. and 55 N. Venice Blvd., Venice; 392–8695. Across the street from the West Beach Café serving French cuisine in the European style, this gallery offers European and American contemporary art with an emphasis on English works. Claims to hold the country's largest collection of graphic arts outside New York City. *Tortue Gallery,* 2197 Santa Monica Blvd., Santa Monica; 828–8878. Features contemporary American art with an emphasis on California painting, sculpture, and drawings. Exhibits change once a month.

GOURMET FOOD AND EQUIPMENT

Los Angeles is a city interested in food, and there are many gourmet markets and stores that attest to this preoccupation. *Montana Mercantile,* at 1324 Montana Ave. in Santa Monica, is an unusual store that offers cooking classes and extremely high-quality cookware, gadgets, and anything else that you need to start a gourmet kitchen. Demonstrations of new equipment often take place, and this is a store in which you can browse for hours.

The Casual Gourmet Galleria, at the Sherman Oaks Galleria, has glassware and china, as well as unusual gourmet foods. It also carries small goods such as place mats and utensils. Coffee beans of all kinds are sold. And at several locations of the *Coffee Bean and Tea Leaf,* coffee beans are the main staple; there are all kinds of coffee and tea pots in stock, as well as unusual teas and herbs.

The *Pottery Barn,* also with many locations, has a wonderful selection of gadgets—all up on one wall; and there is an extensive selection of well-priced glasses, china, vases, salad sets, and so on—everything for the well-equipped kitchen and dining room. *Williams Sonoma,* at the Beverly Center and 438 N. Rodeo Dr., is a well respected name in kitchen wares. They carry gourmet pots and gadgets as well as spices and gourmet foods.

Le Cookery, 13624 Ventura Blvd., Sherman Oaks, is a gourmet cookware store and cooking school. Coffees, teas, jams, and mustards are all available. *Le Petit Four Gourmet Shop and Catering,* 8654 Sunset Blvd., is a comfortable and appealing store. Petit fours, other French pastries, caviars, chocolates from Belgium, and gourmet foods from Fauchon in Paris are enough to make even the most diehard dieter break down. *The Tudor House,* 411 Santa Monica Blvd. in Santa Monica, caters to the transplanted Englishman who cannot survive without his sausage rolls and shortbread. Groceries, sweets, meats, and bakery goods are featured, and there is a little tea room. The mail-order operation ships merchandise anywhere. *Mon Grenier Gourmet Shop,* 22235 Pacific Coast Hwy. in Malibu, has French dishes—smoked fishes, pâtés, croissants, and picnic baskets, to name just a few, to take out.

In Venice are two especially good gourmet markets with a wide range of food and merchandise. At 175 Marine St., off Pacific Ave., *Charmer's Market* is a huge place with the freshest of flowers, one of the largest selections of magazines around, the freshest produce, and much more. There is fresh pasta, delicious tarts and other bakery goods, salads, a tremendous stock of wines—in a wine refrigerator—cheeses, bread, and more. There are tables at which you can have a meal and a cappucino/wine bar where you can also sample the pastries. The *Rose Café,* close by at 220 Rose Ave., is another gourmet's delight. From the large pink rose on the wall of the building to the scrumptious pastries, the Rose attracts people from all around Los Angeles. There is a cafeteria-like section with tables and high stools, and a more formal restaurant (and some outdoor tables) in back. Coffee beans, mustards, and crackers are carried, as is a collection of housewares, such as mugs, dishes, glasses, and so on.

BOOKS

Los Angeles is well represented by the large book chains; there are specialized bookstores geared to many particular interests as well. The following is a selection of both. *B. Dalton/Pickwick* has stores in Beverly Hills, Canoga Park, Costa Mesa, Lakewood, Los Angeles, Palos Verdes, Torrance, and Westwood. This chain has always been interested in promotion, and on any given day you can probably see the author of a newly published book autographing copies. The Hollywood store (6734 Hollywood Blvd.) has some bargains on the second floor, where you will find titles that have been marked down from 50 to 80 percent.

Another well-known chain, *Doubleday,* has stores throughout the city, but the Beverly Hills store is perhaps the most exciting branch. Frequented by authors and stars, this store (9477 Santa Monica Blvd.) is a place to get signed editions of books and to gaze at the stars.

Hunter's Books, Walden Books, and *Brentano's* are other stores with several locations in the L.A. area. *Crown Books* is considered an innovation in the Los Angeles book industry. At any one of its many stores (with more opening all the time) you can get a best seller or a magazine well below list price. Crown features sections with 99-cent and other low-priced books.

One popular independent bookstore is *Small World Books,* 1407 Ocean Front Walk, Venice. Located right near the beach, this is a good place for browsing. There is usually a showing of a local artist to supplement the great selection of books, unusual magazines and newspapers from all over the country.

Papa Bach Bookstore, 11317 Santa Monica Blvd., is named for a well-known figure in the Los Angeles literary world. Open late every night, the store also publishes its own literary magazine—*Bachy.* Because the emphasis is on alternative politics, you will be able to find books on almost any contemporary movement, no matter how obscure. *Westwood Bookstore,* 1121 Gayley Ave., is the epitome of a college-area bookstore. Serious texts abound, as do less scholarly books on contemporary issues. There is also a good selection of magazines, including the more literary "little magazines."

Specialty and unusual bookstores abound in Los Angeles. For metaphysical and religious topics as well as meditation pillows, herbs, and teas there is the *Bodhi Tree Bookstore,* 8585 Melrose Ave., West Hollywood. In the same area, at 9011 Melrose Ave, *George Sand Bookstore* has an impressive selection of books in the areas of dance, music, film, theater, and literature.

An interesting "bookstore cum expresso bar and café" is *Food for Thought* in the Beverly Center. Emphasizing art books, the *Norton Simon Museum Bookstore* is at Colorado and Orange Grove Blvds. in Pasadena. As a nonprofit establishment, this store is able to offer low prices on its high-quality selection of art books.

Los Angeles, in its role as the center of the film industry, has quite a few stores specializing in books on movies and the industry. *Bond Street* at 1638 North Wilcox Ave. in Hollywood is one of these, as is the *Collector's Shop* at 1063 N. Spaulding Ave., in West Hollywood. Another Hollywood "hangout"—the

Larry Edmunds Book Shop at 6658 Hollywood Blvd.—offers many books and photographs relating to cinema and theater. An eye-catching bookstore in a red barn houses maps, new and out-of-print art books, graphics, and more. This store, *Zeitlin and ver Brugge,* at 815 N. La Cienega, also has a wide selection of rare prints and drawings, as the sign in front of the store attests.

The Comic Vendor, as its name implies, provides a wealth of those old comic books that you used to read as a kid. Located at 19800 Hawthorne Blvd., this store carries Superman, Spiderman, and many, more old comics.

Used and antiquarian books also have their providers. *Acres of Books* is a well-known store; it is said to have the most books in one place in Southern California. The store, at 240 Long Beach Blvd., is a huge place in which you will find many obsolete and out-of-print books at reasonable prices. *Butler's Book Store,* in the Boys Market Shopping Center in the Marina, is a great place to discuss favorite "reads"; be sure to check their stack of recommendations.

In the antiquarian field there is also *Bennett and Marshall* at 8214 Melrose Ave. in West Hollywood; they offer rare books and manuscripts. *The Scriptorium,* 427 N. Canon Dr. in Beverly Hills, offers a diverse selection of autographs, manuscripts, and documents. At 6607 Hollywood Blvd. you will find the *Cherokee Book Store,* offering out-of-print books and first editions.

RECORDS

The record shops mentioned in the discount section below are the most popular, but here are a few more:

Nickelodeon, Century City Shopping Center, offers not only records and tapes but is also one of the largest home-entertainment centers in Los Angeles. Video tapes, video discs, video games, songbooks, and accessories are all in abundant supply. *Classical Record Shop,* 366 S. Maple Dr., Beverly Hills, is overflowing with classical music.

Tower Records, in several locations, has its main branch at 8801 Sunset Blvd. This store has been a local institution for years. It has almost every record ever produced; the store is a favorite of local musicians. *Music and Memories,* 10850 Ventura Blvd., Studio City, specializes in those tunes that make you "remember when." It has a good selection of show music, movie music, jazz, and much more.

DISCOUNT SHOPPING

Almost everything is available at a discount in Los Angeles if you look hard enough. The following is a sampling of some of these establishments. (If you explore, you will probably find many more.) Some of the more elegant discount stores are provided in other category listings.

Cameras. *Henry's Camera, Hi Fi, and Video,* 516 W. 8th St., downtown, stocks name-brand camera, stereo, and video equipment and offers prices similar to New York discount prices. It may be a bit of a trauma shopping among the wall-to-wall people, but the large savings are worth it.

Children's Clothing. *The Ridiculous Discount Shop,* 5232 Laurel Canyon Blvd., N. Hollywood, despite its name, has a large selection of clothing for children at up to 50 percent below retail. Mainly geared to girls sized 2 to 14 preteen, there is also a small selection of boys' clothes. *The Stork Shop,* 1868 S. La Cienega Blvd., is an outlet for children's clothes, and up to 40 percent discount is given on clothes from many manufacturers. The shop carries an extremely large regularly changing inventory.

Family Clothing. *Beno's* has more than five Los Angeles locations and offers a very large selection of name-brand clothing discounted at 20 to 60 percent. Levi's is one brand that is consistently stocked. The downtown warehouse, at 1500 Santee St., covers one city block. *Jerry Piller's,* 937 E. Colorado Blvd., Pasadena, and 8163 Santa Monica Blvd., Los Angeles, has a mixture of better garments and footwear for men and women. (The Los Angeles store specializes in ladies wear). There is so much going on in these stores that it is hard for anyone but the seasoned shopper to handle, but your efforts should prove worthwhile. Piller's buys name-brand apparel in lots from some of the finest boutiques in town; designer clothing is discounted up to 50 percent.

Men's Clothing. *Brussell's Gentlemen's Apparel,* at 114 S. Beverly Blvd. in Beverly Hills, caters to the professional man. Stocking Yves Saint Laurent, Ralph Lauren, Pierre Cardin, and other designers, Brussell's suits start from about $100. They also carry slacks, shirts, sweaters, and sports coats. *Dorman–Winthrop* has locations in Culver City, North Hollywood, and Westminister; they offer suits, sport coats, and slacks. Their selection is large and the discounts result in prices about 25 to 40 percent below retail. Styles are current, not closeouts, and they offer an extra two percent discount for cash payments or checks. *Rick Pallack,* at 4554 Sherman Oaks Ave. in Sherman Oaks, has domestic and European sweaters, suits, sports jackets, shirts, and accessories at 25 to 50 percent below retail. The emphasis here is on wardrobe coordination. It is best to shop during the week, when it will be less crowded.

Women's Clothing. *California Apparel and Textile* has three locations. The main store is at 2524 S. Hill St., downtown. This is the outlet for a major manufacturer of women's and girls' clothing, and gigantic sales are held only during the first weekend of each month. Most items sell for about $12.00, and can't be tried on. *Chic Lingerie Outlet,* 693 High Lane, Redondo Beach, and 1126 Santee St., Los Angeles, has quality pajamas, panties, slips, and other intimate apparel. Prices are about 50 percent below retail. *The Fantastic Designer Showroom,* Suite 220, 860 S. Los Angeles St., is among the shops located in the landmark Cooper Bldg. Discounts of from 50 to 75 percent are offered on popular junior lines as well as on designer goods. The regular clothing is in Suite 201, and the designer merchandise is in 220.

The famous *Fredericks of Hollywood* has an outlet, as well as the regular line, at the Hawthorne Plaza Mall, 120 Hawthorne Blvd. This is the place to get those alluring lingerie fashions at low prices. All items have been marked down from one to six times, yielding substantial savings. *Importique,* 16733 Ventura Blvd. in Encino, offers better European fashions—French designer fashions are from 20 to 70 percent less than retail. *Ladies' Apparel,* at 840 S. Los Angeles St., has a large selection from name manufacturers and designers. The same labels that are found in better department stores are here at 20 to 40 percent less.

New Yorkers visiting Los Angeles will surely know this familiar name— *Loehmann's.* This "grandmother of discount stores" has three locations in Los Angeles: 6220 W. 3rd St., 130 Laguna Rd. in Fullerton, and 19389 Victory Blvd. in Reseda. Loehmann's has been offering national brands and designer goods at a discount for over half a century. The secret to shopping here is that you have to be able to recognize designer and manufacturer items that contain no labels. The prices are at least one-third less than retail, and a separate section contains clothing at even greater reductions.

Gifts. *Christine Import Company,* 714 South Hill St., downtown, has porcelain figures and leather goods. There is a good selection, and the prices are extremely low—starting at only 99 cents for some figurines. *The Soap Plant,* 3720 Sunset Blvd., offers items from around the world. Natural soaps start at 70 cents, and there are baskets, wood boxes, toys, fans, stone carvings, kimonos, and more. *The World Center,* at 420 N. Beverly Dr., is a nonprofit UNICEF organization offering international crafts. Dolls are featured; items from the Soviet Union, Mainland China, Africa, and many other countries include wall hangings, jewelry, and almost any handmade item that you can imagine.

Jewelry. *Marvin Hime and Company,* 228 S. Beverly Blvd., Beverly Hills, sells precious stones, metals, and jewelry. It imports many pieces directly from the country of origin and sells wholesale to jewelers as well as to the public. *M. Weinstein, Inc.,* Room 719, 727 W. 7th St., downtown, has been dealing in diamonds and gold jewelry for years. Gems from estates, banks, and other parties getting rid of their holdings are about 30 percent below retail prices.

Pottery. *Camerons,* 1022 S. Sepulveda Ave., Manhattan Beach, has a great selection of Mikasa china and pottery at 15 percent off. There are also closeouts at an 80 percent discount. The *Franciscan Shop,* at 2901 Los Feliz Blvd. in Los Angeles, has a large selection of seconds of Franciscan Earthenware at 40 percent off regular retail prices. Famous patterns, such as Desert Rose, Apple, Ivy, and Hacienda, are available; the shop also carries crystal, candles, place mats, stainless flatware, and other accessories for the home. The *Pottery Barn* outlet, 4729 Alla Rd., Marina del Rey, has great prices on nonreturnable housewares: pots and pans, dishes, glasses. Many of the items are the same as those stocked in regular stores and at considerable savings.

Shoes. *Coast Footwear,* 2016 Lincoln Blvd., Santa Monica, has recent fashions at approximately 20 percent below retail; they carry athletic footwear as well as fashion. *Standard Shoes Stores* are famous throughout the Los Angeles area as *the* place to go for a bargain on the same shoes that you would see in better department stores and boutiques. There are several locations in the area. And for even bigger savings there is the *Standard Shoe Disposal Store* in Culver City, Reseda, and Hawthorne. This is where the inventory from the other stores goes when it is not sold within a certain amount of time; women's shoes start at about $2.00.

Michael's is the well-known discount shoe store for men. There are several locations; the main one is in Beverly Hills at 9551 Wilshire Blvd. Name brands, athletic as well as fashion footwear, are sold here at considerable savings.

The Cinderella Shoe Shop is for women with very small feet, as you might have guessed from the name. Sample sizes 1½ to 5 in dress and casual shoes are available. *Samples Only,* at Loehmann's Plaza, 19367 Victors Blvd., Reseda: Ladies' fashion shoes and purses are sold at this store, which is connected with Loehmann's. Only sizes 4B to 7B are stocked; they are sold at 30 to 60 percent less than retail.

Sporting Goods and Sports Clothing. *Bikecology Bike Shops* are a rare treat to visit for people who have ordered from their catalogues for years. Probably the best-stocked bike stores in the country, they are great for anything from a bike light to an expensive Italian frame. They also carry skates and skating equipment in some of their locations. *Love Tennis,* 4134 Lincoln Blvd. in the Marina, is a good place to find tenniswear and equipment at competitive prices. This large store has a large selection of Head and other name products. The staff is very helpful.

Records. *Licorice Pizza Records and Tapes* has nineteen stores in southern California. Record albums and tapes are discounted by at least 20 percent on all kinds of music from pop to classical. *The Wherehouse,* with more than fifty stores in the area, is well known throughout the country. There are especially low savings; many albums sell for less than $5.00, and the more recent releases sell for $8.98.

Swap Meets. These are special events for Southern Californians. Everyone, from artists to old-book collectors and silver craftsmen to comic-book collectors, sells his or her wares at swap meets around the city. From time to time almost every community has a small swap meet in front of the community center or church, but the following include some of the larger recurring meets: Rose Bowl Flea Market, Rosemont Ave. and Arroyo Blvd., Pasadena; (213) 588–4411; and the San Fernando Valley Swap and Flea Market, 585 Glenoaks Blvd., San Fernando; (213) 670–0660.

Toys. *Toys 'R' Us* is a nationwide chain with more than ten stores in the Los Angeles area; it offers name-brand, widely advertised toys at low prices. This chain advertises quite often in local papers, and you can get a good idea of the recent prices from these ads.

DINING OUT. It wasn't too many years ago that Los Angeles was considered a gastronomic wasteland; if you were in a restaurant and were served a steak the way you ordered it, you were considered a lucky individual. Ethnic restaurants were a rarity, and it was the general consensus that New York was the only city where you could literally eat your way around the world.

In the last decade, there has been a tremendous growth in the restaurant industry of Los Angeles. Chinese restaurants now include Szechuan, Hunan, Cantonese, and Mandarin restaurants, categorized by the region of the country, not just the country as a whole. Italian restaurants also became specialized and now serve either northern or southern Italian cuisine. There grew to be representation of other countries as well: Hungary, Jordan, Israel, Ethiopia, Morocco, Spain, Germany, and Jamaica. Ethnic bistros, offering home-style food at budget prices, much like those in New York City, are now in every corner of the city.

French restaurants have also undergone growth. The classic dishes alone, such as coq au vin or boeuf bourgignon, no longer satisfied a curious and more sophisticated clientele. When nouvelle cuisine became the vogue, French restaurants in Los Angeles, such as Ma Maison and L'Orangerie, offered this cuisine on their menu at practically the same time as the rage hit Paris.

Other restaurants have recently blossomed that tout the California and the New America cuisine. This emphasis on fresh, local foodstuff, usually prepared by grilling, is evident at L.A. Nicola in Las Feliz and Bernie's in Westwood, as well as at many other eateries.

Most of Los Angeles's most distinguished restaurants are within the borders of Hollywood and West Los Angeles, incorporating part of Los Angeles proper, Beverly Hills, and West Hollywood. Such notable restaurants as the Palm, Spago, Ma Maison, and Le St. Germain, all lie within this area, as do hundreds of ethnic cafés. Chinatown offers the highest concentration of Chinese restaurants; Little Tokyo, Japanese restaurants; Little Korea, Korean restaurants. The Fairfax district specializes in Israeli and Jewish-style cafés.

For budget dining, ethnic restaurants offer the best value for your dollar and generally provide warm hospitality in a "Momma–Poppa" family-style operation. Many restaurants offer "early-bird dinners" between the hours of 5:00 P.M. and 6:30 P.M., when you can dine at reduced cost; but it's best to phone ahead to be certain.

In a city well noted for its entertainment industry and celebrities, it is to be expected that there will be many very expensive restaurants that cater to "beautiful people." The Bistro, Ma Maison, Spago, La Serre at lunch, Jimmy's, and many more restaurants offer haute cuisine dining experiences in elegant surroundings with a clientele to match. It's not uncommon to see a plethora of famous faces at these bistros. There's no need to feel intimidated about making a reservation at one of the star-studded restaurants; if you dress appropriately and are prepared to spend money, in nine out of ten cases you'll be treated kindly. If your pocketbook does not match your curiosity, you can have lunch instead of dinner, save 10 to 20 percent of the bill, and still have the same exciting experience.

Dining out at Sunday brunch is a trend in Los Angeles. Traditionally this late morning/early afternoon meal includes breakfast fare as well as light luncheon dishes, either as a buffet or as a sit-down repast. Eggs Benedict, crepes, quiches, and salads are usual brunch items. Several Los Angeles hotel dining rooms offer spectacular brunches, featuring everything from eggs and crepes to crab legs and roast beef. The Westwood Marquis, the Sheraton Universal, and the Century Plaza hotels offer outstanding buffet brunches. The offering at the Fine Affair in Bel Air—an airy restaurant filled with lush greenery, trellises, and mirrors—is representative of a chic California brunch. It serves French/California-style entrees on dainty flowered china. Brunch has become so popular that many Los

Angeles restaurants are beginning to offer a Saturday brunch besides the traditional Sunday one.

The most popular evening dining hours are between 7:00 P.M. and 9:00 P.M.; Friday and Saturday nights are the busiest. Always make a reservation to be certain of getting a table and always check the dress code as well. Many restaurants are closed on Sunday and/or Monday nights.

Price categories are approximate and generally are set for a three-course meal—appetizer, entree, and dessert—per person. The price does *not* include cocktails, wine, tax, tip, or gratuities. Fifteen percent is the expected tip, 20 percent for very fine service or for a dinner at the city's most expensive restaurants, where dining is an evening's experience. An *expensive* dinner runs $30 and up. A *moderate* meal usually costs between $12 and $30 per person. An *inexpensive* dinner runs under $12.

Credit cards are accepted at most restaurants, but inexpensive specialty or ethnic restaurants usually accept cash only. Restaurants' acceptance of credit cards appears at the end of each of the following listings according to the following abbreviations:

AE - American Express
CB - Carte Blanche
DC - Diner's Club
MC - MasterCard
V - Visa

If a listing indicates "No CB," for example, that means the restaurant accepts all credit cards but Carte Blanche.

Restaurants are categorized first by location and then by ethnicity. Sections are broken down within each cuisine according to its price category; entries are in alphabetical order within the price category. Before we begin our formal listings, here are a few notes on additional dining spots that do not fit into our regular categories.

Fast food. Internationally operated restaurants such as *McDonald's, Burger King,* and *Kentucky Fried Chicken* proliferate in Los Angeles. The White or Yellow Pages of the telephone directory will give you the location of one in your vicinity. *Cassell's* and *Fatburgers* in Los Angeles, *Fat Jack's* in Studio City, and *The Apple Pan* in West Los Angeles offer the best hamburgers at fast-food prices. *Pink's Famous Chili Dogs* is indeed the most famous hotdog stand in the city, and *Tail of the Pup* is one hotdog stand that is actually shaped like a hotdog. Mexican taco stands, much like pizza stands in New York, are in abundance. Soft-shell tacos, enchiladas, tostadas, and burritos are popular, inexpensive snacks and are generally freshly prepared. It's hit or miss, but *King Taco* in East Los Angeles, *Burrito King, Campos,* and *Lucie's,* all chains in Los Angeles, offer superior products.

Chains. Several moderately priced chain restaurants, notably *Victoria Station, Charley Brown's, the Velvet Turtle* and *the Hungry Tiger,* all successful in the steak/seafood genre. The *Sizzler* chain steakhouses are inexpensive steak-and-salad-bar restaurants that cater to families.

Twenty-four hour and late-dining stops. There are a few restaurants open twenty-four hours, besides coffee-shop chains such as *Denny's. Vickman's* (1228 E. 8th St.) in downtown Los Angeles opens at 3:00 A.M. to serve fresh pies and Danishes, eggs, and simple American fare. *The Pantry* (877 S. Figueroa) and the *Pacific Dining Car* (1310 W. 6th St.), also located downtown, serve steaks, eggs, and other hearty items twenty-four hours a day. *Roscoe's House of Chicken and Waffles* (1514 N. Gower, in Hollywood) stays open until 3:00 A.M. It serves excellent fresh waffles, crispy fried chicken, and homemade biscuits. *DuPars* is a chain of coffee shops that stays open until the wee hours of the morning and all night at some locations. The shops bake their own pies, cakes, and doughnuts on the premises and use fresh and natural ingredients.

Desserts. Ice cream parlors and chocolate-chip cookie stores are located throughout the city; there is a section for those with sweet tooths at the end of this *Dining Out* section.

LOS ANGELES

African

Red Sea African Cuisine. *Inexpensive.* 8030¾ W. Third St., Los Angeles; 655–3992. East and West African cuisine. Chicken, beef, liver, lamb, injera sauce, dorowot sauce, and tibbswot. Lunch and dinner daily. MC, V.

Walia Ethiopian Cuisine. *Inexpensive.* 5881 W. Pico Blvd., Los Angeles; 933–1215. A restaurant with thatched walls, African-print tablecloths, and walls covered with African woven baskets, mirrors bordered with shells, and Ethiopian travel posters. Dishes are served communal-style; one eats with the aid of *injera,* the Ethiopian flat bread. *Sambusas* are crispy meat-filled turnovers, and entrees include spicy stewed beef in red pepper sauce, chicken stew, raw chopped beef with hot pepper and spicy butter, and a combination vegetable platter. Best to order a combination plate to sample a variety of foods. Try the honey wine; it's homemade with raisins, hops, and honey. It tastes like nectar from the gods. Lunch Tuesday through Friday; dinner daily, except Monday. All major credit cards.

American

Pacific Dining Car. *Expensive-Moderate.* 1310 W. 6th St., Los Angeles; 483–6000. One of Los Angeles's oldest restaurants. Great wine list with low prices. Known for steaks that are aged on the premises and charbroiled. Also good is the boned saddle of lamb and abalone steak. Desserts include a superior cheesecake, hot apple pie, and excellent ice cream. Open 24 hours daily. Valet parking. MC, V.

Lawry's California Center. *Moderate.* 570 West Ave. 26, Los Angeles; 225–2491. One of the most romantic restaurants in the city, with completely alfresco dining. Open May through October only. You'll dine outdoors at tables strategically placed throughout lush gardens of palms and tropical plants. Strolling mariachis serenade. Dinners are charbroiled New York steak, fresh swordfish, salmon, or hickory-smoked chicken. All dinners include salad, corn on the cob, sour cream tortilla casserole, fresh steamed vegetables, and hot herb bread. Strolling through the landscaped gardens is a must, either pre- or postdinner. Located near Dodger Stadium. Dinner Tuesday through Sunday. Reservations accepted for six or more only. AE, MC, V.

Maurice's Snack and Chat. *Moderate.* 5553 W. Pico Blvd., Los Angeles; 931–3877. A tiny, popular soul-food restaurant. Friendly service. The menu features short ribs, smothered pork chops, pan-fried fish, and liver and onions. Black-eyed peas, greens, and candied yams are up to par. Save room for fresh coconut cake; it's worth it. Lunch Monday through Friday; dinner daily. No credit cards.

The New York Company. *Moderate.* 2470 Fletcher Dr., Los Angeles; 665–1115. Despite the out-of-the-way location, this restaurant/saloon, depicting the urban hustle and bustle of New York, creates an unusual ambience. The cuisine is Continental/American and features spinach salad, salmon mousse, prime New York steak, fresh fish, and Provimi veal. It draws an eclectic crowd, particularly in the adjoining bar that has an elaborate video-and-sound system projecting occasional entertainment. Lunch and dinner daily. All major credit cards.

O'Shaughnessy's. *Moderate.* Arco Plaza, 515 S. Flower St., Los Angeles; 629–2565. Located on the "C" level of a modern shopping plaza, this restaurant, stressing the West, features the cuisine of the United States. Appetizers include homemade rabbit pâté and melon with spiced Kentucky ham. Seafood selections take advantage of Lake Superior whitefish, Pacific red snapper, and California sand dabs. Buffalo steak and buffalo stew, as well as roast saddle of rabbit, are highlighted menu items. Less adventurous souls can stick to chicken teriyaki or a T-bone steak. Chocolate fondue laced with Kirsch will please everyone. Unusual coffees with assorted liqueurs. Located close to the downtown Music Center; special dinners before curtain call. Lunch Monday through Friday; dinner Monday through Saturday. Validated parking. AE, DC, V.

Tam O'Shanter Inn. *Moderate.* 2980 Los Feliz Blvd., Los Angeles; 664–0228. The warm ambience of a Scottish inn. The menu features excellent prime rib with the same creamy horseradish sauce as Lawry's Prime Rib. Specials of the day. Lunch menu features sandwiches, salads, omelettes, and fish and chips. Great cole slaw with the interesting addition of chopped peanuts. Recent remodeling includes an upgraded menu. You can count on the success of the Lawry's chain to keep up this restaurant's high standards of cuisine and service. Lunch weekdays, dinner daily. No CB.

Tracton's Restaurant. *Moderate.* 3560 S. La Cienega Blvd., Los Angeles; 931–1581. Also at 16705 Ventura Blvd., Encino; 783–1320. Informal steakhouse atmosphere with kindly service. The portions are enormous and the menu includes Florida stone crabs and huge portions of prime rib au jus. Even the baked potatoes are some of the largest you will have seen. Valet parking. Lunch Monday through Friday; dinner daily. No reservations. All major credit cards.

The Egg and the Eye. *Moderate-Inexpensive.* 5814 Wilshire Blvd., Los Angeles; 933–5596. A luncheon restaurant featuring dozens of varieties of omelettes and homemade desserts. Across from the Los Angeles County Art Museum. Crafts and folk art, which fit right into the cultural mood lingering from a visit to the museum, are exhibited. Lunch Tuesday through Sunday; dinner Friday and Saturday. All major credit cards.

Phillippe's Original Sandwich Shop. *Inexpensive.* 1001 N. Alameda St., Los Angeles; 628–3781. A seventy-year-old cafeteria close to Union Station. Giant haunches of meat rest on a long counter where they are sliced into thick and juicy roast-beef sandwiches. Stew, soup, salads, and chili are also on the menu, but the sandwiches are the real draw. Dining is communal; everyone eats together at long tables. Coffee is still 10 cents a cup! Breakfast, lunch, and dinner daily. No reservations, no credit cards.

Vickman's. *Inexpensive.* 1228 E. Eighth St., Los Angeles; 622–3852. All the action starts here at the improbable hour of 3:00 A.M. when this restaurant opens its doors. It's located by the downtown produce mart, and its customers are truck drivers, delivery men, and insomniacs. The fare is plain and wholesome American food, including an excellent assortment of freshly baked goods. The strawberry pie is not to be missed, and the Danishes are sheer heaven. Ham, omelettes, poached salmon, and stuffed pork chops are satisfying. Monday through Saturday, from 3:00 A.M. to 3:00 P.M. No reservations, no credit cards.

Chinese

Lew Mitchell's Orient Express. *Moderate.* 5400 Wilshire Blvd., Los Angeles; 935–6000. This is no ordinary neighborhood Chinese restaurant. It's chic and sophisticated, with bentwood chairs, a plethora of potted palms, and ivy covered trellises in the windows. In other words, no one will throw you your chopsticks here. Specialties include sesame beef, thin sliced steak glazed with honey and sesame seeds, tea-smoked duck, beggar's chicken, and Peking duck (the latter requiring 24-hour notice). Szechuan dishes are predominant, but Mandarin cooking is featured as well. For the timid there is even a Western-style menu, which boasts a New York steak, mahi mahi, and squab. The dessert menu is eclectic; you can order the traditional lychee fruit or go for an Italian tartufo, a rich ice cream, or cheesecake with raspberry sauce. "Something for everybody" should be their motto. Closed Sunday. AE, V, MC. Lunch and dinner.

Shanghai Winter Garden. *Moderate.* 5651 Wilshire Blvd., Los Angeles; 934–0505. A reliable Oriental restaurant consistently serving Shanghai and Szechuan cuisine prepared authentically. Hot and sour soup is excellent, and the eight-precious duck is not to be overlooked. Kindly service. Open daily, lunch and dinner. Valet parking. All major credit cards.

The Twin Dragon. *Moderate-Inexpensive.* 8597 W. Pico Blvd., Los Angeles; 655–9805. One of top Los Angeles restaurants for Peking, Shanghai, and Szechuan cooking. Shrimp toast and hot and sour soup here are superior; the mu-shu pork and spicy chicken excel. Lunch Monday through Saturday; dinner daily. No CB.

Changsha Restaurant. *Inexpensive.* 1019 N. Broadway, Los Angeles; 227–9945. A busy restaurant serving not only neighborhood clientele but downtown business persons as well. Crispy walnuts and chicken a la viceroy, five-spice beef, eggplant with shredded pork in garlic sauce, and braised meatballs are recommended. Lunch and dinner daily. MC, V.

Chinese Friends Restaurant. *Inexpensive.* 984 N. Broadway, Los Angeles; 626–1837. This restaurant may be minuscule, but the dishes it serves are bold and fiery. The Hunan style of cooking is predominant, and at lunch there is a multitude of tasty noodle dishes. Lunch and dinner daily. MC, V.

Chung Mee Café. *Inexpensive.* 207 Ord St., Los Angeles; 628–5026. Forget the nonexistent decor and concentrate on the excellently prepared Cantonese food. Specialties include steamed pork with fruit peel, oysters, and fried squab. The rice and soup are thrown in at no charge. Dinner daily. Open until 3:00 A.M. No credit cards.

Diamond Seafood Restaurant. *Inexpensive.* 724 N. Hill St., Food Center #131, Los Angeles; 617–0666. Fresh fish, Hong Kong style, is their specialty. Lobster, catfish, and crab are wise choices, and there is also squid with black bean sauce. Dim sum at lunch. Pleasant decor. Lunch and dinner daily. AE, MC, V.

Limehouse. *Inexpensive.* 708 New High St., Los Angeles; 624–2983. A simple Cantonese–American-style restaurant. No ambience, but the paper-wrapped chicken, bird's nest soup, and Chinese okra with chicken are highly recommended. Lunch and dinner daily, except Tuesday. No credit cards.

Mandarin Shanghai Restaurant. *Inexpensive.* 970 N. Broadway, Los Angeles; 625–1195. Located in the Mandarin Plaza (#114), this Shanghai restaurant uses authentic ingredients not always available in this country. Golden fried yellow fish, meats and vegetables simmered in an earthen pot, and shrimps with chives are excellent choices. Lunch and dinner daily. AE, MC, V.

Mon Kee Live Fish and Seafood Restaurant. *Inexpensive.* 679 N. Spring St., Los Angeles; 628–6717. A large, complex menu with extensive seafood offerings. Bare decor, but the fish just can't be beat. Lunch and dinner daily. MC, V.

New Moon. *Inexpensive.* 912 S. San Pedro St., Los Angeles; 622–1091. A Cantonese restaurant located close to the downtown garment district. Steak cubes, shredded chicken salad, lemon chicken, and crystal shrimp. Full bar. Lunch and dinner daily. All major credit cards.

Continental

Perino's. *Expensive.* 4101 Wilshire Blvd., Los Angeles; 383–1221. Almost one-quarter of a century has passed since this restaurant opened, and although it no longer bears the glory of its previous excellent reputation, it still is considered to be one of Los Angeles's premier restaurants. Flowers are everywhere, and the crystal and silver are sparkling. Service is very attentive, and there is still an air of richness and extraordinary luxury. The menu, featuring fresh fish, prime beef, and rich desserts, is Continental and fairly classical. Lunch Monday through Friday; dinner Monday through Saturday. Valet parking. All major credit cards.

Scandia. *Expensive.* 9040 Sunset Blvd., Los Angeles; 278–3555 or 272–9521. This elegant Scandinavian/Continental restaurant has long been a fixture on the Sunset Strip and has been the winner of numerous awards for many years. Different rooms have different themes, from the flowery garden atmosphere of the Belle Terrasse to the Danish Room, with copper utensils decorating the walls. Tables are beautifully and formally appointed, and fresh flowers are everywhere. Hors d'oeuvres include shrimps in dill, miniature pancakes flavored with aquavit and served with sour cream and Danish caviar, and the best gravlax you could hope to try. Entrees feature sauteed spring chicken, saddle of lamb, veal Oskar and kalldolmar, white cabbage filled with veal and pork stuffing. All tables get baskets of excellent assorted fresh breads, including the noted parmesan-crusted pumpernickel bread. A cold, creamy kiwi fruit souffle and Danish rum pudding top the dessert list. From 10:30 P.M. to 1:00 A.M., late night dining with a lighter menu is featured. Jackets required for men. Lunch Tuesday through Sunday; dinner Tuesday through Sunday. Sunday brunch. Valet parking. All major credit cards.

Tower. *Expensive.* 1150 S. Olive St., Los Angeles; 746–1554. Offering one of the best views of the city, this restaurant is located on the 32nd floor of an office building in downtown Los Angeles. You'll have to take two elevators to get there; the last one is the private one that takes you to the top of the building and has its own elevator operator for restaurant clientele. The view at night stretches as far as the eye can see, and it is breathtaking. The Continental/French cuisine features classical dishes: coq au vin, duckling with turnips, sole with pine nuts, and Lyonnaise sausages. Service is very proper, and the tables are well-appointed. Lunch Monday through Friday; dinner daily except Sunday. All major credit cards. Valet parking.

The Windsor. *Expensive-Moderate.* 3198½ W. 7th St., Los Angeles; 382–1261. The winner of many awards, this impeccable restaurant offers classical cuisine in a carefully appointed dining room filled with comfortable, roomy booths. Service is gracious. The menu features stuffed trout monarch, steak Diane, and stuffed squab. There is a fine wine list. Sensational pastries. Dinner daily, except Sunday. Valet parking. AE, MC, V.

At Marty's. *Moderate.* 8657 W. Pico Blvd., Los Angeles; 272–1048. It's great fun to dine At Marty's! The menu, both in size and creativity, is tremendous; it's a series of mimeographed sheets of menu items stapled together. Owner Marty wants to be able to change his menu on a continual basis so he doesn't get bored. The customers certainly aren't. The menu travels the world from the Middle East for a tabouly salad to Italy for spinach lasagna, to say nothing about special entrees for vegetarians and health-food fanatics. Emerald Shrimp is spectacular; jumbo shrimp is baked with a vivid green sauce of puréed spinach and garlic. Also served are lychee chicken, zum-zum sausages, a casserole of three varieties of Latin-style sausage, and many concoctions using veal and beef. The decor is eclectic, and that's fun too, as is Marty's Art-Deco ambience. The waiters are cheerful and energetic. Dinner daily, except Monday. All major credit cards.

The Cove. *Moderate.* 3191 W. 7th St., Los Angeles; 388–0361. A Continental restaurant with a European flair. One walks downstairs to enter a cozy room with dark booths and flocked wallpaper. Soft lamps illuminate the tables. The dinner menu is extensive and features everything from steaks, chops, and seafood to wiener schnitzel, sauerbraten, and boneless squab. Desserts include cherries jubilee, crepes Suzette, and a German chocolate cake with cherries made on the premises. Valet parking. All major credit cards.

Roda Rummet The Red Room. *Inexpensive.* 611 N. La Cienega Blvd., Los Angeles; 855–9444. This tiny but cheerful bistro features authentic Swedish-style cuisine. Various salad plates are artistically arranged portions of herring, a superior liver pâté, Swiss cheese, and hard-boiled eggs. Hot sandwiches include homemade Swedish meatballs and meatloaf. Swedish-style sandwiches are served in traditional open-face fashion on limpa bread. There are some wonderful Swedish desserts, including the Princess Cake, a Swedish torte. Beer only. Lunch and dinner; closed Sunday. Monday evenings also closed. MC, V.

Delicatessen

Canter's. *Inexpensive.* 419 N. Fairfax Ave., Los Angeles; 651–2030. The most renowned Los Angeles deli, located in the Fairfax district close to Farmers Market. The food is not what it used to be, but the name attracts customers on a continual basis. A hangout for entertainers late at night. Near the entrance is a display case filled with home-baked desserts. The waitresses are known to mother customers. Open twenty-four hours. No credit cards.

French

Bernard's. *Expensive.* Biltmore Hotel, 515 S. Olive St., Los Angeles; 624–0183. A renowned Los Angeles restaurant often overlooked owing to its downtown location. The emphasis is on seafood, but there are also such marvels as veal rib eye with marinated corn and roasted squab on country bread. Maine lobster in red wine sauce and red snapper braised in beer exemplify this bistro's creativity. Lunch weekdays, dinner Monday through Saturday. Valet parking. All major credit cards.

François. *Expensive.* 555 S. Flower St., Los Angeles; 680–2727. Close to the Music Center and located in the underground shopping area of ARCO Plaza. The dining room is handsome, restrained dignity. A creative hors d'oeuvre is baked oysters on a bed of creamed spinach. Pepper steak in a Cognac sauce is superb. Also served are turkey breast Oklahoma, sea bass with lemon sauce, and chicken breast stuffed with crab meat. There are always fresh fish and daily specials, as well as special pre-theater dinners at bargain prices. Lunch Monday through Friday; dinner daily except Sunday. All major credit cards.

Le Dome. *Expensive.* 8720 Sunset Blvd., Los Angeles; 659–6919. An elegant French restaurant with a round bar that attracts a show- and music-business crowd. Country French cuisine, including blood sausage, smoked meats, and headcheese, is featured. Fragrant, fresh fruit desserts. Lunch Monday through

Saturday; dinner Monday through Saturday. Valet parking. All major credit cards.

L'Ermitage. *Expensive.* 730 N. La Cienaga Blvd.; 652–5840. One of LA's most refined French restaurants. Brought to great heights by its late owner, Jean Bertranou, L'Ermitage's beautiful ambience is complimented by such entrees as breast of chicken with goose liver and port wine, and sauteed veal loin with green apples. Creativity reigns in chef Michel Blanchet's capable kitchen. Valet parking. Dinner Monday through Saturday. All major credit cards.

L'Orangerie. *Expensive.* 903 N. La Cienega Blvd., Los Angeles; 652–9770. One of Los Angeles's most renowned French restaurants, though it caters largely to a Beverly Hills crowd. The restaurant, with a dining room and a bar that face a formal courtyard, was built along architecturally classic lines. The tables are beautifully appointed. The very French menu includes eggs with caviar, terrine of duck with pistachio, medallions of veal in a three-mustard sauce, and chicken with shallots. Elaborate, freshly prepared desserts include chocolate charlotte and a hot apple tart served with a pitcher of heavy whipped cream. Valet parking. Dinner daily. Jackets for men are required. All major credit cards.

Ma Maison. *Expensive.* 8368 Melrose Ave., Los Angeles; 655–1991. Los Angeles's most star-studded restaurant, in a converted bungalow under a canvas roof. This restaurant is so chic that its phone number is unlisted. Rows of Mercedes and Rolls Royces fill the parking lot. Owner Patrick Terrail is the suave, ever-present host. The cuisine matches the glamour of the clientele. Only the best and the freshest ingredients are chosen for the French-style menu. Excellent wine list. Excellent for people watching. Lunch and dinner Monday through Saturday. No DC.

Entourage. *Expensive-Moderate.* 8450 W. Third St., Los Angeles; 653–1079. This chic French restaurant, located next door to a major recording studio, draws many famous recording artists. Beautiful decor, particularly the sky-lighted garden room in the rear. The menu highlights duckling in pear sauce and trout stuffed with a mousseline in a Cognac-cream sauce. All sauces are silken and rich, and the poultry, fish, and produce are very fresh. Try the escargot wrapped in puff pastry and cloaked with a creamy sauce. Desserts, particularly the chocolate mousse cake topped with shavings of white chocolate, are extra rich. Valet parking. Lunch Monday through Friday; dinner Monday through Saturday. No DC.

La Toque. *Expensive-Moderate.* 8171 Sunset Blvd., Los Angeles; 656–7515. An intimate French bistro with a flair for the unusual. Owner Ken Frank is so creative in the kitchen that he changes his menu daily according to the best of fresh ingredients he sees at the markets. Sauces are silken understatements, and each plate arrives at the table with appeal to both the eye and the senses. Service is kindly, not stuffy. Always fresh fish, excellent soups. Heavy use of native California fish and vegetables. An experience. Valet parking. Dinner Monday through Saturday. No DC.

Greek

Constadina's. *Inexpensive.* 540 S. Vermont Ave., Los Angeles; 388–9478. A restaurant with a schizophrenic personality. By day it's an American coffee shop. By night it is transformed into a Greek restaurant and nightclub. The menu features chicken baked with lemon and oregano, roast leg of lamb, grape leaves, and fresh fried calamari. Expert Greek dancing, and you're invited to join in. Comfortable atmosphere; many booths. Dinner nightly, except Monday. All major credit cards.

Health

Golden Temple of Conscious Cookery. *Inexpensive.* 7910 W. 3rd St., Los Angeles; 655–1891. A vegetarian restaurant with lofty principles. The menu is international in scope, and the food is generally prepared well. Close to Farmers Market and CBS. Many salads; eggplant parmigiana is a specialty. Nightly specials. Lunch Monday through Saturday; dinner Monday through Saturday. MC, V.

Hungarian

Budapest Hungarian Restaurant. *Moderate.* 432 N. Fairfax Ave., Los Angeles; 655–0111. Close to Farmers Market and CBS. A small neighborhood restaurant that caters to an older Jewish and European clientele. Seltzer is served instead of water. Beef goulash, roast goose (in season), stuffed cabbage, and strudel are specialties. The food is not great, but you get bountiful portions, honestly prepared, at low prices, and you can't beat the ambience. Dinner daily, except Monday. No CB.

Indian

Gitanjali India Restaurant. *Moderate.* 414 N. La Cienega Blvd., Los Angeles; 657–2117. Authentic decor in this northern Indian restaurant. Tandoori chicken and marinated tikka dishes. The large menu includes beef, fish, and vegetarian entrees. Attentive service. Wine, beer. Dinner daily. No CB.

Italian

Adriano's Ristorante. *Expensive.* 2930 Beverly Glen Circle, Los Angeles; 475–9807. One of Los Angeles's most distinctive Northern Italian restaurants. The decor is sophisticated; it includes an outdoor patio surrounded by greenery adorned with twinkling lights. Indoors are an intimate bar and a chic dining room with peach-colored walls, green carpeting, and a lot of walnut wood trim. Pastas are all made on the premises. Gnocchi with pesto is good, but even better is the fettuccine Tre 'P'—fettuccine with prosciutto, peas, and grated parmesan combined with a silken, creamy sauce. Roast duck with olives, a casserole of rabbit with polenta, and many veal dishes complete a discriminating menu.

Desserts include fresh berries with cream and fragole gratinate, a velvety custard with ice cream, and marinated strawberries baked in a caramel crust. Good wine list. Attentive service provided by both captains and waiters. Lunch Tuesday through Saturday; dinner Tuesday through Sunday. Sunday brunch. AE, V, MC.

Giuseppei! *Expensive.* 8256 Beverly Blvd., Los Angeles; 653–8025. Very California looking, with chic decor and a plethora of plants. Calamari with marinara sauce is fine, and so is the porterhouse steak, which is well marinated in olive oil and herbs. The best of all is the gnocchi Genovese, a plate of the lightest most tender gnocchi ever in a smooth and fragrant pesto (basil) sauce. Classic souffles and fresh pastries. Lunch Monday through Friday; dinner, Monday through Saturday. Valet parking. AE, MC, V.

Rex Il Ristorante. *Expensive.* 617 S. Olive St., Los Angeles; 627–2300. One of Los Angeles's most respected restaurateurs, Mauro Vincenti, opened this architectural masterpiece featuring sophisticated "nuova cucina" (the new cuisine) Italian dining. The decor features imported French oak, rich carpeting, Italian marble, and a burgundy color scheme, all creating an Art Deco ambience. Every dish is prepared from fresh ingredients. Ice cream, pasta, and bread are made on the premises. All dishes are prepared in copperware only. The wine cellar features over 300 labels of Italian, French, and California wines. An experience. Valet parking evenings only. Lunch Monday through Friday; dinner Monday through Saturday. All major credit cards.

Dan Tana's. *Expensive-Moderate.* 9071 Santa Monica Blvd., Los Angeles; 275–9444. Located close to the Troubadour nightclub; good for celebrity spotting. Cioppino, chicken Florentine with spinach and cheese, and veal rollatini are good here. Valet parking. Dinner daily. All major credit cards.

Alberto's. *Moderate.* 8826 Melrose Ave., Los Angeles; 278–2770. Despite the elegance of this restaurant's appointments, it still has a comfortable neighborhood bistro appeal. Clams oregenata and mozzarella marinara excel as appetizers. and the chicken pappagallo and most veal dishes here can't be beat. Distinctive service. The cheesecake is so rich and creamy that it makes other cheesecakes taste like cardboard. Valet parking. Dinner daily. All major credit cards.

Fellini's. *Moderate.* 6810 Melrose Ave., Los Angeles; 936–3100. Fellini's attracts an artsy crowd to dine amid funky decor and a lot of plants. Light Italian fare, including crepes, omelettes, fresh fish, and pasta. Good cheesecake. Lunch and dinner daily. Open until 2:00 A.M. Valet parking. MC, V.

La Strada. *Moderate.* 3000 Los Feliz Blvd., Los Angeles; 664–2955. The Italian food is good, but it's even better combined with the opera and musical comedy offered. Have you ever tried *La Boheme* with fettuccine? Sometimes there are costumes and scenery, other times singers will serenade you at your table. Veal, fresh fish, daily specials. Valet parking. Lunch Monday through Friday; dinner daily. All major credit cards.

Virgilio's. *Moderate.* 2611 S. La Cienega Blvd., Los Angeles; 559–8532. A sleek Italian restaurant with a wide variety of pastas. Featured are spaghettini with black olives, garlic, and capers; fettuccine; mostacciole; linguini; lasagna.

An elaborate chicken preparation is the Pollo Alla Romana, chicken sauteed with crabmeat, asparagus, and bearnaise sauce. Veal, beef, and sweetbreads round out a well-planned menu. Desserts include Champagne sherbet, souffles, and fresh berries. A delightful after-dinner drink is the Italian coffee spiked with Frangelico. Lunch Monday through Friday; dinner daily. No CB.

Japanese

Eigiku. *Moderate.* 314 E. 1st. St., Los Angeles; 629–3029. Popular downtown Japanese restaurant. Efficient service. Nigiri, tekka, and inari sushi. Full bar. Dinner Tuesday through Sunday. All major credit cards.

Lyon. *Moderate.* 3360 West First St., Los Angeles; 381–5040. A unique restaurant serving a blend of French and Japanese cuisine. Although it's counter service only, the dishes are sophisticated. Rack of lamb in mint sauce, chicken in red wine, snow peas, and teriyaki marinades accent the menu. Soups are prepared daily from stock pot. Stark Oriental decor. Limited wines. The desserts are homemade and include cranberry ice with custard sauce and cheesecake with cranberry custard. Reservations required. Lunch and dinner daily, except Monday. No credit cards.

Ichiban Café. *Inexpensive.* 108 S. San Pedro St., Los Angeles; 622–4453. A tiny downtown bistro catering mostly to Japanese customers. Small sushi bar; table service for tempura, oshinko maki, and nigiri. *Sake,* wine, and beer. Lunch and dinner daily, except Wednesday. MC, V.

Mexican

Antonio's Restaurant. *Moderate-Inexpensive.* 7472 Melrose Ave., Los Angeles; 655–0480. The usual Mexican fare, with the addition of more complex specialties. Jicama salad with fresh exotic fruits and chicken with an intriguing mole sauce excel. Authentic ropa vieja. Mariachi music Wednesday through Sunday. Lunch Tuesday through Friday; dinner Tuesday through Sunday. Valet parking at night only. AE, MC, V.

El Cholo. *Inexpensive.* 1121 S. Western Ave., Los Angeles; 734–2773. Attentive service, a huge menu, and giant portions characterize this comfortable Mexican restaurant. Great for families, starving artists, and virtually everyone who thinks spending a lot of money to eat out is a ridiculous thing to do. Lunch and dinner daily. CB, MC, V.

El Coyote Spanish Café. *Inexpensive.* 7312 Beverly Blvd., Los Angeles; 939–7766. Spartan Mexican decor. Smiling waitresses bring you warm, fresh tortillas the moment you sit down. Traditional Mexican fare: enchiladas, burritos, tostadas, and so on. Lunch and dinner daily. MC, V.

The Gardens of Taxco. *Inexpensive.* 1113 N. Harper Ave., Los Angeles; 654–1746. Mexican food is most popular in Los Angeles, and this restaurant represents the best of Mexico City cuisine. Margaritas, sangria, and Mexican beer will quench your thirst. The quesadillas are splendid, the chicken mole is terrific, and there are at least ten desserts to choose from, including flan and bananas in a creamy custard. Dinner daily, except Monday. AE, MC, V.

Russian

Mischa's. *Moderate.* 7561 Sunset Blvd., Los Angeles; 874–3467. This Russian cabaret restaurant is always alive with the energy of its performers and the enthusiasm of the clientele. The food is in the classical Russian vein and includes chicken Czar Alexander, with a cream sauce accented by mushrooms and cucumbers, a smooth beef Stroganoff, and fresh fish and veal specialties. Fine wine list; many varieties of vodka. Lunch Tuesday through Friday; dinner daily except Monday. All major credit cards.

Seafood

The Fishmarket. *Expensive-Moderate.* 9229 Sunset Blvd., Los Angeles; 550–1544. An elegant seafood restaurant popular for fresh fish flown in from Hawaii. Ulua, ono, mahi mahi, and opaka-paka are featured menu items. You can expect to find fresh catfish, fresh salmon, and abalone—suggested entree selections. Fresh oysters Rockefeller, fresh cherrystone clams, and fresh Blue Point oysters are also popular. Fresh berries are always available; if not in season, they're flown in. Comfortable soft lighted booths and competent service. Lunch Monday through Friday; dinner daily. All major credit cards.

South American

El Cid. *Moderate.* 4212 Sunset Blvd., Los Angeles; 668–0338. A funky cabaret featuring Latin art, flamenco dancers, and the songs of Spain. Notable entrees are shrimp Puerta Vallarta, chicken in mole, and Tampico-style steak. Good quesadillas. Dinner Tuesday through Sunday. AE, MC, V.

El Dorado. *Inexpensive.* 4273 Beverly Blvd., Los Angeles; 660–7746. A tiny bistro serving Colombian food. Flank steak with sauce, blood sausage, bean soup with fried pork skin, and beef tripe soup are all highlighted on the menu. All dishes are unusual and well prepared. Lunch and dinner Tuesday through Sunday. Beer and wine only. CB, MC, V.

Spanish

La Masia. *Moderate.* 9077 Santa Monica Blvd.; Los Angeles; 273–7066. An intimate restaurant with warm ambience. Excellent paella and Spanish-style bouillabaisse. Dinners include salad, vegetables, and rice in the price. A guitar player entertains on weekends. Usually very busy; be sure to make reservations. Dinner daily, except Monday. No CB.

Thai/Southeast Asian

Siam Orchid. *Moderate.* Beverly Center, 8500 Beverly Blvd., Los Angeles; 652–6000. A fortune was spent to build this restaurant out of imported teakwood and carved teak doors. Cascades of Thai lanterns and silk panels add to its authenticity. The kitchen staff, imported from Thailand, prepare stuffed omelets and vegetable soup, glass-noodle salad and roast-duck red curry among many items on the lengthy menu. Lunch and dinner daily. All major credit cards.

Saigon Flavor Restaurant. *Inexpensive.* 1044 S. Fairfax Ave., Los Angeles; 935–1564. A top Vietnamese restaurant; spacious, comfortable booths with friendly service. The seafood specialties are best represented by salted rock crab, crab claws wrapped in shrimp, and shrimp balls on sugar cane. Wine, beer. Lunch and dinner Wednesday through Monday. MC, V.

Siamese Princess. *Inexpensive.* 8048 W. Third St., Los Angeles; 653–2643. A great restaurant for those unfamiliar with Thai food; explanations are written in detail below each featured dish. Strips of beef marinated in coconut milk and spices are charbroiled and served with cucumber relish and a dip of curried peanut butter. Coconut-chicken soup and orange sour soup are other offerings. Quenelles of sea bass in mussel shells and sauteed stuffed squid are even more exotic. Dinner daily. All major credit cards.

Tepparod Tea House. *Inexpensive.* 4645 Melbourne Ave., Los Feliz; 669–9117; or 667–2874. One of the oldest, most successful Thai restaurants in Los Angeles. Try the mee krob, minced pork soup, fried beef sauteed in oyster oil, or the Siamese greens with chicken. Wine, beer. Lunch and dinner daily. No credit cards.

Yugoslavian

Yugoslavian Village. *Inexpensive.* 3365 Barham Blvd., Los Angeles; 876–2063. A comfortable, relaxed ambience, with Yugoslavian and Serbian cuisine. Sarma, musaka, schnitzel, and veal and lamb char broiled as shish kebabs. Soup or salad with dinner; the rolls are homemade, as are the desserts. Dinner Tuesday through Sunday. MC, V.

GLENDALE/PASADENA

Continental

Maldonado's. *Moderate.* 1202 E. Green St., Pasadena; 796–1126. A musical restaurant, Maldonado's features haute cuisine with a side order of opera, musical comedy, and other cabaret entertainment. Appetizers include escargots and a salad of crisp spinach and romaine tossed with crumbled Roquefort. There are always several specials, as well as duckling with sauce Grand Marnier and a kiwi fruit garnish, medallions of lamb sauteed with thyme sauce and artichoke hearts, and an honorable chicken Marengo. Fine wine list. Lunch Tuesday through Friday; dinner daily except Monday. All major credit cards.

Phoenicia. *Moderate.* 343 N. Central Ave., Glendale; 956–7800. Ara Kalfayan and his wife Silva are the two loveliest restaurant owners in town. They go out of their way to make each guest feel at home while dining. Silva goes downtown to the flower market and creates beautiful flower arrangements for each table. Ara is Lebanese, Silva is Russian, and their chef is Swiss, so it's a veritable United Nations in the kitchen. Salmon mousse with Champagne sauce is a smooth and satisfying hors d'oeuvre, as is the mozzarella marinara and the pheasant pâté. Salads are arranged artistically, with fresh spinach, bacon, herbs, and walnuts or hearts of palm with shrimp. Chicken baked in clay is a specialty that has brought the Kalfayans much acclaim. It has to be specially ordered; the chicken is marinated before it is baked and brought tableside, where the clay is then cracked—all the juices are sealed in and the fragrance perfumes the room. Roast quail stuffed with apples and grapes, shish kebab, and veal with avocado, tomatoes, and cheese round out a well-planned menu. The service is impeccable, and the wine list is extraordinary. Lunch Monday through Saturday; dinner daily, except Monday. AE, V, MC, DC.

HOLLYWOOD/LOS FELIZ/WEST HOLLYWOOD

American

Morton's. *Expensive.* 8800 Melrose Ave., West Hollywood; 276–5205. This trendy spot bases its success on grilled chicken, fish, and steaks. Usually crowded with celebrities and Beautiful People. Dinner Monday through Saturday. All major credit cards.

The Palm. *Expensive.* 9001 Santa Monica Blvd., West Hollywood; 550–8811. One branch of a successful national chain. Sawdust on the floors, caricatures on the walls, and a high noise level. It is not uncommon to see celebrities here. The steaks are the best in the city. The lobsters are enormous, usually five pounds and over, but they can be shared. Cheesecake is flown in from New York, and it's thick, creamy, and very, very rich. The fried onions can't be beat. Entrees are served with hunks of sourdough and pumpernickle bread. New York-style waiters, brash but kindly. Valet parking. Lunch Monday through Friday; dinner daily. All major credit cards.

Greenblatt's. *Moderate-Inexpensive.* 8017 Sunset Blvd., Hollywood; 656–0606. A favored deli with the show-biz crowd. Enormous wine selection. Fat sandwiches of pastrami, corned beef, and roast beef are popular. Smoked ribs and ham. Takeout or sit down, but you order at the counter. Catering. Breakfast, lunch, and dinner daily. No reservations. Wines to go only. MC, V.

Roscoe's House of Chicken and Waffles. *Moderate-Inexpensive.* 1514 N. Gower St., Hollywood; 466–7453. A tasty soul-food restaurant that serves mostly breakfast, no matter what time of day. There are hot and fresh biscuits, sinfully smothered chicken livers, and feathery-light waffles made from Roscoe's own mix. Chicken, "fried to the bone," is done properly, and it's served in various combinations with eggs or waffles. Open daily, except Monday, for breakfast, lunch, and dinner. Usually open until 3:00 A.M. No credit cards.

The Hard Rock Café. *Inexpensive.* 8600 Beverly Blvd., West Hollywood; 276–7605. This fifties-style café has a vintage '59 Cadillac jetting out of the roof, *Happy Days'* Fonzie's leather jacket hangs on the wall—as does Elvis's motor cycle—and the waitresses are dressed in appropriate threads of the era. The American menu consists of burgers, baby back ribs basted in watermelon barbecue sauce, and apple pie. The restaurant's message? Rock 'n' roll is here to stay. Fast becoming an L.A. landmark. Open daily, lunch and dinner. V, MC, AE.

Lillian's. *Inexpensive.* 962 N. Cahuenga Blvd., Hollywood; 462–0435. A casual storefront restaurant where just about everything is homemade. The soups, straight from a stockpot, are rich, and dinners include just about every course but the kitchen sink. Lunch Monday through Friday; dinner Monday through Saturday. No credit cards.

California/Continental

Spago. *Moderate.* 8795 Sunset Blvd., West Hollywood; 652–4025. Owner Wolfgang Puck is the "golden chef" of Los Angeles, and this California-style restaurant has helped make Puck shine all the more. It's innovative, creative, and unique, and the menu features produce, poultry, and seafood native to California. Wood-burning ovens cook your meals right in the dining room as a bit of a show. Many unusual combinations of pizza: Did you ever have lox and cream cheese on pizza before? There are also Santa Barbara shrimp, California goat cheese, homemade duck sausage, and pastas with seafood. Ravioli may be filled with lobster, and the fresh fish is served strict and pure, grilled with butter only. The restaurant, decorated in a beige color scheme, has small tables and ice cream parlor chairs and fine art on the walls. You'll see rows of Rolls Royces and Mercedes in the parking lot; this is a restaurant patronized by the elite—great for celebrity spotting. Interesting wine list. The pastry chef prepares flaky tarts, cakes, and other pastries, many with fresh fruit and liqueurs. Valet parking. Dinner nightly. All major credit cards.

Caribbean

T & T Carib. *Inexpensive.* 6547 Santa Monica Blvd., Hollywood; 467–9654. Trinidad and Tobago have their place in the sun right in the heart of Hollywood. Only eight tables, but this bistro is cheerful and service is kindly. This is your chance to order curried goat, but if you're not feeling brave, you can stick to shrimp or egg noodles with vegetables. Fried plantains and an okra and spinach mixture called callaloo are worth trying. Reservations for eight or more only. Lunch and dinner daily, except Monday. No credit cards.

Continental

Trumps. *Expensive.* 8764 Melrose Ave., West Hollywood; 855–1480. Contemporary decor marks this chic and popular Los Angeles restaurant featuring an eclectic Continental menu. Weekday tea is most popular, almost overtaking the lunch hour; Sherry, tea, and assorted tea sandwiches and scones are offered. This kitchen is always inventive, and the food will not disappoint. Lunch Monday through Saturday; tea Monday through Saturday from 3:30 P.M. to 6:00 P.M.; dinner Monday through Saturday. Valet parking. Patio dining. AE, MC, V.

Los Feliz Inn. *Moderate–Expensive.* 2138 Hillhurst Ave., Hollywood/Las Feliz; 663–8001. An emphasis on fresh fish and vegetables. Wild game gets special treatment here. Cozy, neighborhood Old World ambience. Close to

Dodger Stadium, Griffith Park, and the zoo. Lunch Monday through Friday, dinner Monday through Saturday. Valet parking. All major credit cards.

L.A. Nicola. *Moderate.* 4326 Sunset Blvd., Hollywood; 660–7217. Nouvelle cuisine at incredibly reasonable prices. Hi-tech decor. Great hors d'oeuvres, including fried chicken wings with apricot sauce. Chef/owner Larry Nicola excels with fish and chicken dishes. Around the corner from ABC Studios. Features an airy outdoor café. Closed Sundays. Lunch (except Saturday) and dinner. All major credit cards.

English

The Cock 'n Bull. *Moderate.* 9170 Sunset Blvd., West Hollywood; 273–0081. The British pub atmosphere draws many stray Englishmen. Long a fixture on the Sunset Strip, this restaurant features prime rib, steak-and-kidney pie, and other stalwart entrees. Sunday brunch consists of a proper plate of eggs, sausage, finnan haddie, chicken, and fruit. Service is kindly, and although it's buffet service for your entree and vegetables, soup, salad, or Welsh rarebit are served at the table. Valet parking. Lunch Monday through Friday; dinner daily; Sunday brunch. No CB.

Oscar's. *Moderate.* 8210 Sunset Blvd., Los Angeles; 654–3457. A restaurant with a salute to English cooking—and Art-Deco decor. Starters or appetizers include angels on horseback (oysters wrapped in bacon, baked, and served on toast points) and potted shrimp. Entrees featured are chicken parsley pie, quiche, pasta primavera, steak-and-kidney pie, and "bangers and mash"—pork sausages and mashed potatoes with onion gravy. There is always trifle for dessert. You have the option of dining in the jazz room, where soft combos or nostalgia singers perform. Valet parking. Dinner Tuesday through Saturday. All major credit cards.

Franco/Japanese

La Petite Chaya. *Expensive.* 1928 Hillhrst Ave., Hollywood/Los Feliz; 665–5991. Freshly done and highly touted restaurant serving the newest in-vogue cuisine. French-trained Japanese chef is very imaginative, service is impeccable, and decor is simple, yet elegant. Enclosed porch makes for a very romantic dining spot. Near ABC Studios. Lunch Mon. through Friday, dinner Monday through Saturday., closed Sunday. Valet parking. Full bar. All major credit cards.

French

Le St. Germain. *Expensive.* 5955 Melrose Ave., Hollywood; 467–1108. A serene restaurant, decidedly French and decidedly chic. One of the restaurants to see and "be seen" in. The menu is elegant, and the specials of the day are always the best. The service is impeccable. The presentation of the plates is a joy to behold. The surroundings are formal despite a casual ambience. Salmon with a sorrel cream sauce and roast chicken in a Champagne sauce are noted entrees. Fresh berry fruit tarts are the best bet for dessert. Lunch Monday through Friday; dinner Monday through Saturday. No CB.

Greek

Athenian Gardens. *Moderate-Inexpensive.* 1835 N. Cahuenga Blvd., Hollywood; 469–7038. Long a fixture in Hollywood. The menu features moussaka, roast lamb, dolmades, and pastitsio. Greek music and dancing. Dinner Tuesday through Sunday. Valet parking. AE, MC, V.

Health

Old World. *Inexpensive.* 8782 Sunset Blvd., West Hollywood; 652–2520. Also at 1019 Westwood Blvd., Westwood; 208–4033; and 216 N. Beverly Dr., Beverly Hills; 274–7695. The West Hollywood location is the original. All the Old World restaurants feature health-oriented cuisine, including superior hamburgers, Belgian waffles, and homemade soups. Their vegetable platters and vegetarian burgers are not only healthy for you, but they also taste good, too. Breakfast, lunch, and dinner daily. AE, MC, V.

Indian

Bengal Tiger. *Inexpensive.* 1710 N. Las Palmas Ave., Hollywood; 469–1991. This tiny Indian and Pakistani restaurant consistently prepares authentic cuisine from its corner of the world. Mulligatawny soup is a spicy specialty, and curries will be prepared just as hot as you can stand them. Appetizers include *samosas,* the deep-fried pastry pockets filled with meat or vegetables and dipped into a sweet and hot murky sauce. Breads are truly delights; the *poori,* deep-fried puffed wheat bread, and *parathas,* flaky layered, crisp bread stuffed with potatoes or vegetables, are some of the best prepared Indian breads in the city. Wine, beer. Lunch and dinner daily. MC, V.

Bombay Curry. *Inexpensive.* 7617 Sunset Blvd., Hollywood; 876–2799. A simple, Indian-style café featuring traditional Indian cuisine. Specialties include lamb Madras and chicken birani. Entrees come with samosas, mulligatawny soup, rice, chutney, and custard pudding or baklava. Lunch and dinner daily, except Tuesday. MC, V.

Paru. *Inexpensive.* 5140 Sunset Blvd., Hollywood; 661–7600. Southern Indian cuisine that is vegetarian: A lot of rice dishes, lentil soup, and poori bread stuffed with potatoes and curry. Homemade yogurt. Good *lassis,* the yogurt drinks that are flavored with rosewater. Lunch daily, except Wednesday; dinner daily, except Wednesday. Wine, beer. MC, V.

Israeli

Shula and Esther. *Inexpensive.* 519 N. Fairfax Ave., West Hollywood; 852–9154. You could break out in the hora over the good food of this Israeli café. There is a great appetizer plate with a fiery Turkish salad and rich hummus and tahina. Shaslik and schnitzel are quite authentic, and there is also moussaka. No ambience, but a neighborhood hangout for a young Israeli crowd. Breakfast, lunch, and dinner daily. No credit cards.

Tel Aviv Café. *Inexpensive.* 509½ N. Fairfax Ave., West Hollywood; 653–7031. Fine Israeli cuisine in a restaurant that lacks atmosphere. But the clientele is colorful enough, and the steam tables are laden with delicious moussaka, kebabs, and stuffed peppers. There is hot pita bread and the usual Middle Eastern salads. Counter seats only: you will be served quickly, and you can't beat the prices. Lunch and dinner daily, except Sunday. No credit cards.

Italian

Bono's. *Expensive.* 8478 Melrose Ave., West Hollywood; 651–1842. Entertainer Sonny Bono is at the helm of this trendy and celebrity-filled bistro. Antipasto, pasta, and Italian-style seafood. Crowded and noisy. Come for the scene rather than the food and you'll not be disappointed. Valet parking. Lunch, dinner, Monday through Saturday. AE, MC, V.

Japanese

Imperial Gardens. *Expensive-Moderate.* 8225 Sunset Blvd., West Hollywood; 656–1750. A gathering spot for entertainment industry sushi freaks as well as restaurateurs who come here on their nights off. Different dining rooms feature tempura, teriyaki, and shabu-shabu. Tatami room. Valet parking. Dinner daily. All major credit cards.

Amagi. *Moderate.* 6114 Sunset Blvd., Hollywood; 464–7497. The decor isn't much, but the cuisine is authentic. Sushi bar. Ginger crab, steak teriyaki, and lobster Amagi for the less adventurous; teriyaki eel will delight the brave. Lunch and dinner daily. All major credit cards.

Restaurant Katzu. *Moderate.* 1972 N. Hillhurst Ave., Los Feliz; 665–1891. This new entry into the sushi bar/restaurant market is indeed refreshing. A stark hi-tech interior and exterior (no sign indicates that there's a restaurant inside) provides a great showplace for some of the city's most imaginative sushi. Owner/designer/sushi-chef Katzu never compromises on his own tastes; hence all sushi orders are authentic. (No California Roll sushi at Katzu's place.) Richly designed plates and cups in a modern motif mix well with the highly technological chemistry equipment that is used to mix the sauces that must accompany sushi. Wine and beer. Lunch from 11:30 A.M. to 2:00 P.M.; dinner from 5:30 to 9:30 P.M. Closed Sunday. MC, V.

Yamashiro. *Moderate.* 1999 N. Sycamore Ave., Hollywood; 466–5125. This beautiful restaurant in the hills of Hollywood resembles an Oriental palace set amid acres of flowering gardens. At night the view is mind-boggling; you can see almost to the ocean. The menu is Japanese, but there are also Continental offerings such as steak, veal, and fish. The food tends to be uneven; best advice is to order hors d'oeuvres and drinks and enjoy the view. Valet parking. Lunch Monday through Friday; dinner daily. AE, MC, V.

Mediterranean

Espartacus. *Expensive.* 8911 Santa Monica Blvd., West Hollywood; 659–2024. A stylish restaurant/nightclub that features authentic coastal Mediterranean cuisine with dishes from France, Spain, and Italy. Owned by film director Espartaco Santoni, this restaurant's decor is both glamourous and chic. The menu highlights include paella, shrimp with shallots and tomatoes, bouillabaisse, and sweetbreads with wild mushrooms, Marsala, and cream. Entertainment is provided by Spanish flamenco dancers in the Flamenco Cave, and live Latin jazz is featured in the Moorish Bar. Very European–Los Angeles ambience. Valet parking. Lunch Monday through Friday; dinner daily. All major credit cards.

Mexican

La Casita. *Inexpensive.* 6611 Hollywood Blvd., Hollywood; 464–9480. Salvadorian and Mexican cuisine. Steaks, fried fresh fish, and black beans and rice. Wine and beer only. Lunch and dinner daily. No credit cards.

El Conquistador. *Inexpensive.* 3701 Sunset Blvd., Hollywood/Silverlake; 666–5136. Standard Mexican and Cal-Mex cuisine, generally well prepared. Patio dining. Lunch and dinner daily. No CB.

Lucy's El Adobe. *Inexpensive.* 5536 Melrose Ave., Hollywood; 462–9421. An intimate Mexican restaurant that is a music-industry hangout. Reportedly was a rendezvous for Governor Jerry Brown and his ex-girlfriend Linda Ronstadt. Arroz con pollo, enchiladas rancheros, and enchiladas verdes are specialties. Lunch and dinner Monday through Saturday. MC, V.

Moroccan

Dar Maghreb. *Expensive-Moderate.* 7651 Sunset Blvd., Hollywood; 876–7651. A posh Moroccan restaurant with authentic decor. Dine on low benches piled high with cushions, and eat off communal plates set atop ivory-inlaid tables. There is a dramatic interior courtyard with a fountain. Hand-painted tiles, Moroccan rugs, and costumed waiters. Dinners include a choice of chicken, pigeon, lamb, or rabbit. Hands are washed in rose-scented water. *B'stilla,* couscous, mint tea, fruit and nuts, and baklava are all included in the dinner price. Dinner daily. Valet parking. MC, V.

Moun of Tunis. *Moderate.* 7445½ Sunset Blvd., Hollywood; 874–3333. Like your neighborhood casbah. Enter through an arched door leading to small rooms with cushioned benches and round, low tables. Waiters and waitresses are dressed in traditional garb. There are several choices of full-course meals: *b'stilla* is wonderful, as is the lemon chicken with almonds, which literally falls apart in your fingers because it's so moist. A mixed salad plate includes a couple of hot salads; be prepared to breathe fire. Belly dancing on weekends. All major credit cards.

South American

Chile Lindo. *Inexpensive.* 5237 Sunset Blvd., Hollywood; 667–9973. Homestyle Chilean food. Dinners include a hearty homemade soup. Highlights of the menu are the *corvina* (Peruvian fish and rice) and the *lomo con ensalada Chilena* (steak with an onion and tomato salad). Beer and Chilean wine by the glass. Weekend entertainment features live Latino music to an enthusiastic audience. Lunch and dinner daily, except Thursday. MC, V.

Thai

Tommy Tang's. *Moderate.* 7473 Melrose Ave., Hollywood. This trendy Thai bistro caters to the entertainment industry with a punkish flair. Thai cuisine has an American flavor. Try the spicy bbq chicken, squid with mint leaves and chili, and *mee krob.* Upbeat, eclectic atmosphere. Lunch Monday through Friday, dinner daily, closed Sunday. MC, V, AE.

Chao Praya. *Inexpensive.* Corner Yucca and Vine at 6307 Yucca, Hollywood; 464–9652. This earthy restaurant is set smack in the middle of Hollywood, cater-cornered from the Capital Records Building. The delicious Thai cuisine is served in an extremely casual manner. Highlights: beef and pork *stay, mee krob,* barbecued and garlic chicken dishes. Generous portions. Lunch, dinner; closed on Mondays. All major credit cards.

Jitlada. *Inexpensive.* 5233½ Sunset Blvd., Hollywood; 667–9809. In a small shopping center. Specialties include *mee krob,* lemon grass, and prawn soup. Wonderful curries. Lunch and dinner, Tuesday through Sunday. DC, MC, V.

BEVERLY HILLS/CENTURY CITY

American

En Brochette. *Expensive-Moderate.* 9018 Burton Way, Beverly Hills; 276–9990. Two outdoor dining patios, one facing Burton Way where you can watch the shoppers, and the other on the side, gazebo-style. Strolling musicians play classical music. Appetizers include quiche, broiled mushrooms, and guacamole. The featured entrees are skewered beef and chicken and fish served with assorted dipping sauces. Mousse pies for dessert. Lunch and dinner daily. Valet parking. All major credit cards.

Gingerman. *Moderate.* 369 Bedford Dr., Beverly Hills; 273–7585. Patrick O'Neil and Carroll O'Connor own this sleek establishment that is both a pub and a restaurant. The bar area, packed at "happy hour" and into the evening, has become a singles meeting place. The restaurant produces fine fare. Burgers, salads, and omelettes are always right, and there is always a selection of fresh fish. Lunch and dinner daily. Sunday brunch. Valet parking. AE, MC, V.

The Highwayman. *Moderate.* 10250 Santa Monica Blvd., Century City; 552–4505. Located in Century City Mall. A carnivore's delight: juicy, tender charbroiled steaks cooked to your liking. Mushroom steak is very popular. Fresh seafood and fresh desserts. Relaxed service. Lunch and dinner Monday through Saturday. All major credit cards.

Lawry's the Prime Rib. *Moderate.* 55 N. La Cienega Blvd., Beverly Hills; 652–2827. The leading restaurant in Los Angeles for prime ribs. Silver carts are wheeled to your table, where your individual slice of beef is hand carved. Each dinner is served with a salad that is spun on a bed of ice and tossed with Lawry's French dressing. The creamed horseradish sauce, slightly spicy and slightly sweet, is one of the best. Yorkshire pudding, a bit bland, accompanies the dinner. A separate dessert menu, with fresh Hawaiian pineapple, chocolate pecan pie, and a chocolate fantasy cake that is indeed fantastic, is featured. Dinner daily. AE, MC, V.

Lawry's Westside Broiler. *Moderate.* 116 N. La Cienega Blvd., Beverly Hills; 655–8686. A well-designed, casual restaurant with an elegant flair. Steaks are the specialty, and they are thick, tender, and charbroiled. There are some creative appetizers, such as mussels in escargot butter with pistachios. Broiled Indonesian shrimp and chicken tempura are also available for noncarnivores. Their vegetables taste very fresh, as does a creative assortment of desserts. Young, eager—if inexperienced—waiters. Lunch Monday through Friday; dinner nightly. Valet parking. AE, MC, V.

R.J.'s the Rib Joint. *Moderate.* 252 N. Beverly Dr., Beverly Hills; 274–RIBS. A unique restaurant serving bountiful quality food in a relaxed and casual atmosphere. Its "Green Grocery Salad Bar" is tops in the city. An ice-cold cast-iron skillet is your salad plate, and you'll choose from several varieties of lettuce or exotic raw vegetables served with homemade dressings and homemade croutons. Cut your own hunk of bread to take to the table. Ribs are the specialty, and they're generally tender and slightly sweet. Sunday brunch includes the salad bar and a smoked fish platter brought to your table, as well as such items as zucchini bread and fried bagels (fried bagels?). Desserts are slices of cake so big that one slice can easily feed four hungry adults. Valet parking. Lunch Monday through Saturday; dinner daily; Sunday brunch. MC, V.

Nate 'n Al's. *Moderate-Inexpensive.* 414 N. Beverly Dr., Beverly Hills; 274–0101. A home away from home for deli lovers from New York. Some of the best smoked salmon (lox) in town. Fat sandwiches and freshly squeezed orange juice. The potato pancakes are crisp, and the blintzes are good enough to make you plump. Known as a show-biz haunt for deli eaters. Breakfast, lunch, and dinner daily. No reservations. No credit cards.

Chinese

The Mandarin. *Moderate.* 430 N. Camden Dr., Beverly Hills; 272–0267. A sister restaurant of the successful Mandarin in San Francisco. Blue and green tile floors, orange carpeting, and rooms filled with much greenery and gracious antiques. The table settings are elegant, and the waiters are quite competent. Beggar's chicken is a specialty, and their Szechuan shrimp is a delight. Mongolian firepot is featured; guests can cook their own meats, seafood, and vegetables or let the chef do it instead. Good California wine list. Lunch Monday through Friday; dinner daily. Valet parking. All major credit cards.

Monkey West. *Moderate.* 170 N. La Cienega Blvd., Beverly Hills; 652–4188. Mandarin Chinese cuisine in an elegant atmosphere. The ceilings are covered with hanging silk lanterns; the walls are oak paneled and feature illuminated silk screens. On each table rests a vase with a single bud rose—positively romantic. The menu features hot braised Mandarin lobster, sweet and sour cubed fish, Szechuan spicy shrimp, pineapple duckling, and chicken with pinenuts. Peking duck is superior here, as are the many *dim sum* appetizers. Gracious service for a relaxing dining experience. Lunch and dinner daily. All major credit cards.

Continental

The Coterie. *Expensive.* The Beverly Hills Hotel, 9641 Sunset Blvd., Beverly Hills; 276–2251. Cozy booths, attentive captains and waiters, and a motif of browns and bronze characterize this restaurant. The Continental menu highlights filet mignon Coterie, a thick filet cloaked with crispy fried onion strands and sauteed mushrooms. Also popular are lamb sauteed au jus and seasoned with fresh rosemary, veal with sliced apples and apple brandy, and, as an appetizer, a scallop mousse with a watercress sauce. There are souffles on the menu, but the rolling pastry cart stars freshly baked tarts and cakes. A popular dessert is the coconut mousse topped with strawberries and then flambéed. Noted wine cellar. Dinner daily. All major credit cards.

L'Escoffier. *Inexpensive.* Beverly Hilton Hotel, 9876 Wilshire Blvd., Beverly Hills; 274–7777. An elegant penthouse restaurant with a superb view of the city. The color scheme is gray, muted rose, and burgundy, and chairs are upholstered in velvet. An impressive mural of inlaid mosiac, featuring all the signs of the zodiac, covers one wall. Dining is in the tradition of the famed "King of Chefs," Auguste Escoffier, who is renowned for his classical French cuisine. Service is most proper, and the wine list is extensive. Dancing to an orchestra every night but Monday. Jacket and tie required for men. Dinner Monday through Saturday. Validated parking. All major credit cards.

Jimmy's. *Expensive.* 201 S. Moreno Dr., Beverly Hills; 879–2394. A serene and sophisticated restaurant with a country club-like atmosphere. Cold lobster salad is a delight at lunch; veal piccata is excellently light. The French–Continental menu is well-constructed, with an emphasis on the nouvelle. Lunchtime is very hectic, and service can be harried then. Dinner is a more relaxing experience. Lunch Monday through Friday; dinner daily except Sunday. Valet parking. All major credit cards.

The Princess. *Expensive.* 10131 Constellation Blvd., Century City; 553–1770. A first-class enterprise with haute cuisine and a magnificent decor. Many artifacts and objets d'art are set in an interior garden. Homemade pastas, salmon with sorrel, calf's liver with shallots, and grilled beef. Impressive wine list. Lunch and dinner, Monday through Saturday. All major credit cards.

The Vineyard. *Expensive.* Century Plaza Hotel, 2025 Avenue of the Stars, Century City; 277–2000. A dedication to the choicest, freshest ingredients, with a presentation of artistically arranged plates, makes the Vineyard one of Los Angeles's finest restaurants. It is a bit of a well-kept secret, for it is buried within a hotel, and hotels were not associated with fine dining in this city until recently. Captains and waiters here pamper you to almost ridiculous proportions. Appetizers include smoked breast of goose and pâté of wild game with a lingonberry sauce. Daily specials. Regular entrees feature quail with wild rice stuffing and saddle of lamb prepared with chutney, almonds, English mustard, and garlic. Souffle lovers will be pleased to find Grand Marnier and chocolate souffles expertly prepared. Lunch Monday through Friday. Dinner Monday through Saturday. All major credit cards.

Andre's of Beverly Hills. *Moderate.* 8635 Wilshire Blvd., Beverly Hills; 657–2446. Also at West 3rd St. at Fairfax Ave., Los Angeles; 935–1246. Despite the fancy title, this Continental restaurant is truly a bargain. Portions are enormous, and you'll get complete dinners expertly prepared. You'll begin with an appetizer plate filled with assorted salads and pâté, then soup or salad, your entree, and dessert. Entrees include veal parmigiana, coq au vin, roast duck, trout, frog legs, and much more. The ambience is elegant, and the service is swift and efficient. Lunch Tuesday through Friday; dinner daily, except Monday. All major credit cards

Trader Vic's. *Moderate.* 9876 Wilshire Blvd., Beverly Hills; 276–6345. Located in the Beverly Hilton Hotel. Not really Continental, the tropical South Sea Island decor is highlighted by much greenery and wicker chairs and an enormous selection of tropical drinks with such names as Dr. Funk's Son and Missionary's Downfall. The Menu is Polynesian, some Continental and Chinese, including barbecued meats prepared in Chinese clay ovens. The appetizers are renowned, and the clay ovens produce juicy, succulent meats. Valet parking. Dinner daily. All major credit cards, including the Hilton.

French

Le Festival. *Expensive.* 8689 Wilshire Blvd., Beverly Hills; 652–6590. An elegant French restaurant with well-appointed tables and a lot of fresh flowers; very proper service. Lunches feature roasted duck leg, steamed lotte, and grilled chicken breast. Dinners lean toward grilled beef with shallots and noisettes of lamb with truffles. Desserts are made on the premises. Espresso and cappucino. Lunch Monday through Friday; dinner Monday through Saturday. No DC.

Bagatelle. *Moderate.* 8690 Wilshire Blvd., Beverly Hills; 659-0782. A former French charcuterie, this bistro is now a full-scale French restaurant, although takeout, particularly of pâtés and terrines, is still available. Specialties range from rabbit with a wine, cream, and grape sauce to veal chop val-suzon. Desserts are made on the premises; although not elaborate, they are noteworthy. Lunch Monday through Friday; dinner Monday through Saturday. CB, MC, V.

Maison Gerard. *Moderate.* 224 S. Beverly Dr., Beverly Hills; 273-5430. Also at 4100 Cahuenga Blvd., North Hollywood; 766-3841. Long a favorite in Los Angeles for country French cooking at reasonable prices rather than haute French cuisine. Not an experimental menu either, but one of restraint, featuring familiar French entrees. Casual; kindly service. Lunch and dinner Monday through Saturday. All major credit cards.

Italian

La Scala. *Expensive.* 9455 Santa Monica Blvd., Beverly Hills; 275-0579. One of Los Angeles's trend setters in bringing fine Italian cuisine to this city; an elegant northern Italian restaurant decorated Florentine-style with a series of intimate dining areas. Elaborate Italian pottery filled with large bouquets of flowers has been placed throughout the rooms. A smartly dressed Beverly Hills crowd. Specialties include smoked Scottish salmon, zuppa all' Ortolana, fettuccine Leon, calf's liver all' Veneziana, and homemade ice cream. The luncheon menu includes light salads and omelettes as well as veal, pasta, and seafood. Valet parking. Lunch Monday through Friday; dinner daily except Sunday. AE, MC, V.

Harry's Bar. *Moderate.* In the ABC Entertainment Center near the Shubert Theater, Century City; 277-2333. Fashioned after the world-famous restaurant in Florence, Italy. A charming room with warmth and excellent service. The specialties are veal dishes and fettucine Alfredo. Closed on Sundays for lunch. AE, MC, V.

La Scala Boutique. *Moderate.* 475 N. Beverly Dr., Beverly Hills; 550-8288. A less formal and smaller version of La Scala (above). Large glass windows afford terrific people watching, especially of Beverly Hills shoppers. There are cartoons of celebrities on the walls. Specialties include prosciutto and melon, linguini and clams, veal and peppers, and whitefish alla Casalinga. The luncheon menu has salads, sandwiches, and omelettes. Lunch daily except Sunday; dinner daily except Sunday. AE, MC, V.

Japanese

Benihana of Tokyo. *Moderate.* 38 N. La Cienega Blvd., Beverly Hills; 659-1511. Also at 14160 Panay Wy., Marina del Rey; 821-0888. Also at 16226 Ventura Blvd., Encino; 788-7121. One of a chain of restaurants that feature American food prepared Japanese-style by chefs who flash their knives about much like samurai. The tables are round and group together several customers, whether they know each other or not. Chefs stand in the cutout center of the table, where they stir-fry your dinner before your eyes in dramatic fashion on a grill set in the table. Steaks, seafood, and vegetables; good quality maintained. Efficient service. Valet parking. All major credit cards.

Mexican

Acapulco. *Inexpensive.* 134 N. La Cienega Blvd., Beverly Hills; 652-5344. Also at 1109 Glendon Ave., Westwood; 208-3884. One chain restaurant that does not compromise its standards. Gracious Mexican hacienda-style decor and an eighteen-page menu. Friendly service. Their crabmeat enchiladas are really special. Lunch and dinner daily. AE, MC, V.

SAN FERNANDO VALLEY

American

The Beef 'n' Barrel. *Moderate.* 8920 Tampa Ave., Northridge; 885–1055. A value restaurant serving quality food at reasonable prices. There are five dining rooms, each with its own fireplace. Dinners include an above-average salad bar and your own iron kettle of homemade soup. Prime rib, a tender cut served in natural juices with a side of slightly sweet creamy horseradish sauce, is a specialty. Teriyaki sirloin is also of good quality, and there are various combinations of surf and turf (seafood and beef). There is a children's menu. Desserts, not made on the premises, generally consist of mousse pies. A creative variety of mixed drinks highlights liqueur and ice cream. Twilight economy dinners are served between 5:00 P.M. and 6:30 P.M. Lunch Monday through Friday; dinner nightly. AE, MC.

Victoria Station. *Moderate.* 3850 Lankershim Blvd., North Hollywood; 760–0714. Located atop the Universal Studios hill, this chain restaurant has been built to resemble a British railway station. Much memorabilia graces the walls, and you'll feel as if you're dining in a railroad car. The service is young, cheerful, and efficient. Quality top sirloin and good teriyaki steak; gooey, cheesy baked potato skins provide a perfect appetizer. Their ribs are a wee bit greasy but have a nice smoky flavor. There is a great children's menu charging very reasonable prices. Dinners come with soup of the day or a pleasant salad bar and whole-grain bread. Lemon sorbets in minicones provide a refreshing touch. No matter what age you are, don't leave without trying the peanut butter pie. It's a nutty peanut butter filling frozen into a graham cracker crust with whipped cream on top and chocolate hot fudge sauce on the side; sinful. Good value here. Consult the phone directory for other locations. Lunch Monday through Saturday; dinner daily. AE, MC, V.

Dr. Hogly Wogly's Tyler Texas Barbeque. *Moderate-Inexpensive.* 8136 Sepulveda Blvd., Van Nuys; 782–2480. The best barbecue restaurant in the San Fernando Valley. Succulent, lean and tender, smoky ribs are brought to your table. Beef ribs and spareribs are equally good; there are also sliced beef and pork and links. Dinners come with half a loaf of homemade white bread, extra barbecue sauce, and a choice of baked beans, cole slaw, or other salads. Pick the baked beans; they've been simmered for hours, and they're thick, smoky, and slightly sweet with maple syrup. Pecan pie here is just okay; the sweet potato pie fares better. Lunch and dinner daily. No credit cards.

The Melting Pot. *Moderate-Inexpensive.* 16348 Ventura Blvd., Encino; 995–6500. An all-purpose café, equally suitable for breakfast, lunch, or dinner. Computer games and televisions tuned in to soap operas amuse in the waiting area/lounge. The restaurant is decorated with antique mirrors and lush hanging plants. Tables are heavy oak, and the lighting shines through Tiffany-style lamps. The menu moves from salads, such as Chinese chicken, to omelettes, freshly baked waffles, and mushroom burgers. Mexican-style appetizers, terrific taquitos de Machos. Desserts are baked on the premises. Chocolate mousse cake, honey date nut cake, and warm pistachio cake with French vanilla ice cream are hard to pass up. Lunch and dinner daily. Sunday brunch. AE, MC, V.

Otto's Pink Pig. *Moderate-Inexpensive.* 4958 Van Nuys Blvd., Van Nuys; 788–9971. This is a landmark Valley restaurant; they're busy serving the grandchildren of their original customers. The American–Continental-style food is served in generous portions. Owner Fred Nasser cuts his own beef, and the bread served is baked according to an old family recipe. Fresh beef liver, top sirloin steak, several fish entrees, and chicken with fruit sauce are specialties. Don't leave without trying their famous cherry pie. It's got a flaky crust and is plump with ripe cherries; it tastes just like one Aunt Emily in Idaho might make. Lunch and dinner; closed Monday. All major credit cards.

Womphopper's Wagon Works. *Moderate-Inexpensive.* 100 Universal City Plaza, Universal City; 508–3939. A great place to bring the family. MCA built this restaurant adjacent to the Universal Studios Tour and created a legend to go with it. C. L. Womphopper is supposed to have been a wagon salesman who did a lot of wheeling and dealing in the Old West. It cost close to $4 million to build Womphopper's; it is made out of authentic barnwood to resemble an 1880s wagon factory. The restaurant is divided into nine rooms, each with a different theme. Antique lighting fixtures, hooked rugs, and velvet draperies fill the rooms. Buffalo-meat chili is a must to try; it's robust, hearty and rich with spices. There are many barbecued items as well as steaks, salad plates, and sandwiches, on the menu. Their ribs, in a sweet and smoky sauce, are meaty and tender. Hot apple cobbler is made on the premises, and it has a buttery flaky top crust. Country-and-western entertainment after 9:00 P.M. Breakfast during the summer only. Lunch and dinner daily. AE, CB, MC, V.

Art's Delicatessen. *Inexpensive.* 12224 Ventura Blvd., Studio City; 769–9808 or 762–1221. One of the best Jewish-style delicatessens in the city. The sandwiches are mammoth and are made from some of the best corned beef, pastrami, and other cold cuts around. Matzoh-ball soup and sweet-and-sour cabbage soup are specialties. Good chopped chicken liver. Beer. Breakfast, lunch, and dinner Tuesday through Sunday. No credit cards.

Barron's. *Inexpensive.* 4130 W. Burbank Blvd., Burbank; 846–0043. This is a momma–poppa restaurant where the love in the kitchen shows up on your plate. The decor is virtually nonexistent; the place is more like a coffee shop. But the Barrons have brought in their own antique collection of Depression glass and fine china and proudly display them by the front door, which adds warmth and charm. Dinners include soup or salad, baked, mashed, or French fried potatoes, vegetables, bread and butter, beverage, and a choice of home baked desserts. Entrees include roast turkey, baked chicken, roast beef, and roast pork. At this restaurant no one walks out the door hungry. Soups are made daily in a giant stock pot, and desserts are light-as-a-feather marble cakes and pies. The whole family participates in this operation, and it shows. Open weekdays for breakfast, lunch, and dinner. No credit cards.

Hampton's. *Inexpensive.* 4301 Riverside Dr., Burbank; 845–3009. Also at 1342 N. Highland Ave., Los Angeles; 469–1090. A casual café-style restaurant with anything and everything you'd ever want to put on a hamburger—and then some. Would you believe a peanut butter and jelly burger? Only in California! Thick and juicy hamburgers, the meat ground fresh daily. Lunch Monday through Friday, dinner daily in Burbank. Lunch and dinner daily in Los Angeles. Reservations requested for six or more. Valet parking. MC, V.

Paty's. *Inexpensive.* 10001 Riverside Dr., Toluca Lake; 760–9164. Paty's is a place to dine and star gaze and not have to mortgage your home to pay the bill. It's located close to NBC, Warner Brothers, and the Disney Studio, and so you're liable to see top series stars, producers, and even the gaffers dining here. This is an all-American style upgraded coffee shop with a comfortable, eclectic decor. Breakfasts are charming; the omelettes are plump, and the biscuits are homemade and served with high-quality jam. Lunches and dinners include Swiss steak and a hearty beef stew that is served in a hollowed-out loaf of home baked bread. Roast turkey is served with dressing and a moist and sweet loaf of home-baked nut or raisin bread. All desserts are worth saving room for; they're made on the premises and taste sinfully butter rich. New Orleans bread pudding with a hot brandy sauce is popular, and the Danishes are gigantic. Breakfast, lunch, and dinner daily. No credit cards.

Chinese

Fung Lum. *Moderate.* Universal Studios, Universal City; 760–4603. Located in the Universal Studios complex, this ornate Chinese restaurant cost millions to build. It's a replica of a Chinese palace, and the interior design includes handcarved, painted, and embroidered panels, rosewood and teak furniture, and breathtaking, handwoven carpeting. The menu is long and primarily Cantonese. Best to come here in a large group where you can taste a multitude of courses. The minced squab in lettuce leaves is wonderful. Open daily for lunch and dinner. No reservations. AE, MC, V.

Continental

Camille's. *Expensive-Moderate.* 13573 Ventura Blvd., Sherman Oaks; 995–1660. One of the most romantic restaurants in the Valley. Rose-colored walls, an eclectic assortment of antique mirrors and paintings, trailing plants, and a lot of lattice work provide a sentimental Art Deco–Victorian ambience. Here is one restaurant where the cuisine is as charming as the decor. Chef/co-owner Peter Schawalder is Swiss; his creations are individualistic as well as poetic in presentation. Entrees are often garnished with carrot stars, olives hold enoki mushrooms, and strawberries are sculptured into blossoming roses. Entrees include sauteed whitefish and grapefruit, veal steak with mushroom puree, and roasted duckling with apple and chestnut puree. The soup of the day is always fresh, and their desserts are worth giving up a diet for. Closed Sunday and Monday. Dinner only. AE, MC, V.

Four Stages Restaurant. *Moderate.* Sheraton–Universal Hotel; 3838 Lankershim Blvd., Universal City; 980–1212. Imagination takes precedent in a restaurant where the decor carries out the theme of the neighboring movie studio.

There are four authentic movie sets, including a western saloon, a medieval castle, and a courtyard in India. The menu is Continental and well prepared. Best is the Sunday brunch, which is an elegant buffet that includes crab legs and caviar as well as many hot and cold entrees. Lunch Monday through Friday; dinner daily. All major credit cards.

Ingrid and David's Gingerhouse Café. *Moderate-Inexpensive.* 18669 Ventura Blvd., Tarzana; 881–0660. When you walk into this restaurant, you'll feel as if you've walked into an enchanted cottage. It's decorated with white picket fences and Ingrid's original art work. Different rooms have different themes and moods. The menu is highly creative: Have you ever tried veal sautéed with strawberries, blueberries, and banana slices and then covered with Jack cheese and bearnaise sauce? It may sound awful, but it tastes awfully good. Salads, quiches, omelettes, and crepes are the order of the day, but more substantial entrees such as David's seafood sauté or scampi Tekotsky should not be missed. A wide selection of desserts. Palm and tarot-card readers are available for consultation. The nightly entertainment includes everything from Broadway revues to original one-act plays. Lunch and dinner Tuesday through Saturday; Sunday brunch and dinner. MC, V.

French

La Serre. *Expensive.* 12969 Ventura Blvd., Studio City; 990–0500. Undoubtedly the most beautiful restaurant in the San Fernando Valley. The rooms are lattice divided, the floors are brick, and there are fresh flowers and lush greenery everywhere you look. It's a bit like dining in a greenhouse. At lunchtime celebrities flock here in droves, for it is near the Universal, Warner, and Disney studios. Julie Andrews, Lorne Greene, Walter Matthau, and Michael Caine have all been spotted lunching at La Serre. The cuisine is very French and very nouvelle, and it's all served on the finest china with sparkling crystal and silverware. Captains and waiters are most attentive. Valet parking. Lunch Monday through Friday; dinner Monday through Saturday. MC, V.

Aux Delices. *Expensive-Moderate.* 15466 Ventura Blvd., Sherman Oaks; 783–3007. Although this French restaurant is small, it has a decidedly reserved ambience. Its food is superior to most restaurants in the Valley. A mousse of scallops with cream and Cognac is soft, rich, and delicate—an outstanding appetizer. Escargots, onion soup, and duck pâté are equally pleasing. Baked jumbo shrimp with paprika, Cognac, and cream is a gustatory delight. Sauces are always silken and sophisticated without being overwhelming. Other entrees include veal with apples, cider, cream, and Calvados and sweetbreads sauteed in a truffle sauce with goose liver pâté. The bouillabaisse is one of the best in Los Angeles. Specials daily. Good wine list, heavy on French wines. Desserts include the traditional mousse and creme caramel, but the freshly baked, flaky tarts filled with custard and fresh fruit should not be overlooked. This touch of Paris in Sherman Oaks will please even the most discriminating diner. Dinner daily, except Monday. No CB.

Le Café. *Moderate.* 14633 Ventura Blvd., Sherman Oaks; 986–2662. This high-tech café/restaurant provides fine food in a relaxing ambience. Small tables fill one large room with walls papered from French newspapers. The menu, running the gamut from ratatouille omelettes and salad Nicoise to filet mignon in blue cheese sauce and shrimp in a saffron cream sauce, is brasserie-style. Fresh fish is always a wise choice, and the spinach canneloni is hard to beat. Le Café serves Haagen Dazs ice cream; the owner's homemade cheesecake is definitely the best. Lunch Monday through Saturday; dinner daily. AE, MC, V.

Wine Bistro. *Moderate.* 11915 Ventura Blvd., Studio City; 766–6233. A cheerful wine bar with an extensive blackboard menu. The airy decor features butcher block and a lot of plants. Several daily offerings of different California and French wines and Champagnes by the glass. Filet of sole Veronique, salmon with mustard sauce, and daily cream soups are always refreshing and tasty. A giant brass espresso maker produces vibrant cups of cappuccino and espresso. Desserts, usually fruit tarts, are made on the premises. A partially open kitchen provides entertainment, for you can watch the chefs scurry about. Valet parking. Lunch Monday through Friday; dinner daily, except Sunday. All major credit cards.

Epicurean Express. *Moderate-Inexpensive.* 19014 Ventura Blvd., Tarzana; 996–7977. One of the newer and most unique concepts in fast-food gourmet dining. There are only a few tables in this country-French-style restaurant that predominantly features food to go. There's an open kitchen, and chef/owner Joe Donahue is a joy to behold as he madly yet efficiently dashes from pot to pan. Within fifteen minutes, you can be enjoying prime milk-fed veal flamed in Madeira wine and simmered with wild mushrooms and fresh cream. There are always daily specials, and the fresh pastas are not to be missed. Also good is the roast duck that is brushed with rosemary and served with a sauce of the day. There are Cobb salad, spinach salad, or a shellfish salad for those with lighter appetites. One popular dish is the brie-and-almond sandwich: brie cheese melted onto French bread and topped with toasted almonds. Desserts are melt-in-your-mouth pastries and cakes, all baked on the premises. Lunch and dinner daily, except Sunday (dinner only) and Monday (lunch only). MC, V.

German

The Weinstube. *Moderate.* 17739 Sherman Way, Reseda; 345–1994. German food is traditionally supposed to be heavy, but this German restaurant is a happy surprise. Yes, there are smoked pork chops and wiener schnitzel on the menu, but there is also a light entree of veal medallions sauteed in butter and white wine with herbs out of the chef's garden. Also light yet bursting with flavor is a roast loin of milk-fed veal served with imported wild mushrooms. Other dishes include sauerbraten, Chinook salmon poached in a white wine/herb sauce, and roast goose stuffed with apples, potatoes, and goose liver in season. Charming decor; waitresses are garbed in traditional costumes. Cozy booths, softly lighted. Lunch Tuesday through Friday; dinner daily, except Monday. AE, MC, V.

Greek

The Greek Market. *Moderate–Inexpensive.* 9034 Tampa Ave., Northridge; 349-9689. Zorba the Greek himself would love the authentic Greek cuisine served here. Appetizers include the zesty tarmosalata, a salty Greek caviar made with carp roe. Tiropitas, cheese filled phyllo-dough pastries, and fried squid and octopus in red wine sauce are other appetizer selections. Leg of lamb is roasted with cloves of whole garlic, black pepper, and lemon juice, and the moussaka, with its layers of eggplant and ground lamb cloaked in a thick rich bechamel sauce, will not disappoint. All entrees come with the vegetable of the day, rice pilaf, and pita bread. Desserts are made on the premises, and the baklava—layers of phyllo dough and nuts drenched in honey syrup—is luscious. Dancing to live Greek music. If you drink enough ouzo, you might want to throw a plate or two! Lunch and dinner daily, except Sunday. No credit cards.

Health

The Good Earth. *Moderate-Inexpensive.* 17212 Ventura Blvd., Encino; 986-9990; also, 1002 Westwood Blvd., Westwood; 208-8215; 23397 Mulholland Dr., Woodland Hills; 888-6300. Eating healthfully does not have to mean eating a diet of alfalfa sprouts and wheat germ. The menus of this health-oriented chain feature whole-grain breads, desserts baked with honey, and entrees heavy on fruit and vegetables rather than meat. Even the decor, with earth-tone walls and furnishings and macramé and wicker baskets on the walls, is earthy. Breakfast items feature turkey sausages, ten-grain sourdough pancakes, and a choice of omelettes. Vegetarian burgers, curried chicken, and Zhivago's beef Stroganoff are superior. Their yogurt cream pie tastes almost like cheesecake, but the carrot cake is a little heavy, probably because of the whole-grain flour content. Breakfast, lunch, and dinner daily. MC, V.

Chez Natural. *Inexpensive.* 11838 Ventura Blvd., Studio City; 763-1044. It's not easy to find gourmet health food, especially in a restaurant that has an attractive ambience as well as a creative menu. A dinner at Chez Natural includes a fruit cup or soup or salad, lightly steamed fresh vegetables, and homemade, stone-ground whole-grain rolls with sweet butter. Vegetables Chez Natural consists of a popular plate of steamed vegetables on a bed of brown rice covered with melted cheese and sliced almonds. Another successful entree is the breast of chicken (organic, of course) that's boned and stuffed with a blend of pine nuts, cheese, and herbs and then covered with a golden brown nut sauce. There are a lot of California-style salads, omelettes, and quiches on the menu as well. Considering that they contain carob and honey instead of chocolate and sugar, the desserts are superior. It's no Snickers bar, but the Carob Caress is the healthful way to junk-food heaven. Open daily for lunch and dinner. No credit cards.

Italian

Matta's Ristorante. *Moderate.* 21733 Ventura Blvd., Woodland Hills; 704–9191. Everything is soft here. The lighting is soft, the music is soft, and even the waiters speak softly. Very relaxing. This Italian restaurant has a great house salad that includes red cabbage, romaine lettuce, artichoke hearts, hearts of palm, and fresh mushrooms and will make you forget every iceberg lettuce salad you've ever endured. The homemade dressing is a smooth and creamy vinaigrette that is enlivened with fresh herbs. Cucumbered sole is a fresh filet cloaked in a delicate cream sauce that contains the essence of fresh cucumbers; slices of cucumber garnish the fish. Other unusual dishes include chicken with Mandarin orange wedges and green grapes, veal with brandy and water chestnuts, and veal with prosciutto and provolone wrapped around jumbo scampi. Desserts are made on the premises; the chocolate mousse is not to be missed. Lunch and dinner daily. AE, V, MC.

Ameci. *Moderate–Inexpensive.* 18900 Ventura Blvd., Tarzana; 705–8232. New York Italian–style cuisine. Spicy, rich sauces. Generous portions. Southern-Italian cooking. New York subway maps help comprise the decor. Friendly neighborhood bistro. Dinner daily. MC, V.

Japanese

Hatsuhana. *Moderate–Expensive.* 7167 Ventura Blvd., Encino; 789–8287. Plenty of flash at this trendy Japanese restaurant, right down to the rolling sushi bar. High-tech space with a good measure of Japanese influence. Fresh, fresh fish imported from around the world. Try the Hatsuhana special, a combination of sushi and sashimi, salmon teriyaki, tempura, and half a lobster. Parking lot. Lunch (except Saturday) and dinner daily. Closed Monday. All major credit cards.

Teru Sushi. *Moderate.* 11940 Ventura Blvd., Studio City; 763–6201. Entertainment-industry clientele feast on some of the best sushi in town here at a bar where the chefs put on a show. The freshest fish is served. Table service features traditional Japanese fare, especially a tender teriyaki. Lunch Monday through Friday; dinner daily. All major credit cards.

Domo. *Moderate-Inexpensive.* 11680 Ventura Blvd., Studio City; 761–6151. A Japanese restaurant tucked into a small neighborhood shopping center. Japanese kites hang from high-beamed ceilings. Two levels; the tatami room is on the top one. There is a small bar. Dinners come with soup, salad, and rice. Teriyaki and tofu steak are both wise choices. Lunch Tuesday through Friday; dinner Tuesday through Sunday. DC, MC, V.

Moroccan

Marrakesh. *Moderate.* 13003 Ventura Blvd., Studio City; 788–6354. A maze of intimate rooms, much like a Moroccan home. Soft lighting, cushioned benches, and communal plates of *b'stilla*, salads, couscous, and lamb, as well as fish, chicken, or rabbit, are ceremoniously served. The servers are traditionally garbed in robes and will wash your hands and attend you most graciously. It's comfortable, casual, and most unusual. Dinner daily. Valet parking. All major credit cards.

Swiss

St. Moritz. *Moderate.* 11720 Ventura Blvd., Studio City; 980–1122. There aren't too many Swiss restaurants in Los Angeles, but St. Moritz qualifies as one of the best. It's styled a bit like a Swiss chalet, with cozy booths and an Alpine mural on the wall. Ask to sit on the enclosed patio that offers a pretty garden view and a replica of a potbellied stove in the center of the room. Appetizers include a shrimp dish with dill and pernod and a light cannelloni prepared à la Swiss. The salad Neuchatel consists of a heaping plate of Bibb lettuce with sweet bay shrimp and an unusual yogurt-dill dressing. Entrees include the traditional wiener schnitzel and the not-so-traditional shrimp sauteed with almonds, mushrooms, and romaine lettuce. Chicken in a tarragon cream sauce is always a favorite. Some desserts are not made on the premises, but they are purchased from a top Los Angeles bakery. Lunch Tuesday through Friday; dinner Tuesday through Sunday. MC, V.

Thai

Anajuh Thai. *Inexpensive.* 14704 Ventura Blvd., Sherman Oaks; 501–4201. When you walk into this restaurant you might become confused: the walls are baby blue, graceful ferns separate the tables, and each table is appointed with gleaming silver. But despite the tasteful Western decor, you'll still get treated to inexpensive Thai food. Start with the regal barbecue spareribs. It's lick-your-fingers time because these ribs are smoothly coated in a dark reddish-brown sauce that's slightly sweet and slightly spicy. *Tom yum kai* is an intriguing soup that blends chunks of white meat chicken with mushrooms and that exotic Thai herb, lemon grass. There's a lot of curry on the menu, as well as a satisfying rendition of *mee krob,* the popular, sweet and crisp rice noodle dish. Service is kindly. AE, MC, V.

WEST LOS ANGELES/WESTWOOD/SANTA MONICA

American

The Corkscrew. *Moderate.* 11647 San Vicente Blvd., Brentwood; 826–5501. A comfortable neighborhood restaurant featuring steaks, prime rib, and old-fashioned chicken and dumplings. One of the city's best salad bars includes a superior gazpacho soup with assorted toppings. Daily homey specials such as short ribs, lamb shanks, and English-style pot roast. Baked potatoes are à la carte, but they are huge. Crispy onion rings accompany steak orders but can also be ordered à la carte. Booths and tables, low lighting. Lunch Monday through Friday; dinner daily. AE, MC, V.

Junior's. *Moderate-Inexpensive.* 2379 Westwood Blvd., W. Los Angeles; 475 –5771. It may not be New York, but Angelenos take their delis seriously. Your mouth will water before you even get to the reception desk; you'll have to pass glass cases filled with deli meats, breads, and appetizers. The menu is vast, and all sandwiches are jumbo. A pickle barrel is placed on each table, just as in the old days. There is turkey, brisket, roast beef, corned beef, pastrami—you name it. Breakfast can be a real treat; the coffee is strong and the omelettes are plump and light. Open daily for breakfast, lunch, and dinner. MC, V.

Bagel Nosh. *Inexpensive.* 1629 Wilshire Blvd., Santa Monica; 451–8771: also at 9689 Santa Monica Blvd., Beverly Hills; 274–8538. Butcher-block tables and plants fill this cafeteria-style deli, offering several varieties of fresh bagels, deli sandwiches, and omelettes. Breakfast and lunch daily. No credit cards.

California Cuisine

Bernie's. *Moderate.* 911 Broxton Ave., Westwood; 824–5449. A trendsetter. California artists' works are displayed in a high-tech environment. An open kitchen quickly grills chicken, fresh fish, and beef. Santa Barbara fresh shrimp, cold pasta salads, and Bernie's Salad with a raspberry vinaigrette and pine nuts. Lunch Monday through Friday; dinner daily. Sunday brunch. Valet parking. AE, MC, V.

Caribbean

Act I. *Inexpensive.* 2921 S. La Cienega Blvd., Culver City; 558–9314. A touch of the Caribbean in Los Angeles, this Jamaican restaurant features Jamaica's gastronomic specialty, curried goat. There are also Jamaican-style chicken, red snapper, and exotic desserts. Lunch Monday through Saturday; dinner Monday through Saturday. No credit cards.

Continental

The Dynasty. *Expensive.* 930 Hilgard Ave., Westwood; 208–8765. Located in the elegant Westwood Marquis Hotel. The dramatic decor features Chinese artifacts and artwork by Erté. Cozy booths and many live plants, including some breathtaking orchids. The menu is Continental; entrees include fois gras, smoked salmon, and escargots. House specialties are lobster Newburg, veal Marsala, calves liver, veal Oscar, and thick grilled lamb chops. Desserts made on the premises include strawberry and raspberry mousse. Attentive service. Fine, reasonably priced wine list. Valet parking. Dinner nightly. All major credit cards.

French

Au Chambertin. *Expensive.* 708 Pico Blvd., Santa Monica; 392–8738. A formal and chic dining room decorated to reflect impeccable taste. Owned by a Vietnamese family who lend a touch of Oriental artistry to haute French cuisine featuring fresh seafood, veal, filet mignon with herbs, pheasant, and Grand Marnier souffles, in the *nouvelle* slant. Dinner Monday through Saturday. Valet parking. AE, MC, V.

Le Cellier. *Moderate.* 2628 Wilshire Blvd., Santa Monica; 828–1585. Moderate priced but high-quality French food. The ambience is that of a fashionable country inn with soft lighting and French paintings. Dinners include soup and salad. The appetizer list is standard, but the chef comes up with unusual monthly specials that focus on regional French cuisine. Breast of mallard duck with green peppercorn and loin of lamb with crushed pepper, pears, and cabbage are special entrees. Le Cellier's bouillabaisse is always popular, as are its souffles and its rolling dessert cart. Valet parking. Dinner daily, except Monday. All major credit cards.

Café Reni. *Inexpensive.* 2226 Wilshire Blvd., Santa Monica; 829–5303. It's hard to believe that there is any French restaurant you can dine in well and not pay a bill equal to the price of a plane ticket to Paris. But this intimate French café is genuinely inexpensive. There is a fresh soup of the day; entrees all come with crusty French bread. Choose between beef Bourguignon, sand dabs, chicken Florentine, or a creamy blend of crab, shrimp, and other fish. There are always fresh specials listed on the blackboard. The wine list is small. Beer. Lunch Monday through Friday; dinner daily. Sunday brunch. AE, MC, V.

Chez Puce. *Inexpensive.* 318 Santa Monica Blvd., Santa Monica; 393–4454. Some of the best crepes in the city. Many assorted fillings, or you can just have the crepes plain with melted butter. There are dessert crepes and pizza too. Beer and wine. Lunch and dinner Monday through Saturday. MC, V.

Pioneer Boulangerie. *Inexpensive.* 2012 S. Main St., Santa Monica; 399–1405. Close to the ocean, this treasure of a restaurant serves strictly fresh, strictly homemade soups and breads of the French persuasion. There are several soups to choose from daily, as well as hearty stews. French baguettes are made on the premises, and you can buy loaves to take home. Occasionally Pioneer offers some Basque specialties. Lunch and dinner daily. No credit cards.

German

Knoll's Black Forest Inn. *Moderate.* 2454 Wilshire Blvd., Santa Monica; 395–2212. A well-known German bistro. Smoked pork loin is the specialty; there are also sauerbraten, veal, wiener schnitzel, and goose (in season). German beers. Pleasant service. Dinner Tuesday through Saturday. AE, MC, V.

Greek

Skorpios. *Inexpensive.* 1133 Westwood Blvd., Westwood; 208–3480. Mostly a takeout stand, but some tables. Good, home-prepared Greek cooking: souvlaki, gyros, psari, mezedhes, assorted appetizers, and falafel. Lunch and dinner Monday through Saturday. No credit cards.

Health

Meyera. *Inexpensive.* 3009 Main St., Santa Monica; 399–1010. An attractive and cozy health food restaurant; vegetarian cuisine. The breads and pastries are freshly baked. Creative menu. Wine, beer. Dinner daily. MC, V.

Indian

Gypsy's. *Inexpensive.* 1215 4th St., Santa Monica; 451–2841. A tiny Indian restaurant specializing in Eastern Indian cuisine. Homemade chutneys, nice use of spices. Lamb korma and chicken Hyderabad are specialties. Wine, beer. Dinner Tuesday through Sunday. MC, V.

Italian

Valentino. *Expensive.* 3115 Pico Blvd., Santa Monica; 829–4313. Noted as one of Los Angeles's finest restaurants, with an extensive and exciting Italian menu. Chicken in clay, mussels in brandy, osso buco, and fine pastas are a delight. Crema fritta (fried cream) is a splendid dessert with a cup of espresso. Admirable wine list. Attentive service; the tables are well appointed. Valet parking. Dinner daily except Sunday. No CB.

Donatello's Ristorante. *Expensive-Moderate.* 11712 San Vicente Blvd., Brentwood; 820–9719. An intimate European-style bistro featuring northern Italian cuisine. Its long, complex menu includes such appetizers as a galantine of chicken, veal, ham and truffles, vitello tonnato, and every salad you can think of from spinach to roasted green peppers. Their mozzarella marinara is a must; the tomato sauce captures all the essence of fresh ripe tomatoes. They offer many soups besides stracciatella and minestrone. The pasta list is long; try rigatoni with eggplant, string beans and cream, or tortelloni stuffed with veal and vegetables. Risottos, veal, fish, and beef dishes featured. Red snapper wrapped in parchment in a cream and porcini mushroom sauce is a delight. Desserts include two varieties of ice cream, hard and soft, both homemade. Banana sorbet is smooth and rich in flavor. Dinner Monday through Saturday. All major credit cards.

Marquis West. *Expensive-Moderate.* 3110 Santa Monica Blvd., Santa Monica; 828–4567. A warm northern-Italian restaurant, too elegant to be called a neighborhood bistro, yet that feeling of hospitality is ever present. Comfortable booths, soft lighting, thick carpeting, and friendly waiters prevail. Appetizers include mussels marinara, a satisfying mozzarella marinara, and a fine shrimp cocktail. Entrees feature fresh fish in a variety of styles, a big bowl of calamari, frog legs, and linguine al pesto (basil). Tripolino and tartufo are special desserts of rich ice cream and dark, sweet chocolate. Espresso, cappuccino. Valet parking. Lunch and dinner daily. All major credit cards.

Verdi. *Expensive-Moderate.* 1519 Wilshire Blvd., Santa Monica; 393–0706. A unique restaurant with a novel concept—opera while you dine. An excellent ensemble performs arias from several operas, though an occasional Broadway tune is included. The dining room is high-tech; painted murals on the walls depict famous opera scenes. The menu is northern Italian with home-baked sweets. There is a fine antipasto plate and a careful selection of pastas. There are shrimp scampi, veal with cream and mushrooms, and an excellent broiled piece of swordfish marinated with olive oils and herbs. Valet parking. Dinner nightly, except Monday. AE, MC, V.

Anna's. *Moderate.* 10929 West Pico Blvd., W. Los Angeles; 474–0102. Also at 15300 Ventura Blvd., Sherman Oaks; 787-ANNA. Unsophisticated Roman cuisine is the specialty of these sister Italian restaurants. The Los Angeles restaurant features comfortable booths and typical southern Italian ambience. The newer Sherman Oaks restaurant has its main dining room centered on a gazebo. Within and surrounding the gazebo are individual booths, each with its own awning marked for a different Italian city. Portions, featuring linguine, spaghetti, fettuccine, and cannelloni—all at inexpensive prices—are generous. Slightly more expensive are the veal dishes prepared in a variety of styles and the American-style steaks. Desserts include homemade ricotta cheesecake, and on Saturday night you can try the zuppa inglese. Lunch weekdays; dinner daily. All major credit cards.

Casa Monica. *Moderate.* 1110 Montana Ave., Santa Monica; 451–0765. Cozy decor with Continental–Italian cuisine, using milk-fed veal and fresh fish as well as unique appetizers. Desserts, prepared daily, include fresh fruit in cream. Dinner daily. MC, V.

Mangia. *Moderate.* 10543 W. Pico Blvd., West Los Angeles; 470–1952. Elegant café dining and gourmet takeout, including wonderful appetizer selections and luscious desserts. The style of cooking is northern Italian, stressing Tuscan fare. Specialties include boned spring lamb sauteed in wine and black truffles, trout sauteed in Tuscan olive oil, and herbs, and fresh pastas with light home-made sauces. Espresso and flaky croissants are featured all day. Spartan and cheerful décor, very stylish. Interesting wine selection. Lunch and dinner Monday through Saturday. AE, MC, V.

Pontevecchio. *Moderate.* 2518 Wilshire Blvd., Santa Monica; 829–1112. An intimate, warm northern-Italian restaurant, decorated with antiques and plants. Appetizers include mussels marinara, scampi, and a splendid antipasto. Besides the traditional minestrone soup, Roman stracciatella is offered. Pastas are fresh and include vermicelli with red pesto, spaghetti with tomato, cream, and fresh basil, and linguine with shellfish in a white wine-tomato sauce. The veal is milk-fed white veal and is prepared with lemon and butter, sage, and prosciutto or in an osso bucco Milanese. Desserts, made on the premises, are impressive. A perky demitasse of espresso is the perfect accompaniment. Service is attentive. Dinner daily, except Monday. AE, MC, V.

Japanese

Asuka. *Moderate.* 1266 Westwood Blvd., Westwood; 474–7412. One of the largest sushi bars in Los Angeles, offering many varieties. Squeamish customers (and you know who you are) may opt for their good tempura, sukiyaki, or teppanyaki. Lunch Monday through Friday; dinner Monday through Saturday. AE, MC, V.

Hiro Sushi. *Moderate.* 1621 Wilshire Blvd., Santa Monica; 395–3570. The waiting area features video games. As you would expect, Hiro offers an excellent variety of sushi. Again, for those with timid palates, teriyaki, and sukiyaki are also featured. Lunch Monday, Wednesday, and Friday; dinner Wednesday through Monday. MC, V.

Mexican

Verita's La Cantina. *Moderate.* 10323 Santa Monica Blvd., W. Los Angeles; 277–3362. A little shopping center strangely named New England Village is the home of this charming Mexican restaurant with fireplaces and cozy decor. The cooking is Sonora-style, and the menu includes sea bass baked in a corn husk, liver marinated in tequila, and rack of lamb with *salsa borracha* (drunk sauce). Good omelettes, good mole dishes. Occasional mariachi music. Lunch Monday through Saturday; dinner Monday through Saturday. Valet parking. All major credit cards.

Macho's. *Inexpensive.* 939 Broxton Ave., Westwood; 208–8050. Located in the heart of Westwood Village. You don't have to be macho to like the enchiladas, tacos, or the carne en serappi here. AE, MC, V.

Sagebrush Cantina. *Inexpensive.* 9523 Culver Blvd., Culver City; 836–5321. Also at 23527 Calabasas Rd., Calabasas; 888–6062. Always popular as a singles' meeting place for the young set, this restaurant offers pleasant Mexican-style fare as well as steaks, seafood, barbecued chicken, and ribs. Usually a wait for tables, especially on the weekends. Lunch and dinner Monday through Friday in Culver City; Tuesday through Sunday in Calabasas. MC, V.

Middle Eastern

Beach Café. *Inexpensive.* 304 Santa Monica Blvd., Santa Monica; 394–8448. Persian food in a sparkling clean restaurant with excellent service. The steak kebab is tender and is made from filet mignon; lamb simmered with kidney beans and spinach makes a hearty and rich stew. Yogurt soup is accented with cilantro, and all entrees come with hot Persian bread and butter. Lunch and dinner daily. MC, V.

Moroccan

Koutoubia. *Expensive-Moderate.* 2116 Westwood Blvd., Westwood; 475–0729. A touch of Morocco in Westwood. You'll eat with your hands from communal plates on ornate brass tables. The "Wedding Feast" is a romantic, leisurely multicourse dinner featuring soup, salad, *b'stilla,* lemon chicken, and couscous. Waiters will frequently pour water from samovar-style pitchers over your hands to cleanse them. Dishes can be ordered à la carte as well. Dinner daily, except Sunday. All major credit cards.

Seafood

Famous Enterprise Fish Company. *Moderate.* 174 Kinney, Santa Monica; 392–8366. A popular and crowded restaurant serving fresh fish broiled over mesquite charcoal and prepared in an open kitchen. Nautical atmosphere, friendly service. Lunch and dinner daily. No reservations. AE, MC, V.

The **Pelican** Restaurants. *Moderate.* A chain of seafood restaurants specializing in charbroiled fresh fish. Not for indecisive folks; there's usually a choice of twenty varieties. Expertly broiled, your catch of the sea comes with fresh, crisp vegetables and potato chunks, lightly fried. There is excellent sourdough bread with dinner, as well as green salad or chowder. Nautical decor, casual service. Lunch Monday through Friday; dinner daily. Sunday brunch. MC, V. Located at: 1717 Ocean Ave., Santa Monica; 451–0818; 2720 Main St., Santa Monica; 392–5711; 1715 Pacific Ave., Venice Beach; 392–3933; 3801 Highland, Manhattan Beach; 595–6563; 8232 Sepulveda Blvd., Van Nuys; 988–6334; 24454 Calabasas Rd., Calabasas; 710–1550.

The Captain. *Inexpensive.* 1028 Swarthmore Ave., Pacific Palisades; 459–7571. Fresh flowers are on each table, and the walls are covered with murals of the seashore. Fresh seafood is the specialty, but there are also chicken, Swedish meatloaf, a vegetarian platter, and steak. Soup or salad and hot bread are included with each entree. Lunch and dinner daily. No AE.

Spanish

Toledo Restaurant. *Moderate.* 11613 Santa Monica Blvd., West Los Angeles; 477–2400. Castillian cuisine; paella, callos a la Madrilena, garlic soup, and gazpacho are specialties. Wine and beer only. Lunch Tuesday through Friday; dinner Tuesday through Sunday. AE, MC, V.

Thai

Thai Pepper Restaurant. *Inexpensive.* 11480 Lindbrook Dr., Westwood; 208–9140. Authentic ambience and gracious service at this bistro located close to the heart of Westwood. *Mee krob,* beef satay, Thai spring rolls, and ginger chicken are specialties. Lunch Monday through Saturday; dinner daily. MC, V.

BEACHES

Gladstone's 4 Fish. *Moderate.* 17300 Pacific Coast Hwy., Pacific Palisades; GL-4-FISH. This restaurant is located right on the ocean; fresh fish broiled over mesquite charcoal is their specialty. Huge tanks hold live lobster and crab. There are always daily specials, and cioppino and sashimi are also on the menu. All dinners include green salad or chowder, coleslaw, sourdough bread, and a choice of rice, potatoes, or vegetables. Save room for the Works, a gigantic slice of cake loaded with mounds of ice cream, fresh fruit, hot fudge sauce, candies, and whipped cream. After this dessert, go straight to the dentist. Casual nautical decor, slightly noisy because it's always packed. Breakfast, lunch, and dinner daily. MC, V.

Sausalito South. *Moderate.* 3280 N. Sepulveda Blvd., Manhattan Beach; 546–4507. A perfectly decorated restaurant despite its being so close to the sea. There is a lot of greenery and wood with an airy, open flair plus a lot of fresh fish on the menu and a mean Ramos Fizz. A friendly, relaxed atmosphere. Congenial service. Dinner daily. AE, MC, V.

AIRPORT/MARINA DEL REY

Continental

Le Club. *Expensive.* 404 Washington St., Marina del Rey; 822–3939. Decorated in a blue-and-gold motif with original art, wood-burning fireplace, velvet curtains, and Strass chandeliers, located one and one-half blocks from the ocean. Fresh mussels in garlic sauce, salmon in dill sauce, quail with grapes, veal with lemon, and calves liver with onions are only some of the special entrees prepared here. A very good dessert menu, featuring a bavarois Marie Antoinette; it's not off with your head but off with your waistline when you devour one. Valet parking. Lunch Monday through Friday; dinner Monday through Saturday. Piano bar. No CB.

Le Gourmet. *Expensive.* Sheraton Plaza La Reina Hotel, 6101 W. Century Blvd., Los Angeles; 642–1111. This dining room lifts hotel food out of its usual doldrums. The decor is dark green velvety walls with brass accents, etched glass dividers, and peach-tinted mirrors. No dish is precooked. Everything is seared on a flattop stove at superhigh heat. All sauces are naturally reduced. Exciting hors d'oeuvres include quail with julienne of zucchini and potatoes, sashimi with hazelnut oil, and pigeon with truffles. The salads, such as sweetbreads, langostino, or fish salad with Japanese eggplant, are unusual. Entrees include sliced breast of duck with marrow, snapper with black pepper, and quail with prunes. Dinner Monday through Saturday. All major credit cards.

T. J. Peppercorn's. *Moderate.* Hyatt Hotel at Los Angeles International Airport; 6225 W. Century Blvd., Inglewood; 670–9000. A comfortable hotel dining room noted for its excellent duck, prepared rotisserie-style. Also steaks, fresh fish, and veal Oscar. The salad and dessert bars offer a multitude of items. Lunch Monday through Friday; dinner daily. All major credit cards.

Indian

Akbar. *Moderate.* 590 Washington St., Marina del Rey; 822–4116. An intimate dining room featuring mulligatawny soup, vindaloo, curries, and a real Tandoori oven. Akbar's homemade desserts excel. There is soft Indian music in the background. Lunch Monday through Saturday; dinner daily. All major credit cards.

Mexican

Baja Cantina. *Moderate.* 311 Washington St., Marina del Rey; 821–2250. Also at 23410 Civic Center Way, Malibu; 456-2021. Lighthearted Mexican food in a high-energy restaurant. The names of the dishes are whimsical, but don't let that scare you; the preparation is careful and sophisticated. Monday night is all-you-can-eat taco night. Tuesday night has whole Maine lobster as a special, and every night there is a wonderful choice of exotic drinks. Brunch is a real bargain, with a selection of eight egg dishes, Champagne, tortillas, and fresh fruit. Relaxed decor with unusual antiques. Lunch and dinner daily. Sunday brunch. MC, V.

LONG BEACH/SAN PEDRO

Continental

Delius. *Expensive-Moderate.* 3550 Long Beach Blvd., Long Beach; 426–0694. Close to the *Queen Mary.* The price-fixed Continental menu starts with Champagne and includes soup, an appetizer, entree, vegetables, dessert, and coffee. Dinner Tuesday through Saturday. Reservations a must. No credit cards.

Greek

Papadakis Taverna. *Moderate-Inexpensive.* 301 W. 6th St., San Pedro; 548–1186. A kick-up-your-heels Greek taverna. Waiters, cooks, and customers all join in for song and dance up and down the aisles. Their moussaka, pastitsio, and tiropitas will not disappoint. Greek wines. Always a daily special, anything from stuffed eggplant to squid or red snapper Greek style. There are baskets of ferns and prints of the Acropolis on the walls. This is the most authentic Greek restaurant in Los Angeles. Dinner Tuesday through Sunday. MC, V.

Yugoslavian

Paragon Inn. *Moderate.* 660 W. 7th St., San Pedro; 831–2200. Yugoslavian specialties. Located close to the harbor and Ports O'Call Village, Paragon offers shish kebab, sarma, musaka, leg of lamb, fresh fish, and strudel. Yugoslav folk dancing. Wine and beer. Dinner Tuesday through Sunday. CB, MC, V.

DESSERTS. Despite the rumor that Los Angelenos are preoccupied with slim and trim bodies, there is no lack of dessert parlors in this city.

When the craving for sweets strikes after the midnight hour, there is nothing to fear, for *DuPar's* is open until the wee hours of the morning throughout the city. These chain restaurants have in-house bakeries that whip up assorted varieties of buttery Danishes, pies, cakes, and doughnuts. They also brew a strong cup of coffee guaranteed to keep you awake for the drive back to your hotel.

It's natural to assume that in a city with such a moderate climate, ice-cream parlors would abound. *Häagen-Dazs,* offering a superb, rich, hand-packed ice cream in a multitude of flavors, with a choice of freshly prepared fudge and nut toppings, is the king of the chains. *Baskin-Robbins* is a California tradition; they are known for creating 101 different flavors of ice cream. Here's your chance to try bubble-gum flavored ice cream or blueberry cheesecake ice cream from among a rainbow of assorted tastes and colors. *Swenson's* is another popular Los Angeles chain offering a variety of flavors guaranteed to please the true ice-cream connoisseur. All the above chains have various outlets throughout the city.

Bennett's Ice Cream, located in Farmers Market in Los Angeles, has splendid fresh ice cream, ice-cream cakes, and fountain service.

San Fernando Valley visitors need only trek to Encino to discover *Robb's Ice Cream Co.,* 17621 Ventura Blvd., Encino; 784–0867. This intimate parlor features over thirty-five flavors of ice cream, including cinafee (cinnamon and coffee) and banaffee (banana and coffee). A true hedonist will add some M&M and Reese's candy toppings.

The Beverly Hills Hotel, 9641 Sunset Blvd., Beverly Hills; 276–2251. Not usually thought of as a place in which to eat dessert, but its downstairs fountain shop makes a wicked chocolate milk shake—rich, thick, cold, and very chocolaty.

C. C. Brown's Hot Fudge Shoppe, 7007 Hollywood Blvd., Hollywood; 464–9726, is an ice-cream legend in Los Angeles. This Hollywood landmark is renowned for its excellent hot fudge sundaes. Judy Garland was once a waitress here.

Michel Richard, 310 S. Robertson, Los Angeles; 275–5707. This charming bistro is representative of many city cafés specializing in pastries and espresso. A bakery as well, Michel Richard's offers the crème de la crème of fine baking, with tiny tables for enjoying the confections on the premises. Also at 12321 Ventura Blvd., Studio City; 508–9977.

La Fondue Bourguignonne, 13354 Ventura Blvd., Sherman Oaks; 501–0181. This restaurant, specializing in fondue, will, on special order, serve that wonder of wonders, chocolate dessert fondue. Chilled fresh fruits in season, along with marshmallows, are skewered onto long forks and dipped into a pot of warm, fudgy chocolate. If that wasn't heaven enough, you then get to dip the finished product into a bowl of freshly whipped heavy cream.

Miss Grace Lemon Cakes, 443 S. Robertson Blvd., Beverly Hills; 274–2879; also at 16571 Ventura Blvd., Encino; 995–1976. Fabulous cakes to go, made with the freshest, prime ingredients. Their lemon cake is filled with the essence of so many lemons that it will make your mouth pucker with joy. Also chocolate fudge, banana, and carrot cakes as well as chocolate chip cookies.

Freshly baked chocolate-chip cookies have been the rage of Los Angeles cookie eaters for some time. *Famous Amos* started the trend, and many other entrepreneurs have entered the race. Famous Amos, at 7181 Sunset Blvd., Hollywood; 851–6777, still has the original store with which its multimillion dollar business started. Most major shopping malls feature chocolate-chip cookie emporiums, such as the *Original Chocolate Chip Cookie Company* and *David's,* a successful New York cookie company, featuring cookies made with Lindt's imported bittersweet chocolate. David's is located at the Broadway Department Store, Century City.

If you're lucky and it's the spring or summer months, you'll find carts with peddlers selling the latest sweet creation: ice creamwiches. These sinful desserts have chocolate-chip cookie outer shells and ice-cream fillings. They're usually located in the Beverly Hills and Century City areas as well as across from the Los Angeles County Art Museum.

 COFFEEHOUSES AND CAFÉS. Grabbing a quick bite while touring Los Angeles shouldn't be passed off as purely a functional stop. From the uniformity of a hamburger chain to the more particular ambience of a neighborhood café, eating and running (or eating and driving) is part of the Los Angeles experience.

For only cents more than such familiar places as Burger King or Taco Bell, travelers can explore the many walk-up, drive-in, and takeout stands featuring "chili on everything," a California speciality.

The original *Tommy's Hamburgers* near the USC campus (2575 Beverly at Rampart) is a Los Angeles tradition where you'll find students and other devotees scooping up the famous double-chili cheeseburger. Many locations, two in the Valley: in Burbank, 1310 N. San Fernando Blvd., and in Van Nuys, 6180 Van Nuys Blvd. in Van Nuys.

Although it is a professed imitation, try *Tom's #5,* 1544 La Cienega, and *Tom's #5* in Santa Monica at 1906 Ocean Ave. (an easy walk from the Ocean Ave. entrance to Santa Monica Beach at the end of Pico Blvd.) These stands, like Tommy's, satisfy by providing chili on everything for a good price. Open twenty-four hours; tables provided for traffic watching.

Pink's (at Melrose and La Brea) serves a celebrated chili-cheesedog. A favorite for even the most discerning gourmet, Pink's guarantees a full stomach.

A novel setting is *Carney's,* 8351 W. Sunset Blvd. in West Hollywood, and also in Studio City at 12601 Ventura Blvd., between Coldwater Canyon and Whitset. Some of the best hamburgers in town are served from these converted railroad cars. The Hollywood booths face well-lighted Sunset Strip.

Also boating the best burgers around is *Fat Jack's* on Ventura Blvd. in Studio City, located west of Universal Studios, a five-minute drive away.

Tiny Naylor's Coffee Shop and Drive-in has been a Los Angeles landmark since 1926. Of its thirty locations, the Sunset and La Brea restaurant, one of the surviving original drive-ins, is reminiscent of a scene from *American Graffiti* as waitresses hook trays outside car windows twenty-four hours a day. Among special features is a steak, vegetable, and potato dinner at a very reasonable price. Even with a slice of the not-to-be missed cheesecake, visitors can get away for as little as $5.00.

The classic coffee-shop cuisine of the original *Schwab's* in Hollywood at Sunset and Laurel; 656–1212, is matched only by its classic environment. The counter stool where Lana Turner was reputedly discovered years ago is today occupied by another generation of Hollywood hopefuls. Leon Schwab heralds his French toast as "the best in town," and soups are always a specialty here. Chop Suey has been a tradition on Fridays since the chef began serving it thirty-seven years ago. Daily, 7:00 P.M. to 9:00 P.M.

For a more upbeat, contemporary eating experience, Los Angeles offers a number of fine cafés with no set minimum. *Café Beverly Hills* (9725 Wilshire Blvd. at La Cienega; 273–6397), open twenty-four hours a day, is a favorite late-night haunt. The cuisine is straight coffee shop, though beer and wine are served. Prices range to $7.00. Cash only. Parking.

Also competing as the best patio in the West Hollywood area is the enclosed tree-planted area at *Joe Allen,* 8706 W. 3rd St.; 274–7144. The New York theatrical decor features the same checked tablecloths and blackboard menus found at namesake restaurants located in New York, Paris, London, and Toronto. Though reservations are accepted, there is usually a wait, well passed at the lively bar. Daily 11:30 A.M.–2:00 A.M. Price range: $5.00–$12.00 a la carte. MC, V, AE.

El Coyote Spanish Café, 7312 Beverly Blvd.; 939–7766, cannot be beat for its inexpensive Mexican food and festive decor. Costumed waitresses are friendly; the service is great. Daily 11:00 A.M.–10:00 P.M. MC, V. A town favorite, so expect a wait.

170 Café, 170 S. La Brea; 939–0107, is a new entry on the Los Angeles scene. On the second floor of a building that also includes three contemporary art galleries and a bookstore, this neo-Palladian-style lunch spot features nouvelle French cuisine, including pastries, pâté, and pastas. The café itself serves as a viewing space for contemporary and primitive African art.

Where Melrose Ave. begins at Doheny Dr. on the edge of Beverly Hills, so does the real Los Angeles café life. A newcomer worth a look is *Starlight Café* at 7505 Melrose Ave.; 655–1310. An upbeat place, it is equipped with music and disc jockey and some refreshingly updated luncheonette fare, with pizza as a specialty. Sunday through Thursday, noon on (until 3:00 A.M. Friday and Saturday). V, MC. The large bay windows of *Café Figaro,* 9010 Melrose; 274–7664, reveal comfortable coffeehouse surroundings. The healthful food is popular with students and entertainment-industry aspirants. Monday–Thursday 11:30 A.M. –2:00 A.M., Friday and Saturday until 3:00 A.M., Sunday 4:00 P.M.–2:00 A.M. Reservations.

At the entrance of West Hollywood on Melrose are several trendy café and espresso bars. Most popular is *Flamingo Café,* (7212 Melrose Ave.; 939–2420). Always busy, Flamingo is open Monday–Saturday 11:30 A.M.–3:00 P.M. Frequented by comedians and actors from the nearby Improvisation and the Groundlings Theater, its curried chicken salad is a favorite. No reservations, so expect a wait. Cash only.

A short jaunt west amid campy antique stores, you'll find *City Café,* 7407½ Melrose Ave.; 658–7494. The country French cooking features pâtés and cheese platters that can be enjoyed with wine you carry in (it's served for a small corking fee). The specials change daily, but espresso, cappuccino, and pastries are always available. Daily 9:00 A.M.–midnight. V, MC.

A number of French cafés can be found in Los Angeles. The authentic music and Continental waiters at *La Poubelle*, 5909 Franklin, Hollywood; 462–9264, give it a true café atmosphere. Chef's specialties are crepes, quiches, and omelettes, all homemade with fresh ingredients. Reservations. Daily 5:00 P.M.–midnight. No credit cards.

Michel Richard (310 S. Robertson; 275–5707) sets tables just outside the busy baker/restaurant, giving it the most "sidewalk feeling" within Los Angeles. Croissants and coffees are enough for a substantial lunch, though a small menu is offered. The clientele is largely French. (Also in the San Fernando Valley, 12321 Ventura Blvd., Studio City; 508–9977.) MC, V.

Downtown, *Café de Paris* (821 S. Spring opposite Cal Mart; 623–7308) is a tiny hole in the wall offering a big French experience. The freshly baked goods and coffee provide a quick shopping respite. The prices are more than reasonable. Monday–Friday, 8:00 A.M.–4:00 P.M.

Clifton's Cafeteria has six restaurants in the Los Angeles area, but the downtown location (515 W. 7th St. at Olive) has persevered in a Los Angeles landmark building where much of the 1920s decor has been maintained. The fourth generation family-owned-and-operated business serves family-style recipes. Monday–Friday, 7:00 A.M.–3:30 P.M. $3.50 luncheon, $4.50 dinner.

Open twenty-four hours for the past fifty-five years, the *Original Pantry*, 977 S. Figueroa; 972–9272, offers big helpings, strictly of the meat-and-potatoes kind. Though it is always crowded, you can't go wrong here.

The Westside is Los Angeles's best part of town for strolling and café lounging. In Beverly Hills try *Café Rodeo* (360 N. Rodeo Dr.; 273–0300), well worth the $3.50 minimum for its Continental cuisine and stargazing on the famous drive where many celebrities stop for lunch. There is usually a wait for patio dining. Reservations are suggested for dinner. All major credit cards. Daily 7:00 A.M.–midnight. Valet parking.

Nearby is one of three *Santo Pietros* at 340 N. Camden; 274–0248. (The others are at 2954 Beverly Glen Circle, Bel Air; 474–4349, and at 23063 Park Sorrento, Calabasas.) This country Italian café features chopped-antipasto salad, light pastas, pizza, beer, and wine. Desserts are great. Try the pistachio cake. It's definitely a place to see and be seen.

The café/cafeteria style at *Café Casino* (9595 Wilshire, Beverly Hills; 274–0201, and in two other locations at 1299 Ocean Ave., Santa Monica; 394–1135, and in Westwood at 1135 Gayley Ave.; 208–1010) allows for slightly lower prices in this normally high-density eating district. The proprietors are French, as are the fresh croissants, pâtés, salads, and hot entrees. Choose what you like, and carry your tray to the shaded umbrella patio, or take out a fresh pastry from the bakery counter and window shop. Monday–Saturday 7:00 A.M.–10:00 P.M. AE, MC, V.

Thirty varieties of the town's finest cheesecake are found at the *Cheesecake Factory* (364 N. Beverly Dr., Beverly Hills; 278–7270). The $3.00 minimum is easily spent on one of their unique flavors: amaretto, peanut butter, and marble, to name a few, and a cup of steaming espresso. Otherwise, the full menu and salad bar may be enjoyed in the casual, pleasant atmosphere. Monday–Thursday 11:00 A.M.–11:00 P.M., Friday and Saturday 11:00 A.M.–12:30 A.M., Sunday 11:00 A.M.–10:00 P.M.

The contemporary *Cadillac Café*, 359 N. La Cienega Blvd.; 657–4762, is a frequent eating spot for such celebrities as Teri Garr and Steve Martin. The diverse menu features the freshest of salads. Open Monday through Friday, 11:30 A.M. to midnight, Saturday and Sunday, 10:00 A.M. to midnight.

Students frequent the twenty-four-hour *Ships*, 10877 Wilshire Blvd. (at Glendon); 474–5534, popping their bread in the toasters provided at every table.

The more ethnic version of Ship's coffee shop cuisine is *Junior's Deli/Restaurant*, 2379 Westwood Blvd.; 475–5771. Always busy, their Jewish cooking is unrivaled on the Westside. Daily 7:00 A.M.–1:00 A.M. MC, V.

The Hamburger Hamlet, 10943 Weyburn Ave.; 208–8980, serves plump and juicy hamburgers. Lobster bisque and overloaded omelettes are also specialties. Several locations. All major credit cards. Monday–Thursday, 11:30 A.M.–9:00 P.M. Friday–Saturday 11:00 A.M.–11:00 P.M.

D. B. Levy's (10936 Lindbrook Ave.; 208–3773) features 164 sandwiches (at last count), 27 ice-cream creations, homemade soups, and a variety of cheesecakes. The upper level is bright and airy. All major credit cards. Monday–Thursday, 11:30 A.M.–11:00 P.M., Friday and Saturday, 11:30 A.M.–2:00 A.M., Sunday 11:00 A.M.–11:00 P.M.

In West Los Angeles French–California cuisine is served at the *Bicycle Shop Café* (12217 Wilshire Blvd.; 826–7831). Antique bicycles are set among plants and waterfalls. Excellent for after-theater and movie dining. Cary Grant is a frequent customer for their authentic French onion soup. Weekends a fabulous brunch. No minimum, lunch about $7.00, $10.00 for dinner. Daily 11:00 A.M. –2:00 A.M., MC, V.

Get ready for a flash from the past at the *Hardrock Café* 8614 Beverly Blvd., on the ground floor of the Beverly Center shopping mall; 276–7605. Waitresses are known to break into a 50s dance routine in the middle of taking your order.

The most frequented outdoor café in Venice is *The Sidewalk Café* (1401 Ocean Front Walk; 399–5547). From any seat in the patio, diners are treated to the famous Venice charades. Mimes, magicians, acrobats, and roller-skating dancers glide by the busy café. An ocean view, too. Omelettes, salads, and sandwiches. Expect a wait! Daily 8:00 A.M.–1.00 A.M. V, MC.

The Dandelion Café (636 Venice Blvd.) is best known for its omelettes. Vegetable chili and homemade sherry trifle at reasonable prices are also specialties. Tuesday–Sunday 8:00 A.M.–4:00 P.M. No credit cards. Easy parking.

Figtree's Café, 429 Ocean Front Walk; 396–5559, is a warm and friendly natural-foods coffeehouse with vegetarian and espresso specialties. $2.50 minimum on weekends. Parking on Rose Ave. lot.

The Rose (220 Rose Ave., 399–0711) serves an elegant dinner and luncheon menu, but the coffee shop serves croissants and fruit tarts without the $6.00 minimum. Monday–Saturday 8:00 A.M.–11:00 P.M., Sunday 9:00 A.M.–5:00 P.M. MC, V.

In Pasadena don't miss *The Espresso Bar,* 34 S. Raymond Ave.; 356–9095. High vaulted ceilings, Persian rugs, and a fireplace create a unique European café atmosphere. Interesting salads and soups are the specialties. Tuesday through Saturday a Continental breakfast is served, 8:00 A.M.–11:00 A.M., lunch 11:30 A.M.–4:00 P.M. Dinner is served Tuesday through Saturday 7:00 P.M. –10:30 P.M., but open until 2:00 A.M. for espresso, cappuccino, and pastries. Monday night there is jazz in the alcove; wonderful acoustics.

 NIGHT LIFE. Night life in Los Angeles has come to mean anything from catching a comedy act at the Comedy Store to frenetic disco dancing at Chippendales or dreamily listening to a sultry chanteuse at Chez Nora's. This city offers a potpourri of specialized entertainment, not only in the hub of the city but also in the outlying suburban communities.

Despite the diversity of entertainment and the high energy level of the nightlife crowd, Los Angeles nightclubs are not known for keeping their doors open until the wee hours of the morning. This is an early-to-bed city, and it's not unusual to hear the call for "last drinks" at 1:30 A.M. It's safe to say that by 2:00 A.M., most jazz, rock, and disco clubs are closed for the night. Afterhours clubs are few and far between. Perhaps it's because of the temperate climate and the sports orientation of the city. Most Angelenos want to be on the tennis court or out jogging by 9:00 A.M., and so a late night social life is often out of the question.

The accent in this city is on trendy rock clubs, smooth country-and-Western establishments, intimate jazz spots, and laugh-a-minute comedy clubs. City residents generally do not gravitate toward hotels for nighttime entertainment, but you can discover there a quiet evening of soft piano or harp music, often accompanied by sentimental vocalists, for a refreshing change of pace.

The Sunset Strip, running from West Hollywood to Beverly Hills, offers a wide assortment of nighttime diversions. Comedy stores, restaurants with piano bars, cocktail lounges, and hard-rock clubs proliferate.

Westwood, home of UCLA, is a college town, and this section of Los Angeles comes alive at night with rock and new-wave discos and clubs playing the canned and live music. It's one of the few areas in Los Angeles with a true neighborhood spirit. You'll see people of all ages strolling its streets at night, and you can feel the excitement and energy in the air. On the other hand, downtown Los Angeles is generally not the place to be at night. Other than the Dorothy Chandler Pavilion for concerts and theater, downtown night life is virtually nonexistent.

Dress codes vary depending on the establishment you choose to visit. Jackets are expected at the more traditional night entertainment spots, such as cabarets and hotels. Discos are generally quite casual, although some prohibit the wearing of blue jeans. New-wave and punk-rock clubs are the most casual of all— almost anything goes there! The rule of thumb is to phone ahead and check the dress code, but, on the whole, Los Angeles is oriented toward casual wear.

The following night spots are divided according to their orientation: jazz; folk/pop/rock; cabaret; disco/dancing; country; hotel rooms and piano bars; and comedy/magic. Consult *Los Angeles* and *California* magazines for up-to-the-minute listings. The Sunday *Los Angeles Times* Calendar section, the free *Los Angeles Weekly,* and *Los Angeles Reader* also provide wide listings.

Don't think that the suburbs of this city have no night life. Some of Los Angeles's best jazz, discos, and comedy clubs are scattered throughout the San Fernando and San Gabriel valleys. For example, the Baked Potato in Studio City offers dynamic jazz, and the Palomino Club in North Hollywood boasts nationally recognized country-and-western performers.

With a little exploration you will discover that "the City of Angels" can easily bring out a bit of the devil in you.

Key to credit card information following each listing.

AE = American Express
CB = Carte Blanche
DC = Diners Club
MC = MasterCard
V = Visa

Expensive is a charge of $10.00 or more per person; *Moderate* is $5.00–$9.00. *Inexpensive* refers to places where the cover and/or minimum totals less than $5.00. On weekend nights, cover charges at most establishments are usually a few dollars higher than on weeknights.

JAZZ

Concerts by the Sea. 100 Fisherman's Wharf, Redondo Beach; 379–4998. One of Los Angeles's most popular jazz clubs. Many name acts, including Lionel Hampton, Jimmy Smith, and Ramsey Lewis. A wide variety of jazz artists featured. Three shows nightly. Valet parking available. Thursday through Sunday. *Expensive to Moderate.* MC, V.

Nucleus Nuance. 7267 Melrose Ave., Hollywood; 939–8666. This Art Deco restaurant features vintage jazz Friday and Saturday from 10:00 P.M. on. *Moderate to Expensive.* All major credit cards.

Donte's. 4269 Lankershim Blvd., North Hollywood; 877–8347, and 769–1566. A comfortable room featuring a variety of jazz entertainment, including top-name big bands. Many studio musicians and talk-show orchestra members sit in on shows. The dinner menu includes many Continental specialties. Closed Sunday. *Moderate.* All major credit cards.

Jazz Safari. 1119 Queen's Highway, Long Beach; 443–2004. Contemporary jazz fills this club. Junglelike decor: There are ceramic tigers and lions, huge trees, and a forty-gallon fish tank filled with exotic fish. International hamburgers, steak, and scampi are the dining specialties. Open seven days. *Moderate.* All major credit cards.

Le Café. 14633 Ventura Blvd., Sherman Oaks; 986–2662. The Room Upstairs is of high-tech design and features mellow jazz. It's an intimate room; many vocalists, including owner Lois Boileau, are presented. Three shows nightly, Thursday through Saturday. Downstairs is a dynamic restaurant-café offering everything from onion soup to the best fresh duck in town. *Moderate.* AE, MC, V.

Memory Lane. 2323 W. Martin Luther King Jr. Blvd., Los Angeles; 294–8430. Now owned by comedy star Marla Gibbs of "The Jeffersons" fame. Newly remodeled, the club seats 275. This room pops with blues, jazz, and easy listening. Kenny Burrell and Ernie Andrews play here from time to time. A new menu includes roast prime rib of beef and Alaskan King Crab Legs. *Moderate.* AE, CB, DC.

Mulberry Street. 12067 Ventura Pl., Studio City; 980–8405. This joint started out as a great pizza parlor and grew to be a terrific jazz spot. George Segal plays here regularly with his Beverly Hills Unlisted Jazz Band. Many studio musicians frequent this club, and of course so do George Segal devotées. Homemade pasta, pizza, beer, and wine. Closed Monday. *Moderate.* MC, V over $10.00.

Parisian Room. 4960 W. Washington Blvd., Los Angeles; 936–0678. One of Los Angeles's oldest and most established jazz clubs. Etta James and Linda Hopkins are just two of the powerful vocalists who play this room. The cover varies; usually *Moderate.* AE, MC, V.

Pasquale's. 22724 Pacific Coast Hwy., Malibu; 456–2007. The sight of the Pacific Ocean and the sound of top jazz artists characterize this club by the sea. Willie Bobo and the Los Angeles Jazz Choir play here. Seats 100. *Moderate.* MC, V.

Maiden Voyage. 2424 Wilshire Blvd., Los Angeles; 480–9667. Local and top-name jazz artists are featured. Entertainment nightly. Snacks, wine, and cocktails. The cover varies; generally *Moderate to Inexpensive.* MC, V.

The Baked Potato. 3787 Cahuenga Blvd., west, North Hollywood; 980–1615. A tiny club where they pack you in like sardines to hear a powerhouse of jazz. The featured item on the menu is, of course, baked potatoes; they're jumbo and stuffed with everything from steak to vegetables. This intimate, intelligent jazz club usually features Don Randi and Quest, Wednesday through Saturday. *Inexpensive.* MC, V.

Carmelo's. 4449 Van Nuys Blvd., Sherman Oaks; 995–9532, and 784–3268. An intimate club seating no more than 100 people. Dixieland and straightforward jazz is featured. Sarah Vaughan is known to "sit in" on occasion. Dinner can be ordered; Italian and Continental cuisine. *Inexpensive.* AE, MC, V.

Coffee Emporium. 4345 Glencoe Ave., Marina del Rey; 823–4446. This earthy coffeehouse features jazz quartets and quintets on Friday and Saturday evenings from 8:30 P.M. to midnight. It's full of green plants, fresh flowers on oak tables, and a giant espresso machine that brews several varieties of imported coffees. Pastries and cheesecake are specialties. Generally standing room only; come early. *No cover.* MC, V.

Comeback Inn. 1633 W. Washington Blvd., Venice; 396–7255. A showcase for original music. "Fusion," jazz blended with funk, pop, ethnic, and electronic music, is strong here. From April through November are featured outdoor concerts. A European-style bistro with a bohemian flair. The club serves strict vegetarian cuisine. Entertainment nightly and weekend afternoons. *Inexpensive.* No credit cards.

Flying Jib. 17237 Ventura Blvd., Encino; 986–2598. A large room, separate from their Continental-style restaurant. Progressive jazz is highlighted. Munch on potato skins and egg rolls during sets. Open seven days. *Inexpensive.* AE, MC, V.

The Lighthouse. 30 Pier Ave., Hermosa Beach; 372–6911 and 376–9833. One of Los Angeles's finest. A broad spectrum of jazz from progressive to big band. Jam sessions often on weekends. Freddie Hubbard, Woody Herman, and Jimmy Witherspoon have all played here. The decor is of wood, brass, and brick, with a lot of plants. Dine on fettucini, assorted appetizers, or steaks while hearing the sounds. *No cover.* MC, V with a $5.00 minimum.

The Money Tree. 10149 Riverside Dr., Toluca Lake; 766–9891 and 766–8348. A restaurant-jazz club featuring assorted vocalists and small combos. Studio musicians often sit in. Open seven days. *No cover, no minimum.* MC, V.

FOLK/POP/ROCK

The Palace. 1735 N. Vine St., Hollywood; 462–3000 or 462–6031. The in spot for the upwardly mobile. It's plush Art Deco—truely a palace—and boasts live entertainment, a fabulous sound system, full bar and dining upstairs in the L'Élysée Matignon restaurant. Patrons dress to kill. *Expensive.* Tickets available at Ticketron or at the Palace box office. AE, V, MC.

McCabe's Guitar Shop. 3101 Pico Blvd., Santa Monica; 828–4497. Folk, acoustic rock, bluegrass, and soul in an intimate concert-hall setting. Coffee, herb tea, apple juice, and homemade sweets are served during intermission. Friday through Sunday only. *Expensive to Moderate.* All major credit cards.

The Roxy. 9009 Sunset Blvd., West Hollywood; 276–2222. The premier Los Angeles rock club. Classy and comfortable, this intimate club now also offers performance art as well as theatrical productions. Many famous Los Angeles groups got their start here as opening acts. *Expensive to Moderate.* All major credit cards.

The Central. 8852 Sunset Blvd., West Hollywood; 855–9183. A musician's hangout. Road crews, pop-act managers, and famous guitarists alike come to hear live music in the pop, soul, and jazz-fusion genres. Many celebrity musicians attend the Tuesday night jam sessions. *Moderate.* No credit cards.

Club Lingerie. 6507 Sunset Blvd., Hollywood; 466–8557. This exciting Art Deco night spot features everything from reggae to big-band music. Drink prices are fair, and the door varies according to the attraction. *Moderate.* No credit cards.

Gazzari's. 9039 Sunset Blvd., West Hollywood; 273–6606. A Sunset Strip landmark. Pure rock and roll with a 19- early 20's age group. Dress is casual. *Moderate.* No credit cards.

Madame Wong's Restaurant. 949 Sun Mun Way, Los Angeles; 624–5346. A young crowd; new-wave fanatics. Two shows nightly. Also Madame Wong's West, 2900 Wilshire Blvd., Santa Monica; 829–7361. *Moderate.*

Perkins Palace. 129 N. Raymond Ave., Pasadena; 796–7001. Rock-and-roll concerts, Friday and Saturday only. Up-and-coming talent as well as some name acts. *Moderate.*

Relic House. 7140 Reseda Blvd., Reseda; 344–9759. Relics from movies make up the decor. A combination of sounds, from jazz to rhythm-and-blues, is booked. *Moderate.* No credit cards.

At My Place. 1026 Wilshire Blvd.; 451–8596. One of the new LA clubs, this year-old enterprise features a provocative blend of jazz/fusion, pop, and rhythm-and-blues music acts. Comedy performers open the weekend shows, and on Sunday afternoons you can enjoy a 20-piece ensemble playing big-band music. Some of the culinary specialties include quiche and potato skins. There is also a full bar. *Moderate.* V, MC.

Banjo Café. 2906 Lincoln Blvd., Santa Monica; 392–5716. Dixieland, folk, and jazz music are featured. An intimate, casual club with inexpensive, quality food. *Inexpensive* cover for nondiners. MC, V.

Club 88. 11784 Pico Blvd., West Los Angeles; 479–6923. Rock and roll nightly. *Inexpensive.*

Pier 52. 52 Pier Ave., Hermosa Beach; 376–1629. From Tuesday through Sunday there are live dance bands playing pure rock and roll and Top 40s. Monday night is saved for top bands, including new wave and heavy metal. *Inexpensive.* No credit cards.

Sasch. 11345 Ventura Blvd., Studio City; 769–5555. A live band plays Top 40s for the twenty-one to thirty-five age group. Anything goes for dress. *Inexpensive.* All major credit cards.

Sunset Saloon. 1 Washington St., Venice; 396–5914. This club draws a beach crowd with primarily rock and roll entertainment. *Inexpensive.* MC, V with $5.00 minimum.

The Troubador. 9081 Santa Monica Blvd., West Hollywood; 276–1158. In the early 1970s this was one of the hottest clubs in town for major talent. Business then became shaky for a few years as the music industry changed its focus; but now it's rolling again, this time with up-and-coming talent. The adjoining bar is a great place to see and be seen. *Inexpensive.* No credit cards.

Twenty Grand West. 5812 Overland Rd., Los Angeles; 296–3195. This reggae club draws many a homesick Jamaican. Jamaican food is another strong plus here. *Inexpensive.* MC, V.

CABARET

Playboy Club. ABC Entertainment Center, 2020 Ave. of the Stars, Century City; 277–2777. If you want to fork over $25.00 for instant membership, you've got instant admittance to Playboy clubs all over the country. You may bring an unlimited number of guests. Bunnies will provide the drinks; the likes of Lainie Kazan and other chanteuses will provide the entertainment. Closed Sunday. *Expensive to Moderate,* depending on whether you are a member. All major credit cards.

Studio One Backlot. 657 N. Robertson Blvd., West Hollywood; 659–0472. An elegant, classy night spot featuring excellent musical acts, singers, comedians, and dancers. Closed Sunday through Tuesday. *Expensive to Moderate.* AE, MC, V.

Hop Singh's. 4110 Lincoln Blvd., Marina del Rey; 822–4008. Intimate and innovative. Jazz, rock, folk, and comedy—what more could you want? Closed Tuesday. *Moderate.* All major credit cards.

The Horn. 2627 Wilshire Blvd., Santa Monica; 828–7554. A variety nightclub for twenty-eight years; the spotlight is on singers, comedians, and an occasional magic act. Joan Rivers performs here, and Milton Berle and Hal Linden have been known to walk up on stage unannounced. Closed Sunday and Monday. *Moderate.* MC, V.

L.A. Cabaret. 17271 Ventura Blvd., Encino; 501–3737. This new night spot features a variety of comedy acts on weekends and on Wednesday. Often, famous entertainers will make surprise appearances. *Moderate.* AE, V, MC.

La Cage aux Folles. 643 N. La Cienega Blvd., West Hollywood; 657–1091. A cabaret supper club that has a unique angle: female impersonators who do impressions of famous female stars such as Liza Minnelli or Barbra Streisand. The ambience, with a shocking-pink and stark-blue color scheme, resembles a European bistro of forty years ago. An unusual fun nightspot. There is an extensive French–Continental menu. *Moderate* cover charge for diners; *Expensive* for nondiners. AE, MC, V.

Gio's Cabaret. 7574 Sunset Blvd., Hollywood; 876–1120. An eclectic variety of talented Los Angeles artists perform here. One night will feature comedians; another night it's big-band time or jazz quartets or aspiring theatrical talent performing Broadway vignettes. The cabaret menu features sandwiches, calamari fritti (fried squid), and mozzarella marinara. The adjoining restaurant specializes in Brazilian cuisine. *Moderate to Inexpensive.* All major credit cards.

Ingrid and David's Gingerhouse. 18669 Ventura Blvd., Tarzana; 881–0660. An eclectic variety of entertainment in a restaurant that looks like a gingerbread house. Ingrid's original art is everywhere, and there are white picket fences dividing the tables. Singers, mentalists, original short plays, and Broadway revivals are featured. Psychics and tarot-card readings too! *Moderate to Inexpensive.* MC, V.

Chez Nora. 14642 Ventura Blvd., Sherman Oaks; 788–1416. A club for sentimentalists. Nora will sing to you in French while you relax on love seats and settees. Flowered wallpaper and tulip-shaped lamps provide the backdrop for an assortment of jazz, pop, and blues singers. The menu consists of mostly snacks, plus popcorn, peanuts and pretzels. *No Cover.* MC, V.

New Rose Café and Cabaret. 3707 W. Cahuenga Blvd., Studio City; (808) 762–2800. This place is so tiny that it's like having a cabaret in your living room. Music, comedy, and cabaret revues are highlights. You can order hot food up to 2:00 A.M. Closed Monday and Tuesday. Reservations strongly recommended. *No cover.* MC, V.

DISCO/DANCING

Chippendale's. 3739 Overland Ave., West Los Angeles; 202–8850. A popular Los Angeles disco, well-known for its male exotic dancers–waiters who strip down to G-strings for women only from Wednesday through Sunday at the 8:30 P.M. shows. On Tuesday night it's female mud wrestling, and every night it's disco, disco, disco. Loud punk, funk, and new-wave music spills out the doors and into the street. Not for the timid or prudish. The cover varies; usually *Moderate.* Occasional free night for ladies. MC, V.

Osko's Disco. 333 S. La Cienega Blvd., Los Angeles; 652–9333. A leading Los Angeles disco. This multilevel club was featured in the disco film *Thank God It's Friday.* There are female mud wrestlers and male exotic dancers as well as the latest disco singles. *Moderate* cover. All major credit cards.

The Speakeasy. 8531 Santa Monica Blvd., West Hollywood; 657–4777. A softly lighted disco with the latest of disco music pounding the room. Soul-type music predominates. A well-dressed crowd; people really get up and boggie seriously. Cover *Moderate.* MC, V in bar only.

Tennessee Gin and Cotton Co. 19710 Ventura Blvd., Woodland Hills; 347–4044. Two dance floors; one is a disco, and the other has a live rock or Top 40s band for a classy over-twenty-one crowd. Casual but neat dress. *Moderate.* Closed Monday.

Circus Disco. 6648 Lexington Ave., Hollywood; 462–1291. Gay owned and operated, this disco features funk and rock, with new wave exclusively on Thursday nights, all played over a large-scale quadrophonic sound system. Open nightly. *Moderate to Inexpensive.* No credit cards.

Le Hot Club. 15910 Ventura Blvd., Encino; 986–7034. The San Fernando Valley's most chic club. A lot of backgammon tables and a well-dressed crowd of all ages. Music is played by a D.J. with a deference toward all disco factions. *Moderate to Inexpensive.* Closed Monday. AE, MC, V.

Annabelle's. 1700 Pacific Coast Hwy., Redondo Beach; 316–1434. It's jazz until 9:00 P.M., and then disco is king—seven nights a week. *No cover charge.* MC, V.

Beverly Cavern Discotheque. 4289 Beverly Blvd., Los Angeles; 662–6035. Disco and backgammon is popular here. Oldies as well as the latest in disco and rock and roll predominate. *Inexpensive.* No credit cards.

Filthy McNasty's. 11700 Victory Blvd., North Hollywood; 769–2220. McNasty is almost a Hollywood landmark himself, having held court on the Sunset Strip for countless years. He has since moved to the San Fernando Valley for another wild and crazy club. Proceed at your own risk. There is female mud wrestling for male oglers and male exotic dancers for female oglers. Live and canned music. After hours Friday and Saturday until 4:00 A.M. Some nights long-time entrepreneur McNasty himself gets up on stage.

Le Chic. 1717 Silverlake Blvd., Los Angeles; 666–2885. A mixture of Latino, funk, and pop disco. The crowd is of all ages. Backgammon is a popular game

between dances. Free disco lessons on Wednesday and Sunday. *Inexpensive.*
MC, V.

Odyssey I. 8471 Beverly Blvd., West Hollywood; 658–8106. Rock nightly
until 4:00 A.M., Friday and Saturday until 5:00 A.M. Pool table and pinball
machines. *Inexpensive.* No credit cards.

Playboy Club. ABC Entertainment Center, 2020 Ave. of the Stars, Century
City; 277–2777. An instant key costs $25.00 and includes unlimited guests.
Disco in the Living Room from 9:00 P.M. until 2:00 A.M. *Moderate.* All major
credit cards.

The Stop. 12446 Moorpark St., Studio City; 761–8686. Hard rock-and-roll
disco; young, for a twenties crowd. *No cover.* MC, V.

Studio One. 652 N. LaPeer Dr., West Hollywood; 659–0471. Known as Los
Angeles's largest disco, it hosts a predominately gay crowd. Dancing nightly.
Inexpensive. No credit cards.

The Tapestry. 10177 Reseda Blvd., Northridge; 993–7071. Progressive disco
with the very latest of pure disco music. The records that play here are straight
from New York of record distributors. The crowd is eighteen to twenty-five.
Sunday is New-Wave night. *Inexpensive.* Closed Monday. MC, V.

COUNTRY

Little Nashville Club. 13350 Sherman Way, North Hollywood; 764–0420.
Country–Western entertainment and dancing nightly. Free dance lessons
Wednesday and Saturday. *No cover; two-drink minimum.* MC, V.

The Palomino. 6907 Lankershim Blvd., North Hollywood; 764–4010. There
is occasionally a wild crowd at this premier country showcase in Los Angeles.
Good old boys and hip cowboys meet here, and everybody has a good time. The
cover varies between *Moderate and Inexpensive.* All major credit cards.

Womphopper's Wagon Works. 100 Universal City Plaza, Universal City;
508–3939. Live country-Western entertainment at this unique restaurant built
out of barnwood, in an authentic Western motif with painstaking attention to
details. Dancing nightly. Full bar. Try the buffalo-meat chili. All major credit
cards.

HOTEL ROOMS AND PIANO BARS

Alberto's Ristorante. 8826 Melrose Ave., Los Angeles; 278–2770. This piano
bar draws a neighborhood crowd, generally over forty and well-to-do. Excellent
Italian food as well. All major credit cards.

Bel-Air Sands Hotel. 11461 Sunset Blvd., Bel Air; 476–6571. The Bimini Bar
features a singer–pianist who performs songs of the 1940s, 1950s, and 1960s. All
major credit cards.

Beverly Hills Hotel. 9641 Sunset Blvd., Beverly Hills; 276–2251. There is
late supper and after-theater piano entertainment in the Polo Lounge nightly.
This stately old hotel is a celebrity mecca. All major credit cards.

Century Plaza Hotel. 2025 Ave. of the Stars, Century City; 227–2000. The
Lobby Lounge features piano music nightly. All major credit cards.

Hotel Bel Air. 701 Stone Canyon Rd., Bel Air; 472–1211. Entertainment Tuesday through Sunday, alternating between a pianist and a vocalist. This is one of Los Angeles's most famous hotels. All major credit cards.

Hyatt Regency. 711 S. Hope St., Los Angeles; 683–1234. There is a good piano lounge in this spectacularly designed hotel. All major credit cards.

Hyatt Wilshire. 3515 Wilshire Blvd., Los Angeles; 381–7411. There is entertainment in the Café Carnival Lounge. All major credit cards.

Los Angeles Marriott. 5855 W. Century Blvd., Los Angeles; 641–5700. The Hangar Room on the top floor of the hotel offers a panoramic view of the city and especially of the arrival and departure of planes at the Los Angeles International Airport. It's a romantic place to go for a drink and soft piano music accompanied by a soothing vocalist. Both standard and contemporary songs are featured. All major credit cards.

The New Otani Hotel and Garden. 120 S. Los Angeles St., Los Angeles; 629–1200. The Genji Bar of this Japanese-style hotel offers a sentimental vocalist. All major credit cards.

Sheraton–Universal Hotel. 30 Universal City Plaza, North Hollywood; 980–1212. Soft combos perform in the Portuguese Bar. The hotel is convenient to restaurants and the entertainment complex in Universal City. All major credit cards.

Simply Blues. 6290 Sunset Blvd., Hollywood; 466–5239. This has an action-filled bar area; a lot of people crowd into the bar and listen to the soft piano music. All major credit cards.

Smoke House. 4420 Lakeside Dr., Burbank; 845–3731. There is a lounge room with assorted entertainment separate from the restaurant. Many musical acts of the 1950s are featured. All major credit cards.

Sportsmen's Lodge Restaurant. 12833 Ventura Blvd., Studio City; 984–0202. There is a pianist in the lounge connected to the lovely Sportsmen's Lodge Hotel. The setting, with brooks and swan-filled ponds, is pretty. All major credit cards.

S. S. Princess Louise Restaurant. Berth 94, Port of Los Angeles, San Pedro; 831–2341. This ship sails to nowhere but stays afloat with a piano bar and a good restaurant. Enjoy a romantic view of the ocean and the incoming ships. If you get carried away, you can get married at the ship's chapel. All major credit cards.

Tony Roma's. 9404 Brighton Way, Beverly Hills; 278–1207. There is piano entertainment in the lounge nightly. The restaurant is known for moderate-priced but tasty ribs. MC, V.

Westin Bonaventure Hotel. 5th and Figueroa St., Los Angeles; 624–1000. In the Lobby Court there is music nightly. Another room, Top of Five, features two pianists in a revolving lounge, offering breathtaking sights of the whole city. All major credit cards.

Westwood Marquis. 930 Hilgard Ave., Westwood; 208–8765. The Westwood Lounge of this chic hotel offers cozy settees, soft lights, and a piano or a harp player. Occasional vocals. Very relaxing. All major credit cards.

COMEDY AND MAGIC

Comedy Store. 8433 Sunset Blvd., Hollywood; 656–6225. Los Angeles's premier comedy showcase for over a decade. Many famous comedians, such as Robin Williams and Steve Martin, try out routines here. The cover varies; usually *Moderate.* MC, V. Also, the **Comedy Store West,** 1621 Westwood Blvd., Westwood; 477–4751.

The Improvisation. 8162 Melrose Ave., West Hollywood; 651–2583. The Improv is a transplanted New York establishment: eighteen years in the Big Apple, now seven in the Big Orange. Comedy is showcased here, with some vocalists. The Improv was the proving ground for Liza Minelli and Richard Pryor, among others. *Moderate.* No credit cards.

Merlin McFly Magical Bar and Grill. 2702 Main St., Santa Monica; 392–8468. This is one bar where you might see double, and it may not be because of the drinks: magical illusions are featured nightly until midnight. Ladies, watch out for the powder room; lights will dim there, and you'll see a Houdini-like figure with a crystal ball in the mirror. All major credit cards.

The New Ice House Comedy Showroom. 24 N. Mentor Ave., Pasadena; 681–1923. Three-act shows here feature comedians and magicians from Las Vegas as well as from television shows. *Moderate;* special bargain prices include show and dinner. MC, V.

Comedy and Magic Club. 1018 Hermosa Ave., Hermosa Beach; 372–1193. This beachfront club features many magicians and comedians seen on television and in Las Vegas. The Unknown Comic, Elayne Boosler, and Pat Paulsen have all played here. Closed Monday. Reservations are suggested. The menu features light American fare and many appetizers. *Moderate to Inexpensive,* depending on the featured act. MC, V.

Bert's Deli-Smoker. 14513 Ventura Blvd., Sherman Oaks; 990–8650. Sawdust on the floor, big brisket sandwiches—and lots of laughs. This deli turns into a comedy club Thursday through Saturday evenings. Local favorites as well as those trying to get established are featured. *Inexpensive.* MC, V.

L.A. Connection. 13442 Ventura Blvd., Sherman Oaks; 784–1868. Comedy revues and improvisation in a theater setting. *Inexpensive.* Reservations suggested on Saturday and Sunday. No credit cards.

The Laugh Factory. 8001 Sunset Blvd., Hollywood; 656–8860. A variety of comedy acts and improvisation. Closed Sunday. No age limit. Food, drink. *Inexpensive.*

Groundlings Theater. 7307 Melrose Ave., Hollywood; 934–9700. Original skits, music, improvisation with each player contributing his/her own flavor to this most hysterical performance. *Inexpensive to Moderate.* MC, V.

CASINOS. In the late 1930s the famed gambling ship *Rex,* anchored just outside the three-mile limit, catered to Los Angelenos looking for the occasional brief fling with Lady Luck. Each night tuxedoed men and gowned ladies took a motor launch out to the ship for an evening of gaming—blackjack, roulette, craps, or poker. Readers of Raymond Chandler's *Farewell, My Lovely* will recognize the scene.

Today the *Rex* is only a memory perpetuated largely through a restaurant in downtown Los Angeles that bears its name and Art Deco motif. Anyone who lusts for the thrill of "bones" dancing across green felt has to hop a jet to Las Vegas; it's just an hour away.

Poker players, though, don't have to make that trek. Just fifteen miles south of the Los Angeles civic center is the community of Gardena, home of six combination card rooms, restaurants, and cocktail lounges. These are not full gaming casinos, and there are no attached hotels. Although California law now prohibits gambling, Gardena had enacted an ordinance years ago allowing operators to run draw-poker, low-ball, and pan card games.

The six card rooms are fairly standardized, even though the decor varies and limits on maximum bets differ. A card room, for example, can have no more than thirty-five tables. Typically a poker table has eight seats and a designated limit on bets. The minimum bet is $1.00 before the draw and $2.00 after the draw and no limits on the number of raises. Some tables have a "house" dealer; the card room collects a fee, ranging from $1.00 up to $24.00 an hour in the $100–$200 games, from the players every half hour.

Gardena card rooms are open twenty-four hours a day, and you can play as long as your cash and stamina hold out. It is not uncommon to see women in their seventies playing twenty-four hours straight. Card rooms also have surprisingly good food in their restaurants at reasonable prices. Law requires that the bar be separate and outside the building. Usually these bars are unimaginative and rarely offer entertainment, but they are a welcome oasis for someone who thirsts for a gin and tonic after a grueling six hours at the table. You can't have a drink brought to your table.

Don't expect headline entertainers (there is no entertainment other than the excitement of winning a fat pot) and craps, "21," roulette, baccarat, and slot machines are banned. Yet even without the glitter and some of the more alluring games, Gardena is a great break for the $2.00 or $2,000 bettor. All area codes are 213.

The Horseshoe Club. 14305 S. Vermont, Gardena 90247; 327–1900. One of the most famous of the Gardena card rooms, it has $1.00–$2.00 games in poker, low ball, and a special "jackpot" card game. No pan. Co-owner Tom Parks has put in a large screen TV so players can watch sporting events between games. The Horseshoe Restaurant serves a hefty New York Steak for $13.25. The Kings Inn bar is nothing special.

The New Gardena Club. 15046 S. Western Ave., Gardena, 90247; 323–7301. General manager George Ursich claims to have the hottest card action and best restaurant in Gardena. The menu is an amazing combination of Oriental, Mexican, and Continental fare. The filet mignon in orange sauce is only $8.95. The Four Queens cocktail lounge serves $1.75 drinks, and the coffee shop runs breakfast specials from 3:00 A.M. to noon for $1.95. The New Gardena also offers Pan, a combination of gin rummy and poker, where a player wins depending on certain melds. Players can also buy chips and charge them to a Visa or Master Card credit card.

The Eldorado Club. 15411 S. Vermont Ave., Gardena, 90247; 323–2800. This is the high rollers club, and the only card room with a $100–$200 limit game going nonstop. That means that your first bet can be up to $100, and after the draw (cards from the dealer), the maximum bet is $200. With eight players and no limits on the number of times players can raise, pots can easily double or triple. "I've seen $40,000 winners and $40,000 losers," says general manager Peter Ackoury. The food at bargain prices is superb. A lavish luncheon buffet costs $6.00; at night more food is piled on, and the price is bumped up a buck to $7.00. One third of the tables have house dealers. Establish credit and you can cash checks easily, but no credit cards are accepted for chips. The Eldorado Room bar has one of Gardena's only one-man musical shows, nightly 9:00 P.M. to 2:00 A.M.

Normandie Club. 1045 W. Rosecrans, Gardena 90247; 515–1466. This is Gardena's newest club, a European-style card room that opened in October 1980. Most of the table games are $40.00–$80.00 stakes, but some are lower. New players are welcomed. Instruction is offered free by staffers. The Fleur de Lis Room has full Italian dinners at less than $10.00 and the chef is accomplished.

Rainbow Club. 11317 Vermont Ave., Gardena 90247; 323–8150. Opened in 1959, this colorful card room has lower limit games; the biggest bet is $40.00. Pan is played here. Many players favor this club for dinner because its prices are among the best in Gardena; a full prime rib or lobster dinner costs $7.50. There are also a coffee shop and a café; breakfast specials start at $1.19 apiece. The attached Midway Bar is only a run-of-the-mill cocktail lounge.

As this was being written, the *Monterey,* a sister card room next door to the Rainbow, was undergoing remodeling. The owners promise that it will be the most elegant club in Gardena when it opens. Well . . .

BARS. Despite its well-publicized penchant for hedonism, Los Angeles, unlike New York City, Chicago, and San Francisco, is not a saloon town. The practiced art of pubcrawling—barhopping with old friends or in quest of new ones—has never flourished in Los Angeles mainly because the city has no neighborhoods and plenty of freeways. Your favorite Mexican cantina may be in Marina del Rey, or the premier Irish pub may be in Pasadena, 25 miles away.

Even though the sheer sprawl has stunted the growth of a true saloon society, do not conclude that the Women's Christian Temperance Union (WCTU) rules Los Angeles. Far from it. There are hundreds of great cozy bars, lively pubs, and festive watering holes to quench your thirst for conversation and fine spirits.

They are simply not confined to a particular neighborhood. Nor are they dominated by regulars or cliques that often, though unintentionally, give first-time visitors the cold shoulder.

The Los Angeleno, in short, has no real loyalty to any libational hangout. He or she is adventuresome, willing to crisscross the city to try an authentic Piña Colada, or share some suds with a pal at a bar that just opened. The Angeleno is fickle and forever searching for the new spiritual experience, the newest, most "in" bar. Unlike New Yorkers, the Angeleno will not adopt a single saloon as his own home base from which to wander to other saloons to meet and greet his pals. Angelenos are too nomadic.

But that is changing. The price of gasoline and the trend toward close-in living are spawning a new breed of saloongoer. In a town that has lured legions of New Yorkers, Chicagoans, other Midwesterners, and Texans—not to mention Europeans, Asians, and now South Americans—there is a new sociology springing up in saloons. People are getting acquainted not just for the proverbial one-night stand but to form conversational communities of interest. At 5:00 P.M., the cocktail hour, Rive Gauche in Sherman Oaks is as lively as Henry Africa's in San Francisco or Charley O's in Manhattan, but the prices are about $1.00 a drink less, and the proprietors lay out a near-bacchanalian buffet.

The message here is that you as a visitor will still have to venture out on freeway forays to find the bar that you feel most comfortable in. We've compiled a compendium of cantinas, a slice of the saloon scene, but it is by no means complete. Space does not permit a larger listing.

Yet before you begin this expedition, keep these guidelines in mind:

South Bay bars and any place near the water have younger, hipper, more hedonistic crowds. Depending on the establishment, this is more or less the Endless Summer scene. Rugby shirts and cutoffs are commonplace. Oceans of beer flow, and the talk is largely about volleyball, beach parties, real estate syndications, and sports cars.

Westside thirst parlors are typically more trendy. Designer jeans and silk chemises. Again, the open-neck shirt is perfectly acceptable and casual-chic is the watchword. Generally most pub patrons here opt for white wine (French, preferably, if sold by the glass), and the conversation ranges from shrewd investments to the most "in" restaurant. Fighting to be taken seriously as gourmets, West Los Angelenos are now tracking the careers of young European chefs, just as culture buffs follow symphony conductors.

In West Hollywood and Hollywood environs, the attire is even more relaxed: young directors in jogging suits; out-of-work actors in racquetball attire—tense on the inside, laid back on the outside. Here bars buzz with the intoxicating talk of "deals," as in "three-picture deals," "development deals," "book deals," "album deals." Deals are the lifeblood of the entertainment industry. The libational nectars are often European in their roots—Kir (cream de cassis and white wine), Campari, Dubonnet on the rocks, premium Scotch on the rocks, or imported beers and wines. Never rush; that's uncool, and never neck crane if Rod Stewart slides in the front door. Also uncool. Everyone is expected to act as if, "Hey, doesn't he always come in here?" In fact, autograph hounding in Los Angeles bars and bistros is discouraged by owner-managers who are thrilled whenever celebs choose to frequent their places and don't want them to be bothered by some rube's brother-in-law from Dubuque.

Pasadena pubs, once fiercely conservative, have loosened and livened up. But the attire is still traditional—button-down shirts, rep ties, blue blazer—or decidedly preppy—women in corduroy and chino or tailored skirts and suits; men in Polo shirts or sweaters. The three-piece suit is a sartorial staple. Conversation spans the spectrum from business and wise investments to politics, football, and alumni gossip.

The downtown bars are generally a bastion for bankers, brokers, and other business folk, including a burgeoning brigade of import-export executives. Two- and three-piece suits are de rigeur, and the conversation is usually expansionary, as in company acquisitions and conquering global markets. Whiskies (Scotch and Canadian but little American bourbon) are popular, and the dry martini is worshipped. Vodka drinkers have largely switched to wine, and liqueurs are popular during the cocktail hour. Even though California brandy is delicious, the preference is for Cognac.

Naturally, these are generalities, but they are solid ones. As for specific advice, the best wisdom we can offer is to monitor your intake of spirits if you're driving. California has enacted some very tough laws to rid its streets and freeways of intoxicated motorists. Although the laws have yet to be tested in the courts as of this writing, a first-time offender who has more than a 0.1 percent blood-alcohol reading is supposed to get twenty-four hours in jail and a stiff fine. So beware.

Otherwise, welcome to Los Angeles and "Bottoms up!"

DOWNTOWN

Downtown Los Angeles, once a deserted ghost town after dusk, is enjoying a renaissance as a dining, drinking, and socializing center for Angelenos who thirst for the excitement of a city at night. Not exactly a chic complex of bistros and bars, downtown is nevertheless now honeycombed with libational retreats often unfamiliar even to locals. A little exploration will yield a treasure chest of cantinas and cocktail lounges that is sure to delight any visitor who heretofore harbored the notion that Beverly Hills and the Westside are the only places to imbibe.

For starters we recommend what may be Los Angeles's biggest surprise, the five-story Romanesque-style *Variety Arts Theater* at 940 N. Figueroa. Inside this cavernous structure is near nonstop entertainment: vaudevillians, singers, magicians, and comics—plus the fourth-floor W. C. Fields Bar, rescued from a San Pedro waterfront saloon. Enjoy Fields's favorite "martoonie" (a martini with a kumquat), and dance to the dreamy sounds of Art Deco and his orchestra. Kick back with a cool one in Tin Pan Alley, or just wander through fifty years of showbiz memories. Admission is $5.00 at night, free during the day.

A mile north, west of the Harbor Freeway, the venerable *Pacific Dining Car* at 1310 W. Sixth has a tiny bar that serves gourmet hors d'oeuvres nightly at no charge. Choose from beef tartar, paté, stuffed mushrooms, and husky drinks mixed only with premium liquors. A Los Angeles landmark. Beneath the ARCO Towers at 555 Flower, *O'Shaughnessey's* may not be the most authentic Irish pub, but it's one of the most popular. Sample a Bailey's Irish Cream and milk on the rocks to soothe your ulcer. Several streets east, the sleek *Grand Avenue Bar* in the Biltmore Hotel, opposite Pershing Square, serves—and rocks —until 2:00 A.M. Bring money. For serenity amid góthic splendor, the Biltmore's *Lobby Bar* is cheery and cozy. Its perfect Manhattans are renowned among downtowners. Sake or a bottle of brewed-in-Japan Kirin beer at the nearby Bonaventure Hotel's *Inagiku* restaurant bar has become a tradition. But for a sweeping view of the city, hop up to the Bonaventure's *Top of the Fives* after 11:00 P.M., and share a Cognac with a friend while the rotating bar takes you on a leisurely 360-degree trip. Sweet music, too. Not to be outdone, *Angel's Flight*, atop the Hyatt Regency Hotel, 711 S. Hope, is remote and romantic, and it also rotates while you dance cheek to cheek or simply soak up the city lights and expertly mixed cocktails.

Sports buffs shouldn't miss the bar at *Little Joe's,* 900 N. Broadway, across the street from Chinatown. Prices are cheap, the pour is stiff, and the big-screen TV is always tuned to the hottest game. Los Angeles Dodger manager Tommy Lasorda is a regular these days. Bulbous-nosed comic W. C. Fields frequented the bar in the 1930s. The unpretentious bar at *Nikola's,* 1449 W. Sunset Blvd., a ten-minute drive east of downtown, draws Dodger players, sportswriters, and die-hard fans alike. Prices are twenty years behind the times. The bartenders have photographic memories; once they learn your name, they never forget it. Put them to the test. A bit farther east, virtually unknown to tourists, *Taix,* 1911 W. Sunset, will uncork a bottle of good French wine without busting your budget. In the heart of downtown *Casey's Bar,* 613 S. Grand, is probably the area's most popular pub. If you can't strike up a conversation there, join a monastery. Frothy Irish coffees are the specialties. Despite the din, there are plenty of corners for quiet conversation.

Even though downtown Los Angeles is landlocked, you can venture off on a voyage of sorts. *Rex,* on the ground floor of the historic Oviatt Building, 617 S. Olive, radiates the Art-Deco ambience of a 1930s cruise liner. Essentially a fine restaurant, it is an elegant escape, if only for an hour-long cocktail break. Sip slowly and enjoy.

Itching to swap yarns with the world-weary, or looking for a political debate? The gaudy, gabby *Redwood Room* is the hangout for the Los Angeles press corps. Reporters from *The Los Angeles Times* and United Press International pack this place at 316 W. Second St. after 5:00 P.M. to postmortum the day's big stories or to drink their lunch if they're working nightside.

RESTAURANT ROW

Once partly lined with saloons where scantily clad, leg-gartered women swung from the ceiling, La Cienega Blvd. is now bereft of pubs per se. Today the bars are part of the boulevard's restaurants and are usually small alcoves off dining rooms, more European than Californian. The bar at *L'Ermitage*, generally considered one of the five best restaurants in Los Angeles, at 730 N. La Cienega, is intimate, personable, and staffed by a mixologist who takes his time when concocting a cool one. Across the street and down the block is Lou Paciocco's *La Cage Aux Folles*, 643 N. La Cienega, a saucy saloon and cabaret featuring female impersonators romping through an ever-changing revue. The bar is Paris circa 1920, the drinks are a bit steep, and the barkeeps talk your ear off. You can sip and not be pressured to stay for the show. *Ma Maison*, 8368 Melrose, around the corner, is mainly a restaurant, but drop in after 2:00 P.M. or at the cocktail hour, and slip into a Campari and soda or a Kir (white wine and creme de cassis). Host Patrick Terrail has set up a small bar for such intimate imbibing. Or have drinks at a table in the covered patio and while away the afternoon with a friend. Back on the boulevard, the *Tail of the Cock* bar, 477 S. La Cienega, is courtly, comfy, and thoroughly calming. Leather booths ring the room, a pianist takes requests during the cocktail hour, and the gratis munchies compare with canapes offered at an East Hampton garden party. Stout drinks and hearty conversation.

MID-WILSHIRE

Wilshire Blvd. is the umbilical cord linking downtown to Beverly Hills, Santa Monica, and the Pacific Ocean. It's lined with good (some great) bars. *HMS Bounty*, 3357 Wilshire, is an apres-work business person's watering hole; very clubby, very gabby. Premium brands are in the well; order a Scotch and soda or a bourbon and water and rest assured that you'll get a good drink. Across the street, the *Palm Bar* in the Ambassador Hotel, 3400 Wilshire Blvd., is a nostalgia-filled nook off the lobby. Walter Winchell hung out here. Dustin Hoffman rendezvoused with Mrs. Robinson here in the hit film *The Graduate*. Drink here in dignity, and soak up eighty years of elegance. Less pretentious, for it has been a businessman's bar for more than four decades, is the *Bull and Bush*, 3450 Sixth St. Nothing fancy; just a heritage of hefty drinks at fair prices and customers who chat up a storm with total strangers—a rarity today. For a frothy strawberry margarita or some other potent south-of-the-border potable, the *Red Onion* at 3580 Wilshire is a classic cantina, though a chain operation. Packed during happy hour, a throbbing disco later in the evening. *Taylor's Steak House*, 3361 W. 8th St., is known for its thick slabs of aged prime beef. Any sports buff who loves verbally to replay great moments of big games should belly up to Tex Taylor's; there's always one USC Trojan booster on a bar stool. Superb Bloody Marys there, too. Farther West, two of Los Angeles's best Irish pubs, both off Wilshire, can be found. *Tom Bergin's*, 840 S. Fairfax, is plastered with Day-Glo shamrocks perpetuating the names of thousands of the patrons who have passed through the door. The long rectangular bar is well stocked with friendly folks twenty-one to sixty-five. The Irish coffees here aren't imaginative, but they're strong. A few blocks north, *Molly Malone's*, 575 S. Fairfax, is your real Irish pub. Gaelic music on weekends, Harp beer all the time, and a hamburger that is a feast in itself. Small and cozy. Ask for Angela; she'll make you feel you're in Ireland. Rather be in Tahiti? Farther north up Fairfax, across from CBS Television City and the historic Farmers Market, *Kelbo's,* 101 N. Fairfax, is an old Polynesian pub and spare rib house that does wonders with rum. Ask Johnny Carson; when he broke into showbiz doing a five-minute show on Los Angeles's CBS station for sponsor Butter Nut Coffee, Johnny ducked into Kelbo's for an afternoon pick-me-up now and then.

BEVERLY HILLS

Ten years ago you would never have found a corner saloon in Beverly Hills. Too déclassé. But as the world citizenry flocked to this enclave of wealth, they brought with them the customs of the leisurely rich. Add to that the growing affluence of Los Angelenos who had made killings in real estate, television, screenwriting, or stocks. You'll find now that this small city is riddled with libational refuges from the rat race.

If you're looking for a new drink, check out *R. J.'s* at 252 N. Beverly Dr. Behind the oak bar and beyond the brass rail is literally a library of liquor—800 bottles stacked to the ceiling. Barkeeps shinny up a ladder to fill your request. R. J.'s is a hoot. Dip into the barrel of unshelled peanuts, listen to the piano player pound out his favorite ditty, elbow-bend at the bar with a brace of new buddies. Women can enjoy R. J.'s and not be hassled. For an old-style New York saloon, try *Archie's Place,* otherwise known as the Ginger Man, 369 N. Bedford Dr., co-owned by actor Carroll O'Connor. Tile floored, with green shades over small tables, this is the stand-up-and-rap haunt of young execs, lovely women, and O'Connor's pals such as Sammy Davis Jr. On a per square foot basis, the compact bar at the *Rangoon Racquet Club,* 9474 Santa Monica Blvd., may be Beverly Hills' busiest. The house special is a Pimm's Cup served by snappy regimental bartenders. Once you commandeer a stool, don't budge or it will disappear. Manny Zwief, co-owner and maitre 'd, doles out goodies during happy hour. A block away, the *Saloon* has reopened as an American pub with tudor tendencies and a 50-foot bar for lively people watching. *La Scala,* 9455 Santa Monica Blvd., has a quaint bar, but the treasure here is the wine cellar with its immense selection of California and European vintages. Pick one out downstairs; enjoy it upstairs. La Scala is honeycombed with celebrities nightly. At the *Café Swiss* bar, 450 N. Rodeo Dr., the crowd is older and mellower, more self-assured: agents and business managers, chic shopkeepers unwinding with pedigree spirits generously poured. The bar, a throwback to the style of 1940s where gracious bartenders catered to appreciative customers, is dark. A pricier version is the *El Padrino Room* of the Beverly Wilshire Hotel, 9500 Wilshire. Sink into comfortable chairs as attentive waitresses fill your requests. The ambience is one of casual elegance, but you pay for it. A couple of miles away, the *Polo Lounge* of the Beverly Hills Hotel, 9641 Sunset, no longer attracts the superstars and the gossip columnists (Howard Hughes drank here in his prerecluse days when he lived in one of the hotel bungalows). But the room, with its deep forest green decor and tiny bar, has lost none of its cachet. The drinks are made slowly and courteously, and only premium mixers are used. Farther west and past the gated entrance to one of Los Angeles's most exclusive neighborhoods, the bar at the *Bel Air Hotel* is the ultimate hideaway favored by industrialists and producers among others. The banquettes are comfortable. Deferential waiters serve skillfully mixed potables while a piano player works his keyboard magic; everything is soothing, never obtrusive. Back down in Beverly Hills, *Trader Vic's* bar, in the Beverly Hilton Hotel, 9876 Wilshire Blvd., is an opulent version of Don the Beachcombers. Demon rum is poured freely here. After all, Vic invented the Mai Tai, Scorpion, and—probably his most popular creation of all—Tiki Puka Puka, a potent blend of dark rum, orange, and lime. Most exotic drinks are around $4.00 a glass.

CENTURY CITY

Nestled within this sprawling complex of towering office buildings and luxury condominiums, once the back lot of 20th Century Fox, are several good bars and saloons. But do not expect aged wood and venerable barkeeps. Century City is too new to have a heritage. It does have *Harry's Bar & American Grill,* a reasonably authentic version of the famed Florence bar and grill that Hemingway and other rogues of the pen frequented. Sandwiched inside the tri-level ABC Entertainment Center, 2020 Ave. of the Stars, Harry's Bar is unrivaled, from our viewpoint at least, for its potent cappuccino. Across the mall, the *Avenue Saloon* is a central place to meet friends for cocktails before or after the show at the Shubert Theater: warm decor and exceptionally generous drinks, but the bartenders are generally chilly. Elegant and new, the *Bon Soir Lounge* of the Princess Restaurant is a mini-supper club with entertainment and complementary munchies like shrimp salad and quiche. Great hideaway.

WESTWOOD/WESTSIDE

Before the franchisers and mall builders arrived, Westwood Village was your basic quaint college town (something out of a sleepy Midwest hamlet), the front door to UCLA. Now it is still an university town, but it's also a popular hangout for kids of all ages. Order your first drink at *Yesterday's,* 1056 Westwood Blvd., and sit amid three quarters of a million dollars worth of antiques. There's a small bar downstairs, and upstairs is a veranda bar, where you can leisurely sip on a banana daiquiri and listen to a guitarist and other music makers. Two blocks north, inside a tree shaded courtyard, the bantam sized bar at *Stratton's,* 10886 Le Conte, is for stool sitters only. Essentially, this is a restaurant that looks like the inside of an 11th-century castle. The bartenders are unusually loquacious and the drinks imaginative and strong—but prices are semisteep. For free meatballs the size of baseballs, we recommend *Monty's* atop an office building at 1100 Glendon. Pull up a stool and look out over a lush residential neighborhood and beyond to Beverly Hills. Or plop in a comfy couch. A two-piece combo plays from midweek on. Across the street is the *Acapulco,* 1109 Glendon. The Acapulco was once an Irish pub, and the conviviality lives on. There is a good assortment of Mexican beers. A sumptuous spread of nachos, tacquitos, and quesadillas are laid out nightly, and there is an endless supply of free freshly popped popcorn. Dollar for dollar, though, the most inviting bar in Los Angeles could well be inside the *Westwood Marquis Hotel,* 930 Hilgard. A one-time UCLA dorm, this European-style hostelry has turned its bar into a giant living room with pillow-soft sofas, coffee tables, a harpist and a pianist nightly, and silk gowned waitresses serving canapes on sterling silver trays. Favored by chief executive officers, entertainers, and visiting royalty (it's away from the hoopola of Hollywood and Beverly Hills), it is known for its fine French wines served by the glass and its expertly crafted drinks. Another bar that has adopted the homey look is the *Hungry Tiger's* step down saloon, 936 Westwood Blvd. The look evokes the library and playroom of a turn-of-the-century home. Arrive at happy hour, and save half a dollar a drink; feast on hot hors d'oeurves and cheddar cheese. The best bargain in Westwood during happy hour is the elfin size bar (five stools, four small tables) in the *Old World,* 1019 Westwood Blvd. A glass of wine is 75 cents, mixed drinks are $1.25. They've held the prices at that level for 1½ years.

Moving west: The bar stashed inside the *Bel Air Sands Hotel,* 11461 Sunset, is for lovers and anyone who wants to avoid the madding crowds. Sit on the patio out by the pool as the sun sets or inside at night when the piano music starts. Munchies go with the music, and the drinks are hearty. A mile south, in the sylvan community of Brentwood, the *Jumping Frog Saloon,* 11777 San Vicente, well, jumps, mostly with a younger crowd. The reigning singles bar and disco, though, is a place called, of all things, *Hamburger Hamlet,* 11648 San Vicente. For some unfathomable reason, this has become the Westside's hottest meet um 'n mate um bar, so don't walk in looking for solitude. Another happy hunting ground is *Bergen's West,* 11600 San Vicente, the hip Westside cousin of Tom Bergen's Irish pub in mid-Wilshire. Bergen's West is ersatz Irish and jammed with ladies and gents looking for someone to love. A funky version of the traditional fern bar is the *San Francisco Saloon,* 11501 W. Pico Blvd. This is thrift store chic ambience, but the crowd is adventurous, and there are always rabid chess and backgammon players at their boards. The bar provides the boards. Only premium brand liquors (Beefeaters, Jack Daniels, J&B Scotch) are poured in the drinks. A real gritty Mexican cantina is several blocks east at 11751 Pico. Known as *The Talpa,* it has Coors on tap, chips and salsa on the bar, and a color TV on at all times. You know the food is first rate because most of the patrons are Hispanic. A favorite of budget-conscious journalists.

SANTA MONICA AND THE BEACHES

Santa Monica may be the most globally cosmopolitan city in Southern California. The British, for example, love its cool weather and its proximity to the ocean. Not surprisingly then, there are some authentic British pubs in this charming seaside community. Try the *King's Head* at 116 Santa Monica Blvd. for a pint of bitters and a fast game of darts. Appropriately seedy and reeking of brew, it nevertheless is stocked with Brits eager to hear or dispense news from the home front. From there it's a short crawl to *Ye Old Mucky Duck,* 1810 Ocean, where co-owners Frank Green (from Scotland) and Maureen Morrison (from Liverpool) serve up draught Watney's, Guinness, and Bass, plus genuine Scotch eggs and Cornish pastries. *Cheerio's* at 1828 Ocean is more a country inn than pure pub. One feels as if he (or she) is in Nottingham or Yorkshire. Lovely, attentive waitresses purvey powerful potables. Delightful.

Beach bums, barristers, sailors, and superstars (the likes of Warren Beatty, Julie Christie, Ali McGraw) pack themselves nightly into *Chez Jay,* a shack of a saloon (at 1657 Ocean) that has endured for thirty years. Actor/balloonist Jay Fiondello and his mother Alice have a following of loyalists that includes California Governor Jerry Brown. There are superb food and drink at fair prices. Along revitalized Main Street, the tiny bar in the *Galley Steak House* is recommended for nostalgics who want to see Santa Monica circa 1940. Once located at the end of the Santa Monica pier, the Galley, 2442 Main, is thick with nautical mementos and people who appreciate the siren song of the sea, not to mention zesty Bloody Marys. Farther south on Main St., *Willy Tiffany's Saloon,* 2907 Main St., packs in the young professionals and other assorted revelers. It's the closest thing around here to a real New York gin mill. Great hot dogs too. Far flashier is *Merlin McFly's,* 2702 Main, a stained-glass filled Victorian pub with a roving magician who does close-up magic that is as dazzling as the drinks. Pure escape. The secret here is the Chinese chicken salad; a mountain of it on a plate is less than $5.25. Try it with a McFlying Saucer—Amaretto, cream de cocoa, and cream, blended. For a saloon that looks as if it has been trashed rather than decorated, the *Oar House* shouldn't be missed. Located at 2941 Main, it has motorcycles and carriages hanging from the dust covered ceiling. The fact is that something old has been glued or nailed to every square inch of the place. Drinks are downright cheap. This sawdust-on-the-floor joint jumps nightly until 2:00 A.M., seven days a week.

Carlos and Clancy's may be the first (or only) combination Mexican cantina and Irish pub. Perched on the corner of Second and Arizona in Santa Monica, this place is for serious drinkers and fun-loving gringos. Special drinks command a separate menu. The Mexican cappuccino milk shake is a calorie filled treat made with ice cream. Tequila lovers (who aren't driving) might like the Six Shooter—six shots of different gold tequilas. Not that brave? We recommend the Tutti Fruitti margarita in the El Grosso (45 oz) glass. Or choose from twenty-seven coffee and cappuccino drinks.

MARINA DEL REY/VENICE

If you play the ponies, you'll love turtle racing, a parking lot grand prix that is a fixture at *Brennan's,* 4089 Lincoln Blvd. This Irish pub's big open bar makes conversation easy and the powerful drinks make it lively. Down the street a bit, *Casablanca,* 220 Lincoln, sounds as if it should be a Bogey bar. Instead, it is a Mexican bar and grill featuring a woman pounding and cooking tortillas right before your eyes. Order a fresh, hot one, slather it with butter, and wash it down with a cerveza. Cook it again, Maria. For swashbuckling saloongoers, we recommend the *Black Whale,* 3016 Washington Blvd. Plenty of mates ready to swing rum with you. Or sample a little tequila and tonic for a summertime cooler (it's always summer in Los Angeles) at the *Baja Cantina,* 311 Washington St. Beach women love this bar. Fair prices, too.

Inside the marina, the bar at *Fiasco,* 4451 Admiralty Way, draws yachting types and aspiring commodores. The platters of munchies are piled high at cocktail hour, and no one rushes you. A real kick back bar. Nearby the *Warehouse,* 4499 Admiralty Way, has streams stocked with fish, a bar stocked with tourists, and a buffet brunch renowned in these parts. Ex-cinematographer Burt Hixon collected tropical drink recipes on his South Seas forays and whips up one of the most sinfully rich Pina Coladas this side of Samoa. Popular, so get there early. There is also *Don the Beachcomber* in the Marina, 13530 Bali Way, but it's not as comfortable as its half-century old Hollywood counterpart. Even the Marina locals often overlook the intimate *Flagship Lounge* in the Marina International Hotel, 4200 Admiralty Way. Dark and cozy, it is a great place to play footsies with a friend. The piano bar alternates with a guitarist. Parking is free. For pubcrawlers who want to save their energy, the *Red Onion,* 4215 Admiralty Way, has a three-hour happy hour (4:00–7:00 P.M.) during the week and thirty-one flavors of margaritas. Underneath is *Pearl's Harbor,* a wild bar and disco operated by the Red Onion folks. Don't forget *TGI Friday's,* 13470 Maxella Ave., the consummate "meet market." Outside the Marina and before you get to Los Angeles International Airport, the *Admiral's Dingy* at the corner of Pershing and Manchester is well stocked with airline people (yes, some stewardesses, too) who come to party and dance. Circular bar; booths. No cover.

AIRPORT AND SOUTH BAY

The airport has half a dozen hotels vying for the business traveler and his or her expense account, but only one has an outstanding bar—the Hyatt LAX. It's called the *Park at the Top,* 6225 W. Century, and sits twelve stories in the air, providing a sweeping 330 degree view of the airport. This is one you cannot overlook. Each night a mini-Las Vegaslike buffet is served free. Jazz starts at 5:00 P.M. and goes nonstop till midnight. The drinks are robust. Try a Grand Cafe a La Park (Grand Marnier with cream de banana). South of the Airport, at Rosecrans and Sepulveda, Barnabey's Hotel is the home of *Rosie's Pub,* a turn of the century theme bar packed with 19th-century antiques, floor-to-ceiling bookcases, and a forest of ferns. Watney's is on tap. Rosie's Bombay Bomb, a Pina Colada made with Bombay gin, is the specialty.

In Manhattan Beach, the second-story bar at *Orville and Wilbur's* has a spectacular view of the Pacific, and behind the bar are aspiring actresses who don't know how to pour skimpy drinks. You can eat lunch at the bar. The clientele is an eclectic mix of surfers, business folks, and rugby shirted beach rats who live for sunny days and volleyball. A real sundown place.

HOLLYWOOD

The bar and saloon scene in the film capital of the world is no longer the raucous, gin soaked setting that Zelda and Scott Fitzgerald, Errol Flynn, Robert Benchley, and even Sinatra and Burton adored. The great Sunset Strip nightclubs—the Mocambo, Ciro's, Trocadero, Interlude—are gone. The barhopping ritual of the 1940s, crawling down Sunset in a top-down '47 Chrysler convertible in quest of the next Cuba Libre, has been replaced by cruisers who clog that boulevard and others the moment the sun sets. But for the patron of the libational arts who has fond memories of Hollywood past or who might like briefly to relive yesteryear, there are some oases that should be visited.

The bar at *Musso and Franks*, 6667 Hollywood Blvd., once hosted film studio moguls and two-dollar-a-day extras alike. Today the Rob Roys are just as smooth and the clientele just as eclectic. No-nonsense bartenders will give you an oral history of the boulevard; just ask. Overlooking Hollywood is *Yamashiro's*, a Japanese restaurant at 1999 N. Sycamore Ave. A lovely tradition is to meet there at sunset for cocktails on the terrace and gaze down on the city. Or take your drink and wander through the gardens.

Ask around among your friends beforehand to find out whether any are members of the *Magic Castle*. It's the private club for magicians and others right next door to Yamashiro. As a guest of a member, you'll still pay the $5.00 admission at the door, but once you utter the magic words "open sesame" to a blinking owl, a bookcase slides back to reveal a secret panel and a three-level celebration of the magical arts. Watch out for the first bar stool on the left; perch on it and you get this sinking feeling.

Holiday Inns are not exactly known for their imaginative cocktail lounges, but *Windows on Hollywood*, atop the city's Holiday Inn at 1755 N. Highland, is a pub with a panoramic view. Late afternoon is the best time to imbibe. Try their Tequila Sunrise at sunset. Hollywood *is* the city of celluloid and song, and to spot the heavyweights in the film and record business, motor over to *Martoni's*, 1523 Cahuenga, the venerable Italian restaurant launched decades ago by Frank Sinatra's former valet. The cozy bar is packed nightly with agents, studio musicians, and stars on the ascent, all feasting on free pizza, meatballs, and other delicacies dished out to guests around the 5:00 P.M. happy hour. Zesty conversation. Martoni's is several streets west of Vine and about three streets south of Hollywood Blvd., the famed crossroads that is a few steps away from the historic *Brown Derby*, 1628 Vine. Don't expect to see a hat with a front door. That Brown Derby was on Wilshire Blvd., across from the Ambassador Hotel, but was recently demolished. This Derby is the original Hollywood watering hole, where starlets and other pretenders to fame had themselves paged. The feeling in the bar is warm, and the drinks are potent and reasonably priced.

For stargazers who appreciate chatty bartenders and frugally priced drinks, *Nickodell*, 5507 Melrose, next door to Paramount Studios, is a must. Henry ("the Fonz") Winkler and the "Happy Days" cast often drop in after shooting sessions. The TV is always tuned to the hottest sporting event. Nickodell may have the most talented mixologists in town. A few doors down, *Vine Street Bar & Grill*, 1610 N. Vine, re-creates the glamour of Duke Ellington's swingtime '40s. Nostalgic sounds of the Ink Spots and Herb Jeffries float through the Art Deco–style bar. A bit south (and very near the Los Angeles border), the bar attached to the nifty *Fellini's* restaurant, 6810 Melrose Ave., is a cozy *cantina* packed with a young, hip crowd. Good spirits and suds list, including Taddy porter, hearty English brew for discriminating quaffers.

WEST HOLLYWOOD

Carlos and Charlie's, 8240 W. Sunset, is a slick Los Angeles version of the funky cantinas found throughout Mexico under a variety of names (Carlos O'Brian's in Puerto Vallarta, for instance). A beautiful-people hangout complete with tasty hors d'oeurves and steep prices. Big with the record industry crowd. *El Privado,* upstairs, is a throbbing disco. Farther west, at 8720 W. Sunset, is *LeDome's* circular bar offering $3.00 drinks and French "house" wine. It draws the likes of rocker Rod Stewart and actors Michael Caine and Richard (*American Gigolo*) Gere. The best time to visit is after 11:00 P.M., when it *really* starts to jump. Owners Eddie and Michel are usually there nightly. One big fault: the bartenders are aloof and the service ranges from prompt to indifferent. Far friendlier and not as congested is the bar at *Trumps,* 8764 Melrose. Sink into soft sofas, and sip a tall gin and tonic. Moderate to expensive drink prices, but the European ambience—clean, contemporary design—makes you feel like a jet setter. Across the street, *Morton's,* 8800 Melrose Ave., has a small bar (the place is mainly a restaurant) but a big-name clientele. Look hard and you might see the latest James Bond or Jacquie Bissett. Skip, the bartender, keeps up a lively rap with patrons. Another late-night haunt is *Dan Tana's;* again, mainly a restaurant but blessed with a busy bar. Ask Michael, the bartender, to whip up a Gibson Special (cappuccino laced with a generous shot of Napoleon Cognac), named after top record-industry press agent Bob Gibson.

New Yorkers will feel right at home in West Hollywood. The Los Angeles version of the Big Apple's venerable *Palm Restaurant,* 9001 Santa Monica Blvd., is big among Hollywood lawyers, agents, and luminaries such as Farrah Fawcett and Ryan O'Neal (there is always a crowd of tabloid papparazzi milling around out front). But the stellar attraction is Frosty, the bartender, who spins yarns and pours stiff drinks for those who perch on the five bar stools. From there, pubcrawlers can move over to *Joe Allen's,* the Los Angeles clone of the New York saloon of the same name, at 8706 W. Third. The crowd is a mix of showbiz, interior design, and advertising types. The bartenders are young and not too personable. Walk a block west and you're at *Kathy Gallagher's,* a casual-chic bar and bistro that catches the Joe Allen overflow. You'll find a congenial crowd of ex-New Yorkers reminiscing about the excitement of Manhattan, but then they'd never have their year-round tans or wear their open-neck shirts if they still lived and worked there. You can't miss Kathy; she's a former fashion model. A block away, at 8715 Beverly Blvd., *Dominick's* is a virtually unknown, secluded bar and grill frequented by Hollywood heavies, Jack Lemmon, Johnny Carson, and his producer Freddie De Cordova, among others. With wood paneling, traditional pictures, and a staff that's courteous, never obsequious, Dominick's bar is great for a before-dinner dry martini or late evening Cognac and cigars. One of the most comfortable and hospitable thirst parlors in West Hollywood remains the *Cock 'n Bull* at 9170 W. Sunset. A landmark on the strip, it opened in the late 1930s, gained fame as the home of the Moscow Mule (vodka and ginger beer in an iced copper mug), and was the chosen hideaway pub for stars and studio execs for decades. Even today the bar is filled with character actors whose faces are instantly recognizable, though their names may mean nothing to you. You can always find a partner here for a chess game. Cock and Bull may have the best buffet lunch in Los Angeles. Several blocks east, *Scandia* remains quiet, dignified, and tranquilizing. The house special is a Danish Mary—tomato juice and Aquavit, wickedly spiced. Walk in tired and come out a Viking. Celebrity watching is a polished art at *Spago*, 8795 W. Sunset. The tiny bar tucked away inside this ultrachic bistro is immensely popular; consider yourself fortunate if you can stake out a bar stool. The host/chef is Wolfgang Puck, a charming, chatty chap.

PASADENA

Pasadena is the closest thing in Los Angeles to a traditional Eastern or Midwestern city. Famed worldwide for the Rose Bowl game and the New Year's Day Rose Parade, it also boasts some of the friendliest bars and pubs in southern California. First stop for any first timer should be *Monahan's Pub*, 110 S. Lake Ave., where host Peter Monahan whips up a frothy Irish coffee and cheery conversation. Single women can comfortably perch on a bar stool in this warm, woodsy setting and not be hassled. Why? Many of the patrons are off-duty police who favor it because best-selling author and ex-cop Joe Wambaugh elbow-bends there regularly. A few blocks south is the *Chronicle*, 897 Granite Dr., essentially a restaurant and the site of a congenial horseshoe-shaped bar stocked with preppies in their mid thirties and their families. You feel as if you're drinking in an old turn-of-the-century mansion. Friendly bartenders and generous drinks.

Pasadena's best hideaway bar is the *Tap Room* of the Huntington Sheraton Hotel, tucked away in this graceful hostelry and a popular retreat for more than fifty years. Debs and dowagers alike, plus business folks, nibble on thick roast beef sandwiches and drink cold beers. One of the bartenders has been there twenty-seven years. Comfortable captains chairs and tables, rich woods, munchies in the afternoon. Pasadena politicos and business leaders flock after work to *Fanny's*, a turn-of-the-century Victorian bar, the lower level of the Pasadena Hilton, 150 S. Los Robles. Visit during the 4:30–7:00 P.M. "happy hour" for free hors d'oeuvres and relatively cheap drinks. Fernando presides over the bustling bar. If you feel like dancing, shoot upstairs to *Slick's*, the top floor speakeasy/disco. No little old ladies from Pasadena here; action central.

A mellow saloon steeped in history is *Josephina's*, 110 E. Holly, festooned with fresh ferns, fly fans, and antiques. You can dine and drink on a budget in this restored relic of Pasadena's past. Or try *Maldonado's* tiny European-style bar attached to one of Pasadena's finest restaurants at 1202 E. Green. Perch on a bar stool, order a glass of French wine, and enjoy live opera and Broadway show tunes. No Muzak here. For a fast game of darts and a pint of Watney's or Courage, check out the *John Bull* in Old Pasadena, a British pub that looks as if it is straight out of London. Proprietress Delyse Sharp is always on the premises giving the latest news of the mother country. At 103 S. Fair Oaks.

Apres-work unwinding spots include *Beckham Place,* 77 W. Walnut, a rather fancy "Olde English" pub known for its huge drinks, free roast beef sandwiches, and wingback chairs around a roaring fire. Packed with engineers and science buffs; the conversation is heady, the serving wenches friendly. *Vinchenzo's,* 901 E. Del Mar, is said to be the reigning Pasadena semisingles bar, especially on Friday night. Get there early for thick margaritas and gratis finger foods.

SAN FERNANDO VALLEY

The San Fernando Valley, once known for acres of tract houses supplanting fields of orange trees, is rapidly becoming a sophisticated suburban bedroom community, especially the southern (closer to Ventura Blvd.) slice of this 1.2-million-person mini-megalopolis. Commuters traverse the Ventura Freeway east to west and often stop off to dine and drink at a potpourri of French, Italian, Asian, and trendy American bistros. Some are old favorites; others are daring discoveries. In Calabassas, a one-time stagecoach stop complete with a hanging tree, the *Sagebrush Cantina* (23527 Calabassas Rd.), is an indoor-outdoor saloon, sort of the Valley version of the Via Veneto café scene. Motorcycle hippies mix comfortably with computer moguls and showbiz folk including a platoon of stunt people. Margaritas fetch a buck during happy hour; so do house drinks and beer. Great for table hopping. Country-pop entertainment nightly. For sophisticated saloonophiles and civilized conversationalists, the venerable *Tail o' the Cock* restaurant in Studio City (12950 Ventura) has a discreet, dark-paneled pub and piano bar. Vested bartenders pour healthy drinks and spin fascinating yarns of the Valley from a simpler era. Favored by film and TV producers and actors. *Houlihans,* 17150 Ventura Blvd., Encino, is one of the better antique-crammed, fern-filled "meet market" bar-restaurants proffering less-than-a-dollar beer, wine, and single mixed drinks in the late afternoon and early evening. Stick around at night and boogie in the disco. Plenty of people and fun.

OUTSIDE
LOS ANGELES

NORTH ALONG THE COAST

Malibu to Hearst Castle

by
JANE LASKY and MARY JANE HORTON

Jane Lasky is a contributor to the Los Angeles Times Syndicate, a columnist for the in-flight magazines for Republic and Continental airlines, and a regular contributor to Travel Agent, Bon Appetit, Palm Springs Life, *and many other consumer magazines. Mary Jane Horton writes about fitness, fashion, and travel for various national publications; she lives in Santa Monica.*

Twenty-seven miles of picturesque beaches and mountain peaks ranging over 2,000 feet are the essence of the colony of Malibu, just up the coast from Los Angeles, a spectacular sight from sunrise to sunset.

327

The canyons and summits of the Santa Monica Mountains provide not only an amazing background for the sea but also countless opportunities for adventure and exploration.

Hikers, horseback riders, and bicyclists will be pleased at the number of trails available throughout the area, Malibu Creek Park, Topanga State Park, and Point Mugu State Park among them. Camping and picnic sites abound within the area as well. For the less ambitious, a drive along any of the major canyon roads provides unforgettable views of Santa Monica Bay and the mountains on one side and the San Fernando Valley on the other.

But Malibu pays a price for its beauty: This exquisite topography is susceptible to natural disasters. Along the coastline, landslides are common occurrences. The problem becomes especially severe during heavy rainstorms, often making it necessary to close off traffic on the Pacific Coast Hwy. (Route 1), the main thoroughfare along the coast. Mountain and canyon areas are prone to fires during the summer months; plants and shrubbery become so dry that even the slightest spark can cause a major brush fire.

Despite Malibu's numerous hazards, the community is one that many hope some day to call home. Homes range from no less than two hundred fifty thousand dollars to more than six million dollars; a three-million-dollar abode is considered a bargain. Thus such household names as Burt Reynolds, Johnny Carson, Neil Diamond, and Dudley Moore have come to live in this central coastline community.

The Malibu Beaches

Most of the beaches in Malibu are privately owned by those who live there, but coastal accessways every few miles allow visitors to stroll along the beaches, perhaps even relax and take a swim, and get a close-up of the houses and their occupants. However, there are no lifeguards or restrooms around, so water sports are not recommended.

Malibu's reputation as a surfer's paradise, stemming from the old Beach Boys songs and Frankie Avalon movies, is just a small but noticeable part of what Malibu really is. Several public beaches stretch along the Malibu coast, providing the type of sun and fun that everyone across the country once dreamed about. The four most popular of these beaches are Topanga Canyon Beach, Malibu Surfrider Beach, Zuma Beach, and Leo Carillo State Beach. All offer swimming and limited areas for surfing, both body and board. Surfrider attracts board-riders from the world in September, when the annual International Surfing Contest takes place. During this time waves reach from three to five feet. Zuma Beach is the largest of the four, running over three miles long. Leo Carillo Beach has some rocky caves to explore, as well as camping facilities right on the beach. Lifeguards and restrooms are also provided. Easy parking make Zuma and Leo Carillo more convenient than the others, where unloading your vehicle can be a big problem.

Fishing, boating, and scuba diving are also everywhere to be found in Malibu. Boats can be rented at Paradise Cove or at the Malibu pier. Sport fishing boats leave the pier twice daily, or you can fish off the pier itself. From March through August, when these small fish come up on the beach to spawn, searching for grunion is a favorite sport in Malibu.

To add to all its natural attractions, Malibu also offers a variety of cultural experiences. The J. Paul Getty Museum, located on the Pacific Coast Hwy., one mile north of Sunset Boulevard, houses fine collections of Greek and Roman antiquities as well as Renaissance and Baroque paintings. The museum also features decorative arts made for Frenchmen from Louis XIV to Napolean. The building itself is modeled on an ancient Roman country house called the Villa dei Papiri, located outside the city of Herculaneum. The villa, destroyed during the eruption of Vesuvius in A.D. 79, was discovered in the 18th century. Getty decided to model his building on this classic. The museum itself contains one of the most important private art collections in the United States.

Another of Malibu's cultural havens is Pepperdine University where, along with other intellectual opportunities, various programs in art and music are offered. High-caliber concerts and shows are frequently presented there.

For jazz lovers Pasquales, a jazz club located on the Pacific Coast Hwy, features up-and-coming as well as established jazz artists.

Restaurants along the Malibu coast offer wonderful food in a perfect setting. Ranging in price from moderate to expensive, most of the colony's restaurants are situated right on the beach. Malibu is a favorite dinner spot for residents and visitors alike.

Oxnard and Ventura

Farther north, Oxnard is a small city on the Pacific with interesting motels and recreational facilities. A new attraction, Fisherman's Wharf, is reminiscent of New England, with shops, restaurants, and a seafood market located at Channel Islands Harbor.

Seaside Ventura is known as Poinsettia City. If you are there in winter, you will see the crimson blooms everywhere in long hedges and giant clumps sprouting as high as the bungalow eaves. Millions of beautiful Monarch butterflies come to the city and surrounding countryside in October to stay the winter.

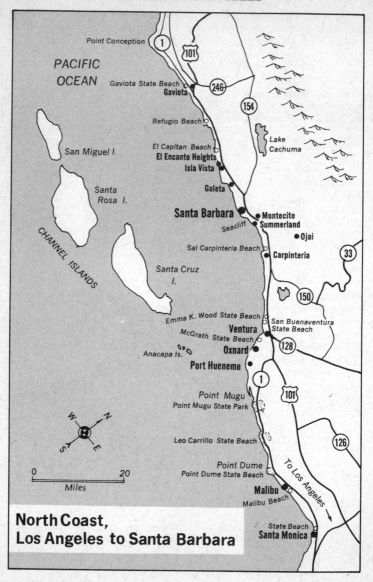

PACIFIC OCEAN

Point Conception

Gaviota State Beach
Gaviota

Refugio Beach

El Capitan Beach
El Encanto Heights
Isla Vista

Goleta

San Miguel I.

Santa Rosa I.

CHANNEL ISLANDS

Santa Cruz I.

Santa Barbara ● **Montecito**
Seacliff   **Summerland**
● **Ojai**

Sal Carpinteria Beach ○ **Carpinteria**

Lake Cachuma

Emma K. Wood State Beach ○
Ventura   San Buenaventura State Beach

McGrath State Beach
Anacapa Is.   **Oxnard**
Port Hueneme

Point Mugu
Point Mugu State Park

Leo Carrillo State Beach

Point Dume
Point Dume State Beach

To Los Angeles

Malibu
Malibu Beach

State Beach
Santa Monica

W—N—S—E

0   20
Miles

North Coast, Los Angeles to Santa Barbara

Oxnard's Mission San Buenaventura was founded in 1782. Its museum is excellent; the city is developing the entire site into an archeological park. Lake Casitas, eight miles north, has fishing and boats for rent.

Lemon groves cover the valley a few miles inland. Lemon trees like even milder weather than oranges do. They are known as the "hardest working" trees because they bear sweet-smelling blossoms and ripen fruit simultaneously, year round. Lemons are picked every six weeks; in a year a single, well-bearing tree may produce 3,000 lemons. The "square" trees you see, giving you the impression that you could walk across the flat top of a grove, are trimmed to increase the yield. The world's largest lemon grove (1,800 acres) is near Paul, which is known as the Lemon Capital.

The Channel Islands

Around Ventura, north of Oxnard, look out toward the Pacific and feast your eyes on the Channel Islands of Anacapa, Santa Barbara, Santa Cruz, Santa Rose, and San Miguel—part of California's extensive national park system. In all, the Channel Islands National Park consists of about 18,000 acres, although the two largest islands, Santa Cruz and Santa Rosa, within the park boundary, remain private property.

Ocean mist softens the contours of the Channel Islands, making it hard to identify those gentle, luminous shapes on the horizon or to judge their true distance from shore. Lying from 11 to 40 miles off the coast, these islands loom tantalizingly close one moment and then ebb into the fog the next. They have been labeled America's Galapagos, where many plants and several animal species have evolved into unique states.

Reachable only by boat, the islands offer perhaps the ultimate close-to-home getaway for Southern California and a revelation for others. You'll find no high-rise hotel or posh resorts on the islands; in fact, you'll find no modern comforts at all. All discoveries will be in the form of wave-walled coves, congregations of sea lions, trails to dramatic vantage points, fossils, and some of North America's oldest traces of man.

All-day boat trips are scheduled from the Center Harbor in Ventura aboard Island Packer Cruises (P.O. Box 993, Ventura, CA 93001; 805-642-1393).

Ojai

Up the coast highway is Ojai (pronounced Oh-hi), a small town surrounded by mountains, shaded by oak trees, with many streams flowing through it. The name Ojai, which means "the nest," was given to the valley by its first inhabitants, the Chumash Indians, because of its location deep in the midst of peaked mountains.

Ojai's natural beauty is enhanced by its architecture, mostly early 1900s Spanish style. The artists, of course, have even further contributed to the town's elegance by displaying their wares throughout the area.

Many artists open their homes and galleries to visitors. The pottery studios of world-famous Beatrice Wood, 8560 Hwy. 150, and Vivika and Otto Heino, 971 McAndrew Rd., are two of the most popular galleries in town. The Gallery of Historical Figures, on McNell at Reeves Rd., features sculptures of personalities who have shaped all phases of history. Ojai's artists and craftspeople display and sell their creations *en masse* every Sunday in the parking lot of the Security Pacific Bank.

Boutiques, shops, and galleries abound throughout Ojai. The Arcade, Ojai's downtown shopping center, is a historical site as well, for its architecture is patterned after that of the old California missions. And Meiners Oaks, a country village on the outskirts of Ojai off Hwy. 33, is a unique shopping area. Once a huge ranch, the stores of this village are interspersed between trees and citrus groves. The setting lends itself to a relaxing and unusual shopping spree.

For antique hunters, Ojai has more than ten shops well worth your while. Winkworth Antiques, 310 E. Matilija, not only offers exquisitely displayed furniture from all over the world, but has a library right in the store where art objects and old pieces can be researched.

The relaxed, trusting attitude in Ojai is epitomized in Bart's Bookstore, 302 W. Matilija, where you're left on your honor when the store closes. If you see a book you'd like, throw the coins into the grillwork on the patio and it's yours.

Ojai's serenity attracts various holistic groups, students of spirituality, and meditators from all around. World University, Meditation Mount, and the Krotona School of Theosophy, offering programs in religion, philosophy, meditation, yoga, and astrology, among others, are all located here. The Krotona Library is one of the largest spiritual libraries in the country. Check the local newspaper and visitor guides for special programs.

Relaxation is an integral part of the life-style in Ojai—and you'll relax completely at Matilija Hot Springs, where, since the days of the Chumash Indians, people have been enjoying the natural mineral waters. Today the twenty-six natural mineral waters are pumped into a bathhouse for all to benefit.

Despite all its calm, Ojai is also a place that can be enjoyed by the very active. Its golf courses are noted for their charming settings. Ojai's two eighteen-hole courses abound in oak trees, presenting a great challenge to golfers.

Public and countless private tennis courts are also located all over town. The Ojai Valley Tennis Tournament, the oldest in the country, takes place each April in Libbey Park in the center of town.

For serious hikers, hundreds of miles of trails are featured throughout Los Padres National Forest. For not-so-serious hikers who want to enjoy mild exercise and beautiful views, Ojai's mountains, valleys, canyons, and parks offer countless trails (Sisar Canyon, Sulphur Mountain Road, and the Sespe are just a few). Horseback riding trails are also featured throughout the valley.

Bicycle rides are lovely along any of the town's winding roads and parks, often leading to streams, citrus groves, and stands of giant oak trees. Scenic drives from 5 to 50 miles in and around Ojai Valley offer spectacular views from your car. Perhaps you might stop for a picnic along the way. If you go East on Ojai Ave. and then up the hill, you will see the valley of "Shangri-La" as Ronald Coleman saw it in the movie *Lost Horizon.*

Boating is popular at Lake Casitas, off Hwy. 150. The lake is enclosed by almost 100 miles of shoreline and is recognized as a prime location by boat enthusiasts. In fact, the lake was chosen as the site of the 1984 Rowing Olympics. Lake Casitas is a prime fishing area, abounding in trout, bass, and sunfish. Fishing is also available throughout Ojai Valley's miles of stocked streams.

If you're interested in physical fitness, stay at The Oaks at Ojai, 122 East Ojai Ave., Ojai, CA 93033; (803) 646–5573), which features a full fitness program that will whip you right into shape.

Ojai is the center of many annual events. The Ojai Folk Dance Festival and the yearly Arts and Crafts Festival attract people from all around the state. The end of May brings the Annual Ojai Music Festival in Libbey Park's outdoor Festival Bowl. For three days the festival presents tunes ranging from classical to jazz and rock, both old and new.

Montecito, Santa Barbara, and San Marcos Pass

At the southern approach to Santa Barbara, wealthy Montecito covers the lower mountain slopes and canyons with wooded estates. A palm-fringed beach and yacht harbor are to the left and fruit groves to the right. To many the stretch of freeway entering the city rates as one of the most beautifully landscaped in California.

The lagoon and many park areas afford ideal picnic areas where once the social center of Old Spanish California thrived. Today's residents, many of them wealthy retired Easterners, strive to retain the old atmosphere.

Discovered in 1542 by a Portuguese navigator, Santa Barbara derives its name from a second landing in 1602 on the feast day of St. Barbara. The city's heritage combines the early Indian and later Spanish, Mexican, and American cultures. Today much of its past glory is reflected in a distinct artistic ambiance among relics of earlier civilizations.

Many Indian-built Spanish adobes in the city were made of massive bricks from local adobe clay. Rounded red clay rood tiles were molded on the thighs of Indian women. Numerous adobes are in active community use today. Although Victorian buildings are abundant, perhaps the predominant architecture of the twenties and thirties is still Spanish Colonial. Many streets bear Spanish names, such as Indio Muerte (dead Indian) and Camino Cielo (Street of the Sky).

A good way to tour Santa Barbara is to follow the local Chamber of Commerce's convenient visitor signposts; one set is designed for those on foot, and the other for visitors in cars. The "red tile" walking tour takes in the tropical gardens and the stately Spanish–Moorish County Courthouse, perhaps one of the most beautiful public buildings in North America; the Santa Barbara Museum of Art is noted for its Greek, Roman, and Egyptian sculptures set in the central gallery and highlighted by natural light from skylights, as well as for its rich glassware collection; the Carriage Museum; and many old residences built around peaceful, landscaped parks. The picturesque El Paseo Arcade, also a stop on the tour, offers the opportunity for antique hunters to shop for bargains.

A more extensive motor tour, the Scenic Drive, headlines fifteen main points of interest, including Mission Santa Barbara, the only Californian mission with twin towers, regarded by many as being the most beautiful mission of them all. Since the mission's founding in 1786, the altar light has never been extinguished. Brothers garbed in brown lead guided tours upon request, or visitors may opt for a self-guided tour available for fifty cents.

Also en route are natural landmarks, such as the nation's largest fig tree at Chapala and Montecito Sts. Visits to the sixty-acre Botanic Gardens (particularly in spring), the Andree Clark Bird Refuge, and the Child's Estate Zoo are all worthwhile. At one point the tour follows the wharf and beach areas before winding back through luxurious residential areas into the wild foothills that harbor several ranches and private clubs. Both circuitous tours can be picked up at any point along

Santa Barbara

the route and can be accomplished in a day. The Santa Barbara Chamber of Commerce can also arrange air, land, or sea tours; cars, mopeds, bikes, and roller skates can be rented, as can horses for the more adventurous.

According to the Ornithological Society, there have been more bird sightings in Santa Barbara than in any other U.S. city. The endangered California condor haunts the San Rafael Wilderness's Sisquoc Sanctuary (closed to the public) of Los Padres National Forest.

Many hiking trails run through the hills. Camping equipment can be rented for use at two privately owned trailer parks within the city limits. (It is illegal to camp or park trailers at city parks or beaches.) Along the beach are state park campgrounds within easy driving distance of the city—10 to 20 miles, north or south. Moderately priced accommodations can be found near the highway every weekend.

The city is most renowned for its art. Every Sunday an arts and crafts show held along Cabrillo Blvd. exhibits local handicrafts that are also available in many local stores. Annual concert seasons feature the Los Angeles Philharmonic and Santa Barbara Symphony Orchestra; drama, music, and dance are presented at the Arlington Theater. A packed annual program caters to all tastes, the highlight being the Wednesday-to-Sunday "Old Spanish Days" fiesta from the first week of July to August 3. February is the start of seasonal flower, cat, dog, and horse shows. In July "Semana Nautica" opens a week of mainly water sports, followed by a Summer Music Festival Series held at the Lobera Theater and the spectacular September Concours d'Elegance antique-car parade. October is the third annual week-long arts festival with a host of fine arts. A number of events are free, and main theaters and art galleries feature special showings.

In addition to its many cinemas and discotheques, Santa Barbara boasts, by its own reckoning, more restaurants per capita than any other U.S. city. The fishing port has many excellent seafood restaurants. Elsewhere cuisines range from hamburger, omelettes, and health-food specialties to Mexican, Japanese, Cantonese, Italian, Swiss, French, Belgian, German, and Greek styles. Wineries offer samplings of local wines.

A few miles up the coast, the architecturally interesting University of California campus overlooks the sea at Goleta. Numerous art exhibits and dramas are staged by the students in the campus theater. A tour of Dos Pueblos Orchid Ranch in Goleta is free.

San Marco Pass is an easy jump inland, with panoramic marine views over the coast and Channel Island Chain, opening to the Santa Ynez Valley, where palamino parade horses were first bred systematically at Rancho San Fernando Rey.

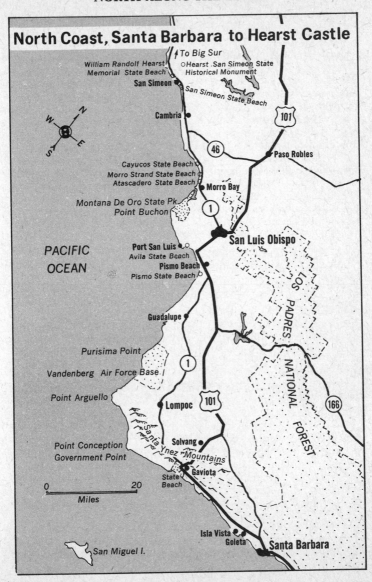

North Coast, Santa Barbara to Hearst Castle

To Big Sur

William Randolf Hearst
Memorial State Beach

Hearst San Simeon State
Historical Monument

San Simeon

San Simeon State Beach

101

Cambria

46

Paso Robles

Cayucos State Beach
Morro Strand State Beach
Atascadero State Beach

Morro Bay

Montana De Oro State Pk.
Point Buchon

1

San Luis Obispo

PACIFIC
OCEAN

Port San Luis
Avila State Beach
Pismo Beach
Pismo State Beach

LOS PADRES

Guadalupe

Purisima Point

Vandenberg Air Force Base

1

Point Arguello

101

Lompoc

NATIONAL

166

Point Conception
Government Point

Solvang

Santa Ynez Mountains

FOREST

Gaviota

State
Beach

0   20
Miles

Isla Vista
Goleta

Santa Barbara

San Miguel I.

Solvang

Solvang, a small town in the Santa Ynez Valley, is known as Little Denmark, U.S.A., and it's not hard to see why. In its architecture, windmills, and its gas street lamps (some actually imported from Copenhagen), Solvang looks exactly like a Danish town. Many Solvang residents still speak Danish, making the place *sound* like a Danish town. And the alluring aroma of its food and pastries gives it the scent of its Scandinavian sister.

Solvang was founded around 1910 by a group of Danes from the Midwest. The group, searching for a site on which to build a special Danish folk school, came upon the area and named it Solvang, which means "sunny field." Since then Danes from across the country as well as from Denmark have been flocking to the area.

Today Solvang is a great tourist attraction that preserves its heritage to a very large degree. Windmills can be seen all over town. The Wulff Windmill, the oldest of all, is located on Fredensborg Canyon Road, northwest of Solvang. Not so accessible to tourists, this windmill is a historical landmark and was actually used at one time to pump water and grind grain.

The food and pastries in Solvang are prepared from old Danish recipes and are a real treat. For those who only occasionally go off a diet, plan to do it in Solvang.

Solvang's shops along Copenhagen Dr. carry imported items from Denmark (where else?) as well as other parts of the world, making it an excellent town for gift purchasing. Pewter, cloth items, tiles, and household accessories, including cuckoo clocks, abound in the town's countless shops.

During the summer months an outdoor Theaterfest presented for evening entertainment features five plays. Critics nationwide have applauded performances since 1974.

Real Danish tradition is demonstrated in Solvang with the celebration of Denmark's Independence Day each September. Residents dress in traditional costume for the three-day festival, which includes authentic food, music, and dance, resulting in lots of fun, Danish style.

The Fastelavn is another Danish tradition commemorated each February in honor of the coming of Lent (before Ash Wednesday). For one day the entire town bursts into a celebration much the same as a Mardi Gras.

Long before the Danish got hold of the town, Solvang was the site of the Santa Ines Mission. Founded by the Spaniards in 1804, the mission was one of the twenty-one settled throughout California. Today this is one of the best preserved of all the missions; the church, chapel, and gardens are open to visitors. A mission museum presents historical and other interesting facts about the site. While you're in the neighborhood, don't miss the Bethania Lutheran church with its Danish provincial architecture and its nearby chiming wind harp.

Natural beauty abounds not only in Solvang but throughout the Santa Ynez Valley. Nojoqui Falls Park, only six miles south of Solvang, features a flowing waterfall within its eighty-four acres of greenery and is the site of much Indian legend and lore.

Only fourteen miles southeast of Solvang is Lake Cachuma, the largest man-made, fresh-water lake in southern California. The lake offers boating and fishing and is the site for sailboat races during the summer months. Horseback riding is also available.

The Santa Ynez Valley is proud of its vineyards and wineries. Many offer tours and wine tasting. Ballard Canyon Winery in Solvang is just one that's open to visitors. An appointment is necessary, so call first; (805) 688-2069.

San Luis Obispo, Pismo Beach, and Morro Bay

For a bit of California history preserved in a modern-day setting, stop at the city of San Luis Obispo, slightly inland along the central California coast. Located almost halfway between Los Angeles and San Francisco, San Luis Obispo is the home of the fifth of the twenty-one Spanish Franciscan missions.

Mission San Luis Obispo de Tolosa, founded in 1772, still stands today. The original adobe building houses Indian relics and is located on the lush grounds of the Mission Plaza, the site of many concerts, festivals, and weekly events. With the San Luis Creek running along one side of the plaza, the area provides a relaxing setting.

Beginning at the mission, a two-mile tour (marked on the streets by a green line) takes you on a trip through history. It features preserved adobes, Victorian-style homes of the 1800s, and even an old train depot, built by the Southern Pacific Railroad Company in 1889.

The downtown area of San Luis Obispo also exemplifies the old preserved in the new. Businesses, minimalls, shops, and boutiques featuring the latest fashions are housed in architectural designs representing the city's past.

A tour of San Luis Obispo is incomplete without a stop at the world famous Madonna Inn, 100 Madonna Rd. The Madonna Inn, referred to as an architectural fantasyland by *The New York Times,* has 104 rooms, each addressing an individual—if rather garish—theme. With one room designed as a cave, another as a mining area, and still another with a Cinderella scene in mind, the inn is a novelty that will both amaze and amuse you. Some of the rooms are carved out of rocks, and the men's urinal is an actual waterfall. If you can't stay there, at least grab a bite to eat at the coffee shop, or have dinner in the one-of-a-kind dining room.

San Luis Obispo abounds in natural beauty and agriculture. Vineyards, first introduced in the area by Spanish missionaries, continue to flourish today, producing some of California's best wines. Stop in at the Chamisal Vineyard on Rte. 3, Orcutt Road, or at the Lawrence Winery, one mile off Edna Rd. on Corbett Canyon Rd. These are just two of the vineyards offering tours and tasting rooms to delight the traveler.

For the physically active, San Luis Obispo offers hiking trails in the Santa Lucia Mountains, as well as in Montaña de Oro State Park west of the city. Hard-core hikers can climb one of the city's seven volcanic peaks.

Laguna Lake Park features a lake that is well stocked with trout. Fishing in this area can be both relaxing and fruitful. The park also has a nine-hole golf course open to the public. And for those who enjoy touring by bike, San Luis Obispo is filled with a network of bicycle paths for exploring.

Two picturesque college campuses put forward many cultural as well as educational programs. California Polytechnic State University and Cuesta College are both open for public enjoyment. Visitors' passes are available at the Administration Building.

The city of San Luis Obispo is a great home base for exploring the rest of the county. Pack your bags and visit Pismo Beach to the south. Famous for its dunes but even more so for its clams, this area was originally harvested for chicken and hog feed. Today no clam less than five inches in diameter may be taken.

Also on the southerly route is Diablo Canyon Nuclear Plant in Avila Beach. Tour the place at either 10:00 A.M. or 2:00 P.M., courtesy of the Pacific Gas and Electric Company. Also in Avila Beach are plenty of beach sports, golf, and natural spring baths. Port Luis is a renowned sport fishing center where boats can be rented.

Morro Bay, to the north of San Luis Obispo along Hwy. 1, boasts 576-foot-high "Morro Rock," the second largest monolith in the world. Hundreds of artists display their work in the shops and galleries along the Embarcadero in the town of Morro Bay. At the Museum of Natural History are interesting displays, lectures, and movies, concentrating on the local area.

Cambria and Hearst Castle

Farther north along the coast is Cambria, where "the pines meet the sea." Located six miles south of Hearst Castle, it represents the peaceful coexistence of the old and the new.

Old Cambria continues its gentle expansion as a haven for artists as well as for being a resort colony. Within the confines of the community, San Simeon State Beach offers a pleasant refuge of campsites and picnic areas. William R. Hearst Memorial State Beach Park is lovely for daytime use only, as is nearby Shamel Park.

This area is terrific for ocean viewing; numerous vista sites are arranged in formal pull-offs overlooking the beach and ocean on Hwy. 1, an overwhelmingly picturesque route that skirts blue-green coves and rocky headlands.

Just up the coast from Cambria is the fabulous Hearst Castle.

The former owners called Hearst Castle simple "the ranch." Guests and people who lived in the San Luis Obispo area called it La Casa Grande. The state of California's Department of Parks and Recreation staff who now administer this lavish historic monument call it Hearst-San Simeon State Historical Monument, or Hearst Castle. Whatever anybody calls it—this place on Enchanted Hill is fantastic.

Designed by architect Julia Morgan, whose works are carefully treasured in Berkeley and San Francisco, the home of the late newspaper magnate was once a working ranch that covered a ridgetop encompassing more than 253,000 acres. Its site is high in the Santa Lucia Mountains, 45 miles northwest of San Luis Obispo.

Grazing on these vast lands, during Hearst's lifetime, were hundreds of horses—including prize Arabians—cattle and farm animals as well as a "zoo" of free-roaming wild animals. The wild animals were shipped to the ranch from all over the world, from all parts of the United States, as well as from wilderness areas nearby. Steam schooners from Monterey, for example, once hauled to the Hearst San Simeon estate a load of wild elk that had been rounded up on the 17-Mile Drive in Pebble Beach.

The impressive main buildings on Enchanted Hill have been deeded to the state, but many of the houses, barns, the airport, and other land surrounding the castle remain private holdings. Zebras—seldom seen now—are the only creatures remaining from Hearst's former wild animal "park" that was once the largest private zoo in the world.

Built in 1919, the twin-towered Spanish-style castle includes an eclectic and seemingly endless collection of rare *objets d'art,* sculpture, tapestries, rugs and carpets, antique furniture, and remarkable treasures representing all periods of civilization. Museum curators from around the globe—as well as visitors from everywhere—are dazzled by the original paintings, one-of-a-kind ceilings, beautiful fireplaces, classic pools.

Work was still ongoing at the Castle when Mr. Hearst died in 1941. He dedicated much of his life to gathering these treasures and to building the Castle that now houses them. Experts say he spent more than one million dollars each year—over a period of fifty years—on the fabulous art collection now open for public viewing at San Simeon. There is no way to estimate the value of this incomparable collection today. The castle was donated to the state in 1958 as a memorial to William Randolph Hearst and also honors his mother, Phoebe Apperson Hearst.

There are four Castle tours offered by the state parks. It is important to make reservations for the tours of your choice through the Ticketron outlets throughout the state. (Some people do take the big chance of buying their tickets at the castle, but it is a real risk that you won't get on a convenient tour.) Tickets for each tour cost $8.00 for adults and $4.00 for children aged six through twelve. Each tour lasts about two hours, and it is not advisable to take more than two tours in one day because this treasure house that mixes examples of art from all over the world is almost overwhelming. Tour One, the best for first-time visitors, includes the Castle's lower floors and one guest house. Tour Two gives visitors a chance to see the bedrooms, Hearst's offices, as well as the guest cottage, Casa Del Monte, and buildings on the grounds. The third tour focuses on the new wing, built in the years from 1945 to 1947. Tour Four, the newest, was created for those who want to see, and hear more about, the lovely gardens that surround the Castle. Also included: a peak at the vaults where luxurious furs were kept and the wine cellars and engine room.

Wear comfortable shoes; there are many stairs on all tours. Cameras are allowed, but gadget bags, tripods and flash equipment are not permitted. Pets cannot enter the grounds. To protect the Castle, the state does not allow any smoking or food on the tours, although there is a pleasant outdoor snack bar located at the visitors' center at the bottom of the hill. There is also a museum shop and bookstore in this complex. The bookstore stocks a wide variety of excellent works on the Castle and its collection.

Many children take the tours and appear to savor the grandeur and opulence of the art and the architecture, but parents should be aware that they cannot wander unescorted through the grounds or the Castle with their children. It is a place where the young or restless can experience "museum fatigue" because there is so much to see in such a short time. On very hot days, some people might find the Castle uncomfortable. But—in spite of a certain regimentation that is necessary for protection of the estate and efficiency—more than one million people a year visit the Castle. Seeing Hearst Castle is an exhilarating educational experience; the gift of the Hearst family is one in which the state and its citizens take great pride.

PRACTICAL INFORMATION FOR
NORTH ALONG THE COAST

 HOW TO GET THERE. By car. Most of the cities from Malibu north to Cambria can be reached directly via the Pacific Coast Hwy. (Route 1), one of the country's most scenic highways. If you are entering Malibu from the north, Hwy. 101 meets Rte. 1 near Ventura. The exit to each city or community from there on is clearly marked.

A quicker route that leads right into Ojai is by taking the Ventura Fwy. (101) north to Highway 33. This leads right into town. For a more scenic route to Ojai, take 101 N. to Hwy. 150 around Lake Casitas and then take 33 into Ojai. For a scenic way to get to Solvang, take the Ventura Fwy. (Hwy. 101) to Hwy. 154 around Lake Cachuma. This leads right into town. To Pismo Beach, U.S. 101 N. is the most direct route. The same is true in order to reach Santa Barbara. San Luis Obispo is just four hours from Los Angeles along Highway 101.

By bus. Greyhound Bus Lines and Great American Stage Lines travel between Oxnard and Los Angeles on eight round trips each day. From Malibu north, Greyhound service is also available on a limited basis.

By train. Downtown Los Angeles's Union Station at 800 N. Alameda offers train service to Santa Barbara, Oxnard, and San Luis Obispo. The station—an attraction itself with its 52-foot-high ceilings and beautiful carved wood—is a good example of one of the last grand railroad stations in this country. For Amtrak scheduling and information in Los Angeles, call (213) 624-0171.

By air. For general air transportation to the area, see Los Angeles "Practical Information." The Ventura County Airport is in Oxnard and is served by Golden West Airlines with flights from Los Angeles that continue to other major cities. Santa Barbara is accessible by air through two airlines: Golden West Airlines travels from LAX to Santa Barbara Airport, as does Apollo Airlines. San Luis Obispo Airport is served by Imperial and Wings West airlines.

By boat. To get to the Channel Islands, commercial boat service is available. Public transportation to the islands is available from many Southern Californian ports, though presently there is only one charter operation running on a regular basis (Island Packer Cruises, P.O. Box 993, Ventura, CA 93001; 805-642-1393).

 TELEPHONES. The area codes for the cities north along the coast from Malibu to Paso Robles vary. In Malibu the area code is 213; north from there, beginning in Oxnard, the area code is 805. You do not need to dial the area code if it is the same as the one from which you are calling. Information (known as directory assistance) is 411. When dialing a long-distance number from any of these cities, you must dial the number 1 (one) *before* you dial the area code and the number itself. An operator will assist you with person-to-person, credit card, and collect calls if you dial 0 first. Pay telephones still start at 10 cents.

 HOTELS AND MOTELS. Sleeping accommodations along the coast, although very lovely, are not as plentiful as you would find south of Los Angeles. Therefore, it's a good idea to plan ahead, especially during the high seasons of the spring, summer (in particular), and fall. Many of the hotels and motels are oceanside, and many operate swimming pools. Many establishments have seasonal rates, so during winter months you can often find a bargain. Some of the more exclusive properties require a certain length of stay during their busy season—three days must often be booked in the summer. To be on the safe side, be sure to call well ahead of your intended visit.

The Santa Barbara area also has several bed-and-breakfast establishments. Some of the more reputable ones have formed a guild—Bed & Breakfast Inn-keepers Guild of Santa Barbara. For further information, write P.O. Box 20246, Santa Barbara, CA 93120.

The following is a **selection** of hotels and motels in the area. Price categories for double-occupancy rooms in this region are: *Deluxe,* $60.00 and up; *Expensive,* $50.00–$59.00; *Moderate,* $40.00–$49.00; *Inexpensive,* $40.00 and under. For a more complete explanation of categories, refer to the *Facts At Your Fingertips* section at the front of this book.

MALIBU (213)

Casa Malibu. *Deluxe.* 22752 W. Pacific Coast Hwy; 456–2219. Located right on the ocean, this property contains twenty-one units, eight of which are on the sand. Low winter rates. MC, V.

Shangri-La Hotel. *Deluxe–Expensive.* 1301 Ocean Ave.; 394–2791. Streamlined modern in its design, this hotel is extremely quaint and charming. Movie stars frequent this property. Multilingual staff, laundry facilities, room service, restaurants, banquet and meeting rooms surrounded by garden patios. Free parking is available at the hotel. 70 rooms. V, MC, AE.

Tonga Lei Motor Hotel. *Expensive.* 22878 Pacific Coast Hwy; 456–6444. A nine-unit motel right on the sand. Polynesian-style architecture. V, ME, AE.

Malibu Surfer. *Moderate.* 22541 W. Pacific Coast Hwy; 456–6169. Across the street from the beach, in a nice section of Malibu. 16 units. V, MC.

Malibu Riviera Motel. *Moderate–Inexpensive.* 28920 Pacific Coast Hwy.; 457–9503. Color TV, health spa, and sundeck, Located between Malibu Beach and Point Dume in the heart of the beach community. Free parking for guests. 12 rooms. V, MC, AE.

Malibu Shore Hotel. *Inexpensive.* 23033 Pacific Coast Hwy; 456–6559. Moments from the beach, the hotel is easily spotted because of its Spanish design. Color TV, laundry. Spanish is spoken. Plenty of free parking. 18 rooms. V, MC.

OXNARD (805)

Casa Firena Marina Hotel. *Deluxe.* 3605 Peninsula Rd., Channel Islands Harbor; 985–6311. Attractive accommodations overlooking the marina. Suites and efficiency units. Lobster Trap restaurant. Complimentary coffee. Room service. The hotel recently added a 100-room wing with convention facilities. Pool, sauna, jacuzzi, tennis courts, game room, fishing. 274 rooms. All major credit cards.

Hilton Inn. *Moderate.* 600 Esplanade Dr.; 485–9666. Near beach, boating, and golf, this hotel boasts tennis, a swimming pool, and a whirlpool. Café and room service, with entertainment on Sunday nights. Convention facilities. Sundries, shopping arcade. 155 rooms. All major credit cards.

Vagabond Motor Hotel. *Moderate.* 1245 N. Oxnard Blvd.; 983–0251. Cheerful, pleasant rooms; color TV, playground. Coin laundry. Centrally located. All major credit cards.

VENTURA (805)

Holiday Inn. *Deluxe.* 450 E. Harbor Blvd.; 648–7731. Balconies with ocean view on the beach. Revolving rooftop room. Sauna, pool. The café is open from 7:00 A.M. to 9:00 P.M.; the bar from 12:00 noon to 1:30 A.M. Meeting rooms. Family rates available. 260 rooms. All major credit cards.

Best Western Inn of Ventura. *Moderate.* 708 E. Thompson Blvd.; 648–3101. This two-story building has air conditioning, color TV, pool; there is a café adjacent to the property. The beach is only two blocks away. 75 rooms. All major credit cards.

Pierpont Inn. *Moderate.* 550 Sanjon Road; 643–6144. 80 units. Walking distance to the beach, excellent restaurant, balconies, tennis at adjacent racquet club. Built in 1908. MC, V, AE.

OJAI (805)

Ojai Valley Inn and Country Club. *Deluxe-Expensive.* Country Club Dr.; 646–5511. Prices, although on the upper scale, include three square meals a day. Rooms in a number of buildings spread across the magnificent grounds and are surrounded on three sides by a beautiful golf course, site of an annual tournament. Tennis courts, as well as riding stables, are also available. 115 rooms. No credit cards.

Capri Motel. *Inexpensive.* 1180 E. Ojai Ave.; 646–4305. A panoramic view of the mountains is afforded from this property, which is near a golf course. Two pools, jacuzzi, and cable color TV. Air conditioning. 30 units. V, MC. AE.

Ojai Rancho Motel. *Inexpensive.* 615 W. Ojai Ave.; 646–3907. The rooms are wood paneled from ceiling to floor, giving a rustic feel to the place. Twelve of the sixteen units feature kitchens. Large heated pool, outdoor barbecue, cable color TV, air conditioning. V, MC, AE.

SANTA BARBARA (805)

Marriott's Santa Barbara-Biltmore. *Deluxe.* 1260 Channel Dr.; 969–2261. Luxurious accommodations in a traditional, elegant style. Hotel rooms and cottages; private beach across the street. Two pools, complimentary bicycles. Golf and tennis privileges arranged at the property. Lovely setting. 169 rooms, 11 cottages. All major credit cards.

San Ysidro Guest Ranch. *Deluxe.* 900 San Ysidro Lane; 969–5046. Superelegant hideaways; white cottages, fireplaces. Riding, hiking, tennis, and pool on 500 acres of lush land. No TVs in rooms because the theme is restful seclusion. 38 units, 5 kitchen units. MC, V, AE.

Santa Barbara Miramar Hotel-Resort. *Deluxe-Expensive.* 1555 S. Jameson Lane; 969–2203. Near the Pacific, this tranquil property is set in subtropical gardens, complete with two swimming pools, tennis, private beach, and a terraced dining room. There is a golf course three miles away. 195 units; 35 with kitchens. All major credit cards.

El Encanto Hotel. *Deluxe.* 1900 Lasuen Rd.; 687–5000. On ten acres of lushly landscaped grounds overlooking the Channel Islands. Despite the Spanish name, this hotel is really a French country inn equipped with its own chef, who originally worked in Maxims. Cocktail lounge. All major credit cards.

La Casa Del Mar. *Expensive-Moderate.* 28 W. Cabrillo Blvd.; 966–6337. This hotel faces the beach and has such amenities as ping pong, shuffleboard, and a sun patio. Seasonal rates. 35 rooms. AE, MC, V.

Ambassador by the Sea. *Moderate.* 202 W. Cabrillo Blvd.; 965–4577. This motel opposite the beach and the yacht harbor has a heated pool and sun decks and features a free Continental breakfast. 32 rooms. All major credit cards.

El Escorial Hotel. *Moderate.* 625 Por la Mar Circle; 966–4101 or 963–9302. Situated within a two-minute walk of Santa Barbara's best beach, it's also one mile from an excellent golf course. Tennis courts, pool, Jacuzzi, billiards, sauna, and gym. 312 suites, all with balconies, ocean view. All major credit cards.

Bayberry Inn. *Expensive-Moderate.* 111 West Valerio St.; 682–3199. Once a boarding school. New England decor. Croquet on the lawn. Piano in the garden room. Full breakfast included. AE, V, MC.

Santa Barbara Inn. *Moderate.* 435 Milpas St.; 966–2285. Distinctively decorated rooms with balconies. Don the Beachcomber Restaurant on premises features entertainment and dancing. Room service. Pool with food service right on the deck. Game rooms. Wheelchair unit. All major credit cards.

The Bath Street Inn. *Expensive-Moderate.* 1720 Bath Street; 682–9860. A Queen Anne Victorian house build more than 100 years ago. Flower-filled patios and brick courtyards. Quaint rooms. Continental breakfast. Six rooms. MC, V.

The Glenborough Inn. *Expensive-Moderate.* 1327 Bath St.; 966–0589. Charming inn. Beautiful antiques and decor. Complimentary breakfast of fresh juices and fresh-baked breads. Enclosed outdoor hot tub. Immaculate rooms. MC, V.

The Parsonage. *Expensive–Moderate.* 1600 Olive St.; 962–9336. Built in 1892 as a parsonage. Exquisite antique decor. Private solarium. View of the harbor. Breakfast included.

The Old Yacht Club Inn. *Expensive–Moderate.* 431 Corona Del Mar; 962–1277. One half block from the beach. Fresh flowers and sherry in each room. Continental breakfast included. Dinner offered; not included in room price. AE, V, MC.

SOLVANG (805)

Chimney Sweep Inn. *Moderate.* 1554 Copenhagen Dr.; 688–2111. A quaint retreat with a café across the street (café open from 6:00 A.M. to 10:00 P.M.). Color TV and a whirlpool on premises; room service from 8:00 A.M. 22 rooms. MV, V.

Solvang Inn. *Moderate.* 485 Alisal Rd.; 688–3248. This two-story property offers a free Continental breakfast along with a pool; café adjacent. 38 rooms. AE, MC, V.

Royal Copenhagen. *Moderate-Inexpensive.* 1579 Mission Dr.; 688–5561. A Danish motif sets the mood in this 23-room motel, which features free airport and bus-depot transportation and offers a pool and nearby café. AE, MC, V.

PISMO BEACH (805)

Best Western Shore Cliff Lodge. *Moderate.* 2555 Price St.; 773–4671. These accommodations are complete with private patios, refrigerators, and a spiral staircase to the beach. Other amenities include a whirlpool, sauna, pool, and lighted tennis courts. 99 rooms. All major credit cards.

Sea Gypsy. *Moderate.* 1020 Cypress at Wadsworth; 773–1801 or (800) 592–5923. The rooms boast private patios and balconies and are located on the beach, with lovely ocean view from each. A walkway on the property leads to the beach. Pool, whirlpool; café in the neighborhood. All major credit cards.

Arroyo K Lodge. *Inexpensive.* In Arroyo Grande, 611 E. Camino Real; 489–9300. A nice property, with pool, convention rooms, and free coffee in each room. Near a café, which is open twenty-four hours a day. 42 rooms. MC, V.

SAN LUIS OBISPO (805)

San Luis Bay Inn. *Deluxe.* Avila Beach, Box 189; 595–2333. A classic seaside resort with rooms and suites offering a breathtaking view, private balconies, spacious baths with sunken tubs. Pool, tennis, fishing, and 18-hole golf course. 76 rooms. Restaurant and cocktail lounge. V, MC.

Country House Inn. *Expensive.* 91 Main St., P.O. Box 179 in Templeton 93465; 434–1598. Built in 1886, this quaint village inn boasts 11-foot ceilings and is filled with antiques and fresh flowers. Wine and tea are served in the parlor. Lovely gardens. Personal check or cash only.

Heritage Inn. *Expensive.* 978 Olive St.; 544–7440. This turn-of-the-century bed-and-breakfast establishment offers rooms filled with antiques. Homemade breakfasts. 8 rooms, V, MC.

Madonna Inn. *Expensive.* 100 Madonna Rd.; 543–3000. A fantasy oriented establishment, each of the rooms here has a different if rather garish theme. Whether it's a cave in which you'd like to hibernate or a room fit for Cinderella, this place has got it. Restaurant and coffee shop. 109 rooms. No credit cards, but personal checks are accepted.

Campus Motel. *Moderate.* 404 Santa Rosa St.; 544–0881. The property features a playground for the kids and free coffee in the rooms. Café in the neighborhood. 28 rooms. All major credit cards.

Heritage Inn Bed & Breakfast. *Moderate.* 978 Olive St.; 544–7440. This old Victorian inn is off Hwy. 1 and 101. Facility has nine rooms and offers a Continental breakfast. All major credit cards.

MORRO BAY (805)

Anchor Inn Motel. *Inexpensive.* 220 Beach St.; 772–3333. 33 Units. Sun deck, on the bluff overlooking the bay. All major credit cards.

Breakers. *Expensive–Moderate.* 780 Market St.; 772–7317. Directly on the water and facing the famed Morro Rock, this hotel is only one block from the Pacific. Many rooms afford views and have fireplaces. Pool; café in area. 25 rooms. All major credit cards.

San Marcos. *Expensive–Moderate.* 250 Pacific St.; 772–2248. This three-story building offers balconies, and some rooms feature ocean views. Located two blocks from the ocean, there is a café nearby. 32 rooms. All major credit cards.

Best Western Bay View. *Moderate.* 225 Harbor St.; 772–2771. Kitchens are available, and some rooms have a view. King- and queen-size beds. 22 units. All major credit cards.

Fireside Inn. *Moderate.* 730 Morro Ave.; 772–2244. Rooms feature electric fireplaces, some with refrigerators and all with color TV. Near a café that's open from 6:00 A.M. to 10:00 P.M. 17 rooms. All major credit cards.

CAMBRIA (805)

Cambria Shores. *Deluxe.* 6276 Moonstone Beach Dr.; 927–8644. Views of the ocean are available from this hotel, which is opposite the beach and Hearst Castle. Café down the street. 24 rooms. AE, MC, V.

Castle In by the Sea. *Deluxe.* 6620 Moonstone Beach Dr.; 927–8605. This two-story building offers many amenities, including a pool, putting green, rooms with ocean views, and some oversize beds. 31 rooms. AE, MC, V.

Fireside Inn by the Sea. *Deluxe.* 6700 Moonstone Beach St.; 927–8661. Fireplace, Jacuzzi, TV, pool. All major credit cards.

HOW TO GET AROUND. Because Southern California coastal cities are spread out, the best way to get around is by car. All major car rental firms and several local concerns are represented in the Los Angeles area. Check directory assistance or the Yellow Pages for telephone numbers.

Public bus service is available, but it is severely limited. Western Greyhound lines offers public transportation around the Santa Ynez Valley, making two stops daily along the east side of Solvang Park and a few stops in Bulleton. In Oxnard South Coast Area Transit provides bus service throughout the city. RTD runs through Malibu.

 TOURIST INFORMATION. Visitor bureaus and chambers of commerce in the beach cities and communities can be helpful with specific questions and information. In Malibu the Chamber of Commerce is located at 22653 Pacific Coast Hwy., 90265; (213) 456–9025.

The Oxnard Convention and Visitors' Bureau is located at 228 South A St., Oxnard 93030; (805) 485–8833.

The Ventura Visitors' Bureau is at 785 Seaward Ave., 93003; (805) 648–2075. Information is available at this location for the city of Ventura and also for the Channel Islands.

To visit the two privately owned Channel Islands, a permit (which is free) is required for entry. To visit Santa Rosa, write to 123 W. Padre St., Santa Barbara 93105; (805) 682–7645; open during the day. To visit Santa Cruz, write the Santa Cruz Island Co., 515 S. Flower St., Los Angeles 90071; (213) 485–9208.

To visit the islands of Santa Barbara and San Miguel, permits are also required. Free, they may be obtained by writing to 1901 Spinnaker Dr., Ventura, CA 93001.

The Ojai Valley Chamber of Commerce is located at 338 E. Ojai Ave.; (805) 646–3000.

For information on Santa Barbara, contact Santa Barbara Beautiful, P.O. Box 299, Santa Barbara 93102; (805) 965–3021.

Solvang's Chamber of Commerce is located at 1623 Mission Dr., Solvang, CA 93463; (805) 688–3317.

San Luis Obispo Chamber of Commerce is at 1039 Chorro St., San Luis Obispo, CA 93401; (805) 543–1323.

Pismo Beach Chamber of Commerce is at 581 Dolliver St.; (805) 773–4382 or (805) 773–1661.

Morro Bay information is available from Morro Bay Chamber of Commerce, P.O. Box 876, 385 Morro Bay Blvd.; (805) 772–4467.

In Cambria, contact the Cambria Chamber of Commerce, 767 Main St.; (805) 927–3624.

SEASONAL EVENTS. Many events in the area are scheduled at the last moment, preventing us from including them. One of the best ways to find out about such happenings is to check the local newspaper in each individual city. The following are established annual events.

January. *The Ken McMullen and Jim Colborn Golf Tournament* is presented at the Ojai Valley Inn's eighteen-hole championship course.

February. Another of the many Danish traditions in Solvang takes place in honor of the coming of Lent before Ash Wednesday. This Danish service, called the *Fastelavns Fest,* is held at the Bethania church, followed by a day of partying similar to that of Mardi Gras.

April. In San Luis Obispo the spring brings *Poly Royal,* a country fair sponsored by Cal Poly University. This two-day event, held the last weekend in the month, presents rodeos, livestock judgings, and concerts, as well as various food sampling. If you plan to visit the area during this time, be sure to reserve hotels in advance; the city gets very crowded. The *Ojai Valley Tennis Tournament* is held the last week in April in the center of town in Libbey Park. The tournament, the oldest in the country, has a traditional tea tent, where hot tea and cookies are served during the games.

May. *La Fiesta,* San Luis Obispo's annual tribute to Spanish culture, is a three-day event held the third weekend in May. Traditional food and festivities highlight the celebration. The end of May brings the annual *Ojai Music Festival* in Libbey Park. The three-day event features classical, rock, and jazz music and is held outdoors under the park's festival bowl. In the *Paso Robles Wine Festival,* the bouquets of California's finest wines mingle in an air of enchanting excitement as the area's finest libations are presented.

June. *Semana Nautica Summer Sports Festival* is a highlight in Santa Barbara. The sports include everything from speedboat races to sports car racing.

July. Morro Bay's Independence Day Weekend explodes with a colorful *Morro Bay parade.* It marks the opening of three days of arts-and-crafts shows, a Morro Bay tradition for more than 20 years.

August. The *Mozart Festival* in San Luis Obispo takes place the first week of this month in various indoor and outdoor locations throughout the city. Performances include local as well as guest musicians. Morro Bay's annual *three-day antique show* is held in the Veterans Memorial Building, 209 Surf St., the first weekend in August. Santa Barbara's *Old Spanish Days Fiesta* is held for five days beginning the first Wednesday of the month at Earl Warren Showgrounds. During this time the city's history, beginning with the days of the Indians and ending with the arrival of American troops, is recreated.

September. Malibu attracts surfers from all over the world during the month to Surfrider Beach for the annual *International Surfing Contest.* Winners get the chance to compete in national and world championships. In Ojai this month the *Mexican Fiesta* is held, with funds going toward scholarships for Mexican-American students. Food, dancing, crafts, mariachis, and entertainment are featured. Solvang celebrates *Denmark's Independence Day* with festivities taking place for three days. Residents dress in their native costumes. Authentic food, drink, music, and dance give you a taste of what a real Danish life-style is like. The *Eighth Annual Fireman's Challenge* in Morro Bay is a competitive event between fire departments from northern and southern California counties (Sept. 15–16).

 TOURS. To visit any of the Channel Islands, your best bet is to join an organized expedition. On any of the following tours that you may choose, be sure to travel prepared for the environment: Wear rubber-sole shoes and plenty of clothing, for it will turn chilly before the return to port.

These are some of the organizations from which to choose; reservations are assured when fees are received by the company selected.

American Cetacean Society, Los Angeles Chapter, Box 2698, San Pedro 90731; (213) 548–6279; *Island Packers Co.,* Box 993, Ventura 93002; (805) 642–1393; *Santa Barbara Island Cruises,* c/o Sea Landing Sport Fishing, Breakwater, Santa Barbara 93109; (805) 963–3522; *Pacific Adventures,* Box 5041, Riverside, CA 92517; (714) 684–1227.

Another source is the City of San Buenaventura Department of Parks and Recreation, Box 99, Ventura, CA 93002; (805) 644–7421. They suggest reservations a month in advance, and that you visit various islands.

For bird-watchers seeking satisfaction from the Channel Islands, the *Los Angeles Audubon Society* runs a trip that circles the best bird-watching locations. Write to them at Audubon House, Plummer Park, 7377 Santa Monica Blvd., Los Angeles, CA 90046; (213) 876–0202.

Tour the city of Solvang in a streetcar resembling the kind found along the streets of Copenhagen between 1860 and 1915. Guided tours are available beginning at Alisal and Copenhagen Dr.

VINEYARD AND WINERY TOURS

Santa Ynez Valley in Santa Barbara County is becoming increasingly prominent in the world of wine. About a dozen vineyards and eight thousand acres of grapes now dot this thirty-mile area over the Santa Ynez Mountains from Santa Barbara and adjacent to President Reagan's "Rancho del Cielo" retreat.

Many of the vineyards in this area are family owned; all offer tours, which should be arranged beforehand.

Among them:

Among them:

The *Santa Ynez Valley Winery,* 365 N. Refugio Rd.; (805) 688–8381; *Vega Vineyards,* 9496 Santa Rosa Rd., Buellton, 93427; (805) 688–2415; *Firestone Vineyard,* Los Olivos, Jaca Station Rd., P.O. Box 244, 93441; (805) 688–3940; *Zaca Mesa Winery,* Foxen Canyon Rd., in Los Olivos (mailing address is P.O. Box 547, Los Olivos, CA 93144); (805) 688–3310.; (805) 688–4632; *Sanford and Benedick Vineyards,* ten miles west of Buellton; (805) 688–8314; the *J. Carey Cellars,* between Solvang and Los Olivos, at 1711 Alamo Pintado Rd., Solvang; (805) 688–8554; *Ballard Canyon Winery,* 1825 Ballard Canyon Rd., Solvang;

(805) 688–7585; *Rancho Sisquoc Winery,* 1711 Foxen Canyon Rd., Solvang; (805) 937–3616; *Santa Barbara Winery,* 202 Anacapa St.; (805) 962–3812.

The Pine & the Palm, a local tour operator, offers tours of many of the area's wineries. P.O. Box 40426, Santa Barbara, CA 93103; (805) 962–9624.

Vineyards also abound through San Luis Obispo County. Within the San Luis Obispo city limits, the following are open for touring: *Chamisal Vineyard,* Rte. 3, Orcutt Rd.; (805) 544–3576; *Lawrence Winery,* one mile off Edna Rd. on Corbett Canyon Rd.; (805) 544–5800.

SPECIAL-INTEREST TOUR

The Pacific Gas and Electric Company, 592 San Luis Obispo Street, offers motor coach tours to *Diablo Canyon Nuclear Plant* at Avila Beach, seven miles south of the city. The tour includes a video presentation on the workings of a nuclear plant, a demonstration of energy conservation, and other exhibits. Buses leave from the Pacific Gas and Electric Company's visitors' center at 10:00 A.M. and 2:00 P.M. daily. Located five miles south of Pismo Beach on Hwy 101.

GARDENS. *Santa Barbara Botanic Gardens,* 1212 Mission Canyon Rd., a mile and a half from the mission, is made up of sixty magnificent acres; so plan to spend at least an hour taking a leisurely self-guided tour through the grounds—three miles of easy-to-walk nature trails. Plants and trees indigenous to California—colorful wild flowers, redwoods, brilliantly flowering shrubs and desert plants—grow in this natural setting. Trail directions can be obtained at the Information Center. There is a guided tour on Thursday.

Downtown Santa Barbara boasts the *Alice Keck Park Memorial Garden,* a full square block of delight, with pond, gazebo, and the native flowers and shrubs of California.

At Cal Poly University in San Luis Obispo, this school's renowned Agricultural Development offers public access to its *All American Garden,* a testing ground for the flower-seed industry. The university's Ornamental Horticulture Department has many greenhouses and a flower shop. To get on campus, obtain a visitor's permit at the Administration Building.

In Ojai, the *Biblical Gardens,* 304 N. Foothill Rd., are located at the Presbyterian church. Plants mentioned in the Bible thrive in this lush paradise.

PARKS. In **Ojai,** *Dennison Park* offers beautiful views of the valley. Camping is available amid the oak and pine trees. *Libbey Park,* Ojai's civic center park, is the site of festivals and tennis tournaments. *Soule Park,* Boardman Rd., Ojai, is a great place for family picnics. There are tennis courts and horseshoe pits as well. *Lake Casitas,* site of the 1984 Rowing Olympics, is a must-see, with camping, horseback riding, fishing, and boating enclosed by 100 miles of park shoreline.

In **San Luis Obispo** *Mission Plaza Park* on the grounds of Mission San Luis Obispo de Tolosa in the downtown area is the site of many annual activities and concerts. The San Luis Creek, with small cafés and boutiques located across a footbridge, is located in the park.

Other parks within the San Luis Obispo city limits and ideal for a pleasant afternoon stroll are *Sinsheimer Park* near Orcutt Rd.; *Meadow Park* near Meadow and South Sts.; *Mitchell Park* near the downtown area; and *Santa Rosa Park* near California Polytechnic University.

Laguna Lake Park, at the southwest end of the city along Madoon Rd., is a large recreational area with a lake for fishing as well as a golf course. *Montana de Oro* State Park is located outside the city to the west. Situated along the coast, this park offers hiking and camping, among other activities.

Hearst-San Simeon State Historical Monument is off Hwy. 1 just north of the town of San Simeon Village, about sixty-six miles south of Big Sur and about thirty miles north of **Morro Bay**. There are four two-hour tours of the famed William Randolph Hearst estate. *Tour I* features the main floor of the main house, one guest house, and some of the gardens. There is about a half-mile of walking and 150 steps. This tour is a good introduction to the monument. *Tour II* covers the upper floors of the main house; about 300 steps. Included are the kitchen and library. *Tour III* covers the newer wing and emphasizes guest bedrooms furnished with fine works of art and furniture, about 300 steps. All three tours include the Roman and Neptune pools with their modern and ancient statuary. *Tour IV* offers a behind-the-scenes tour of the gardens, vaults, wine cellars, and engine room. Tours are $8.00 for adults, $4.00 for children ages six to twelve. Tours are generally sold out, although a few tickets are often available if you reach the ticket office at the castle when it opens (8:00 A.M., June 1 to August 31; 8:30 A.M. the rest of the year). Reservations are *strongly* recommended and can be made through Ticketron. The toll-free number for ticket information (in California) is (800) 952-5580. From outside the state the non-toll free number is (805) 927-4621.

In **Solvang**, *Lake Cachuma Recreation Area*, located on Hwy. 154 (fourteen miles southeast of the city), offers boating and fishing all day long. Camping, horseback riding, and picnicking are also available. A recreation center in the park provides a swimming pool and skating rink.

Nojogui Falls Park is located six miles south of Solvang on Alisal Rd. The area is good for picnics and barbecues. The park, featuring a beautiful flowing waterfall, covers eighty-four acres.

Hans Christian Andersen Park is located off Atterdag Rd. in Solvang. Tennis courts, barbecues, and picnic facilities, as well as children's play attractions, are found there.

Topanga State Park, off Topanga Canyon Rd. at 20825 Entrada Rd. in **Malibu** (455-2465), offers hiking and self-guided trails. Beautiful ocean views can be seen from its peaks. The park is 9,000 acres.

Malibu Creek State Park, 28754 Mulholland Dr.; 991-1827, has one of its entrances through Malibu Canyon. Hiking is available among the trees, rocks, and waterways.

Point Mugu State Park, across from the Leo Carillo State Beach; 457–5538, offers close to seventy miles of trails as well as camping facilities. Reservations for camping are necessary.

 BEACHES. All along the coast, beaches of varying description can be found, becoming the center of attention for these resort areas. The farther north you travel, the rockier the coastline becomes—and as the rocks become increasingly jagged, the wind starts to gust at high speeds, making water sports almost impossible.

Ventura County beaches begin about a mile west of Leo Carillo State Beach on a narrow strip of sand called the *County Line* by neighborhood surfers. Open turf to all who wanted to brave its waters, in the last few years, the beach has been taken over by the state.

Just across the road is Neptune's Net (42505 Pacific Coast Highway; 805/488–1302), a seafood lover's paradise, where you can choose live lobsters or crabs from large saltwater tanks. While you wait, try the clams, which are steamed before your eyes.

Point Magu State Beach is a relatively new park south of Oxnard. Noted in and around the park are one hundred open-beach campsites, with facilities for restrooms, cold showers (no hook-ups, sorry), and a recreational vehicle sanitation station called La Jolla Beach. Fishing is usually quite good here, but unless the day is particularly calm, swimming is not.

Fifty more comfortable campsites are located in Big Sycamore Canyon. A path leading under the highway ends up in *Sycamore Cove,* a beautifully landscaped area, boasting grassy picnic grounds and a lifeguard beach.

South of Oxnard is Port Hueneme, which is home to a small fishing fleet and some of the U.S. Navy. For those who enjoy looking at fishing boats, you can often witness cargo ships unloading here while oil company boats run in and out, carrying equipment to tend the offshore oil rigs. Bus #10 makes a convenient stop here.

Ventura Marina is a quiet, peaceful yacht harbor with plenty of greenery and only a few commercial fishing boats. Currently under construction is an imitation of a New England village. Take Bus #4 to reach this point.

Marina Park, directly west of Ventura Marina's West Channel, is a new, charming park for the whole family. A small sand play area features a life-sized bronze dolphin that sprays water from its spout to dampen the sand for castle-builders. Small sailboats are available here, and there's a bicycle path that follows the water line. For old-fashioned flavor, the park is lit by antique street lamps.

San Buenaventura State Beach is a two mile-sandy stretch of land safe for swimming since the sand drops off at a gradual level. This beach also offers surfing and fishing in an aesthetically pleasing environment. Admission is free at this park, where plush picnic grounds are surrounded by lovely tall pine trees, providing an abundance of shade. Skateboarders and rollerskaters love the smooth concrete walkways. Fishers can catch bonita, shark, bass, surf perch, and corbina, and San Buenaventura is an excellent grunion-run beach. (March to August; license required).

Located in front of the Ventura County Fairgrounds, west of the pier is *Surfer's Point.* This is an excellent place to learn to surf. Rest rooms and showers are available. Entrance is at Harbor and Figueroa Street.

Emma Wood State Beach is notorious for its big winter waves. Many tents and campers enjoy the environment as they set up their temporary homes along windy parking lots.

This beach, with its nice tidepool, raccoons and many different types of birds, is also noted for the lovely rock formations it boasts. Catch perch, bass, capezon and corbina here.

Up the coast and closer to Point Conception, the Channel Islands and the Santa Ynez Mountains, the water becomes much bluer while the sand becomes smoother and whiter.

Off the shoreline from Ventura to *Rincon Beach County Park* are houses which seem to hug the shoreline. Here, some of the best winter big wave surf in California rolls in on the east side of the point. Also available are new picnic tables and barbecues.

Carpinteria State Beach has it all. This beach is frequented by some 700,000 visitors a year, and due to its sheltered position, is a choice spot in the winter. Surrounded by magnificent trees, this park offers campgrounds, bicycle renting, recreational vehicles, and pine-covered dunes for a day-use picnic area.

Next door, *Carpinteria's City Beach* has the same safe swimming and mat surfing. This beach is slowly becoming as active as neighboring areas since many apartment complexes are springing up in the neighborhood. A slew of vacation apartment rentals are within walking distance of the beach.

Moving west, take the Summerland Freeway exit to the residential beaches of *Loon Beach.* This is a local favorite for nude swimmers and sunbathers.

Also at Summerland, *Lookout Point* is a grassy retreat with barbecues, a play area and a trail leading to a wide sandy beach.

SANTA BARBARA BEACHES

The lazy community feeling of Santa Barbara flows from the downtown area to the beaches, waterfront and harbor. Many escape from Los Angeles for the weekend, and for just dollars they can travel on Amtrak and return on Sunday, avoiding coastal traffic.

The beginning of Santa Barbara city beaches starts just west of the Old Biltmore at *Montecito Shores.* Often at low tide, clean sand greets the waves and ends up at the yacht harbor.

Opposite Andree Clark Bird Refuge is *East Beach.* A bicycle path leads around the Marsh Lake to the Child's Estate Zoo just off Andree Clark. The famous Santa Barbara volleyball tournaments are held here, and just a short walk around the point west of the courts is Butterfly Beach, perfect for sunbathing.

The Cabrillo Youth Center is located west of the volleyball courts. *Palm Beach* (not to be confused with the Florida resort town) is noted for its formal line of palms that line a grassy park strip.

West Beach is sheltered from the constant westerly winds by the harbor and breakwater. Banos del Mar is the city swimming pool at West Beach, open to the public in summer. Artists line the street along Cabrillo Blvd. next to the beach on the weekends, exhibiting their wares.

The Santa Barbara Harbor is a complete opposite to Marina del Rey. Small and old fashioned, this charming town offers a traditional bait and tackle store. Beyond the harbor is *Leadbetter Beach,* known for great swimming and good board surfing.

One of Southern California's nicest natural beaches is *Arroyo Burro Beach County Park* on *Hendrey's Beach,* located on Clift Drive two miles out of town. Along the miles of beach perfect for sunbathing, jogging, and walking are a picnic area, swimming, and good surfing and diving.

Goleta Beach Park is the fishing enthusiast's dream. Off the pier, find sportfishing boats, boat launching, speedboat rentals, and jetski. The community beaches at Isla Vista are usually saturated with students in good weather.

BEACHES NORTH TO MORRO BAY

Just north of Santa Barbara are three older, more established beaches: *El Capitan, Refugio,* and *Gaviota Beach State Parks.* Set in a natural environment, these beaches are excellent for family camping or weekends of surf fishing, snorkeling, swimming, and surfing—all in crystal-clear water. Reservations are needed in the summer and on holiday weekends. (Call 805/968–1411 for El Capitan, 805/968–1350 for Refugio, and to reach Gaviota, call the local operator and ask for Gaviota Toll Station Number 5.)

Jalama Beach is located just south of Lompoc, off a road running through a series of ranches. This beach is famous for its extraordinary sunsets and fishing. Although swimming and surfing are not allowed at Jalama due to the powerful waves, walk for miles along the sand, cast a line for rockfish or halibut, or spend some time looking for fossils.

Surf Beach is at the end of Highway 246 and runs through Vandenberg Air Force Base. Heavy winds usually prevail here, thus isolating the area. Rough waters make swimming dangerous except on calm days.

Farther north along the coast, the highway runs into *Oceano County Park,* with the largest Dune Buggy Area on the California coast. Swimming is safe, along with other activities at the clamming beaches, a fishing lake, picnic and barbecue area and even a swimming pool open in the summer.

Pismo Beach State Park runs from Oceano to Pismo Beach. Quite the setting for fishers, since this park has six miles of sandy beach and its own fishing pier which is floodlit at night. Perch and other surf fish are often caught. The campsites are great for kids who love sliding around in the dunes; any corrugated cardboard box makes an excellent sled.

Also noteworthy for fishing are the floodlit piers at Avila Beach and Port San Luis. Sportfishing boats sail out to sea for rockfish, salmon, cod, and blue bass. Usually the waters here are calm, and warm enough for swimming—but this beach is especially popular with sunbathers and socializers.

Farther north, *Montana de Oro State Park* is sheltered from the damp wind and fog by large green pines. Safe swimming is found in a protected cove near park headquarters. When the tide moves out, shell hunting and tidepooling are always quite beautiful.

Morro Bay is situated halfway between San Francisco and Los Angeles with an enormous stretch of interesting shoreline. One can find pretty much every activity with camping, fishing, surfing, clamming, boating within the bay, bird-watching, and even golf—located within the super state parks which also offer clean, public beaches.

Morro Bay State Park Sand Split Wild Area, a bit farther north, is a sandy peninsula that protects Morro Bay from the ravages of storm and wind surf. Sand dunes rise as high as 85 feet. Morro Bay State Park is located in front of the bay and with its 135 campsites is a haven for campers since each site has tables, a stove and a food locker. Restrooms have hot showers and laundry tubs. For those out for the day is *Morro Strand State Beach,* which has several miles of sandy shoreline but no facilities except restrooms.

CHILDREN'S ACTIVITIES. *Child's Estate Zoological Gardens,* 1300 E. Cabrillo Blvd., Santa Barbara, is a unique eighty-one-acre park, playground, and zoo that was once the site of a Chumash Indian village. Popular is the Sealarium, with underwater portholes for viewing. A miniature railroad rides around the park. Hours: 10:00 A.M. to 8:00 P.M., Monday through Friday; Admission: adults, $2.50; teenagers, $1.25, children two-twelve, $1.00. Call (805) 962-6310.

PARTICIPANT SPORTS. Sports activities in the areas north of Los Angeles to Cambria are as varied as the cities along the way. The following is a sample of what this section of California has to offer in the way of participant sports:

Water sports. The Pacific is really too cool for swimming except during the summer, but other activities keep sports fanatics busy along the coastal waters. At Morro Bay, dig for clams; for giant clams try Pismo Beach; snatch grunion (bare hands and fishing license required) as the tiny fish spawn at low tide during the full moon from March through August.

Surfing. Surfing has become a big sport in California in recent years. There are more than seventy-five beaches between Cambria and Los Angeles. For exciting observation or participation in the skills of surfing and the "surfing scene," head out to the beaches bright and early (best time is between 6:00 and 9:00 A.M.). Expert surfers follow the tide and swell conditions in choosing their beach. During the winter surfing is year round at Rincon in Ventura, where some of the world's best surfers ride huge Hawaii-style waves. Santa Barbara Jalama State Park has waves so large that dozens of ships have crashed on the rocks, not a pleasant thought for seagoers but a very exciting place to watch surfing. (For Malibu information, see the Los Angeles *Beaches* section.)

Fishing. Oxnard is a favorite port for fishing the Channel Islands for halibut, the size fishers tell tall tales about. Bass, swordfish, and even shark are taken offshore. Surf fishing is popular up and down the coast.

Ocean sport fishing services are offered by H and M Sport Fishing, Breakwater, Santa Barbara. Contact Sea Landing; (805) 963–3564. Other boats leave from Avila Beach, Morro Bay, and Ventura. There is good sport fishing at Catalina Island (see the *Long Beach to San Clemente* section, below).

In San Luis Obispo fishing for trout is located at the southwest end of the city along Madonna Rd. In Malibu fish off Malibu pier, or take a sport fishing boat, which leaves from there or Paradise Cove twice daily.

Lake Casitas in Ojai, with an abundance of bass, trout, and catfish, is also a fishers' haven. Bait and boats are available for rental. Lake Cachuma, Solvang, the largest man-made lake in Southern California, offers fishing, too.

Golf. In Ojai golf is available at *Soule Park's* eighteen-hole course (call 805–646–5633), and at the *Ojai Valley Inn* on Country Club Lane, the site of annual golfing tournaments. In Solvang the *Alisal Golf Course* at the Alisal Guest Ranch is open to members and guests.

In Santa Barbara public courses include the *Santa Barbara Community Course,* an eighteen-hole course at Las Positas Rd. and McCaw Ave., open 6:00 A.M. to dark; (805) 687–7087. *Fairview Community Golf Course,* a nine-hole, par-3 course plus driving range at 6034 Hollister Ave., Goleta, open 8:00 A.M. to 10 P.M.; (805) 964–1414. *San Marcos Pass Course,* a nine-hole course at 1187 Via Chaparall, open 7:00 A.M. to 6:30 P.M.; (805) 967–3901; *Ocean Meadows Golf Course,* a nine-hole course at Storke Rd. south of Hwy. 101; open from 8:00 A.M. until dark on weekdays and 6:30 A.M. until dark on weekends; (805) 968–6814. *Sandpiper Golf Course,* eighteen holes at 7925 Hollister Ave., Goleta; open 7:30 A.M. until dark during the week and from 6:30 A.M. until dark on weekends and during holidays; (805) 968–6814. For putting greens in Santa Barbara, try *Spencer Aams Park* and the *Fairview Golf Center.*

Horseback Riding. Santa Barbara has many pleasant trails to explore. For rentals try *Cachuma Trails Riding Stable* at Cachuma Lake. Closed Tuesday. For reservations, (805) 688–3018. *San Ysidro Stables,* 900 San Ysidro Lane; by reservation only; (805) 969–5046. *Gene O'Hagan Stables* at Circle Bar B Ranch; take Refugio Canyon exit from Highway 101. For reservations call (805) 968–5929. *Rancho Oso Stables;* take Hwy. 154 across Cold Spring Arch Bridge to Paradise Rd., then turn right five miles to the ranch. Evening dinner rides featured; (805) 967–4155.

Horses may be rented at *Lake Cachuma* in Solvang. In Ojai the sport is popular throughout the valley. Rent horses at the *Ojai Valley Stables* on Hermosa Rd.; (805) 646–2837. There are also horse rentals at Lake Casitas.

Bicycling. In Santa Barbara rent bikes at *Beach Rentals,* 8 W. Cabrillo Blvd. near the beach (rollerskates also available there); (805) 953–2524. Mopeds and bicycles are available for rent at *Moped City Rentals,* 336 N. Milpas St., Santa Barbara; (805) 962–7467.

San Luis Obispo has an intricate bike path that takes you all through the area and is a lovely way to experience the city.

Hiking. In San Luis Obispo, hiking is available through the Santa Lucia Mountains for those who want to exert varied amounts of energy. For more vigorous hikers, there are seven volcanic mountain peaks that will give a real workout. Also Montana de Oro State Park, west of the city, offers hiking trails. In the Ojai area, hiking trails, some reaching close to 7,000 feet in elevation, abound in Los Padres National Forest. The U.S. Forest Service, 1190 E. Ojai Ave., has free hiking maps.

Tennis. In Santa Barbara courts are available at both private tennis clubs and at many schools and parks. Night-lighted courts include *Municipal Courts,* near Salinas St. and Hwy. 101, access off Old Coast Hwy., *Oak Park; Las Positas Municipal* Courts, 1002 Las Positas Rd. In San Luis Obispo, the *City High School,* 1350 California Blvd., and *California Polytechnic State University.*

Racquet Ball. In Santa Barbara at *Los Carneros Court Club,* 170 Los Carneros in Goleta; (805) 968–7480. In San Luis Obispo at the *YMCA Fitness Center,* 1020 Southwood Dr.; (805) 541–1816.

Shuffleboard. In Santa Barbara at *Spencer Adams Park,* open daily from 9:00 A.M. to 5:00 P.M. Free.

Ice Skating. In Santa Barbara at *The Ice Patch,* an indoor ice-skating rink, 1933 Cliff Dr.; (805) 963–0833.

Lawn Bowling. In Santa Barbara at *Spencer Adams Park,* Tuesday, Thursday, Saturday, and Sunday; 12:30–4:30 P.M.; $1.00. *MacKenzie Park,* Monday, Wednesday, Friday, and Saturday; 12:30–4:30 P.M.; $1.00.

SPECTATOR SPORTS. One of the best polo playing fields in the United States is the Santa Barbara Polo and Racquet Club, located just ten miles south of Santa Barbara. Trophy matches are played there most Sundays. (A number of thoroughbred horse ranches are found in Montecito and neighboring Santa Ynez Valley.) At 3375 Foothill Rd., Carpinteria (just south of Montecito); for schedules, call (805) 684–5819. Admission: $2.50 adults, $1.00 students, children under twelve admitted free.

HISTORICAL SITES. In Solvang the *Old Wulff Windmill* on Fredensborg Canyon Rd. is the oldest mill in town. At one time actually used to pump water and grind grain, the Wulff Windmill was dedicated as an historical landmark on October 5, 1980.

The *Bethania church* on Atterdag Rd. is Danish provincial in architecture and resembles a typical country church in Denmark.

Point Dume, **Malibu,** located at the tip of a now-residential area jutting into the ocean, was named in honor of Father Dumetz, one of the Franciscan fathers at the Ventura Mission, in 1794. The once-jagged point has been excavated for building purposes. Point Dume is located in the Malibu Riviera region.

Ojai. *City Hall,* located at Blanche and Santa Ana St. in downtown Ojai, is the old ranching estate of the Hobson–Smith family. The Spanish-style house and grounds have remained basically unchanged. The *Arcade,* Ojai's downtown shopping center, preserves history in its early 1900s architectural style, which is that of the old California missions. It is considered a historical landmark.

Santa Barbara. The *Santa Barbara County Courthouse* on the 1100 block of Anacapa St., is a superior Spanish–Moorish palace surrounded by lawns and vast tropical gardens.

Part of the original Presidio Real or royal fortress founded in 1782, the *El Cuartel* is located at State Historial Park, 122 E. Canon Perdido St.

Also in Santa Barbara *El Paseo,* or "the street" in Spanish, is reminiscent of just that, with a shopping arcade built around the adobe home of the historic De la Guerra family (circa 1827).

San Luis Obispo has preserved its homes and architecture so that historic sites can be seen at all times while strolling the streets. *Heritage Homes,* built in the late 1800s, are spread throughout the city. These feature primarily Victorian-style homes with ornate design.

Beginning at the *Mission Plaza* in the downtown area, a two-mile tour, marked by a green line through the city, takes you to various historic spots, including old adobe homes of prominent people, an old train depot, and a Bull and Bear Pit, where California's early inhabitants used to engage in the spectator sport of pitting a bull and bear against each other.

See *Parks* for information on Hearst–San Simeon estate.

OLD MISSIONS

In 1768, when the Russian interest in Alaska was seen as a possible prelude to southward expansion, King Charles of Spain ordered the colonization of California. The king's decree launched the missions, which provided the seminal growth for California.

Under the astute leadership of Father Junipero Serra and Father Fermin Lausen (each founded nine missions), the gray-robed Franciscans moved slowly northward. By 1823 a chain of twenty-one missions extended 600 miles from San Diego to Sonoma. Approximately a day's travel apart (thirty miles in those days), the missions dotted the coastal route called El Camino Real. Today U.S. Rte. 101 parallels the historic Mission Trail, one of the state's most popular tourways.

Six of these missions are in the area north of Los Angeles from Malibu to Cambria:

Mission Santa Buenaventura is located in Ventura at 211 E. Main St. It was the ninth mission founded and the last to be dedicated by the Franciscan padre, Father Serra. The date was Easter Sunday 1782, two years before his death.

The doors of the mission, carved with the River of Life design and studded with handmade nails, are replicas of the originals. The original baptismal font is still in use in the baptistry. Some of the original Indian paintings are on display at the arched baptistry entrance. At the Mission Museum, old records and books—two of which are the baptismal and death records written and signed by Father Junipero Serra—are on display. Also, there are original confessionals showing Indian handiwork. Hours: 10:00 A.M. to 5:00 P.M., daily. Free.

Mission Santa Barbara is located at the upper end of Laguna St. in Santa Barbara. Called the Queen of the Missions because of its graceful beauty, it was founded in 1786 and is still used as a parish church; it is the only one of Calfornia's missions never abandoned by the Franciscans. A candle has been burning on the altar since December 4, 1786. This mission is considered the state's most photographed building and is set in a dramatic pose as it overlooks its city namesake. Remnants of the aqueduct exist on the hill north of the mission. The garden and the museum are outstanding. Gift shop. Hours: 9:00 A.M. to 5:00 P.M., Monday through Saturday; 1:00 P.M. to 5:00 P.M., Sunday. Admission: 50 cents adults; children under sixteen free.

Mission Santa Ines is located thirty-five miles north of Santa Barbara, only a bell's call from the Danish inspired town of Solvang. It was the nineteenth of the twenty-one Franciscan missions and is today one of the most well preserved. Santa Ines was founded in 1804 and dedicated to the martyred Saint Agnes. It housed California's first seminary, the College of Our Lady of Refuge.

Still in use are carved wooden crucifixes, hand hammered copper and silver altar pieces, and other religious articles crafted on the premises by Indian neophytes. The original mural decorations are rivaled only by those at San Miguel. Hours: 9:30 A.M. to 5:00 P.M. daily.

Mission La Purisma Concepcion is located in Lompoc in Santa Barbara County; (805) 733–3713. This mission is a faithful restoration of the impressive structure it once was before being sadly neglected after the Mexicans sold it at auction in 1845 for $1,000. When the mission was being restored in the 1930s, young men of the Civilian Conservation Corps (CCC) molded more than 100,-000 adobe bricks in the manner of the original Indian builders.

The mission was founded in 1787, but the original buildings were destroyed in a devastating 1812 earthquake. The hero of the earthquake, Father Marinao Payeros, is buried on the premises.

Mission San Luis Obispo de Tolosa is located in downtown San Luis Obispo on the beautiful grounds of the Mission Plaza. It was Father Serra's fifth mission, dedicated in 1772. It is believed that tile roofs had their beginning here after the flaming arrows of Indians continually set fire to the original roofs of tule or rush. Father Serra's vestments and other rare religious items are preserved in the mission museum. Open daily summer 9 A.M. to 5 P.M.; winter 9 A.M. to 4 P.M.

Mission San Miguel is located about forty miles north of San Luis Obispo in Paso Robles, adjacent to the town of San Miguel. Noted for its murals, arches, and for a donkey named Ramona, this mission was founded in 1797, the sixteenth of the twenty-one that were built. The frescoes on the walls of the church are still intact. Never having been restored, the frescoes offer a unique look at history. Open daily 9 A.M. to 5 P.M.

LIBRARIES. In Santa Barbara's public library, paintings are displayed in the Faulkner Gallery, a nice public venue showing off selections of art made by the Santa Barbara Art Association. All kinds of art can be seen in this changing exhibit hall. Located at 40 E. Anapamu St. in the central branch of the public library, directly across the street from the county courthouse; (805) 962–7653.

The Krotona Library in Ojai Valley is the largest library of the occult on the West Coast. The library contains books on religion, spirituality, meditation, and similar subjects. Hours: 1:00 P.M. to 4:00 P.M., daily; (805) 646–2653.

MUSEUMS. San Luis Obispo. *San Luis Obispo County Historical Museum,* 696 Monterey St. at Broad; (805) 543–0638. Full of Californian and Indian artifacts and relics from San Luis Obispo's past. In the old Carnegie Free Library. Open Wednesday through Sunday, 10:00 A.M. to 4:00 P.M. Free.

The Shakespeare Press Museum, on the campus of California Polytechnic University at the north end of town; (805) 546–1108. Houses antique press equipment. Tours are possible through the campus Graphics Communication Department. Free.

The San Luis Obispo Art Center, 1010 Broad St., (805) 543–8562, displays works of art by local artists as well as those from out of town. Hours: Noon to 5:00 P.M., Tuesday through Sunday. Free.

Malibu. *The J. Paul Getty Museum,* 17985 Pacific Coast Hwy.; (213) 454–6541. Precisely modeled on an ancient Roman villa, the Villa dei Papiri, once situated in the old city of Herculaneum. The villa was destroyed in A.D. 79 when Mount Vesuvius erupted. In making his decision to replicate the villa, Getty didn't miss a thing. Everything (from the colonnades and the frescoes to the gardens) resembles the original. The museum itself is one of the most important in the country as far as private art collections are concerned. Greek and Roman antiquities, fine Rennaisance and Baroque paintings, and decorative arts from eighteenth- and nineteenth-century France abound within the museum.

Hours: Monday through Friday, from mid-June to mid-September; Tuesday through Saturday the balance of the year; 10:00 A.M. to 5:00 P.M. Free but reservations are recommended for parking. (For more details on the J. Paul Getty Museum, see Los Angeles "Practical Information," *Museums.*)

Ojai. *The Ojai Valley Museum,* 109 S. Montgomery St.; (805) 646–2290. Artifacts of the Oak Grove and Chumash Indian tribe, the area's first residents, are on display.

The California Oil Museum, 1003 E. Main St.; (805) 525–6672 (in Santa Paula). One of the two oil museums in the country. Learn all about oil production; scenes from the movie *Oklahoma Crude* were shot at this site. Hours: Wednesday through Sunday, 10:00 A.M. to 4:30 P.M. Free.

Oxnard. *CEC/Seabee Museum.* At the Naval Construction Battalion Center, Channel Islands Blvd. and Ventura Rd; (805) 982–5103. Uniforms and other memorabilia of the U.S. Navy Seabees. Hours: Monday through Friday, 8:00

A.M. to 4:30 P.M.; Saturday 9:00 A.M. to 4:30 P.M.; Sunday 12:30 P.M. to 4:30 P.M. Free.

Santa Barbara. *Santa Barbara Historical Society Museum,* 136 E. De la Guerra Street; (805) 966–1601. Reflections of Santa Barbara's past exist here in the form of documents, paintings, costumes, and a number of rare mementos from Indian, Spanish, Mexican, and American eras. Guided tours available at 1:30 P.M., Wednesday and Sunday. Open: Noon to 5:00 P.M., Tuesday through Friday; 1:00 P.M. to 5:00 P.M., Saturday, Sunday. Free.

Museum of Natural History, Puesta del Sol Rd., two blocks north of the mission; (805) 682–4711. Features exhibits on mammals, birds, fish, reptiles, plant life, and geology of the Pacific Coast and Channel Islands. Planetarium. Open 9:00 A.M. to 5:00 P.M.; summer hours begin at 10:00 A.M. Free.

Santa Barbara Museum of Art, 1130 State St.; (805) 963–4364. Changing exhibits are dominant in this small but cheerful art museum. Permanent exhibits include ancient sculpture, oriental art, and an American art collection. On weekends films are shown. Free guided tour, Tuesday through Friday 1:30 P.M., Saturday and Sunday 2:00 P.M. Open Tuesday through Saturday 11:00 A.M. to 5:00 P.M.; Sunday noon to 5:00 P.M. Free.

MUSIC. The *Ojai Music Festival* takes place each May in Libbey Park, Ojai, offering three days of music ranging from classical to rock and jazz.

San Luis Obispo's *County Symphony* performs classical as well as contemporary productions throughout the year.

San Luis Obispo's *Mozart Festival* is held in early August. The settings vary: The Mission San Luis Obispo de Tolosa, the Cal Poly Theater, and the Mission San Miguel in Cambria are among them. Besides the concerts and recitals by professionals and well-known visiting guest artists, there are seminars, workshops, and outdoor concerts involving local musicians as well as guest artists. The main concerts are held evenings as well as afternoons, with some candlelight programs in the evenings at the missions. Not all the music is Mozart; there are Haydn and other classical composers as well. Individual tickets range from $6.00–$13.50. Write the San Luis Obispo Mozart Festival at P.O. Box 311, San Luis Obispo, CA 93406, or call (805) 543–4580.

San Luis Obispo's *Civic Ballet* puts on a performance of the *Nutcracker Suite* every Christmas season. Exact dates and ticket information can be obtained from the Chamber of Commerce; (805) 543–1323.

In Santa Barbara annual concert seasons are presented by the *Los Angeles Philharmonic* and *Santa Barbara Symphony Orchestras.* The LA Philharmonic plays in Santa Barbara at the Arlington Theater, 1317 State Street; (805) 965–5392. The Santa Barbara Symphony plays in Santa Barbara at the Arlington Theater in April and November. In Ojai, the Santa Barbara Symphony plays at Libbey Mall.

STAGE. Santa Barbara is the center of theatrical life in this section along the coast. On the site of the city's first theater, built about 1873 by Jose Lobero, is its present county-owned playhouse, the *Lobero Theater,* 33 E. Canon Perdido St. This house presents local products as well as national touring groups.

The Arlington Center for the Performing Arts, a grandiose Spanish-style theater, features leading performers in music, drama, and dance. For information regarding productions, prices, and times on either Santa Barbara theater, call (805) 963–0761.

SHOPPING. San Luis Obispo has much to offer in the way of shopping. Stores are located throughout the city and are housed in buildings that are historic sites. This offers a combination of shopping and sightseeing.

The downtown area is the city's main shopping district. Two minimalls are located there. One, *The Network,* houses twenty-two stores and was once a department store in the 1900s. The other, *The Creamery,* was used as just that in the early 1900s. *Madonna Road Plaza,* with large department stores, restaurants, and supermarkets, is the largest shopping center in the area. On Madonna Rd.

Ojai is known for its small shops, boutiques, and antique shops. *The Arcade,* downtown Ojai, built in early 1900 Spanish-style architecture, is the main shopping center. A variety of stores is available there. *Meiners Oaks,* past Ojai off Hwy. 33, is an eighty-year-old ranch site with stores dispersed among the trees and fruit orchards. Shopping can be accomplished in a relaxed environment. *Winkworth Antiques,* 310 E. Matilija, has furniture from around the world and a research library in the back room, while *Hodge Podge Antiques and the Doll Doctor,* 209 N. Montgomery, has a display of antique dolls, along with its furniture. *Bart's Books,* 302 W. Matilija, is a world-famous outdoor bookstore and flower shop. After hours you're left on your honor. If you see something you like, you're expected to throw some coins into the patio grillwork.

Solvang is lined with stores featuring products imported from Denmark as well as other European countries. The town is superb for gift buying, with Danish products sold in almost every store.

About twenty antique shops with great bargains can be found in **Cambria.**

Malibu has various shops within its boundaries: clothing (especially beach wear), antiques, and gifts. They are found both along the coast and within the canyons.

DINING OUT. Restaurants north along the coast are about as varied as the coastal communities that thrive there. From small cafés to grand dining establishments, there's something for everyone. Price ranges are as follows (per person, with no wine or tip included; for more information see "Facts at Your Fingertips"): *Expensive,* $25.00 and up; *Moderate,* $10.00–$25.00; *Inexpensive,* below $10.00.

MALIBU
Area Code 213

Sandcastle Restaurant. 28128 W. Pacific Coast Hwy. in Paradise Cove; 457–2503. *Expensive to Moderate.* Situated right on the sand, this restaurant offers excellent seafood and Continental cuisine. Open daily for breakfast, lunch, and dinner. Major credit cards.

Moonshadows. 20356 Pacific Coast Hwy.; 456–3010. Steak and seafood are specialties in this restaurant. A lot of wood and hanging plants give the restaurant a rustic yet elegant look. Prices for dinner range from $8.95 to $19.95. Located right on the beach. Reservations recommended. Major credit cards.

The Chart House. 18412 Pacific Coast Hwy; 454–9321. Features steak and lobster in a rustic setting on the ocean. Reservations are necessary, especially on the weekends. Prices range from $8.45 a dinner to $17.95 for lobster. No CB.

La Scala Malibu. *Expensive-Moderate.* 3835 Cross Creek Rd; 456–1979. The tables are arranged informally for relaxed dining by the beach. There is an enclosed patio with a decorated Florentine tile floor. Specialties include roasted red peppers, gazpacho, rigatoni "Malibu," and pollo al forno. Excellent wine list. Cappuccino and espresso; light desserts. Lunch, Tuesday through Friday; dinner, daily except Monday. AE, MC, V.

Nantucket Light. 22706 Pacific Coast Hwy.; 456–3105. *Moderate.* Offers ocean-view dining. The fare is basically seafood. Salad bar. Reservations recommended. AE, MC, V.

Something's Fishy. 18753 Pacific Coast Hwy; 459–3192. *Moderate.* An excellent sushi bar features extremely fresh fish. Steak and tempura dishes are available as well. A very popular place. AE, MC, V.

OXNARD/VENTURA/CHANNEL ISLANDS
Area Code 805

Port Royal. *Expensive-Moderate.* 3900 Bluefin Circle, Channel Islands Harbor; 984–1919. A haute gourmet menu, starring flaming desserts. Entertainment nightly. Lunch and dinner daily. Sunday brunch. AE, MC, V.

Castagnola's. *Moderate.* Fisherman's Wharf, 3910 Channel Islands Blvd.; 985–3922. Dine on the docks with a pleasant view of the harbor. Many fresh seafood selections amid nautical decor. Breakfast, lunch, and dinner daily. Major credit cards.

Lobster Trap. *Moderate.* Casa Sirena Marina Hotel, 3605 Peninsula Rd., Channel Islands Harbor; 985–6361. Seafood is the specialty; all baking is done on the premises. Steak and prime ribs are also featured. Lunch Monday through Saturday; dinner daily. Sunday brunch. Major credit cards.

The Whale's Tail. *Moderate.* 3950 Bluefin Circle, Channel Islands Harbor; 985–2511. Fresh fish, prime steaks, and an elaborate salad boat. Entertainment nightly. Lunch Monday through Saturday; dinner daily. Major credit cards.

Dominick's Italian Restaurant. *Moderate-Inexpensive.* 477 N. Oxnard; 483–7933. Italian cuisine. Dinner daily. MC, V.

Maykro Restaurant. *Moderate-Inexpensive.* 115 Esplanade Dr.; 485–9511. Danish-style liver and onions and carrot cake. Unusual. Lunch Monday through Saturday; dinner Monday through Friday. MC, V.

OJAI
Area Code 805

The Ranch House. 102 Besant Rd.; 646–2360. *Expensive–Moderate.* This superb restaurant, hidden on a back street, bakes all its bread right on the premises and grows its own herbs. Known as a gourmet garden restaurant, The Ranch House has received the Holiday Magazine award. Reservations recommended.

Antonio's Mexican Restaurant. *Moderate.* 106 S. Montgomery; 646–6353. Authentic Mexican food and drink. Open Tuesday through Sunday for lunch and dinner. Located in downtown Ojai across from the Art Center. Open 11:30 A.M.–9:00 P.M. MC, V.

L'Auberge Restaurant. *Moderate.* 314 El Paseo St.; 646–2288. French cuisine cooked to perfection. Extensive wine selection. Open for dinner every day except Tuesday; lunch weekends. Reservations recommended. MC, V.

The Gaslight Restaurant. *Moderate.* 11432 N. Ventura Ave.; 646–5990. Veal, steak, fresh seafood, and German dishes are the specialties. Prime ribs served on Saturday. Excellent cocktail lounge. Reservations recommended. Open Tuesday–Sunday 5:00 P.M.–10:00 P.M. AE, MC, V.

Ojai Valley Inn and Country Club. Country Club Dr.; 646–5511. *Moderate.* American cuisine served in a country club-style dining room. Open for breakfast, lunch, and dinner daily. Closes at 9:00 P.M. Reservations recommended. No credit cards.

MONTECITO
Area Code 805

Olive Mill Bistro. *Expensive-Moderate.* 1295 Coast Village Rd.; 969–4900. A comfortable dining room serving Continental dishes. Nice curry Bombay. Dinner daily. Valet parking. AE, MC, V.

Café del Sol. *Moderate–Inexpensive.* 516 San Ysidro Rd.; 969–0448. This café is designed in Mexican Motifs and is set amid a complex of sophisticated boutiques. Good salads and Mexican- and Spanish-style dishes. Outdoor patio. Sunday brunch. Lunch and dinner daily. AE, MC.

SANTA BARBARA
Area Code 805

La Chaumiere. *Expensive.* 1305 State St.; 962–5607. A tiny French restaurant with typical French specialties. A small but good menu. Lunch Tuesday through Friday; dinner Tuesday through Saturday. Major credit cards.

Talk of the Town. *Expensive.* 123 W. Gutierrez; 966–4910. A sophisticated Continental menu. Strict dress code: coats and ties for men, dresses for women. An extensive menu and a strong wine list. Lunch Monday through Friday; dinner daily. Major credit cards.

The Harbor Restaurant. *Expensive–Moderate.* 210 Stearns Wharf; 963–3311. On the wharf, specializing in local seafood and Maine lobster. Outdoor patio, cocktail lounge. AE, MC, V.

Casa de Sevilla. *Moderate.* 428 Chapala St.; 966–4370. Comfortable dining featuring Spanish-style as well as other Continental cuisines. Lunch and dinner Tuesday through Saturday. No DC.

Metro Café. *Moderate.* 734 State St.; 965–5942. This contemporary café features a wine bar with more than 2,000 wines. Lunches served on the patio and inside. AE, MC, V.

Suishin Sukiyaki. *Moderate.* 511 State St.; 962–1495. A soothing Japanese atmosphere, with a sushi bar as well as tatami rooms. Traditional Japanese dishes are featured. Dinner daily. Major credit cards.

Wine Cask. *Moderate.* 813 Anacapa St.; 966–9463. Wine bar for sampling best of the area as well as other California wines. Creative menu for light eating. All major credit cards.

The Eggception. *Inexpensive.* 1208 State St.; 965–7942. One hundred varieties of omelettes, plus other light items. Breakfast and lunch daily. MC, V.

SOLVANG
Area Code 805

The Danish Inn. *Moderate.* 1547 Mission Drive; 688–4813. Open daily, this restaurant, serving gourmet dishes prepared by award-winning chefs, is one of Solvang's most prestigious. A smorgasbord is served daily. A charming old windmill out front is its trademark. No DC.

Ballard's Store. *Moderate.* 2449 Baseline, Solvang; 688–5319. This restaurant was formerly a country store; it now boasts an international menu. Specialties include Long Island duckling and beef roulade. Budget price children's dinners. Home-baked breads and desserts. Dinner in the $10.00–$15.00 range from Tuesday through Saturday. MC, V.

Belle Terrass. *Moderate–Expensive.* 1564 Copenhagen; 688–2762. Northern-Italian cuisine. Veal dishes great. Lunch, dinner daily. All major credit cards.

The Belgian Café. *Inexpensive.* 475 First St.; 688–6316. Modeled on a European sidewalk café, this restaurant offers Belgian waffles as its specialty. Solvang fruit wines are served here. Open daily 8:00 A.M.–5 P.M. Breakfast and lunch. No dinner. AE, MC, V.

Mollekroen Restaurant. *Inexpensive.* 435 Alisal Road; 688–4555. Open for lunch and dinner, the Mollekroen features a daily smorgasbord of close to thirty dishes. Major credit cards.

PISMO BEACH
Area Code 805

F. McLintock's Saloon and Dining House. *Moderate–Expensive.* 750 Mattie Rd., Shell Beach; 773–1892. Specializing in barbecued steaks and ribs as well as seafood. Western ambiance, ocean view. Reasonable children's menu. Dinner daily; Sunday breakfast. No reservations on Friday and Saturday nights. MC, V.

Trader Nicks. *Moderate.* 1601 Price St., Pismo Beach; 773–4711 or 773–5432. Ocean view dining in Polynesian atmosphere. Sunday champagne brunch. Entertainment and dancing nightly. Breakfast, lunch, and dinner daily.

Plessas Tavern. *Moderate-Inexpensive.* 891 Price St., Pismo Beach; 773–2060. A Continental menu served in a Mediterranean decor. Special children's menu. Lunch and dinner daily, except Tuesday. No credit cards.

Heidi's Delicatessen. *Inexpensive.* 323 Five Cities Dr., Pismo Beach; 773–1696. Authentic German home cooking. Imported and domestic beer and wine. Lunch and dinner.

SAN LUIS OBISPO
Area Code 805

Apple Farm Restaurant. *Moderate.* 2015 Monterey St.; 544–6100. The slogan here says it all, "Homemade Food Served with Country Charm." Open daily for breakfast, lunch, and dinner, this restaurant features freshly baked cornbread, homemade soup, and an array of meals cooked in an old-fashioned manner. No credit cards. No reservations.

Le Croissant. *Inexpensive.* 1117 Chorro St.; 541–8086. Specializing in all types of croissants. No credit cards.

1865. *Moderate-Expensive.* 1865 Monterey Street; 544–1865. Elegant decor creates a fine dining atmosphere. Open for lunch and dinner, daily. Prime rib is the specialty. Reservations are recommended. AE, MC, V.

William Randolf. *Moderate–Expensive.* 1850 Monterey St.; 543–3333. Named after the man himself. Interior is decorated in theme of Hearst's animal collection, with flamingo motifs adorning the walls. Open daily for dinner. AE, V, MC, CB, DC.

San Luis Bay Inn. *Moderate.* Avila Rd., Avila Beach; 595–2097. From your table you can watch the moonbeams dance across the ocean. Cuisine is delicious, prepared with skill and affection. More than 400 California and imported wines. Serves all three meals. MC, V.

Los Hermanos. *Inexpensive.* 736 Osos Street; 544–5198. Open for lunch and dinner, this restaurant features a large selection of authentic Mexican food.

Entertainment Sunday, Monday, and Wednesday nights. Reservations are recommended. Major credit cards.

Madonna Inn. *Moderate-Inexpensive.* 100 Madonna Road; 543–3000. Located in the world-famous Madonna Inn, this restaurant is open for breakfast, lunch, and dinner, and features a varied menu offering everything from eggs Benedict to filet mignon. No credit cards, but they do accept personal checks.

Café Roma. *Moderate-Inexpensive.* 1819 Osos Street; 541–6800. Spotlights authentic Northern Italian cooking in an elegant setting. Lunch is served Monday through Friday, dinner Monday through Saturday. Reservations are recommended. MC, V.

MORRO BAY
Area Code 805

The Galley. *Expensive-Moderate.* 899 Embarcadero; 772–2806. There's a lot of fresh fish on this menu, as well as simply grilled chicken and steak. Deep-fried oysters are a specialty. There is a large wine selection, plus ports and sherries by the glass. Good view. Lunch and dinner daily; breakfast on weekends. No credit cards.

Dorns. *Moderate.* 801 Market St.; 772–4415. This cheerful bistro offers a splendid view of Morro Bay. Breakfast specials include buttermilk pancakes, pecan waffles and fresh vegetable omelettes. Fresh local fish is broiled or fried and treated properly. The wine list is small. Breakfast, lunch, and dinner. No credit cards.

Dutch's Griddle House. *Moderate.* 2738 N. Main St.; 772–8645. This restaurant was built out of original Morro Bay stone. More gourmet than most in the area, serving such specialties as sauteed Morro Bay oysters in cream sauce atop fresh spinach. Dinners include soup and salad. Small wine list. Lunch and dinner. MC, V.

Grey Heron. *Moderate.* 901 Embarcadero; 772–5467. Louisiana Creole cooking. All major credit cards.

Harbor Hut. *Moderate.* 1205 Embarcadero; 772–2255. Live entertainment combined with seafood and steaks. Dine over the waters. Lunch and dinner. Open 7 days. All major credit cards.

Mister K's Anchorage. *Moderate.* 998 Embarcadero; 772–2424. Seafood specialities. Lobster. MC, AE.

The Fondue Pot. *Inexpensive.* 213 Beach St.; 772–8900. Fine salads and homemade soups. The best freshly baked breads and pastries in the area. Shrimp and beef bourguignonne as well as cheese fondue bourguignonne. Excels in down-home, hearty breakfast. Breakfast, lunch, and dinner. DC, MC, V.

CAMBRIA
Area Code 805

Brambles Dinner House. *Moderate–Expensive.* 4005 Burton Dr.; 927–4716. Fresh seafood and steaks featured in a Victorian atmosphere. Children's menu. Dinner daily. AE, MC, V.

Grey Fox Inn. *Moderate.* 4095 Burton Dr. at Center St.; 927–3305. A Continental menu, with fresh seafood and prime ribs. Brunch Saturday and Sunday. Patio dining facilities. Dinner daily. MC, V.

 NIGHT LIFE. The largest concentration of nightlife activities in the area is of course in nearby Los Angeles, but there is also a blend of night-owl activities in most of the coastal cities, with a definite emphasis on the more subdued atmosphere, except in Malibu and Santa Barbara, which are a little more lively.

Santa Barbara. Disco is big at *Peppers,* 27 Canon Perdido Rd.; for bar life, try *Joe's Café,* 512 State St.; a fifty-year-old place with a casual dinner atmosphere. For more activity, visit *Maggie McFly's* at 536 State St.; a funky bar and restaurant especially intriguing to *Casablanca* fans because of the movie's memorabilia that decorate the place. *Flapper Alley,* at 217 State Street (963–6608), offers a unique roaring-20s atmosphere close the beach. Dancing Tuesday through Saturday. Full-service bar.

A night spot popular with singles in Santa Barbara is *1129,* at 1129 State St. Besides being a fine restaurant offering Continental cuisine from a large menu of fish, chicken, and beef dishes, crepes, quiches, and salads, the bar beckons many to hang out until all hours with lures of live music and outdoor patio out front, complete with Spanish flavor; a favorite place to be during Santa Barbara's Fiesta Days in August, when margaritas are cheap and mariachi bands liven up the place even more.

In **Malibu,** *Pasquales,* 22724 W. Pacific Coast Hwy., is a jazz club featuring up-and-coming as well as established artists. The club is located right at the beach. *Topanga Corral,* 2034 S. Topanga Canyon Blvd., offers country and western music as well as rock n' roll and the blues. Dinner is also available.

Oxnard. *Whale's Tail,* at 3950 Bluefin Circle at the marina in Channel Islands Harbor, has entertainment nightly. This night spot overlooks the harbor and specializes in seafood and beef dishes.

In **Solvang** visit the Ranch House, 102 Besant Rd., which offers a Continental menu in an outdoor setting with live chamber music.

San Luis Obispo. At the *San Luis Bay Inn,* Avila Beach, entertainment and dancing are offered every night.

Pismo Beach. *F. McLintock's Saloon and Dining House* at 750 Mattee Rd. on Shell Beach offers entertainment nightly. A popular local hangout, this saloon is set in an Old West atmosphere, with a view of the ocean.

In **Morro Bay,** try the *Golden Tee,* at 19 Country Club Rd., which features Fletcher Peek on Sunday evenings performing, among other tunes, his original song about Morro Bay. For some live jazz, there's the *Hungry Tiger,* 781 Market St. And for something romantic and different, come aboard the *Tiger's Folly,* 1205 Embarcadero, a cruiser that offers cocktails, food, and a thrilling moonlight ride. The *Folly* departs from the harbor four times each evening, daily, June through September; weekends only, October through May.

In **Cambria** take in the Hearst Castle Show, Box 1796 in Cambria, which is located in the showroom of the *San Simeon Restaurant.* The show covers more of the newspaper magnate's memorabilia. A must for those who have yet to go on the Hearst Castle tour.

THE HIGH SIERRAS

The name Sierra Nevadas was placed on a map for the first time by a Franciscan missionary, Pedro Font, a member of the Anza expedition that went overland from Mexico to establish a settlement on San Francisco Bay. From a hill near the mouth of the Sacramento River he beheld a scene in east central California that he described in his journal in 1776 as " . . . a great, snow covered range (*una gran sierra nevada*) which seemed to me to run from south-southeast to north-northwest."

The great Sierra Nevada mountain range is a westward tilted fault-block of granite about 450 miles long and 60 to 80 miles wide. Contained within the range, as its southern end, are two great national parks, Sequoia National Park and Kings Canyon National Park. The two parks embrace more than 1,300 miles of spectacular granite mountains, deep canyons, and magnificent forests, lakes, and waterfalls.

Two features especially distinguish these parks from others in the world: their forests of gigantic sequoia trees and their extensive lofty mountains. The Sierra Crest rises to its highest point at Mount Whitney (14,495 feet), the highest peak in the United States outside Alaska. Here, too, is "the largest living thing" in the world: the General Sherman giant sequoia tree, biggest of all the sequoias (274.9 ft above the base).

Sequoia Park's General Sherman Tree is estimated to be 3,500 years old. An adult human could comfortably lie crosswide on several of its massive branches. The tree's weight has been estimated at 2,145 tons—as heavy as a small oceangoing steamship. It also has been estimated that the General Sherman Tree could produce 600,000 board feet of lumber—enough to build a small town.

Kings Canyon Park also boasts giant sequoias. Its General Grant Tree is only five feet shorter than the Sherman Tree and exceeds the Sherman's base circumference by six feet. In 1965 Kings Canyon was greatly enhanced when President Johnson signed into law the dream of naturalist John Muir, adding the Cedar Grove tract and the Tehipite Valley to the national park area.

Other notable sights in these parks include Tharp Log, where the road goes through rather than around the trunk; Moro Rock, climbed by a safe, 300-foot stairway for a view over the Great Western Divide; and Crystal Cave, a marble cave with elaborate limestone formations.

Both parks offer an abundance of hiking and camping possibilities, and tours are available. From Southern California, the gateway city to the national parks is Visalia, county seat of Tulare County.

Tulare County is America's third highest-ranking county in agricultural income. The snow pack in its nearby mountains yields thousands of acres of feet of water each year, which is delivered through an extensive network of dams and canals to the farms and ranches in the San Joaquin Valley—one of the world's richest agricultural basins. Thousands of acres of grapes head Tulare's list of cash income, followed by citrus crops, olives, walnuts, plums, peaches, and nectarines.

Visalia is located close to the foothills of the Sierra Nevada mountain range, where Hwy. 198 (General's Hwy.), gateway to the Sequoias, meets U.S. Hwy. 99. Day tours from Visalia to Kings Canyon and Sequoia National Parks are available through Visalia's Rucksack Mountain Shop.

Inyo-Mono, at the eastern slope of the Sierra Nevada Range, bears the imprint of yesterday's grizzled fortune seeker—an imprint still found today in such mining ghost towns as Bodie. Both Inyo and Mono counties are part of the Owens Valley, the most important watershed for Los Angeles; it yields 80 percent of the city's water supply and a significant portion of its clean hydroelectric power.

Bishop, a major Inyo city, is an outfitting center for hunters and fishers who cast in the area's roughly 2,000 trout-filled lakes and

Southern Part of the High Sierras

streams. Every notch in the great nearby mountain wall is marked by a trout stream trickling down to the highway. The prized golden trout, found in few other locales, is caught in the higher waters. The area abounds in game birds and deer during open-hunting season.

Bishop is also the site of the Laws Railroad Museum and historical site. Independence, the county seat forty miles south, is home to the Inyo County Museum, also known as the Eastern California Museum.

The Eastern High Sierras are well known for their Alpine skiing conditions in winter. Chair and gondola facilities, in addition to classes for a wide range of abilities, are provided at both the Mammoth and June Mountain ski areas. A wide range of excellent accommodations and restaurants can be found in these villages.

The Palisade Glaciers overlooking Big Pine, twenty-eight miles north of Independence, are small as glaciers go but have the distinction of being the southernmost "living" glaciers on this continent. (A "living" glacier is one that is continually cracking off and melting at its lowest fringe, supplied anew at its upper level by the winter snows.) These glaciers cover about two square miles and are located at about the same latitude as the palm trees in the San Joaquin Valley on the other side of the Sierra Nevada range.

PRACTICAL INFORMATION FOR
THE HIGH SIERRAS

 HOW TO GET THERE. From Los Angeles take Interstate 5 (Golden Gate Fwy.) to Hwy. 99. Follow 99 north to Tulare and then Highway 63 north to Visalia. Then take 198 east into the park (General's Hwy.). The trip is 220 miles (five hours) to Lodgepole Visitors' Center, 250 miles (six hours) to Grant Grove Visitors' Center, 280 miles (seven hours) to Cedar Grove Visitors' Center.

General's Hwy.—the main road that connects Sequoia and Kings Canyon National Parks—is closed from November through the end of April. The highway winds through the scenic sequoia belt for forty-six miles. It's a two-hour drive from Sequoia's Ash Mountain entrance to Grant Grove in Kings Canyon National Park.

TELEPHONES. The High Sierras region is served by two area codes: 619 covers the southern portion, as far north as Visalia; 209 includes Visalia and the area north of it as far as Stockton.

HOTELS AND MOTELS. Visalia. *Holiday Inn.* 9000 Airport Dr; (209) 733–9000. 260 units. TV, indoor and outdoor pool, coffee shop, and dining room. Pets allowed.

Best Western Visalia Inn Motel. 623 W. Main St; (209) 732–4561. Forty units, TV, pool. Small pets invited.

Lamp Liter Inn. 3300 W. Mineral King Ave.; (209) 732–4511. 100 units. TV, pool, coffee shop, and dining room. Dancing.

TraveLodge Motel. 4645 W. Mineral King Ave.; (209) 732–5611. Seventy-eight rooms, some with kitchen units in a two-story property. All have TV. Pool, coffee shop, and dining rooms. Pets welcome.

Bishop. *High Sierra Lodge.* 1005 N. Main; (619) 873–8426. Fifty-one rooms, heated pool, indoor spa, fishing facilities.

Best Western Westerner Motel. 150 E. Elm St.; (619) 873–3564. Fifty-five rooms and suites. Pool, color TV. Some waterbeds.

Best Western Holiday Lodge. 1025 N. Main St.; (619) 873–3543. Pool, spa, restaurant on premises. Fish cleaning, freezer facilities.

Sequoia National Park. *Stony Creek Lodge.* For information, call (209) 565–3373.

Kings Canyon National Park. *Wilsonia Lodge.* For information, call (209) 335–2310.

HOW TO GET AROUND AND TOURS. Preferably by car, but bus tours from Visalia to the national parks are available through the Rucksack Mountain Shop, 1043 S. Mooney; (209) 732–4404. Tours are conducted on a charter basis only and cover all the outlying areas except Yosemite; the fee is $1.00 per mile. The parks also offer package bus tours for up to three days and two nights. For information and reservations, call (209) 565–3373.

TOURIST INFORMATION. All chambers of commerce in the area, unfortunately, offer minimal information. But try anyway. *Visalia Chamber of Commerce,* 720 W. Mineral King Ave., Visalia, CA 93277; (209) 734–5876.

Tulare County Chamber of Commerce, Room 100, Courthouse, Visalia, CA 93277; (209) 733–6513.

Bishop Chamber of Commerce, 690 N. Main St., Bishop, CA 93514; (619) 873–8405.

Mammoth Lakes Chamber of Commerce is especially informative about ski conditions in the area. Contact Mammoth Lakes Chamber of Commerce, P.O. Box 123, Mammoth Lakes, CA 93540; (714) 934–2712.

Inyo-Mono Interagency Visitor Center is also helpful. At P.O. Box 889, Lone Pine, CA 93545; (714) 876–4252.

For *Sequoia* and *Kings Canyon National Park,* general information is available by calling (209) 565–3341, ext. 15 (Address: Three Rivers, CA 93271), and lodging information is obtained from the hospitality service there at (209) 565–3306.

At Sequoia, Ash Mountain Visitor Center at (209) 565–3341 is open daily from 8:00 A.M. to 4:30 P.M. Information includes books, maps, and general pamphlets on the area, plus wilderness permits.

Lodgepole Visitor Center, also at Sequoia, can be reached by calling (209) 565–3364. Open daily from 9:00 A.M. to 5:00 P.M., this information booth has pamphlets, maps, exhibits, and books on the area. Wilderness permits may also be obtained there.

Grant Grover Visitor Center in Kings Canyon is open daily from 8:00 A.M. to 5:00 P.M. and offers information, maps, and a free eleven-minute slide program on the area. For specific information by phone, call (209) 335–2315 about activities and road and weather conditions in the area. After 5:00 P.M., call (209) 335–2511 for a recorded message on conditions.

 CAMPING. Sequoia and Kings Canyon National Parks. Campsites are available only on a first-come, first-served basis, except for Lodgepole Campground. From Memorial Day weekend through Labor Day weekend, Lodgepole campsites can be reserved up to eight weeks in advance at any California Ticketron outlet for a nominal charge. Campsites cost $5.00 per campsite, per night, May 15–October 15; free camping the remainder of year.

Reservations can be made only in person or by mail. No electrical, water, or sewer hookups are available in any campground. The concessionaire has pay showers available in the following areas: Giant Forest, Stony Creek, Grant Grove, and Cedar Grove. For information, call (209) 565–3341, or write Sequoia and Kings Canyon National Parks, Three Rivers, CA 93271.

Inyo-Mono. In the heart of the Mammoth Lakes area and throughout both counties many campgrounds, ranging from undeveloped tent sites to improved RV campgrounds and parks with complete hookups, are available. In the Mammoth area, Camp High Sierra, open for family vacations from mid-June to early September, features hot showers, toilets, and a recreation lodge. For information call (213) 485–4853 (Los Angeles).

 STATE AND NATIONAL PARKS. Sequoia and Kings Canyon National Parks are located in the southern part of the Sierra Nevada of California. The geologic story of the mountain range and therefore of the two parks covers a period of about 400 million years and begins in the Paleozoic Era. The parks' three Visitor Centers feature exhibits portraying the history and local geology of the area. The three Visitor Centers are Ash Mountain (south entrance), Lodgepole (Giant Forest), and Grant Grove (north entrance). Sequoia and Kings Canyon National Parks are accessible only from the west via Visalia, Fresno, and Bakersfield.

MUSEUMS. *Eastern California Museum* (Inyo County Museum), 155 Grant St., Independence; (619) 878–2010. Founded in 1928, this is a frontier-style museum located in a picturesque high-desert setting. The museum features exhibits of Native American and pioneer artifacts, photographs, documents, and scientific data. Free.

Laws Railroad Museum and Historical Site, Bishop; (619) 873–5950. The museum is built on the site of the Old Laws Railroad Depot and agent's house. The depot is filled with many artifacts of the old railroad days, including "Locomotive Number 9" and its little strings of cars standing on the original tracks, plus switches and bunkers. Other buildings that can be viewed include the original Laws Post Office, the Wells Fargo Building, and the Assay Office, all filled with antiques. Free.

Tulare County Museum in Mooney Grove near Visalia, 27000 Mooney Blvd.; (209) 733–6613. A large, 150-acre oak grove boasts ten buildings bursting with historical exhibits of Indian artifacts and early farm equipment. Of particular interest is an antique gun collection and a fully functional log cabin. The entrance fee is fifty cents.

 DINING. Visalia. *Finni's Ristorante.* 3016 S. Mooney. Italian cuisine, steaks, cocktails. All major credit cards.

Hong Kong Restaurant. 417 E. Center. Chinese fare. No credit cards.

Vintage Press. 216 N. Willis. Lunch, dinner, and cocktails. All major cards.

Bishop. *La Pinata.* 106 MacIver. Lunch and dinner of fine Mexican cuisine. MC, V.

Enrico's. 1015 N. Main. American and Italian cuisine. Steak, veal, lasagna, manicotti, and pizza are specialties. MC, V.

 SKI RESORTS. Inyo National Forest. *Mammoth Mountain,* off U.S. Hwy. 395. The closest first-class ski area to Los Angeles and one of the most popular, with 23 lifts. Excellent springtime skiing. Longest run is 2½ miles, with a 3,100-foot vertical drop. Eating facilities. Open November–June. Phone (619) 934–2571 or write Mammoth Mountain, P.O. Box 24, Mammoth Lakes 93546.

Sequoia National Park. *Giant Forest,* off State Hwy. 198, 56 miles east of Visalia. Downhill skiing at Wolverton; cross-country skiing at Giant Forest Village. Open November–May. Phone visitors' center at (209) 565–3341.

Sierra National Forest. *China Peak,* on State Hwy. 168, 62 miles northeast of Fresno. Downhill skiing and marked cross-country trails. Restaurant, bar, heated swimming pool. Open mid-November–mid-April. Phone (209) 893–3316.

Yosemite National Park. *Badger Pass,* on Glacier Point Rd., 21 miles from Yosemite Valley. The state's oldest established ski area has slopes for beginning and intermediate skiers, plus marked ski touring trails through the woods.

Snack bar. Phone (209) 372–4691. *June Mountain,* four miles from U.S. Hwy. 395, off the June Lake exit. Downhill ski runs for all levels of expertise; 2,560 feet of vertical drop. Peanutsville area for young children learning to ski. Eating facilities, bar. Open mid-November–mid-April. Phone (619) 648–7733 or write June Mountain, P.O. Box 146, June Lake 93529.

THE MOJAVE DESERT AND
DEATH VALLEY

by
DIANA RICO

*Diana Rico is a Hollywood-based journalist specializing in the arts.
Her articles have appeared in* California, Architectural Digest, Arts &
Architecture, *the* Los Angeles Herald Examiner, *the* L.A. Reader, *and
many other publications. She has a special interest in the Mojave/Death
Valley area.*

John Steinbeck called it "a great and mysterious wasteland, a sun-
punished place. It is a mystery, something concealed and waiting."
Steinbeck was writing of his crossing of the great Southern California

desert, and although his travels with his dog Charley took place over twenty years ago, not much has changed. The desert today still seems at once frighteningly brutal and hauntingly calm, still evokes mystery and encourages meditation, still appears astoundingly beautiful in its harsh starkness.

Steinbeck was driving across the Mojave, a vast, arid stretch that begins just north of the San Bernardino Mountains along the northern edge of Los Angeles and extends north 100 miles into the Eureka Valley and east 200 miles to the Colorado River, forming a gigantic L. Located in the northeast crook of the L is Death Valley, aptly named by a party of white settlers who crossed it on their way to the California gold fields in 1849. Death Valley is bounded on the west by the Panamint Range and on the east by the Grapevine, Funeral, and Black Mountains. Both the Mojave and Death Valley are places of rare natural beauty, where life has adapted to the most brutal conditions imaginable and where "at night in [the] waterless air," as Steinbeck observed, "the stars come down just out of reach of your fingers."

Mojave, the "High Desert"

The Mojave is known as the High Desert because of its high elevations, which range from 3,000 to 5,000 feet above sea level. Broad, sandy basins alternate with bleached salt flats and rough mountain terrain. Daytime temperatures reach over 100 degrees Fahrenheit in the summer and hover around 50 or 60 degrees in the winter, and rainfall is sparse—a scant five inches per year.

Flora and fauna have had to adapt in unusual ways in order to survive in this unfriendly clime. Plant life has developed ways of living for long periods of time without water—the creosote bush gathers the scarce moisture by growing its roots close to the surface of the earth; mesquite drops its roots as deep as 60 feet in order to tap underground water; cacti store water in their thick stems. Animals are mostly nocturnal; the kangaroo rat, the desert tortoise, jackrabbits, snakes, and coyotes have learned to avoid the killing daytime sun.

Traveling North

Take California State Hwy. 14 north through Antelope Valley, the corner of the L shape that forms the Mojave Desert. Three miles north of the Los Angeles County line you'll find Rosamond, a small town dating to the cattle and mining days of the late nineteenth century. Gold Panning Days are celebrated in Rosamond the first weekend in March; the festivities include a gold panning contest, a deep-pit barbecue, and a burro claim-staking race. Rosamond is of particular interest

The Mojave Desert Area

to rockhounds, who can find petrified wood, palm root, green agate, and green jasper in the surrounding area.

Five miles west of Rosamond is the historic Burton's Tropico Gold Mine and Mill, Southern California's largest standing gold mill. Tons of the ore were taken from this mine between 1894, when owner Ezra M. Hamilton first struck pay dirt, and 1956, when the local mining district was shut down. Today visitors can take guided tours through a 900-foot shaft, see original mining tools and drills in place, and have the milling process explained in detail. Below the mine stands the original gold mill, a rickety network of corrugated metal buildings and wooden catwalks clinging tenaciously to the side of a hill.

North of Rosamond, where Hwy. 58 cuts into Hwy. 14 from the east, the town of Mojave nestles in the foothills of the Sierra Nevada Mountains. Mojave started out as a rough-and-ready railroad center in 1876, and it quickly became a gathering point for the wagons hauling ore from the many outlying mining areas. The famous twenty-mule teams used to bring in ten tons of borax per wagon from the Harmony Works in Death Valley 165 miles away. Gold was discovered in 1894, and from then until the government closed the mines in 1942 Mojave lived through cycles of mining booms broken by periodic calm.

The old mining days are commemorated by the Mojave Twenty-Mule Team Borax Terminus, a historical marker in front of the Mojave County Building, the original unloading site for the Death Valley borax.

At Edwards Air Force Base, just southeast of Mojave, thousands gathered to watch the Columbia Space Shuttle make two landings in 1981 and a third in 1982. The country's second largest air force base is used for the testing of experimental rocket and jet craft; each May, on Armed Forces Day, civilians can catch a glimpse of what goes on when the Edwards Flight Line is opened to the public.

Mojave is well known to Los Angelenos for a phenomenon that one can witness only in the spring: the wild flowers in bloom. Around the end of March and the beginning of April, the usually brown desert undergoes a dazzling change. Heliotrope and fiddler's neck, California poppies and red maidens, desert candles and yellow coreopsis make a fabulous display against the hills surrounding the town.

Another popular site for nature lovers and camera buffs is the brilliantly colored Red Rock Canyon, where many Westerns have been filmed. Located on Hwy. 14 about twenty-five miles north of Mojave, this State Recreation Area consists of 4,000 acres of uplifted lake bottom, sandy rolling hills, and clay cliffs eroded by hundreds of years of wind and sand into fabulous, weird shapes. In the early morning and late afternoon sun, the coloring of the cliffs is at its most spectacular.

Northeast of Mojave, on Hwy. 395, lies the historic Rand Mining District, an area still dotted with old abandoned mines and what's left of the original mining equipment. Consisting of the towns of Randsburg, Red Mountain, and Johannesburg, the Rand Mining District was the scene of major tungsten, gold, and silver strikes. The most famous was the 1895 gold discovery at the Yellow Aster Mine, which had miles of tunnels and produced $16 million worth of the precious metal in its day.

The nearby China Lake Naval Weapons Center is breathtaking, unspoiled desert country at its finest. Although most of the year it is closed to the public, hunting is allowed for a limited period in the fall, and two campsites are provided for overnight visitors.

From China Lake, Hwy. 178 meanders northeast into Death Valley. This route is studded with old ghost towns, the best of which is Ballarat, 100 miles from China Lake. Ballarat's heyday was at the turn of the century, when the little town served as a supply center for prospectors from the Panamint Valley. Today the visitor can see the remains of old cabins and adobe buildings—truly the ghost of what was once a bustling, brawling frontier town.

Death Valley

An examination of the topography of Death Valley National Monument is like a minilesson in geology. Two hundred million years ago, seas covered the area, depositing layers of sediment and fossils. Between five and thirty-five million years ago, faults in the earth's crust and folding and volcanic activity caused the mountain ranges to rise and the valley floor to drop. Later the valley was filled periodically by lakes, which eroded the surrounding rocks into fantastic formations and deposited the salts that now cover the floor of the basin.

Today Death Valley is the lowest spot in the continental United States, as well as one of the driest and one of the hottest—temperatures commonly reach over 120 degrees on summer days. November through March are the best months to visit the valley, when temperatures are at a more comfortable 60 or 70 degrees; in fact, the valley has become a popular winter vacation spot. It is an area characterized by variety: the landscape ranges from the arid alkali flats of the basin to the subalpine peaks of the Panamint Mountains, and about 600 species of plants and trees can be found. As in the Mojave, wildlife is primarily nocturnal, although in the mountain areas one can sometimes glimpse bighorn sheep and wild burros during the day.

At the northernmost tip of the monument, off Hwy. 190, is Scotty's Castle, an eccentric Spanish–Moorish conglomeration strangely at variance with its desolate locale. This $2.5 million mansion, begun in

1924 and never completed, takes its name from Walter Scott, better known as Death Valley Scotty, a legendary adventurer who, as the story goes, financed his shenanigans with mysterious gold taken from a secret mine. In actuality, Scott was financially backed by a Chicago millionaire named Albert Johnson, and the castle (although Scotty claimed to be its owner) was Johnson's winter vacation home. Guides tell tales of Scotty's exploits and explain the castle's unusual design on tours through the interiors; guests can also stroll through the surrounding grounds and outbuildings.

Death Valley was the original site of the Harmony Borax Works, from which the renowned twenty-mule teams hauled borax to the railroad town of Mojave. Those teams were a sight to behold: twenty mules hitched up to a single wagon whose rear wheels measured seven feet across and front wheels measured five, carrying a load of ten tons of borax to a terminus 165 miles away through burning desert! The mule teams hauled borax between 1884 and 1888, when the Harmony Works was closed down. Today you can visit the Harmony Borax Works Ruins, located on a spur road off State Hwy. 190 about fifty miles south of Scotty's Castle—the center of Death Valley National Monument. The remains of the refinery, outlying buildings, and mounds of borax give some idea of the activity that went on during the processing days. The nearby Borax Museum houses original mining machinery and historical displays in a building that used to serve as a boardinghouse for miners; the adjacent structure is the original twenty-mule team barn.

Near the Harmony Borax Works Ruins is Furnace Creek, where a visitor's center provides exhibits, an hourly slide program, evening naturalist programs, guided walks, and a variety of publications to help orient the traveler to the surrounding sights.

When you travel through Death Valley, be prepared to see landscapes unlike those anywhere else in the world. Marble Canyon, formed by water cutting deeply into the Cottonwood Mountains, has sheer walls of polished black limestone on which one can find petroglyphs etched long ago by the Native Americans who once inhabited the area. For face paint they used the red clay at the mouth of Golden Canyon, so called because in the late afternoon the canyon's walls glow a deep gold and red. Also beautiful in the late afternoon sun is Artists Drive, where the clay deposits of an alluvial fan have oxidized into a rainbow of colors.

Hikers will be especially interested in Telescope Peak, the highest point in the monument and certainly one of the most visually spectacular. From the summit both the highest point (Mount Whitney) and the lowest (the area near Badwater) in the country can be seen. Bristlecone pines, the world's oldest living things, flourish here at elevations above 10,000 feet.

To the east of the 11,000-foot-high Telescope Peak is Badwater, at 279.8 feet below sea level the lowest point in the United States accessible by car. The high amounts of chloride, sodium, and sulfate found in the spring-fed pool give Badwater its name. In the summer the surrounding region commonly reaches over 120 degrees, making it one of the hottest spots in the world.

Badwater is located about fifteen miles south of Furnace Creek on Hwy. 178. To exit from Death Valley, take either Hwy. 178 southeast or Hwy. 190 east to Hwy. 127 and then travel south on the 127 into the San Bernardino County section of the Mojave Desert—the east-west leg of the Mojave L.

West Through Mojave

To the east of Hwy. 127 as one leaves Death Valley are the Dumont Dunes, a popular area with offroad vehicle enthusiasts from both California and Nevada. For travelers whose style does not include recreational vehicles but does include nature observation and perhaps photography, the Kelso Sand Dunes, off Kelbacker Rd. south of Hwy. 127 and the Interstate 15 junction, offer some of the most fabulous landscapes in the California desert. These dunes are located at the east end of a desolate, windswept plain called, appropriately, Devil's Playground.

Also off Kelbacker Road is the Providence Mountains State Recreation Area, where one can see weird limestone formations—stalactites, stalagmites, cave coral, flowstone—as well as the remains of Native American habitats in Mitchell Caverns. The area has six campsites for overnight campers.

Either Interstate 15 or Interstate 40 will take the traveler west to the city of Barstow. Barstow was established in 1886 when a subsidiary of the Atchison, Topeka, and Santa Fe Railroad began construction of a depot, hotel, and eating house at this junction of AT&F tracks and the 35th parallel transcontinental lines. The Barstow Way Station contains exhibits about desert ecology, wild flowers, wildlife, hazards, and other features of the desert environment. Also located in Barstow is the Mojave River Valley Museum, which collects and displays information and artifacts concerning the history of the area as far back as 50,000 years and as recent as the space program. Geologists and rockhounds will be interested in the museum's collection of local gemstones and materials.

Twelve miles from the Barstow Way Station is the world's most famous ghost town, Calico, which was restored by Walter Knott (of

Knott's Berry Farm fame) in 1951. Calico dates to a rich silver strike of 1881. In a very active fifteen-year period the area yielded more than eighty-six million dollars in silver and borax. Today visitors can tour many of the original buildings and mines and get a real feeling for what the old mining towns were like.

Near Daggett, twelve miles southeast of Barstow, is Solar One, the world's largest solar-powered electrical generating station. With its 1,818 computer-controlled mirrors arranged in concentric circles to gather the sun's rays, Solar One resembles a science-fiction vision of the future.

From Barstow two routes lead back to Los Angeles. The first continues southwest on Interstate 15. This takes you through Victor Valley, where, just south of the town of Victorville, you'll see some of the desert's best displays of the exotic Joshua tree. The Joshua tree has thick, erratically angled branches ending in bunches of swordlike spikes and, in the spring, huge cream-colored blossoms. These thirty- and forty-foot giants were named by Mormon settlers, who were reminded by the trees' strange branches of Joshua raising his arms to heaven.

The other route back to Los Angeles follows State Hwy. 58 straight west, passing through a real rockhounds' paradise: the Kramer District, located just six miles east of the town of Boron. Palm fiber and palm root, jasper agate, and opalite are among the local minerals one will come across in this brilliantly hued landscape. Continue on to Boron to see the largest open-pit mining operation in the world—2,000 feet long and 310 feet deep. You'll understand why Boron is known as the borax capital of the world. From Boron it is thirty miles to the town of Mojave, from which State Hwy. 14 cuts south into Los Angeles.

PRACTICAL INFORMATION FOR
MOJAVE DESERT AND DEATH VALLEY

 HOW TO GET THERE. By Car. The vast *Mojave Desert* is shaped like a gigantic L, with one leg traveling north and the other heading east. State Hwy. 14 enters the Mojave just north of the Los Angeles County line at Antelope Valley and goes straight north through Rosamond, Mojave, Red Rock Canyon State Recreation Area, and China Lake. An alternate route is U.S. Hwy. 395, which travels north through Victor Valley, Boron, and the Rand Mining District, meeting up with Hwy. 14 northwest of China Lake. To travel east through the Mojave Desert, take either State Hwy. 14 or U.S. Hwy. 395 north to State Hwy. 58, which then cuts east to Barstow, or take I-15 north to

Barstow. From Barstow two routes go straight east: I-40, which passes through the mountainous areas of San Bernardino County, whisks by the Providence Mountains, and enters Arizona at the town of Needles; or the more northerly I-15, which passes south of Calico, near Devil's Playground and the Kelso Sand Dunes, and northeast into Nevada.

Death Valley National Monument can be entered from the southeast or the southwest. From the southwest: Take State Hwy. 190 or 178 through the Mojave Desert to the monument. From the southeast: Take Hwy. 127 north from I-15 and then link up with either Hwy. 178, which travels east into the valley and then cuts north past Funeral Peak, Badwater, Dante's View, and Zabriskie Point before meeting up with Hwy. 190 at Furnace Creek, or continue on Hwy. 178 north for twenty-eight miles and then take Hwy. 190 east straight into the middle of Death Valley.

TELEPHONES. Mojave Desert has three different area codes. 805 covers the area just north of Los Angeles and around the town of Mojave; 714 covers the San Bernardino area; 619 covers Death Valley and all other points.

HOTELS AND MOTELS. Overnight accommodations are rare in the Mojave Desert. Death Valley, however, has become a popular winter vacation spot and has several comfortable establishments. In-season reservations should be made two months in advance.

DEATH VALLEY

Furnace Creek Inn. *Deluxe.* (619) 786–2345. 67 rooms and suites. Heated pool, tennis courts, golfing, riding, dining rooms, cocktail lounge, entertainment. Open October 16–April 30. All major cards.

Furnace Creek Ranch. *Expensive.* (619) 786–2345. 216 units; some cottages available; newer section has very good rooms. Originally crew headquarters for a borax company. Pool, putting green, playground, tennis courts, golfing, riding, coffee shop, steak house, cocktail lounge, general store. Open all year. All major cards.

Stove Pipe Wells Village. *Moderate.* State Hwy. 190; tel.: Dial 0 and ask for Stove Pipe Wells No. 1. Seventy-four units. Heated mineral pool, cocktail lounge, grocery store, dining room. Open all year. MC, V.

CAMPERS AND TRAILER TIPS. The Mojave Desert and Death Valley have about two dozen campgrounds in a variety of desert settings; listed below is a sampling of what is available. For further information, the following booklets are useful: *High Desert Recreation Resource Guide* from the Mojave Chamber of Commerce, P.O. Box 818, Mojave, CA 93501; *San Bernardino County Regional Parks* from the Regional Parks Department, 825 E. Third St., San Bernardino, CA 92415.

Death Valley. *Mahogany Flat,* E. of Hwy. 178. Ten well-shaded tent spaces in a forest of juniper and pinon pine. Tables, pit toilets, no water. Open April through November only. *Mesquite Springs,* Hwy. 190, near Scotty's Castle. Sixty tent or RV spaces, some shaded, with stoves or fireplaces, tables, flush toilets, water. *Wildrose,* W. of Hwy. 178. 39 tent or RV sites, some shaded, in a canyon. Stoves or fireplaces, tables, water, pit toilets.

Mojave Desert. *Mid Hills Campground,* 123 miles E. of Barstow via I-40. Hiking, horseback riding, sightseeing in a wooded setting. Thirty campsites, pit toilets, water. *Mojave Narrows,* I-15. Eighty-seven camping units, hot showers. Secluded picnic areas and two lakes surrounded by cottonwoods and cattails make this a lovely camping spot. Fishing, rowboat rentals, bait shop, specially designed trail for handicapped. *Owl Canyon Campground,* 12 miles N. of Barstow and 1 mile E. of Rainbow Basin, named for its richly colored sedimentary layers. Thirty-one camping units, cooking grills, vault toilets, water.

HISTORIC SITES. Barstow. *Calico Ghost Town,* I-15. An authentically restored 1881 mining town. Original buildings, silver, and borax mines, shops, restaurants, weekend street entertainment, and a twenty-four hour campground.

Death Valley. *Harmony Borax Works Ruins,* State Hwy. 190. Abandoned refinery and outbuildings used to process borax from 1882 to 1889. *Scotty's Castle,* junction of State Hwy. 190 and Grapevine Canyon. This extravagant Spanish-Moorish mansion, never completed, was named after legendary adventurer Walter ("Death Valley Scotty") Scott. Unusual design, well-crafted furnishings.

Rosamond. *Burton's Tropico Gold Mine and Mill,* five miles W. of Rosamond off Rosamond Blvd. Tours of southern California's largest gold mill and a historic mine. Displays include firearms, photographs, antique household equipment, and clothing.

MUSEUMS. Barstow. *Barstow Way Station,* 831 Barstow Rd. This Bureau of Land Management facility houses displays about the desert's natural history. Publications available. *Mojave River Valley Museum,* corner Barstow Rd. and Virginia Wy. Artifacts and information concerning prehistory and history of the area through today. Collection of local gemstones and minerals.

Daggett. *Solar One,* off Hwy. 40. Giant model of the world's largest solar-powered electrical generating station, plus exhibits and movies explaining solar and other forms of energy.

Death Valley. *Visitor Center Museum,* State Hwy. 190. Exhibits and slide programs on natural and historic points of interest. Evening naturalist programs, guided walks, and trips also offered. There is a good selection of sightseeing literature.

Randsburg. *Desert Museum.* Historical items on display. The focal point for the restoration of Randsburg.

LAS VEGAS

by
MURRAY HERTZ AND STEPHEN ALLEN

Murray Hertz is a long-time resident of Nevada and a member of the Society of American Travel Writers, and has contributed articles to many national magazines. He is editor of What's On in Las Vegas *magazine in Las Vegas. Stephen Allen is the managing editor of* What's On *magazine.*

Few persons would dispute Las Vegas' claim to being the "Entertainment Capital of the World." A ride down its famous three-and-one-half-mile Strip at any time of the year reveals more headliner stars on the marquees of the hotel-casinos than can be found anywhere else in the world.

Actually, there are two Las Vegases. While the Strip—with its hotel-casinos, such as Caesars Palace, the MGM Grand, the Tropicana, the Sands, the Flamingo, the Desert Inn, and the Sahara—is the more famous of the two, the downtown Glitter Gulch area (also called Casino Center) is more often photographed. It has provided the backdrop for numerous movies.

Glitter Gulch is only four blocks long (Fremont Street between South Main Street and Las Vegas Boulevard), but the light is so bright there that one so inclined can easily read a newspaper on the street at 3:00 A.M.!

Las Vegas is a town that never shuts down. It is the world's only 24-hour-a-day town. All of the casinos are open round-the-clock, and so are many of the restaurants; for local residents, nearly all of the supermarkets and convenience stores are open day and night. Because of this 24-hour-a-day nature, many Las Vegas residents are at work at any given hour of the day, and the supermarkets are as crowded at 4:00 A.M. as they are at 4:00 P.M.

The casinos reinforce this atmosphere, for they don't have windows and you will see no clocks. Many of the people playing at the tables at 6:00 A.M. do not have any notion of what time it is.

Las Vegas did not build hotels such as Caesars Palace and the MGM Grand by sending people home with more money than they had when they came. On the other hand, people are constantly plunking a couple of dollars into the "progressive" slot machines and walking away with a quarter of a million dollars or more. It happens several times a year at the large hotels.

Which games have the best odds? If you know what you are doing, the best odds are to be found at the craps and baccarat tables—but every year fewer and fewer people are playing craps, since it does not seem to be taught on the streets anymore.

For the average player, the best odds are to be found at the blackjack table. The worst odds are at keno or the big wheel.

Is the gambling in Las Vegas honest? Matter of fact, it is. The gambling is tightly controlled by the Nevada Gaming Commission, and any hotel would be in danger of losing its license if it deliberately tried anything fancy. On the other hand, individuals will be individuals, and it is a good idea always to keep your eyes open.

Is Las Vegas really Sin City? Sin City is a term of the past; "the Entertainment Capital of the World" describes today's city. Of course if you compare Las Vegas with Komical Korners, Kansas, then it is Sin City. You can gamble and drink around the clock in Las Vegas, and Nevada is one of the few states where brothels are still legal. They are not legal in Clark County, of which Las Vegas is part, but they are legal in Nye County, 65 miles to the north.

Most people think of Las Vegas as an entity in itself, but it also is a jumping-off point for many other attractions. Among them are: Hoover Dam, 25 miles away, and Lake Mead, one of the largest man-made lakes in the world, created by Hoover Dam; Death Valley, 137 miles; Grand Canyon, 300 miles (you can take scenic flights from Las Vegas over and through the canyon); Disneyland, 290 miles; Lake Havasu City, today the home of the famous original London Bridge, 145 miles; Palm Springs, 280 miles.

As incredible as it may sound, some fine skiing also may be found near this desert city. Lee Canyon Ski Resort at Mt. Charleston is just 36 miles away. If you badly enough wanted to, during certain times of the year you could go snow-skiing in the morning at Lee Canyon, return to Las Vegas for lunch, then go water-skiing in the afternoon at Lake Mead; both are about 35 miles away.

While most of the big development of Las Vegas has occurred within the past 30 years, this desert resort city began to develop in 1931, when the Nevada legislature made gambling legal in an effort to solve the economic problems of the Great Depression. The area also received a financial boon when construction on Hoover Dam began the same year. Construction on the dam lasted until 1935; after that nothing much happened until the end of World War II, when mobster Benjamin "Bugsy" Siegel "had a dream" and built the Flamingo resort hotel in Las Vegas. The Flamingo proved to be a financial flop, and Siegel subsequently met his end in typical gangland fashion in Beverly Hills at the home of his girlfriend. But a seed had been planted that eventually took root and blossomed.

If you do not lose too much money gambling, Las Vegas actually can be one of the best vacation bargains in America. You can have a big breakfast anywhere in town for around $1, and a huge buffet dinner anywhere in town costs $4 or less. At one hotel, you can both see a Broadway play with a well-known star and enjoy dinner for just $11.95.

PRACTICAL INFORMATION FOR LAS VEGAS

 HOW TO GET THERE. By air. Airlines flying to Las Vegas are: American, Continental, Delta, Eastern, Frontier, Northwest Orient, Pan Am, PSA, Republic, TWA, United, and Western.

By car. Interstate 15 from San Diego goes all the way to Las Vegas. From Los Angeles, take Interstate 10 until it reaches Interstate 15.

By bus. Greyhound and Trailways from San Diego or Los Angeles.

Resort Hotels and Casinos

1) Tropicana
2) Marina
3) Aladdin
4) MGM Grand
5) Barbary Coast
6) Flamingo Hilton
7) Maxim
8) Imperial Palace
9) Holiday Inn & Casino
10) Sands
11) Desert Inn
12) Riviera
13) El Rancho
14) Sahara
15) Las Vegas Hilton
16) Landmark
17) Nevada Palace
18) Hacienda
19) Holiday Inn
20) Dunes
21) Caesar's Palace
22) Castaways
23) Frontier
24) Silver Slipper
25) Stardust
26) Circus-Circus
27) Showboat
28) Sam's Town

Downtown Hotels and Casinos

29) Vegas World
30) Union Plaza
31) Golden Gate Casino
32) Golden Nugget
33) Four Queens
34) Sundance
35) Las Vegas Club
36) Mint
37) Horseshoe
38) Fremont
39) Holiday Inn
40) California Hotel
41) Lady Luck Casino
42) El Cortez
43) Western Hotel

By train. Amtrak from Los Angeles to Las Vegas (the train continues on to Salt Lake City, and from there to Chicago).

CLIMATE. Las Vegas has fair weather year-round, with spring and fall temperatures averaging in the mid-70's. Winter weather fluctuates between 55° and 65°, so snow is seldom, if ever, seen. Summer temperatures can soar up to about 100°, but the extremely low humidity makes the high temperatures much more tolerable than those of the tropics. Even so, air conditioners are an integral part of Las Vegas life. Be on the lookout for nighttime drops in temperature, since it may fall as much as 20° to 30° after the sun goes down. Annual precipitation is less than four inches.

TELEPHONES. The area code for the entire state of Nevada is 702. From outside the area, directory information can be obtained toll-free by dialing (702) 555-1212. Dial (800) 555-1212, directory information nationwide for tollfree 800 numbers, to see if there is an 800 number for the business or hotel you want to reach.

HOW TO GET AROUND. By car. All major car rentals at the airport and along the Strip.

By bus. The Strip bus leaves every 15 minutes from the Hacienda hotel, located at the lower end of the Strip; it runs up the Strip to the downtown Casino Center. 90 cents.

TOURIST INFORMATION SERVICES. The Las Vegas Tourist Center, Hwy. 95 south of town; 736-7671. The Greater Las Vegas Chamber of Commerce, 2301 E. Sahara; 457-4664. The Las Vegas Welcome Center, 4825 Boulder Hwy.; 451-7648.

SEASONAL EVENTS. Desert Inn National Pro-Am Golf Tournament, mid-March; Alan King Tennis Classic, mid-April; Mint 400 Off-Road Race, beginning of May; Helldorado (Western events), mid-May; Jaycee State Fair, mid-September; Circus Circus Chili Cookoff, mid-December.

RECOMMENDED READING. *Inside Las Vegas,* by Mario Puzo (an Ace paperback).

TOURS. American Sightseeing, Gray Line, and Transportation Unlimited all operate bus tours of Las Vegas, its nightclubs, Hoover Dam, Death Valley, and the Grand Canyon. Scenic Airlines (739-1900) flys tours to and through the Grand Canyon. Deluxe air-ground tour $158; four-hour air tour $128.

 ARCHITECTURE. The Las Vegas Strip is considered one of the architectural wonders of the modern world because of its lavish hotels, such as Caesars Palace, and because of its imaginative use of light and neon.

 SPORTS. Skiing. At Lee Canyon (Mt. Charleston), 36 miles from Las Vegas.

Boating, swimming, water-skiing, houseboat rentals. On Lake Mead, about 36 miles to the east.

Golf. Many of the major hotels have their own golf courses, but public courses also are available. Among the best of both are: Sahara Country Club, Tropicana Country Club, Desert Inn Country Club, Dunes Country Club, Winterwood, Craig Ranch, Las Vegas City, and Paradise Valley.

Fishing. On Lake Mead: bass, bluegill, crappie, strippers, Coho and rainbow trout. License $7.50 for a special three-day permit; $10 for ten days; $20 annually.

Horseback riding. At Mt. Charleston, 35 miles from Las Vegas.

 NATIONAL PARKS. *Toiyabe National Forest,* about 40 miles west of Las Vegas. Camp and picnic grounds from May to October, and a popular ski area from December to March.

 STATE PARKS. *Valley of Fire.* A wonderland of rock formations that resemble elephants, dragons, and anything else you can imagine, in red sandstone that changes hues with the passage of the day. Indian petroglyphs and rock carvings. About 45 miles north of Las Vegas, and a pleasant trip through the beautiful desert.

 CAMPING OUT. Lake Mead National Recreation Area, 35 miles to the east of the city, open all year. Campsites at Boulder Beach, Overton Beach, Callville Bay, and Echo Bay. Mt. Charleston, about 35 miles to the northwest, has several major campgrounds under the jurisdiction of the National Forest Service. The closest campgrounds there are at Kyle Canyon. Others are at Hill Top, Mahogany, Deer Creek, and McWilliams. Campgrounds also are available at Valley of Fire, 45 miles north of Las Vegas.

WHAT TO DO WITH THE CHILDREN. In Las Vegas, children enjoy the live circus acts at the Circus Circus hotel and the large game mezzanine there. They also like *Omnimax,* a futuristic wraparound theater at Caesars Palace that is most inexpensive. Outside of the city, the Hoover Dam tour is worth a visit. Old Nevada, a replica of an old Western town, complete with shoot-outs, is just 40 minutes from Las Vegas out W. Charleston Blvd. Old Las Vegas, the replica of an early fort, is on Hwy. 93, a few miles east of the city.

 MUSEUMS. The *Desert Research Institute,* at the University of Nevada, Las Vegas. The *Museum of Natural History,* also at the University. The *Las Vegas Art Museum,* 3333 W. Washington.

 SHOPPING. *The Fashion Show,* a luxurious mall right on the Strip at Spring Mountain Rd. Lavish department stores, including Neiman-Marcus, Saks Fifth Avenue, Bullock's, and Goldwater's. *The Meadows Mall,* an attractive complex of 140 stores several miles from the Strip. *The Boulevard Mall,* a collection of 90 stores only two miles from the Strip.

 HOTELS AND MOTELS. Las Vegas has some of the most lavish and luxurious hotels in the world, and the hotel-filled 3½-mile Strip is an architectural wonder. Most of the Las Vegas luxury hotels are located along the Strip. Those in the downtown Glitter Gulch area tend to be less expensive, since they do not feature big-name entertainment. Prices quoted are double-occupancy, in-season rates; winter rates are slightly lower. *Deluxe,* $60 and up; *Expensive,* $50–$60; *Moderate,* $30–$50; *Inexpensive,* under $30.

THE STRIP AND VICINITY

Caesars Palace. *Deluxe.* 3570 Las Vegas Blvd.; 731-7110. Luxurious rooms. The ultimate in service and atmosphere. Spacious grounds with many fountains and statues. Superstar entertainment, fine restaurants, *Omnimax* theater.

Las Vegas Hilton. *Deluxe.* 3000 Paradise Rd.; 732-5111. Largest resort hotel in the world. Home of the progressive slots. Top entertainment, fine restaurants, Benihana Village, tennis courts, health club, and sauna. Youth hotel with recreation facilities for children. Next to Las Vegas Convention Center.

MGM Grand. *Deluxe.* 3645 Las Vegas Blvd.; 739-4111. The world's largest luxury hotel, costing over $100 million. Hollywood's idea of what a great hotel should be, and even named after a movie. Superstar entertainment, jai alai, fine restaurants (including *Cafe Gigi*), theater showing old MGM movies.

Aladdin. *Expensive.* 3667 Las Vegas Blvd.; 736-0111. A large complex of hotel rooms and villas. Olympic-size pool. Theater for the Performing Arts.

Barbary Coast. *Expensive.* 3595 Las Vegas Blvd.; 737–7111. Right across the street from the MGM Grand and Caesars Palace. Turn-of-the-century decor, Dixieland music.

Circus Circus. *Expensive.* 2880 Las Vegas Blvd.; 734-0410. Circus atmosphere, with live circus acts performing over the heads of the casino players. The only hotel on the Strip that caters to families with children. Large camperland.

Desert Inn. *Expensive.* 3145 Las Vegas Blvd.; 734–4444. Among the most beautiful grounds in Las Vegas, and the former home of Howard Hughes. Large country club, garden rooms. Superstar entertainment.

Dunes. *Expensive.* 3650 Las Vegas Blvd.; 737–4110. Three fine restaurants including the *Top O' The Strip,* with the best view in Las Vegas. Attractive grounds, 18-hole championship golf course.

Flamingo Hilton. *Expensive.* 3555 Las Vegas Blvd.; 733–3111. One of the largest Strip hotels. Attractive grounds—and do not miss Bugsy Siegel's Rose Garden. The old Flamingo was the first big hotel built in Las Vegas; this one is all new.

Frontier. *Expensive.* 3120 Las Vegas Blvd.; 734–0110. Western motif. Superstar entertainment.

Imperial Palace. *Expensive.* 3535 Las Vegas Blvd.; 731–3311. Chinese decor, with one of the most beautiful casinos in Las Vegas.

Landmark. *Expensive.* 364 Convention Center Dr.; 733-1110. Hexagon-shaped hotel. Outside elevator; dining and drinking at the top with a wonderful view. Large pool with a waterfall. Across from the Convention Center.

Marina. *Expensive.* 3805 Las Vegas Blvd.; 739-1500. Attractive casino.

Maxim. *Expensive.* 160 E. Flamingo.; 731-4300. Across from the MGM Grand. Attractive casino area.

Riviera. *Expensive.* 2901 Las Vegas Blvd.; 734-5110. Beautiful grounds, excellent restaurants, superstar entertainment.

Sahara. *Expensive.* 2535 Las Vegas Blvd.; 737–2111. Space Center for conventions; excellent restaurants, 18-hole golf course.

Sands. *Expensive.* 3355 Las Vegas Blvd.; 733–5000. Original home of the "Rat Pack" of the fifties. Attractive accommodations, famous *Regency* restaurant.

Tropicana. *Expensive.* 3801 Las Vegas Blvd.; 739–2222. Newly and lavishly redecorated, with a new tower. Near the airport; large country club with 18-hole golf course. American home of the *Folies Bergere.*

Hacienda. *Moderate.* 3950 Las Vegas Blvd.; 739-8911. At the lower end of the Strip. Garden rooms. Large camperland, new tower.

Holiday Casino. *Moderate.* 2375 Las Vegas Blvd.; 732-2411. Right on the Strip and a favorite gambling place among locals, who believe the odds are better here.

Royal Las Vegas. *Moderate.* 99 Convention Center Dr.; 735–6117. Near the Convention Center.

Stardust. *Moderate.* 3000 Las Vegas Blvd.; 732–6111. Convenient location right in the heart of the Strip. American home of the *Lido de Paris.* Large camperland.

Bali Hai. *Inexpensive.* 336 Desert Inn Rd.; 734-2141. Conveniently located only a block from the Strip.

Las Vegas Strip TraveLodge. *Inexpensive.* 2830 Las Vegas Blvd. 735-4222. In the center of the Strip.

Motel 6. *Inexpensive.* 195 E. Tropicana; 736-4904. Near the Strip and the airport.

Vagabond Motel. *Inexpensive.* 3688 Las Vegas Blvd.; 736–0991. Right next to the Dunes.

DOWNTOWN AND ELSEWHERE

California. *Moderate.* 12 Ogden; 385-1222. In the downtown area; the only hotel in Las Vegas where you can take a picture in the casino.

Four Queens. *Moderate.* 202 E. Fremont St.; 385-4011. In the heart of downtown's Glitter Gulch. All rooms the same price.

Golden Nugget. *Moderate.* 129 E. Fremont St.; 385-7111. Attractive turn-of-the-century decor.

Mint. *Moderate.* 100 Fremont St.; 385-7440. In the heart of the downtown area. Home of the Mint 400 Desert Off-Road Race in May. Glass-enclosed elevator to dining at the top.

Sam's Town. *Moderate.* 5111 Boulder Hwy.; 456-7777. A quaint western atmosphere, popular with locals; largest Western-goods store in the world. Out-of-the-way location.

Sundance. *Moderate.* 301 E. Fremont St.; 382-6111. In the center of the downtown Glitter Gulch area. Largest building in the state of Nevada. New Tower.

Union Plaza. *Moderate.* 1 Main St.; 386–2110. At the heart of the downtown area. Home of the Las Vegas Amtrak station. Famous for its dinner-theater and New Year's Eve fireworks.

Fremont. *Inexpensive.* 200 E. Fremont; 385-3232. In the downtown area; large sports book.

Holiday Inn Downtown. *Inexpensive.* 300 N. Main St.; 385-1500. Conveniently located in the downtown area.

Showboat. *Inexpensive.* 2800 E. Fremont; 385-9123. In an out-of-the-way location, but a large and friendly hotel, popular with families. 110 lanes of bowling.

Travel Inn. *Inexpensive.* 217 Las Vegas Blvd. N.; 384-3040. One block from the downtown area.

TraveLodge Downtown. *Inexpensive.* 2028 Fremont St.; 384–7540.

 CASINOS. All of the hotels have their own casinos; basically they look the same, and all are open 24 hours a day. The most lavish are at Caesars Palace and the MGM Grand.

NIGHTCLUBS. All of the major Strip hotels feature either headliners such as Frank Sinatra or spectaculars such as the MGM Grand's "Jubilee!" The average cost for the major performers is $30–$40, but this usually includes dinner or at least drinks. The cost of seeing someone like Frank Sinatra can go as high as $50 person, and you are expected to tip the maitre d' and the waitress as well. On the other hand, many smaller shows in Las Vegas come in at no more than $5.95, and at the Union Plaza Hotel in the downtown area, you can see a Broadway play with a major star, dinner included, for $11.95. Hotels in the downtown area do not feature name entertainers, but all have live music. All major hotels also have lounge shows, and they can be a real bargain; usually, the only cost there is a two-drink minimum.

DRINKING LAWS. Liquor can be sold and consumed round-the-clock in Las Vegas. The drinking age is 21, as is the gambling age. You are not even supposed to be in a casino if you are under 21, although of course you are allowed to be in the hotel.

BUFFETS. Nearly all of the major hotels maintain elaborate breakfast, lunch, and dinner buffets, and they are among the best dining bargains in town. Figure on about $2 for breakfast or lunch and about $4 for dinner.

DINING OUT. Las Vegas has some of the finest restaurants in America, with prices for dinner ranging from as much as $100 for two all the way down to $6 for two at one of the hotel buffets. Dining out in Las Vegas may mean dining plus entertainment, since many of the hotels still offer dinner with the entertainment—although there are fewer of these every year. The most reasonable dining will be found at the hotel buffets. *Deluxe,* $20 and up; *Expensive,* $15–$20; *Moderate,* $10–$15; *Inexpensive,* under $10. These ranges do not include drinks, tips, tax.

Bacchanal. *Deluxe.* In Caesars Palace. A Roman feast, with beautiful, lightly clad maidens to pour your wine. The most unusual restaurant in Las Vegas and a feast for the gourmand as well as the gourmet.

Cafe Gigi. *Deluxe.* In the MGM Grand. Were it not for the casino sounds outside, you might think you were in an 18th-century French drawing room. Actually you are in a Hollywood set.

Palace Court. *Deluxe.* In Caesars Palace. Probably the best restaurant in Las Vegas. A lavishly praised culinary wonder, in a setting of trees and bushes beneath a glass dome. Continental dining, impeccable service.

Regency Room. *Deluxe.* In the Sands Hotel. One of the most highly-praised restaurants in Las Vegas. Gourmet French food, dependably excellent.

Ah-So. *Expensive.* In Caesars Palace. A Japanese feast prepared on a tabletop hibachi; the chef is all the entertainment you need.

Benihana Village. *Expensive.* In the Las Vegas Hilton. A collection of wonderful Oriental restaurants surrounding a waterfall, with thunder, lightning, and rain—all in the hotel!

Dome of the Sea. *Expensive.* In the Dunes Hotel. May have the best seafood in Las Vegas, and a harpist plays while you eat.

House of Lords. *Expensive.* In Sahara Hotel. American food in an elegant European setting.

Spanish Steps. *Expensive.* In Caesars Palace. Wide variety of Spanish dishes.

Sultan's Table. *Expensive.* In the Dunes Hotel. Continental dining to the accompaniment of more strolling violinists than you can count.

Top O' The Strip. *Expensive.* In the Dunes Hotel. Continental dining, with the finest view in Las Vegas, overlooking the Strip.

Alpine Village. *Moderate.* 3003 Paradise Rd. Swiss-German food with wonderful ambiance, and there is singing in the Rathskeller. Across from the Las Vegas Hilton.

Backstage. *Moderate.* In the Union Plaza Hotel, downtown. Where all the showfolk go. Terrific sandwiches and an "in" place to gather.

Battista's Hole in the Wall. *Moderate.* 4041 Audrie St.; 732-1424. Right across the street from the MGM Grand. An unusual and colorful atmosphere, with fine Italian food and more fun than a barrel of opera singers.

The Tillerman. *Moderate.* 2245 E. Flamingo; 731-4036. A favorite of the locals. Consistently good seafood and consistently friendly service.

Top of the Mint. *Moderate.* In the Mint Hotel, downtown. One of the best views in Las Vegas, and you go up in a glass-enclosed elevator.

Cafe Cortez. *Inexpensive.* In the El Cortez Hotel, downtown; 385-5200. May be the least expensive good steak dinner in town. Popular with locals.

Cattleman's. *Inexpensive.* 2625 S. Maryland Pkwy.; 732-7726. "Early Bird Specials," served from 4:00 to 7:00 P.M. for only $5.95 per dinner, are popular with tourists trying to save a dollar. Good food, large restaurant.

Cosmos Underground. *Inexpensive.* 32 E. Fremont St.; 382-0330. Excellent and inexpensive Italian food in a convenient downtown location.

Empress Gardens. *Inexpensive.* 1155 E. Sahara. Excellent Mandarin, Szechuan, and Cantonese food.

Old Heidelberg. *Inexpensive.* 604 E. Sahara, near the Sahara Hotel; 731-5310. Authentic homemade Bavarian food. Friendly staff. German deli and gift shop at the front.

Ricardo's. *Inexpensive.* 2380 E. Tropicana. May serve the best Mexican food in the city. Large and attractive.

PALM SPRINGS

Glamorous Desert Resort

by
JANE LASKY

Jane Lasky is a contributor to the Los Angeles Times Syndicate and a contributing editor to Travel Agent *magazine, and has written for* Bon Appetit, Working Woman, Palm Springs Life, Los Angeles *magazine, and many in-flight and trade magazines.*

Nestled beneath the 10,831-foot Mount San Jacinto is the desert resort community of Palm Springs, a celebrity playground attracting visitors from all over the world. Why has a suburban resort like this drawn so many visitors, from almost all nationalities, age groups, and economic brackets, for over 50 years?

Why indeed? Palm Springs has more than its share of luxurious hotels, dramatic restaurants, chic boutiques, and vast recreation areas for tennis, golf, swimming, skiing, and hiking. By virtue of its location, nature has guaranteed this corner of the desert a life of constant sunshine—with snow-capped mountaintops only 15 minutes away. You can spend the day cross-country skiing, then enjoy a quick dip in one of the desert floor's 7,000 swimming pools before sunset.

With an average daytime temperature of 88° and a nighttime average of 55°, Palm Springs has an ideal climate for outdoor sports enthusiasts. There is horseback riding, 35 miles of bicycle trails, over 300 tennis courts, and more than 40 golf courses within a 20-mile radius (no wonder this small city is nicknamed "the winter golf capital of the world"). Those who unwind with a fishing rod are happy too: both freshwater and saltwater fishing are available. Baseball fans should note that the California Angels spend time at Palm Springs' Angel Stadium each spring, training and performing exhibition games.

Year-round, Palm Springs is both a vacation retreat and a residence for celebrities and famous politicians. Bob Hope is the city's honorary mayor, and Gene Autry, Frank Sinatra, Gerald Ford, and scores of other luminaries can be spotted in supermarkets, restaurants, and on the golf course. This resort area is not new territory to celebrity visitors either: Esther Williams once practiced her strokes at the El Mirador pool, Spencer Tracy once played chess at the Racquet Club, and Joan Bennett once pedalled her bicycle down Palm Canyon Drive.

Palm Springs became a retreat for the Hollywood crowd in 1930, after the arrival of noted silent film stars Charlie Farrell and Ralph Bellamy. For thirty dollars an acre, the two actors bought 200 acres of land on which they planned to build tennis courts. This was the beginning of the Palm Springs Racquet Club, which soon listed Ginger Rogers, Humphrey Bogart, and Clark Gable among its members.

The number of celebrities who have graced Palm Springs must surely rival the number who parade through Beverly Hills. For the curious, tour groups are organized to drive past these stars' estates. Celebrity Tours offers guided treks to take a glimpse at both current and past celebrity homes.

One reason celebrities are drawn here is the area's sophistication. The palm-tree-lined main thoroughfare, Palm Canyon Drive, offers more than one mile of dazzling boutiques and galleries. Palm Springs' answer to New York's Fifth Avenue, this is the home of Rolls-Royce and Mercedes dealerships, a Saks Fifth Avenue department store, and countless designer and custom-wear shops. Desert Inn Fashion Plaza, on Palm Canyon Dr., and Palm Springs Mall, on Tahquiz-McCallum Way near the airport, are the city's major enclosed shopping centers.

PALM SPRINGS

Points of Interest

1) Ariel Tramway
2) California Angels Stadium
3) City Center
4) Community Swim Center
5) DeMuth Park
6) Desert Botanical Gardens
7) Desert Inn Fashion Plaza
8) Desert Museum
9) Fairchild Bel Aire Greens
10) Indian Canyons
11) Mac's Bike Rentals
12) Municipal Golf Course
13) Palm Springs Convention & Visitors Bureau
14) Palm Springs Mall
15) Palm Springs Tennis Center
16) Public Library
17) Ruth Hardy Park
18) Smoke Tree Stables
19) Smoke Tree Village

In addition, the Vineyard, on Palm Canyon Drive, offers about a dozen shops in a gardenlike mall.

The most powerful drawing card of all is the supreme beauty of Palm Springs. Nature has not taken a second seat here to urban growth; instead, it dominates the area. City buildings are restricted to a height of 30 feet; flashing, moving, and neon signs are prohibited by law, preserving an intimate village feeling; 50 percent of the land consists of open spaces with palm trees and desert vegetation. Wherever you go in Palm Springs, you'll feel the splendor of nature's artistry.

This beauty is particularly felt in Palm Springs' surrounding canyons. Lush Tahquitz Canyon, one of five canyons that line the San Jacinto Mountains, was the setting for the original version of "Lost Horizon," a movie set in paradise. Centuries ago, the original inhabitants of these rock canyons were the Cahuilla Indians. Their descendants were named Agua Caliente—or "hot water"—Indians, as a tribute to the hot mineral springs that flowed throughout their reservation. These springs were thought to wield magical healing powers.

The canyons begin five miles south of downtown Palm Springs. An Indian toll collector accepts a nominal fee at the entrance of this Indian-owned sanctuary. Once inside, visitors gaze upon pictographs, bedrock mortar holes for grinding grain, and stone houses and shelters built high atop cliff walls, all relics of ancient Indian history. Streams of icy mountain water wind through the dense growth of willows, sycamores, and mesquite, as well as groves of stately Washingtonia palms. Bands of wild ponies roam through Murray Canyon, while Andreas Canyon has towering rock faces and mysterious crevices and caves. Palm Canyon has more than 3,000 palm trees, which exist alongside its wildlife; visitors experience the awesome sensation of slipping through a time warp into a prehistoric era.

The Agua Caliente Indians have leased eight acres of their land to create the Palm Springs Spa Hotel. Its mineral waters are the hotel's main attraction, and the two-million-dollar spa draws those who wish to experience the relaxation and tranquility of the baths. The spa is open year-round to Palm Springs' guests and residents. Today, the Agua Caliente tribe still owns approximately 30,000 acres of Palm Springs desert, making them one of the richest Indian tribes in the country.

Aside from its Indian heritage, this city also offers a historical wealth. In 1885, "Judge" John McCallum, a San Francisco attorney, brought his family to this area hoping to restore the health of his son, who had been stricken during a typhoid epidemic. The adobe home McCallum built for his family, now the oldest building in the center of town, is today a museum, filled with the area's antiques and artifacts. In 1894, the Cornelia White House was built from railroad ties and was inhabited in 1912 by Cornelia White and her two sisters. This house now stands as a museum in the Village Green; inside are such historical items as the first telephone in Palm Springs.

Southeast of Palm Springs, along Palm Canyon Drive, parallel to I-10, you will come to three satellite areas in succession: Cathedral City, Rancho Mirage, and Palm Desert.

As suggested in the film "Lawrence of Arabia," as well as in other movies set in the desert, dates are a dietary staple of desert life. Palm Springs is often referred to as the "Arabia of America," and will tempt you with its many varieties of sweet, luscious dates that grow atop clusters of towering palms. Many date ranches, open to the public, feature outdoor tables for snacking on homemade date cakes and date shakes. Harvesting is in November and December, and each date must be painstakingly hand-picked. Feel free to feast on this wonderful fruit; surprisingly, they contain only 21 calories each.

Dates are not the sole culinary delight of this vacation retreat. French, Mexican, Chinese, Japanese, English, and Yugoslavian restaurants proliferate. Many are consistent award-winners for dining excellence. Dine one night on couscous and mint tea while being entertained by exotic belly dancers in a reproduction of a Moroccan palace at Dar Maghreb. Give one day's notice for whole roast suckling pig at Bob Sipovac's Adriatic restaurant. Hard-core fast-food fanatics will rejoice in the 1982 opening of McDonald's. Just don't look for the proverbial golden arches—Palm Springs wouldn't allow any McDonald's in the area until recently, and when it did, it was on the condition that the building blend into the city's prevailing architectural theme.

Eating isn't the only nighttime activity in Palm Springs. No need to head straight to bed after a sumptuous dinner. Discos, Las Vegas-style floor shows, hotel piano bars, mariachi music, and a comedy nightclub provide a rich assortment of exciting entertainment into the early morning hours.

PRACTICAL INFORMATION FOR PALM SPRINGS

HOW TO GET THERE. Since Palm Springs attracts visitors from all over the world, all modes of transportation are available, providing easy access to the area.

By car. Palm Springs is about a two-hour drive east of Los Angeles and a three-hour drive northeast of San Diego. Highway 111 brings you right on to Palm Canyon Drive, the main thoroughfare in Palm Springs. *From Los Angeles,* the San Bernardino Freeway (Interstate 10 East) makes a direct connection with Highway 111, making the trip virtually a straight ride. *From San Diego,* Interstate 15 North connects with the Pomona Freeway (60 East), leading to the San Bernardino Freeway (10 East).

If you're coming from the Riverside area, you might want to try the Palms-to-Pines Highway (74). This 130-mile scenic route crosses desert country and mountain forests. The route begins in Hemet and connects directly with Highway 111.

By air. Seven major airlines serve the Palm Springs Municipal Airport. They include American Airlines, Alaska Airlines, Trans World, Western, Frontier, Republic, and Pacific Express. Sun Aire and Air Irvine are commuter airlines to the area.

Most hotels provide pick-up service to and from the airport, located only 2.1 miles from the town's main intersection.

By bus. Greyhound Bus Service is available in Palm Springs, providing transportation and connections to major destinations around the country.

By train. Amtrak passenger trains service the Indio area, only 20 miles east of Palm Springs. From there, the Greyhound bus will take you right into the Palm Springs area.

TELEPHONES. The area code for all of Palm Springs is 619. You do not need to dial the area code if it is the same as the one from which you are calling. Information (known as directory assistance) is 411. When direct-dialing a long-distance number from anywhere in Palm Springs, you must dial the number "1" (one) *before* you dial the area code and the number itself. An operator will assist you on person-to-person, credit-card, and collect calls if you dial "0" first. Pay telephones still start at 10 cents.

CLIMATE. Palm Springs has sunny, warm, clear, dry weather year-round, and basking in the sun is its main attraction. Temperatures range from a high of 91° to a low of 70° during winter days. Winter evenings are refreshingly cool, with temperatures ranging from the low 40's to the upper 50's.

From June through September, the summer weather is extremely hot, often reaching temperatures of 110° during the day. But low humidity, air conditioning, and the abundance of pools make the hot weather an enjoyable treat. Summer evenings are comfortably warm, usually reaching about 70°.

There are normally only 15 to 20 days of annual rainfall in Palm Springs.

If you're planning to take a ride on the Aerial Tramway to the top of Mount San Jacinto, you'll need some warm clothing. The climate there is usually 40 degrees lower than it is in the desert, with snow falling from November through April.

HOTELS. In Palm Springs, there is no such thing as a motel. However, there is a full array of resorts, inns, clubs, spas, manors, and lodges. The range is extraordinary; visitors have their choice, and may spend less than $20 a night to as much as $300 or more. Most hotels have at least one swimming pool; some have two or three, in addition to hot tubs, jacuzzis, and saunas. Many properties boasts tennis courts and golf courses, too.

Don't attempt to visit this famous resort during the holiday season without advance reservations. There are reduced rates and many units available in the summer, from June 1 through September 15. Call (800) 854–4325 (nationwide) or (800) 472–4387 (in California). Locally, call 325–1577, the Palm Springs Chamber of Commerce's special reservations and information number.

Listings are in order of price category. Based on double occupancy, price categories and ranges are as follows: *Super Deluxe,* $90 and up; *Deluxe,* $75–$90; *Expensive,* $50–$75; *Moderate* $35–$50; and *Inexpensive,* up to $35. For a more complete explanation of hotel categories, see the "Facts at Your Fingertips" section at the beginning of this volume. The following is a *selection* of hotels and resorts.

Canyon Hotel Racquet and Golf Resort. *Super Deluxe.* 2850 S. Palm Canyon Dr.; 323–5656. This luxurious resort offers three swimming pools, a sauna, an 18-hole private golf course, horseback riding, tennis. All suites have a mini-kitchen and wet bar. Restaurants and cocktail lounges with entertainment. Barber shop, beauty salon, and other fine shops. All major credit cards.

La Mancha Resort. *Super Deluxe.* 444 N. Avenida Caballeros; 323–1775. Privacy and casual luxury in a 33-villa resort; half of the villas have private swimming pool with jacuzzi. Fully equipped kitchens, fireplaces, widescreen TV, video disc players with full library in each villa. Nine-hole golf course, gym, sauna, 65-foot-long pool, and night-lighted tennis. Gourmet dining at the club. AE, V, MC.

Racquet Club of Palm Springs. *Super Deluxe.* 2743 N. Indian Ave.; 325–1281. 120 rooms. Built by Charlie Farrell and Ralph Bellamy in 1933, the Racquet Club marked the beginning of Palm Springs' glamour era. Swimming pool, therapy pool, sauna, tennis courts, cocktail lounge. AE, MC, V.

La Siesta Villas. *Super Deluxe.* 247 W. Stevens Rd.; 325–2269. 19 luxurious one- and two-bedroom villas in a tropical setting. Pool and jacuzzi. No credit cards, cash only.

Spa Hotel and Mineral Springs. *Super Deluxe.* 100 N. Indian Ave.; 325–1461. Therapeutic mineral springs, four indoor-outdoor pools, 35 swirlpool tubs, gym, and tennis are the big attractions here. Coffee shop, dining room, cocktail lounge with entertainment. All major credit cards.

Sundance Villas. *Super Deluxe.* 378 Cabrillo Rd.; 325–3888. Beautifully decorated, spacious suites include fireplace, wet bar, kitchen, and private patio for dining or sunning. Each villa has a private pool or jacuzzi. Tennis courts. AE, V, MC.

The Tennis Club and Hotel. *Super Deluxe.* 701 W. Baristo Rd.; 325–1441. Beautifully done appointments and spacious, attractive rooms. Full-fledged tennis club, pool; mountain setting; close to town. V, MC only.

Gene Autry Hotel. *Deluxe.* 4200 E. Palm Canyon Dr.; 328–1171. Six tennis courts, three swimming pools, and two therapy spas. Horseback riding, hiking, desert tours. Dining and entertainment nightly. Closed in summer. All major credit cards.

Ingleside Inn. *Deluxe.* 200 W. Ramon Rd.; 325–0046. Hacienda-style inn with 26 rooms furnished with antiques. Swimming pool, therapeutic pool, and sauna. All major credit cards.

Ocotillo Lodge. *Deluxe.* 1111 E. Palm Canyon Dr.; 327–1141. At the foot of the San Jacinto mountains, this beautifully landscaped lodge offers 114 suites, bungalows, and villas. Pool, therapeutic pool, and tennis. Dining, entertainment, and dancing nightly. No children. All major credit cards.

Palm Springs Biltmore Hotel Resort. *Deluxe.* 1000 E. Palm Canyon Dr.; 323–1811. Garden setting on 12 acres. 72 cottages and bungalows, some with kitchens, fireplaces; minutes from shopping, dining, and theaters. Pool, jacuzzi, tennis, and shuffleboard; golf nearby. Excellent dining with award-winning menu. Saturday-Sunday Champagne brunch. All major credit cards.

Palm Springs Hilton Riviera Hotel. *Deluxe.* 1600 N. Indian Ave.; 327–8311. 500 luxurious rooms. Olympic-size pool, therapy pool, tennis (lighted for night). Dining and entertainment. All major credit cards.

Sheraton Plaza. *Deluxe.* 400 E. Tahquitz-McCallum Way; 320–6868. New 1980-built property on a 13-acre site. The 250-room hotel is a complete resort complex. All major credit cards.

Sheraton Oasis Hotel. *Deluxe–Moderate.* 155 S. Belardo Rd.; 325–1301. Elegantly furnished rooms in a motel, and pleasant older rooms in two-story buildings across the road. Suites. Nicely landscaped grounds. Two pools, therapy pools. Restaurant, bar. All major credit cards.

Tuscany Manor Apartment-Hotel. *Expensive.* 350 Chino Canyon Rd.; 325–2349. Lovely apartments, pool, and therapeutic pool. V, MC only.

Canyon Plaza Hotel and Spa. *Expensive–Moderate.* Hydrotherapy pool, sauna; Palm Springs golf course right next door. Coffee shop, dining room, entertainment, dancing. All major credit cards.

Tiki Spa Hotel and Apartments. *Expensive–Moderate.* 1910 S. Camino Real; 327–1359. Sauna, hot tub; family-owned business, with small restaurant, serves breakfast and lunch. No credit cards; check or cash.

Seven Springs Hotel. *Moderate.* 1269 E. Palm Canyon Dr.; 323–2775. Quiet, relaxing hotel offers swimming pool, jacuzzi. Convenient to shopping centers and downtown. Dining room and 24 hour coffee shop. AE, V, MC.

Westward Ho Seven Seas Hotel. *Moderate.* 701 E. Palm Canyon Dr.; 327–1531. 209 rooms. Swimming pool, therapy pool, and cocktail lounge grace this modest property. AE, V, MC.

The Monkey Tree Hotel. *Inexpensive.* 2388 E. Racquet Club Rd.; 327–1504. 18 units with kitchens. Swimming pool. Pets allowed. V, MC only.

HOW TO GET AROUND. By car. The easiest way to get around in Palm Springs is by automobile. There are many rental agencies, with rates starting at about $10 per day plus mileage. Companies include Ajax Rent-A-Car, 1800 E. Palm Canyon Dr. in the International Hotel Resort Lobby, 320–7441; Avis Rent-A-Car, 1090 N. Palm Canyon Dr., Palm Springs Airport, 325–1331; Aztec Rent-A-Car, 450 N. Indian Ave., three blocks north of the Spa Hotel, 325–2294; Budget Rent-A-Car, Palm Springs Airport, 327–1404; Dollar Rent-A-Car, Palm Springs Airport, 325–7334; Hertz Rent-A-Car, 244 N. Indian Ave., 325–7175 or at the Palm Springs Airport, 327–1523; and Select Rent-A-Car, Palm Springs Airport, 320–5781.

By limousine. Several services are available. Carey of Palm Springs Limousine Service, 325–1505; Celebrity Limousine, 325–2682; and Skyview Palm Springs—Los Angeles Limousine Service, (213) 459–1923, or 327–8816 locally.

By taxi. Call either Caravan Yellow Cab, 346–2981, or Desert Cab, 324–8233.

TOURIST INFORMATION. The Palm Springs Convention and Visitors Bureau (at 327–8411) has set up shop at the Palm Springs Airport for quick and easy reference to all activities and attractions in and around Palm Springs. Pick up a hotel guide, guide to dining, tour availability, and a host of other useful information at their convenient counter in the midst of the airport's main terminal building.

Palm Springs Life magazine also has useful visitor information, as does the *Palm Springs Life Guide,* a free monthly publication found in all hotels, most restaurants, and other area outlets.

SEASONAL EVENTS. Annual golf and tennis championships are among the major reasons for Palm Springs' popularity, but throughout the year special events in other areas entertain and excite visitors. Phone numbers cited below are all in the 619 area code. (714 until Nov. 6.)

January. The *National Collegiate Tennis Classic* gathers together the country's top women's and men's collegiate teams to compete for the championship at Rancho Las Palmas Country Club, Rancho Mirage; call 568–2727. The popular *Annual Sled Dog Races* at Palm Springs Aerial Tramway means long lines to reach the top of Mt. San Jacinto and a cross-country-style race; call 325–1391. Golf's longest tournament, the 90-hole *Bob Hope Desert Classic,* is played over five days at four courses. Followed by traditional Classic Ball. Palm Springs *Mounted Police Rodeo of Stars,* with bareback competition, steer wrestling, and saddle bronc riding, capped off by largest equestrian parade in California; at Angel Stadium.

February. *Riverside County National Date Festival* at Indio Fairgrounds. 10-day celebration, with camel races, Diaper Derby, Bearderino Contest, newspaper fold and toss contest, beauty pageant, and carnival. Entertainment, flower and garden show; call 347–8247 or 347–0676.

March. *Desert Circus:* This parade down Palm Canyon Dr. includes a hat contest. The *California Angels* play at Angel Stadium.

April. The *Dinah Shore Championship,* the richest tournament on LPGA tour. Sponsored by Nabisco Brands, Inc., it attracts many show business personalities; at Mission Hills Country Club; call 324–1727.

July. *Miss Tramway Beauty Pageant* at the top of the Palm Springs Aerial Tram; call 325–1391.

TOURS. Several companies offer tours of the city and the surrounding desert area. *Palm Springs Celebrity Tours* allows the visitor to see the homes of 65 to 70 movie stars, celebrities, and politicians, as well as country clubs, the Eisenhower Medical Center, and the desert and its fascinating wildlife. Pick it up at any hotel in Palm Springs or at the Chamber of Commerce. Rates vary; reservations required. One to six hours in length. Call 325–2682.

Aerial tours of Palm Springs are offered by Ron Barkmeyer at *Aerial Photographic Excursions.* You will get a view of the city—with its palatial homes of great and famous people—that only the birds have seen. Advance reservations are required; call 327–4300. Also of note are helicopter tours, a unique aerial tour of Palm Springs and the surrounding desert. (Custom tours are available from *Landells Aviation,* which has two sightseeing helicopters for trips above the area. Call 329–6338.)

If floating over the desert and mountains sounds more your style, *Sunrise Balloons* has private and group flights available. Write P.O. Box 571, Palm Desert, 92261; call 346–7591.

A *Gray Lines Tour* via air-conditioned motor coach takes tourists to the Palm Springs Aerial Tramway, Living Desert Reserve, and to view dozens of celebrity homes. Other tours visit Joshua Tree National Monument, date gardens, and other southern California attractions. Call 325–0972 for information and reservations. Hotel pick-up available.

Palm Springs Safari Tours of the Desert visits homes of the celebrities, museums, landmarks. Tour takers also attend fashion shows and health spas, as well as wineries of the area. Call 320–4664.

GARDENS. From cactus to dates, Palm Springs' desert environment creates a perfect setting for some of the country's most unusual garden spots.

At *Moorten Botanical Garden,* plants from the world's great deserts are grown in special sections to simulate their original environment. Indian artifacts as well as rock, crystal, and wood forms are exhibited. Guided tours available. Moorten Botanical Garden is located at 1701 South Palm Canyon Dr.; 327–6555. Open daily, 9:00 A.M. to 5:00 P.M.

The Coachella Valley is known as the Date Capital of the World, since many varieties of dates are grown here. Palm groves have been abundant in this desert area since the late 1800s. Today, many date ranches are open for viewing. At both *Laflin Date Gardens* (in Thermal; 399–5665) and *Indian Wells Date Gardens* (on Hwy. 111 in Palm Desert; 346–2914), outdoor tables among the date groves offer a garden setting in which to drink up delicious date shakes. At *Shields Date Gardens* (80–225 Highway 111, Indio; 347–0996), watch a 30-minute color-slide show on the cultivation and history of dates. Several varieties on display. Free admission, open daily, 8:00 A.M. to 6:00 P.M.

HEALTH SPAS. For centuries, Palm Springs has been famous for its "healing" hot mineral waters. First discovered by the Cahuilla Indians, these therapeutic pools are situated beneath land that is still owned by the tribe. Today, eight acres of the land have been leased from the Indians; this is the site of the *Palm Springs Spa Hotel,* a two-million-dollar structure located at 100 North Indian Ave.; 325–1461.

A treatment here begins with a good workout in the gym, followed by a seven-minute visit to the inhalation room. Here, soothing menthol vapors relax the bronchial tubes and sinuses.

Next stop is the sauna. Three to four minutes there and your temperature rises, opening your pores in preparation for the mineral bath.

Upon exiting the sauna, you are assisted into your own private mineral pool, where you can actually feel the tension leave your body amidst the whirling waters. Ten minutes later, an escort appears to help you out of the pool, wrap you in a towel, and take you to the cooling room where you can actually go to sleep. When you awaken, take a brisk shower and be newly invigorated.

Facials and massage are also available. The spa is open daily from 9:15 A.M. to 6:00 P.M. Prices begin at $9.00.

Dennis' Canyon Villas Spa and Health Resort (520 Murray Canyon Dr.; 320–6841) is another popular spot in the desert. Guests are kept busy with daily exercises that include swimming, aerobics, horseback riding, tennis, golf, yoga, and hiking. Saunas, steam baths, massages, a mineral pool, and a skin-and-hair-care beauty center are also available. Rates range between $60 to $200, per day.

The Palms at Palm Springs (572 N. Indian Ave.; 325–1111) operates out of the old Howard Manor. Activities center around a large pool, two saunas, and nearby golf courses and tennis courts. Guests take body-contouring, yoga, and dance classes as they practice a low-calorie diet of around 800 calories a day. Rates range from $64 to $94 a day. Owner Sheila Cluff suggests packing casual clothes to visit the Palms. For reservations, call (805) 646–5573.

CHILDREN'S ACTIVITIES. For children, as well as adults, a ride on the *Palm Springs Aerial Tramway* is usually a special thrill. Located at Highway 111 and Tramway Rd.; a cable car carries you more than 8,500 feet to the top of Mount San Jacinto. Upon arrival, a restaurant and well-stocked game room that features computer games and pinball machines will surely put a smile on your child's face. During the winter months, the snow-covered mountains offer cross-country skiing and sleigh riding. Skis, shoes, and sleds can be rented at the ski center. There are also hiking trails for active families.

The *Living Desert Reserve* offers an enjoyable learning experience for children. Located in Palm Desert, there is a six-mile nature walk, as well as a walk-through aviary, coyote grotto, desert reptile exhibition, and flock of bighorn sheep in their natural habitat. The grounds are open daily, from 9:00 A.M. to 5:00 P.M. The reserve is closed during June, July, and August.

The *Agua Caliente Indian Canyons,* located six miles south of Palm Springs, offer hiking and picnic areas for family fun.

Perhaps your child will make some new friends at the *Palm Springs Swim Center* on Sunrise Highway and Ramon Rd. An Olympic-size public swimming pool has a separate swimming section for children only. Swimming instruction is available for all ages. An entrance fee is charged.

Gray Line Sightseeing Tours features a full-day excursion every Wednesday and Friday to *Disneyland,* California's most complete amusement park, home of Snow White, Cinderella, and Mickey Mouse. On Tuesday and Thursday, Gray Line ventures to *Sea World* in San Diego. A marine-life park, Sea World features a killer whale, dolphins, seals, and many aquatic shows.

Bike riding along the city's 35 miles of bike paths can make for an exciting family outing. So can horseback riding along the many equestrian trails. For details on horse and bicycle rentals, please consult the Sports section.

PARTICIPANT SPORTS. For those of you who like to play in the sun as well as bask in it, Palm Springs has much to offer in the way of sports.

Sunning is a sport in itself in Palm Springs. Here, the sun usually shines 350 days a year, making it the ideal place to get a tan, whatever the season.

When it gets too hot to sun, you can dive into one of the city's 7,000 pools. **Swimming** is a favorite pastime for Palm Springs visitors and residents alike. An Olympic-size swimming pool is available to the public at the Palm Springs Swim Center, located at Sunrise Way and Ramon Rd.; admission fee.

Palm Springs is known as the winter **"golf** capital of the world"; the city has 40 golf courses within its limits. Of the 40, 13 are open to the public. Among these are the Palm Springs Municipal Golf Course, 1885 Golf Club Dr., 328–1005; and Fairchilds Bel Aire Greens, 1001 El Cielo Road, 327–0332. Many politicians and Hollywood stars are seen on the greens and have helped elevate the status of golf in the area.

Equally popular is **tennis,** also a favorite of Hollywood's brightest stars. More than 300 tennis courts exist in the area, including 27 municipal courts. Two popular tennis centers are the *Palm Springs Tennis Courts,* 1300 Baristo Rd., 325–1381, which offers nine lighted courts, and *DeMuth Park,* 4375 Mesquite Ave., which offers four.

Why not see the city by **bicycle?** There are over 35 miles of bike trails, with five mapped-out city tours. You can rent a bike at *Mac's Bike Rental,* 700 E.

Palm Canyon, and *Burnett's Bicycle Barn,* 429 S. Sunrise Way. (Maps and rentals are available at any of the bicycle shops in town.)

Horseback riders will be pleased to hear of the miles of equestrian trails through the Indian Canyons. Horses may be rented at *Smoke Tree Stables,* 2500 Toledo, and are available during the winter and spring months. Overnight pack trips can be arranged. Mule rides are available during the summer months in Mount San Jacinto. To get there, take the Palm Springs Aerial Tramway, located at Highway 111 and Tramway Rd.

You'll find it hard not to catch a rainbow trout when **fishing** at Whitewater Trout Farm, just 10 miles north of Palm Springs.

Boating and **water-skiing** are available at the Salton Sea, a unique beach area smack in the middle of the desert. The Salton Sea is 47 miles southeast of Palm Springs on Highway 111.

Hiking in nature trails, camping, and backpacking are available in some of the *Ancient Indian Canyons. Mt. San Jacinto State Park and Wilderness* also offers these activities for those who love adventure. The Palm Springs Aerial Tramway carries you up more than 8,500 feet, where the trails begin. The little town of Idyllwild, up in the San Jacinto Mountains, is a delight, though the town—many degrees cooler than the desert floor—is a fair hike from the tramway top. The *Living Desert Reserve,* located two miles from the center of Palm Desert, offers six miles of nature trails in the serenity of the desert.

During the winter months, the Palm Springs Aerial Tramway will lead you to a snow-covered wonderland, where cross-country **skiing** and sleigh riding are available. Ski, snowshoe, and sled rentals are available at the ski center.

 SPECTATOR SPORTS. A variety of spectator sports are available in Palm Springs.

Baseball. For baseball fans, the *California Angels* do their annual spring training in Palm Springs for one full month every year. Held at Angel Stadium, east of Sunrise Way near Ramon Rd., pre-season exhibition games are played with rivals such as the San Francisco Giants, the Chicago Cubs, the Cleveland Indians, the San Diego Padres, and the Oakland As.

Golf. Over 100 golf tournaments are presented in Palm Springs: the two most popular are the *Bob Hope Desert Classic* (January) and the *Dinah Shore Championship* (April). Both have been held annually for a number of years.

Tennis. The *National Collegiate Tennis Classic* (January) is now in its seventh year, attracting men and women collegiate tennis players annually. The competition is held at Rancho Las Palmas Country Club in Rancho Mirage. Other annual tennis matches include the *James Franciscus Celebrity Tennis Classic* and the *Association of Tennis Professionals Match.*

Rodeos, horse shows, parades, the Desert Circus, and fashion shows are presented annually in Palm Springs.

Consult the *Desert Sun* or *Palm Springs Guide* magazine for scheduled events.

HISTORIC SITES. In the early days, the home-sites of the Cahuilla Indians were embedded in the Ancient Indian Canyons, where today you can still find old Indian relics. The *Agua Caliente Canyons* begin five miles south of Palm Springs on Palm Canyon Dr. Upon arriving at the reservation, an Indian tollkeeper collects a nominal fee at the gate.

Palm Canyon, the most frequently visited canyon, is noted for its lovely palm trees, which were planted centuries ago. The site has been used as a setting for several movies. A cold-water stream flows through the area. The canyon is open for hiking and picnicking, October through June.

Andreas Canyon abounds with tribal lore and history. Its richly scenic bridal trail is most popular with desert riders.

The band of wild ponies that inhabits Murray Canyon is supposedly related to early canyon animals. It is the least accessible and most primitive of the canyons.

The beautiful falls of Tahquitz Canyon have made it the location for several motion picture scenes, including the original version of "Lost Horizon."

Tahquitz, Murray, and Andreas canyons may be closed to visitors at certain times of the year; information is always posted at the main entrance to the canyons.

Just north of Palm Springs you will find *Cabot's Old Indian Pueblo Museum,* 67616 E. Desert View Ave. in Desert Hot Springs. This Indian pueblo, featuring a Hopi-style design, was built by one man, Cabot Yerxa. Starting in 1941, it took him 20 years to complete. The structure has 35 rooms, 150 windows, and 65 doors. Original desert paintings are exhibited in the art gallery, while the museum and trading post feature Indian relics and artifacts.

In 1884, "Judge" John McCallum, a San Franciscan, was the first white settler in Palm Springs. Today, his adobe home has been restored and stands in the center of town. Referred to as the *McCallum Adobe Museum,* it houses rare photographs, paintings, and artifacts representing this early period. The museum is located at the Village Green Heritage Center, 221 S. Palm Canyon Dr., and is open Wednesday through Sunday.

Next door to the museum you'll find the *Cornelia White House,* a restored version of an original house built in 1894 that belonged to one of Palm Springs' earliest settlers. Purchased by the Whites in 1912, the house is constructed of rail ties from the Old Palmdale Railway. It displays antiques and relics, and is also open Wednesday through Sunday.

The *Palm Springs Historical Society,* housed in a turn-of-the-century log cabin, preserves and displays historical artifacts of the town. It's located at the Village Green near the Vineyard on South Palm Canyon Dr.

The *Spa Hotel,* the home of the famed Palm Springs mineral baths, is located on land leased from the Agua Caliente Indians and has been deemed a state historical site.

LIBRARIES. Palm Springs' main library branch is housed in the Library Center, 300 S. Sunrise Way. The library has more than 78,000 volumes, 250 current magazines, and audio-visual aids, and also offers an unusual "loan-out" art and sculpture service.

At the Welwood Murray Branch, located downtown at 100 S. Palm Canyon Dr., Palm Springs residents relax over a newspaper or a game of chess.

 MUSEUMS AND ART GALLERIES. A full spectrum of art, from avant garde and modern to traditional, can be seen at the newly expanded *Palm Springs Desert Museum,* located on Museum Dr. between Tahquitz-McCallum Way and Andreas Rd. In addition to art, the museum concentrates on natural science and the performing arts. Nationally and internationally famed artists are featured at the museum, as well as classical ballet, choral activities, chamber music, and ethnic dance. All can be seen (or heard) in the 450-seat Annenberg Theater. Open 10:00 A.M. to 5:00 P.M.; closed Monday. Call 325–7186.

Cabot's Old Indian Pueblo Museum is a four-story Hopi-Indian-style structure with 35 rooms, 150 windows, and 65 doors. It was constructed single-handedly by Cabot Yerxa over a 20-year period. The museum contains many Indian artifacts and relics from the early days. Located at 67616 East Desert View Ave., Desert Hot Springs, just minutes north of Palm Springs. Call 329–7610.

The *Village Green Heritage Center* comprises two 19th-century pioneer homes. The McCallum Adobe, built in 1884, and Miss Cornelia's "Little House," built in 1894, represent the pioneer era in Palm Springs. Open Wednesday through Saturday, 10:00 A.M. to 4:00 P.M. and Sundays from 1:00 to 4:00 P.M. $1.00 admission to both homes. Located at 221 South Palm Canyon Dr.

Palm Springs boasts many art galleries that carry a wide variety of work, ranging from Indian, desert, and western art to lithographs and oriental pieces. Most of the galleries are located on Palm Canyon Dr. in the center of town.

 MUSIC. The desert offers a dazzling calendar of musical events. The *Palm Springs Friends of the Los Angeles Philharmonic* provide a consistently rewarding repertoire of classical works. The Sunday afternoon concert series—highly regarded in Southern California—includes dance groups, chamber orchestras, and soloists. The organization sponsors 10 events a year on selected Sundays in the Desert Museum's Annenberg Auditorium. During March, the *Palm Springs Opera Guild* presents an extravagant program, including touring companies from the major civic centers.

The *Palm Springs Desert Museum* sponsors a somewhat lighter selection, including programs by Benny Goodman and his orchestra and the Los Angeles Chamber Orchestra.

SHOPPING. If it weren't for the 1,200 palm trees lining the boulevard, you might think you were strolling down the Rue du Faubourg-St. Honoré in Paris instead of Palm Canyon Drive in Palm Springs. The many custom boutiques and elegant art galleries provide hours of shopping pleasure, not only on Palm Canyon Drive but throughout the Palm Springs area. This resort community also has several large air-conditioned indoor malls that offer not only chic boutiques and fast-food restaurants, but major department stores as well. Nearby Palm Desert's El Paseo seeks to rival Palm Canyon Drive, with its original art galleries, antiques stores, and designer boutiques.

Palm Canyon Drive is Palm Spring's most popular shopping destination. It began as a dusty two-way dirt road, and is now a one-way, three-lane thoroughfare with parking on both sides. Its shopping core extends from Alejo Road on the north to Ramon Road on the south. The street's architecture is an eclectic blend of Spanish and modern. Individual shopping arcades are a street tradition, each with its own distinctive flavor. Expect to find everything your heart desires —though your pocketbook may or may not agree with your selections. Furs, jewelry, sportswear, books, home furnishings, ice cream parlors, shoe stores, and craft shops will tempt you on this busy street.

Highlights of the boulevard are *Bullocks Wilshire,* an exclusive department store; *Adagio Galleries,* featuring original paintings, graphics and sculptures, and *James Callahan,* an interior-design showroom of furniture and artwork from all over the world. At night, many of the palm trees are illuminated, creating a relaxed ambiance as you window-shop. Bob Hope has even been seen strolling down Palm Canyon Drive in the evening.

El Paseo Village is touted as a true shopping experience rather than a shopping center. Unique stores are architecturally designed with a Spanish motif, and are clustered among flower-lined paths, fountained courtyards, and gently flowing lakes. *Crock-R-Box* is the collected artistry of over 100 professional American craftspeople. A zoo of animals can be found at the *D'Cooper Galleria,* where an array of elephants, birds, and other wildlife is reproduced in copper, brass, papier-maché, paintings, and prints. Be sure to stop at *Whatever:* it's like visiting Greenwich Village and Santa's Workshop at the same time; the wearable art, unusual greeting cards, and gourmet jelly beans here are a bountiful feast for the eye as well as the stomach.

A major shopping center is the *Rancho Las Palmas* on Highway 111 and Bob Hope Drive, Rancho Mirage. Its shops feature specialty floral arrangements, gourmet kitchen ware, imported chocolate and confections, and antiques, and there are fine restaurants.

With seemingly endless opportunities for diversified shopping, Palm Springs surely competes with almost any major shopping capital in the world. The glamour and individuality of its boutiques appeal to a wide cross-section of consumers.

DINING OUT. Culinary experiences in Palm Springs vary with your mood, for everything is available in this rather small city and the area surrounding it. Eating out isn't always necessary for visitors, though, because a good number of hotel properties (particularly the smaller, less expensive ones) have their own kitchens and, occasionally, an outdoor barbecue. Supermarkets nearby carry just about anything desired.

But for those who like to dine out, Palm Springs has it all: from French, Italian, and American cuisine to the more exotic Indian, Moroccan, and Japanese menus. We've provided a sampling of area eateries; for a more complete selection, see the Palm Springs Convention and Visitors Bureau staff at the Palm Springs airport for one of their dining guides.

Establishments are categorized according to the price of a dinner from the middle range of their menus. Price categories may be interpreted as follows: *Expensive*, $25 and above; *Moderate*, $10–$25; and *Inexpensive*, below $10. Not included are drinks, tip, and tax. A more complete explanation of price categories can be found in the Facts at Your Fingertips section at the front of this guide.

Expensive

Alberto's Ristorante. 71416 Highway 111, Rancho Mirage; 346-3221. This Northern Italian restaurant is the sister to the ever-popular Alberto's in West Hollywood. Veal piccata, scampi fra diavalo, and chicken papagallo are special favorites. Pastas are either imported or homemade and cooked *al dente*. Cheesecake is made fresh daily from an old family recipe, and is only one step away from heaven. Service is most attentive and the decor is comfortable and elegant. Full bar. Semi-dressy. V, MC.

Etienne's. 72–281 Highway 111, Palm Desert; 340-1888. An upper-echelon restaurant founded in Scottsdale, Arizona, is bound for success in its second home in the desert. The cuisine is authentically and aristocratically French. Canard a l'orange, beef and seafood filets, and elaborate French pastries are featured. The wine selection is extensive, featuring a good blend of both California and French vintages. Cocktail lounge. Dinner from 6:00 P.M., Monday through Saturday. Dressy. All major credit cards.

La Cave. Located below the Medium Rare on Restaurant Row, Rancho Mirage; 324-4673. A French restaurant designed to pamper your individual whims and desires. The menu changes daily according to the fresh ingredients available; fresh fish is flown in daily. Imagine fresh flowers, linen tablecloths, and sterling silver and you've got the picture. Soft piano music while you dine. Dinner from 6:00 P.M.; closed Sundays. Dressy. All major credit cards.

Le Vallauris. 385 W. Tahquitz-McCallum, Palm Springs; 325-5059 or 325-5050. An exclusive French restaurant that celebrates nouvelle French cuisine. Mousseline de trois poissons aux asperges and tarte tatin are two popular specialties. Provisional membership is $5 for the host, valid one month, or yearly at $50. Entertainment includes piano. Dressy. Reservations necessary. Noon to 2:00 P.M., Tuesday through Friday and Sunday. Dinner from 6:00 P.M., Tuesday through Sunday. All major credit cards.

Melvyn's Restaurant. 200 W. Ramon Rd., Palm Springs; 325-2323. A gathering place for celebrities, including Frank Sinatra, this restaurant is snugly nestled in the pretty gardens of the Ingleside Inn in the heart of Palm Springs. The cuisine is continental and the motif is Old World. Live entertainment and dancing. Saturday and Sunday brunch on the patio is a Palm Springs tradition, from 9:00 A.M. to 3:00 P.M. Noon to 3:00 P.M., Monday through Friday, and dinner from 6:00 P.M. to 11:00 P.M., daily. Dressy. No DC.

Riccio's. 2155 N. Palm Canyon Dr., Palm Springs; 325-2369. Tony Riccio, formerly of the Marquis in Beverly Hills and Martoni's of Hollywood, is becoming famous all over again with this relatively new restaurant. Fresh seafood dishes, imported pasta, and milk-fed veal are renowned specialties. Most appetizers are guaranteed to be outstanding. Easy listening music at the piano. Semi-dressy. 5:00 P.M. to 1:00 A.M., daily. No DC or CB.

Tapestry Room. Sheraton Plaza–Palm Springs. 450 E. Tahquitz-McCallum, Palm Springs; 320-6868. This hotel dining room spares no expense. Located in this city's first new hotel in 15 years, it focuses on food, beverages, and service of the highest quality. The menu is Continental, the decor is elaborate, and the wine list goes on and on. Perfect for a very special occasion. Dressy. Sunday brunch, 10:00 A.M. to 2:00 P.M. Monday through Saturday, noon to 2:00 P.M. Dinner nightly, 6:00 P.M. to 10:30 P.M. All major credit cards.

Moderate

Adriatic. 71–877 Highway 111, Rancho Mirage; 346-0252. A rare sight in the desert, a restaurant featuring Yugoslavian food. Chicken paprikash, scampi Dalmatian-style, and a fish-of-the-day are house specialties. Try the calamari (squid) appetizer. The octopus salad may sound awful, but is really good. Cheese and meat bureks are flaky pastry appetizers. Children's menu. Cocktails and extensive wine list. Casual or semi-dressy. No DC.

Agua Room. Palm Springs Hotel, 100 N. Indian Ave., Palm Springs; 325-1461. A Palm Springs landmark restaurant. The menu is comprehensive Continental, served with impeccable style in an old-world ambiance. Roast rack of lamb bouquetiere is a house specialty. Vegetables are very fresh and French pastries a sophisticated treat. Entertainment and dancing. Dressy for dinner. Valet parking. 7:30 A.M. to 11:00 P.M., daily. All major credit cards.

The Fountain Room. Chaparral Country Club. 42–555 Portola, Palm Desert; 340-1893. American and Continental menu specializing in fresh fish entrees flown in daily from Pacific and Delta waters. Steaks, veal, chicken, and prime rib are also featured. Desserts are made on the premises. 11:30 A.M. to 2:30 P.M., 5:00 P.M. to 10:00 P.M., Tuesday through Sunday; Sunday brunch 10:30 A.M. to 2:30 P.M. Semi-dressy. All major credit cards.

Kiyosaku. 1563 S. Palm Canyon Dr., Palm Springs; 327-6601. The only authentic Japanese restaurant in Palm Springs. Tempura, sukiyaki, and teriyaki dishes are most popular. Its sushi bar is now becoming the rage. Complimentary glass of sweet plum wine with dinner. 11:30 A.M. to 2:30 P.M. and 5:30 P.M. to 10:30 P.M., Tuesday through Saturday. Beer and wine. V, MC.

Las Casuelas Nuevas. 70–050 Highway 111, Rancho Mirage. Fine Mexican cuisine served in a Spanish courtyard atmosphere. Guitar players and mariachis are featured nightly. Open daily for lunch. MC, V, and AE.

Medium Rare. 70–064 Highway 111, Rancho Mirage; 328-6563. Modern English pub decor with Continental menu. Located on Restaurant Row. Four theme dining rooms feature prime rib of beef, rack of lamb, and scampi from Costa del Sol. Spinach salads and individual loaves of seven-grain bread are noted specialties. 11:30 A.M. to 2:45 P.M., Monday through Friday; dinner from 5:00 P.M., Monday through Saturday. Semi-dressy. All major credit cards.

1000 East. Biltmore Hotel, 1000 E. Palm Canyon Dr., Palm Springs; 323-1811. Continental cuisine is well-prepared in a low-keyed atmosphere. Restaurant overlooks splendid landscaped gardens. Eastern seafood, live Maine lobster, and Italian and French specialties. Saturday and Sunday Champagne brunch. Cocktails and piano music. 7:00 to 3:00 P.M. Monday through Friday; 10:00 A.M. to 3:00 P.M., Saturday and Sunday; 6:00 P.M. to 11:00 P.M., daily. All major credit cards.

Perrina's. 340 N. Palm Canyon Dr.; 325–6544. Continental-Italian cuisine; atmosphere is warm and intimate, food cooked to order. Piano bar, entertainment. Dinner served. Closed Monday and Tuesday. All major credit cards except AE.

The Rusty Pelican. Highway 111 at Rancho Mirage and Palm Desert border, Palm Desert; 346-8065. It's not a mirage, there is an oasis in the desert at this nautical restaurant. There's even a boat in dry dock on the premises. Fresh seafood is their specialty, and Rusty's Oyster Bar shucks to order. The clam chowder is popular. Cocktails. Live entertainment and dancing, Tuesday through Saturday. Casual. No DC.

Tai Ping. 45–299 Lupine Lane on El Paseo, Palm Desert; 340-1836. Elegant Chinese restaurant with favorites of toss-shredded hot chicken salad, jumbo prawn tempura and Indian curry. Enjoyable selection of Polynesian drinks in cocktail lounge. Happy hour. Semi-dressy. 5:00 P.M. to 10:00 P.M., daily except Monday. No DC.

Inexpensive

Di Amico's Steak House. 1180 S. Palm Canyon Dr., Palm Springs; 325-9191. Hearty eaters will enjoy dining at this Early California-style restaurant. The menu focuses on prime Eastern cornfed beef, with seafood specialties too. Look for a liver steak vaquero and "son-of-a-gun stew" as special entrees. You've heard of a three-martini lunch; how about a salad bar and a martini-burger? Casual. Open daily, lunch 11:00 A.M. to 3:00 P.M., and dinner 5:00 P.M. to 11:00 P.M. Piano bar in cocktail lounge except Monday. V, MC.

Elmer's Pancake and Steak House. 1030 E. Palm Canyon Dr., Palm Springs; 327-8419. Forget about Aunt Jemima. Elmer's offers 25 varieties of pancakes and waffles, including buckwheat, cakes, German, and Swedish pancakes, and blueberry roll-ups. There are steaks, chicken, and seafood on the dinner menu. Children's menu too. Casual; the atmosphere is colonial-style. 7:00 A.M. to 9:00 P.M., Sunday through Thursday; 7:00 A.M. to 10:00 P.M., Friday and Saturday. V, MC.

House of Lamb. Highway 111 and Grove, Cathedral City; 328-7518. Owner-chef Arthur Morris loves lamb, and he prepares a menu full of it, both American and Greek-style: rack of lamb, leg of lamb, lamb shanks, lamb stew, shish kabob, and lamb patties are specialties. Dinner prices include homemade soup, complete salad bar, home-baked bread, entree, beverage, and home-baked dessert. Seats 65. Casual. Beer and wine. 4:00 P.M. to 9:00 P.M., Tuesday through Saturday, 3:00 P.M. to 9:00 P.M., Sunday. V, MC.

Louise's Pantry. 124 S. Palm Canyon Dr., Palm Springs; 325-5124. A Palm Springs landmark, located in the center of the downtown district for 32 years. Features down-home cooking: specialties are chicken and dumplings, petrale sole, and short ribs of beef. For less than $7 you will get soup, salad, entree, beverage, and dessert. Home-baked sweet rolls for breakfast, moist cakes and flaky pies for lunch and dinner; they're kinda like Mama used to make before Duncan Hines came along. Casual. 7:00 A.M. to 10:00 P.M., daily. No credit cards.

Nate's Deli. 283 N. Palm Canyon Dr., Palm Springs; 325-3506. There are 100 sandwich combinations on this menu and they are piled as high as their list is long. Nate's nickname is "Mr. Corned Beef of Palm Springs," so we'll let you figure out their specialty. Rye bread is outstanding, so is the borscht. Come between 4:00 and 6:00 P.M. for special nine-course dinners that include fried chicken and brisket of beef. 8:00 A.M. to 8:30 P.M., daily. Take-out service available. Casual. Wine and beer. V, MC.

Old World Restaurant. 262 S. Palm Canyon Dr., Palm Springs; 325-5502. Organic-style restaurant chain. Fresh-squeezed juices, Belgian waffles, garden-fresh salads, and preservative-free meats are main attractions. Don't feel guilty if you enjoy one of their desserts; they're prepared with health in mind, too. Patio dining. Casual. 9:00 A.M. to 10:00 P.M., daily. No DC.

Tony Roma's. 450 S. Palm Canyon Dr., Palm Springs; 320-4297. The place for ribs: crisp, tender, and relatively ungooey. The sauce is slightly sweet. Baby back ribs and barbecued chicken are specialties of the house. Try the irresistible onion-ring loaf. Great fun; entertainment nightly. Casual. 11:00 A.M. to 2:00 A.M., Monday through Friday; noon to 2:00 A.M., Saturday; and 3:00 P.M. to 2:00 A.M., Sunday. No reservations. Cocktails. Valet parking. V, MC.

 NIGHT LIFE. Whether your mood calls for a quiet evening or the pulsating beat of a disco, Palm Springs offers a vast array of "after dark" activities.

Live entertainment, ranging from soft dinner music to a Las Vegas-style floor show, is found in a number of the city's hotels and restaurants. The *Hilton Riviera,* 1600 N. Indian Ave., 327-8311, features a spectacular nightly floor show that rivals any in Las Vegas. Big-band music is showcased every Monday night.

Piano bar music, often accompanied by a vocalist, can be heard at *Harry's Bar* at the Sheraton Plaza, 400 E. Tahquitz-McCallum Way, 320–6868, and at a number of restaurants, such as *Banducci's Bit of Italy,* 1260 S. Palm Canyon Dr., 325–2537, *Tony Roma's,* 450 S. Palm Canyon Dr. (great prime rib), 320–

4297 or *One Thousand East*, at the Biltmore Hotel, 1000 E. Palm Canyon Dr. 323–1811—where some of the best lobster in town is served, incidentally.

At *Las Casuelas Terraza*, 222 South Palm Canyon Dr., 325–2794, guitar players and mariachis entertain you while you dine.

A number of nightclubs and discos offer dancing, with music to satisfy people of all ages and tastes.

You can enjoy dancing while dining Continental-style at the *Buss Stop* in the Ocotillo Lodge, 1111 E. Palm Canyon Dr., 327–1141. This restaurant is owned by Jerry Buss, who also owns the Los Angeles Lakers, the Kings, and the Los Angeles Forum. *Melvyn's Ingleside Inn*, 200 West Ramon Rd., 325–2323, is a celebrity favorite, featuring live dance music nightly. Some of the finest haute cuisine in the valley is served here. The *Agua Room* in the Spa Hotel, 100 N. Indian Ave., 325–1461, features excellent Continental cuisine with live dance music in the bar.

Raffles, at the Canyon Hotel Bar, 2850 S. Palm Canyon Dr., 323–7188, delivers everything from rock to slow dancing nightly.

If it's disco you're looking for, *Cecil's* (1775 E. Palm Canyon Dr., 320–4202) is the place. Backlit Chinese artifacts and mirrored palm trees flash on and off to the music, creating the obligatory wild effect. Cecil's also features a separate dining room where slow dancing is standard. *Zelda's*, 169 N. Indian Ave. (across from the Spa Hotel), 325–2375, is another disco that attracts a full house with its mirrors and chrome floors. Or you can try *Ichabod's* (450 S. Palm Canyon Dr.) for more dancing to the disco beat.

For those who like country-western dancing, *Bronco Billie's* (68623 Perez Rd. in Cathedral City, 324–9595) features live music, dancing, and for brave souls, a mechanical bull, à la "Urban Cowboy."

If you're in the mood for a good laugh, the place to go is *The Laff Stop*, 217 N. Palm Canyon Dr., 320–6918. Some of the country's funniest established and up-and-coming comedians perform here nightly. And the *Comedy Haven* (1445 N. Sunrise, 320–7855) offers American-Italian fare along with its laughs.

Two good sources for finding current nightlife attractions are the *Desert Sun*, (the local newspaper) and *Guide* magazine, a monthly publication distributed free at every downtown merchant's counter.

SOUTH ALONG THE COAST

We divide the area south of Los Angeles into two sections. The first is what might be called "Central Orange County," centered around Anaheim (Disneyland; Knott's Berry Farm just to the north)—and not including any of the coastal areas of the county. This central part of Orange we cover as Anaheim/Orange County.

The second area begins at Long Beach, on the coast of Orange County just south of Los Angeles, skips over to Santa Catalina Island, then back to the coast and on down through Newport Beach and Laguna Beach to San Clemente. (South of San Clemente is Camp Pendleton and San Diego County, covered in Fodor's *San Diego*.)

ANAHEIM/ORANGE COUNTY

by
JANE LASKY and MARIE MONEYSMITH

Jane Lasky, a Los Angeles resident, is a contributor to the Los Angeles Times Syndicate. She also writes a food column for Country Gentleman *magazine and is a contributing editor of* Travel Agent *magazine. She has also written for* Bon Appetit, Working Woman, *and many in-flight magazines. Marie Moneysmith has written for the new* Saturday Evening Post, New West *magazine, and the* Los Angeles Times.

Along 42 miles of sun-drenched southern California coastline, between the counties of Los Angeles and San Diego, Orange County extends some 25 miles inland across rolling farmland, strawberry fields, and orange groves. At the eastern end lie the canyons and largely uninhabited mountain wilderness of the Santa Ana Mountains. The county's population of nearly two million is contained primarily in the cities in the northwest corner and along the coast. This section of our guide covers the northwestern and central parts, not the coast or the east.

In the 1600s, the Spaniards discovered this area—now known as Orange County—and colonized it, basking in the new-found land rich with ranching and farming possibilities. Land was not parceled out in small units, but rather divided into six rambling ranches, where oranges, walnuts, strawberries, and flowers flourished in the lush valley between the ocean and the mountains.

The original land grants have changed hands, of course, but most of the land parcels have remained intact, never having been subdivided by the individual owners. In fact, three quarters of Orange County is privately owned by a few landholders, with most of the industrial and urban growth having been achieved on leased land—a peculiarity indigenous to Orange County in the United States.

Anaheim

Once a part of these Spanish land grants, Anaheim—or "the home by the river"—was named by early German settlers who bought the land for two dollars an acre in the mid-1800s. German colonists immigrated to the region to grow grapes and seek their fortunes producing wine. In fact, for many years, Anaheim was the state's wine capital. But in the 1880s, blight completely wiped out the vineyards, ending the new wine industry.

Undaunted, colonists looked to their citrus crops, which were perfectly suited to the area's climate. Extensive groves were planted and a prosperous orange industry was soon developed. The years that followed were a time of ever increasing expansion and development for the young city of Anaheim.

Then, in 1955, Walt Disney opened the doors of his magic kingdom, Disneyland; tourism came to the area, forever changing the face of Anaheim and Orange County.

Anaheim is a prime world-class visitor destination today. It is the headquarters of almost all the area amusement parks: besides Disneyland, there are Knott's Berry Farm and attractions such as Six Flags' Movieland Wax Museum. In fact, this city has the unusual distinction of being able to claim two of the three most popular amusement parks in the nation. Anaheim's world-famous Disneyland, visited by more than ten million each year is, of course, first, followed in third place by Knott's Berry Farm, host annually to nearly five million people (Florida's Disney World is number two).

Disneyland

At Disneyland, visitors will find the fruits of Walt Disney's dream; this fantasy-maker had hopes of creating the "happiest place on earth," and there are literally millions who agree that he did just that. From the entrance into Main Street, a typical turn-of-the-century American thoroughfare, the various "lands" of Disneyland—Tomorrowland, Frontierland, Fantasyland, Adventureland—open up.

Tomorrowland offers a glimpse into the future as a monorail whisks passengers around the park, giving them an unhindered view of the many attractions. On a miniature reproduction of the freeways of the future, scale automobiles can be driven. Other forms of transportation include a sky ride and a rocket trip to the moon. Space Mountain is a fast-paced journey hurtling through space.

Fantasyland has been updated, and many attractions altered. Pinocchio's Daring Journey is a new character ride; ocean waves and a fly-through waterfall have been added to the Peter Pan Flight; and logs turn into crocodiles in Snow White's Scary Adventures.

Sporting a new snowcap and with a new bobsled, the Matterhorn is for the brave, who careen through snowstorms, fog, icy caverns, and an encounter with the Abominable Snowman.

In Frontierland, visitors can step back into America's yesteryear. Passengers experience Wild West adventures in southwestern terrain, complete with mining tunnels, caverns, earthquakes, and avalanches. One of Disneyland's newest rides, Big Thunder Mountain, a runaway mine train, whips down a spine-tingling roller-coaster track as it travels along twisting mountain paths. The sternwheeler *Mark Train* and the sailing vessel *Columbia* take passengers aboard to explore the rivers of America and the popular Tom Sawyer's Island. Ride on rafts, just as Tom and Huck Finn did, or seek out caves to explore and burros to ride. During the summer season, entertainers on the dock and on the two boats cruise this early American western lagoon.

In Adventureland, the Jungle Cruise takes passengers through swamplike jungles, where they must be ever watchful for snapping alligators or crocodiles. Jungle sounds screech as rampaging rhinos and other menacing animals appear in the thick tropical foliage. For every swashbuckler, young and old alike, an adventure with the Pirates of the Caribbean satisfies the renegade in all. Another favorite for the kids is a climb into a tremendous tree, similar to one in Disney's Swiss Family Robinson movie. This tree has *three* tree houses to rummage through.

Throughout the park are curio shops, some with inexpensive keepsakes, some with exquisite mementos. And Disneyland has restaurants of all descriptions, ranging from expensive full-course dining rooms to snack and refreshment stands.

There seems to be no end to enjoyment in this vast theme park, no matter when you come; winter (open weekends only) or summer, Disneyland is always fresh and clean. One of the surprising, if not well-known features, is the park's spotless reputation. Everything in Disneyland is wholesome (no drinking of alcohol on the premises) and everywhere bright, polite, cheerful attendants give each and every visitor a warm welcome to Walt Disney's "happiest place on earth!"

Knott's Berry Farm

A ten-acre fruit patch, Knott's Berry Farm, on Beach Boulevard in Buena Park, began entertaining visitors several decades ago as a re-created ghost town. Additions and expansions have resulted in today's Knott's Berry Farm, a 150-acre complex, featuring more than 20 restaurants, 40 shops, and 100 rides and attractions. Among them are the Calico Mine ride, which brings back the flavor of the Old West, and the Roaring '20s section, with its old-time airfield and some very zippy rides. Fiesta Village, one of Knott's older attractions, has recently been refurbished and now includes a Soapbox Races ride, plus the Dragon Boat, a ride that recalls the days of Viking exploration. For fearless visitors, there are two attractions unsurpassed for thrills: the Cork-

ARTESIA FRWY.

Movieland
Wax Museum
Alligator
Farm

Lakewood

SAN GABRIEL RIVER FRWY.

LA PALMA AVE.

Knotts
Berry
Farm

Buena Park
Shopping
Center

LINCOLN AVE.

Long Beach

VALLEY VIEW ST.

KNOTT ST.

MAGNOLIA AVE.

405

605

SAN DIEGO FRWY.

KATELLA AVE.

22

405

22

Marina
Pacific
Shopping
Center

Seal Beach

SAN DIEGO FRWY.

PACIFIC COAST HWY.

Westminster
Mall Shopping
Center

BOLSA CHICA RD.

MAGNOLIA ST.

Anaheim
Bay

Huntington
Shopping
Center

WEST ST.

Sunset Beach

Huntington
Beach

GOLDEN ST.

PACIFIC OCEAN

CENTRAL ORANGE COUNTY

screw and Sky Jump parachute rides. For those who prefer vicarious thrills, a 180-degree Omnivision Theater shows films of the more treacherous rides. During the summer, Knott's also hosts an ice-skating show with talented performers. In addition, there is live rock music and dancing nightly.

A new addition to the park, Camp Snoopy, has 30 rides and attractions. Included are: a mule-powered merry-go-round, a Red Baron plane ride, and a wheeler steamboat.

Because of Knott's Berry Farm, Disneyland, and other area attractions—not to mention the city's proximity to many popular nearby beaches—Anaheim has become a natural site for conventions of all description. More than 650,000 delegates travel there annually to meet in the newly expanded Anaheim Convention Center, an ultramodern facility with 35 spacious meeting rooms and an arena that easily seats more than 9,000.

More visitors than ever, from all over the world, are expected to make their way to Orange County when the summer Olympics are held in Los Angeles in 1984. This surge of visitors will be met with open arms. Guests will choose from all manner of overnight accommodations; the more than 16,000 rooms here range from family-oriented units for the budget conscious to elegant, full-service luxury hotels.

To make room for new activities and forms of recreation, several projects are already underway. A 2,189-seat performing arts theater is set to open in Anaheim, and a 1,422-seat equestrian arena, The Kingdom of Dancing Stallions, featuring 32 highly trained horses—reminiscent of the famed white Lippizaner horses of Vienna—has been constructed and recently opened in Buena Park. And the 19,000-seat Pacific Amphitheater is new at the Orange County Fairgrounds.

Annual festivals in major Orange County cities feature almost everything, from local arts-and-crafts exhibits to the area's own special brand of attractions. Most of Orange County's cities—Anaheim, Orange, Fullerton, Santa Ana, and Garden Grove—are undergoing restoration of their original turn-of-the-century downtown buildings.

Restaurants in the area have begun to rival those of more populated Los Angeles, with every type of cuisine imaginable. Shopping in the County is also quite distinct; nearly every community has a shopping area, whether it be an enclosed mall, a boardwalk village, or a collection of more sophisticated international shops. With all of these offerings, Orange County continues to beckon visitors to its vacation wonderland, promising them all sorts of adventures.

PRACTICAL INFORMATION FOR
ORANGE COUNTY

HOW TO GET THERE. By air. Some 35 miles from downtown Anaheim, Los Angeles International Airport (LAX) is easily accessible by ground transportation from the Orange County area. LAX can be reached from any point in the United States; the airport is serviced by more airlines than any other in the world. The most frequent long-distance direct flights are offered by American, Continental, Delta, Eastern, National, Northwest Orient, TWA, United, and Western. From Honolulu, Pan Am also has service; from Canada, you may fly either Air Canada or Western. From Mexico, Aeromexico, Mexicana de Aviacion, and Western offer flights. From Europe, you may fly Pan Am, British Airways, Lufthansa, Air France, or KLM. From the Pacific, you may take Japan Airlines, Air New Zealand, UTA, or Qantas.

The John Wayne Orange County Airport is 14 miles south from centrally located Anaheim, with daily local flights from San Diego, Los Angeles, Denver, Salt Lake City, Seattle, Phoenix, and other major cities. The airport services American, Aircal, Frontier, Golden West, Pacific Southwest Airlines (PSA), and Republic.

By train. Amtrak offers six departures daily from Los Angeles, south to San Diego, with stops in Fullerton, Santa Ana, San Clemente, and San Juan Capistrano. Fullerton or Santa Ana stops are convenient and easily accessible from Anaheim.

By car. Interstate Highways 5 and 405 travel north-south through the county, intersecting with Highways 22, 55, and 91, which travel east to the mountains and west to the beaches. U.S. 5 goes directly south to San Diego.

TELEPHONES. In 1982 Orange County was split into two area codes, 714 and 619. The majority of numbers in this section are in the central and coastal areas of the county, 714; the 619 code covers the eastern area of the county. If in doubt, check with the operator. You do not need to dial the area code if it is the same as the one from which you are calling, although you must dial "1" (one) for some city-to-city calls. Information (known as directory assistance) is 411. When direct-dialing a long-distance number from anywhere in Orange County, you must dial the number "1" (one) *before* you dial the area code and the number itself. An operator will assist you on person-to-person, credit card, and collect calls if you dial "0" first. Pay telephones still start at 10 cents.

Fantasyland

1) Motor Boat Cruise
2) "It's A Small World"
3) Mr. Toad's Wild Ride
4) Fantasyland Autopia
5) Matterhorn Bobsleds
6) Storybook Land
7) Snow White's Adventures
8) Mad Tea Party
9) Dumbo Flying Elephants
10) Casey Jr. Circus Train
11) King Arthur Carrousel
12) Peter Pan Flight
13) Alice in Wonderland

Tomorrowland

14) Skyway to Fantasyland
15) America the Beautiful
16) People Mover
17) America Sings
18) Rocket Jets
19) Submarine Voyage
20) Tomorrowland Monorail
21) Mission to Mars
22) Tomorrowland Autopia
23) Adventure Thru Inner Space
24) Space Mountain

Tomorrowland

Grand Canyon
Diorama

Primeval
World

DISNEYLAND

Disneyland
Kennel Club

Stroller and
Wheelchair
Rentals

Disneyland
Monorail System

Entrance

Street

Square

Castle

New Orleans Square
25) Pirates of the Caribbean
26) Haunted Mansion

Frontierland
27) Explorer Canoes
28) Columbia Sailing Ship
29) Tom Sawyer's Island
30) Golden Horseshoe
31) Keel Boats and Tom Sawyer Rafts
32) Shooting Gallery
33) Mark Twain Steamboat

Main Street
34) Penny Arcade
35) Main Street Cinema
36) The Walt Disney Story and "Great
Moments With Mr. Lincoln"

Adventureland
37) Big Game Shoot
38) Swiss Family Tree House
39) Jungle Cruise
40) Enchanted Tiki Room

CLIMATE. Orange County boasts a year-round temperate climate ranging from a low of 45 degrees in the winter to a high of 79 degrees in the summer. Average annual rainfall is 15 inches, which includes some April showers. Come early fall, the Santana (or Santa Ana) Winds invade the area, causing September and the first part of October to be the hottest and most uncomfortable months of the year. These winds, which Californians have come to know as the cause of their Indian Summer, create a very dry and windy climate—and inevitably take a turn for the better, making the end of October and November a most attractive time to visit Orange County.

Because temperatures in this area tend to drop dramatically in the evening, a sweater or light overcoat is recommended.

HOTELS & MOTELS. Orange County's overnight facilities are plentiful, especially with Anaheim's recent convention industry boom. More than ten million worldwide visitors annually come to the Anaheim/ Orange County area seeking adventure at Disneyland and other attractions. You are likely to find accommodations easily adaptable to any budget, from the elaborate to the bargain. (Two new super-deluxe hotels are scheduled to open in the summer of 1984: the Anaheim Hilton and the Emerald of Anaheim. See FODOR'S LOS ANGELES 1985 for descriptions of both.) Take note: Even though more than 16,000 rooms are available, reservations are necessary year-round. Based on double occupancy, price categories are as follows: *Super Deluxe,* $75 and up; *Deluxe,* $60–$75; *Expensive,* $42–$60; *Moderate,* $30–$42; and *Inexpensive,* $18–$30. Listings are divided by price range category. For more details, see the "Facts at Your Fingertips" section.

ANAHEIM

Deluxe

Disneyland Hotel. 1150 West Cerritos Ave.; (714) 778–6600. Connected to Disneyland by monorail, this 1,000-room hotel is actually a 60-acre resort. Choose accommodations in one of the tropical villages, or perch in the spacious towers. Shop at the waterfront bazaar, with ports-of-call shops specializing in exotic wares from Hong Kong, Australia, Mexico, or Tahiti. Swim in one of three pools or walk the sandy shores of the hotel's cove. For exercise, pedal-boat on the marina. Ten lighted tennis courts, fourteen (yes!) restaurants.

Grand Hotel. 1 Hotel Way; (714) 772-7777. Adjacent to Disneyland with a free shuttle. Boutiques and gift shop keep guests happy. Special entertainment features dinner theater. Dining room, coffee shop, pool. No pets.

Hyatt Anaheim. 1700 S. Harbor Blvd.; (714) 772–5900. Near Disneyland; heated pool, suites available, restaurant and discotheque. Wheelchair units available. No pets.

Hilton at the Park. 1855 S. Harbor Blvd.; (714) 750–1811. Private balconies overlook the man-made Matterhorn at Disneyland and the God-made Santa

Ana Mountains. Heated pool. Suites available. Restaurant and coffee shop; lounge with entertainment.

Marriott Hotel. 700 W. Convention Way.; (714) 750–8000. Adjacent to the Convention Center, two blocks from Disneyland, this new hotel caters to the convention visitor with its outstanding meeting facilities and quality service. Special suites for the busy executive or the lively family. Gift shops, hair salon, heated swimming pool, elegant dining in *JW's,* plus two additional restaurants, lounge entertainment. 1050 rooms.

Quality Inn. 616 Convention Way; (714) 750–3131. Close to Disneyland; heated pool, saunas, bar, restaurant; suites available. 285 rooms.

Sheraton-Anaheim Motor Hotel. 1015 W. Ball Rd.; (714) 778–1700. Close to Disneyland, free shuttle. This Tudor-style motel has large, well-decorated rooms, heated pool; suites available; restaurant, bar, dancing; wheelchair units available. 370 rooms.

Expensive

Anaheim TraveLodge. 1166 W. Katella Ave.; (714) 774–7817. Close to Disneyland, attractive; restaurant nearby; heated pool. 57 rooms.

Anaheim Viking TraveLodge. 505 W. Katella Ave.; (714) 774–8710. Near Disneyland; heated pool; coffee shop adjacent. 51 rooms.

Best Western Apollo Inn. 1741 S. West St.; (714) 772–9750. Heated pool, laundry, sauna, whirlpool; restaurant adjacent. Bus to Disneyland. 135 rooms.

Best Western Cosmic Age Lodge. 1717 S. Harbor Blvd.; (714) 635–6550. Heated pool, Jacuzzi, large units for families, babysitters available, restaurant. Free shuttle bus to Disneyland. 156 rooms.

Best Western Fabulous Space Age Lodge. 1176 Katella Ave.; (714) 776–0140. Heated pool, restaurant; shopping center adjacent. Laundry, beauty salon, barber shop, family accommodations, babysitting available, pets accepted; free shuttle to Disneyland. 100 rooms.

Best Western Galaxy Motel. 1735 S. Harbor Blvd.; (714) 772–1520. Heated pool; restaurant adjacent; laundry, large family suites; free shuttle to Disneyland. 93 rooms.

Best Western Inn of Tomorrow. 1110 W. Katella Ave.; (714) 778–1880. Unique garden of topiary trees, heated pool, sauna and Jacuzzi, laundry, closed circuit TV to watch kids at pool, over 800 works of art, restaurant. 200 units.

Captain's Quarters. 620 Orangewood Ave.; (714) 638–1590. Heated pool, whirlpool, 63 rooms.

Conestoga Inn TraveLodge. 1240 S. Walnut.; (714) 535–0300. Heated pool, Jacuzzi, suites, restaurant, and coffee shop, bar. 255 rooms.

Desert Inn Motel. 1600 S. Harbor Blvd.; (714) 772–5050. Heated pool, Jacuzzi, large family units available, coffee shop adjacent. 21 rooms.

Holiday Inn. 1850 S. Harbor Blvd.; (714) 750–2801. Heated pool, laundry, Jacuzzi, suites, dining room, coffee shop, cocktails, entertainment. 313 rooms available.

Howard Johnson's Motor Lodge. 1380 S. Harbor Blvd.; (714) 776–6120. Two heated pools, laundry, Jacuzzi, suites, restaurant, bar. 320 rooms.

Moderate

Admiral's Cove Friendship Inn. 1028 W. Ball Road; (714) 774–1650. Heated pool, sauna, Jacuzzi, spacious rooms, large family units available, two efficiency apts.; restaurant opposite. 61 rooms.

Akua Best Western Motor Hotel. 1018 E. Orangethorpe Ave.; (714) 871–2830. Heated pool, four two-room units. 63 rooms.

Alamo Motor Lodge. 1140 W. Katella Ave.; (714) 635–8070. Heated pool, no pets. 50 rooms.

Alpine Motel. 715 W. Katella Ave.; (714) 535–2186. Heated pool, steam baths, family units available; restaurant; substantial rate reductions September 8 to May 26. 41 rooms.

Anaheim Friendship Inn. 426 W. Ball Road; (714) 774–3882. Small heated pool, laundry, Jacuzzi, four efficiency apts. Restaurant adjacent. 33 rooms.

Anaheim Park Motor Inn. 915 S. West Street; (714) 778–0350. Heated pool, Jacuzzi. Lower winter rates. 114 rooms.

Best Western Stardust Holiday Motel. 1057 W. Ball Road; (714) 774–7600. Heated pool; restaurant adjacent, water slide nearby. 35 rooms.

Cavalier Motor Lodge. 11811 Harbor Blvd.; (714) 750–1000. Heated pool, jacuzzi. 93 rooms.

Concord Inn. 1111 S. Harbor Blvd.; (714) 533–8830. Heated pool, Jacuzzi, one large kitchen unit. Free bus to Disneyland. 82 rooms.

Harbor Inn TraveLodge. 2171 S. Harbor Blvd.; (714) 750–3100. Heated pool, Jacuzzi; coffee shop adjacent. Deluxe rooms with kitchenettes available. 128 rooms.

Jolly Roger Inn Hotel. 640 W. Katella; (714) 772–7621. Two heated pools, Jacuzzi; suites available, one suite with private pool. Dining room, dancing, entertainment; beauty salon, dress shop, liquor and sundries shop; free shuttle to Disneyland. 180 rooms.

Kona Kai Motel. 1820 S. West St.; (714) 971–5506. Heated pool, aqua-slide; family suites with kitchenettes available; restaurant adjacent. 21 rooms.

Lamplighter Motel. 1759 S. West St.; (714) 774–2136. Heated pool, refrigerators, family units, laundry; restaurant adjacent; shopping center nearby. Free morning coffee. Low rates Labor Day to May 22. 55 units.

Magic Lamp Motel. 1030 W. Katella; (714) 772–7242. Heated pool, laundry, 15 efficiency apartments available; restaurant adjacent. Lower winter rates. 39 rooms.

Park Vue Motel. 1570 S. Harbor Blvd.; (714) 772–5721. Heated pool, family units, kitchen apartments, laundry, sundeck, restaurant. Lower winter rates. 90 rooms.

Penny Sleeper Inn. 1441 S. Manchester Ave.; (714) 991–8100. Heated pool, laundry, game room. 206 rooms.

Saga Motel. 1650 S. Harbor Blvd.; (714) 772–0440. Heated pool, laundry, Jacuzzi; coffee shop adjacent. Lower winter rate; AAA discount prices. 102 rooms.

Sandman Inn. 921 S. Harbor Blvd.; (714) 956–5730. Heated pool; coffee shop adjacent. No pets. 74 rooms.

The Sands Motel. 1520 S. Harbor Blvd.; (714) 774–1324. Heated pool, family units. 24 rooms.

Inexpensive

Ana-Lin Motel. 2123 W. Lincoln Ave.; (714) 535–8446. Midway between Disneyland and Knott's Berry Farm. Heated pool, no pets; three efficiency apartments; restaurants and shopping nearby. Lower winter rates. 23 rooms.

Anchor Motel. 1538 E. Lincoln Ave.; (714) 533–3972. Heated pool, some refrigerators. 20 rooms.

Ha' Penny Inn. 2630 W. Lincoln Ave.; (714) 821–3690. All suites with kitchenettes, heated pool; free shuttles from Amtrak station and airport.

Mecca Motel. 1544 S. Harbor Blvd.; (714) 533–4581. Two heated pools, laundry; efficiency apartments available. Restaurant adjacent. Lower winter rates. 96 rooms.

The Mediterranean Inn. 733 S. Beach Blvd.; (714) 761–3111. Heated pool, no pets. 29 rooms.

Polynesian Motel. 641 S. Brookhurst Street; (714) 778–6892. Heated pool; efficiency units available; coffee shop nearby; low winter rates. 28 rooms.

BUENA PARK

Deluxe

Buena Park Hotel. 7675 Crescent Ave.; (714) 995–1111. Heated pool, suites; dining room and coffee shop, cocktails, entertainment. 320 rooms.

Holiday Inn. 7000 Beach Blvd.; (714) 522–7000. Heated pool, laundry, jacuzzi, kennels, suites, dining room, coffee shop, bar entertainment. 250 units.

Expensive

Best Western Aztec Motel. 7620 Beach Blvd.; (714) 522–8433. Near Knott's Berry Farm. Heated pool, laundry, eight kitchenettes, family units. Excellent restaurant next door. Winter rates. 50 units.

Buena Park TraveLodge. 7640 Beach Blvd.; (714) 522–8461. Heated pool, pets allowed; kitchenettes and family units available. Restaurant across the street. 68 rooms.

Moderate

Buena Park Quality Inn. 7555 Beach Blvd.; (714) 522–7360. Heated pool, sauna, jacuzzi, current movies; restaurant nearby. 152 rooms.

Farm De Ville Motel. 7800 Crescent Ave.; (714) 527–2201. Two heated pools, sauna, suites, efficiency apts., laundry. Coffee shop close by. 130 rooms.

Inexpensive

Capri Motel. 7860 Beach Blvd.; (714) 522–7221. 400 feet to Knott's Berry Farm. Heated pool, kitchenettes, family units. Restaurant adjacent. 30 rooms.

Covered Wagon Motel. 7830 Crescent Ave.; (714) 995–0033. Heated pool, family units. Opposite southern entrance to Knott's Berry Farm. 20 rooms.

Gaslite Motel. 7777 Beach Blvd.; (714) 522–8441. Pool, laundry, kitchenettes; coffee shop nearby. 77 rooms.

Siesta International Motel. 7930 Beach Blvd.; (714) 522–2422. Heated pool, 40 efficiency units, family units, some refrigerators, laundry; coffee shop adjacent. 80 rooms.

COSTA MESA

The Westin South Coast Plaza. *Super Deluxe.* 666 Anton Blvd.; (714) 540–2500. The Westin South Coast Plaza Hotel is a modern 400-room hotel with a variety of sports facilities. Volleyball, shuffleboard, putting green, swimming pool, and tennis courts are all on the grounds. There is an additional restaurant, three bars, and live entertainment nightly. A special weekend plan is available— everything, including the room, is up to 50% less than the regular rates.

FULLERTON

Willow Tree Lodge. *Moderate.* 1015 S. Harbor Blvd.; (714) 871–5430. Heated pool, family units available. 61 rooms.

IRVINE

Irvine Marriott. *Super Deluxe.* 1800 Von Karman; (714) 851–1100. This brand-new hotel, the third Marriott property in Orange County, has 501 guest rooms. Indoor-outdoor swimming pool, lighted tennis courts, game rooms. Restaurants, lounge, entertainment. AE, CB, DC, MC, V.

The Registry Hotel. *Super Deluxe.* 18800 MacArthur Blvd.; (714) 752–8777. Accessibility is a main feature of this hotel. It is right across from the John Wayne Orange County Airport, four miles from the ocean, and 15 to 20 minutes from Disneyland. The 300-room hotel has a swimming pool, tennis courts, a Jacuzzi, and complimentary coffee and *Wall Street Journal* are offered. Le Chardonnay dining room offers dining and dancing nightly, and the Gazebo Restaurant is open from 6 A.M. until 2 A.M. daily for lighter fare. Special weekend packages. Complimentary limousine service from the airport.

Airporter Inn Hotel. *Deluxe–Expensive.* 18700 MacArthur Blvd.; (714) 833–2770. Heated pool, dining room, cocktails, entertainment, suites, one room with private pool. Opposite John Wayne Orange County Airport.

Irvine Host-Best Western. *Moderate.* 1717 E. Dyer Rd.; (714) 540–1515. Heated pool, sauna, Jacuzzi. Restaurant adjacent. 150 rooms.

ORANGE

Best Western El Camino. *Moderate.* 3191 N. Tustin Ave.; (714) 998-0360. Centrally located about twenty minutes from Disneyland or Knott's Berry Farm. Heated pool, efficiency apts., steam baths, Jacuzzi. 56 rooms.

El Matador Motel. *Moderate.* 1300 E. Katella Ave.; (714) 639–2500. Small pool; restaurant close to hotel. 29 rooms.

Orange TraveLodge. *Moderate.* 1302 W. Chapman Ave.; (714) 633–7720. Pool. 32 rooms.

SANTA ANA

Ramada Inn. *Expensive.* 1600 E. First St.; (714) 835–3051. Heated pool, sauna, Jacuzzi, restaurant and coffee shop. 150 rooms.

El Cortez. *Moderate.* 1503 E. First St.; (714) 835–2585. Heated pool; coffee shop nearby. 60 rooms.

Orange Tree Motel. *Moderate.* 2720 N. Grand Ave.; (714) 997–2330. Small pool; restaurant adjacent. 48 rooms.

Vagabond Motor Hotel. *Moderate.* 1519 E. First St.; (714) 547–9426. Pool, children's playground, coffee shop, family units. 52 rooms.

TRABUCO CANYON

Coto de Caza. *Deluxe.* P.O. Box 438, Trabuco Canyon; (714) 586–0761. This resort community is at the base of the Saddleback Mountains. The 5,000-acre valley will serve as the site for the Modern Pentathlon during the 1984 Olympics. Available in the complex are swimming pool, whirlpool, gym, tennis, bowling, horseback riding, billiards, racquetball, dining facilities, and shops.

HOW TO GET AROUND. By car. Avis, Budget, and Hertz have offices at both Los Angeles International Airport and John Wayne County Airport.

By taxi. Taxis are available, as are limousine services offering full transportation from all airports, harbor areas, and other locations on request. *Luxe Livery Service,* toll-free in California (800) 422–4267 or from other areas (800) 854–8171; *Green Flag Airport Shuttle,* (714) 991–5660.

By bus. *Continental Trailways* and *Greyhound* operate out of the central bus terminal in Los Angeles, servicing major cities in Orange County. There are convenient shuttle buses and comfortable air-conditioned motor coaches traveling from both airports to designated stops and hotels in Orange County. *Airport Service Motor Coach,* (714) 776–9210.

Locally, the Orange County Transit District operates buses daily throughout the county; call (714) 636–7433 for route information.

TOURIST INFORMATION SERVICES. Most cities in Orange County have Chamber-of-Commerce bureaus. These organizations are more than happy to assist out-of-town guests.

In Anaheim, contact the *Anaheim Area Visitor and Convention Bureau,* 800 W. Katella Ave., Anaheim, CA 92803; (714) 999–8999. The Automobile Club of Southern California, for members only, provides maps, brochures, booklets, and information on many special events, fishing, hunting, and camping. The Anaheim Automobile Club of Southern California is located at 150 W. Vermont Ave., Anaheim; (714) 774–2392.

In Buena Park, stop by the *Buena Park Visitor's Bureau* at 6696 Beach Blvd. for information on the immediate area. Maps, restaurant guides, hotel brochures and more. Call (714) 994–1511.

 SEASONAL EVENTS. The events listed are for inland Orange County only. For coastal events, of which there are many, please refer to the "Long Beach to San Clemente" section.

April–September. Major league *baseball season,* with season opener the California Angels vs. the Los Angeles Dodgers at Anaheim Stadium.

April. *A Night in Fullerton,* an annual festival featuring arts, crafts, shows, and exhibits.

May. Memorial Day Weekend. Annual *Strawberry Festival* celebrates the annual harvest of strawberries; Garden Grove.

July–August. *Orange Country Fair,* Fairgrounds, Costa Mesa.

August–December. *National Football League* season, with the Los Angeles Rams at home in Anaheim Stadium.

September. Labor Day Weekend. *International Street Fair,* a festival featuring different international foods and art; at Orange Circle in the city of Orange.

 TOURS. Special sightseeing tours operate daily out of Anaheim to such varied places as Universal Studios, the many beach areas, Six Flags' Magic Mountain, Catalina Island, Hollywood, San Juan Capistrano Mission, San Diego, RMS *Queen Mary,* and Mexico and Las Vegas. Contact the Anaheim Area Visitor Bureau for information.

In Anaheim, a free *Fun Bus* tours the area from hotels to amusement sights several times daily, leaving its own terminal at 304 Katella Way in Anaheim. Fun Bus tour routes include Disneyland, the Anaheim Convention Center, Anaheim Stadium, Knott's Berry Farm, Movieland Wax Museum, and the Buena Park Shopping Center. For information on hotel pickups, call (714) 635–1390.

 SPECIAL-INTEREST TOURS. Tucker Wildlife Preserve, in Modjeska Canyon, is 17 miles southeast of the city of Orange, a pleasant drive through rolling hills and farmland. At live-oak-lined Modjeska Canyon, you'll find a bird watcher's haven (or heaven), nestled in the foothills of the Santa Ana Mountains. The preserve features more than 50 bird species, most of which are migratory. Colorful resident hummingbirds are plentiful and delightful to watch. An observation porch aids in sighting and an attendant is available daily for help in identification.

Brookside Vineyards, 711 South Brookhurst Rd, Anaheim (714–778–9933), boasts wine-tasting daily, with more than 100 wines, and an imaginative, well-stocked gift shop.

PARKS. The foothills of the Santa Ana Mountains offer several excellent, conveniently located recreation areas; the best two are:

The *Irvine Regional Park*, once a part of the Mexican land grant, Rancho Lomas de Santiago, that belonged to the Yorba family. In 1876, James Irvine bought the ranch to raise sheep. The area has always been a popular picnic site. Now the vast park—located seven miles east of Orange—boasts 477 acres of picnic grounds, a boating lagoon, hiking trails, an amphitheater, a small petting zoo, and pony stables.

Irvine Lake Park. About 15 miles southeast of Orange, on the Santiago Reservoir, this recreational lake sports boating and swimming.

 CAMPING. Camping is limited in the inland Orange County area. The coastline, however, has abundant and excellent camping sites. (Please refer to the Long Beach to San Clemente section.) A few lovely campsites, however, are available in the Santa Ana Mountains. These are full-service, state-owned campsites, offering showers, stoves, tables, drinking water, and toilets.

Trabuco Canyon. O'Neill Regional Park offers camping among live oaks in the Cleveland National Forest, with 350 campsites available; 13 full-service rest rooms throughout. Trailer space available.

Featherly Regional Park. Up Santa Ana Canyon, this park has more than 200 campsites, trailer spaces available, and ample restrooms throughout.

For further information on camping and campsites, contact the California State Department of Parks and Recreation, P.O. Box 2390, Sacramento 95811, or call (213) 620–3342 or (619) 427–5133.

RV parks are abundant in Orange County. Here is a partial listing: *Anaheim Vacation Park* (311 N. Beach Blvd.); *KOA Campground* (1221 S. West St., Anaheim); *Orangeland RV Park* (1600 W. Struck Ave., Orange); *Tratel Garden Grove Trailer Park* (13190 Harbor Blvd., Garden Grove); *Travelers World RV Park* (333 W. Ball Rd., Anaheim); *Vacationland RV Park* (1343 S. West St., Anaheim).

CHILDREN'S ACTIVITIES. Orange County is a family paradise with more family-oriented activities in a single area than anywhere else in the United States.

Disneyland, 1313 Harbor Blvd., Anaheim; 999–4565. 27 miles southeast of downtown Los Angeles via Santa Ana Freeway. This "Magic Kingdom," the late Walt Disney's legacy to the Southland's amusement and entertainment world, now boasts of seven lands of Fantasy—about $200,000,000 worth of magic. Ride mules or space ships, but plan at least a six-hour visit starting on Main Street with its turn-of-the-century nostalgia. (For a fuller description, see the Orange County introductory section, above).

Disneyland is the center of an immense vacation playground that includes Knott's Berry Farm, California Alligator Farm, Movieland Wax Museum and Palace of Living Art, and Anaheim Stadium.

Admission to Disneyland is $12.00 for adults and $9.00 for children 3 to 11; for information, call (714) 999–4565. Hours are as follows: Monday through Friday, 10 A.M. to 7 P.M.; Saturday, 9 A.M. to 12 midnight; and Sunday, from 9 A.M. to 7 P.M., except during the summer when from June 19th until the middle of September the park stays open from 9 A.M. to 12 midnight all week long.

How to get there from Los Angeles: Take the #5 Freeway south or the San Diego #405 Freeway south to #5 north to Harbor Blvd. Disneyland will be on the right side of the boulevard.

Knott's Berry Farm, 8039 Beach Blvd., Buena Park; 952–9400. A family fun place with an atmosphere of the Old West and Gold Rush eras. Visitors pan for gold, ride ore cars, stagecoaches, a narrow-gauge railroad, burros, and eat finger-lickin' chicken dinners. 180-degree omnivision theater, showing films of thrill rides. Ice-skating show, live rock music and dancing in the summer.

Admission is $10.95; $8.95 for children; parking is free. Summer hours are Monday through Thursday, 9 A.M. to 12 midnight, and Friday to Sunday from 9 A.M. to 1 A.M. Winter season hours are weekends from 10 A.M. to 9 P.M., and weekdays from 10 A.M. to 6 P.M. Closed Wednesdays and Thursdays during the winter except for holiday and vacation periods. Also closed Christmas Day. American Express, Visa, and MasterCard accepted.

To get there: Take the #5 to #91 East to Beach Blvd; turn right to La Palma and Beach.

Lion Country Safari, 8800 Irvine Center Drive, Laguna Hills; (714) 837–1200. If you think a wildebeest is a mythical creature from Shakespeare or early Arthurian tales, you're in for a surprise. This African wildlife preserve features not only lions, rhinos, cheetahs, zebras, and giraffes, but such interesting and exotic creatures as the oryx, gazelle, eland, gnu, aoudad, and, yes, the wildebeest. Take an hour and drive through this 500-acre mini-African veldt watching the uncaged animals roam.

Admission is $7.25 for adults; $4.50 for children. Open every day, 9:45 A.M. to 5 P.M.

How to get there from Los Angeles: Take the San Diego Freeway #405 south to Irvine Center Drive, turn right.

Raging Waters, 150 East Puddingstone Rd., San Dimas; (714) 592–5302. The newest addition to Orange County's theme parks, this 30-acre attraction has water slides, the Wave Pool with waves breaking on a sandy beach, and a splash pool for "little dippers." Lifeguards are on duty. Open 10:00 A.M. to 10:00 P.M., June through August; from 10:00 A.M. to 7:00 P.M., starting in September. Admission is $8.50 for adults; $7.00 for children 4 to 11; younger than 4, free; $5.00 for seniors. After 5:00 P.M. admission is $5.00 for adults. Season passes and group rates are available.

Movieland Wax Museum and Palace of Living Art, 7711 Beach Blvd., Buena Park.; (714) 522–1154. Inside a modern, white building with elegant gold trim are more than 200 wax figures depicting famous and infamous movie and television stars of all eras. This 20-year-old shrine to these memorable personalities, both living and dead, show off our favorite characters in interesting ways. Walk through the original set of Doctor Zhivago or stroll down the Yellow

Brick Road with Dorothy and the Tin Man. Strike a pose with John Wayne or flirt with *Happy Days'* The Fonz. A new attraction, the Black Box, takes visitors through lifelike scenes from *Halloween, Alien,* and *Altered States.*

Admission is $7.50 for adults; $4.50 for children 4 – 11, and children under four are admitted free. Open daily, 9:00 A.M. to 9:00 P.M. (summer); 10:00 A.M. to 10:00 P.M. the rest of the year.

How to get there from Los Angeles: Take the #5 Freeway South and exit right on Knott Ave. Turn left on Orange Thorpe Ave. and right on Beach Blvd.

California Alligator Farm, 7671 La Palma, Buena Park.; (714) 522–2615. Across the street from Knott's Berry Farm, this farm is the home of hundreds of reptiles and other scaly creatures. Many of the more than 3,000 alligators, crocodiles, snakes, lizards, turtles, and tortoises have been featured in motion pictures; now they put on regular demonstrations at the farm. Besides scheduled tours, there is a winter wonderland extravaganza during the Christmas holidays.

Admission, $4.95 for adults, $2.95 for children. Open every day from 10:30 A.M. to 6 P.M., with later hours during July and August.

Kingdom of Dancing Stallions, 7662 Beach Blvd, Buena Park (one block north of Knott's Berry Farm). This exciting arena is primarily a showplace for 32 of the finest and most highly trained horses of Spain, Mexico, and Australia which perform in the tradition of the amazing white Lippizaner horses of Vienna.

Ornate stables are the proper setting for these amazing animals. During off-hours each horse stands in a stall topped with solid brass, curved railings. A plaque hanging on the outside of each stall reviews the animal's ancestry, which is inevitably illustrious.

Performances include beautifully choreographed production numbers and solos to the tunes of Fiesta, Capriole, and Pas de Deux. Also on the grounds, which cover some 6½ acres, is an Antique Carriage Museum, packed with fully-restored horse-drawn carriages assembled from all over the world.

To further enhance a walking tour of the stables and Carriage Museum, cassette tapes are available in several languages.

Admission is $6.00 for adults, $4.00 for children 12 and under, and $4.00 for senior citizens (60 and over). Group rates available. For further information, call (213) 546–4366 or (714) 546–4366—(that's easy numbers to remember since the last seven digits spell out KINGDOM).

PARTICIPANT SPORTS. Outdoor recreation activities are many and varied in the region, thanks to a near-perfect climate. **Golf** courses include: *Anaheim Hills Public Country Club,* 6501 E. Nohl Ranch Rd., Anaheim; *Rancho San Juaquin Golf Course,* Irvine; *H.G. "Dad" Miller Public Golf Course,* centrally located between Anaheim and Buena Park; *Mile Square Golf Course,* Fountain Valley. For a more detailed list, see the *Participant Sports* section for Long Beach to San Clemente, below.

For **tennis,** try the *Tennisland Racquet Club,* 1330 S. Walnut St., Anaheim, which offers tennis lessons. For water sports, see the Orange County Coast section (Long Beach to San Clemente).

SPECTATOR SPORTS. Featured are the *California Angels* professional baseball team April through September. At times, the *Los Angeles Rams* NFL football team shares Anaheim Stadium with the Angels, since the Rams season runs August through December.

Horse racing is a popular attraction at *Los Alamitos Race Course,* at 491 Katella Ave., Los Alamitos. Night racing features quarter horses May through August, and Orange County Fall Fair thoroughbreds late October through early November. Quarter horses run from early November to mid-January, and harness racing lasts from February to May.

HISTORICAL SITES. Visit the *Heritage House Museum* at California State University in Fullerton. Built in 1894, this former residence and office of a once-prominent area physician, Dr. Clark, is restored to its Victorian elegance. Of special interest is the doctor's office and parlor, fully restored, with instruments and furniture actually used for turn-of-the-century medical practice.

Also worth a stop is the *Mother Colony House* (West and Sycamore Sts. in Anaheim). This restored Victorian home once belonged to early German settlers and includes many German artifacts that they brought to this country, plus interesting historical items from Orange County and early Anaheim.

ARCHITECTURE. Take a trip to *Crystal Cathedral,* 12141 Lewis Street, Garden Grove. Philip Johnson, world-famous architect, designed this bold, theatrical auditorium for Robert Schuller's Garden Grove Community Church. The Crystal Cathedral seats 3,000 people in the all-glass, star-shaped structure, which rises 124 feet. Concerts, lectures, and tours are held inside.

LIBRARIES. Open to the public, the California State University Library in Fullerton houses a "Freedom Center," where political pamphlets and dogmatic literature of every sort reside, from interests far left to far right. The library also has an extensive collection of government documents on every subject imaginable.

MUSEUMS. Besides entertainment, the Spanish heritage and early industries of Orange County are remembered in the area's many museums.

The Bowers Museum. 2002 N. Main St., Santa Ana; 547–8304. Built to resemble a Spanish hacienda, this excellent museum features a fine collection of Indian artifacts and early Orange County historical items on permanent display. The museum also owns outstanding works of pre-Columbian art from Mexico and Central America, which are on display periodically.

Movieland of the Air. John Wayne Orange County Airport; 545–1193. This unique museum houses one of the largest collections of antique aircraft in the country. It is an "active" museum, as many of the WWI and WWII aircraft replicas are loaned to movie and television studios for use on historical projects. Admission: $2.25 adults; $1.00 juniors; $.50 children.

Villa Bianchi Winery Museum. 2045 S. Harbor Blvd., Anaheim 750–4503. A small museum devoted to the early wine industry, with various photos, distilleries, bottles, labels. Free admission.

Movieland Wax Museum. Beach Blvd, Buena Park; 522–1154. This intriguing collection of stars' likenesses, all created out of wax, features more than 200 such replicas. Original costumes and props are displayed on sets that recreate some famous roles. Both classical and contemporary films are represented here and nearly all are enhanced with special animation, lights, and sound effects.

Another section of the museum, the Palace of Living Arts, displays replicas of famous statues, again in wax, along with 3-D reproductions of well-known paintings. An added treat is to be found at the California Plaza, where visitors walk through the upside-down ship used in the film *The Poseidon Adventure*. $7.50 for adults, $4.50 for children under 11.

Museum of North Orange County. 301 Pomona Ave., Fullerton; 738–6545. This museum features a variety of interesting traveling exhibits, covering prehistoric presentations to the space age. Donation.

Museum of World Wars. 649 N. Euclid, Anaheim; 956–0300. Houses one of the largest collections of military uniforms and vehicles in the country; featuring WWI and WWII photos and artifacts. Of special interest: Hermann Goering's personal items are on display.

Hobby City Doll Museum. 1238 S. Beach Blvd., Anaheim; 527–2323. Fifty-seven years of collecting dolls from all over the world has resulted in this fascinating doll museum, featuring ancient Egyptian dolls, Indonesian and Chinese miniatures, and space-age Star Trek dolls. Free admission.

 MUSIC. *Irvine Meadows Amphitheater* (8800 Irvine Center Dr., Laguna Hills) is an open-air structure offering a variety of musical events from May through October. The amphitheater features special general-admission "meadow seating" and a large, sloping, grass lawn for viewing concerts behind served seating. For information, call (714) 855–8095.

At *Anaheim Stadium,* specialty concerts are performed throughout the year. For information, call (714) 634–2000. The *Pacific Amphitheater* is a recent addition to the music scene in Orange County. On the Orange County Fairgrounds, Costa Mesa, this facility will offer musical entertainment as well as stage plays, from May through October.

SHOPPING. Orange County offers abundant and distinctive shopping for every taste. There are convenient shopping plazas in every area, not to mention the many small specialty shops and larger department stores.

Anaheim's major enclosed mall, *Anaheim Plaza,* has more than 72 shops, boutiques, restaurants, and services. As a convenience for visitors, the Plaza Express Bus Service travels from over a dozen Anaheim hotel/motel locations to the mall; call 635–3431. Hotels with service are: Sheraton Anaheim Hotel, Conestoga Motor Inn, Disneyland Hotel, Apollo Motor Inn, Marriott Hotel, Inn At The Park, Quality Inn, Holiday Inn, Hamburger House (at Harbor and Katella), Hyatt Hotel, Grand Hotel, Park Vue Hotel, Tropicana Motor Inn, Anaheim Plaza.

South Coast Plaza Village, Sunflower and Bear Sts., Santa Ana, is an unusual shopping village with unique, quality merchandise. Gifts from most European countries are available, and six international restaurants and sidewalk cafés make shopping easier.

The mammoth *South Coast Plaza Shopping Center,* at 3333 South Bristol Street in Costa Mesa, also has an interesting variety of shops, restaurants, and theaters.

More than 90 stores and services operate at *The City Shopping Center* (2 City Blvd., Orange), where landscaping, fountains, and courtyards add to shopping pleasure. The large *Buena Park Mall* in Buena Park guarantees shopping enjoyment near Knott's Berry Farm.

DINING OUT in Orange County can be a rewarding experience. Restaurants are beginning to follow Los Angeles's lead in offering especially fresh food creatively prepared. There is some ethnic diversity of cuisine and its sophistication of preparation is a growing trend in a growing community. Within a few years, Orange County will undoubtedly become a miniature version of Los Angeles in gastronomy. Dress is usually casual; where it is more formal we'll say so.

Establishments are categorized here according to the price of a dinner from the middle range of their menus. Price categories may be interpreted as follows: *Expensive,* $25 and above; *Moderate,* $10–$25; and *Inexpensive,* below $10. Not included are drinks, tip, and tax. A more complete explanation of price categories can be found in "Facts at Your Fingertips" at the front of this guide.

ANAHEIM

Bessie Wall's. *Moderate.* 1704 N. Tustin Ave.; (714) 630–2812. In 1927, John Wall built a mansion for his bride Bessie. Now it's a lovingly restored restaurant;

Bessie's upstairs bedroom has been converted into a cocktail lounge. Authentic photographs of the Wall family and other memorabilia grace the walls. Early California food is featured, including chicken and dumplings, rabbit Madeira, and crab enchiladas topped with sour cream. Casual. No DC.

Mr. Stox. *Moderate.* 1105 E. Katella Ave.; (714) 634–2994. A Continental à la carte menu is kept simple here, with fresh fish, aged beef, and live lobster. There is a cocktail lounge with entertainment, and non-smokers have their own "pure air" section. One of Orange County's best wine lists. Semi-dressy. Valet parking. All major credit cards.

Overland Stage and Territorial Saloon. *Moderate.* 1855 S. Harbor Blvd.; (714) 750–1811. The theme here is what California was like in the days of the Wild West. Roast buffalo is served nightly; boar, bear, elk, and pheasant are standard specials. The bar is from a Mississippi steamboat, and an actual Overland Stage rests atop the restaurant (this *is* Southern California, after all). Happy hour; Sunday brunch and magic acts during lunch. Casual. All major credit cards.

Acapulco. *Inexpensive.* 1410 S. Harbor Blvd.; (714) 956–7380. One of a chain of Mexican restaurants that excel in quality. Owner Ray Marshall wins a lot of awards for authentic Mexican cuisine, as well as for his creative concoctions. The cold avocado soup is a winner, the crabmeat enchiladas are a renowned specialty. Also in Garden Grove and Santa Ana. Casual. No DC.

COSTA MESA

Alfredo's. *Moderate.* The South Coast Plaza Hotel, 666 Anton Blvd.; (714) 540–1550. Set in an intimate garden courtyard, Alfredo's offers a wide selection of Italian and Continental cuisine. Veal dishes are the specialty; also featured are beef and pasta dishes. Over 200 varieties of premium California, French, and Italian wines are offered. Live entertainment. Reservations recommended. All major credit cards.

La Cuisine Newport. *Moderate.* 1400 Bristol St.; (714) 546–4000. French cuisine is served here in an elegant setting with white linen table cloths and fine china and crystal. Nouvelle and classic dishes are all prepared with the freshest ingredients—imported and domestic. Specialties of the house include an appetizer of puff pastry filled with scallops and spinach, and Escalops de Veau aux Bananes—veal and bananas sauteed in cognac. Reservations recommended. All major credit cards.

FULLERTON

The Cellar. *Expensive.* 305 N. Harbor Blvd.; (714) 525–5682. This elegant Continental restaurant is impeccably European, both in cuisine and ambiance. Featured entrees are a blend of classical Escoffier and adventurous nouvelle. An outstanding wine list. Dressy. Dinner only. All major credit cards.

Mandarin Pavillion. *Inexpensive.* 1050 Valencia; (714) 870–7950. A Chinese restaurant explosion has hit Orange County, and this place is at the forefront. Specializes in Shanghai, Peking, Szechuan, and Hunan cuisine. The wine list is good for a Chinese restaurant. There is a sister restaurant, equally good: **Mandarin Gourmet** in Costa Mesa. All major credit cards.

IRVINE

Chanteclair. *Expensive.* 18912 MacArthur Blvd.; (714) 752–8001. They seek to overwhelm. The setting is beautiful, the service is very attentive, and the wine list includes an impressive 100 labels. The cuisine is haute Continental, with an emphasis on French. The menu is à la carte. Dressy; jackets required. Dinner only. All major credit cards.

Le Chardonnay. *Expensive.* In the Registry Hotel, 18800 MacArthur Blvd.; (714) 752–8777. A new name and a new restaurant replace the Grand Portage. La Chardonnay, as its name suggests, is a French restaurant. Soft, muted colors and a European atmosphere make this an enjoyable dining experience. Open for lunch, dinner, and Sunday brunch. All major credit cards.

Gulliver's. *Moderate.* 18482 MacArthur Blvd.; (714) 833–8411. Part of a small quality-oriented chain. Picture yourself in jolly old England at the time of Jonathan Swift. Waitresses are "wenches" and busboys are "squires." Walls are adorned with artifacts and old prints. If you can put yourself in this picture, you'll enjoy the food. The single entree is prime rib, and it's roasted tender and juicy; you choose how thick and how well done. The service is youthful and friendly, very California. Casual. Dinner only. MC, V.

The White House. *Moderate.* 887 South Anaheim Blvd.,; (714) 772–1381. In a turn-of-the-century home, recently converted for dining. Features fresh fish, prime ribs, and baby-back pork ribs. Dessert specialties are Amaretto and Grand Marnier mousses. Open for lunch during the week, for dinner daily. Closed Monday. Sunday brunch from 10:00 A.M. All major credit cards.

Houlihan's Old Place. *Inexpensive.* 4880 Campus Dr.; (714) 752–6023. Lots of green plants and a cozy atmosphere; American-style food. Many seafood specialties and ethnic appetizers. Have you ever had pita bread pizza before? Various omelette choices, salad selections, and big juicy hamburgers. Casual. All major credit cards.

ORANGE

Chez Cary. *Expensive.* 571 S. Main St.; (714) 542–3595. The reputation of this Continental restaurant extends far past Orange County. Not only is the food exquisite, but the table settings include the very best china, crystal, and silver. Elegant as well as luxurious, personalized attention is the specialty. If you're a wine enthusiast, you'll love this restaurant—the wine list has 600 labels. Strolling violinist. Dressy. Dinner only. Valet parking. All major credit cards.

The Hobbit. *Expensive.* 2932 E. Chapman Ave.; (714) 997–1972. Dine your way through a charming house. Start in the wine cellar, with Champagne and hors d'oeuvres as you mingle with other guests. Dinner is a Continental multi-course affair, and your table may be in one of many different rooms. There is an intermission, so stroll through the restaurant's own art gallery, and then go on to other courses, such as New York steak with Madeira sauce and a crêpe de maison. Great fun. Dinner only. So popular that reservations must usually be made four to five months in advance. MC, V.

La Brasserie. *Moderate.* 202 S. Main St.; (714) 978–6161. This restaurant is French all the way. A multi-level house with a library-dining room. The accent is on veal and fresh fish. Always fresh vegetables and always homemade soup. A relaxed atmosphere that will not intimidate even those uninitiated in French cuisine. Semi-dressy. No DC.

SANTA ANA

Saddleback Inn. *Inexpensive.* 1660 E. 1st St.; (714) 835–3311. A hacienda-style restaurant, with the decor a blend of Old Spain, Mission California, and modern Orange County. The dining rooms are decorated individually, with a touch of nostalgia. Baby back pork ribs, basted with barbecue sauce, and slow-cooked barbecued beef roast are the house specialties. Filet of sole almandine, barbecued baked chicken, and filet mignon with Bordelaise sauce are other possibilities. Vegetarians, take note: a vegetarian plate will be created upon request. Casual. All major credit cards.

 NIGHT LIFE AND ENTERTAINMENT. Concerts, dinner theaters, and a wide variety of musical entertainment are to be found in the Anaheim area, as well as several discos and Country-and-Western bars. Most major hotels have entertainment. For listings in all Orange county cities, check with the Anaheim Area Visitors Bureau, the Sunday *Los Angeles Times*' Calendar section, *Los Angeles Magazine,* and *California Magazine.*

Of particular note in the area is *J.W.'s Cowboy,* a combination disco and country bar complete with large Texas-style room, dance floor, and a game room. At 1721 South Manchester Ave., Anaheim, near Katella; (714) 956–1410.

The best Orange County happy hour (an import from San Diego), weekdays but especially Friday late afternoons, is at *Rusty Pelican* seafood restaurant, 1830 Main St., Irvine; (714) 545–4774. Take the MacArthur exit from #405; the place is right across from John Wayne Orange County Airport, and is an odd building with an Aztec pyramid look. Another good drinking and meeting place is the *Crazy Horse Saloon,* visible from the Newport Freeway (#55) near #405.

Area dinner theatres include: *Curtain Call Dinner Theater,* 690 El Camino Real, in Tustin (714–838–1540); *The Grand Dinner Theater,* Grand Hotel, 7 Freeman Way, Anaheim (714–772–7710); and *Harlequin Dinner Playhouse,* 3503 S. Harbor Blvd., Santa Ana (714–979–5511).

The *South Coast Repertory Theater,* 655 Town Center Drive, in Costa Mesa (714–957–4033) presents plays in two different theaters—the Main Stage and the Second Stage. The professional theater company offers two seasons of plays each year. The Main Stage seats 507 people and presents 6 plays—general theater fare for the whole family, and a Christmas show each year. The Second Stage is more experimental, offers five shows each year, and seats 161 people.

New shows are featured, many by local writers, and this theater has recently begun commissioning new works. The Second Stage has also received a Drama Critics Circle Award for fostering the production of new plays.

For new wave and rock concerts, try *The Woodstock Concert Theater,* 951 S. Knott Ave., Anaheim (714–761–9840). Jazz groups and choirs can be heard at *The Bridges Auditorium,* The Claremont Colleges, 4th and College Way, Claremont (714–621–8032).

LONG BEACH SOUTH TO SAN CLEMENTE

The Coast North of San Diego County

by
MARY JANE HORTON

Mary Jane Horton writes about fitness, fashion, and travel for various national publications; she lives in Santa Monica.

South from Los Angeles, the Pacific coast has often been termed the American Riviera—but it's really something quite different. Coastal communities still almost in their infancy are growing in individuality and prosperity with each passing year. These cities once resembled "Small Town, U.S.A.," with their overabundance of fast-food establishments mixed in with a smattering of stores, one movie theater, a market—and not much more. But with Los Angeles spreading by leaps and bounds, the coastal communities have now taken on some of the richer qualities of urban life.

Beginning with Long Beach, each offers attractions and activities—cultural, historical, and physical—to please all tastes. To contrast with its unique view of technology afforded by offshore oil rigs, Long Beach is a modern, industrial city surrounded by fascinating symbols of the past. Rancho Alamitos, California's oldest standing Spanish ranch, is just a stone's throw from the innovative Long Beach Convention and Entertainment Complex.

Santa Catalina Island, 22 miles off the coast of Long Beach, is an entity unto itself—in many ways, a throwback to simpler days. A short plane ride or a four-hour boat trip takes the traveler to Catalina and a view of the way things must have been in all of southern California before its growth—clean air, green grass, and white picket fences.

Back on the mainland: Coastal Orange County boasts 42 miles of sandy beaches, secluded coves, and sheltered harbors. The "beach boy" atmosphere is prevalent starting in Huntington Beach, where visitors get a feel for this phenomenon whenever the ocean swells: Warm or cold, winter or summer, fair-haired boys and girls of all ages run to the waves with their surf boards ready.

Alongside many of the beaches are new cultural establishments. Some of the coastal cities have their own museums; more and more art

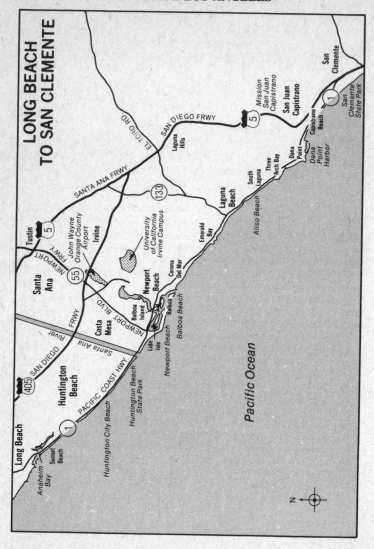

LONG BEACH
TO SAN CLEMENTE

galleries and small theater groups are popping up all the time. Fanciful recreations of fishing villages are also in good supply—take a look at Ports O' Call Village in San Pedro, Fisherman's Village (under construction in Long Beach), and the Dana Point Harbor.

Farther down the coast, the cities of Newport Beach and Laguna Beach, although smaller than Long Beach, have an important role. They are the "big cities" of their area, surrounded by much smaller communities. Newport has an impressive roster of businesses—retail, industrial, and financial—and Laguna Beach has long been known as an artists' colony. Dana Point, just south of Laguna, is an up-and-coming area as it starts to catch some of Laguna's overflow visitors and residents. San Juan Capistrano takes us back in time again, with its inspiring mission. And San Clemente is, of course, well known as the site of Richard Nixon's Western White House, Casa Pacifica.

Long Beach

Long Beach, at present, is undergoing a dramatic facelift. In a surge of redevelopment, six city blocks have been removed to make way for a hundred-million-dollar shopping mall; this is only part of a rejuvenation project totaling more than one billion dollars. The plan will eventually produce one-and-one-half million square feet of office and retail space, hotels, and residential projects.

Part of the redevelopment has resulted in the creation of two new marinas. One contains 1,700 boat slips and the other 131. Both marinas are located adjacent to the Long Beach Convention and Entertainment Center. Shoreline Village, which opened in June, 1983, is a large attraction with restaurants, shops, and a restored carousel dating back to 1906. Slips are available for cruise-up shoppers. Shoreline Park completes the picture with fishing, boat rentals, jogging and bicycle paths, and a seaside RV campground.

The Long Beach Convention and Entertainment Center was recently refurbished and now houses one of the major performing arts facilities in Southern California, with its gigantic Terrace Theater, the smaller, elegant Center Theater, and an expansive 100,000-square-foot exhibition hall. In 1984 the center will host two Olympic events—volleyball and fencing. Howard Hughes's famous huge flying boat, the *Spruce Goose,* is another addition to the city of Long Beach, housed alongside the formidable *Queen Mary* in a 12-story aluminum dome. The seaplane, which was hidden for nearly 40 years, is wood and has a wing span of 319 feet. Multimedia displays surrounding the plane explain its history; Howard Hughes memorabilia are also on view.

So much for the new. Throughout the city, one can look at the architecture and feel the flavor of the Spanish California of yesterday.

Points of Interest

1) Spruce Goose
2) Queen Mary
3) Long Beach Catalina Cruises
4) Department of Fish and Game Headquarters
5) Harbor Scenic Drive
6) Port of Long Beach Administration Building
7) Long Beach Arena
8) Long Beach Convention Entertainment Center

LONG BEACH

Fine examples of Spanish residential architecture line Ocean Boulevard —pink and white stucco buildings with immaculately groomed grounds. Two traditional Spanish ranches are open to the public: Rancho Los Alamitos, the oldest standing adobe structure of its type in California, which was built in 1806, and Casa Rancho Los Cerritos, constructed in 1844, which is now a museum/reference library furnished with pieces dating back to the early 1800s.

In nearby San Pedro, visitors get a taste of the world's most famous seaports, such as Singapore and Marseilles, at Ports O'Call Village; the Whale's Wharf is a replica of a New England seaport with quaint cobblestone streets and shops brimming with exotic fare.

Of course, no description of Long Beach is complete without mention of the venerable *Queen Mary*. This most luxurious of luxury liners (built in 1934 at a cost of 48 million dollars) is completely intact, from the extensive wood paneling to the gleaming nickel- and silver-plated handrails and the hand-cut glass. Once the largest, fastest ocean liner on the seas, the *Queen* is now permanently moored at the southern end of the Long Beach Freeway. Tours through the ship are available; guests are invited to browse the 12 decks and witness close-up the bridge, the staterooms, officer's quarters, and engine rooms. Also aboard the *Queen* is The Living Sea, a marine museum created by Jacques Cousteau, where visitors share Cousteau's vision for a futuristic undersea city. Long Beach is also the starting point for a restful and luxurious cruise to Mexico, on the S.S. *Azure Seas,* if one is so inclined.

Palos Verdes Peninsula, a bit north of Long Beach, offers a special treat for the kids: Marineland of the Pacific is a unique park located on a particularly scenic stretch of the coast on Palos Verdes Drive South. In the Family Adventure Swim, the first of its kind in any park, guests paddle among 4,000 fish in a half-million gallon tank. Sea lions romp at Sea Lion Point, and the new Touch Tank allows visitors to feel sea anemones, starfish, sea urchins, and more. Killer whales, dolphins, pilot whales, and sea lions star in regularly scheduled shows.

Santa Catalina Island

On a clear day, if you look out to sea from Long Beach, you'll be able to pinpoint a gleaming spot in the Pacific. This gem is Santa Catalina Island, only 22 miles from Long Beach and, therefore, easily accessible by plane or boat. (See *How to Get There* below.) Originally named San Salvador, this island was discovered and claimed for Spain by Cabrillo in 1542. In 1892, San Salvador was purchased and incorporated into the Santa Catalina Company; present ownership stems from stock purchases made by William Wrigley, Jr., in 1919. The Santa Catalina Island Conservancy, a nonprofit foundation, acquired title to

42,135 acres, or 86 percent of Catalina, in 1974. Through this agreement the island's natural resources are preserved and conserved while public access to recreational opportunities is increased. Hopefully, the agreement will also help to preserve the fresh, old-fashioned country flavor that still pervades the island.

Avalon is the island's only city; Avalon Bay is the site of its most famous attraction—the Casino Building (constructed in 1929 by William Wrigley, Jr.), housing an art gallery, museum, motion picture theater, and ballroom. Guided tours are offered daily.

An array of outdoor activities awaits Catalina visitors. Coastal cruises around the island often pass Seal Rock, where the mammals bark and ham it up for their audience. A glass-bottom boat tour cruises the California State Marine Preserve for a look at the local undersea life, which includes foot-long saltwater goldfish, electric perch, and other unusual species of fish. From May through September, divers take a closer glance at what these waters have to offer.

May through September is also flying-fish season. On another tour, which can be arranged by the local Chamber of Commerce (213–510–1520), a boat equipped with 40-million-candlepower searchlights allows the best view of Catalina's beautiful iridescent flying fish. Soaring out of the water—sometimes as much as 75 yards—these flying fish even land in passing boats from time to time.

Bus tours view other parts of the island, including the 66 square miles of mountainous interior; El Rancho Escondido features performances by pure-bred Arabian horses and wild animals—buffalo, deer, goat, and boar—that wander unhindered in the interior. A tour of the Wrigley Memorial and Botanical Garden is available. Some visitors pursue golf, tennis, fishing, boating, diving, and hiking, while others just take it easy soaking up the sun. Any visit to Catalina is also usually filled with much rambling down the main street sampling the taffy, frozen bananas and other treats.

Huntington Beach

Back on the mainland, and traveling south: The first city you encounter is Huntington Beach. If you come from inland, you'll know you're close when you see the oil derricks. Surfers flock to Huntington Beach; the long pier is a good vantage point from which to watch these dare-devils. This city is also the site of annual surfing competitions in September. Huntington Harbor boasts Orange County's first marina-city: eight separate islands are bordered by concrete bulkheads. The novel waterfronts and water-view homes are a delight to see.

Nearby, Bolsa Chica Ecological Reserve is a must-see for an education on the area's natural environment. Under the management of the

California Department of Fish and Game, Bolsa Chica is a protected wetland where visitors witness nature at her best. On Pacific Coast Highway, two miles north of the Golden West exit off the San Diego Freeway (Route 405), the reserve has a mile-long loop trail. The Amigos de Bolsa Chica give tours October through March on the first Saturday of the month.

The coastal wetland, or salt marsh, is home to 100 different animal species. Among various birds are such unlikely sounding creatures as the great blue heron and the common egret. Five endangered species are protected here as well: the light-footed clapper rail, the brown pelican, the peregrine falcon, the California least tern, and the Beldings Spanish sparrow. Some of these birds nest on the two man-made islands. The reserve is still undergoing a restoration, and eventually a total of 150 acres will be turned back to tidelands. At the end of the reserve, you may fish for round stingrays, smooth-hounded shark, topsmelt, and yellow-finned croaker.

Newport Beach

Newport Beach, one of Orange County's oldest communities, is the area's bastion of high society. Numerous yacht and country clubs host a wealth of debutante balls, weddings, and charity functions. Newport began as a small shipping center and vacation spot, but today it is world famous as a recreational community. Newport Harbor is one of the world's busiest small-boat harbors, home to more than 9,000 pleasure crafts.

Many integral parts of Newport's history are still alive today. A 3-car ferry still shuttles cars and passengers between Balboa Island and the peninsula—the Balboa Island Ferry, a bit of history and novelty in Orange County, crosses the main channel from Palm Street to Agate Street and vice versa. Service first began in 1909 due to the necessity of transportation and convenience for the locals. It was then owned and operated by the Wilson Brothers, and was eventually purchased by Joseph Beck, whose family still owns the ferry.

Tourists and locals alike make use of this mode of transportation because it cuts driving distances down 6½ miles and, rather than walking across the Balboa Island Bridge, it gives a scenic main view of the harbor.

Cost is 45 cents for car and driver; 15 cents for each additional adult passenger, and 5 cents for each child. Detailed information on the ferry is available by calling (714) 673–1070.

To get to Balboa Island from Los Angeles, take either the #5 or #405 Freeway south to Newport Beach Freeway #55 west. Then take the Pacific Coast Highway south to Jamboree, and right entering Bal-

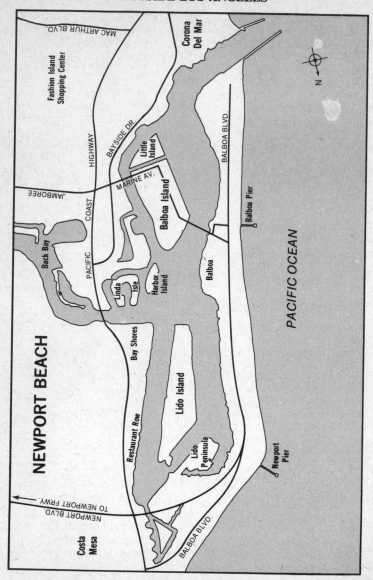

boa Island. On Balboa Island frozen banana stands thrive on every corner. (It is said that the frozen banana, dipped in chocolate and rolled in nuts, originated here.)

Another remaining bit of the past is the Dory Fishing Fleet, which still operates at its turn-of-the-century location at Newport Pier. The completely restored Balboa Pavilion serves as a terminal for steamers delivering people to and from Santa Catalina Island. The former South Coast Ship Yard has also been restored as a bayside restaurant; and the Newport Harbor Yacht Club is the oldest sailing club on the harbor.

Before its growth, this area was a cattle ranch above an uncharted estuary, and the Balboa Peninsula was a natural landlocked harbor. It was not until Spanish land grants were sold in the 1860s that this sleepy area began to change. In 1879, Newport received more attention when the sternwheeler, the *Vaquero* from San Diego, started making local stops to take on hide, tallow, livestock, and grain from the Irvine Ranch. Captain S.S. Dunnels is credited with naming the community "New Port."

In 1876, the jetty area was dredged, making it easier for boats to enter the channel, and in 1888, today's Newport Pier was built. In the 19th century, the Santa Ana River was diverted from the lower bay; deep channels and turning basins were dredged, marshlands filled, and the entrance stabilized by two jetties. In 1906, Newport Beach was incorporated as a city.

Today, Newport Beach has more than 60,000 permanent residents, with summer visitors averaging between 20,000 and 100,000 a day. Newport encompasses a total area of 37.5 square miles: 15.5 square miles of land, 1.9 square miles of bay, and 20.1 square miles of ocean.

During the Christmas holidays, a spectacular boat parade finds vessels ablaze with lights and holiday decorations. Balboa Pavilion is the hub of activity. To get there from Los Angeles, take the San Diego Freeway #405 to the Newport Freeway #55 south to the end. This freeway will eventually become Newport Boulevard. Take Newport Boulevard to the end, and bear left onto Balboa Boulevard. Drive two miles to Main Street and turn left. Balboa Pavilion is straight ahead. For information, call (714) 673–5245.

The annual Flight of the Snowbirds in Newport Harbor, the largest small boat race on earth, has been dazzling Pavilion-goers since the first regatta in 1926. Now held in June, this race includes about 150 little Snowbird-class catboats, usually skippered by young people.

The Pavilion was also a hot spot during the days of the big bands— Count Basie, Benny Goodman, and Stan Kenton all played there. An annual dance, the Balboa Hop, commemorates all the "swingers" that once graced the dancing hall.

Sportfishing in modern, comfortable boats is available daily at the Pavilion. And December through February, passengers aboard the whale-watching boats witness the giant gray whale as he passes by on his migratory route. On these trips other marine creatures, such as seagulls, pelicans, pilot whales, and porpoises, can be seen as well. During the summer, the *Pavilion Queen* riverboat leaves each day for a fully narrated cruise of the harbor. Smaller skiffs may be hired for individual rentals throughout the year.

Corona del Mar, just south of Newport Center, is a quaint little town with a lovely state beach. The shopping area, on Coast Highway, has a nautical flavor, and the renovated Eaglet building boasts new, fanciful shops. Sherman Library and Gardens, down the road a bit, is an unusual little stop; this "library cum botanical garden," extremely inviting for browsing, is also the site of many chic social gatherings.

Laguna Beach

Nestled along the shore, among the cliffs, Laguna Beach, with its Saint-Tropez-like flavor, is perhaps the most beautiful of all southern California cities. Bounded by beach for about five miles, the city's 3,328 acres provide a panoramic setting for hillside residents and beauty-seeking travelers.

Entering from the north, you can imbibe one of the most enchanting views of the Pacific; at the same time, stop at the Sunshine Cove roadside stand for a luscious date shake, which may quench your physical thirst with flair. As you travel along Pacific Coast Highway, the ocean glistens on the right. Waves pound against rocks, and the memory of the colorful homes chiseled into the surrounding hills will stay with you forever. On the approach to town lie two of Laguna's most prestigious ocean-side residential areas, Irvine Cove and Emerald Bay.

Farther along, Heisler Park is among the cliffs above the ocean; the Laguna Beach Museum of Art adjacent to the park. Walking south from the park takes you to Main Beach and the center of town. The blue-and-white lifeguard stand and boardwalk are landmarks among the exciting boutiques that fill the streets to the north, east, and south of Laguna's Main Beach.

Laguna's name was applied to this area in the late 1800s by the Indians; *lagonas* means lake, and so the community was named after the town's two freshwater lagoons. Since its incorporation as a city in 1827, Laguna has been widely known as an artists' colony. The Festival of the Arts, an annual event (July and August) that began 40 years ago, insures the city's long-time reputation as a thriving environment for artists and craftspeople.

In the 1960s the city was a haven for hippies; Timothy Leary and other period celebrities hung out at the Taco Bell on Pacific Coast Highway. To this day, a unique mixture of people is drawn to Laguna; the 18,000 permanent residents range in type from rich and famous to countercultural and eccentric.

An enormous likeness of "town greeter" Eiler Larson lends a pleasant historical touch. For years, this friendly man stood on the Coast Highway at the edge of town shouting salutations to everyone who passed by. His "How are you?" and "Leaving so soon?" could be heard eight hours a day as Larson did his job for "the love of Laguna." After his death six years ago, a statue was erected showing his hands eternally outstretched to Laguna visitors. Remarkably enough, a new greeter, looking amazingly like the original, has recently appeared at the entrance to town.

To the outside world, much of Laguna's popularity is linked to the different festivals presented throughout the year. The Festival of the Arts, and the Pageant of the Masters—a human recreation of famous paintings—run concurrently with the Sawdust Festival and Art-a-Fair for six weeks in July and August. All these events combine to present myriad arts and crafts at various prices. February's Winter Festival offers an artist and craftsman fair, a poetry festival, and the Patriot's Day Parade.

Even when no events are scheduled, there's always something to do in Laguna. Quaint boutiques and small malls, packed full with unique stores, prove more than a worthwhile investment of time for those who like to shop. Prices are not always a bargain, but an abundance of items are available that otherwise may be difficult to find. The antique shops, bookstores, craft shops, and art galleries are outstanding, and more goldsmiths and jewelers per square foot fill Laguna than in any other city in the country. As far as restaurants go, there is one for every taste and pocketbook from one end of town to the other.

In the summer, when the crowds gather, a free cable-car-inspired bus runs the length of town. Visitors arrive from all corners of the country, and for this reason it's a good idea to book hotel rooms as far ahead of the busy season as possible.

The Laguna Beach Museum of Art, built in 1972, is a regional institution concerned with community needs. An outgrowth of the Laguna Beach Art Association, founded in 1918, it also tries to carry on that organization's promise: "to advance knowledge of and interest in art, to maintain a permanent art collection, and to create a spirit of cooperation and fellowship between painter and the public"—a truly southern California credo. The art highlights California and the Pacific Coast from 1900 to the present. Since the museum has quite a large collection, and space is limited, exhibitions are frequently changed.

Visit the shoreline to see what inspired much of this scenic art. Exploring the town's beaches and coves, you will learn the different areas and their different purposes. Main Beach is the center of downtown activity, usually teeming with interesting people from around the world. To get away from the crowds, there is Woods Cove—with rocks to hide behind, to climb on, and to use as a look-out for lurking crabs.

Climbing the steps from Wood's Cove, look up: You'll see a stunning English-style mansion, once the home of film star Bette Davis. When the surf's up, find Salt Creek—that's where the action is. And, for some general relaxation in the sun and sand, you've got quite a choice: A beach or cove awaits you at the end of almost every east-west street in Laguna.

Dana Point

Dana Point is the next stop as you travel south along the coast. A city on the rise, this community is growing in popularity partially because it's so close to Laguna Beach.

Richard Henry Dana, Jr., the city's namesake, tells a bit of history in his book, *Two Years Before the Mast,* as he recalls how cattle hides tossed over surrounding cliffs by Spanish Californian rancheros and Capistrano mission padres were loaded onto trade ships, thus giving the port its start.

Dana also describes the beautiful cove, now the setting of Dana Point Harbor: "There was a grandeur in everything around . . . as refreshing as a great rock in a weary land . . . I experienced a glow of pleasure in finding what of poetry and romance I ever had in me." Dana ended a long ocean voyage at the Point in the 1830s; a bronze statue of the author-seaman sits alongside the harbor today.

When square-rigged sailing ships were in port, Dana Point was the major trading post between Santa Barbara and San Diego. Its new reincarnation has once again taken shape in an enchanting trading port. Mariner's Village sits on the harbor with the backdrop of colorful boats and unique Dana Wharf shops. They share the waterfront with a sportfishing fleet, seagulls, and pelicans. Two marinas are home port to more than 2,500 yachts; for sailors, this is one of southern California's easiest and least crowded marinas to navigate—despite the numerous seals who play on a buoy not far from the harbor.

On the sandy, siltwater swimming beach, kyacks and paddleboats are available for rent. The Orange County Marine Institute conducts tours and offers educational information on tide pools in the area; a replica of Richard Henry Dana's ship, the *Pilgrim,* is on hand to explore. The Dana Point Lighthouse boasts nautical memorabilia. From December through March, whale watching is a popular pastime.

Next to the harbor, Doheny State Beach's expansive campgrounds border excellent picnic areas and a picturesque park perfect for long walks or extensive bicycle treks.

San Juan Capistrano

Well known for its historic Mission San Juan Capistrano, this city is also blessed with a breathtaking coastline. The imposing Spanish mission, not far from the coast, is summer home to millions of migrating swallows; these famous birds arrive around St. Joseph's Day, March 19, and go on their way around St. John's Day, October 23. It's a mystery of nature why these swallows unerringly return to Capistrano each year after wintering in Argentina; it has been that way, though, since the mission was built in 1776 by Father Junipero Serra.

Seventh in a chain of California missions established by Franciscan friars, Mission San Juan Capistrano served as the focal point for local Juanero Indians, who were converted to Christianity and taught to raise crops and tend livestock. Because of increasing activity there, by 1797 the mission had outgrown its first chapel and thus the Stone Church was erected. This structure's architecture was awesome: It was said to have had seven domes and a belltower rising from an ornately arched roof. Sadly, the church was destroyed by an earthquake only a few years after its completion. Although Stone Church has never been rebuilt, there is now ongoing construction at the site; completion date for the new church is set for the end of July, 1984.

After Mexico received its independence from Spain in 1821, the mission was confiscated. The ceding of California to the U.S., the gold rush, and California's statehood in 1850 brought about many more changes. The Catholic Church requested the return of Mission San Juan Capistrano and was granted such by Abraham Lincoln in 1865. (The original grant is stored safely in the Mission archives, but a copy is on display in the vestment room.) In 1895, a Los Angeles historical club reroofed the remaining buildings to prevent further decay, but the real restoration came in 1910 with the arrival Father John O' Sullivan. New gardens were planted and foundations and walkways were built. The Serra Chapel was restored in 1924; it now holds a gilded altar from Barcelona.

In November, 1976, in honor of the mission's 200th birthday, and coinciding with the nation's bicentennial, the entire west wing of Mission San Juan Capistrano's quadrangle was rebuilt.

The mission's almost mystical atmosphere must have been the same throughout history. The sheer tranquility and simple character of mission life in old Spanish California comes to life as you walk through the grounds and buildings. Excavation on mission grounds continues to unearth other elements of the past; artifacts, tools, and vestments from these diggings are shown in the vestment room and museum. Self-guided tours by tape-recorder are available, and a visitors bureau with extensive information on the area has recently been established inside the mission.

Swallows arriving from their long journey add even another element of beauty to this enchanted place. The first official mention of the swallows is an entry in the Mission Archives, dated St. Joseph's Day, 1777: "Today, the *pjaritos* returned to the area. The Indians, being joyous over their return, put part of their welcoming ceremony into their evening singing in the neighboring village."

The swallows arrive like clockwork each March; they stay throughout the summer to bear their young and teach them to fly. In October, they're off again to Argentina where it's springtime. One popular legend about the swallows says that these birds come from the Holy Land, carrying in their beaks twigs that are used as a kind of open-air aviary to rest on the ocean, mid-flight. The popular song, *When the Swallows Return to Capistrano,* written by Leon Rene in 1939, etched the mission and its famous swallows into the minds of people throughout the world.

San Juan Capistrano has other historical attractions besides the mission. A restored Santa Fe railroad station, circa 1895, serves as the combination Amtrak terminal and restaurant, the Capistrano Depot. Old adobe buildings, such as the Los Rios Adobe, are also abundant in the area.

San Clemente

As they pass the awesome San Onofre nuclear plant on the coast between San Juan Capistrano's beautiful old mission and San Clemente, travelers may get a strange feeling that the future is, indeed, here. Surfers in the water near the plant confirm that this is, for certain, Southern California.

The San Onofre Nuclear Information Center is a fascinating stop for those interested in learning more about the mechanics of nuclear energy. Displays and self-operated exhibits explain the conversion of an atom into the generation of electricity. Uses of nuclear energy are shown in a film.

San Clemente is probably best remembered as the site of President Nixon's Western White House. This residence, Casa Pacifica, regularly made the news during Nixon's years in office. A Nixon library is slated to be built nearby.

San Clemente also offers more of what makes the beach cities of Southern California proud: lots of sun, fun, and sports activities. Swimming, surfing, sailing, fishing, golfing, and tennis reign among other

recreational activities throughout the city. Skeet and trap shooti
lawn bowling, and picnicking are also popular.

The next 20 miles down the coast are lined with the Marine barracks
of Camp Pendleton, the country's largest Marine Corps base. Training
here involves offshore landing; overland treks are conducted through
the camp's three mountain ranges, five lakes, and more than 250 miles
of roads. Camp Pendleton was a troop take-off point for the Pacific in
World War II, and during the Korean and Vietnam wars.

The next town south is Oceanside, in San Diego County.

PRACTICAL INFORMATION FOR LONG BEACH
SOUTH TO SAN CLEMENTE

HOW TO GET THERE. By car. From Los Angeles, the
San Diego Freeway (Interstate 405) is the fastest way to
get to the coastal cities. There is an exit—or multiple
exits—for each city; the way to each city is clearly
marked. Long Beach has more than nine exits. Huntington Beach can be
reached by going west on Beach Blvd. (Route 39) off Route 405. Newport Beach
is accessible from the freeway at the Newport Freeway (Route 55), again west.
For Laguna Beach, exit at Laguna Canyon Road (Route 133) and go west.
Pacific Coast Highway (Route 1) follows the coast, and is probably the easiest
way to get to the cities south of Laguna. (It joins U.S. 5—freeway to San
Diego—going south at Capistrano Beach.) From San Diego, get off U.S. 5 onto
Rte. 1 at Capistrano Beach. For people who like a leisurely drive along stretches
of some of the country's most magnificent scenery, Pacific Coast Highway (Rte.
1) follows the coast through all of these cities.

By train. Downtown Los Angeles' Union Station, at 800 North Alameda,
offers train service to both Santa Ana and San Juan Capistrano. The station—an
attraction itself with its 52-foot-high ceilings and beautiful carved wood—is one
of the last grand railroad stations in this country. For Amtrak scheduling and
information in Los Angeles, call (213) 624–0171; in San Diego, call (714)
239–9021 for information on Orange County coastal destinations.

By bus. From Santa Ana, the Orange County Transit Department (OCTD)
(714–636–7433) has bus service to Newport Beach. From San Juan Capistrano,
there's a southbound bus that stops in San Clemente. Southern California Rapid
Transit buses leave the downtown Los Angeles terminal (at 6th and Los Angeles
Sts.) for various southern destinations. To travel to Long Beach, get the #456
going east on 7th St., or in Beverly Hills, take the #20, which goes west on
Wilshire Blvd. To go farther south from the downtown Los Angeles terminal,
take bus #800. This leaves approximately 10 and 40 minutes after each hour.
The #800 takes you to Knott's Berry Farm, and from there take the #29 bus

to Beach Blvd. West. The #29 travels to Huntington Beach. To go south from there, take the #1 bus south.

For private bus information, call *Greyhound* at (213) 394–5433 (Los Angeles) or (714) 235–0691 (San Diego) or *Gray Line* at (213) 481–2121 (Los Angeles) or (714) 231–9932 (San Diego).

By boat. Boats to Catalina Island run from San Pedro and Long Beach. Call Catalina Cruises at (213) 775–6111. Service is also available from Newport Beach through Catalina Passenger Service at (714) 673–5245, leaving from Balboa Pavilion.

By air. Catalina is accessible by air on a regularly scheduled basis. Call Catalina Airlines at (213) 548–1314. Charter services are available at the airport as well.

For more information on general air transportation to the area, see the "How to Get There" section for the City.

TELEPHONES. The area code for the cities south along the coast from Long Beach to San Clemente vary. In Long Beach and Santa Catalina Island, the area code is 213; south from there, in Huntington Beach, Newport Beach, Laguna Beach, Dana Point, San Juan Capistrano and San Clemente, the area code is 714. Parts of the county, however, have been changed to a 619 area code; if in doubt, check with the operator.

You do not need to dial the area code if it is the same as the one from which you are calling. For directory assistance, dial 411. When direct-dialing a long-distance number from any of these cities, you must dial the number "1" (one) *before* you dial the area code and the number itself. An operator will assist you on person-to-person, credit cards, and collect calls if you dial "0" first. Pay telephones still cost 10 cents.

CLIMATE. The coastal area boasts the best of southern California's renowned weather. Devoid of the city smog, this area is also quite a few degrees cooler than inland areas when summer temperatures rise. Also cooler in the winter, the coast can be brisk in the first three months of the year—almost like the New England seaside at times. Temperatures can drop as low as the high 30s and low 40s, especially in the evenings, so be sure to bring a warm sweater or jacket this time of year. However, winter days can also be temperate, climbing up into the 60s. The ususal temperature for other times of year ranges from the mid-60s to mid-70s (with occasional overcast periods during late spring).

The hottest and most uncomfortable weather is definitely a product of a local weather phenomenon called the Santa Ana winds. These dry winds which blow in September and early October create a bothersome dry, hot condition. The line "it never rains in southern California" is not totally true; yet there are some years in which hardly any rain falls. Rainstorms are heaviest in January and February, and sometimes it can storm continuously for a week at a time. June, which some might think to be the beginning of summer, can be disappointing by the coast. Foggy mornings can be deceptive, but often the sun comes burning through around mid-day. The water temperature is cool until July and then stays in the area of the mid-60s until October.

HOTELS AND MOTELS. Since Southern California is the perfect vacation spot, hotels and motels of all description are plentiful. Many are on the ocean, and most operate swimming pools, year-round. Many establishments have seasonal rates, so during winter months you can often find a bargain. Some properties also require a certain length of stay during the busy season—a minimum of three days often must be booked in the summer. To be on the safe side, be sure to call well ahead of your intended visit.

The following is a selection of hotels and motels in the area. Price categories for double occupancy rooms in this region are: *Super Deluxe,* over $70; *Deluxe,* $50–$69; *Expensive,* $40–$49; *Moderate,* $30–$39; and *Inexpensive,* $30 and under. For a more complete explanation of categories refer to the "Facts at Your Fingertips" section at the front of this book.

In making reservations, please note: Some cities run centralized reservation services that can quote rates and availability for a selection of different establishments. In Catalina, call the Chamber of Commerce's "One Call Does It All" number, (213) 510–1520.

LONG BEACH

Queen Mary Hotel. *Super Deluxe.* Pier J, at the end of the Long Beach Fwy.; (213) 435–4747 or (800) 421–3732. The *Queen Mary,* one of the most luxurious of luxury liners, has been moored and now serves as a hotel. Staterooms on the ship are guest rooms; guests feel as if they are traveling far and wide though they never leave the pier. The view of the Long Beach skyline is also spectacular. Several restaurants offer gourmet cuisine. Cocktail lounges, entertainment, and shops.

Queensway Bay Hilton. *Super Deluxe.* 700 Queensway Dr.; (213) 435–7676. With its own marina, this hotel has moorings for 100 boats; an additional 100 are planned for the near-future. Many rooms have partial or full marina views. *Adolph's Restaurant* at the hotel is one of the most popular in town. Nightly entertainment. Swimming pool.

Hyatt Regency Long Beach. *Deluxe.* 200 S. Pine Ave.; (213) 491–1234; (800) 228–9000. This new resort, across from the downtown marina, has pool, spa, restaurant, and lounge. Business services are also available.

Hyatt Edgewater at Long Beach Marina. *Deluxe.* 6400 E. Pacific Coast Hwy.; (800) 228–9000 or (213) 434–8451. A new section of this hotel offers first-floor rooms with beautiful garden views. The marina-hotel has a coffee shop, restaurant, and lounge.

Golden Sails Inn (Best Western). *Expensive.* 6285 E. Pacific Coast Hwy.; (800) 528–1234 or (213) 596–1631. Close to the marina, this hotel has a 24-hour restaurant, the *Olive Tree,* and a restaurant-lounge with entertainment. Swimming pool.

Ramada Inn. *Expensive.* 5325 E. Pacific Coast Hwy.; (800) 228–2828 or (213) 597–1341. This member of the familiar chain is close to the ocean. The *Governor's Restaurant* features a piano bar. Swimming pool.

Rochelle's Motel. *Expensive.* 3333 Lakewood Blvd.; (213) 421–8215. Kitchen facilities come with many of the rooms at this motel. Restaurant, entertainment, and swimming pool.

SANTA CATALINA ISLAND

Las Casitas. *Deluxe.* P.O. Box 4215, Long Beach 90804; (213) 599–1010. In Avalon, adjacent to the golf course, this hotel is made up of 34 individual studio, one- and two-bedroom cottages or casitas. All units offer full kitchens. Pool, tennis courts, color television.

Hotel Catalina. *Expensive.* 129 Whittley Ave., Avalon; (213) 510–0027. In a residential area, half a block from the beach, the Hotel Catalina offers a choice of rooms and cottages. The charming old-style inn also has a spa, spacious sun patio, free movie theater, and free baggage storage and change lockers.

Sacri's Hotel. *Expensive.* 111 Crescent; (213) 510–0555. Often called the best-designed hotel in Avalon, this hotel boasts a restaurant, sun deck, and art gallery. It is a popular honeymoon retreat with appropriate accommodations for newly-married couples.

Zane Grey Pueblo Hotel. *Expensive.* P.O. Box 216, Los Angeles 90704; (213) 510–1520. Former home of the famous novelist; the view is fantastic from this hotel. Swimming pool, complimentary toast and coffee, courtesy bus, and television in lobby.

Atwater Hotel. *Moderate.* P.O. Box 4215, Long Beach 90804; (213) 599–1010. Avalon's largest hotel, with 100 rooms. Family oriented; half block from the beach.

Bay View Hotel. *Inexpensive.* 124 Whittley Ave., (213) 510–0600. A half-block from the bay; many of the rooms overlook the water. Jacuzzi, barbecue, and patio.

Cloud "7" Hotel. *Inexpensive.* 137 Marilla, (213) 510–0454. Some rooms have ocean views in Avalon's newest motel. Centrally located, with courtesy bus service from boat and air terminals. Coffee and refrigerators.

Hermosa Hotel and Cottages. *Inexpensive.* 131 Metropole St.; (213) 510–1010. With cottages and rooms, there are about 100 units here. Some have kitchens. Courtesy coffee.

HUNTINGTON BEACH

Huntington Beach Inn. *Deluxe.* 21112 Ocean Ave.; (714) 536–1421. This inn is across the street from the beach, complete with a pool, a restaurant and lounge, and a three-par golf course.

Huntington Shores Motor Hotel. *Moderate.* 21002 Ocean Ave. (on California Route 1); (714) 536–8861. Pleasant rooms can be found in this motel, which is located across from the beach. Some rooms face the Pacific. Restaurant nearby; heated pool.

Sun 'N Sands. *Moderate.* 1102 Pacific Coast Hwy.; (714) 536–2543. Opposite the beach, this motel operates a café and a pool.

NEWPORT BEACH

Marriott Hotel and Tennis Club. *Super Deluxe.* 900 Newport Center Dr.; (714) 640–4000. A beautiful atrium surrounded by fountains is the trademark of this hotel. A large swimming pool overlooks an adjacent golf course that can be used by guests. Ocean view from the pool as well as from some of the rooms. Fashion Island, a popular shopping area, is across the street. Ten lighted tennis courts, Jacuzzi, two restaurants, a lounge, and entertainment.

The Newporter Resort. *Super Deluxe.* 1107 Jamboree Rd.; (714) 644–1700. Guests have access to the John Wayne Tennis Club on the grounds of the hotel; there are 16 lighted tennis courts in all. Other sports facilities include a three-par, nine-hole golf course, a game field for exercising, jogging paths, shuffleboard, and two large swimming pools. A $12-million renovation has taken place here. Art work by Jim Dine and Kenneth Price in a palm motif is echoed by exotic horticulture spread over 26 acres. Restaurants, lounges, and entertainment.

Sheraton Newport Beach. *Expensive.* 4545 MacArthur Blvd.; (714) 833–0570. One of the newest hotels in this area. Features pool, Jacuzzi, and tennis courts. Also free *Wall Street Journal* and coffee. Restaurant, lounge, and entertainment.

Newport Channel Inn. *Moderate.* 6030 S. West Coast Hwy.; (714) 642–3030. This small, cozy inn on the water has 30 rooms.

LAGUNA BEACH

Surf and Sand Hotel. *Super Deluxe.* 15555 S. Coast Hwy.; (714) 497-4477. The largest hotel in town, the Surf and Sand is much like a little city. It has a complete shopping area with clothing stores, antiques, shops, and boutiques right on the premises. Private beach, swimming pool, ocean-view lounge, two restaurants, and entertainment.

Hotel San Maarten. *Super Deluxe.* 696 S. Coast Hwy.; (714) 494–9436. This is one of Laguna's newest hotels, and it is stunning. An atrium and garden decorate the middle of the hotel, with surrounding rooms accented by calicos and antiques. Pool, sauna, restaurant, lounge; Continental breakfast.

The Carriage House. (Bed-and-Breakfast) *Deluxe.* 1322 Catalina St.; (714) 494–8945. A beautiful garden surrounds this charming New Orleans-style house. Stay in the Lilac Suite, the Time Suite, or the Green Palms Suite. Complimentary breakfast, family-style. Welcome gifts of fresh California fruit and wine.

The Inn at Laguna. *Deluxe.* 211 N. Coast Hwy.; (714) 484–7535. This comfortable inn is on the beach, near Main Beach and Heisler Park. Pool, some oceanfront rooms; Continental breakfast.

The Reef. *Deluxe.* 30806 S. Coast Hwy.; (714) 499–2227. This hotel is close to the beach, and has an impressive botanical garden brimming with exotic plants. Color television and current-run movies. Swimming pool, sauna, jacuzzi. Continental breakfast served in the summer.

Eiler's Inn. (Bed-and-Breakfast) *Super Deluxe.* 741 S. Coast Hwy.; (714) 494–3004. A beautifully renovated bed-and-breakfast inn featuring a flower-laden atrium and fountain. Continental breakfast is served in this setting; on summer weekends, wine and cheese combines with afternoon entertainment. With only 13 rooms and a loyal following, it is important to book here well in advance.

Hotel Laguna. *Expensive.* 425 S. Coast Hwy.; (714) 494–1151. The oldest hotel in Laguna is smack in the middle of town, with easy beach access. A patio overlooks a charming garden and the beach for sunbathing. Restaurant, lounge, entertainment.

Seacliff Motel. *Moderate.* 1661 S. Coast Hwy.; (714) 494–5892. Under the same management for 15 years, the Seacliff has many rooms overlooking the Pacific. Private sun decks, heated pool, in-room coffee.

Vacation Village. *Moderate.* 647 S. Coast Hwy.; (714) 494–8566. Good beach location with pool and Jacuzzi. Restaurant next door.

DANA POINT

Marina Inn Best Western. *Moderate.* 34902 Del Obispo St.; (714) 496–1203 (call collect). This lovely marina hotel has a pool and sauna.

SAN JUAN CAPISTRANO

Country Bay Inn. *Deluxe.* 34862 Pacific Coast Hwy.; (714) 496–6656. Wood-burning fireplaces grace each room in this inn, located across from a sandy beach. Gracious hospitality is also a plus. The rooms are all differently decorated, some with brass headboards, patios, and balconies. Complimentary Continental breakfast. Jacuzzi.

Capistrano Inn (Best Western). *Expensive.* 27174 Ortega Hwy; (714) 494–5661. This rambling, comfortable motel is conveniently located. Swimming pool, Jacuzzi; restaurant next door.

Mission Inn Motel. *Expensive.* 26891 Ortega Hwy.; (714) 493–1151. Next door to the mission, this motel stands right in the middle of an orange grove. Restaurant next door.

HOW TO GET AROUND. Since Southern California coastal cities are so spread out (there are 44 miles between Long Beach and San Clemente), by far the best way to get around is by car. All major car rental firms and a number of local concerns are represented in the Los Angeles/Long Beach and San Diego areas. Check directory assistance or the Yellow Pages for telephone numbers. Public bus service is available, but it is severely limited.

TOURIST INFORMATION. The Chambers of Commerce of the beach cities can be helpful with information on specific questions. In Long Beach, the Convention and Tourism Bureau is at 300 East Ocean Blvd., Long Beach, CA 90802; (213) 436–3645. In Santa Catalina Island, contact the Chamber of Commerce, P.O. Box 217, Avalon, CA 90702; (213) 510–1520.

In Huntington Beach, the chamber is located at 18582 Beach Blvd., Huntington Beach, CA 92648; (714) 962–6661. In Newport Beach, the Convention and Visitors Bureau is at 1470 Jamboree Rd., Newport Beach, CA 92660; (714) 644–8211.

For Laguna Beach information, contact the Laguna Beach Chamber of Commerce and Civic Association, P.O. Box 396, Laguna Beach, CA 92652; (714) 494–1018. For Dana Point, contact the Chamber of Commerce at P.O. Box 12, Dana Point, CA 92629; (714) 496–1555.

San Juan Capistrano has a brand new Visitor's Center inside the mission. For information, contact the Visitor's Center, Mission San Juan Capistrano, Suite 218, San Juan Capistrano, CA 92674; (714) 493–1414. The San Juan Capistrano Chamber of Commerce is located at 31882 Camino Capistrano, San Juan Capistrano, CA 92675; (714) 493–1171. The San Clemente Chamber can be contacted at P.O. Box 338, San Clemente, CA 92672; (714) 492–1131.

SEASONAL EVENTS. Many events in the area are scheduled at the last moment, making it impossible for us to include them. One of the best ways to find out about such happenings is to check the local newspaper in each individual city. The following are established annual events.

January. *Whale watching* begins from the harbors at Dana Point and Newport Beach.

February. The *Laguna Beach Winter Festival,* usually held mid-month, includes a crafts fair and a poetry festival. The *Laguna Beach Patriot's Day Parade.*

March. March 19th is *St. Joseph's Day* when, annually, *the swallows return to Capistrano.* Daylong festivities include Mexican and Indian dances, mariachi music, and other entertainment. In mid-March there is a *Festival of the Swallows,* "Fiesta de la Golindrinas," with a week-long celebration capped off with a parade. Annual *All-City Kite Tournament,* Long Beach.

April. The *Long Beach Grand Prix*—the only formula-one race through the streets of a North American city. Weeklong activities include a chili cook-off, bike race, celebrity race, and a 10,000-meter foot race.

May. Cinco de Mayo, *Mexican Independence Day,* is celebrated with festivals throughout the Southland, on May 5th.

July. Through August, the *Festival of the Arts* is held in Laguna Beach. Included in this popular event is the Sawdust Festival, the Art-a-Fair, and the Pageant of the Masters. On the *Fourth of July,* many coastal cities sponsor fireworks; there is a parade and celebration in Huntington Beach.

August. *California International Sea Festival,* Long Beach. *Character Boat Parade,* Newport Beach.

September. *Newport Harbor Art Museum Antique Show,* Sept. 16–18. *Huntington Beach Annual Surf Championship.*

October. *Sandcastle Contest,* Corona del Mar, Newport Beach.

December. *Christmas Parade,* San Pedro. *Boat parades* in Newport Beach and Dana Point.

 TOURS. In **Long Beach,** tours to the *Queen Mary* (berth J at the southern end of the Long Beach Freeway) include a look at the ship from stem to stern, plus a stop at the *Living Sea* underwater exhibit created by Jacques Cousteau. Summer: daily, 10:00 A.M.–4:30 P.M.; winter: Monday through Friday, 10:00 A.M.–3:30 P.M.; weekends: 10:00 A.M.–4:30 P.M.; (213) 435–4733. The *Spruce Goose* is on view from 10:00 A.M. to 6:00 P.M. Call (213) 435–5671 for further information. *La Casa de Ranchos Los Cerritos* (4600 Virginas Rd., Long Beach), a Spanish house built in 1844, is open to tour daily, Wednesday through Sunday, 1:00–5:00 P.M., (213) 424–9423. *Rancho Los Alamitos* (6400 Bixby Rd., Long Beach), one of the oldest adobe structures in California, also has organized tours. Open daily, Wednesday through Sunday, 1:00–5:00 P.M.; (213) 431–2511. For those who wish to venture out to sea, the S.S. *Azure Seas* might be just the thing. Operated by Western Cuisine Lines, this ship combines an exciting escape, with a large informal party and a chance to see the sights "down Mexico way." For information on the three- and four-night cruises call (800) 421–5866 or (213) 548–8411.

Catalina Island. Various tours are offered around the island. Included are the glass-bottom boat tour, the casino tour, the coastal cruise, skyline cruise, flying-fish boat tour, and the inland motor tour. For information, call (213) 510–2500.

Wrigley Memorial and Botanical Gardens, 1400 Avalon Canyon Road, Avalon, Catalina Island; (213) 510–2288 or (213) 510–1520. This showcase for Catalina Island's native plants comprises more than 37 acres. Grounds are open seven days a week, 8 A.M. to 5 P.M. Admission is 50 cents; children under 12 free. Group tours are available. Tram service is provided between Island Plaza and Wrigley Memorial and Botanical Gardens.

Newport Beach. From the Balboa Pavilion, visitors can take advantage of many tours. Among them: sportfishing (714) 673–1434, and whale-watching and harbor cruises (714) 673–5245.

San Juan Capistrano. Walking tours are conducted each Sunday at 1:00 P.M. to take in the seven remaining adobes built as part of *Mission San Juan Capistrano,* the mission itself, and other historical sights in this quaint town. Those wishing to participate should meet at El Peon across from the mission on Ortega Bay. In **San Clemente,** tour the San Onofre Nuclear Energy Information Center; (714) 492–5272.

BEACHES. In addition to city beaches in each community, there are also state- and county-run beaches and recreation areas.

Huntington Beach State Beach is on Pacific Coast Hwy. (near Beach Blvd.). It runs into the city-run beach, and offers miles and miles of coast. Picnic facilities and fire rings for barbecues are available. **Bolsa Chica State Beach** is close to Huntington. This beach also has fire rings for barbecues; it's across the street from the Bolsa Chica Ecological Reserve.

A bit south of Newport Beach, **Corona Del Mar** boasts one of the best walks around, on a rock pier jutting out into the ocean. **Aliso County Park** in south Laguna Beach is a recreation area with a fishing pier. Adjacent to the Dana Point Marina, **Doheny State Park Beach** has a good marine recreation facility for swimming, fishing, and picnicking. Camping is also available here. (For camping information, call 714–496–6171.)

San Clemente State Beach also has camping facilities; for information, call (714) 492–5171. This spot is particularly lovely.

 FISHING AND BOAT CHARTERS. Fishing is available in most coastal cities and can run the gambit from a day of leisurely pier fishing to out-and-out deep-sea fishing. No licenses are needed to fish off any public piers in California.

Visit *Belmont Pier,* the place to fish in Long Beach. The pier goes a full half mile into the bay. Half- and full-day deep-sea fishing charters can be arranged at Queen's Wharf Sportsfishing (213) 432–8993, or call Belmont Pier Sportsfishing at (213) 432–6784.

Catalina is an excellent fishing spot; rent large or small craft in Avalon at *Avalon Boat Stand Co.;* call (213) 510–1097. *Huntington Pier* in Huntington Beach is frequented by casual and die-hard fishermen alike.

At Newport Beach's *Balboa Pavilion,* more than 40 skiffs and outboard motors are available for full- or half-day fishing. These boats seat four and are equipped with built-in live bait tanks. For information, call (714) 673–1431. Also from Newport, enjoy a day of deep-sea fishing aboard modern boats; rental equipment, license, and anything else you may need is provided at the Pavilion landing; call (714) 673–1434. *Aliso Beach Park* in south Laguna has a fishing pier, as does *Dana Point. Doheny State Beach* boasts surf-fishing.

 CAMPING. Camping areas along the beach are filled with recreation opportunities. The following are campsites along or close to the coast:

Newport Dunes Travel Trailer Park. Newport Beach at 1131 Back Bay Dr.; (714) 644–0510. All year; fee $13.00, reservation required. Deposit $13.00, pets an additional $1.00. 151 campsites, all with electrical, water, and sewage hook-up. Sanitary disposal, water, toilets, showers, cooking, tables, swimming, fishing, playground, propane, groceries, laundry.

Doheny State Beach. 2 miles south of San Juan Capistrano; (714) 496–6171. Open all year. Fee $6.00, reservation deposit required; pets allowed for $1.00. 114 tent and recreation vehicle (RV) spaces; 28 days maximum stay for RVs. Sanitary disposal station, water, toilets, showers, cooking facilities, tables, swimming, fishing.

San Clemente State Beach. 2 miles south of San Clemente off I–5; (714) 492–3156. Year-round, fee $6.00; $1.00 for pets. 65 tent spaces, 72 RV spaces, 35 days maximum stay for RVs. Sanitary disposal, water, toilets, showers, cooking facilities, tables, and propane; groceries and laundry nearby.

San Onofre State Beach. 3½ miles south of San Clemente, off I–5; (714) 492–4872. Year-round, fee $6.00. Reservation deposit required; fee for pets, $1.00. 57 tent spaces. Sanitary disposal, water, toilet, showers, cooking facilities, tables, swimming, fishing; groceries nearby.

CHILDREN'S ACTIVITIES. Kids will enjoy almost anything grownups enjoy in this area, especially beach activities (swimming and surfing) and biking. Most of the theme parks for which southern California is world famous are located in inland Orange County (see the *Orange County* section above).

Marineland, however, is one exception. The adventure-filled Family Swim is new at Marineland. Here, guests can swim in a half-million-gallon tank with 4,000 fish. At Sea Lion Point, visitors will observe a rare colony of sea lions in their natural environment. Performing whales, dolphins, and sea lions star in regularly scheduled shows. Another attraction at Marineland is the Sky Tower: A glass enclosed bi-level elevator revolves slowly as it takes passengers above Marineland; from the top is a great view of the Palos Verdes Peninsula, and on a clear day, you can see Catalina Island. Marineland is located at Palos Verdes Dr. S., in Palos Verdes Hills; call (213) 377–1571. The park is open daily, 10:00 A.M. to 7:00 P.M. except from mid-April to mid-June, when it is open from 10:00 A.M. to 6:00 P.M., and, until September, from 10:00 A.M. to 7:00 P.M.

While in Laguna Beach, take the children to the *Laguna Moulton Playhouse,* 606 Laguna Canyon Rd.; 494–0743. A special children's theater is sure to entertain the younger members of the family. Open year-round; box office open 1:00–5:00 P.M., Tuesday through Saturday. How to get there: Take San Diego #405 Freeway south or the Santa Ana #5 Freeway south to the Laguna Freeway. The Laguna Freeway ends and becomes Laguna Canyon Road. The playhouse is at the Laguna Festival Grounds, about three miles away. Laguna Moulton Playhouse, 606 Laguna Canyon Rd., closed Sunday and Monday.

PARTICIPANT SPORTS: Southern California is one of the world's most active playgrounds. From walking on the beach and swimming, to wind-surfing and biking, there is a sport for everyone.

Swimming. All beaches mentioned above under *Beaches* are open for swimming; those used to swimming in warm ocean water, however, may think the Pacific a bit brisk in the winter.

Surfing. For those daring enough to try this typically Californian sport, here are some of the popular spots: *Seal Beach*, between the pier and the jetty, is good for morning surfing; *Huntington Beach*, right near the pier, is popular for surfers as well as spectators; in *Newport Beach*, "the Wedge" is known world wide as one of the most treacherous surfing spots—certainly not for beginners, but great for interested spectators; and in *San Clemente*, surfers practice right across from the San Onofre nuclear reactor—an interesting juxtaposition. There is surfing at many more locations; just look for other surfers, gather as much courage as you need, and hit the waves.

Snorkeling. *Corona del Mar*, with its two colorful reefs, is a popular place for snorkeling because it is off limits to boats. In *Laguna Beach*, there is good snorkeling along the whole length of the beach; be sure not to disturb the marine life, though, for it is part of a protected ecological reserve.

Biking. To help bikers throughout California, Caltrans (California Department of Transportation) has a listing of bike paths; call (213) 620–3550. Usually, the bike paths follow the ocean whenever possible, for an indescribably beautiful ride. For weekend and longer trips, call L.A. Wheelman at (213) 533–1687 for planning information.

Golf. Southern California has more than its share of golf courses. There are more through inland Orange County than in the coastal area. Private clubs often honor other memberships. Some of the major courses include:

In Orange County: *Buena Park:* Los Coyotes Country Club (private) (714) 521–6171.

Costa Mesa: Costa Mesa Public Golf & Country Club (714) 540–7500; and Mesa Verde Country Club (private) (714) 549–0377.

Fountain Valley: Mile Square Golf Course (714) 545–3726.

Los Alamitos: Los Alamitos Country Club (semi-private) (714) 821–5990.

Placentia: Alta Vista Country Club (private) (714) 528–1185.

Santa Ana: River View Golf Course (714) 543–1115; Santa Ana Country Club (private) (714) 556–3000; and Willowick Golf Course (par 3) (714) 531–0678.

From Long Beach to San Clemente: *Catalina:* Catalina Island Golf Course (par 3) (213) 510–0530.

Huntington Beach: Huntington Seacliff Country Club (714) 536–7575; and Meadowlark Golf Course (714) 846–1364.

Irvine: Rancho San Joaquin Golf Course (714) 551–5522.

Laguna Hills: Laguna Hills Golf Course (private) (714) 837–7630.

Laguna Niguel: El Niguel Country Club (private) (714) 496–5767.

Mission Viejo: Costa del Sol Golf Course (par 3) (714) 581–9040; and Mission Viejo Country Club (private) (714) 831–1550.

Newport Beach: Big Canyon Country Club (private) (714) 644–5404; Irvine Coast Country Club (private) (714) 644–9550; and Newport Beach Golf Course (par 3) (714) 751–4344.

Long Beach: El Dorado Golf Course (213) 430–3089; Heartwell Golf Park (par 3) (213) 421–8855; Recreational Park Municipal Golf Course (213) 438–4012; Skylinks Golf Course (213) 421–3388; and Virginia Country Club (private) (213) 427–0924.

San Clemente: San Clemente Municipal Golf Course (714) 492–7602.

San Juan Capistrano: San Juan Hills Country Club (714) 837–0361.

Seal Beach: Old Ranch Country Club (private) (213) 596–4425.

South Laguna: Aliso Creek Golf Course (par 3) (714) 499–1919.

Tennis. Southern California also has thousands of tennis courts, many lighted for evening play. These range from the most exclusive private clubs to public tennis courts; check the Yellow Pages in each area for the latter. Some of the major courts include:

Long Beach: The Billie Jean King Tennis Center, 1040 Park Ave., (213) 433–9294, has eight courts which can be rented for a fee of $2.00 an hour without reservations and $3.00 an hour with reservations. Six courts, at California State University at Long Beach, 1250 Bellflower Blvd, (213) 498–4111, are open to the public. No reservations here—first come first served.

Catalina: Tennis courts at Las Casitas are open to the public with reservations, for a fee of $6.00 an hour. The hotel has three courts and is located two blocks from the Avalon marina. Call (213) 510–2226 for information and reservations. Catalina Island Tennis Courts has two courts available for $4.00 an hour. The club is located two and a half blocks from Avalon Harbor on Country Club Road; for reservations call (213) 510–0530.

Huntington Beach: Four courts are offered on a first come, first served basis at the Edison Community Center, 21366 Magnolia St. (Magnolia and Hamilton), (714) 960–8870. The fee is $2.00 an hour, and reservations can be made as far as 48 hours in advance. At the Murdy Community Center, 7000 Norma Dr. (off Golden West St., north of Warner), (714) 960–8895, four courts are available for free. No reservations are necessary.

Newport Beach: The Corona del Mar High School, 2101 East Bluff Dr., has eight courts for public use. The Recreation Department uses the courts, so it is best to call and find out when they are free—for the Recreation Department call (213) 640–2271. The same number should be used for information on tennis courts at San Joaquin Road and Crown Drive N. Four courts are available at this location, and can be used for free.

Laguna Beach: In Laguna the tennis courts are located at the Laguna Beach High School on Park Ave. There are eight courts and they are metered. Additional courts are available on Mondays, Wednesdays, and Fridays at the Irvine Bowl, 650 Laguna Canyon Rd. No reservations and no fees are required for these courts.

San Clemente: Four courts are open to the public at San Luis Rey Park, on Avenue San Luis Rey, off El Camino Real; and another two courts are located at Bonita Canyon Park at the corner of El Camino Real and Calle Valley. All of these courts are available for free on a first come, first served basis. For more information call the Recreation Department at (714) 492–5101.

Water Sports. Sailboat, windsurfing, and other nautical rentals are generally available at or near the piers in each beach city. Some of the major rental groups are:

Long Beach: Bayshore Boat Rentals, at Marina Park Beach (2nd St. and Appian Way), has Hobie Catamarans and Sunfish sailboats for rent. The Hobies are $20.00 for the first hour and $15.00 for each subsequent hour. A Sunfish can be rented for $10.00 an hour or $30.00 a half a day. Sailing experience is necessary, and lessons are available for $20.00 an hour. Reservations can be made in person, or through the mail by writing to Bayshore Boat Rentals, 317 Colorado Place, Long Beach, CA 90804. Call (213) 433-3435 for recorded information. Matlack Windsurfing, 4726 East 2nd St., in Belmont Shores (213) 430-3000, rents windsurfers for $6.00 an hour. They also offer a lesson-and-equipment package for $45.00, as well as individual lessons by the hour.

Newport Beach: Balboa Boat Rentals, Palm and Edgewater, next to the Balboa Ferry, (714) 673-1320, offers 21-foot Victory sailboats for a rental fee of $13.00 an hour. The boats are for use in the bay only.

Dana Point: Sailboat rentals are available from Embarcadero Marina, adjacent to the launching ramp at Dana Point Harbor, (714) 496-6177. Boat sizes range from 14 feet to 23 feet for all-day rentals.

SPECTATOR SPORTS. Because southern California is such an active place, sports activities you might want to take part in outnumber those you just want to watch. However, at the spectator events that take place each year you can be assured that you'll witness some amazing athletics.

Racing. Long Beach is the scene of a grand prix formula-one race in early spring. This race, The *Long Beach Grand Prix,* lures thousands to Long Beach streets for a truly exciting day.

Boating. The *Flight of the Snowbirds Regatta* is held annually at Balboa Pavilion in Newport Beach.

Surfing. In September, an annual *surfing competition* is held in Huntington Beach.

HISTORICAL SITES. With the Spanish influence so prevalent in southern California, historical remnants of the Spanish residents are popular attractions. *La Casa de Rancho Los Cerritos* is one of these. The adobe house dates back to 1844. It's located at 4600 Virginas Rd., Long Beach and is open Wednesday through Sunday, from 1:00 to 5:00 P.M.; (213) 424-9423.

Rancho Alamitos at 6400 Bixby Rd., Long Beach, (213) 431-2511, is one of the oldest adobe structures. Open Wednesday through Sunday, 1:00 to 5:00 P.M.

MISSIONS. Many areas of California boast old Spanish missions, but probably none are as awesome or well known as *Mission San Juan Capistrano.* This historical fortress, sometimes called The Jewel of the Missions, is known the world over for its swallows, which return faithfully every St. Joseph's Day (March 19). The classic beauty of the mission, its gardens and its flock of white pigeons, attract some 300,000 visitors and photographers each year. Because of this large influx of tourists, the mission has recently opened a Visitor Information Center inside Mission San Juan Capistrano at Suite 218, San Juan Capistrano, CA 92675; (714) 493–1424. The mission itself is located at Camino Capistrano and Ortega Hwy.

MUSEUMS. The cultural focus is growing here by leaps and bounds. In addition to museums, tiny art galleries are plentiful in most of the cities.

    Long Beach Museum of Art, 2300 East Ocean Blvd.; (213) 439–2119. Emphasizing art in California, the museum is housed in a beautiful brick-and-lava-stone mansion on a bluff overlooking the ocean in Long Beach. Open Wednesday through Sunday, 12 noon to 5:00 P.M.

    In San Pedro, **Cabrillo Marine Museum,** 3720 Stephen White Dr.; (213) 548–7562. Boasts of more than 15,000 foreign and local shells as well as diverse species of fish and other marine life. Open weekdays, 12 noon to 5:00 P.M.; weekends 10:00 A.M. to 5:00 P.M. Closed Monday.

    Newport Harbor Art Museum, at 850 San Clemente Dr.; 759–1122. Newport Beach. Concentrates on "the art of our time," with an emphasis on the last three decades. Open daily from 11:00 A.M. to 5:00 P.M.; Friday from 11:00 A.M. to 9:00 P.M.; closed Sundays.

    Laguna Beach Art Museum, 307 Cliff Dr.; 494–6531. Contains art that highlights the area. Exhibitions held of early and present-day California artists. Because of limited space, displays change often. Open weekdays from 11:30 A.M. to 4:30 P.M.; Fridays, in the summer from 11:30 A.M. to 9:00 P.M.; closed Fridays.

MUSIC. The *Long Beach Convention and Entertainment Center,* 300 East Ocean Blvd.; (213) 436–3636, offers a selection of different music throughout the year. The Terrace Theater opened in 1978, with a performance by the Long Beach Symphony Orchestra featuring Van Cliburn on piano. Eugene Ormandy, former conductor of the Philadelphia Orchestra, has called the acoustics at the Terrace "absolutely first-class." A 24-hour event line, (213) 432–2233, is available for information on current productions.

    The *Golden Bear,* directly across the street from the Huntington Beach Pier, is a popular showcase for bands and musical groups.

STAGE. The *Long Beach Convention and Entertainment Center* has a continuing theater program at the Center Theater. The arena presents extravaganzas such as the Ice Capades. The *Long Beach Community Playhouse* offers outstanding comedy and drama; call (213) 438–0536.

At Laguna Beach, the *Laguna Moulton Playhouse,* 494–0734, offers first-rate plays for children as well as adults. *Sebastian's West Dinner Playhouse* in San Clemente often attracts older, well-known stars such as Kathryn Grayson and Caesar Romero; for information call (714) 492–9950.

SHOPPING. California is the land of the mall; in most areas, all popular department stores, as well as smaller boutiques, are well represented under one roof. Otherwise, look for clusters of stores, usually located in the center of town.

Long Beach. The *Marina Pacifica* shopping center on Pacific Coast Hwy., just north of Second St., is a captivating little shopping area on the water. Redwood buildings and the parklike atmosphere make this an exciting place to shop. *Lakewood Center,* at Lakewood and Del Amo Blvds., is an indoor mall housing more traditional department stores—May Co., Montgomery Ward, J.C. Penny's, Buffums, and Bullocks. *The Market Place,* at the intersection of Pacific Coast Hwy. and Second St., surrounds a lake with theaters, boutiques, and restaurants. *Ports O' Call Village,* in San Pedro, is an "old-fashioned" waterfront complex in one of the world's busiest harbors.

Newport Beach. *Fashion Island* in Newport Center has a multitude of prestigious department stores and boutiques.

Laguna Beach. This small town is unanimously voted the most interesting place to shop in the area, with its tiny malls set off from the street, and more stores than you would ever imagine could fit into such a small town. Laguna offers incredibly diverse items, ranging from silk flowers (at *As Things Are,* in the new Bluebird Canyon Shopping Center) to aloe vera products (at the *Palm Springs Perfume and Cosmetics Company,* in the Lumber Yard Plaza on Forest Ave). Dozens of intriguing art galleries include the renowned *Vorpal Gallery,* 326 Glennyere; the *Watercolor Gallery,* 1416 S. Coast Hwy.; the *Tree of Life Studio Gallery,* 751 Rembrandt; and *Gallery Xyst,* 1412 S. Coast Hwy., just to name a few of the more than 40 galleries. Antiques shops are also abundant in Laguna; there is *Richard Yeakal,* on Coast Hwy., for fine American and European antiques (at very high prices); the *Queen's Head,* at 250 Broadway, with a wide selection for the dollar-wise buyer; *Mage Wind* in the Lumber Yard, which offers antiques as well as contemporary items; and *Off the Wall,* at 950 Glenneyre, with some unusual architectural antiques such as clawfoot bathtubs, brass hardware, mantles, and pedestal sinks. Some of the more out-of-the-ordinary stores include: *Chicken Little Emporium,* Coast Hwy., with whimsical gifts and clothes; *South Seas Rag Co.,* 279 S. Coast Hwy., with some of the barest fashions around; and *Khyber Pass,* at 384 Forest Ave., which features unusual gifts from Afghanistan and the Middle East. *Peppertree Lane* is an adorable shopper's alley at 448 Coast Hwy.; it includes a woman's clothing store, a sweet shop, and an antiques shop, all designed to take you back to simpler, less hectic shopping days, amid trees, white wrought-iron benches, and an array of flowers.

DINING OUT. Restaurants along the Orange County coast are about as varied as the people who live here. This is a high-priced area in general, so the restaurants are fairly expensive. Dining in this area is usually a casual and informal affair; when there *is* a dress code we'll mention it. For those on a budget, there are many coffee shops and cafés. Price ranges are as follows (per person, with no wine or tip included—for more information see "Facts at Your Fingertips"): *Expensive,* $25 and up; *Moderate,* $10–$25; and *Inexpensive,* below $10.

LONG BEACH

Adolph's. *Moderate.* 700 Queensway Dr.; (213) 437–5977. In the Queensway Hilton, this restaurant is located in the marina, allowing a beautiful view of the *Queen Mary.* The decor is tropical, with hanging plants and wicker chairs. Seafood is the house specialty. All major credit cards.

Bobby McGee's Conglomeration. *Moderate.* 6501 East Pacific Coast Hwy.; (213) 594–8627. Looking like an old English farmhouse from the outside, this Elizabethan-style restaurant is filled with antiques and mirrors. The staff is dressed in costumes, each depicting a different storybook character. Choose from a variety of seafood, steak, and prime rib dishes. A discotheque features big band to contemporary music nightly until 2:00 A.M. Restaurant open from 5:00–10:00 P.M. weekdays, until midnight on weekends. All major credit cards.

Domenico's Belmont Shore. *Moderate.* 5339 E. 2nd St.; (213) 439–0261. This restaurant, in the popular Belmont Shores area, has Italian specialties from braciole to fettucine, in a friendly atmosphere. Open for lunch and dinner. All major credit cards.

Hamburger Henry's. *Moderate.* 4700 East 2nd St.; (213) 433–7070. A choice of 38 different hamburgers here; from plain to a polar burger topped with ice cream. Full salad bar; steak, fish, and chicken dishes. A heated patio allows outdoor dining year-round. Open 24 hours, every day. Beer and wine. MC, V.

Houlihan's Old Place. *Moderate.* 6272 A East Pacific Coast Hwy.; (213) 598–9638. Located in the Marina Pacifica Shopping Center, this restaurant offers an interesting setting with a potpourri of old and contemporary posters on the wall. The menu includes burgers and omelettes, as well as duck, shrimp, and fettucine, plus unusual appetizers and desserts. Full bar open until 1:30 A.M., every night. Open weekdays, 11:30 A.M. to 10:30 P.M.; weekends until 11:30 P.M. Sunday brunch from 10:00 A.M. Major credit cards.

Le Bistro. *Moderate.* 3222 East Broadway (in Belmont Shores); (213) 434–3003. Fine French cuisine. Fresh flowers, candlelight, and classic art add to the mood in this café-style restaurant. Fresh fish every day. Closed Monday. All major credit cards.

La Grotte. *Moderate.* 529 East Seaside Way; (213) 437–2119. Located near the Long Beach Convention and Entertainment Center. French and Continental cuisine served in an intimate, European atmosphere. Veal dishes are their specialty, though there is a good selection of seafood. Closed Sunday and holidays. Dinner from 5:30 to 10:00 P.M. weekdays; to 11:00 P.M. weekends. All major credit cards.

Panama Joe's Cafe and Bar. *Moderate.* 5100 East 2nd St.; (213) 434–7417. More than 50 exciting Mexican dishes are available at this local favorite. Antiques, ceiling fans, and Tiffany lamps adorn the restaurant, lending a 1900s flavor. A 20-foot oak bar dominates the scene; sporting photos and hunting gear clutter the walls. Try the arroz con pollo (chicken and rice), made with pineapple. Music at the bar nightly. Open daily from 11:00 A.M. to 11.00 P.M., Sunday brunch at 10:00 A.M. (The bar closes at 1:30 A.M.) Major credit cards.

Prince of Whales. *Moderate.* 6790 Long Beach Blvd.; (213) 632–1366. Fifty-two years ago this Scottish-style restaurant opened, at the time seating only eight. Now, 150 seats later, the decor remains Scottish, with an array of crests and swords. Strictly a seafood restaurant, the fresh fish is prepared in a Scottish batter, the recipe of which was brought to the States by the owner himself. Halibut and shrimp have been a favorite for 45 years. Beer and wine only. Open Monday through Thursday. 11:00 A.M.–2:00 P.M. and 4:00–8:45 P.M. Open weekends, 11:00 A.M. to 8:45 P.M.; closed Sunday. All major credit cards.

The Crab Shell. *Moderate.* 5372 East 2nd St.; (213) 434–1865. Fresh seafood is charbroiled or deep-fried here and served in a casual setting. The large windows and greenery make you feel as though you are dining outdoors. Open Sunday through Thursday, 11:30 A.M. until 10 P.M.; open until 11 P.M. on weekends. MC, V.

SAN PEDRO

Papadakis Tavern. *Moderate.* 301 West 6th St.; (213) 548–1186. The tavern is full of Greek festivity and spirit; decor includes hanging Greek rugs, bronze statues, and marble pillars. Taped music plays continuously as waiters break into Greek dancing throughout the evening. Traditional Greek fare; specialties include lamb wrapped in pastry. Extensive list of Greek and California wines. Open for lunch Tuesday through Friday, 11:30 A.M. to 2:00 P.M. Dinner on Tuesday through Thursday, from 5:00 to 9:00 P.M.; on Friday and Saturday, from 5:00 to 9:45 P.M.; and on Sunday, from 5:00 to 8:45 P.M. Closed Monday. Reservations a must. MC, V.

SANTA CATALINA ISLAND (AVALON)

Carlos O'Malley's. *Moderate.* 693 Crescent; (213) 510–1218. Primarily Northern Italian cuisine (believe it or not). On the waterfront in an intimate setting. Beer and wine. Open all year; Fridays through Tuesday in the winter. Open on weekdays from 5:00 to 9:00 P.M.; on weekends until 10 P.M. AE, MC, V.

Flying Yachtsman. *Moderate.* 403 Crescent St.; (213) 510–9177. Situated on the waterfront; a nautical motif prevails here. Variety of seafood, steak, and prime ribs. Open year-round. Lunch, 11:00 A.M. to 2:00 P.M.; dinner, 5:00 to 10:00 P.M. (five nights off season, seven nights in season). AE, MC, V.

Mr. Gee's Restaurant and Bar. *Moderate.* 888 Los Lomas; (213) 510–1327. Both Continental and Chinese fare. Full bar, entertainment in the summer. Open year-round, 5:00 to 10:00 P.M. for dinner; from 8:30 A.M. to 3:00 P.M. in season. AE, MC, V.

The Upstairs Place. *Moderate.* 417 Crescent; (213) 510–0333. Located right on the water; arched windows overlook the bay. Fresh seafood dinners. Beer, wine. Open 5:30 to 9:00 P.M. daily during the summer (June to September), weekends only the rest of the year. MC, V.

El Galleon Restaurant. *Inexpensive.* 411 Crescent; (213) 510–1188. A variety of fish, locally caught. The decor is nautical, with portholes and ship rigging. Full bar with nightly entertainment May through October. Dinner, year-round, served from 5:00 P.M. to 9:00 P.M. (11:00 P.M. in season.) Lunch served all seasons. All major credit cards.

HUNTINGTON BEACH

Jeremiah's. *Moderate.* 8901 Warner Ave.; (714) 848–2662. Relax in this lush atmosphere, filled with plants, redwood, and leaded glass. Prime rib, fresh seafood, chicken, and steak served in this multi-level restaurant. Guitar music Wednesday through Saturday; disco dancing with live music on weekends. Open 5:00 to 11:00 P.M. on weekends.

Maxwell's. *Moderate.* 317 Pacific Coast Hwy.; (714) 536–2555. A beautifully decorated restaurant right on the ocean near Huntington Beach pier. Large selection of seafood: local fish and fish from the East coast; live Maine lobster a specialty. Beef and prime rib are also available. One of the largest wine lists around. Breakfast, 8:00–11:30 A.M.; lunch, 11:30 to 4:00 P.M.; dinner Sunday through Thursday, until 10:00 P.M. Sunday buffet brunch from 10:00 A.M. to 2:30 P.M. All major credit cards.

Tibbie's Music Hall. *Moderate.* 16360 Coast Hwy.; (714) 840–5661. A musical revue by the young Americans' Song and Dance Company entertains while you dine on prime rib or chicken. Also a selection of seafood appetizers. Two dinner shows nightly from Tuesday through Saturday at 5:45 and 8:45 P.M.; one seating Sunday at 5:00 P.M. AE, MC, V.

The Golden Bear. *Inexpensive.* 306 Pacific Coast Hwy.; (714) 536–9600; for reservations, call (714) 960–5436. Live entertainment is the primary reason for going to The Golden Bear—food secondary. Sandwiches, salad, chicken, and steak are served during the performances that take place from 8:30 to 10:30 P.M. No credit cards accepted.

NEWPORT BEACH

Ambrosia. *Expensive.* 501 Thirtieth St.; (714) 673–0200. Has a formal dining room—complete with high-backed wing chairs of red velour, crystal chandeliers, and silver flatware. French cuisine served to the tune of strolling violinists. The wine list shows 800 domestic and imported wines. Jacket and tie required; reservations necessary. Open 7 days. All major credit cards.

The Wine Cellar (in The Newporter Resort). *Expensive.* 1107 Jamboree Rd.; (714) 644–1700. Strolling guitarists (why not?) serenade diners in this French restaurant. Seating is from 7:00–8:30 P.M., Tuesday through Saturday. Reservations required, jackets requested. Major credit cards.

Cano's. *Expensive.* 2241 West Coast Hwy.; (714) 631–1381. On Newport Beach's seafood restaurant row south of the junction of the Coast Hwy. with Rte. 55, Cano's is supposed to be a Mexican seafood place, but has more of an eclectic Continental menu. Yachts are moored right outside the windows. The customers are rather dressy; the bar is spacious and slick. Reservations recommended. Valet parking. AE, MC, V.

The Ritz. *Expensive.* 880 Newport Center Dr.; (714) 720–1800. Just as the name suggests, this restaurant is grand. Brass and glass accentuate the richness of the atmosphere, and the food is also first-rate. Specialties include grilled calf's liver and roast duck, and many unusual appetizers are featured, such as steamed mussels and fried oysters. Open for lunch and dinner. All major credit cards.

Amelia's. *Moderate.* 311 Marine Ave., Balboa Island; (714) 673–6580. For 20 years, Amelia and her family have been entertaining visitors (well-known celebrities among them) in the Newport area. This warm and friendly restaurant on the main street of Balboa Island is now a landmark. Fresh fish is a specialty; Italian cuisine is also served. Reservations a must. Open for dinner only from Tuesday through Sunday. MC, V.

Baxter's Street. *Moderate.* 4647 MacArthur Blvd.; (714) 540–2475. A turn-of-the-century San Francisco street is the setting for this restaurant. Dinner features steak, fresh fish, pasta, and barbecued ribs. Dinner shows nightly by the talented Baxter's Street Singers. Open for lunch, Monday through Friday. Reservations necessary. AE, MC, V.

Capriccio Café (in the Marriott Hotel and Tennis Club). *Moderate.* 900 Newport Center Dr.; (714) 640–4000. An elegant dining room and terrace with a spectacular ocean view. Specialties include crepes, unique sandwiches, and an array of fine desserts. Piano bar. Open daily for breakfast, lunch, and dinner. All major credit cards.

Le Biarritz. *Moderate.* 414 North Old Newport Blvd.; (714) 645–6700. A friendly French restaurant, well known around town for award-winning provincial cuisine. Lunch begins at 11:00 A.M.; treats from 2:00 to 5:00 P.M.; dinner until 11:00 P.M.; Sunday brunch from 10:00 A.M. to 3:00 P.M. AE, MC, V.

La Palme. *Moderate.* In the Newporter Inn, 1106 Jamboree Rd.; (714) 640–4182. Seasonal foods are the specialty in this bright, airy restaurant. Diners can overlook a green garden, and fresh flowers add color to the tables. The chef, trained at the famous Bernard's (under the same management), is innovative; some dishes he has offered include oysters with caviar, and grilled prawns with lime and ginger. Open Monday through Friday for lunch and dinner, weekends for dinner only. All major credit cards.

Rusty Pelican. *Moderate.* 2735 West Coast Hwy.; (714) 642–3431. This restaurant, located right at the water's edge, has a fantastic view. The menu offers a wide selection of fresh fish, as well as prime rib. On the second level is a lounge and oyster bar, with entertainment nightly. Open for lunch, dinner, and Sunday brunch. All major credit cards.

The Bistro (in The Newporter Resort). *Moderate.* 1107 Jamboree Rd.; (714) 644–1700. This Parisian café features French onion soup, quiches, and fresh fish. Lovely, casual atmosphere. Open daily for breakfast, lunch, and dinner. All major credit cards.

The Cannery. *Moderate.* 3010 Lafayette Ave.; (714) 675–5777. An authentic cannery overlooking the harbor in old Newport's Cannery Village. This historic landmark restaurant features waterfront views and outdoor dining alongside local fishing boats. The menu features a wide variety of select seafood and steak entrees. Entertainment. Lunch, Monday through Saturday, 11:30 A.M. to 3:00 P.M.; dinner from 5:00 to 10:00 P.M. Sunday brunch from 9:00 A.M. to 2:30 P.M. All major credit cards.

Villa Nova. *Moderate.* 3131 West Coast Hwy.; (714) 642–7880. Since 1933, the Villa Nova on Newport Bay has been serving fine cuisine from central and northern Italy. The versatile menu includes osso buco and mozzarella marinara. Fine wines. Piano bar. Open daily for dinner. Full menu until 1:00 A.M. All major credit cards.

Warehouse. *Moderate.* 3450 Via Osporo; (714) 673–4700. Typical American-style eats with some foreign entries on a gimmicky menu, but here the place is the thing: right at the water. The bar is lively, the waitresses are everyone's idea of young California women. Reserve for large parties only. Major credit cards.

The Crab Cooker. *Inexpensive-Moderate.* 2200 Newport Blvd.; (714) 673–0100. The concept here is to serve very fresh fish, very simply prepared. Your fish is cooked right in front of you over charcoal in this cafeteria-style restaurant. Fresh fish choices include salmon, oysters, sea bass, and crab, and there's shrimp, lobster, and crab claws as well. Entrees come with rice or potato and tomato slices or cole slaw. Comfortable, casual decor with an attention-getting white shark mounted on the ceiling in the center of the room. The shark was caught off the coast of Newport Beach—now that's food for thought! The nautical decor continues with sea-faring pictures, wood carvings and crabs decorating the walls. No reservations. Lunch and dinner, daily. No credit cards.

CORONA DEL MAR

The Five Crowns. *Expensive.* 3801 East Coast Highway; (714) 760–0331. An authentic reproduction of Ye Old Bell, the oldest inn in England, located just outside London. Heavy leaded glass windows, flower boxes, and manicured shrubs adorn the exterior while intimate dining rooms filled with one-of-a-kind antiques and a cozy fireplace complete the interior. Captains, waitresses, and bartenders are garbed in traditional English costumes, including white bonnets for the ladies and knee pants for the gents! Roast prime ribs of beef is the house specialty, carved to your preference. Creamed spinach, a marvelous horseradish sauce, and Yorkshire pudding complete the plate. Other entrees include sauteed prawns with white wine and garlic, Dover sole Varonique and center-cut pork chops finished with brandy, heavy cream, and pink peppercorns. Excellent wine list with over 400 selections. Sunday and Monday nights feature entertainment, from Broadway tunes to pop and opera. Dinner nightly. AE, MC, V.

Hemingway's. *Expensive.* 2441 East Coast Hwy.; (714) 673–0120. This recently refurbished restaurant offers nouvelle cuisine in a warm, intimate atmosphere. Choose fresh seafood, game birds, or veal. Dinner, Tuesday through Sunday, 5:30 to 11:00 P.M.; Sunday brunch from 10:00 A.M. to 3:00 P.M. All major credit cards.

The Quiet Woman. *Moderate.* 3224 East Coast Hwy.; (714) 640–7440. Famous for its Continental cuisine and friendly atmosphere; a local favorite. Specialties: rack of lamb, veal Oscar, fondue, and charbroiled swordfish. Entertainment. Full bar until 2:00 P.M. Major credit cards.

LAGUNA BEACH

Las Brisas. *Moderate to Expensive.* 361 Cliff Drive, right off the Coast Hwy. north of the junction with Rte. 133; (714) 497–5434. On the cliffs at the north end of the central beach, overlooking the ocean, the beach, and much of the town nestled in the hills, this is a spectacularly sited restaurant, and the Mexican-style seafood in which it specializes is delicious. There is an outside patio that is more or less an adjunct to the bar. All in all a delightful experience, especially at sunset and in the early evening. Both dressy and casual. Brunch on Sunday. Major credit cards.

Ben Brown's. *Moderate.* 31106 Coast Hwy.; (714) 499–2663. Breakfast, lunch, and dinner served in Alisio Canyon, overlooking a 9-hole golf course. Dinner specialties include bouillabaisse, scampi, and veal scallopini. Full bar, cocktail lounge. Open daily. MC, V.

The Beach House. *Moderate.* 619 Sleepy Hollow Lane; (714) 494–9707. With a white-water view of the ocean from every table, this eaterie offers fresh fish, lobster, and steamed clams. Breakfast, 8:00 to 11:30 A.M.; lunch until 2:00 P.M.; and dinner nightly. AE, MC, V.

The Cottage. *Moderate.* 308 North Coast Hwy.; (714) 494–3023. It once was "the thing" to wait on the lovely lawn of this quaint cottage for a table; that was before the establishment started taking reservations. The 70-year-old landmark building, formerly the residence of a pioneer developer, is beautifully landscaped. Daily fresh entree: fish, meat, and vegetarian dishes. Breakfast from 8:00 A.M. to 3:00 P.M.; lunch and dinner from noon to 10:00 P.M., until midnight on Friday and Saturday. Now serving wine and beer. No credit cards.

Jeani's Kitchen. *Moderate.* 1223 N. Coast Hwy.; (714) 497–4700. Try the fresh banana pancakes for breakfast, or top-grade hamburgers on a sourdough roll for lunch. Dinner blackboard menu changes regularly. Open from 7:00 A.M. to 2:30 P.M. and from 5:30 to 9:30 P.M. No credit cards accepted.

Partners Bistro. *Moderate.* 448 South Coast Hwy.; (714) 497–441. An extremely popular local spot. Exquisitely decorated with antiques, beautiful wood, cut glass, and bronze. Favorites include tournedos of beef, veal, and some of the finest fish around. Reservations except Friday and Saturday. Lunch, 11:30 A.M. to 3:00 P.M.; dinner, 5:30 to 11:00 P.M.; Sunday brunch, 10:00 A.M. to 3:00 P.M. MC, V.

The Place Across From the Hotel Laguna. *Moderate.* 440 South Coast Hwy.; (714) 497-2625. This restaurant in the middle of town has a woodsy interior. Homemade pastas, vegetarian dishes, omelettes. Open daily, MC, V, DC.

Poor Richard's Kitchen. *Moderate.* 1198 South Coast Hwy.; (714) 497-1667. In the Village Faire mall, this is a comfortable restaurant. Fine soup-and-salad bar. Patio dining with ocean view. Beer and wine. Open daily, 8:00 A.M. to 9:00 P.M. All major credit cards.

The Terrace. *Moderate.* 448 South Coast Hwy.; (714) 497-6769. A new upstairs, outside addition to the popular dining spot, *Partners* (see above). Lattice and greenery are everywhere; pleasant menu as well. Heat lamps take away the outdoors chill. Lunch daily, from 11:00 A.M. to 5:00 P.M. Dinner, Friday and Saturday until midnight. Sunday brunch. MC, V.

The Towers (atop the Surf and Sand Hotel). *Expensive.* 1555 South Coast Hwy.; (714) 497-4477. One of the best views of Laguna Beach awaits diners in this sophisticated restaurant. Open for breakfast, lunch, and dinner. All major credit cards.

The White House. *Moderate.* 340 S. Coast Hwy.; (714) 494-8089. A Laguna institution, newly decorated. The menu here is extensive—salads, crepes, pastas, and sandwiches are some of the offerings. Open for breakfast, lunch, and dinner. Entertainment nightly. All major credit cards.

Tortilla Flats. *Inexpensive.* 1740 South Coast Hwy.; (714) 494-6588. Since 1959, Maria Aquilar has prepared the same delicious Sonora-style food at this remodeled Laguna Beach landmark. Tequila flows freely in the upstairs cantina. The architecture reflects the warm welcome of a hacienda—and the view of the Pacific is stunning. Tamales a specialty. Open daily from 11:30 A.M.; Sunday brunch, 11:00 A.M. to 3:00 P.M. AE, MC, V.

DANA POINT

Quiet Cannon. *Moderate.* 34344 Green Lantern; (714) 496-6146. Sitting on a bluff overlooking the marina, the view here is *spectacular*. This woody, split-level restaurant serves prime rib, steak, and seafood. Open seven days. Lunch Monday through Friday from 11:30 A.M. to 3:30 P.M. Dinner Monday through Thursday, 5:00 to 10:00 P.M.; open until 11:00 P.M. Friday and Saturday and on Sunday from 4:30 to 10:00 P.M. Reservations recommended. AE, MC, V.

Wind and Sea Restaurant. *Moderate.* 25152 Del Prado; (714) 496-6500. Steak and seafood served in a rustic atmosphere with high beamed ceilings, hanging plants, and redwood decor. The house specialty is Alaskan king crab. Full bar with entertainment, Wednesday through Sunday. Open Monday to Friday, 5:30 until 10:00 P.M., and from 4:30 to 11:00 P.M. Saturday and Sunday. AE, MC, V.

SAN JUAN CAPISTRANO

L'Hirondelle French Cuisine. *Moderate.* 31631 Camino Capistrano; (714) 661–0425. This casual French inn has only 12 tables, so a reservation is imperative, especially on weekends. The menu is typically French. Duckling is the specialty, and it is served three ways. Beer and wine. Open from 4:30 to 10:00 P.M. weekends, and until 9:00 P.M. weekdays. Closed Monday and Tuesday. MC, V.

El Adobe. *Inexpensive-Moderate.* 31891 Camino Capistrano; 714–493–1163. The early American setting here highlights a Mexican/American cuisine restaurant packed with Richard M. Nixon memorabilia. Mariachi band entertains on the weekends. MC, V, AE.

Swallows Inn. *Inexpensive.* 31786 Camino Capistrano; (714) 493–3188. A local hangout, this Mexican eaterie is decorated Western style, complete with sawdust on the floor. Two bars, live entertainment Wednesday through Sunday. Open seven days from 6:30 to 10:00 P.M. Bar open until 2:00 A.M. No credit cards.

Walnut Grove Restaurant. *Inexpensive.* 26871 Ortega Hwy.; (714) 493–1661. Steak, seafood, and salads in a Spanish-style setting. All baking done on premises. Beer, wine. Open seven days for breakfast, lunch, and dinner. AE, MC, CB, V.

SAN CLEMENTE

Andreino's. *Moderate.* 1925 South El Camino Real; (714) 492–9955. This restaurant is full of antiques, flowers, and lace curtains. Italian cuisine, extensive wine list. Open seven days; Monday through Friday, dinner only. MC, V.

San Clemente Inn. *Moderate.* 125 Avenida Esplanadian; (714) 492–6103. Seafood, steak, and chicken are served here in a casual setting. Piano bar. The chicken Jerusalem—chicken sauteed in a white wine and cream sauce—is a favorite. Open daily. All major credit cards.

Swiss Chalet. *Moderate.* 216 North El Camino Real; (714) 492–7931. Swiss-German cuisine served in an authentic atmosphere. Tables surround a fireplace for a cozy setting. Chef's specialty is veal. Open Tuesday through Saturday: lunch from 11:30 A.M. to 2:30 P.M.; dinner from 5:00 to 9:00 P.M. Closed Sunday and Monday. MC, V.

The Fish Tale. *Moderate.* 111 West Palizada; (714) 498–6072. This seafood restaurant features fresh fish carefully prepared. Turn-of-the-century decor. A full bar stocks 50 different imported beers. Open seven days from 11:00 A.M. to 3:00 P.M. for lunch; dinner from 3:00 to 10:00 P.M. Sunday through Thursday, until 11:00 P.M., Friday and Saturday. Reservations recommended. MC, V.

NIGHT LIFE. The largest concentration of night life activities is in nearby Los Angeles, but there is also a blend of night-owl activities in all of the coastal cities.

Long Beach. *Bobby McGee's Conglomeration* is one of

the best discos around. Located in the Market Place, you can feel the pound of dancing feet as soon as you enter.

In **Huntington Beach,** *Maxwell's* is a disco with an ocean view—right on the pier.

In **Newport Beach** several restaurants accommodate night owls with various types of music. At the *Rusty Pelican,* 2735 W. Coast Hwy., Peterson, Paul, and May perform Monday through Saturday. The *Cannery Restaurant,* 3010 Lafayette Ave., offers live bands with top 40s and rock music nightly and for Sunday brunch. The *Studio Café* at 100 Main St. on the Balboa Peninsula presents jazz nightly. The *Red Onion,* 2406 Newport Blvd., presents a live band that plays top 40s and a little bit of everything else. *Quiet Woman,* 3224 E. Coast Hwy., Corona del Mar, has live mellow music and sometimes they add something special, such as a 1950s music night. And finally: *Bobby McGee's,* 353 E. Coast Hwy., has a disc jockey who plays easy-listening music in the early evening and top 40s for disco dancing later.

In **Laguna Beach,** the *White House,* at 340 S. Coast Hwy., has nightly entertainment featuring rock, jazz, and funk. *The Sandpiper,* 1183 S. Coast Hwy., offers the music of some of the best local groups around; people flock here from miles away.

In **San Juan Capistrano,** the *Depot,* at 26701 Verdugo Ave., features country, pop, or jazz every night.

INDEX

**(The letters H and R indicate
Hotel and Restaurant listing.)**

LANGUAGE/30

For the Business or Vacationing International Traveler

In 24 languages! A basic language course on 2 cassettes and a phrase book . . . Only $14.95 ea. + shipping

Nothing flatters people more than to hear visitors try to speak their language and LANGUAGE/30, used by thousands of satisfied travelers, gets you speaking the basics quickly and easily. Each LANGUAGE/30 course offers:

- approximately 1½ hours of guided practice in greetings, asking questions and general conversation
- special section on social customs and etiquette

Order yours today. Languages available:

ARABIC	GREEK	JAPANESE	RUSSIAN
CHINESE	HEBREW	KOREAN	SERBO-CROATIAN
DANISH	HINDI	NORWEGIAN	SPANISH
DUTCH	INDONESIAN	PERSIAN	SWAHILI
FRENCH	ITALIAN	PORTUGUESE	SWEDISH
GERMAN	TURKISH	VIETNAMESE	TAGALOG

To order send $14.95 per course + shipping $2.00 1st course, $1 ea. add. course. In Canada $3 1st course, $2.00 ea. add. course. NY and CA residents add state sales tax. Outside USA and Canada $14.95 (U.S.) + air mail shipping: $8 for 1st course, $5 ea. add. course. MasterCard, VISA and Am. Express card users give brand, account number (all digits), expiration date and signature.
SEND TO: FODOR'S, Dept. LC 760, 2 Park Ave., NY 10016-5677, USA.